UNIX Internals

The New Frontiers

UNIX Internals

The New Frontiers

Uresh Vahalia
EMC Corporation
Hopkinton, MA

An Alan R. Apt Book

Prentice Hall
Upper Saddle River, New Jersey 07458

Library of Congress Cataloging-in-Publication Data

Vahalia, Uresh.
    UNIX internals : the new frontiers / Uresh Vahalia.
        p.   cm.
    Includes index.
    ISBN 0-13-101908-2
    1. UNIX (Computer file)   2.   Operating systems (Computers)
I. Title.
QA76.76.063V33   1996   95-25213
005.4´3--dc20   CIP

Acquisitions editor: Alan Apt
Editorial assistant: Shirley McGuire
Editorial/production supervision: Spectrum Publisher Services
Full service coordinator: Irwin Zucker
Buyer: Donna Sullivan
Cover designer: Joseph Sengotta
Cover illustrator: Don Martineti
Cover art director: Amy Rosen

UNIX is a registered trademark licensed exclusively by X/Open Co., Ltd. SunOS and Solaris are registered trademarks of Sun Microsystems, Inc. Digital UNIX is a trademark of Digital Equipment Corporation. Other designation used by vendors as trademarks to distinguish their products may appear in this book. In all cases where the publisher is aware of a current trademark claim, the designations have been printed in initial capitals or all capitals.

 © 1996 by Prentice-Hall, Inc.
Simon & Schuster/A Viacom Company
Upper Saddle River, New Jersey 07458

The author and publisher of this book used their best efforts in preparing this book. These efforts include the development, research, and testing of the theories and programs to determine their effectiveness. The author and publisher make no warranty of any kind, expressed or implied, with regard to these programs or the documentation contained in this book. The author and publisher shall not be liable in any event for incidental or consequential damages in connection with, or arising out of, the furnishing, performance, or use of these programs.

Printed in the United States of America

10 9 8 7 6 5 4 3 2 1

ISBN 0-13-101908-2

Prentice-Hall International (UK) Limited, *London*
Prentice-Hall of Australia Pty. Limited, *Sydney*
Prentice-Hall Canada Inc., *Toronto*
Prentice-Hall Hispanoamericana, S.A., *Mexico*
Prentice-Hall of India Private Limited, *New Delhi*
Prentice-Hall of Japan, Inc., *Tokyo*
Simon & Schuster Asia Pte. Ltd., *Singapore*
Editora Prentice-Hall do Brasil, Ltda., *Rio de Janeiro*

To Bhinna, whose memory will be forever in my heart,
to Rohan, for his laughter and enthusiasm,
and to Archana, for her love and encouragement.

Foreword

Peter H. Salus
Managing Editor—Computing Systems

There are more flavors of UNIX than of most brands of ice cream. Despite the industrial impetus on the part of X/Open and its members, the single UNIX specification appears to be ever-further from our grasp. In fact, it may not be an important goal. Ever since Interactive Systems produced the first commercial UNIX system and Whitesmiths produced the first UNIX clone, the user community has been confronted by a variety of implementations running on multiple platforms.

Created in 1969, UNIX was not even a decade old when versions began to proliferate. Before it was 20 years old, there were rival consortial (the Open Software Foundation and UNIX International) and a large number of versions. The two main streams were those of AT&T (now Novell) and the University of California at Berkeley. Descriptions of those UNIXes were made easily available by Maurice Bach [Bach 86] and Sam Leffler, Kirk McKusick, Mike Karels, and John Quarterman [Leff 89].

No single book offered the interested student a view of the UNIX Operating System's various implementations. Uresh Vahalia has now done this. He has gone boldly where none have gone before and elucidated the internals of SVR4, 4.4BSD, and Mach. Even more, he presents elaborate discussions of both Solaris and SunOS, Digital UNIX, and HP-UX.

He has done so clearly and without the bias that some writers have displayed toward this UNIX or that. With relatively new UNIX clones such as Linux already developing variants and even Berkeley derivatives diverging from one another, a book like this, which exposes the internals and principles that motivated UNIX's growth and popularity is of exceptional value.

On June 12, 1972, Ken Thompson and Dennis Ritchie released the *UNIX Programmer's Manual,* Second Edition. In its Preface the authors remark: "The number of UNIX installations has grown to 10, with more expected." They could never have expected what has actually happened.

I have traced the paleontology and history of the system elsewhere [Salu 94], but Vahalia has given us a truly original and comprehensive view of the comparative anatomy of the species.

References

[Bach 86]   Bach, M.J., *The Design of the UNIX Operating System,* Prentice-Hall, Englewood Cliffs, NJ, 1986.

[Leff 89]   Leffler, S.J., McKusick, M.K., Karels, M.J., and Quarterman, J.S., *The Design and Implementation of the 4.3 BSD UNIX Operating System,* Addison-Wesley, Reading, MA, 1989.

[Salu 94]   Salus, P.H., *A Quarter Century of UNIX,* Addison-Wesley, Reading, MA, 1994.

[Thom 72]   Thompson, K., and Ritchie, D.M., *UNIX Programmer's Manual,* Second Edition, Bell Telephone Laboratories, Murray Hill, NJ, 1972.

Preface

Since the early 1970s, the UNIX system has undergone considerable metamorphosis. It started as a small, experimental operating system distributed freely (almost) by Bell Telephone Laboratories to a growing band of loyal followers. Over the years, it absorbed contributions from numerous members of academia and industry, endured battles over ownership and standardization, and evolved into its current state as a stable, mature operating system. Today there are several commercial and research variants of the UNIX system, each different from the other in many respects, yet all similar enough to be recognizable as different members of the same family. A UNIX programmer who has gained experience on one specific UNIX system can be productive on a number of different hardware platforms and UNIX variants without skipping a beat.

Hundreds of books have described various features of the UNIX system. Although most of them describe user-visible aspects such as the command shell or the programming interface, only a small number of books discuss UNIX internals. UNIX internals refers to a study of the UNIX kernel, which comprises the heart of the operating system. To date, each book on UNIX internals has focused on one specific UNIX release. Bach's *The Design of the UNIX Operating System* [Bach 86] is a landmark book on the System V Release 2 (SVR2) kernel. Leffler et al.'s *The Design and Implementation of the 4.3BSD UNIX Operating System* [Leff 88] is a comprehensive description of the 4.3BSD release by some of its principal designers. Goodheart and Cox's *The Magic Garden Explained* [Good 94] describes the internals of System V Release 4.0 (SVR4).

Design Perspectives

This book views the UNIX kernel from a system design perspective. It describes a number of mainstream commercial and research UNIX variants. For each component of the kernel, the book explores its architecture and design, how the major UNIX systems have chosen to implement the component, and the advantages and drawbacks of alternative approaches. Such a comparative treatment gives the book a unique flavor and allows the reader to examine the system from a critical viewpoint. When studying an operating system, it is important to note both its strengths and its weaknesses. This is only possible by analyzing a number of alternatives.

UNIX Variants

Although this book gives most attention to SVR4.2, it also explores 4.4BSD, Solaris 2.*x*, Mach, and Digital UNIX in detail. Further, it describes interesting features of a number of other variants, including some research that has not yet made it into commercial releases. It analyzes the major developments in UNIX from the mid-1980s to the mid-1990s. For completeness it includes a brief description of traditional UNIX functionality and implementation. Where necessary, it provides an historical treatment, starting with the traditional approach, analyzing its drawbacks and limitations, and presenting the modern solutions.

Intended Audience

UNIX Internals is useful for university courses and as a professional reference. As a university text, it is suitable for an advanced undergraduate or graduate course on operating systems. It is not an introductory book and assumes knowledge of concepts such as the kernel, processes, and virtual memory. Each chapter contains a set of exercises designed to stimulate further thought and research, and to provide additional insight into the system design. Many of the exercises are open-ended, and some require additional reading on the part of the student. Each chapter also has an exhaustive list of references, which should be useful for the student seeking to explore further.

    UNIX Internals is also suitable as a professional reference for operating system developers, application programmers, and system administrators. Operating system designers and architects can use it to study the kernel architecture in contemporary systems, evaluate the relative merits and drawbacks of different designs, and use the insight to develop the next generation of operating systems. Application programmers can use the knowledge of the system internals to write more efficient programs that take better advantage of the characteristics of the operating system. Finally, system administrators can do a better job of configuring and tuning their systems by understanding how various parameters and usage patterns affect the system behavior.

Organization of the Book

Chapter 1, "Introduction," traces the evolution of the UNIX system and analyzes the factors that have influenced major changes in the system. Chapters 2 through 7 describe the process subsystem. In particular, Chapter 2 describes the process and kernel architecture in traditional UNIX systems (SVR3, 4.3BSD, and earlier variants). Chapters 3 through 7 describe features of modern UNIX systems such as SVR4, 4.4BSD, Solaris 2.*x,* and Digital UNIX. Chapter 3 discusses threads and how they are implemented in the kernel and in user libraries. Chapter 4 describes signals, job control, and login session management. Chapter 5 describes the UNIX scheduler and the growing support for real-time applications. Chapter 6 deals with interprocess communications (IPC), including the set of features known as System V IPC. It also describes the Mach architecture, which uses IPC as the fundamental primitive for structuring the kernel. Chapter 7 discusses the synchronization frameworks used in modern uniprocessor and multiprocessor systems.

The next four chapters explore file systems. Chapter 8 describes the file system interface as seen by the user, and the vnode/vfs interface that defines the interactions between the kernel and the file system. Chapter 9 provides details of some specific file system implementations, including the original System V file system (s5fs), the Berkeley Fast File System (FFS), and many small, special-purpose file systems that take advantage of the vnode/vfs interface to provide useful services. Chapter 10 describes a number of distributed file systems, namely Sun Microsystems' Network File System (NFS), AT&T's Remote File Sharing (RFS), Carnegie-Mellon University's Andrew File System (AFS), and Transarc Corporation's Distributed File System (DFS). Chapter 11 describes some advanced file systems that use journaling to provide higher availability and performance, and a new file system framework based on stackable vnode layers.

Chapters 12 through 15 describe memory management. Chapter 12 discusses kernel memory allocation and explores several interesting allocation algorithms. Chapter 13 introduces the notion of virtual memory and uses the 4.3BSD implementation to illustrate several issues. Chapter 14 describes the virtual memory architecture of SVR4 and Solaris. Chapter 15 describes the Mach and 4.4BSD memory models. It also analyzes the effects of hardware features such as translation look-aside buffers and virtually addressed caches.

The last two chapters address the I/O subsystem. Chapter 16 describes the device driver framework, the interaction between the kernel and the I/O subsystem, and the SVR4 device driver interface/driver kernel interface specification. Chapter 17 talks about the STREAMS framework for writing network protocols and network and terminal drivers.

Typographical Conventions

I have followed a small set of typographical conventions throughout this book. All system calls, library routines, and shell commands are in italics (for instance, *fork, fopen,* and *ls −l*). The first occurrence of any term or concept is also italicized. Names of internal kernel functions and variables, as well as all code examples, are in fixed-width font, such as `ufs_lookup()`. When specifying the calling syntax, the system call name is italicized, but the arguments are in fixed-width font. Finally, all file and directory names are in bold face (for instance, **/etc/passwd**). In the figures, solid arrows represent direct pointers, whereas a dashed arrow implies that the relationship between the source and destination of the arrow is inferred indirectly.

Despite my best efforts, some errors are inevitable. Please send me all corrections, comments, and suggestions by electronic mail at **vahalia@acm.org**.

Acknowledgments

A number of people deserve credit for this book. First of all, I want to thank my son, Rohan, and my wife, Archana, whose patience, love, and sacrifice made this book possible. Indeed, the hardest thing about writing the book was justifying to myself the weekends and evenings that could have been spent with them. They have shared my travails with a smile and have encouraged me every step of the way. I also thank my parents for their love and support.

Next, I want to thank my friend Subodh Bapat, who gave me the confidence to undertake this project. Subodh has helped me maintain focus throughout the project and has spent countless hours advising, counseling, and encouraging me. I owe him special thanks for access to the tools, templates, and macros used for his book, *Object-Oriented Networks* [Bapa 94], for his meticulous reviews of my drafts, and for his lucid discourses on writing style.

A number of reviewers contributed an incredible amount of their time and expertise to improve the book, going through several drafts and providing invaluable comments and suggestions. I want to thank Peter Salus, for his constant encouragement and support, and Benson Marguiles, Terry Lambert, Mark Ellis, and William Bully for their in-depth feedback on the content and organization of my work. I also thank Keith Bostic, Evi Nemeth, Pat Parseghian, Steven Rago, Margo Seltzer, Richard Stevens, and Lev Vaitzblit, who reviewed parts of my book.

I want to thank my manager, Percy Tzelnic, for his support and understanding throughout my project. Finally, I want to thank my publisher Alan Apt, both for proposing the book and for helping me at every stage, and the rest of the team at Prentice-Hall and at Spectrum Publisher Services, in particular, Shirley McGuire, Sondra Chavez, and Kelly Ricci, for their help and support.

References

[Bach 86]   Bach, M.J., *The Design of the UNIX Operating System,* Prentice-Hall, 1986.

[Bapa 94]   Bapat, S.G., *Object-Oriented Networks,* Prentice-Hall, 1994.

[Good 94]   Goodheart, B., and Cox, J., *The Magic Garden Explained—The Internals of UNIX System V Release 4, An Open Systems Design,* Prentice-Hall, 1994.

[Leff 89]   Leffler, S.J., McKusick, M.K., Karels, M.J., and Quarterman, J.S., *The Design and Implementation of the 4.3 BSD UNIX Operating System,* Addison-Wesley, 1989.

Contents

1

Introduction

1.1 Introduction

In 1994 the computer industry celebrated the twenty-fifth birthday of the UNIX operating system. Since its inception in 1969, the UNIX system has been ported to dozens of hardware platforms, and has been released in many forms by commercial vendors, universities, and research organizations. Starting as a small collection of programs, it has grown into a versatile operating system used in a wide range of environments and applications. Today, versions of UNIX run on platforms ranging from small embedded processors, to workstations and desktop systems, to high-performance multi-processor systems serving a large community of users.

The UNIX system consists of a collection of user programs, libraries, and utilities, running on the UNIX operating system, which provides a run-time environment and system services for these applications. This book examines the design and implementation of the operating system itself, and does not describe the applications and tools that run on it. While UNIX began life in Bell Telephone Laboratories (BTL), which was responsible for all its early releases, it has since been embraced by several companies and universities. This has led to a proliferation of UNIX variants in the marketplace. All these variants loosely support a core set of interfaces, applications, and features routinely expected from a "UNIX system." They differ in their internal implementation, detailed semantics of the interfaces, and the set of "value-added" features they provide. This book devotes greater attention to baseline releases such as Novell, Inc.'s *System V Release 4 (SVR4),* The University of California's *Berkeley Software Distribution (4.xBSD),* and Carnegie-Mellon University's *Mach.* It also discusses a number of commercial implementations such as *SunOS* and *Solaris* from

Sun Microsystems, *Digital UNIX* from Digital Equipment Corporation, and *HP-UX* from Hewlett-Packard Corporation.

This chapter introduces the UNIX operating system. It begins with a brief history of the birth, maturation, and industry acceptance of the UNIX system. It then discusses the factors that have influenced the evolution of the system. Finally it discusses directions in which UNIX may continue to evolve.

1.1.1   A Brief History

Before embarking on a detailed study of the design of the UNIX system, it is useful to review its history and evolution. In the following sections, we trace the growth of the UNIX system from its modest beginnings with AT&T to its current, somewhat chaotic, state as a multiplatform, multivendor, and multivariant group of operating systems. There are several excellent sources that provide a more detailed history, such as *A Quarter Century of UNIX* by Peter Salus [Salu 94]. This chapter summarizes the important events.

1.1.2   The Beginning

In the late 1960s Bell Telephone Laboratories was involved in a project with General Electric and the Massachusetts Institute of Technology to develop a multiuser operating system called *Multics* [Orga 72]. When the Multics project was canceled in March 1969, some of its principal developers at BTL were searching for other interesting projects to pursue. One of them, Ken Thompson, wrote a game program called *Space Travel* and found a little-used *PDP-7* computer (manufactured by Digital Equipment Corporation) on which to run it. The PDP-7 lacked a program development environment. Thompson had to cross-assemble the program on a different machine, a Honeywell 635 running the *GECOS* operating system, and then hand carry the program on paper tape to the PDP-7.

To facilitate the development of Space Travel, Thompson, along with Dennis Ritchie, began developing an operating environment for the PDP-7. The first component was a simple file system, which evolved into an early version of what is now known as the *System V file system (s5fs)*. They soon added a process subsystem, a simple command interpreter called the *shell* (which evolved into the Bourne shell [Bour 78]), and a small set of utilities. The system became self-supporting, and did not need the GECOS environment. They named this new system *UNIX* as a pun on the name Multics.

The following year Thompson, Ritchie, and Joseph Ossanna persuaded BTL to purchase Digital's *PDP-11* machine to use as a text-processing system for the patent department at BTL. They ported UNIX to the PDP-11, and added several text-processing utilities including the *ed* editor and versions of the *runoff* text rendering tool. Thompson also developed a new language called *B* (an offshoot of an earlier language called *BCPL* [Rich 82]) and used it to write some early assemblers and utilities. B was an interpretive language, and hence suffered from poor performance. Eventually, Ritchie evolved it into the *C* language, which was compilable and supported data types and data structures. The success of *C* has far surpassed that of UNIX.

UNIX became popular within BTL, and many others contributed to its development. In November 1971, Ritchie and Thompson, urged by Doug McIlroy, published the first edition of the

UNIX Programmer's Manual. Since then, there have been a total of ten editions of this manual, corresponding to ten versions of UNIX released by BTL.

The first several releases were strictly internal to BTL. The third edition, in February 1973, included *cc,* the *C* compiler. That same year, UNIX was rewritten in *C* (resulting in version 4 in November 1973), a step that had a tremendous impact on its future success. Thompson and Ritchie co-authored the first UNIX paper, *The UNIX Time Sharing System* [Thom 74]. It was presented at the *ACM Symposium on Operating Systems (SOSP)* in October 1973 and published in the *Communications of the ACM* in July 1974.[1] This paper gave the outside world its first look at UNIX.

1.1.3   Proliferation

In 1956, as a result of antitrust litigation by the Department of Justice against AT&T and the Western Electric Company,[2] AT&T signed a "consent decree" with the federal government. The terms of this agreement prevented AT&T from manufacturing any equipment not related to telephone or telegraph services, or engaging in business other than furnishing "common carrier communication services."

As a result, AT&T took the view that it could not market computing products. On the other hand, the SOSP presentation resulted in numerous requests for UNIX software and sources. AT&T provided the UNIX system to universities for educational and research purposes, royalty-free and under simple licensing agreements. It did not advertise or market the system and did not support its releases. One of the earliest such licensees was the University of California at Berkeley, which obtained the UNIX system in December 1973.

Under these conditions UNIX systems quickly proliferated throughout the world. By 1975 they had spread to sites as far apart as the Hebrew University of Jerusalem, the University of New South Wales in Australia, and the University of Toronto in Canada. The first UNIX port was to the *Interdata* machine. The port was completed independently by the University of Wollongong in 1976, and again by Ritchie and Steve Johnson at BTL in 1977.

Version 7 UNIX, released in January 1979, was the first truly portable UNIX system, and greatly influenced future development of UNIX. Its initial release ran on the PDP-11 and the Interdata 8/32. It was both more robust and provided significantly greater functionality than version 6; it was also considerably slower. Several UNIX licensees responded by improving its performance in several areas; AT&T incorporated many of these improvements in future releases. This spirit of co-operation between its keepers and users (which, unfortunately, deteriorated considerably once UNIX became commercially successful) was a key factor in the rapid growth and rising popularity of UNIX.

Soon UNIX was ported to several other architectures. Microsoft Corporation and the Santa Cruz Operation (SCO) collaborated to port UNIX to the Intel 8086, resulting in *XENIX,* one of the earliest commercial UNIX variants. In 1978 Digital introduced the 32-bit VAX-11 computer. After being turned down by Ritchie, Thompson, and Johnson, Digital approached a group in the Holmdel, New Jersey, branch of BTL to port UNIX to the VAX. This was the first port to a 32-bit machine,

---

[1]   It was later revised and reprinted as [Ritc 78].

[2]   Western Electric was a wholly owned subsidiary of AT&T that was later dissolved. Bell Telephone Laboratories was jointly owned by AT&T and Western Electric.

and the resulting version was called *UNIX/32V*. This version was sent to the University of California at Berkeley, where it evolved into *3BSD* in 1979.

1.1.4   BSD

The University of California at Berkeley obtained one of the first UNIX licenses in December 1974. Over the next few years, a group of graduate students including Bill Joy and Chuck Haley developed several utilities for it, including the *ex* editor (which was later followed by *vi*) and a Pascal compiler. They bundled these additions into a package called the *Berkeley Software Distribution (BSD)* and sold it in the spring of 1978 at $50 per license. The initial BSD releases (version 2 was shipped in late 1978) consisted solely of applications and utilities, and did not modify or redistribute the operating system. One of Joy's early contributions was the *C shell* [Joy 86], which provided facilities such as job control and command history not available in the Bourne shell.

In 1978 Berkeley obtained a VAX-11/780 and the UNIX/32V that had been ported to it by the BTL group in Holmdel, New Jersey. The VAX had a 32-bit architecture, allowing a 4-gigabyte address space, but only 2 megabytes of physical memory. Around the same time, Ozalp Babaoglu designed a paging-based virtual memory system for the VAX, and incorporated it into UNIX. The result, released as 3BSD in late 1979, was the first operating system release from Berkeley.

The virtual memory work prompted the Defense Advanced Research Projects Agency (DARPA) to fund the development of UNIX systems at Berkeley. One of the major goals of the DARPA project was to integrate the Transmission Control Protocol/Internet Protocol *(TCP/IP)* network protocol suite. With DARPA funding, Berkeley produced several BSD releases collectively called *4BSD: 4.0BSD* in 1980, *4.1BSD* in 1981,[3] *4.2BSD* in 1983, *4.3BSD* in 1986, and *4.4BSD* in 1993.

The Berkeley team was responsible for many important technical contributions. Besides virtual memory and the incorporation of TCP/IP, BSD UNIX introduced the *Fast File System (FFS)*, a reliable signals implementation, and the sockets facility. 4.4BSD replaced the original virtual memory design with a new version based on Mach (see Section 1.1.7), and added other enhancements such as a log-structured file system.

The work on UNIX at Berkeley was performed by the Computer Science Research Group (CSRG). With 4.4BSD, CSRG decided to close shop and discontinue UNIX development. The major reasons cited [Bost 93] were:

- Scarcity of grants and funds.
- BSD features were now available in a number of commercial systems.
- The system had become too large and complex for a small group to architect and maintain.

A company called Berkeley Software Design, Inc. (BSDI) was formed to commercialize and market 4.4BSD. Since most of the original UNIX source code had been replaced with new code developed at Berkeley, BSDI claimed that the source code in its *BSD/386* release was completely free of AT&T licenses. UNIX System Laboratories, the AT&T subsidiary responsible for UNIX development, filed a lawsuit against BSDI and the Regents of the University of California, claiming

---

3   There were three separate releases of 4.1BSD—4.1a, 4.1b, and 4.1c.

copyright infringement, breach of contract, and misappropriation of trade secrets [Gerb 92]. The lawsuit was sparked by BSDI's use of the phone number 1-800-ITS-UNIX to sell the source code. The university countersued, and the resulting litigation delayed the release. On February 4, 1994, the case was settled out of court, with all parties dropping their claims. BSDI announced the availability of *4.4BSD-lite*, sold with unencumbered source code, for around $1000.

1.1.5   System V

Going back to AT&T, its legal battles with the Justice Department culminated in a landmark decree in 1982. As a result of this decree, Western Electric was dissolved, the regional operating companies were divested from AT&T and formed the "Baby Bells," and Bell Telephone Laboratories was separated and renamed AT&T Bell Laboratories. Also, AT&T was allowed to enter the computer business.

While the research group at BTL continued to work on UNIX, the responsibility for external releases shifted from them to the UNIX Support Group, then to the UNIX System Development Group, and then to AT&T Information Systems. Among them, these groups released *System III* in 1982, *System V* in 1983, *System V Release 2 (SVR2)* in 1984, and *Release 3 (SVR3)* in 1987. AT&T marketed System V aggressively, and several commercial UNIX implementations are based on it.

System V UNIX introduced many new features and facilities. Its virtual memory implementation, called the *regions* architecture, was quite different from that of BSD. SVR3 introduced an interprocess communication facility (including shared memory, semaphores, and message queues), remote file sharing, shared libraries, and the *STREAMS* framework for device drivers and network protocols. The latest System V version is *Release 4 (SVR4),* which will be discussed in Section 1.1.10.

1.1.6   Commercialization

The growing popularity of UNIX attracted the interest of several computer companies, who rushed to commercialize and market their own versions of UNIX. Each began with a base release of UNIX from either AT&T or Berkeley, ported it to their hardware, and enhanced it with their own *value-added* features. In 1977 Interactive Systems became the first commercial UNIX vendor. Their first release was called *IS/1* and ran on the PDP-11s.

In 1982 Bill Joy left Berkeley to cofound Sun Microsystems, which released a 4.2BSD-based variant called *SunOS* (and later, an SVR4-based variant called *Solaris*). Microsoft and the SCO jointly released XENIX. Later, SCO ported SVR3 onto the 386 and released it as SCO UNIX. The 1980s saw a number of commercial offerings, including *AIX* from IBM, *HP-UX* from Hewlett-Packard Corporation, and *ULTRIX* (followed by *DEC OSF/1,* later renamed to *Digital UNIX*) from Digital.

The commercial variants introduced many new features, some of which were subsequently incorporated in newer releases of the baseline systems. SunOS introduced the *Network File System (NFS),* the *vnode/vfs interface* to support multiple file system types, and a new virtual memory architecture that was adopted by SVR4. AIX was among the first to provide a commercial journaling file system for UNIX. ULTRIX was one of the first multiprocessor UNIX systems.

1.1.7   Mach

A major reason for the popularity of the UNIX system was that it was small and simple, yet offered many useful facilities. As the system incorporated more and more features, the kernel became large, complex, and increasingly unwieldy. Many people felt that UNIX was moving away from the principles that had made it elegant and successful.

In the mid-1980s researchers at Carnegie-Mellon University in Pittsburgh, PA, began working on a new operating system called *Mach* [Acce 86]. Their objective was to develop a *microkernel,* which provides a small set of essential services and a framework for implementing other operating system functions at the user level. The Mach architecture would support the UNIX programming interface, run on uniprocessor and multiprocessor systems, and be suitable for a distributed environment. By starting afresh, they hoped to avoid many of the problems afflicting UNIX at the time.

The basic approach was to have the microkernel export a few simple abstractions, and to provide most of the functionality through a collection of user-level tasks called *servers*. Mach held another advantage—it was unencumbered by AT&T licenses, making it attractive to many vendors. *Mach 2.5* is the most popular release, and commercial systems like *OSF/1* and *NextStep* have been based on it. The early versions of Mach featured monolithic kernels, with a higher-level layer providing a 4BSD UNIX interface. *Mach 3.0* was the first microkernel implementation.

1.1.8   Standards

The proliferation of UNIX variants led to several compatibility problems. While all variants "looked like UNIX" from a distance, they differed in many important respects. Initially, the industry was torn by differences between AT&T's System V releases (the official UNIX), and the BSD releases from Berkeley. The introduction of commercial variants worsened the situation.

System V and 4BSD differ in many ways—they have different, incompatible physical file systems, networking frameworks, and virtual memory architectures. Some of the differences are restricted to kernel design and implementation, but others manifest themselves at the programming interface level. It is not possible to write a complex application that will run unmodified on System V and BSD systems.

The commercial variants were each derived from either System V or BSD, and then augmented with value-added features. These extra features were often inherently unportable. As a result, the application programmers were often very confused, and spent inordinate amounts of effort making sure their programs worked on all the different flavors of UNIX.

This led to a push for a standard set of interfaces, and several groups began working on them. The resulting standards were almost as numerous and diverse as the UNIX variants. Eventually, most vendors agreed upon a few standards. These include the *System V Interface Definition (SVID)* from AT&T, the IEEE *POSIX* specifications, and the *X/Open Portability Guide* from the X/Open Consortium.

Each standard deals with the interface between the programmer and the operating system, and not with how the system implements the interface. It defines a set of functions and their detailed semantics. Compliant systems must meet these specifications, but may implement the functions either in the kernel, or in user-level libraries.

The standards deal with a subset of the functions provided by most UNIX systems. Theoretically, if programmers restrict themselves to using this subset, the resulting application should be portable to any system that complies with the standard. This precludes the programmer from taking advantage of added features of a particular variant, or making optimizations based on specific hardware or operating system peculiarities, without compromising the portability of the code.

The SVID is essentially a detailed specification of the System V programming interface. AT&T published three versions—*SVID, SVID2,* and *SVID3* [AT&T 89], corresponding to SVR2, SVR3, and SVR4, respectively. They allowed vendors to call their operating systems "System V" only if they conformed to the SVID. AT&T also published the *System V Verification Suite (SVVS),* which verifies if a system conforms to the SVID.

In 1986 the IEEE appointed a committee to publish a formal standard for operating system environments. They adopted the name POSIX (Portable Operating Systems based on UNIX), and their standard approximates an amalgam of the core parts of SVR3 and 4.3BSD UNIX. The *POSIX1003.1* standard, commonly known as *POSIX.1,* was published in 1990 [IEEE 90]. It has gained wide acceptance, in part because it does not align itself closely with a single UNIX variant.

X/Open is a consortium of international computer vendors. It was formed in 1984, not to produce new standards, but to develop an open *Common Applications Environment (CAE)* based on existing *de facto* standards. It published a seven-volume *X/Open Portability Guide (XPG),* whose latest release is *Issue 4* in 1993 [XPG4 93]. It is based on a draft of the POSIX.1 standard, but goes beyond it by addressing many additional areas such as internationalization, window interfaces, and data management.

1.1.9   OSF and UI

In 1987 AT&T, facing a public outcry against its licensing policies, announced the purchase of 20% of Sun Microsystems. AT&T and Sun planned to collaborate in the development of SVR4, the next release of AT&T's System V UNIX. AT&T said that Sun would receive preferential treatment, and Sun announced that unlike SunOS, which was based on 4BSD, their next operating system would be based on SVR4.

This produced a strong reaction from other UNIX vendors, who feared that this would give Sun an unfair advantage. In response, a group of major companies, including Digital, IBM, HP, Apollo, and others, joined hands in 1988 to announce the formation of the Open Software Foundation (OSF). OSF would be funded by its founder companies, and chartered to develop an operating system, user environment, and a distributed computing environment, all of which would eventually be free of AT&T license encumbrances. It would make *Requests for Technology (RFT)* from its members, and choose the best solutions from those submitted, through a vendor-neutral process.

In retaliation, AT&T and Sun, along with other vendors of System V-based systems, immediately formed an organization called UNIX International (UI). UI was dedicated to marketing SVR4, and was supposed to define the direction of UNIX System V. In 1990 UI released the *UNIX System V Road Map,* which outlined the future directions for UNIX development.

In 1989 OSF released a graphical user interface called *Motif,* which was very well received. Soon after, it released initial versions of its operating system, called *OSF/1*. The first release of OSF/1 was based on Mach 2.5, with 4.3BSD compatibility and some features of IBM's AIX operating system. It contained many advanced features not found in SVR4, such as complete multiprocessor support, dynamic loading, and logical volume management. The plan was for its founding members to develop commercial operating systems based on OSF/1.

OSF and UI began as great rivals, but were quickly faced with a common outside threat. The economic downturn in the early 1990s, along with the surge of Microsoft Windows, jeopardized the growth, and even survival, of UNIX. UI went out of business in 1993, and OSF abandoned many of its ambitious plans (such as the Distributed Management Environment). *DEC OSF/1,* released by Digital in 1993, was the only major commercial system based on OSF/1. Over time, though, Digital removed many OSF/1 dependencies from their operating system, and in 1995, changed its name to *Digital UNIX.*

1.1.10   SVR4 and Beyond

AT&T and Sun jointly developed System V Release 4 (SVR4), first released in 1989. SVR4 integrated features from SVR3, 4BSD, SunOS, and XENIX. It also added new functionality, such as real-time scheduling classes, the *Korn shell,* and enhancements to the STREAMS subsystem. The following year, AT&T formed a software company called UNIX Systems Laboratories (USL) to develop and sell UNIX.

In 1991 Novell, Inc., maker of the PC-based network operating system called Netware, purchased part of USL, and formed a joint venture called Univel. Univel was chartered to develop a desktop version of SVR4, integrated with Netware. This system, known as *UnixWare,* was released in late 1992. Since then, there have been several newer releases of SVR4. The latest, *SVR4.2/ES/MP,* provides enhanced security and multiprocessor support.

In 1993 AT&T sold the rest of its interest in USL to Novell. Later that year, Novell released the UNIX trademark and conformance certification to X/Open. In 1994, Sun Microsystems bought the right to use SVR4 code from Novell, freeing themselves of royalty and conformance requirements. Sun's SVR4-based release is called *Solaris.* Its latest revision is *Solaris 2.5.* Solaris provides many advanced features including a fully preemptible, multithreaded kernel, and comprehensive support for multiprocessors.

1.2   The Mandate for Change

UNIX has evolved considerably in the past twenty-five years. What started as a basic operating environment for a small group in a laboratory has now evolved into a major operating system, marketed in various flavors by numerous vendors. It is used on a wide variety of systems ranging from small, embedded controllers to huge mainframes and massively parallel systems. It is used in a wide variety of application domains—in offices as a desktop system, in the financial world to manage large databases, or in particle physics laboratories for high-speed number crunching.

The UNIX system has had to change and grow considerably to meet the new challenges it has faced. While it is now a mature operating system, it is not immune to further change. This ongoing evolution does not imply a poor initial design. On the contrary, the ease with which new technology has been incorporated into the UNIX system is a tribute to its original architecture. Rather than having preconceived and inflexible notions about the purpose, form, and functions of the operating system, its originators began with a simple, extensible framework that was built upon incrementally by contributions from all over—from the industry, academia, and enthusiastic users.

It is useful to examine the factors that motivate change and growth in an operating system. In this section we look at the main factors that have influenced the growth of the UNIX system, and speculate about the direction of its future growth.

1.2.1 Functionality

The biggest motivation for change is adding new features to the system. In the beginning, new functionality was provided mainly by adding user-level tools and utilities. As the system matured, its developers added many features to the UNIX kernel itself.

Much of the new functionality helps support more complex programs. The primary example is the System V Interprocess Communications (IPC) suite, consisting of shared memory, semaphores, and message queues. Together, they allow cooperating processes to share data, exchange messages, and synchronize their actions. Most modern UNIX systems also provide several levels of support for writing multithreaded applications.

IPC and threads help the development of complex applications, such as those based on a client-server model. In such programs, the server usually sits in a loop, waiting for client requests. When a request arrives, the server processes it and waits for the next one. Since the server may have to service several clients, it is desirable to handle multiple requests concurrently. With IPC, the server may use a different process for each request, and these processes can share data and synchronize with one another. A multithreaded system can allow the server to be implemented as a single process with multiple, concurrently executing threads sharing a common address space.

Perhaps the most visible part of an operating system is its file system, which too has incorporated many new features. These include support for first-in, first-out (FIFO) files, symbolic links, and files larger than a disk partition. Modern UNIX systems support file and byte-range locks, access-control lists, and per-user disk quotas.

1.2.2 Networking

The part of the kernel that has undergone the greatest change is the networking subsystem. The early UNIX systems ran standalone and could not communicate with other machines. The proliferation of computer networks made it imperative for UNIX to support them. The first major undertaking was at Berkeley, where DARPA funded the project to integrate the TCP/IP suite into 4BSD. Today UNIX systems support a number of network interfaces (such as ethernet, FDDI, and ATM), protocols (such as TCP/IP, UDP/IP,[4] and SNA[5]), and frameworks (such as sockets and STREAMS).

The ability to connect to other machines impacted the system in many ways. Soon users wanted to share files among connected machines and run programs on remote nodes. To meet this challenge, UNIX systems evolved in three directions:

---

[4] User Datagram Protocol/Internet Protocol.
[5] IBM's System Network Architecture.

- Many new distributed file systems were developed, which allow almost transparent access to files on remote nodes. The most successful of these are Sun Microsystems' *Network File System (NFS),* Carnegie-Mellon University's *Andrew File System (AFS),* and Transarc Corporation's *Distributed File System (DFS).*

- A number of distributed services allow sharing of information in a network. These are normally implemented as user-level programs based on a client-server model, and use remote procedure calls to invoke operations on other machines. Some examples are Sun Microsystems' *Network Information Service (NIS)* and the Open Software Foundation's *Distributed Computing Environment (DCE).*

- Distributed operating systems such as Mach, *Chorus,* and *Sprite* provided varying amounts of UNIX compatibility and were marketed as base technologies on which to build future versions of distributed UNIX systems.

1.2.3   Performance

Improving system performance is a constant motivation for change. Competing UNIX vendors make great efforts to demonstrate or claim that their system performs better than that of their rivals. Nearly every kernel subsystem has seen major changes solely to improve performance.

In the early 1980s Berkeley introduced the Fast File System, which took advantage of intelligent disk block allocation policies to improve performance. Faster file systems followed, using extent-based allocation and journaling techniques. Performance improvements also motivated many developments in the areas of interprocess communications, memory management, and multi-threaded processes. One processor was insufficient for many applications, and vendors developed multiprocessor UNIX systems, some with hundreds of CPUs.

1.2.4   Hardware Changes

UNIX systems must keep up with new advances in computer hardware technology. Often this means porting the operating system to newer and faster processors. Since UNIX is largely written in C, the port is relatively easy. In recent years developers have expended considerable effort in isolating hardware-dependent code into separate modules, so that only those modules need be changed when porting to a new machine. Usually these modules deal with interrupt handling, virtual address translation, context switching, and device drivers.

In some cases, the operating system requires major surgery to run on the new hardware. The most obvious case is with multiprocessor systems. The traditional UNIX kernel is designed to run on a single processor and lacks the ability to protect its data structures from concurrent access by multiple processors. Several vendors have developed multiprocessor UNIX systems. Many have taken a traditional UNIX kernel and added locks to protect global data structures. This approach is called parallelization. A few others have built new kernels from the ground up and integrated existing subsystems using the new primitives.

At a more subtle level, an imbalance in the rate of progress of different hardware technologies has profound influence on the operating system design. Since the first UNIX system was built for the PDP-7, the CPU speed of an average UNIX machine has increased by a factor of about a hundred. Memory sizes and the disk space per user have grown by more than a factor of twenty. Memory and disk speeds, on the other hand, have barely doubled.

In the 1970s, UNIX performance was limited by the processor speed and memory size. Hence the UNIX kernel made heavy use of techniques such as swapping and (later) paging to juggle a number of processes in the small memory. As time progressed, memory and CPU speed became less of an issue, and the system became I/O-bound, spending much of its time moving pages between the disks and main memory. This provoked considerable research in file system, storage, and virtual memory architectures to reduce the disk bottleneck, leading to the invention of *Redundant Arrays of Inexpensive Disks (RAID)* and the proliferation of log-structured file systems.

1.2.5   Quality Improvement

Functionality and speed are of little use if the system is error-prone. Many changes have been motivated by the need to make the system more robust and to allow existing software to work better and more reliably.

The initial signal mechanism was unreliable and deficient in many respects. First Berkeley and then AT&T revised this implementation to provide a robust signaling facility, aptly known as *reliable signals*.

Both the System V and the BSD file systems were vulnerable to system crashes. UNIX systems buffer data in memory rather than write all changes synchronously to disk. Consequently, they may lose some data in the event of a crash and leave the file system in an inconsistent state. Traditionally, UNIX provides a utility called *fsck(8)*, which examines and repairs damaged file systems. This is a time-consuming operation, which may require tens of minutes for a large server with many disks. Many modern UNIX systems provide file systems that use a technique called journaling to eliminate the need for *fsck*, thereby increasing system availability and robustness.

1.2.6   Paradigm Shifts

The last three decades have seen major changes in the ways in which people use computers. In the 1970s the typical configuration was a large, centralized computer, about the size of a room, supporting many users through terminals connected over serial lines. The system was time-sharing—the computer distributed CPU time among all its users. User terminals were "dumb," providing little more than a text-based display system.

The 1980s witnessed the rise of the *workstation*, with a high-speed, bitmapped display and the ability to divide it into multiple windows, each running a UNIX shell. This provided an ideal facility for interactive use, and enough processing power for running typical user applications. The workstation was normally used by one user at a time, though it could support multiple users. High-speed networks allowed workstations to communicate with each other and with other computers.

Soon a new model of computing was born, known as *client-server computing*. One or more powerful, centralized machines, known as *servers,* provide a variety of services to individual workstations, or *clients*. *File servers* provide common storage for user files, and users access them through a number of different protocols. *Compute servers* are machines with one or more powerful processors to which users can submit batch jobs involving extensive computations (such as scientific number-crunching applications). *Database servers* run a database engine and handle queries and transactions submitted by clients. The servers are powerful, high-end machines with fast processors, and plenty of memory and disk space. The client workstations have relatively less processing power, memory, and storage, but have good display and interactive features.

As workstations grew more powerful, the differences between clients and servers began to blur. Moreover, centralizing important services on a small number of servers led to network congestion and server overload. The result was one more paradigm shift, this time to *distributed computing*. In this model, a number of machines collaborated to provide a network-based service. For instance, each node might have a local file system, which it makes available to other nodes. Hence each node acts as a server for its local files, and a client for files on other nodes. This avoids network congestion and single points of failure.

The UNIX system has adapted to the different models of computing. For instance, early UNIX releases had only a local file system. The support for network protocols was followed by the development of distributed file systems. Some of these, such as early versions of AFS, required centralized, dedicated servers. In time, they evolved into distributed file systems, where a single machine could be both a client and a server.

1.2.7   Other Application Domains

The UNIX system was designed initially for simple, time-sharing environments such as research laboratories and universities. It allowed a number of users to run simple programs such as text processing, editing, and numerical computations. As UNIX became successful, people tried to use it for a much wider range of applications. In the early 1990s UNIX was used in particle physics and aerospace laboratories, multimedia workstations running audio and video applications, and embedded controllers for mission-critical systems.

Each application domain placed different types of requirements on the UNIX system, which had to incorporate several changes to meet these demands. Multimedia and embedded applications required guarantees of resource availability and bounded response times. Scientific applications required simultaneous use of a number of processors. This led to the introduction of several real-time features in modern UNIX systems, such as fixed-priority processes, gang scheduling of processors, and the ability to lock data in memory.

1.2.8   Small is Beautiful

One of the greatest virtues of the original UNIX system was that it was small, simple, and had a small set of basic abstractions. The basic paradigm was to provide simple tools that could be combined in flexible ways using facilities such as pipes. The traditional UNIX kernel, however, was monolithic and not easily extensible. As more functionality was added, it became larger and more complex, growing from less than a hundred thousand bytes to several megabytes in size. Vendors and users ignored this at first, since computer memories were also increasing. It was more of a problem on low-end platforms, and made UNIX less viable for small personal computers and laptop systems.

Many people felt that the change was not entirely for the better, and that the system had become large, cluttered, and disorganized. This led to many efforts to rewrite the system, or to write a new operating system that was based on the original UNIX philosophy, but was more extensible and modular. The most successful of these was Mach, which was the basis of commercial implementations such as OSF/1 and NextStep. Mach migrated to a microkernel architecture (see Section 1.1.7), in which a small kernel provides the framework for running programs, and user-level server tasks provide other functions.

Efforts at controlling the kernel size have been only moderately successful. Microkernels have never been able to provide performance comparable to the traditional, monolithic kernel, primarily due to the overhead of message passing. Some less ambitious efforts have been more beneficial, such as modularization (see Section 1.2.9), pageable kernels, and dynamic loading, which allows some components to be loaded into and out of the kernel as necessary.

1.2.9   Flexibility

In the 1970s and the early 1980s UNIX kernels were not very versatile. They supported a single type of file system, scheduling policy, and executable file format (Figure 1-1). The only flexibility was offered by the block and character device switches, which allow different types of devices to be accessed through a common interface. The development of distributed file systems in the mid-1980s made it essential for UNIX systems to support both remote and local file systems. Similarly, features such as shared libraries required different executable file formats. The UNIX system had to support these new formats, as well as the traditional *a.out* format for compatibility. The coexistence of multimedia and real-time applications with normal interactive programs required scheduler support for different classes of applications.

In summary, the broadening use of UNIX systems required a more flexible operating system that could support several different methods of performing the same task. This need instigated the development of many flexible frameworks, such as the vnode/vfs interface, *exec* switch, scheduling classes, and segment-based memory architecture. The modern UNIX kernel is very similar to the system shown in Figure 1-2. Each of the outer circles represents an interface that may be implemented in a number of ways.

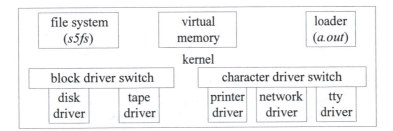

Figure 1-1. Traditional UNIX kernel.

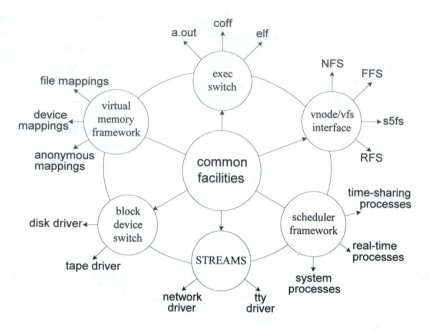

Figure 1-2. Modern UNIX kernel.

1.3   Looking Back, Looking Forward

The UNIX system advanced greatly since its inception. Despite its humble beginnings, it has become extremely popular. In the mid-to-late 1980s, it became the operating system of choice for a
wide variety of commercial, university, and research environments. Often, the only serious choice
buyers faced was which flavor of UNIX to buy. Lately, its position of eminence has been challenged
by Microsoft's *Windows* and *Windows/NT* operating systems. In the low-end, desktop market,
UNIX appears to have lost the battle. In this section, we examine the reasons for its success and
popularity, as well as the factors that have prevented its domination of the computer world.

1.3.1   What was Good about UNIX?

UNIX became enormously successful, probably much more so than its creators envisioned. One of
the primary reasons for its success was the way in which it was initially distributed. Bound by the
consent decree, AT&T chose to give away UNIX licenses and source code for very low fees. This
encouraged people from all parts of the world to acquire and run the system. Since the source code
was available as well, the users experimented with it, improved it, and told others about their
changes. AT&T incorporated many of these changes into its future releases.

The efforts at Berkeley furthered this trend. Overall, UNIX evolved through an extremely open process (or lack of process). Contributions to the operating system came from academia, industry, and enthusiastic hackers from several different countries and continents. Even when UNIX became commercialized, many vendors recognized the value of open systems and made their innovations accessible to others, creating open specifications such as NFS.

The original UNIX system was very well designed and formed a successful basis for a number of later versions and offshoots. One of its greatest strengths was its adherence to the "Small is Beautiful" philosophy [Allm 87]. A small kernel provided a minimal set of essential services. Small utilities performed simple manipulations of data. The *pipe* mechanism, along with the programmable shell, allowed users to combine these utilities in many different ways to create powerful tools.

The UNIX file system exemplified the small, simple approach. Unlike other contemporary operating systems, which had complex file access methods such as *Indexed Sequential Access Method (ISAM)* or *Hierarchical Sequential Access Method (HSAM)*, UNIX treated files as merely a sequence of bytes. Applications could impose any structure on the file's contents and devise their own access methods, without the file system getting in their way.

Most system applications used lines of text to represent their data. For instance, important system databases such as the **/etc/passwd**, **/etc/fstab**, and **/etc/ttys** files were ordinary text files. While it may have been more efficient to store the information in structured, binary format, the text representation allowed users to read and manipulate these files without special tools. Text is a familiar, universal, and highly portable data form, easily manipulated by a variety of utilities.

Another outstanding feature of UNIX was its simple, uniform interface to I/O devices. By representing all devices as files, UNIX allows the user to use the same set of commands and system calls to manipulate and access devices as well as files. Developers can write programs that perform I/O without having to check if the I/O is performed to a file, user terminal, printer, or other device. This, along with the I/O redirection features of the shell, provides a simple and powerful I/O interface.

A key to the success and proliferation of UNIX is its portability. The bulk of the kernel is written in the C language. This allows it to be ported to new machines with relatively little effort. It was first available on the popular PDP-11, and then ported to the VAX-11, also a popular machine. Many vendors could develop new machines and simply port UNIX to them, rather than having to write new operating systems.

1.3.2 What is Wrong with UNIX?

There are two sides to every picture. While it is nice to extol the virtues of UNIX, it is important not to lose sight of its drawbacks. One of the most objective reviews of UNIX came from none other than Dennis Ritchie himself. Speaking at a UNIX Retrospective session at the January 1987 USENIX conference, Ritchie analyzed many of its drawbacks [Ritc 87], which are summarized below.

Although UNIX was initially a simple system, it did not remain that way. For instance, AT&T added the standard I/O library to buffer data for efficiency and to make programs portable to non-UNIX systems. The library grew more complex than the underlying system call interface. For example, while the *read* and *write* system calls are atomic (indivisible) operations on the file, the buffering in the I/O library loses the atomicity.

While UNIX is an excellent operating system, most users want not an operating system, but simply the ability to do a particular task. These users are not interested in the elegance of the underlying file system structure or process model. They want to run specific applications (such as editors, financial packages, drawing programs) with a minimum of expense and bother. The lack of a simple, uniform (and preferably graphical) user interface in early UNIX systems was a major deterrent to its acceptance among the masses. In Ritchie's words, "*UNIX is simple and coherent, but it takes a genius (or at any rate, a programmer) to understand and appreciate its simplicity.*"

The building-block approach to tools is as much a bane as it is a boon. While elegant and aesthetically pleasing, it requires creativity and imagination to use effectively. Many users prefer the integrated, do-it-all programs such as those available for personal computers.

In some ways UNIX was a victim of its own success. Its simple licensing terms and portability encouraged uncontrolled growth and proliferation. As people tinkered with the system, each group changed it in a different way, often with incompatible results. At first there were two major strains—AT&T and BSD, each with a different file system, memory architecture, and signal and terminal handling framework. Soon many vendors released their own variants, trying for some level of compatibility with both AT&T and BSD versions. The situation became more chaotic, and many application developers had to spend great effort porting their programs to all the different flavors of UNIX.

The standardization efforts were only partly successful, since they met with opposition from the very people contributing to the process. This is because vendors needed to add unique features for "product differentiation," to show that their product was different from, and superior to, that of their competitors.

Richard Rashid, one of the principal developers of Mach, offers further insight into the failures of UNIX. In the introductory talk of the *Mach Lecture Series* [Rash 89], he explains how the motivation for Mach grew out of observations on the evolution of the UNIX system. UNIX has a minimalist, building-block approach to tool building. Large, complex tools are created by combining small, simple ones. Yet the same approach is not carried over to the kernel.

The traditional UNIX kernel is not sufficiently flexible or extensible, and has few facilities for code reuse. As UNIX grew, developers simply added code to the kernel, which became a "dumping ground" for new features. Very soon the kernel became bloated, unmodular, and complex. Mach tries to solve these problems by rewriting the operating system from the ground up, based on a small number of abstractions. Modern UNIX systems have tackled this problem differently, adding flexible frameworks to several subsystems, as described in Section 1.2.9.

1.4   The Scope of this Book

This book describes modern UNIX systems. For completeness and to provide historical context, it also summarizes many features of older UNIX releases. There are many UNIX systems currently in the market, each unique in its own way. We can divide these systems into two types—baseline systems and commercial variants. The baseline systems include System V, 4BSD, and Mach. The variants are derived from any one of the baseline systems and contain value-added features and enhancements from the vendor. These include Sun Microsystem's SunOS and Solaris 2.*x,* IBM's AIX, Hewlett-Packard's HP-UX, and Digital's ULTRIX and Digital UNIX.

This book does not focus on a specific release or variant of the UNIX system. Instead, it examines a number of important implementations and compares their architecture and approach to many important problems. SVR4 receives the most attention, but there is ample coverage of 4.3BSD, 4.4BSD, and Mach. Among commercial variants, the book gives maximum coverage to SunOS and Solaris 2.*x,* not only because of their importance in the UNIX market, but also because Sun Microsystems has been responsible for many technical contributions that have subsequently been integrated into the baseline releases, and because of the plethora of published work on their systems.

Often the book makes generic references to traditional UNIX or modern UNIX. By traditional UNIX we mean SVR3, 4.3BSD, and earlier versions. We often discuss features or properties of traditional systems (for instance, "traditional UNIX systems had a single type of file system"). While there are many differences between SVR3 and 4.3BSD in each subsystem, there is also a lot of common ground, and such generic discussions focus on these common themes. When talking about modern UNIX systems, we mean to SVR4, 4.4BSD, Mach, and systems derived from these. Again, general comments, such as "Modern UNIX systems provide some kind of a journaling file system," describe features available in a large number of modern systems, but not necessarily in all of them.

1.5   References

[Acce 86]   Accetta, M., Baron, R., Golub, D., Rashid, R., Tevanian, A., and Young, M., "Mach: A New Kernel Foundation for UNIX Development," *Proceedings of the Summer 1986 USENIX Technical Conference,* Jun. 1986, pp. 93–112.

[Allm 87]   Allman, E., "UNIX: The Data Forms," *Proceedings of the Winter 1987 USENIX Technical Conference,* Jan. 1987, pp. 9–15.

[AT&T 89]   American Telephone and Telegraph, *The System V Interface Definition (SVID),* Third Edition, 1989.

[Bost 93]   Bostic, K., "4.4BSD Release," *;login,* Vol. 18, No. 5, Sep.-Oct. 1993, pp. 29–31.

[Bour 78]   Bourne, S.R., "The UNIX Shell," *The Bell System Technical Journal,* Vol. 57, No. 6, Part 2, Jul.-Aug. 1978, pp. 1971–1990.

[Gerb 92]   Gerber, C., "USL Vs. Berkeley," *UNIX Review,* Vol. 10, No. 11, Nov. 1992, pp. 33–36.

[IEEE 90]   Institute for Electrical and Electronic Engineers, *Information Technology—Portable Operating System Interface (POSIX) Part 1: System Application Program Interface (API) [C Language],* 1003.1–1990, IEEE, Dec. 1990.

[Joy 86]   Joy, W.N., Fabry, R.S., Leffler, S.J., McKusick, M.K., and Karels, M.J., "An Introduction to the C Shell," *UNIX User's Supplementary Documents,* 4.3 Berkeley Software Distribution, Virtual VAX–11 Version, USENIX Association, 1986, pp. 4:1–46.

[Orga 72]   Organick, E.J., *The Multics System: An Examination of Its Structure,* The MIT Press, Cambridge, MA, 1972.

[Rash 89]   Rashid, R.F., "Mach: Technical Innovations, Key Ideas, Status," *Mach 2.5 Lecture Series,* OSF Research Institute, 1989.

[Rich 82]   Richards, M., and Whitby-Strevens, C., *BCPL: The Language and Its Compiler,* Cambridge University Press, Cambridge, UK, 1982.

[Ritc 78]   Ritchie, D.M., and Thompson, K., "The UNIX Time-Sharing System," *The Bell System Technical Journal,* Vol. 57, No. 6, Part 2, pp. 1905–1930, Jul.-Aug. 1978.

[Ritc 87]   Ritchie, D.M., "Unix: A Dialectic," *Proceedings of the Winter 1987 USENIX Technical Conference,* Jan. 1987, pp. 29–34.

[Salu 94]   Salus, P.H., *A Quarter Century of UNIX,* Addison-Wesley, Reading, MA, 1994.

[Thom 74]   Thompson, K., and Ritchie, D.M., "The UNIX Time-Sharing System," *Communications of the ACM,* Vol. 17, No. 7, Jul. 1974, pp. 365–375.

[XPG4 93]   *The X/OPEN Portability Guide (XPG),* Issue 4, Prentice-Hall, Englewood Cliffs, NJ, 1993.

2

The Process and the Kernel

2.1   Introduction

The principal function of an operating system is to provide an execution environment in which user programs *(applications)* may run. This involves defining a basic framework for program execution, and providing a set of services—such as file management and I/O—and an interface to these services. The UNIX system presents a rich and versatile programming interface [Kern 84] that can efficiently support a variety of applications. This chapter describes the main components of the UNIX systems and how they interact to provide a powerful programming paradigm.

There are several different UNIX variants. Some of the important ones are the System V releases from AT&T (SVR4, the latest System V release, is now owned by Novell), the BSD releases from the University of California at Berkeley, OSF/1 from the Open Software Foundation, and SunOS and Solaris from Sun Microsystems. *This chapter describes the kernel and process architecture of traditional UNIX systems,* that is, those based on SVR2 [Bach 86], SVR3 [AT&T 87], 4.3BSD [Leff 89], or earlier versions. Modern UNIX variants such as SVR4, OSF/1, 4.4BSD, and Solaris 2.*x* differ significantly from this basic model; the subsequent chapters explore the modern releases in detail.

The UNIX application environment contains one fundamental abstraction—the *process*. In traditional UNIX systems, the process executes a single sequence of instructions in an *address space*. The address space of a process comprises the set of memory locations that the process may reference or access. The *control point* of the process tracks the sequence of instructions, using a hardware register typically called the *program counter (PC)*. Many newer UNIX releases support multiple control points (called *threads* [IEEE 94]), and hence multiple instruction sequences, within a single process.

The UNIX system is a multiprogramming environment, i.e., several processes are active in the system concurrently. To these processes, the system provides some features of a *virtual machine*. In a pure virtual machine architecture the operating system gives each process the illusion that it is the only process on the machine. The programmer writes an application as if only its code were running on the system. In UNIX systems each process has its own registers and memory, but must rely on the operating system for I/O and device control.

The process address space is virtual,[1] and normally only part of it corresponds to locations in physical memory. The kernel stores the contents of the process address space in various storage objects, including physical memory, on-disk files, and specially reserved *swap areas* on local or remote disks. The memory management subsystem of the kernel shuffles *pages* (fixed-size chunks) of process memory between these objects as convenient.

Each process also has a set of registers, which correspond to real, hardware registers. There are many active processes in the system, but only one set of hardware registers. The kernel keeps the registers of the currently running process in the hardware registers and saves those of other processes in per-process data structures.

Processes contend for the various resources of the system, such as the processor (also known as the Central Processing Unit or *CPU*), memory, and peripheral devices. An operating system must act as a resource manager, distributing the system resources optimally. A process that cannot acquire a resource it needs must *block* (suspend execution) until that resource becomes available. Since the CPU is one such resource, only one process can actually run at a time on a uniprocessor system. The rest of the processes are blocked, waiting for either the CPU or other resources. The kernel provides an illusion of concurrency by allowing one process to have the CPU for a brief period of time (called a *quantum,* usually about 10 milliseconds), then switching to another. In this way each process receives some CPU time and makes progress. This method of operation is known as *time-slicing.*

From another perspective, the computer provides several facilities to the user, such as the processor, disks, terminals, and printers. Application programmers do not wish to be concerned with the low-level details of the functionality and architecture of these components. The operating system assumes complete control of these devices and offers a high-level, abstract programming interface that applications can use to access these components. It hides all the details of the hardware, greatly simplifying the work of the programmer.[2] By centralizing all control of the devices, it also provides additional facilities such as access synchronization (if two users want the same device at the same time) and error recovery. The *application programming interface (API)* defines the semantics of all interactions between user programs and the operating system.

---

[1] There are some UNIX systems that do not use virtual memory. These include the earliest UNIX releases (the first virtual memory systems appeared in the late 1970s—see Section 1.1.4) and some real-time UNIX variants. This book deals only with UNIX systems that have virtual memory.

[2] The UNIX system takes this too far in some cases; for example, its treatment of tape drives as character streams makes it difficult for applications to properly handle errors and exceptional cases. The tape interface is inherently record-based and does not fit nicely with the UNIX device framework [Allm 87].

We have already started referring to the operating system as an entity that *does things*. What exactly is this entity? On one hand, an operating system is a program (often called the *kernel*) that controls the hardware and creates, destroys, and controls all processes (see Figure 2-1). From a broader perspective, an operating system includes not just the kernel, but also a host of other programs and utilities (such as the shells, editors, compilers, and programs like *date, ls,* and *who*) that together provide a useful work environment. Obviously, the kernel alone is of limited use, and users purchasing the UNIX system expect many of these other programs to come with it. The kernel, however, is special in many ways. It defines the programming interface to the system. It is the only indispensable program, without which nothing can run. While several shells or editors may run concurrently, only a single kernel may be loaded at a time. This book is devoted to studying the kernel, and when it mentions the *operating system,* or UNIX, it means the kernel, unless specified otherwise.

To rephrase the earlier question, "What exactly is the kernel?" Is it a process, or something distinct from all processes? The kernel is a special program that runs directly on the hardware. It implements the process model and other system services. It resides on disk in a file typically called **/vmunix** or **/unix** (depending on the UNIX vendor). When the system starts up, it loads the kernel from disk using a special procedure called *bootstrapping*. The kernel initializes the system and sets up the environment for running processes. It then creates a few initial processes, which in turn create other processes. Once loaded, the kernel remains in memory until the system is shut down. It manages the processes and provides various services to them.

The UNIX operating system provides functionality in four ways:

- User processes explicitly request services from the kernel through the *system call interface* (see Figure 2-1), the central component of the UNIX API. The kernel executes these requests on behalf of the calling process.
- Some unusual actions of a process, such as attempting to divide by zero, or overflowing the user stack, cause *hardware exceptions*. Exceptions require kernel intervention, and the kernel handles them on behalf of the process.

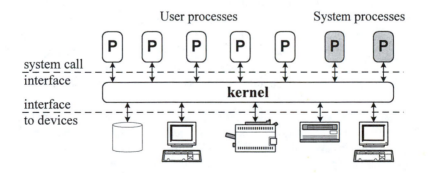

Figure 2-1. The kernel interacts with processes and devices.

- The kernel handles hardware *interrupts* from peripheral devices. Devices use the interrupt mechanism to notify the kernel of I/O completion and status changes. The kernel treats interrupts as global events, unrelated to any specific process.
- A set of special system processes, such as the *swapper* and the *pagedaemon,* perform system-wide tasks such as controlling the number of active processes or maintaining a pool of free memory.

The following sections describe these different mechanisms and define the notion of the execution context of a process.

2.2   Mode, Space, and Context

In order to run UNIX, the computer hardware must provide at least two different *modes of execution*—a more privileged *kernel mode,* and a less privileged *user mode*. As you might expect, user programs execute in user mode, and kernel functions execute in kernel mode. The kernel protects some parts of the address space from user-mode access. Moreover, certain privileged machine instructions, such as those that manipulate memory management registers, may only be executed in kernel mode.

Many computers have more than two execution modes. The Intel 80x86 architecture, for example, provides four *rings of execution*—the innermost being the most privileged. *UNIX, however, uses only two of these rings*. The main reason for having different execution modes is for protection. Since user processes run in the less privileged mode, they cannot accidentally or maliciously corrupt another process or the kernel. The damage from program errors is localized, and usually does not affect other activity or processes in the system.

Most UNIX implementations use *virtual memory*. In a virtual memory system the addresses used by a program do not refer directly to locations in physical memory. Each process has its own *virtual address space,* and references to virtual memory addresses are translated to physical memory locations using a set of *address translation maps*. Many systems implement these maps as *page tables,* with one entry for each *page* (a fixed-size unit of memory allocation and protection) of the process address space. The *memory management unit (MMU)* of the computer typically has a set of registers that identifies the translation maps of the currently running process (also called the *current process*). When the current process yields the CPU to another process (a *context switch*), the kernel loads these registers with pointers to the translation maps of the new process. The MMU registers are privileged and may only be accessed in kernel mode. This ensures that a process can only refer to addresses in its own space and cannot access or modify the address space of another process.

A fixed part of the virtual address space of each process maps the kernel text and data structures. This portion, known as *system space* or *kernel space,* may only be accessed in kernel mode. There is only one instance of the kernel running in the system, and hence all processes map a single kernel address space. The kernel maintains some global data structures and some per-process objects. The latter contain information that enables the kernel to access the address space of any process. The kernel can directly access the address space of the current process, since the MMU registers have the necessary information. Occasionally, the kernel must access the address space of a process other than the current one. It does so indirectly, using special, temporary mappings.

While the kernel is shared by all processes, system space is protected from user-mode access. Processes cannot directly access the kernel, and must instead use the system call interface. When a process makes a *system call,* it executes a special sequence of instructions to put the system in kernel mode (this is called a *mode switch*) and transfer control to the kernel, which handles the operation on behalf of the process. After the system call is complete, the kernel executes another set of instructions that returns the system to user mode (another mode switch) and transfers control back to the process. The system call interface is described further in Section 2.4.1.

There are two important per-process objects that, while managed by the kernel, are often implemented as part of the process address space. These are the *u area* (also called the *user area*) and the *kernel stack.* The u area is a data structure that contains information about a process of interest to the kernel, such as a table of files opened by the process, identification information, and saved values of the process registers when the process is not running. The process should not be allowed to change this information arbitrarily, and hence the u area is protected from user-mode access. (Some implementations allow the process to read, but not modify, the u area.)

The UNIX kernel is *re-entrant,* meaning that several processes may be involved in kernel activity concurrently. In fact, they may even be executing the same routine in parallel. (Of course, only one process can actually run at a time; the others are blocked or waiting to run.) Hence each process needs its own private kernel stack, to keep track of its function call sequence when executing in the kernel. Many UNIX implementations allocate the kernel stack in the address space of each process, but do not allow user-mode access to it. Conceptually, both the u area and the kernel stack, while being per-process entities in the process space, are *owned* by the kernel.

Another important concept is the *execution context.* Kernel functions may execute either in *process context* or in *system context.* In process context, the kernel acts on behalf of the current process (for instance, while executing a system call), and may access and modify the address space, u area, and kernel stack of this process. Moreover, the kernel may block the current process if it must wait for a resource or device activity.

The kernel must also perform certain system-wide tasks such as responding to device interrupts and recomputing process priorities. Such tasks are not performed on behalf of a particular process, and hence are handled in system context (also called *interrupt context*). When running in system context, the kernel may not access the address space, u area, or kernel stack of the current process. The kernel may not block when executing in system context, since that would block an innocent process. In some situations there may not even be a current process, for example, when all processes are blocked awaiting I/O completion.

This far, we have noted the distinctions between user and kernel mode, process and system space, and process and system context. Figure 2-2 summarizes these notions. User code runs in user mode and process context, and can access only the process space. System calls and exceptions are handled in kernel mode but in process context, and may access process and system space. Interrupts are handled in kernel mode and system context, and must only access system space.

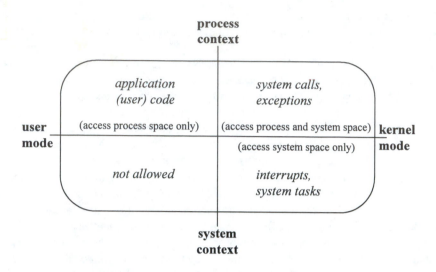

Figure 2-2. Execution mode and context.

2.3   The Process Abstraction

What exactly is a UNIX process? One oft-quoted answer is, "A process is an instance of a running program." Going beyond perfunctory definitions, it is useful to describe various properties of the process. A process is an entity that runs a program and provides an execution environment for it. It comprises an address space and a control point. The process is the fundamental scheduling entity— only one process runs on the CPU at a time. In addition, the process contends for and owns various system resources such as devices and memory. It also requests services from the system, which the kernel performs on its behalf.

The process has a definite lifetime—most processes are created by a *fork* or *vfork* system call and run until they terminate by calling *exit*. During its lifetime, a process may run one or many programs (usually one at a time). It invokes the *exec* system call to run a new program.

UNIX processes have a well-defined hierarchy. Each process has one *parent*, and may have one or more *child* processes. The process hierarchy can be described by an inverted tree, with the *init* process at the top. The *init* process (so named because it executes the program **/etc/init**) is the first user process created when the system boots. It is the ancestor of all user processes. A few system processes, such as the *swapper* and the *pagedaemon* (also called the *pageout daemon*), are created during the bootstrapping sequence and are not descendants of *init*. If, when a process terminates, it has any active child processes, they become *orphans* and are inherited by *init*.

2.3.1   Process State

At all times, UNIX processes are in some well-defined *state*. They move from one state to another in response to various events. Figure 2-3 describes the important process states in UNIX and the events that cause *state transitions*.

The *fork* system call creates a new process, which begins life in the *initial* (also called *idle*) state. When the process is fully created, *fork* moves it to the *ready to run* state, where it must wait to be scheduled. Eventually, the kernel selects it for execution, and initiates a context switch. This invokes a kernel routine (typically called swtch()) that loads the hardware context of the process (see Section 2.3.2) into the system registers, and transfers control to the process. From this point, the new process behaves like any other process, and undergoes state transitions as described below.

A process running in user mode enters kernel mode as a result of a system call or an interrupt, and returns to user mode when that completes.[3] While executing a system call, the process may need to wait for an event or for a resource that is currently unavailable. It does so by calling

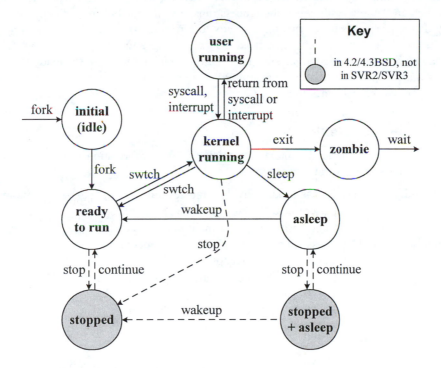

Figure 2-3. Process states and state transitions.

---

[3]   Interrupts can also occur when the system is in kernel mode. In this case, the system will remain in kernel mode after the handler completes.

sleep(), which puts the process on a queue of sleeping processes, and changes its state to *asleep*. When the event occurs or the resource becomes available, the kernel wakes up the process, which now becomes *ready to run* and waits to be scheduled.

When a process is scheduled to run, it initially runs in kernel mode (*kernel running* state), where it completes the context switch. Its next transition depends on what it was doing before it was switched out. If the process was newly created or was executing user code (and was descheduled to let a higher priority process run), it returns immediately to user mode. If it was blocked for a resource while executing a system call, it resumes execution of the system call in kernel mode.

Finally, the process terminates by calling the *exit* system call, or because of a *signal* (signals are notifications issued by the kernel—see Chapter 4). In either case, the kernel releases all the resources of the process, except for the *exit status* and *resource usage* information, and leaves the process in the *zombie* state. The process remains in this state until its parent calls *wait* (or one of its variants), which destroys the process and returns the exit status to the parent (see Section 2.8.6).

4BSD defines some additional states that are not supported in SVR2 or SVR3. A process is *stopped,* or *suspended,* by a *stop* signal (SIGSTOP, SIGTSTP, SIGTTIN, or SIGTTOU). Unlike other signals, which are handled only when the process runs, a *stop* signal changes the process state immediately. If the process is in the running or ready to run state, its state changes to stopped. If the process is asleep when this signal is generated, its state changes to asleep and stopped. A stopped process may be resumed by a *continue* signal (SIGCONT), which returns it to the ready to run state. If the process was stopped as well as asleep, SIGCONT returns the process to the asleep state. System V UNIX incorporated these features in SVR4 (see Section 4.5).[4]

2.3.2   Process Context

Each process has a well-defined context, comprising all the information needed to describe the process. This context has several components:

- **User address space:** This is usually divided into several components—the program text (executable code), data, user stack, shared memory regions, and so on.
- **Control information:** The kernel uses two main data structures to maintain control information about the process—the u area and the proc structure. Each process also has its own kernel stack and address translation maps.
- **Credentials:** The credentials of the process include the user and group IDs associated with it, and are further described in Section 2.3.3.
- **Environment variables:** These are a set of strings of the form

    variable=value

    which are inherited from the parent. Most UNIX systems store these strings at the bottom of the user stack. The standard user library provides functions to add, delete, or modify these variables, and to translate the variable and return its value. When invoking a new

---

[4] SVR3 provides a *stopped* state for the process solely for the purpose of *process tracing* (see Section 6.2.4). When a traced process receives *any* signal, it enters the stopped state, and the kernel awakens its parent.

program, the caller may ask *exec* to retain the original environment or provide a new set of variables to be used instead.

- **Hardware context:** This includes the contents of the general-purpose registers, and of a set of special system registers. The system registers include:

  - The *program counter (PC)*, which holds the address of the next instruction to execute.
  - The *stack pointer (SP)*, which contains the address of the uppermost element of the stack.[5]
  - The *processor status word (PSW)*, which has several status bits containing information about the system state, such as current and previous execution modes, current and previous interrupt priority levels, and overflow and carry bits.
  - *Memory management registers*, which map the address translation tables of the process.
  - Floating point unit (FPU) registers.

The machine registers contain the hardware context of the currently running process. When a context switch occurs, these registers are saved in a special part of the u area (called the *process control block, or PCB*) of the current process. The kernel selects a new process to run and loads the hardware context from its PCB.

2.3.3   User Credentials

Every user in the system is identified by a unique number called the *user ID,* or *UID.* The system administrator also creates several user groups, each with a unique *user group ID,* or *GID.* These identifiers affect file ownership and access permissions, and the ability to signal other processes. These attributes are collectively called the *credentials.*

The system recognizes a privileged user called the *superuser* (normally, this user logs in with the name *root*). The superuser has a UID of 0, and GID of 1. The superuser has many privileges denied to ordinary users. He or she may access files owned by others, regardless of protection settings, and may also execute a number of privileged system calls (such as *mknod,* which creates a special device file). Many modern UNIX systems such as SVR4.1/ES support *enhanced security* mechanisms [Sale 92]. These systems replace the single superuser abstraction with separate privileges for different operations.

Each process has two pairs of IDs—real and effective. When a user logs in, the login program sets both pairs to the UID and GID specified in the *password database* (the **/etc/passwd** file, or some distributed mechanism such as Sun Microsystems' *Network Information Service (NIS)*). When a process *forks,* the child inherits its credentials from the parent.

The *effective UID* and *effective GID* affect file creation and access. During file creation, the kernel sets the owner attributes of the file to the effective UID and GID of the creating process. During file access, the kernel uses the effective UID and GID of the process to determine whether it

---

[5] Or lowermost, on machines where the stack grows downward. Also, on some systems, the stack pointer contains the address at which the next item can be pushed onto the stack.

can access the file (see Section 8.2.2 for more details). The *real UID* and *real GID* identify the real owner of the process and affect the permissions for sending signals. A process without superuser privileges can signal another process only if the sender's real or effective UID matches the real UID of the receiver.

There are three system calls that can change the credentials. If a process calls *exec* to run a program installed in *suid mode* (see Section 8.2.2), the kernel changes the effective UID of the process to that of the owner of the file. Likewise, if the program is installed in *sgid mode,* the kernel changes the effective GID of the calling process.

UNIX provides this feature to grant special privileges to users for particular tasks. The classic example is the *passwd* program, which allows the user to modify his own password. This program must write to the password database, which users should not be allowed to directly modify (to prevent them from changing passwords of other users). Hence the *passwd* program is owned by the superuser and has its SUID bit set. This allows the user to gain superuser privileges while running the *passwd* program.

A user can also change his credentials by calling *setuid* or *setgid*. The superuser can invoke these system calls to change both the real and effective UID or GID. Ordinary users can use this call only to change their effective UID or GID back to the real ones.

There are some differences in the treatment of credentials in System V and BSD UNIX. SVR3 also maintains a *saved UID* and *saved GID,* which are the values of the effective UID and GID prior to calling *exec*. The *setuid* and *setgid* calls can also restore the effective IDs to the saved values. While 4.3BSD does not support this feature, it allows a user to belong to a set of *supplemental groups* (using the *setgroups* system call). While files created by the user belong to his or her *primary group,* the user can access files belonging either to the principal or to a supplemental group (provided the file allows access to group members).

SVR4 incorporates all the above features. It supports supplemental groups, and maintains the saved UID and GID across *exec*.

2.3.4   The u Area and the proc Structure

The control information about a process is maintained in two per-process data structures—the u area and the proc structure. In many implementations, the kernel has a fixed-size array of proc structures called the *process table*. The size of this array places a hard limit on the maximum number of processes that can exist at a time. Newer releases such as SVR4 allow dynamic allocation of proc structures, but have a fixed-size array of pointers to them. Since the proc structure is in system space, it is visible to the kernel at all times, even when the process is not running.

The u area, or user area, is part of the process space, i.e., it is mapped and visible only when the process is running. On many implementations, the u area is always mapped at the same fixed virtual address in each process, which the kernel references simply through the variable u. One of the tasks of the context switch is to reset this mapping, so that kernel references to u are translated to the physical location of the new u area.

Occasionally, the kernel may need to access the u area of another process. This is possible, but must be done indirectly using a special set of mappings. These differences in access semantics govern what information is stored in the proc structure and what is stored in the u area. The u area contains data that is needed only when the process is running. The `proc` structure contains information that may be needed even when the process is not running.

The major fields in the u area include:

- The process control block—stores the saved hardware context when the process is not running.
- A pointer to the `proc` structure for this process.
- The real and effective UID and GID.[6]
- Arguments to, and return values or error status from, the current system call.
- Signal handlers and related information (see Chapter 4).
- Information from the program header, such as text, data, and stack sizes and other memory management information.
- Open file descriptor table (see Section 8.2.3). Modern UNIX systems such as SVR4 dynamically extend this table as necessary.
- Pointers to *vnodes* of the *current directory* and the *controlling terminal*. Vnodes represent file system objects and are further described in Section 8.7.
- CPU usage statistics, profiling information, disk quotas, and resource limits.
- In many implementations, the per-process kernel stack is part of the u area.

The major fields in the `proc` structure include:

- Identification: Each process has a unique *process ID (PID)* and belongs to a specific *process group*. Newer releases also assign a *session ID* to each process.
- Location of the kernel address map for the u area of this process.
- The current process state.
- Forward and backward pointers to link the process onto a scheduler queue or, for a blocked process, a sleep queue.
- Sleep channel for blocked processes (see Section 7.2.3).
- Scheduling priority and related information (see Chapter 5).
- Signal handling information: masks of signals that are ignored, blocked, posted, and handled (see Chapter 4).
- Memory management information.
- Pointers to link this structure on lists of active, free, or zombie processes.
- Miscellaneous flags.
- Pointers to keep the structure on a *hash queue* based on its PID.
- Hierarchy information, describing the relationship of this process to others.

Figure 2-4 illustrates the process relationships in 4.3BSD UNIX. The fields that describe the hierarchy are p_pid (process ID), p_ppid (parent process ID), p_pptr (pointer to the parent's `proc` structure), p_cptr (pointer to the oldest child), p_ysptr (pointer to next younger sibling), and p_osptr (pointer to next older sibling).

---

[6] Modern UNIX systems such as SVR4 store user credentials in a dynamically allocated, reference-counted data structure, and keep a pointer to it in the `proc` structure. Section 8.10.7 discusses this arrangement further.

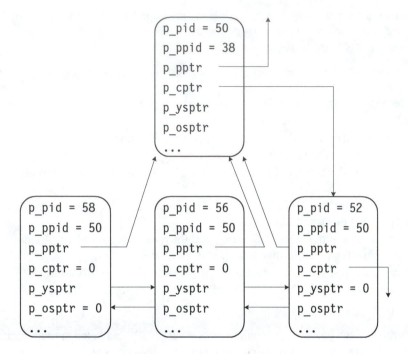

Figure 2-4. A typical process hierarchy in 4.3BSD UNIX.

Many modern UNIX variants have modified the process abstraction to support several threads of control in a single process. This notion is explained in detail in Chapter 3.

2.4   Executing in Kernel Mode

There are three types of events that cause the system to enter kernel mode—device interrupts, exceptions, and traps or software interrupts. In each case, when the kernel receives control, it consults a *dispatch table,* which contains addresses of low-level routines that handle these events. Before calling the appropriate routine, the kernel saves some state of the interrupted process (such as its program counter and the processor status word) on its kernel stack. When the routine completes, the kernel restores the state of the process and changes the execution mode back to its previous value (an interrupt could have occurred when the system was already in kernel mode, in which case it would remain in kernel mode after the handler returns).

It is important to distinguish between interrupts and exceptions. Interrupts are asynchronous events caused by peripheral devices such as disks, terminals, or the hardware clock. Since interrupts are not caused by the current process, they must be serviced in system context and may not access the process address space or u area. For the same reason, they must not block, since that would block an arbitrary process. Exceptions are synchronous to the process and are caused by events related to the process itself, such as attempting to divide by zero or accessing an illegal address. The exception handler therefore runs in process context; it may access the address space and u area of the process and block if necessary. Software interrupts, or traps, occur when a process executes a special instruction, such as in system calls, and are handled synchronously in process context.

2.4.1   The System Call Interface

The set of system calls defines the programming interface offered by the kernel to user processes. The standard C library, linked by default with all user programs, contains a *wrapper routine* for each system call. When a user program makes a system call, the corresponding wrapper routine is invoked. This routine pushes the system call number (which identifies the particular system call to the kernel) onto the user stack and then invokes a special *trap* instruction. The actual name of the instruction is machine-specific (for example, syscall on the MIPS R3000, chmk on the VAX-11, or trap on the Motorola 680x0). The function of this instruction is to change the execution mode to kernel and to transfer control to the system call handler defined in the dispatch table. This handler, typically called syscall(), is the starting point of all system call processing in the kernel.

The system call executes in kernel mode, but in process context. It thus has access to the process address space and the u area. Since it runs in kernel mode, it uses the kernel stack of the calling process. syscall() copies the arguments of the system call from the user stack to the u area and saves the hardware context of the process on the kernel stack. It then uses the system call number to index into a system call dispatch vector (usually called sysent[]) to determine which kernel function to call to execute that particular system call. When that function returns, syscall() sets the return values or error status in the appropriate registers, restores the hardware context, and returns to user mode, transferring control back to the library routine.

2.4.2   Interrupt Handling

The primary function of interrupts on a machine is to allow peripheral devices to interact with the CPU, to inform it of task completion, error conditions, or other events that require urgent attention. Such interrupts are generated asynchronous to regular system activity (i.e., the system does not know at what point in the instruction stream the interrupt will occur) and are usually unrelated to any specific process. The function that is invoked to service an interrupt is called the *interrupt handler* or *interrupt service routine*. The handler runs in kernel mode and system context. Since the process that was interrupted usually bears no relation to the interrupt, the handler must be careful not to access the process context. For the same reason, interrupt handlers are not permitted to block.

There is, however, a small impact on the interrupted process. The time used to service the interrupt is charged to the time slice of this process, even though the activity was unrelated to the process. Also, the clock interrupt handler charges the clock tick (the time between two clock interrupts) to the current process, and thus needs to access its proc structure. It is important to note that the process context is not explicitly protected from access by interrupt handlers. An incorrectly written handler has the power to corrupt any part of the process address space.

The kernel also supports the notion of software interrupts or traps, which can be triggered by executing specific instructions. Such interrupts are used, for example, to trigger a context switch or

Table 2-1. Setting the interrupt priority level in 4.3BSD and SVR4

4.3BSD	SVR4	Purpose
spl0	spl0 or splbase	enable all interrupts
splsoftclock	spltimeout	block functions scheduled by timers
splnet		block network protocol processing
	splstr	block STREAMS interrupts
spltty	spltty	block terminal interrupts
splbio	spldisk	block disk interrupts
splimp		block network device interrupts
splclock		block hardware clock interrupt
splhigh	spl7 or splhi	disable all interrupts
splx	splx	restore *ipl* to previously saved value

schedule low-priority clock-related tasks. While these interrupts are synchronous to normal system activity, they are handled just like normal interrupts.

Since there are several different events that may cause interrupts, one interrupt may occur while another is being serviced. UNIX systems recognize the need to prioritize different kinds of interrupts and allow high-priority interrupts to preempt the servicing of low-priority interrupts. For example, the hardware clock interrupt must take precedence over a network interrupt, since the latter may require a large amount of processing, spanning several clock ticks.

UNIX systems assign an *interrupt priority level (ipl)* to each type of interrupt. Early UNIX implementations had *ipl*s in the range 0–7. In BSD, this was expanded to 0–31. The *processor status register* typically has bit-fields that store the current (and perhaps previous) *ipl*.[7] Normal kernel and user processing occurs at the base *ipl*. The number of interrupt priorities varies both across different UNIX variants and across different hardware architectures. On some systems, *ipl 0* is the lowest priority, while on others it is the highest. To make things easier for kernel and device driver developers, UNIX systems provide a set of macros to block and unblock interrupts. However, different UNIX variants use different macros for similar purposes. Table 2-1 lists some of the macros used in 4.3BSD and in SVR4.

When an interrupt occurs, if its *ipl* is higher than the current *ipl*, the current processing is suspended and the handler for the new interrupt is invoked. The handler begins execution at the new *ipl*. When the handler completes, the *ipl* is lowered to its previous value (which is obtained from the old processor status word saved on the interrupt stack), and the kernel resumes execution of the interrupted process. If the kernel receives an interrupt of *ipl* lower than or equal to the current *ipl*, that interrupt is not handled immediately, but is stored in a saved interrupt register. When the *ipl* drops sufficiently, the saved interrupt will be handled. This is described in Figure 2-5.

The *ipl*s are compared and set in hardware in a machine-dependent way. UNIX also provides the kernel with mechanisms to explicitly check or set the *ipl*. For instance, the kernel may raise the *ipl* to block interrupts while executing some critical code. This is discussed further in Section 2.5.2.

---

[7]   Some processors, such as the Intel 80x86, do not support interrupt priorities in hardware. On these systems, the operating system must implement *ipl*s in software. The exercises explore this problem further.

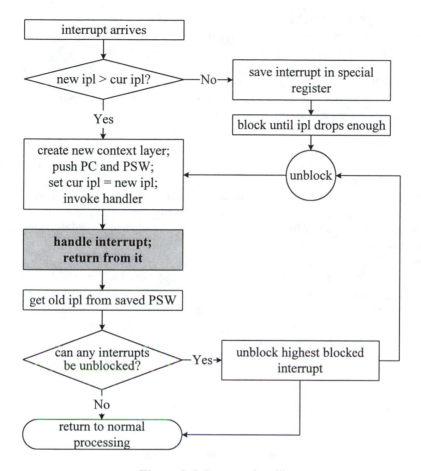

Figure 2-5. Interrupt handling.

Some machines provide a separate global *interrupt stack* used by all the handlers. In machines without an interrupt stack, handlers run on the kernel stack of the current process. They must ensure that the rest of the kernel stack is insulated from the handler. The kernel implements this by pushing a *context layer* on the kernel stack before calling the handler. This context layer, like a stack frame, contains the information needed by the handler to restore the previous execution context upon return.

2.5 Synchronization

The UNIX kernel is re-entrant. At any time, several processes may be active in the kernel. Of these, only one (on a uniprocessor) can be actually running; the others are blocked, waiting either for the

CPU or some other resource. Since they all share the same copy of the kernel data structures, it is necessary to impose some form of synchronization, to prevent corruption of the kernel.

Figure 2-6 shows one example of what can happen in the absence of synchronization. Suppose a process is trying to remove element **B** from the linked list. It executes the first line of code, but is interrupted before it can execute the next line, and another process is allowed to run. If this second process were to access this same list, it would find it in an inconsistent state, as shown in Figure 2-6(b). Clearly, we need to ensure that such problems never occur.

UNIX uses several synchronization techniques. The first line of defense is that the UNIX kernel is nonpreemptive. This means that if a process is executing in kernel mode, it cannot be preempted by another process, *even though its time quantum may expire*. The process must voluntarily relinquish the CPU. This typically happens when the process is about to block while waiting for a resource or event, or when it has completed its kernel mode activity and is about to return to user mode. In either case, since the CPU is relinquished voluntarily, the process can ensure that the kernel remains in a consistent state. (Modern UNIX kernels with real-time capability allow preemption under certain conditions—see Section 5.6 for details.)

Making a kernel nonpreemptive provides a broad, sweeping solution to most synchronization problems. In the example of Figure 2-6, for instance, the kernel can manipulate the linked list without locking it, if it does not have to worry about preemption. There are three situations where synchronization is still necessary—blocking operations, interrupts, and multiprocessor synchronization.

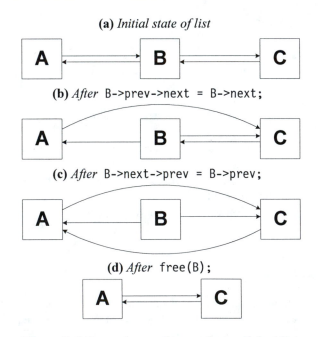

Figure 2-6. Removing an element from a linked list.

2.5.1   Blocking Operations

A *blocking operation* is one that blocks the process (places the process in the *asleep* state until the operation completes). Since the kernel is nonpreemptive, it may manipulate most objects (data structures and resources) with impunity, knowing that no other process will disturb it. Some objects, however, must be protected across a blocking operation, and this requires additional mechanisms. For instance, a process may issue a *read* from a file into a disk block buffer in kernel memory. Since disk I/O is necessary, the process must wait until the I/O completes, allowing other processes to run in the meantime. However, the kernel must ensure that other processes do not access this buffer in any way, since the buffer is in an inconsistent state.

To protect such an object, the kernel associates a *lock* with it. The lock may be as simple as a single bit-flag, which is set when locked and clear when unlocked. Any process that wants to use the object must first check if it is locked. If so, the process must block until the object is unlocked. If not, it locks the object and proceeds to use it. Normally, the kernel also associates a *wanted* flag with the object. This flag is set by a process that wants the object but finds it locked. When a process is ready to release a locked object, it checks the object's *wanted* flag to see if other processes are waiting for the object and, if so, awakens them. This mechanism allows a process to lock a resource for a long period of time, even if it had to block and allow other processes to run while holding the lock.

Figure 2-7 describes the algorithm for resource locking. The following points must be noted:

- A process blocks itself when it cannot obtain a resource, or when it must wait for an event such as I/O completion. It does so by calling a routine called sleep(). This is called *blocking on* the resource or event.
- sleep() puts the process on a special queue of blocked processes, changes its state to asleep, and calls a function called swtch() to initiate a context switch and allow another process to run.
- The process releasing the resource calls wakeup() to wake *all* processes that are waiting for this resource.[8] wakeup() finds each such process, changes its state to runnable, and puts it on a scheduler queue, where it now waits to be scheduled.
- There can be a substantial delay between the time a process is awakened and the time it is scheduled to run. Other processes may run in the meantime, and may even lock the same resource again.
- Thus upon waking up, the process must check once again if the resource is actually available, and go back to sleep if not.

2.5.2   Interrupts

While the kernel is normally safe from preemption by another process, a process manipulating kernel data structures may be interrupted by devices. If the interrupt handler tries to access those very data structures, they may be in an inconsistent state. This problem is handled by blocking interrupts while accessing such critical data structures. The kernel uses macros such as those in Table 2-1 to

---

[8]   Recent versions of UNIX offer several alternatives to wakeup(), such as wake_one() and wakeprocs().

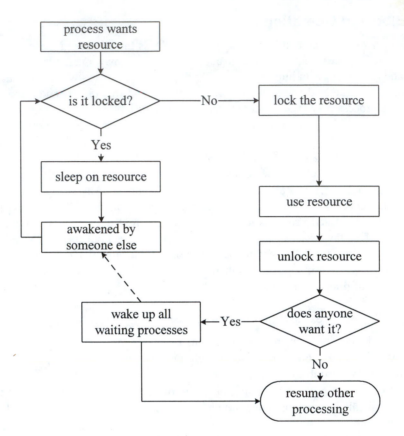

Figure 2-7. Algorithm for resource locking.

explicitly raise the *ipl* and block interrupts. Such a region of code is called a *critical region* (see Example 2-1).

```
int x = splbio();          /* raises ipl, returns previous ipl */
modify disk buffer cache;
splx(x);                   /* restores previous ipl */
```

Example 2-1. Blocking interrupts in a critical region.

There are several important considerations related to interrupt masking:

- Interrupts usually require rapid servicing, and hence should not be interfered with excessively. Thus, critical regions should be few and brief.
- The only interrupts that must be blocked are those that may manipulate the data in the critical region. In the previous example, only the disk interrupts need to be blocked.

- Two different interrupts can have the same priority level. For instance, on many systems both terminal and disk interrupts occur at *ipl* 21.
- Blocking an interrupt also blocks all interrupts at the same or lower *ipl*.

> **Note:** *The word* block *is used in many different ways when describing the UNIX subsystem. A process* blocks *on a resource or event when it enters the asleep state waiting for the resource to be available or the event to occur. The kernel* blocks *an interrupt or a signal by temporarily disabling its delivery. Finally, the I/O subsystem transfers data to and from storage devices in fixed-size* blocks.

2.5.3 Multiprocessors

Multiprocessor systems lead to a new class of synchronization problems, since the fundamental protection offered by the nonpreemptive nature of the kernel is no longer present. On a uniprocessor, the kernel manipulates most data structures with impunity, knowing that it cannot be preempted. It only needs to protect data structures that may be accessed by interrupt handlers, or those that need to be consistent across calls to sleep().

On a multiprocessor, two processes may execute in kernel mode on different processors and may also execute the same function concurrently. Thus any time the kernel accesses a global data structure, it must lock that structure to prevent access from other processors. The locking mechanisms themselves must be multiprocessor-safe. If two processes running on different processors attempt to lock an object at the same time, only one must succeed in acquiring the lock.

Protecting against interrupts also is more complicated, because all processors may handle interrupts. It is usually not advisable to block interrupts on every processor, since that might degrade performance considerably. Multiprocessors clearly require more complex synchronization mechanisms. Chapter 7 explores these issues in detail.

2.6 Process Scheduling

The CPU is a resource that must be shared by all processes. The part of the kernel that apportions CPU time between processes is called the *scheduler*. The traditional UNIX scheduler uses *preemptive round-robin scheduling*. Processes of equal priority are scheduled in a round-robin manner, each running for a fixed quantum of time(typically 100 milliseconds). If a higher priority process becomes runnable, it will preempt the current process (unless the current process is running in kernel mode), even if the current process has not used up its time quantum.

In traditional UNIX systems, the process priority is determined by two factors—the *nice value* and the *usage factor*. Users may influence the process priority by modifying its nice value using the *nice* system call (only the superuser may increase the priority of a process). The usage factor is a measure of the recent CPU usage of the process. It allows the kernel to vary the process priority dynamically. While a process is not running, the kernel periodically increases its priority. When a process receives some CPU time, the kernel reduces its priority. This scheme prevents starvation of any process, since eventually the priority of any process that is waiting to run will rise high enough for it to be scheduled.

A process executing in kernel mode may relinquish the CPU if it must block for a resource or event. When it becomes runnable again, it is assigned a kernel priority. Kernel priorities are higher than any user priorities. In traditional UNIX kernels, scheduling priorities have integer values between 0 and 127, with smaller numbers meaning higher priorities. (As the UNIX system is written almost entirely in C, it follows the standard convention of beginning all counts and indices at 0). In 4.3BSD, for instance, the kernel priorities range from 0 to 49, and user priorities from 50 to 127. While user priorities vary with CPU usage, kernel priorities are fixed, and depend on the reason for sleeping. Because of this, kernel priorities are also known as *sleep priorities*. Table 2-2 lists the sleep priorities in 4.3BSD UNIX.

Chapter 5 provides further details of the UNIX scheduler.

2.7   Signals

UNIX uses *signals* to inform a process of asynchronous events, and to handle exceptions. For example, when a user types control-C at the terminal, a SIGINT signal is sent to the foreground process. Likewise, when a process terminates, a SIGCHLD signal is sent to its parent. UNIX defines a number of signals (31 in 4.3BSD and SVR3). Most are reserved for specific purposes, while two (SIGUSR1 and SIGUSR2) are available for applications to use as they wish.

Signals are generated in many ways. A process may explicitly send a signal to one or more processes using the *kill* system call. The terminal driver generates signals to processes connected to it in response to certain keystrokes and events. The kernel generates a signal to notify the process of a hardware exception, or of a condition such as exceeding a quota.

Each signal has a default response, usually process termination. Some signals are ignored by default, and a few others suspend the process. The process may specify another action instead of the default by using the *signal* (System V), *sigvec* (BSD), or *sigaction* (POSIX.1) calls. This other ac-

Table 2-2. Sleep priorities in 4.3BSD UNIX

Priority	Value	Description
PSWP	0	swapper
PSWP + 1	1	page daemon
PSWP + 1/2/4	1/2/4	other memory management activity
PINOD	10	waiting for inode to be freed
PRIBIO	20	disk I/O wait
PRIBIO + 1	21	waiting for buffer to be released
PZERO	25	baseline priority
TTIPRI	28	terminal input wait
TTOPRI	29	terminal output wait
PWAIT	30	waiting for child process to terminate
PLOCK	35	advisory resource lock wait
PSLEP	40	wait for a signal

tion may be to invoke a user-specified signal handler, or it may be to ignore the signal, or even to revert to the default. The process may also choose to block a signal temporarily; such a signal will only be delivered to a process after it is unblocked.

A process does not instantaneously respond to a signal. When the signal is generated, the kernel notifies the process by setting a bit in the pending signals mask in its proc structure. The process must become aware of the signal and respond to it, and that can only happen when it is scheduled to run. Once it runs, the process will handle all pending signals before returning to its normal user-level processing. (This does not include the signal handlers themselves, which run in user mode.)

What should happen if a signal is generated for a sleeping process? Should the signal be kept pending until the process awakens, or should the sleep be interrupted? The answer depends on why the process is sleeping. If the process is sleeping for an event that is certain to occur soon, such as disk I/O completion, there is no need to wake up the process. If, on the other hand, the process is waiting for an event such as terminal input, there is no limit to how long it might block. In such a case, the kernel interrupts the sleep and aborts the system call in which the process had blocked. 4.3BSD provides the *siginterrupt* system call to control how signals should affect system call handling. Using *siginterrupt,* the user can specify whether system calls interrupted by signals should be aborted or restarted. Chapter 4 covers the topic of signals in greater detail.

2.8 New Processes and Programs

UNIX is a multiprogramming environment, and several processes are active in the system at any time. Each process runs a single program at a time, though several processes may run the same program concurrently. Such processes may share a single copy of the program text in memory, but maintain their own individual data and stack regions. Moreover, a process may invoke a new program at any time and may run several programs in its lifetime. UNIX thus makes a sharp distinction between the process and the program it is running.

To support such an environment, UNIX provides several system calls to create and terminate processes, and to invoke new programs. The *fork* and *vfork* system calls create new processes. The *exec* call invokes a new program. The *exit* system call terminates a process. Note that a process may also terminate if it receives a signal.

2.8.1 *fork* and *exec*

The *fork* system call creates a new process. The process that calls *fork* is the parent, and the new process is its child. The parent-child relationship creates the process hierarchy described in Figure 2-4. The child process is almost an exact clone of the parent. Its address space is a replica of that of the parent, and it also runs the same program initially. In fact, the child begins user mode execution by returning from the *fork*.

Because the parent and child both return from the *fork* and continue to execute the same program, they need a way to distinguish themselves from one another and act accordingly. Otherwise, it would be impossible for different processes to do different things. For this reason, the *fork* system call returns different values to the parent and child—*fork* returns *0* to the child, and the child's PID to the parent.

Most often, the child process will call *exec* shortly after returning from *fork,* and thus begin executing a new program. The C library provides several alternate forms of *exec,* such as *execve, execve,* and *execvp.* Each takes a slightly different set of arguments and, after some preprocessing, calls the same system call. The generic name *exec* refers to any unspecified function of this group. The code that uses *fork* and *exec* looks resembles that in Example 2-2.

```
if ((result = fork()) == 0) {
    /* child code */
    ...
    if (execve ("new_program", ...) < 0)
        perror ("execve failed");
        exit(1);
} else if (result < 0)  {
    perror ("fork");      /* fork failed */
}
/* parent continues here */
...
```

Example 2-2. Using *fork* and *exec.*

Since *exec* overlays a new program on the existing process, the child does not return to the old program unless *exec* fails. Upon successful completion of *exec,* the child's address space is replaced with that of the new program, and the child returns to user mode with its program counter set to the first executable instruction of the new program.

Since *fork* and *exec* are so often used together, it may be argued that a single system call could efficiently accomplish both tasks, resulting in a new process running a new program. Older UNIX systems [Thom 78] also incurred a large overhead in duplicating the parent's address space for the child (during *fork*), only to have the child discard it completely and replace it with that of the new program.

There are many advantages of keeping the calls separate. In many client-server applications, the server program may *fork* numerous processes that continue to execute the same program.[9] In contrast, sometimes a process wants merely to invoke a new program, without creating a new process. Finally, between the *fork* and the *exec,* the child may optionally perform a number of tasks to ensure that the new program is invoked in the desired state. These tasks include:

- Redirecting standard input, output, or error.
- Closing open files inherited from the parent that are not needed by the new program.
- Changing the UID or *process group.*
- Resetting signal handlers.

A single system call that tries to perform all these functions would be unwieldy and inefficient. The existing *fork-exec* framework provides greater flexibility and is clean and modular. In

---

[9] Modern multi-threaded UNIX systems make this unnecessary – the server simply creates a number of threads.

Section 2.8.3 we will examine ways of minimizing the performance problems associated with this division.

2.8.2 Process Creation

The *fork* system call creates a new process that is almost an exact clone of the parent. The only differences are those necessary to distinguish between the two. Upon return from *fork*, both parent and child are executing the same program, have identical data and stack regions, and resume execution at the instruction immediately following the call to *fork*. The *fork* system call must perform the following actions:

1. Reserve swap space for the child's data and stack.
2. Allocate a new PID and `proc` structure for the child.
3. Initialize the child's `proc` structure. Some fields (such as user and group ID, process group, and signal masks) are copied from the parent, some set to zero (resident time, CPU usage, sleep channel, etc.), and others (such as PID, parent PID, and pointer to the parent `proc` structure) initialized to child-specific values.
4. Allocate address translation maps for the child.
5. Allocate the child's u area and copy it from the parent.
6. Update the u area to refer to the new address maps and swap space.
7. Add the child to the set of processes sharing the text region of the program that the parent is executing.
8. Duplicate the parent's data and stack regions one page at a time and update the child's address maps to refer to these new pages.
9. Acquire references to shared resources inherited by the child, such as open files and the current working directory.
10. Initialize the child's hardware context by copying a snapshot of the parent's registers.
11. Make the child runnable and put it on a scheduler queue.
12. Arrange for the child to return from *fork* with a value of zero.
13. Return the PID of the child to the parent.

2.8.3 *fork* Optimization

The *fork* system call must give the child a logically distinct copy of the parent's address space. In most cases, the child discards this address space when it calls *exec* or *exit* shortly after the *fork*. It is therefore wasteful to make an actual copy of the address space, as was done in older UNIX systems.

This problem has been addressed in two different ways. The first is the *copy-on-write* approach, first adopted by System V and now used by most UNIX systems. In this method, the data and stack pages of the parent are temporarily made read-only and marked as copy-on-write. The child receives its own copy of the address translation maps, but shares the memory pages with the parent. If either the parent or the child tries to modify a page, a page fault exception occurs (because the page is marked read-only) and the kernel fault handler is invoked. The handler recognizes that this is a copy-on-write page, and makes a new writable copy of that single page. Thus only those pages that are modified must be copied, not the entire address space. If the child calls *exec* or *exit,* the pages revert to their original protection, and the copy-on-write flag is cleared.

BSD UNIX provided another solution—a new *vfork* system call. A user may call *vfork* instead of *fork* if he or she expects to call *exec* shortly afterward. *vfork* does no copying. Instead, the parent loans its address space to the child and blocks until the child returns it. The child then executes using the parent's address space, until it calls *exec* or *exit,* whereupon the kernel returns the address space to the parent, and awakens it. *vfork* is extremely fast, since not even the address maps are copied. The address space is passed to the child simply by copying the address map registers. *It is, however, a dangerous call, because it permits one process to use and even modify the address space of another process.* Some programs such as *csh* exploit this feature.

2.8.4 Invoking a New Program

The *exec* system call replaces the address space of the calling process with that of a new program. If the process was created by a *vfork, exec* returns the old address space to the parent. Otherwise, it frees the old address space. *exec* gives the process a new address space and loads it with the contents of the new program. When *exec* returns, the process resumes execution at the first instruction of the new program.

The process address space has several distinct components:[10]

- **Text:** Contains the executable code, and corresponds to the text section of the program.
- **Initialized data:** Consists of data objects explicitly initialized in the program, and corresponds to the initialized data section of the executable file.
- **Uninitialized data:** Historically called the *block static storage (bss)* region, consists of data variables declared, but not initialized, in the program. Objects in this region are guaranteed to be zero-filled when first accessed. Because it is wasteful to store several pages of zeroes in the executable file, the program header simply records the total size of this region and relies on the operating system to generate zero-filled pages for these addresses.
- **Shared memory:** Many UNIX systems allow processes to share regions of memory.
- **Shared libraries:** If a system supports dynamically linked libraries, the process may have separate regions of memory containing library code and data that may be shared with other processes.
- **Heap:** Source for dynamically allocated memory. A process allocates memory from the heap by making the *brk* or *sbrk* system calls, or using the *malloc()* function in the standard C library. The kernel provides each process with a heap, and extends it when needed.
- **User stack:** The kernel allocates a stack for each process. In most traditional UNIX implementations, the kernel transparently catches stack overflow exceptions and extends the user stack up to a preset maximum.

Shared memory is standard in System V UNIX, but is not available in 4BSD (through release 4.3). Many BSD-based commercial variants support both shared memory and some form of

---

[10] This division is simply functional in nature; the kernel does not recognize so many different components. SVR4, for instance, views the address space as merely a collection of shared and private mappings.

shared libraries as value-added features. In the following description of *exec,* we will consider a simple program that uses neither of these features.

UNIX supports many executable file formats. The oldest is the *a.out* format, which has a 32-byte header followed by text and data sections and the symbol table. The program header contains the sizes of the *text, initialized data,* and *uninitialized data* regions, and the *entry point,* which is the address of the first instruction the program must execute. It also contains a *magic number,* which identifies the file as a valid executable file and gives further information about its format, such as whether the file is demand paged, or whether the data section begins on a page boundary. Each UNIX variant defines the set of magic numbers it supports.

The *exec* system call must perform the following tasks:

1. Parse the pathname and access the executable file.
2. Verify that the caller has execute permission for the file.
3. Read the header and check that it is a valid executable.[11]
4. If the file has SUID or SGID bits set in its mode, change the caller's effective UID or GID respectively to that of the owner of the file.
5. Copy the arguments to *exec* and the *environment variables* into kernel space, since the current user space is going to be destroyed.
6. Allocate swap space for the data and stack regions.
7. Free the old address space and the associated swap space. If the process was created by *vfork,* return the old address space to the parent instead.
8. Allocate address maps for the new text, data, and stack.
9. Set up the new address space. If the text region is already active (some other process is already running the same program), share it with this process. Otherwise, it must be initialized from the executable file. UNIX processes are usually demand paged, meaning that each page is read into memory only when the program needs it.
10. Copy the arguments and environment variables back onto the new user stack.
11. Reset all signal handlers to default actions, because the handler functions do not exist in the new program. Signals that were ignored or blocked before calling *exec* remain ignored or blocked.
12. Initialize the hardware context. Most registers are reset to zero, and the program counter is set to the entry point of the program.

2.8.5   Process Termination

The `exit()` function in the kernel terminates a process. It is called internally when the process is killed by a signal. Alternatively, the program may invoke the *exit* system call, which calls the `exit()` function. The `exit()` function performs the following actions:

---

[11] *exec* can also invoke shell scripts whose first line is

  `#!shell-name`

in which case, it invokes the program specified by `shell-name` (usually the name of a shell, but could be any executable file) and passes it the name of the script as the first argument. Some systems (such as UnixWare) require a space before the `shell-name`.

1. Turns off all signals.
2. Closes all open files.
3. Releases the text file and other resources such as the current directory.
4. Writes to the accounting log.
5. Saves resource usage statistics and exit status in the proc structure.
6. Changes state to SZOMB (zombie), and puts the proc structure on the zombie process list.
7. Makes the *init* process inherit (become the parent of) any live children of the exiting process.
8. Releases the address space, u area, address translation maps, and swap space.
9. Notifies the parent by sending it a SIGCHLD signal. This signal is ignored by default, and thus has an effect only if the parent wants to know about the child's death.
10. Wakes up the parent if it is asleep.
11. Finally, calls swtch() to schedule a new process to run.

When exit() completes, the process is in the zombie state. *exit* does not free the proc structure of the parent, because its parent may want to retrieve the exit status and resource usage information. The parent is responsible for freeing the child's proc structure, as described below. When that happens, the proc structure is returned to a free list, and the cleanup is complete.

2.8.6   Awaiting Process Termination

Often a parent process needs to know when a child terminates. For instance, when the shell spawns a foreground process to execute a command, it must wait for the child to complete, and then prompt for the next command. When a background process terminates, the shell may want to notify the user by printing an informational message on the terminal. The shell also retrieves the exit status of the child process, so that the user may take different actions based on its success or failure. UNIX systems provide the following calls to await process termination:

```
wait (stat_loc);                        /* System V, BSD, and POSIX.1 */
wait3 (statusp, options, rusagep);      /* BSD*/
waitpid (pid, stat_loc, options);       /* POSIX.1 */
waitid (idtype, id, infop, options);    /* SVR4[12] */
```

The *wait* system call allows a process to wait for a child to terminate. Since a child may have terminated before the call, *wait* must also handle that condition. *wait* first checks if the caller has any deceased or suspended children. If so, it returns immediately. If there are no deceased children, *wait* blocks the caller until one of its children dies and returns once that happens. In both cases, *wait* returns the PID of the deceased child, writes the child's exit status into stat_loc, and frees its proc structure (if more than one child is dead, *wait* acts only on the first one it finds). If the child is being traced, *wait* also returns when the child receives a signal. *wait* returns an error if the caller has no children (dead or alive), or if *wait* is interrupted by a signal.

---

[12] SVR4 supports *wait3* and *waitpid* as library functions.

4.3BSD provides a *wait3* call (so named because it requires three arguments), which also returns resource usage information about the child (user and system times of the child and all its deceased children). The POSIX.1 standard [IEEE 90] adds the *waitpid* call, which uses the pid argument to wait for a child with a specific process ID or process group. Both *wait3* and *waitpid* support two options: WNOHANG and WUNTRACED. WNOHANG causes *wait3* to return immediately if there are no deceased children. WUNTRACED also returns if a child is suspended or resumed. The SVR4 *waitid* call provides a superset of all the above features. It allows the caller to specify the process ID or group to wait for and the specific events to trap, and also returns more detailed information about the child process.

2.8.7   Zombie Processes

When a process exits, it remains in zombie state until cleaned up by its parent. In this state, the only resource it holds is a proc structure, which retains its exit status and resource usage information.[13] This information may be important to its parent. The parent retrieves this information by calling *wait,* which also frees the proc structure. If the parent dies before the child, the *init* process inherits the child. When the child dies, *init* calls *wait* to release the child's proc structure.

A problem may arise if a process dies before its parent, and the parent does not call *wait.* The child's proc structure is never released, and the child remains in the zombie state until the system is rebooted. This situation is rare, since the shells are written carefully to avoid this problem. It may happen, however, if a carelessly written application does not wait for all child processes. This is an annoyance, because such zombies are visible in the output of *ps* (and users are vexed to find that they cannot be killed—*they are already dead*). Furthermore, they use up a proc structure, thereby reducing the maximum number of processes that can be active.

Some newer UNIX variants allow a process to specify that it will not wait for its children. For instance, in SVR4, a process may specify the SA_NOCLDWAIT flag to the *sigaction* system call to specify the action for SIGCHLD signals. This asks the kernel not to create zombies when the caller's children terminate.

2.9   Summary

We have described the interactions between the kernel and user processes in traditional UNIX kernels. This provides a broad perspective, giving us the context needed to examine specific parts of the system in greater detail. Modern variants such as SVR4 and Solaris 2.*x* introduce several advanced facilities, which will be detailed in the following chapters.

2.10   Exercises

1.   What elements of the process context must the kernel explicitly save when handling (a) a context switch, (b) an interrupt, or (c) a system call?

---

[13] Some implementations use a special zombie structure to retain this data.

2. What are the advantages of allocating objects such as proc structures and descriptor table blocks dynamically? What are the drawbacks?

3. How does the kernel know which system call has been made? How does it access the arguments to the call (which are on the user stack)?

4. Compare and contrast the handling of system calls and of exceptions. What are the similarities and differences?

5. Many UNIX systems provide compatibility with another version of UNIX by providing user library functions to implement the system calls of the other version. Why, if at all, does the application developer care if a function is implemented by a library or by a system call?

6. What issues must a library developer be concerned with when choosing to implement a function in the user library instead of as a system call? What if the library must use multiple system calls to implement the function?

7. Why is it important to limit the amount of work an interrupt handler can do?

8. On a system with n distinct interrupt priority levels, what is the maximum number of interrupts that may be nested at a time? What repercussions can this have on the sizes of various stacks?

9. The Intel 80x86 architecture does not support interrupt priorities. It provides two instructions for interrupt management—CLI to disable all interrupts, and STI to enable all interrupts. Write an algorithm to implement interrupt priority levels in software for such a machine.

10. When a resource becomes available, the wakeup() routine wakes up all processes blocked on it. What are the drawbacks of this approach? What are the alternatives?

11. Propose a new system call that combines the functions of *fork* and *exec*. Define its interface and semantics. How would it support features such as I/O redirection, foreground or background execution, and pipes?

12. What is the problem with returning an error from the exec system call? How can the kernel handle this problem?

13. For a UNIX system of your choice, write a function that allows a process to wait for its *parent* to terminate.

14. Suppose a process does not wish to block until its children terminate. How can it ensure that child processes are cleaned up when they terminate?

15. Why does a terminating process wake up its parent?

2.11   References

[Allm 87]   Allman, E., "UNIX: The Data Forms," *Proceedings of the Winter 1987 USENIX Technical Conference,* Jan. 1987, pp. 9–15.

[AT&T 87]   American Telephone and Telegraph, *The System V Interface Definition (SVID),* Issue 2, 1987.

[Bach 86]   Bach, M.J., *The Design of the UNIX Operating System,* Prentice-Hall, Englewood Cliffs, NJ, 1986.

[Kern 84]   Kernighan, B.W., and Pike, R., *The UNIX Programming Environment,* Prentice-Hall, Englewood Cliffs, NJ, 1984.

[Leff 89]   Leffler, S.J., McKusick, M.K., Karels, M.J., and Quarterman, J.S., *The Design and Implementation of the 4.3 BSD UNIX Operating System,* Addison-Wesley, Reading, MA, 1989.

[IEEE 90]   Institute for Electrical and Electronic Engineers, *Information Technology—Portable Operating System Interface (POSIX) Part 1: System Application Program Interface (API) [C Language],* 1003.1–1990, IEEE, Dec. 1990.

[IEEE 94]   Institute for Electrical and Electronic Engineers, POSIX P1003.4a, *Threads Extension for Portable Operating Systems,* 1994.

[Sale 92]   Salemi, C., Shah, S., and Lund, E., "A Privilege Mechanism for UNIX System V Release 4 Operating Systems," *Proceedings of the Summer 1992 USENIX Technical Conference,* Jun. 1992, pp. 235–241.

[Thom 78]   Thompson, K., "UNIX Implementation," *The Bell System Technical Journal,* Vol. 57, No. 6, Part 2, Jul.-Aug. 1978, pp. 1931–1946.

3

Threads and Lightweight Processes

3.1 Introduction

The process model has two important limitations. First, many applications wish to perform several largely independent tasks that can run concurrently, but must share a common address space and other resources. Examples of such applications include server-side database managers, transaction-processing monitors, and middle- and upper-layer network protocols. These processes are inherently parallel in nature and require a programming model that supports parallelism. Traditional UNIX systems force such applications to serialize these independent tasks or to devise awkward and inefficient mechanisms to manage multiple operations.

Second, traditional processes cannot take advantage of multiprocessor architectures, because a process can use only one processor at a time. An application must create a number of separate processes and dispatch them on the available processors. These processes must find ways of sharing memory and resources, and synchronizing their tasks with each other.

Modern UNIX variants address these problems by providing a variety of primitives in the operating system to support concurrent processing. The lack of standard terminology makes it difficult to describe and compare the wide assortment of intraprocess parallelization mechanisms. Each UNIX variant uses its own nomenclature, including terms such as *kernel threads, user threads, kernel-supported user threads, C-threads, pthreads,* and *lightweight processes*. This chapter clarifies the terminology, explains the basic abstractions, and describes the facilities provided by some important UNIX variants. Finally, it evaluates the strengths and weaknesses of these mechanisms. We begin by investigating the necessity and benefits of threads.

3.1.1 Motivation

Many programs must perform several largely independent tasks that do not need to be serialized. For instance, a database server may listen for and process numerous client requests. Since the requests do not need to be serviced in a particular order, they may be treated as independent execution units, which in principle could run in parallel. The application would perform better if the system provided mechanisms for concurrent execution of the subtasks.

On traditional UNIX systems, such programs use multiple processes. Most server applications have a *listener process* that waits for client requests. When a request arrives, the listener *forks* a new process to service it. Since servicing of the request often involves I/O operations that may block the process, this approach yields some concurrency benefits even on uniprocessor systems.

Next, consider a scientific application that computes the values of various terms in an array, each term being independent of the others. It could create a different process for each element of the array and achieve true parallelism by dispatching each process to run on a different computer, or perhaps on different CPUs of a multiprocessor system. Even on uniprocessor machines, it may be desirable to divide the work among multiple processes. If one process must block for I/O or page fault servicing, another process can progress in the meantime. As another example, the UNIX *make* facility allows users to compile several files in parallel, using a separate process for each.

Using multiple processes in an application has some obvious disadvantages. Creating all these processes adds substantial overhead, since *fork* is usually an expensive system call (even on systems that support *copy-on-write* sharing of address spaces). Because each process has its own address space, it must use interprocess communication facilities such as message passing or shared memory. Additional work is required to dispatch processes to different machines or processors, pass information between these processes, wait for their completion, and gather the results. Finally, UNIX systems have no appropriate frameworks for sharing certain resources, e.g., network connections. Such a model is justified only if the benefits of concurrency offset the cost of creating and managing multiple processes.

These examples serve primarily to underscore the inadequacies of the process abstraction and the need for better facilities for parallel computation. We can now identify the concept of a fairly independent computational unit that is part of the total processing work of an application. These units have relatively few interactions with one another and hence low synchronization requirements. An application may contain one or more such units. The *thread* abstraction represents a single computational unit. The traditional UNIX process is single-threaded, meaning that all computation is serialized within the same unit.

The mechanisms described in this chapter address the limitations of the process model. They too have their own drawbacks, which are discussed at the end of the chapter.

3.1.2 Multiple Threads and Processors

For parallelized, compute-bound applications, the advantages of multithreaded systems are most apparent when combined with multiprocessor architectures. By running each thread on a different processor, an application can achieve true parallelism. If the number of threads is greater than the number of processors, the threads must be multiplexed on the available processors.[1] Ideally, an application will have *n* threads running on *n* processors and will finish its work in $1/n^{th}$ the time required by a single-threaded version of the program. In practice, the overhead of creating, managing, and synchronizing thread, and that of the multiprocessor operating system, will reduce the benefit well below this ideal ratio.

Figure 3-1 shows a set of single-threaded processes executing on a uniprocessor machine. The system provides an illusion of concurrency by executing each process for a brief period of time *(time slice)* before switching to the next. In this example the first three processes are running the server side of a client-server application. The server program spawns a new process for each active client. The processes have nearly identical address spaces and share information with one another using interprocess communication mechanisms. The lower two processes are running another server application.

Figure 3-2 shows two servers running in a multithreaded system. Each server runs as a single process, with multiple threads sharing a single address space. Interthread context switching may be handled by either the kernel or a user-level threads library, depending on the operating system. For both cases, this example shows some of the benefits of threads. Eliminating multiple, nearly identical address spaces for each application reduces the load on the memory subsystem. (Even modern systems using *copy-on-write* memory sharing must manage separate address translation maps for each process.) Since all threads of an application share a common address space, they can use efficient, lightweight, interthread communication and synchronization mechanisms.

The potential disadvantages of this approach are evident. A single-threaded process does not have to protect its data from other processes. Multithreaded processes must be concerned with every

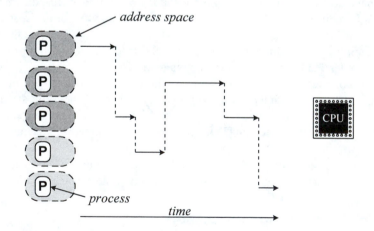

Figure 3-1. Traditional UNIX system—uniprocessor with single-threaded processes.

---

[1] This means using each available processor to service the runnable threads. Of course, a processor can run only one thread at a time.

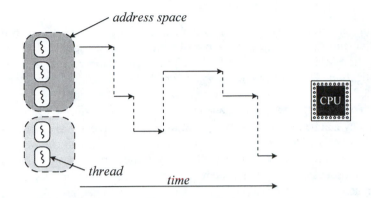

Figure 3-2. Multithreaded processes in a uniprocessor system.

object in their address space. If more than one thread can access an object, they must use some form of synchronization to avoid data corruption.

Figure 3-3 shows two multithreaded processes running on a multiprocessor. All threads of one process share the same address space, but each runs on a different processor. Hence they all run concurrently. This improves performance considerably, but also complicates the synchronization problems.

Although the two facilities combine well together, they are also useful independently. A multiprocessor system is also useful for single-threaded applications, as several processes can run in parallel. Likewise, there are significant benefits of multithreaded applications, even on single-processor systems. When one thread must block for I/O or some other resource, another thread can be scheduled to run, and the application continues to progress. The thread abstraction is more suited for representing the intrinsic concurrency of a program than for mapping software designs to multi-processor hardware architectures.

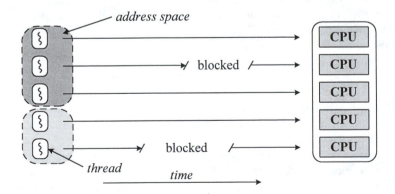

Figure 3-3. Multithreaded processes on a multiprocessor.

3.1.3   Concurrency and Parallelism

To understand the different types of thread abstractions, we must first distinguish between concurrency and parallelism [Blac 90]. The *parallelism* of a multiprocessor application is the actual degree of parallel execution achieved and is therefore limited by the number of physical processors available to the application. The application's *concurrency* is the maximum parallelism it can achieve with an unlimited number of processors. It depends on how the application is written, and how many threads of control can execute simultaneously, with the proper resources available.

Concurrency can be provided at the system or application level. The kernel provides *system concurrency* by recognizing multiple threads of control (also called *hot threads*) within a process and scheduling them independently. It then multiplexes these threads onto the available processor(s). An application can benefit from system concurrency even on a uniprocessor, because if one thread blocks on an event or resource, the kernel can schedule another thread.

Applications can provide *user concurrency* through user-level thread libraries. Such user threads, or *coroutines* (also called *cold threads*), are not recognized by the kernel and must be scheduled and managed by the applications themselves. This does not provide true concurrency or parallelism, since such threads cannot actually run in parallel. *It does, however, provide a more natural programming model for concurrent applications.* By using nonblocking system calls, an application can simultaneously maintain several interactions in progress. User threads simplify programming by capturing the state of such interactions in per-thread local variables (on that thread's stack) instead of in a global state table.

Each of the concurrency models has limited value by itself. Threads are used both as organizational tools and to exploit multiple processors. A kernel threads facility allows parallel execution on multiprocessors, but is not suitable for structuring user applications. For example, a server application may want to create thousands of threads, one for each client. Kernel threads consume valuable resources such as physical memory (since many implementations require thread structures to be memory resident), and hence are not useful for such a program. Conversely, a purely user-level facility is only useful for structuring applications and does not permit parallel execution of code.

Many systems implement a *dual concurrency* model that combines system and user concurrency. The kernel recognizes multiple threads in a process, and libraries add user threads that are not seen by the kernel. User threads allow synchronization between concurrent routines in a program without the overhead of making system calls, and are therefore desirable even in systems with multithreaded kernels. Moreover, it is always a good idea to reduce the size and responsibilities of the kernel, and splitting the thread support functionality between the kernel and the threads library is consistent with that strategy.

3.2   Fundamental Abstractions

A process is a compound entity that can be divided into two components—a set of *threads* and a collection of resources. The *thread* is a dynamic object that represents a control point in the process and that executes a sequence of instructions. The resources, which include an address space, open files, user credentials, quotas, and so on, are shared by all threads in the process. In addition, each thread has its private objects, such as a program counter, a stack, and a register context. The traditional UNIX process has a single thread of control. Multithreaded systems extend this concept by allowing more than one thread of control in each process.

Centralizing resource ownership in the process abstraction has some drawbacks. Consider a server application that carries out file operations on behalf of remote clients. To ensure compliance with file access permissions, the server assumes the identity of the client while servicing a request. To do so, the server is installed with superuser privileges, and calls *setuid, setgid*, and *setgroups* to temporarily change its user credentials to match those of the client. Multithreading this server to increase the concurrency causes security problems. Since the process has a single set of credentials, it can only pretend to be one client at a time. Hence the server is forced to serialize (single-thread) all system calls that check for security.

There are several different types of threads, each having different properties and uses. In this section, we describe three important types—*kernel threads, lightweight processes,* and *user threads.*

3.2.1 Kernel Threads

A *kernel thread* need not be associated with a user process. It is created and destroyed as needed internally by the kernel and is responsible for executing a specific function. It shares the kernel text and global data, and has its own kernel stack. It can be independently scheduled and uses the standard synchronization mechanisms of the kernel, such as `sleep()` and `wakeup()`.

Kernel threads are useful for performing operations such as asynchronous I/O. Instead of providing special mechanisms to handle this, the kernel can simply create a new thread to handle each such request. The request is handled synchronously by the thread, but appears asynchronous to the rest of the kernel. Kernel threads may also be used to handle interrupts, as discussed in Section 3.6.5.

Kernel threads are inexpensive to create and use. The only resources they use are the kernel stack and an area to save the register context when not running (we also need some data structure to hold scheduling and synchronization information). Context switching between kernel threads is also quick, since the memory mappings do not have to be flushed.

Kernel threads are not a new concept. System processes such as the *pagedaemon* in traditional UNIX kernels are functionally equivalent to kernel threads. Daemon processes such as *nfsd* (the Network File System server process) are started at the user level, but once started, execute entirely in the kernel. Their user context is not required once they enter kernel mode. They too are equivalent to kernel threads. Since traditional systems lacked a separate abstraction to represent kernel threads, such processes were encumbered with the unnecessary baggage associated with a traditional process, such as `proc` and `user` structures. Multithreaded kernels allow these daemons to be implemented more simply as kernel threads.

3.2.2 Lightweight Processes

A *lightweight process (LWP)* is a kernel-supported user thread. It is a higher-level abstraction based on kernel threads; hence a system must support kernel threads before it can support LWPs. Every process may have one or more LWPs, each supported by a separate kernel thread (Figure 3-4). The LWPs are independently scheduled and share the address space and other resources of the process.

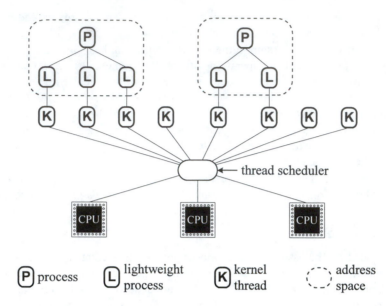

Figure 3-4. Lightweight processes.

They can make system calls and block for I/O or resources. On a multiprocessor system, a process can enjoy the benefits of true parallelism, because each LWP can be dispatched to run on a different processor. There are significant advantages even on a uniprocessor, since resource and I/O waits block individual LWPs, not the entire process.

Besides the kernel stack and register context, an LWP also needs to maintain some user state. This primarily includes the user register context, which must be saved when the LWP is preempted. While each LWP is associated with a kernel thread, some kernel threads may be dedicated to system tasks and not have an LWP.

Such multithreaded processes are most useful when each thread is fairly independent and does not interact often with other threads. User code is fully preemptible, and all LWPs in a process share a common address space. *If any data can be accessed concurrently by multiple LWPs, such access must be synchronized.* The kernel therefore provides facilities to lock shared variables and to block an LWP if it tries to access locked data. These facilities, such as mutual exclusion *(mutex)* locks, semaphores, and condition variables, are further detailed in Chapter 7.

It is important to note the limitations of LWPs. Most LWP operations, such as creation, destruction, and synchronization, require system calls. System calls are relatively expensive operations for several reasons: Each system call requires two *mode switches*—one from user to kernel mode on invocation, and another back to user mode on completion. On each mode switch, the LWP crosses a *protection boundary.* The kernel must copy the system call parameters from user to kernel space and validate them to protect against malicious or buggy processes. Likewise, on return from the system call, the kernel must copy data back to user space.

When the LWPs frequently access shared data, the synchronization overhead can nullify any performance benefits. Most multiprocessor systems provide locks that can be acquired at the user level if not already held by another thread [Muel 93]. If a thread wants a resource that is currently unavailable, it may execute a busy-wait (loop until the resource is free), again without kernel involvement. Busy-waiting is reasonable for resources that are held only briefly; in other cases, it is necessary to block the thread. *Blocking an LWP requires kernel involvement* and hence is expensive.

Each LWP consumes significant kernel resources, including physical memory for a kernel stack. Hence a system cannot support a large number of LWPs. Moreover, since the system has a single LWP implementation, it must be general enough to support most reasonable applications. It will therefore be burdened with a lot of baggage that many applications do not need. LWPs are unsuitable for applications that use a large number of threads, or that frequently create and destroy them. Finally, LWPs must be scheduled by the kernel. Applications that must often transfer control from one thread to another cannot do so easily using LWPs. LWP use also raises some fairness issues—a user can monopolize the processor by creating a large number of LWPs.

In summary, while the kernel provides the mechanisms for creating, synchronizing, and managing LWPs, it is the responsibility of the programmer to use them judiciously. Many applications are better served by a user-level threads facility, such as that described in the next section.

> **Note:** *The term* LWP *is borrowed from the SVR4/MP and Solaris 2.x terminology. It is somewhat confusing, since version 4.x of SunOS [Kepe 85] uses the term* LWPs *to refer to the user-level threads described in the next section. In this book, however, we consistently use* LWP *to refer to kernel-supported user threads. Some systems use the term* virtual processor, *which is essentially the same as an LWP.*

3.2.3 User Threads

It is possible to provide the thread abstraction entirely at the user level, without the kernel knowing anything about them. This is accomplished through library packages such as Mach's *C-threads* and POSIX *pthreads*. Such libraries provide all the functions for creating, synchronizing, scheduling, and managing threads with no special assistance from the kernel. Thread interactions do not involve the kernel and hence are extremely fast.[2] Figure 3-5(a) illustrates such a configuration.

Figure 3-5(b) combines user threads and lightweight processes to create a very powerful programming environment. The kernel recognizes, schedules, and manages LWPs. A user-level library multiplexes user threads on top of LWPs and provides facilities for interthread scheduling, context switching, and synchronization without involving the kernel. In effect, the library acts as a miniature kernel for the threads it controls.

The implementation of user threads is possible because the user-level context of a thread can be saved and restored without kernel intervention. Each user thread has its own user stack, an area to save user-level register context, and other state information, such as signal masks. The library

---

2 Many threads library features require the kernel to provide facilities for asynchronous I/O.

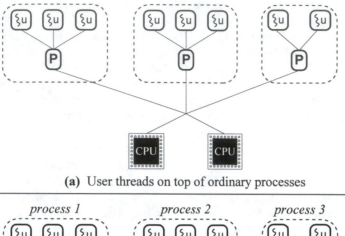

(a) User threads on top of ordinary processes

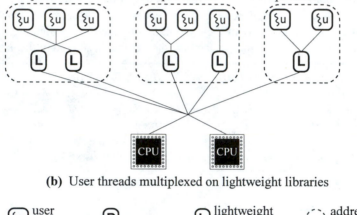

(b) User threads multiplexed on lightweight libraries

| $\{u$ user thread | P process | L lightweight process | address space |

Figure 3-5. User thread implementations.

schedules and switches context between user threads by saving the current thread's stack and registers, then loading those of the newly scheduled one.

The kernel retains the responsibility for process switching, because it alone has the privilege to modify the memory management registers. User threads are not truly schedulable entities, and the kernel has no knowledge of them. The kernel simply schedules the underlying process or LWP, which in turn uses library functions to schedule its threads. When the process or LWP is preempted, so are its threads. Likewise, if a user thread makes a blocking system call, it blocks the underlying LWP. If the process has only one LWP (or if the user threads are implemented on a single-threaded system), all its threads are blocked.

The library also provides synchronization objects to protect shared data structures. Such an object usually comprises a type of lock variable (such as a semaphore) and a queue of threads blocked on it. Threads must acquire the lock before accessing the data structure. If the object is already locked, the library blocks the thread by linking it onto its blocked threads queue and transferring control to another thread.

Modern UNIX systems provide asynchronous I/O mechanisms, which allow processes to perform I/O without blocking. SVR4, for example, offers an IO_SETSIG *ioctl* operation to any STREAMS device. (STREAMS are described Chapter 17.) A subsequent *read* or *write* to the stream simply queues the operation and returns without blocking. When the I/O completes, the process is informed via a SIGPOLL signal.

Asynchronous I/O is a very useful feature, because it allows a process to perform other tasks while waiting for I/O. However, it leads to a complex programming model. It is desirable to restrict asynchrony to the operating system level and give applications a synchronous programming environment. A threads library achieves this by providing a synchronous interface that uses the asynchronous mechanisms internally. Each request is synchronous with respect to the calling thread, which blocks until the I/O completes. The process, however, continues to make progress, since the library invokes the asynchronous operation and schedules another user thread to run in the meantime. When the I/O completes, the library reschedules the blocked thread.

User threads have several benefits. They provide a more natural way of programming many applications such as windowing systems. User threads also provide a synchronous programming paradigm by hiding the complexities of asynchronous operations in the threads library. This alone makes them useful, even in systems lacking any kernel support for threads. A system can provide several threads libraries, each optimized for a different class of applications.

The greatest advantage of user threads is performance. User threads are extremely lightweight and consume no kernel resources except when bound to an LWP. Their performance gains result from implementing the functionality at user level without using system calls. This avoids the overhead of trap processing and moving parameters and data across protection boundaries. A useful notion is the *critical thread size* [Bita 95], which indicates the amount of work a thread must do to be useful as a separate entity. This size depends on the overhead associated with creating and using a thread. For user threads, the critical size is of the order of a few hundred instructions and may be reduced to less than a hundred with compiler support. User threads require much less time for creation, destruction, and synchronization. Table 3-1 compares the latency for different operations on processes, LWPs, and user threads on a SPARCstation 2 [Sun 93].

On the other hand, user threads have several limitations, primarily due to the total separation of information between the kernel and the threads library. Since the kernel does not know about user threads, it cannot use its protection mechanisms to protect them from each other. Each process has its own address space, which the kernel protects from unauthorized access by other processes. User

Table 3-1. Latency of user thread, LWP, and process operations on SPARCstation 2

	Creation time (microseconds)	Synchronization time using semaphores (microseconds)
User thread	52	66
LWP	350	390
Process	1700	200

threads enjoy no such protection, operating in the common address space owned by the process. The threads library must provide synchronization facilities, which requires cooperation from the threads.

The split scheduling model causes many other problems. The threads library schedules the user threads, the kernel schedules the underlying processes or LWPs, and neither knows what the other is doing. For instance, the kernel may preempt an LWP whose user thread is holding a spin lock. If another user thread on a different LWP tries to acquire this lock, it will busy-wait until the holder of the lock runs again. Likewise, because the kernel does not know the relative priorities of user threads, it may preempt an LWP running a high-priority user thread to schedule an LWP running a lower-priority user thread.

The user-level synchronization mechanisms may behave incorrectly in some instances. Most applications are written on the assumption that all runnable threads are eventually scheduled. This is true when each thread is bound to a separate LWP, but may not be valid when the user threads are multiplexed onto a small number of LWPs. Since the LWP may block in the kernel when its user thread makes a blocking system call, a process may run out of LWPs even when there are runnable threads and available processors. The availability of an asynchronous I/O mechanism may help to mitigate this problem.

Finally, without explicit kernel support, user threads may improve concurrency, but do not increase parallelism. Even on a multiprocessor, user threads sharing a single LWP cannot execute in parallel.

This section explains three commonly used thread abstractions. Kernel threads are primitive objects not visible to applications. Lightweight processes are user-visible threads that are recognized by the kernel and are based on kernel threads. User threads are higher-level objects not visible to the kernel. They may use lightweight processes if supported by the system, or they may be implemented in a standard UNIX process without special kernel support. Both LWPs and user threads have major drawbacks that limit their usefulness. Section 3.5 describes a new framework based on *scheduler activations,* which addresses many of these problems. First, however, we examine the issues related to LWP and user thread design in greater detail.

3.3   Lightweight Process Design—Issues to Consider

There are several factors that influence the design of lightweight processes. Foremost is the need to properly preserve UNIX semantics, at least for the single-threaded case. This means that a process containing a single LWP must behave exactly like a traditional UNIX process. (Note again that the term *LWP* refers to kernel-supported user threads, not to the SunOS 4.0 lightweight processes, which are purely user-level objects.)

There are several areas where UNIX concepts do not map easily to a multithreaded system. The following sections examine these issues and present possible solutions.

3.3.1   Semantics of *fork*

System calls in a multithreaded environment have some unusual implications. Many calls that deal with process creation, address space manipulation, or operating on per process resources (such as open files) must be redesigned. There are two important guidelines. First, the system call must satisfy traditional UNIX semantics in the single-threaded case; second, when issued by a multithreaded process, the system call should behave in a reasonable manner that closely approximates the single-threaded semantics. With that in mind, let us examine some important system calls that are affected by the multithreading design.

In traditional UNIX, *fork* creates a child process, which is almost an exact clone of the parent. The only differences are those necessary to distinguish the parent from the child. The semantics of fork are clear for a single-threaded process. In the case of a multithreaded process, there is an option of duplicating all LWPs of the parent or only the one that invokes the *fork*.

Suppose *fork* copies only the calling LWP into the new process. This is definitely more efficient. It is also a better model for the case where the child soon invokes another program by calling *exec*. This interface has several problems [Powe 91]. LWPs are often used to support user-level thread libraries. Such libraries represent each user thread by a data structure in user space. If *fork* duplicates only the calling LWP, the new process will contain user-level threads that do not map to any LWP. Furthermore, the child process must not try to acquire locks held by threads that do not exist in the child, because this could result in deadlock. This may be difficult to enforce, because libraries often create hidden threads of which the programmer is unaware.

On the other hand, suppose *fork* duplicates all the LWPs of the parent. This is more useful when *fork* is used to clone the entire process, rather than to run another program. It also has many problems. An LWP in the parent may be blocked in a system call. Its state will be undefined in the child. One possibility is to make such calls return the status code EINTR (system call interrupted), allowing the LWP to restart them if necessary. An LWP may have open network connections. Closing the connection in the child may cause unexpected messages to be sent to the remote node. Some LWP may be manipulating an external shared data structure, which could become corrupted if *fork* clones the LWP.

Neither solution handles all situations correctly. Many systems compromise by offering two variants of *fork*, one to duplicate the whole process and the other to duplicate a single thread. For the latter case, these systems define a set of safe functions that may be called by the child prior to the *exec*. Another alternative is to allow the process to register one or more *fork handlers,* which are functions that run in the parent or the child, before or after the *fork,* as specified during registration.

3.3.2 Other System Calls

Many other system calls must be modified to work correctly in a multithreaded system. All LWPs in a process share a common set of file descriptors. This causes a conflict if one LWP closes a file that another is currently reading or writing. The file *offset pointer* is also shared through the descriptor, so an *lseek* done by one LWP will affect all others. Figure 3-6 illustrates the problem. LWP **L1** wants to read data from a file starting at offset *off1* and issues an *lseek* followed by a *read*. Between the two calls, **L2** issues an *lseek* to the same file, specifying a different offset. This causes **L1** to read the wrong data. The application could solve the problem directly by using some file locking protocol. Alternatively, the kernel could provide mechanisms to perform random I/O atomically (see Section 3.6.6).

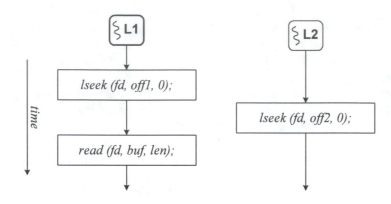

Figure 3-6. Problems with concurrent access to a file.

Likewise, the process has a single current working directory and a single user credentials structure. Since the credentials may change at any time, the kernel must sample them atomically, only once per system call.

All LWPs of a process share a common address space and may manipulate it concurrently through system calls such as *mmap* and *brk*. These calls must be made thread-safe so that they do not corrupt the address space in such situations. Programmers must be careful to serialize such operations, otherwise the results may be unexpected.

3.3.3   Signal Delivery and Handling

In UNIX, signals are delivered to and handled by processes. A multithreaded system must decide which LWP of the process should handle the signal. The problem also applies to user threads, since once the kernel delivers the signal to an LWP, the threads library can direct it to a specific thread. There are several possible answers:

1. Send the signal to each thread.
2. Appoint a master thread in each process to receive all signals.
3. Send the signal to any arbitrarily chosen thread.
4. Use heuristics to determine the thread to which the signal applies.
5. Create a new thread to handle each signal.

The first is highly expensive, not to mention incompatible with most normal applications of signals. It is, however, useful in certain situations. For instance, when a user presses *control-Z* at the terminal, he may wish to suspend all threads of the process. The second leads to an asymmetric treatment of threads, which is incompatible with the modern approach and with the symmetric multiprocessing systems often associated with multithreaded kernels. The fifth solution is reasonable for some specific situations only.

The choice between the remaining two alternatives depends on the nature of the generated signal. Some signals, such as SIGSEGV (segmentation fault) and SIGILL (illegal exception), are caused by a thread itself. It makes more sense to deliver such a signal to the thread that caused it. Other signals, such as SIGTSTP (stop signal generated from the terminal) and SIGINT (interrupt signal), are generated by external events and cannot logically be associated with any particular thread.

Another related issue is that of signal handling and masking. Must all threads share a common set of signal handlers, or can each define its own? Although the latter approach is more versatile and flexible, it adds considerable overhead to each thread, which defeats the main purpose in having multithreaded processes. The same considerations do not hold for signal masking. Signals are normally masked to protect critical regions of code. Hence it is better to allow each thread to specify its own signal mask. The overhead of per-thread masks is relatively low and acceptable.

3.3.4   Visibility

It is important to decide to what extent an LWP is visible outside the process. The kernel undoubtedly knows about LWPs and schedules them independently. Most implementations do not allow processes to know about or interact with specific LWPs of another process.

Within a process, however, it is often desirable for the LWPs to know about each other. Many systems therefore provide a special system call that allows one LWP to send a signal to another specific LWP within the same process.

3.3.5   Stack Growth

When a UNIX process overflows its stack, it results in a segmentation violation fault. The kernel recognizes that the fault occurred in the stack segment and automatically extends the stack[3] instead of signaling the process.

A multithreaded process has several stacks, one for each user thread. These threads are allocated at the user level by the threads library. It is therefore incorrect for the kernel to try to extend the stack, since that might conflict with the operation of the stack allocator in the user threads library.

Therefore in multithreaded systems, the kernel has no knowledge of user stacks.[4] There may not be a special stack region, and stacks may be allocated by the user from the heap area (part of the data region). Usually, a thread will specify the size of the stack it needs, and the library may protect against overflow by allocating a write-protected page just beyond the end of the stack. This causes a protection fault when the stack overflows, and the kernel responds by sending a SIGSEGV signal to the appropriate thread. It is the thread's responsibility to extend the stack or handle the overflow in another manner.[5]

---

[3] Up to a configurable limit. In SVR4, the stack size is limited by the value RLIMIT_NOFILE. This value comprises a *hard limit* and a *soft limit*. The *getrlimit* system call retrieves these limits. The *setrlimit* call may lower the hard limit, or lower or raise the soft limit so long as it does not exceed the hard limit.

[4] Some multithreaded systems, such as SVR4.2/MP, provide facilities for automatic extension of a user thread stack.

[5] Of course, this signal must be handled on a special stack, since the normal stack has no room for the signal handler to operate. Modern UNIX systems provide a way for an application to specify an alternate stack for signal handling (see Section 4.5).

3.4   User-Level Threads Libraries

The design of a user-level threads package must address two important issues—what kind of programming interface the package will present to the user, and how it can be implemented using the
primitives provided by the operating system. There are many different threads packages, such as in
Chorus [Arma 90], Topaz [Vand 88], and Mach's *C threads* [Coop 90]. More recently, the P1003.4a
IEEE POSIX standards group has generated several drafts of a threads package known as *pthreads*
[IEEE 94]. Modern UNIX versions strive to support the *pthreads* interface to comply with this standard (see Section 3.8.3).

3.4.1   The Programming Interface

The interface provided by a threads package must include several important facilities. It must provide a large set of operations on threads, such as

- creating and terminating threads
- suspending and resuming threads
- assigning priorities to individual threads
- thread scheduling and context switching
- synchronizing activities through facilities such as semaphores and mutual exclusion locks
- sending messages from one thread to another

    The threads package strives to minimize kernel involvement, because the overhead of
switching back and forth between user and kernel modes can be significant. Therefore the threads
library provides as many facilities as possible. The kernel generally has no explicit knowledge of
user threads, but the threads library may use system calls to implement some of its functionality.
This has some important implications. For instance, the thread priority is unrelated to the kernel
scheduling priority, which is assigned to the underlying process or LWP. It is simply a process-
relative priority used by the *threads scheduler* to select a thread to run within the process.

3.4.2   Implementing Threads Libraries

The implementation of the library depends on the facilities for multithreading provided by the kernel. Many packages have been implemented on traditional UNIX kernels, which offer no special
support for threads. Here, the threads library acts as a miniature kernel, maintaining all the state information for each thread and handling all thread operations at the user level. Although this effectively serializes all processing, some measure of concurrency is provided by using the asynchronous
I/O facilities of the system.

    In many modern systems, the kernel supports multithreaded processes through LWPs. In this
case, user threads libraries have a choice of implementations:

- Bind each thread to a different LWP. This is easier to implement, but uses more kernel resources and offers little added value. It requires kernel involvement in all synchronization
  and thread scheduling operations.

- Multiplex user threads on a (smaller) set of LWPs. This is more efficient, as it consumes fewer kernel resources. This method works well when all threads in a process are roughly equivalent. It provides no easy way of guaranteeing resources to a particular thread.
- Allow a mixture of bound and unbound threads in the same process. This allows the application to fully exploit the concurrency and parallelism of the system. It also allows preferential handling of a bound thread, by increasing the scheduling priority of its underlying LWPs or by giving its LWP exclusive ownership of a processor.

The threads library contains a scheduling algorithm that selects which user thread to run. It maintains per-thread state and priority, which has no relation to the state or priority of the underlying LWPs. Consider the example in Figure 3-7, which shows six user threads multiplexed onto two LWPs. The library schedules one thread to run on each LWP. These threads (**u5** and **u6**) are in the *running* state, even though the underlying LWPs may be blocked in the middle of a system call, or preempted and waiting to be scheduled.

A thread (such as **u1** or **u2** in Figure 3-7) enters the *blocked* state when it tries to acquire a synchronization object locked by another thread. When the lock is released, the library unblocks the thread, and puts it on the scheduler queue. The thread (such as **u3** and **u4** in Figure 3-7) is now in the *runnable* state, waiting to be scheduled. The threads scheduler selects a thread from this queue based on priority and LWP affiliation. *This mechanism closely parallels the kernel's resource wait and scheduling algorithms.* As mentioned previously, the threads library acts as a miniature kernel for the threads it manages.

[Doep 87], [Muel 93] and [Powe 91] discuss user threads in more detail.

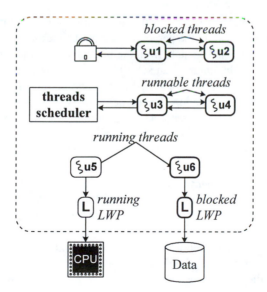

Figure 3-7. User thread states.

3.5   Scheduler Activations

Sections 3.3 and 3.4 describe the benefits and drawbacks of LWPs and user threads. Neither model
is entirely satisfactory. Application developers want the performance benefits and flexibility of user
threads. At the same time, user threads cannot match the functionality of LWPs due to lack of integration with the kernel. [Ande 91] describes a new threads architecture that combines the advantages of both models. This framework has gained acceptance in the operating systems community
and is emerging in commercial threads implementations by vendors such as SGI [Bita 95].

The basic principle is to have close integration between user threads and the kernel. The kernel is responsible for processor allocation, the threads library for scheduling. The library informs the
kernel of events that affect processor allocation. It may request additional processors or relinquish a
processor that it owns. The kernel controls processor allocation completely and may randomly preempt a processor and allocate it to another process.

Once the library is given some processors, it has complete control over which threads to
schedule on them. If the kernel takes away a processor, it will inform the library, which reassigns
the threads appropriately. If a thread blocks in the kernel, the process does not lose the processor.
The kernel informs the library, which immediately schedules another user thread onto that processor.

The implementation requires two new abstractions—an *upcall* and a *scheduler activation*.
An upcall is a call made by the kernel to the threads library. The scheduler activation is an execution
context that may be used to run a user thread. It is similar to an LWP and has its own kernel and
user stacks. When the kernel makes an upcall, it passes an activation to the library, which the latter
uses to process the event, run a new thread, or invoke another system call. The kernel does not time-
slice activations on a processor. At any time, a process has exactly one activation for each processor
assigned to it.

A distinctive feature of the scheduler activations framework is its handling of blocking operations. When a user thread blocks in the kernel, the kernel creates a new activation and upcalls to
the library. The library saves the thread state from the old activation and informs the kernel that the
old activation may be reused. The library then schedules another user thread on the new activation.
When the blocking operation completes, the kernel makes another upcall to notify the library of the
event. This upcall requires a new activation. The kernel may assign a new processor to run this activation, or preempt one of the current activations of this process. In the latter case, the upcall notifies
the library of two events—one, that the original thread may be resumed, and two, that the thread
running on that processor has been preempted. The library puts both threads on the ready list, and
then decides which to schedule first.

Scheduler activations have many advantages. They are extremely fast, since most operations
do not require kernel involvement. Benchmarks described in [Ande 91] show that a threads package
based on activations performs comparably to other user threads libraries. Since the kernel informs
the library of blocking and preemption events, the library can make intelligent scheduling and synchronization decisions, and avoid deadlocks and incorrect semantics. For instance, if the kernel preempts a processor whose current thread holds a spin lock, the library can switch the thread onto another processor and run it there until it releases the lock.

The rest of this chapter describes the threads implementation in Solaris, SVR4, Mach, and Digital UNIX.

3.6   Multithreading in Solaris and SVR4

Sun Microsystems introduced kernel support for threads in Solaris 2.*x*.[6] UNIX Systems Laboratories adopted the Solaris threads design for SVR4.2/MP. The architecture provides a wide variety of primitives, both at the kernel and user levels, allowing the development of powerful applications.

Solaris supports kernel threads, lightweight processes, and user threads. A user process may have several hundred threads, truly mapping the inherent parallelism of the program. The threads library will multiplex these threads onto a small number of LWPs. The user can control the number of LWPs to best utilize the system resources and can also bind some threads to individual LWPs (see Section 3.6.3).

3.6.1   Kernel Threads

The *kernel thread* in Solaris is a fundamental lightweight object that can be independently scheduled and dispatched to run on one of the system processors. It need not be associated with any process and may be created, run, and destroyed by the kernel to execute specific functions. As a result, the kernel does not have to remap the virtual address space when switching between kernel threads [Kepp 91]. Hence context switch to a kernel thread is less expensive than a switch to a new process.

The only resources used by a kernel thread are a small data structure and a stack. The data structure contains the following information:

- Saved copy of the kernel registers.
- Priority and scheduling information.
- Pointers to put the thread on a scheduler queue or, if the thread is blocked, on a *resource wait* queue.
- Pointer to the stack.
- Pointers to the associated `lwp` and `proc` structures (NULL if thread is not bound to an LWP).
- Pointers to maintain a queue of all threads of a process and a queue of all threads in the system.
- Information about the associated LWP, if there is one (see Section 3.6.2)

The Solaris kernel is organized as a set of kernel threads. Some run LWPs, while others execute internal kernel functions. The kernel threads are fully preemptible. They may belong to any of the scheduling classes of the system (see Section 5.5), including the real-time class. They use special versions of the synchronization primitives (semaphores, conditions, etc.) that prevent *priority inversion,* a situation where a low-priority thread locks a resource needed by a higher-priority thread, thus impeding its progress. These features are described in Section 5.6.

---

[6]   Kernel threads were introduced in Solaris 2.0 and the user-visible interface in Solaris 2.2.

Kernel threads are used to handle asynchronous activity, such as deferred disk writes, STREAMS service procedures, and *callouts* (see Section 5.2.1). This allows the kernel to associate a priority to each such activity (by setting the thread's priority), and thus schedule them appropriately. They are also used to support lightweight processes. Each LWP is attached to a kernel thread (although not all kernel threads have an LWP).

3.6.2   Lightweight Process Implementation

Lightweight processes provide multiple threads of control within a single process. They are scheduled independently and may execute in parallel on multiprocessors. Each LWP is bound to its own kernel thread, and the binding remains effective throughout its lifetime.

The traditional `proc` and `user` structures are inadequate for representing a multithreaded process. The data in these objects must be separated into per-process and per-LWP information. Solaris uses the `proc` structure to hold all per-process data, including the process-specific part of the traditional u area.

A new `lwp` structure contains the per-LWP part of the context. It includes the following information:

- Saved values of user-level registers (when LWP is not running).
- System call arguments, results, and error code.
- Signal handling information.
- Resource usage and profiling data.
- Virtual time alarms.
- User time and CPU usage.
- Pointer to the kernel thread.
- Pointer to the `proc` structure.

The `lwp` structure can be swapped out with the LWP, and hence information that must not be swapped out, such as some signal masks, is kept in the associated thread structure. The Sparc implementation reserves the global register **%g7** for holding a pointer to the current thread, thus allowing quick access to the current LWP and process.

The synchronization primitives available to LWPs (and to kernel threads) are mutex locks, condition variables, counting semaphores, and reader-writer locks. These facilities are described in Chapter 7. Each synchronization facility can exhibit different types of behavior. For example, if a thread tries to acquire a mutex that is held by another thread, it may either busy-wait (spin) or block until the mutex is released. When a synchronization object is initialized, the caller must specify which behavior is desired.

All LWPs in a process share a common set of signal handlers. Each, however, may have its own signal mask, deciding which signals to ignore or block. Each LWP may also specify its own alternate stack for handling signals. Signals are divided into two categories—traps and interrupts. *Traps* are synchronous signals generated by the actions of the LWP itself (e.g., SIGSEGV, SIGFPE, and SIGSYS). These are always delivered to the LWP that caused the signal. *Interrupt signals* (e.g., SIGSTOP and SIGINT) can be delivered to any LWP that has not masked the signal.

LWPs have no global name space and hence are invisible to other processes. *A process cannot direct a signal to a specific LWP in another process or know which LWP sent a message to it.*

3.6.3   User Threads

User threads are implemented by the *threads library*. They can be created, destroyed, and managed without involving the kernel. The threads library provides synchronization and scheduling facilities. This allows a process to use a large number of threads without consuming kernel resources and without excessive system call overhead. Although Solaris implements user threads on top of LWPs, the threads library hides these details, and most application writers deal solely with user threads.

By default, the library creates a pool of LWPs for the process and multiplexes all user threads on top of it. The size of the pool depends on the number of processors and user threads. An application may override the default and specify the number of LWPs to create. It may also require the system to dedicate an LWP to a specific thread. Hence a single process may have two types of user threads—threads *bound* to an LWP, and *unbound* threads that share the common LWP pool (Figure 3-8).

Multiplexing many threads on a small number of LWPs provides concurrency at a low cost. For instance, in a windowing system, each object (window, dialog box, menu, icon, etc.) may be represented by a thread. Only a few windows are active at any given instant, and only those threads need to be supported by LWPs. The number of LWPs determines the maximum parallelism the application can achieve (provided there are at least as many processors). It also limits the number of blocking operations the process may have outstanding at any time.

Sometimes, having more threads than LWPs is a disadvantage. For example, when computing the inner product of two two-dimensional arrays, we could assign a different thread to compute each element of the resulting array. If the number of processors is small, then this method might be counterproductive, because the library might waste a lot of time in context switching between threads. It might be more efficient to create one thread for each row of the product array and bind each thread to an LWP.

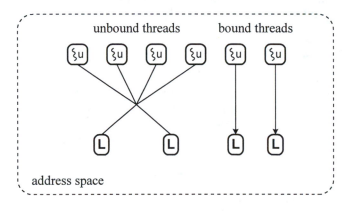

Figure 3-8. The process abstraction in Solaris 2.*x*.

Having bound and unbound user threads in the same application can be very useful in situations that involve time-critical processing. Such processing can be handled by threads bound to LWPs that are assigned a real-time scheduling priority, whereas other threads are responsible for lower-priority background processing. In the previous windowing example, a real-time thread can be assigned to respond to mouse movements, since those must be reflected immediately on the display.

3.6.4   User Thread Implementation

Each user thread must maintain the following state information:

- **Thread ID** — this allows threads within a process to communicate with each other through signals, and so forth.
- **Saved register state** — this includes the program counter and the stack pointer.
- **User stack** — each thread has its own stack, allocated by the library. The kernel does not know about these stacks.
- **Signal mask** — each thread may have its own signal masks. When a signal arrives, the library will route it to an appropriate thread by examining these masks.
- **Priority** — the user thread has a process-relative priority used by the threads scheduler. The kernel is unaware of this priority and only schedules the underlying LWPs.
- **Thread local storage** — each thread is allowed some private storage (managed by the library), to support reentrant versions of the C library interfaces [IEEE 94]. For example, many C library routines return the error code in a global variable called errno. This can lead to chaos if multiple threads invoke such routines concurrently. To avoid these problems, the multithreaded libraries place errno in the thread's local storage [Powe 91].

Threads use the synchronization facilities provided by the library, which are similar to their kernel counterparts (semaphores, conditions, etc.). Solaris allows threads in different processes to synchronize with each other, simply by using synchronization variables placed in shared memory. Such variables may also be placed in files and accessed by mapping the file via *mmap*. This allows the synchronization objects to have a lifetime beyond that of the creating process and to be used to synchronize threads in different processes.

3.6.5   Interrupt Handling

Interrupt handlers often manipulate data shared by the rest of the kernel. This requires the kernel to synchronize access to shared data. In traditional UNIX, the kernel achieves this by raising the *interrupt priority level (ipl)* to block relevant interrupts while executing code that accesses such data. Often, the object being guarded is extremely unlikely to be accessed by the interrupt. For instance, the lock on a *sleep queue* must be protected from interrupts, even though most interrupts would not access that queue.

This model has many drawbacks. On many systems, raising or lowering the *ipl* is expensive and requires several instructions. Interrupts are important and urgent events, and blocking them degrades performance in many ways. On multiprocessor systems, these problems are magnified. The kernel must protect many more objects and usually must block interrupts on all processors.

Solaris replaces the traditional interrupt and synchronization model with a new implementation [Eykh 92, Klei 95] that aims to improve performance, particularly for multiprocessors. To begin with, it does not utilize IPLs to protect from interrupts. Instead, it uses a variety of kernel synchronization objects, such as mutex locks and semaphores. Next, it employs a set of kernel threads to handle interrupts. These *interrupt threads* can be created on the fly and are assigned a higher priority than all other types of threads. They use the same synchronization primitives as other threads and thus can block if they need a resource held by another thread. The kernel blocks interrupts only in a few exceptional situations, such as when acquiring the mutex lock that protects a *sleep queue*.

Although the creation of kernel threads is relatively lightweight, it is still too expensive to create a new thread for each interrupt. The kernel maintains a pool of interrupt threads, which are preallocated and partially initialized. By default, this pool contains one thread per interrupt level for each CPU, plus a single systemwide thread for the clock. Since each thread requires about 8 kilobytes of storage for the stack and thread data, the pool uses a significant amount of memory. On systems where memory is scarce, it is better to reduce the number of threads in this pool, since all interrupts are unlikely to be active at once.

Figure 3-9 describes interrupt handling in Solaris. Thread **T1** is executing on processor **P1** when it receives an interrupt. The interrupt handler first raises the *ipl* to prevent further interrupts of the same or lower level (preserving UNIX semantics). It then allocates an interrupt thread **T2** from the pool and switches context to it. While **T2** executes, **T1** is *pinned,* which means it may not run on another CPU. When **T2** returns, it switches context back to **T1**, which resumes execution.

The interrupt thread **T2** runs without being completely initialized. This means it is not a full-fledged thread and cannot be descheduled. Initialization is completed only if the thread has a reason to block. At this time, it saves its state and becomes an independent thread, capable of running on any CPU. If **T2** blocks, it returns control to **T1**, thus unpinning it. This way, the overhead of complete thread initialization is restricted to cases where the interrupt thread must block.

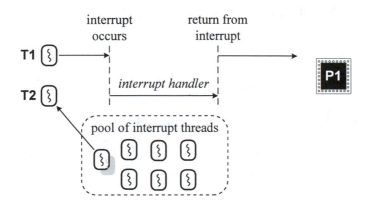

Figure 3-9. Using threads to handle interrupts.

Implementing interrupts as threads adds some overhead (about 40 instructions on the Sparc). On the other hand, it avoids having to block interrupts for each synchronization object, which saves about 12 instructions each time. Since synchronization operations are much more frequent than interrupts, the net result is a performance improvement, as long as interrupts do not block too frequently.

3.6.6   System Call Handling

In Solaris, the *fork* system call duplicates each LWP of the parent in the child. Any LWPs that were in the middle of a system call return with an EINTR error. Solaris also provides a new *fork1* system call; it is similar to *fork,* but only duplicates the thread that invokes it. *fork1* is useful when the child process expects to invoke a new program shortly afterward.

Solaris 2.3 addresses the issue of concurrent random I/O to a file (see Section 3.3.2) by adding the *pread* and *pwrite* system calls, which take a seek offset as an argument. Unfortunately, it does not provide equivalent calls to substitute for *readv* and *writev,* which perform scatter-gather I/O (see Section 8.2.5).

In conclusion, Solaris provides a rich set of programming interfaces with this two-layered model. Having both user threads and LWPs allows us to distinguish between what the programmer sees and what the operating system provides. *Programmers can write applications using only threads, and later optimize them by manipulating the underlying LWPs to best provide the real concurrency needed by the application.*

3.7   Threads in Mach

Mach was designed as a multithreaded operating system from the outset. It supports threads both in the kernel and through user-level libraries. It provides additional mechanisms to control the allocation of processors to threads on multiprocessors. Mach provides full 4.3BSD UNIX semantics at the programming interface level, including all system calls and libraries.[7] This section describes the threads implementation of Mach. Section 3.8 discusses the UNIX interface in Digital UNIX, which is derived from Mach. Section 3.9 describes a new mechanism called *continuations*, which was introduced in Mach 3.0.

3.7.1   The Mach Abstractions—Tasks and Threads

The Mach kernel provides two fundamental abstractions—the *task* and the *thread* [Teva 87]. The *task* is a static object comprising an address space and a collection of system resources called *port rights* (see Section 6.4.1). By itself it is not an executable entity; it is merely an environment in which one or more threads can execute.

The *thread* is the fundamental execution unit and runs within the context of a task. Each task may contain zero or more threads; they all share the resources of the task. Each thread has a kernel

---

[7]   The Mach 2.5 implementation itself provides 4.3BSD functionality within its kernel. Mach 3.0 provides this functionality as a server program at the application level.

stack, used for system call handling. It also has its own computation state (program counter, stack pointer, general registers, etc.) and is independently scheduled by the processor. Threads that belong to user tasks are equivalent to lightweight processes. Pure kernel threads belong to the *kernel task*.

Mach also supports the notion of *processor sets,* which are further described in Section 5.7.1. The available processors in the system can be divided into nonoverlapping processor sets. Each task and thread can be assigned to any processor set (many processor set operations require superuser privilege). This allows dedicating some CPUs of a multiprocessor to one or more specific tasks, thus guaranteeing resources to some high-priority tasks.

The `task` structure represents a *task,* and contains the following information:

- Pointer to the address map, which describes the virtual address space of the task.
- The header of the list of threads belonging to the task.
- Pointer to the processor set to which the task is assigned.
- Pointer to the `utask` structure (see Section 3.8.1).
- Ports and other IPC-related information (see Section 6.4).

The resources held by the task are shared by all its threads. Each thread is described by a `thread` structure, which contains:

- Links to put the thread on a scheduler or wait queue.
- Pointers to the `task` and the processor set to which it belongs.
- Links to put the thread on the list of threads in the same task and on the list of threads in the same processor set.
- Pointer to the *process control block (PCB)* to hold its saved register context.
- Pointer to its kernel stack.
- Scheduling state (*runnable, suspended, blocked,* etc.).
- Scheduling information, such as priority, scheduling policy, and CPU usage.
- Pointers to the associated `uthread` and `utask` structures (see Section 3.8.1).
- Thread-specific IPC information (see Section 6.4.1).

Tasks and threads play complementary roles. The task owns resources, including the address space. The thread executes code. A traditional UNIX process comprises a task containing a single thread. A multithreaded process consists of one task and several threads.

Mach provides a set of system calls to manipulate tasks and threads. The *task_create, task_terminate, task_suspend,* and *task_resume* calls operate on tasks. The *thread_create, thread_terminate, thread_suspend,* and *thread_resume* calls operate on threads. These calls have the obvious meanings. In addition, *thread_status* and *thread_mutate* allow reading and modification of the register state of the thread, and *task_threads* returns a list of all threads in a task.

3.7.2   Mach C-threads

Mach provides a C-threads library, which provides an easy-to-use interface for creating and managing threads. For example, the function

```
cthread_t cthread_fork (void* (*func)(), void* arg);
```

creates a new thread that invokes the function func(). A thread can call

```
void* cthread_join (cthread_t T);
```

to suspend itself until the thread T terminates. The caller receives the return value of T's top-level function or the status code with which thread T explicitly called cthread_exit().

The C-threads library provides mutexes and condition variables for synchronization. It also provides a cthread_yield() function that requests the scheduler to allow another thread to run instead. This function is only necessary for the coroutine implementation discussed below.

There are three implementations of the C-threads library. An application can choose the one best suited to its requirements:

- **Coroutine-based** — Multiplexes user threads onto a single-threaded task (UNIX process). These threads are nonpreemptive, and the library will switch to a different thread only in synchronization procedures (when the current thread must block on a mutex or semaphore). Besides this, it relies on threads calling cthread_yield() to prevent other threads from starving. This implementation is useful for debugging, because the order of thread context switching is repeatable.
- **Thread-based** — Each C-thread uses a different Mach thread. These threads are preemptively scheduled and may execute in parallel on a multiprocessor. This is the default implementation and is used in production versions of C-thread programs.
- **Task-based** — Employs one Mach task (UNIX process) per C-thread, and uses Mach virtual memory primitives to share memory among threads. This is used only when specialized memory-sharing semantics are necessary.

3.8   Digital UNIX

The Digital UNIX operating system, formerly known as DEC OSF/1, is based on the Mach 2.5 kernel. From an application programmer's perspective, it provides a complete UNIX programming interface. Internally, many of the UNIX features are implemented using Mach primitives. This work is based on Mach's 4.3BSD compatibility layer, extended by the Open Software Foundation to be compatible with SVR3 and SVR4 as well. This approach has had a profound effect on its design.

Digital UNIX provides an elegant set of facilities that extend the process abstraction [OSF 93]. Multithreaded processes are supported both by the kernel and by POSIX-compliant threads libraries. The UNIX process is implemented on top of the task and thread abstractions of Mach.

3.8.1   The UNIX Interface

While tasks and threads adequately provide the Mach program execution interface, they do not fully describe a UNIX process. A process provides several facilities that have no Mach counterpart, such as user credentials, open file descriptors, signal handling, and process groups. Furthermore, to avoid rewriting the UNIX interface from scratch, the code was ported from the 4.3BSD compatibility layer in Mach 2.5, which in turn was ported from the native 4.3BSD implementation. Likewise, many device drivers were ported from Digital's ULTRIX, which also is BSD-based. The ported code makes extensive references to the proc and user structures, making it desirable to preserve these interfaces.

There are two problems with retaining the user and proc structures in their original forms. First, some of their functionality is now provided by the task and thread structures. Second, they do not adequately represent a multithreaded process. For instance, the traditional u area contains the *process control block,* which holds the saved register context of the process. In the multithreaded case, each thread has its own register context. Thus these structures must be modified significantly.

The u area is replaced by two objects—a single utask structure for the task as a whole, and one uthread structure for each thread in the task. These structures are no longer at fixed addresses in the process and are not swapped out with the process.

The utask structure contains the following information:

- Pointers to vnodes of the current and root directories.
- Pointer to the proc structure.
- Array of signal handlers and other fields related to signaling.
- Open file descriptors table.
- Default file creation mask (*cmask*).
- Resource usage, quotas, and profiling information.

If one thread opens a file, the descriptor is shared by all threads in the task. Likewise, they all have a common current working directory. The uthread structure describes the per-thread resources of a UNIX process, which include:

- pointer to saved user-level registers
- pathname traversal fields
- current and pending signals
- thread-specific signal handlers

To ease the porting effort, references to fields of the old u area have been converted to references to utask or uthread fields. This conversion is achieved by macros such as:

```
#define u_cmask      utask->uu_cmask
#define u_pcb        uthread->uu_pcb
```

The proc structure is retained with few changes, but much of its functionality is now provided by the task and thread structures. As a result, many of its fields are unused, although they are retained for historical reasons. For instance, the fields related to scheduling and priority are unnecessary because Digital UNIX schedules each thread individually. The Digital UNIX proc structure contains the following information:

- Links to put the structure on the allocated, zombie, or free process list.
- Signal masks.
- Pointer to the credentials structure.

- Identification and hierarchy information—PID, parent PID, pointers to parent, siblings, children, and so forth.
- Process group and session information.
- Scheduling fields (unused).
- Fields to save status and resource usage when exiting.
- Pointers to the task and utask structure, and to the first thread.

Figure 3-10 describes the relationship between the Mach and UNIX data structures. The task maintains a linked list of its threads. The task structure points to the utask, and each thread structure points to the corresponding uthread. The proc structure has pointers to the task, utask, and first thread. The utask points back to the proc, and each thread points back to the task and the utask. This allows for rapid access to all the structures.

Not all threads have a user context. Some threads may be created directly by the kernel to perform system functions such as page replacement. Such threads are associated with the kernel task, which has no user address space. The kernel task and threads have no associated utask, uthread, and proc structures.

3.8.2   System Calls and Signals

The *fork* system call in Digital UNIX creates a new process that has a single thread, a clone of the thread that initially issued the *fork*. There is no alternative call that duplicates all the threads.

As in Solaris, signals are classified as synchronous signals or *traps,* and asynchronous signals or *interrupts*. A trap is delivered to the thread that caused it. Interrupt signals are delivered to any thread that has enabled them. Unlike Solaris, however, all threads in a process share a single set of signal masks, which is stored in the proc structure. Each thread is allowed to declare its own set of handlers for synchronous signals, but they all share a common set of handlers for asynchronous signals.

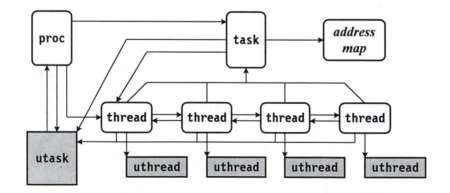

Figure 3-10. Digital UNIX data structures for tasks and threads.

3.8.3   The *pthreads* Library

The *pthreads* library provides a POSIX-compliant, user-level programming interface to threads that is simpler than Mach system calls. The library associates one Mach thread with each *pthread*. Functionally, *pthreads* are similar to C threads or other threads libraries, but they implement an interface that has become an accepted standard.

The *pthreads* library implements the asynchronous I/O functions defined by the POSIX standard. For instance, if a thread calls the POSIX function *aioread()*, the library creates a new thread to issue the read synchronously. When the read completes, the kernel wakes up the blocked thread, which in turn notifies the calling thread via a signal. This is illustrated in Figure 3-11.

The *pthreads* library provides a complete programming interface, including signal handling and scheduling functions and an assortment of synchronization primitives. Synchronization between threads can be implemented at the user level, but the kernel must be involved if an LWP needs to block.

Digital also provides a proprietary *cma_threads* library, which provides some additional features [DEC 94]. Programs using this library will work on Digital's VMS and Windows/NT platforms, but not on other UNIX systems.

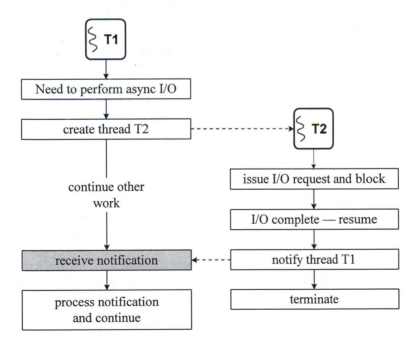

Figure 3-11. Implementing asynchronous I/O by creating a separate thread.

3.9   Mach 3.0 Continuations

Although a kernel thread is more lightweight than a process, it still consumes a large amount of kernel memory, mainly for its stack. Kernel stacks typically consume a minimum of 4K bytes of memory, which is almost 90% of the kernel space used by a thread. On a system with a large number (hundreds) of threads, this overhead becomes excessive and degrades performance. One solution is to multiplex user threads onto Mach threads or lightweight processes, thus avoiding the requirement of one kernel stack per thread. This approach has its disadvantages: user threads can not be scheduled independently and hence do not provide the same level of concurrency. Moreover, because kernel threads do not cross task boundaries, each task must contain at least one kernel thread, creating problems on systems with many active tasks. In this section we examine how Mach 3.0 addresses these issues via a kernel facility called *continuations*.

3.9.1   Programming Models

The UNIX kernel uses a *process model* of programming. Each thread has a kernel stack, used when it traps into the kernel for a system call or exception. When the thread blocks in the kernel, the stack contains its execution state, including its call sequence and automatic variables. This has the advantage of simplicity, as kernel threads can block without having to explicitly save any state. The main drawback is the excessive memory consumption.

Some operating systems, such as QuickSilver [Hask 88] and V [Cher 88] use an *interrupt model* of programming. The kernel treats system calls and exceptions as interrupts, using a single per-processor kernel stack for all kernel operations. Consequently, if a thread needs to block while in the kernel, it must first explicitly save its state somewhere. The kernel uses this saved information to restore the thread's state the next time it runs.

The main advantage of the interrupt model is the memory saved by having a single kernel stack. The main drawback is that a thread must save its state explicitly for each potentially blocking operation. This makes the model difficult to program, because the information that must be saved may span module boundaries. Hence if a thread blocks while in a deeply nested procedure, it must determine what state is needed by all functions in the call chain.

The conditions under which a thread must block dictate which model is more suitable. If a thread blocks deep inside a call chain, it will benefit from the process model. If, however, the thread has little state to save when it blocks, the interrupt model will work better. Many server programs, for instance, repeatedly block in the kernel to wait for a client request, and then process the request when it arrives. Such a program does not have much state to maintain in the kernel and can easily relinquish its stack.

The Mach 3.0 continuations facility combines the advantages of the two models, and allows the kernel to choose the blocking method depending on the circumstances. We now examine its design and implementation.

3.9.2 Using Continuations

Mach uses the `thread_block()` function to block a thread. Mach 3.0 modifies the function to accept an argument, and the new syntax is

```
thread_block (void (*contfn)());
```

where `contfn()` is the *continuation function* to be invoked the next time the thread runs. Passing a NULL argument indicates that traditional blocking behavior is required. This way, the thread can choose to use continuations selectively.

When a thread wishes to use a continuation, it first saves any state that might be needed after resuming. The thread structure contains a 28-byte scratch area for this purpose; if more space is needed, the thread must allocate an additional data structure. The kernel blocks the thread and recaptures its stack. When the thread is resumed, the kernel gives it a new stack and invokes the continuation function. This function recovers the state from where it was saved. This requires that both the continuation and the calling function must have a detailed understanding about what state was saved and where.

The following example illustrates the use of continuations. Example 3-1 uses the traditional approach to blocking a thread:

```
syscall_1 (arg1)
{

    ...
    thread_block();
    f2 (arg1);
    return;
}

f2 (arg1)
{

    ...
    return;
}
```

Example 3-1. Blocking a thread without continuations.

Example 3-2 shows how a thread is blocked using continuations:

```
syscall_1 (arg1)
{

    ...
    save arg1 and any other state information;
    thread_block (f2);
    /* not reached */
}
```

```
f2 ()
{
    restore arg1 and any other state information;
    ...
    thread_syscall_return (status);
}
```

Example 3-2. Blocking a thread using continuations.

Note that when `thread_block()` is called with an argument, it does not return to the caller; when the thread resumes, the kernel transfers control to `f2()`. The `thread_syscall_return()` function is used to return to the user level from a system call. The entire process is transparent to the user, who sees only a synchronous return from the system call.

The kernel uses continuations when only a small amount of state must be saved when blocking. For instance, one of the most common blocking operations occurs during page fault handling. In traditional implementations, the handler code issues a disk read request and blocks until the read completes. When this happens, the kernel simply returns the thread to user level, and the application can resume. The work that must be done after the read completes does requires little saved state (perhaps a pointer to the page that was read in, and the memory mapping data that must be updated). This is a good example of how continuations are useful.

3.9.3   Optimizations

The direct benefit of continuations is to reduce the number of kernel stacks in the system. Continuations also allow some important optimizations. Suppose, during a context switch, the kernel discovers that both the old and new threads have used continuations. The old thread has relinquished its kernel stack, and the new thread does not have one. The kernel can directly transfer the stack from the old thread to the new, as shown in Figure 3-12. Besides saving the overhead of allocating a new stack, this also helps reduce the cache and *translation lookaside buffer (TLB)* misses (see Section 13.3.1) associated with a context switch, since the same memory is reused.

The Mach IPC (interprocess communication) implementation (see Section 6.4) takes this one step further. A message transfer involves two steps—a client thread uses the *mach_msg* system call to send a message and wait for a reply, and a server thread uses *mach_msg* to send replies to clients and wait for the next request. The message is sent to and received from a port, which is a protected queue of messages. The sending and receiving are independent of each other. If a receiver is not ready, the kernel queues the message on the port.

When a receiver is waiting, the transfer can be optimized using a continuation. If the sender finds a receiver waiting, it hands off its stack to the receiver and blocks itself with a `mach_msg_continue()` continuation. The receiving thread resumes using the sender's stack, which already contains all the information about the message to be transferred. This avoids the overhead of queuing and dequeuing the message and considerably speeds up the message transfer. When the server replies, it will hand off its stack to the client thread and resume it in a similar fashion.

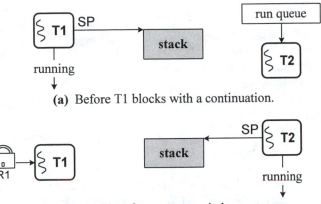

(a) Before T1 blocks with a continuation.

(b) After context switch.

Figure 3-12. Stack handoff using continuations.

3.9.4 Analysis

Continuations have proved extremely effective in Mach. Because their use is optional, it is unnecessary to change the entire programming model, and their use can be extended incrementally. Continuations greatly reduce the demands placed on kernel memory. Performance measurements [Drav 91] determined that on average, the system required only 2.002 kernel stacks per processor, reducing the per-thread kernel space from 4664 to 690 bytes.

Mach 3.0 is particularly well suited for continuations, since it is a microkernel that exports only a small interface and has a small number of abstractions. In particular, the UNIX compatibility code has been removed from the kernel and is provided by user-level servers [Golu 90]. As a result there are only about 60 places where the kernel can block, and 99% of the blocks occur at just six "hot spots." Concentrating on those provides a large benefit for a small programming effort. Traditional UNIX systems, in contrast, may block at several hundred places and have no real hot spots.

3.10 Summary

We have seen several different ways of designing multithreaded systems. There are many types of thread primitives, and a system can combine one or more of them to create a rich concurrent programming environment. Threads may be supported by the kernel, by user libraries, or by both.

Application developers must also choose the right blend of kernel and user facilities. One problem they face is that each operating system vendor provides a different set of system calls to create and manage threads, making it difficult to write portable multithreaded code that efficiently uses the system resources. The POSIX 1003.4a standard defines the threads library functions, but does not address the kernel interfaces or implementation.

3.11   Exercises

1. For each of the following applications, discuss the suitability of lightweight processes, user threads, or other programming models:
    (a) The server component of a distributed name service.
    (b) A windowing system, such as the *X server*.
    (c) A scientific application that runs on a multiprocessor and performs many parallel computations.
    (d) A *make* utility that compiles files in parallel whenever possible.
2. In what situations is an application better off using multiple processes rather than LWPs or user threads?
3. Why does each LWP need a separate kernel stack? Can the system save resources by allocating a kernel stack only when an LWP makes a system call?
4. The proc structure and the u area contain process attributes and resources. In a multithreaded system, which of their fields may be shared by all LWPs of the process, and which must be per-LWP?
5. Suppose one LWP invokes *fork* just at the same instance that another LWP of the same process invokes *exit*. What would be the result if the system uses *fork* to duplicate all LWPs of the process? What if *fork* duplicates only one LWP?
6. Would the problems with *fork* in a multithreaded system be addressed by having a single system call to do an atomic *fork* and *exec?*
7. Section 3.3.2 described the problems with having a single shared set of resources such as file descriptors and the current directory. Why should these resources not be per-LWP or per-user-thread? [Bart 88] explores this idea further.
8. The standard library defines a per-process variable called errno, which contains the error status from the last system call. What problems does this create for a multithreaded process? How can these problems be solved?
9. Many systems classify library functions as thread-safe or thread-unsafe. What causes a function to be unsafe for use by a multithreaded application?
10. What are the drawbacks of using threads to run interrupt handlers?
11. What are the drawbacks of having the kernel control LWP scheduling?
12. Suggest an interface that would allow a user to control which of its LWPs is scheduled first. What problems can this cause?
13. Compare the multithreading primitives of Solaris and Digital UNIX. What are the advantages of each?

3.12   References

[Ande 91]   Anderson, T.E., Bershad, B.N., Lazowska, E.D., and Levy, H.M., "Scheduler Activations: Effective Kernel Support for the User-Level Management of Parallelism," *Proceedings of the Thirteenth Symposium on Operating System Principles,* Oct. 1991, pp. 95–109.

[Arma 90]   Armand, F., Hermann, F., Lipkis, J., and Rozier, M., "Multi-threaded Processes in Chorus/MIX," *Proceedings of the Spring 1990 European UNIX Users Group Conference,* Apr. 1990.

[Bart 88]   Barton, J.M., and Wagner, J.C., "Beyond Threads: Resource Sharing in UNIX," *Proceedings of the Winter 1988 USENIX Technical Conference, Jan. 1988,* pp. 259–266.

[Bita 95]   Bitar, N., "Selected Topics in Multiprocessing," *USENIX 1995 Technical Conference Tutorial Notes,* Jan. 1995.

[Blac 90]   Black, D.L., "Scheduling Support for Concurrency and Parallelism in the Mach Operating System," *IEEE Computer,* May 1990, pp. 35–43.

[Cher 88]   Cheriton, D.R., "The V Distributed System," *Communications of the ACM,* Vol. 31, No. 3, Mar. 1988, pp. 314–333.

[Coop 90]   Cooper, E.C., and Draves, R.P., "C Threads," Technical Report CMU–CS–88–154, Department of Computer Science, Carnegie Mellon University, Sep. 1990.

[DEC 94]   Digital Equipment Corporation, DEC OSF/1 — Guide to DECthreads, Part No. AA–Q2DPB–TK, July 1994.

[Doep 87]   Doeppner, T.W., Jr., "Threads, A System for the Support of Concurrent Programming," Brown University Technical Report CS–87–11, Jun. 1987.

[Drav 91]   Draves, R.P., Bershad, B.N., Rashid, R.F., and Dean, R.W., "Using Continuations to Implement Thread Management and Communication in Operating Systems," Technical Report CMU–CS–91–115R, Department of Computer Science, Carnegie Mellon University, Oct. 1991.

[Eykh 92]   Eykholt, J.R., Kleiman, S.R., Barton, S., Faulkner, R., Shivalingiah, A., Smith, M., Stein, D., Voll, J., Weeks, M., and Williams, D., "Beyond Multiprocessing: Multithreading the SunOS Kernel," *Proceedings of the Summer 1992 USENIX Technical Conference,* Jun. 1992, pp. 11–18.

[Golu 90]   Golub, D., Dean, R., Forin, A., and Rashid, R., "UNIX as an Application Program," *Proceedings of the Summer 1990 USENIX Technical Conference,* Jun. 1990, pp. 87–95.

[IEEE 94]   Institute for Electrical and Electronic Engineers, *POSIX P1003.4a, Threads Extension for Portable Operating Systems,* 1994.

[Hask 88]   Haskin, R., Malachi, Y., Sawdon, W., and Chan, G., "Recovery Management in QuickSilver," *ACM Transactions on Computer Systems,* Vol. 6, No. 1, Feb. 1988, pp. 82–108.

[Kepe 85]   Kepecs, J., "Lightweight Processes for UNIX Implementation and Applications," *Proceedings of the Summer 1985 USENIX Technical Conference,* Jun. 1985, pp. 299–308.

[Kepp 91]   Keppel, D., "Register Windows and User-Space Threads on the SPARC," Technical Report 91–08–01, Department of Computer Science and Engineering, University of Washington, Seattle, WA, Aug. 1991.

[Klei 95]   Kleiman, S.R., and Eykholt, J.R., "Interrupts as Threads," *Operating Systems Review,* Vol. 29, No. 2, Apr. 1995.

[Muel 93]   Mueller, F., "A Library Implementation of POSIX Threads under UNIX," *Proceedings of the Winter 1993 USENIX Technical Conference*, Jan. 1993, pp. 29–41.

[OSF 93]   Open Software Foundation, *Design of the OSF/1 Operating System—Release 1.2*, Prentice-Hall, Englewood Cliffs, NJ, 1993.

[Powe 91]   Powell, M.L., Kleiman, S.R., Barton, S., Shah, D., Stein, D., and Weeks, M., "SunOS Multi-thread Architecture," *Proceedings of the Winter 1991 USENIX Technical Conference*, Jan. 1991, pp. 65–80.

[Sun 93]   Sun Microsystems, *SunOS 5.3 System Services*, Nov. 1993.

[Teva 87]   Tevanian, A., Jr., Rashid, R.F., Golub, D.B., Black, D.L., Cooper, E., and Young, M.W., "Mach Threads and the UNIX Kernel: The Battle for Control," *Proceedings of the Summer 1987 USENIX Technical Conference*, Jun. 1987, pp. 185–197.

[Vand 88]   Vandevoorde, M., and Roberts, E., "WorkCrews: An Abstraction for Controlling Parallelism," *International Journal of Parallel Programming*, Vol. 17, No. 4, Aug. 1988, pp. 347–366.

4

Signals and Session Management

4.1 Introduction

Signals provide a mechanism for notifying processes of system events. They also function as a primitive mechanism for communication and synchronization between user processes. The programming interface, behavior, and internal implementation of signals differ greatly from one version of UNIX to another, and also, for any single variant, from one release to another. To make matters more confusing for the programmer, the operating system provides additional system calls and library routines to support earlier interfaces and maintain backward compatibility.[1]

The original System V implementation of signals was inherently unreliable and defective. Many of its problems are addressed in 4.2BSD UNIX (with further enhancements in 4.3BSD), which introduced a new, robust signal mechanism. The 4.2BSD signal interface, however, is incompatible with the System V interface in several respects. This causes problems both for application developers, who wish to write portable code, and for other UNIX vendors, who want their version of UNIX to be compatible with both System V and BSD.

The POSIX 1003.1 standard [IEEE 90] (also known as POSIX.1) imposes some order amid the chaos created by the plethora of signal implementations. It defines a standard interface that all compliant implementations must support. POSIX standards, however, do not regulate how the interface must be implemented. The operating system is free to decide whether to provide the implementation in the kernel, through user-level libraries, or through a combination of both.

---

[1] This creates other problems. If a library using one set of signal interfaces is linked with an application using another, the program may behave incorrectly.

83

The developers of SVR4 introduced a new, POSIX-compliant signals implementation that incorporates many features of BSD signals. Nearly all modern UNIX variants (such as Solaris, AIX, HP-UX, 4.4BSD, and Digital UNIX) provide a POSIX-compliant signals implementation. The SVR4 implementation also preserves backward compatibility with all earlier System V releases.

This chapter first explains the basic notion of signals and analyzes the problems with the original System V implementation. It then shows how these problems are addressed in modern UNIX systems that provide reliable signals. Finally, it looks at the issue of job control and session management, which is closely related to signals.

4.2   Signal Generation and Handling

Signals provide a way for a procedure to be called when one of a defined set of events occurs. The events are identified by integers and are commonly referred to by symbolic constants. Some of the events are asynchronous notifications (for example, when a user sends an interrupt signal to a process by pressing control-C at the terminal), while others are synchronous errors or exceptions (for example, accessing an illegal address).

There are two phases in the signaling process—generation and delivery. A signal is generated when an event occurs that requires a process to be notified of it. It is delivered, or handled, when the process to which the signal has been sent recognizes its arrival and takes some appropriate action. In between these two events, the signal is said to be pending to the process.

The original System V implementation defined 15 different signals. Both 4BSD and SVR4 support 31 signals. Each signal is assigned a number between 1 and 31 (setting signal number to zero has special meanings for different functions, such as "no signal"). The mapping of signals to signal numbers is different for System V and BSD UNIX (for example, SIGSTOP is 17 in 4.3BSD, but 23 in SVR4). Moreover, many commercial UNIX variants (such as AIX) support more than 31 signals. Hence, programmers use symbolic constants to identify the signals. POSIX 1003.1 specifies the symbolic names for all the signals it defines. The names are portable at a minimum to all POSIX-compliant implementations.

4.2.1   Signal Handling

Each signal has a *default action,* which is what the kernel does if the process has not specified an alternative. There are five possible default actions:

abort	Terminates the process after generating a *core dump,* that is, writing the contents of the process's address space and register context in a file called **core** in the current directory of the process.[2] This file can later be analyzed by debuggers and other utilities.
exit	Terminates the process without generating a core dump.
ignore	Ignores the signal.

---

[2] 4.4BSD calls this file **core.***prog*, where *prog* is the first 16 characters of the program that the process was executing when it received the signal.

stop	Suspends the process.
continue	Resumes the process, if suspended (or else, ignores the signal).

A process may choose to override the default and specify another action for any signal. This alternative action could be to ignore the signal or to invoke a user-defined function called a *signal handler*. At any time, the process may specify a new action or reset the action to default. A process may block a signal temporarily (not in SVR2 or earlier versions), in which case the signal will not be delivered until it is unblocked. The SIGKILL and SIGSTOP signals are special—users cannot ignore, block, or specify a handler for them. Table 4-1 lists the complete set of signals, their default actions, and other restrictions.

It is important to note that any action, including process termination, can only be taken by the receiving process itself. This requires, at the very least, that the process be scheduled to run. On a busy system, if this process has a low priority, this may take quite some time. There may be further delay if the process is swapped out, suspended, or blocked in an uninterruptible way.

The receiving process becomes aware of the signal when the kernel calls the issig() function on its behalf to check for pending signals. The kernel calls issig() only at the following times:

- Before returning to user mode from a system call or interrupt.
- Just before blocking on an interruptible event.
- Immediately after waking up from an interruptible event.

If issig() returns TRUE, the kernel calls the psig() function to dispatch the signal. psig() terminates the process, generating the core file if necessary, or calls sendsig() to invoke the user-defined handler. sendsig() returns the process to user mode, transfers control to the signal handler, and arranges for the process to resume the interrupted code after the handler completes. Its implementation is very machine-specific since it must manipulate the user stack and save, restore, and modify the process context.

Signals generated by asynchronous events may occur after any instruction in the code path of the process. When the signal handler completes, the process resumes from where it was interrupted by the signal (Figure 4-1). If the signal arrived when the process was in the middle of a system call, the kernel usually aborts the call and returns an error of EINTR. 4.2BSD introduced the automatic restarting of certain system calls after a signal (see Section 4.4.3). 4.3BSD provides a *siginterrupt* call that disables this feature on a per-signal basis.

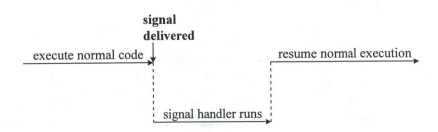

Figure 4-1. Signal handling.

Table 4-1. UNIX signals

Signal	Description	Default Action	Available In	Notes
SIGABRT	process aborted	abort	APSB	
SIGALRM	real-time alarm	exit	OPSB	
SIGBUS	bus error	abort	OSB	
SIGCHLD	child died or suspended	ignore	OJSB	6
SIGCONT	resume suspended process	continue/ignore	JSB	4
SIGEMT	emulator trap	abort	OSB	
SIGFPE	arithmetic fault	abort	OAPSB	
SIGHUP	hang-up	exit	OPSB	
SIGILL	illegal instruction	abort	OAPSB	2
SIGINFO	status request (control-T)	ignore	B	
SIGINT	tty interrupt (control-C)	exit	OAPSB	
SIGIO	async I/O event	exit/ignore	SB	3
SIGIOT	I/O trap	abort	OSB	
SIGKILL	kill process	exit	OPSB	1
SIGPIPE	write to pipe with no readers	exit	OPSB	
SIGPOLL	pollable event	exit	S	
SIGPROF	profiling timer	exit	SB	
SIGPWR	power fail	ignore	OS	
SIGQUIT	tty quit signal (control-\)	abort	OPSB	
SIGSEGV	segmentation fault	abort	OAPSB	
SIGSTOP	stop process	stop	JSB	1
SIGSYS	invalid system call	exit	OAPSB	
SIGTERM	terminate process	exit	OAPSB	
SIGTRAP	hardware fault	abort	OSB	2
SIGTSTP	tty stop signal (control-Z)	stop	JSB	
SIGTTIN	tty read from background process	stop	JSB	
SIGTTOU	tty write from background process	stop	JSB	5
SIGURG	urgent event on I/O channel	ignore	SB	
SIGUSR1	user-definable	exit	OPSB	
SIGUSR2	user-definable	exit	OPSB	
SIGVTALRM	virtual time alarm	exit	SB	
SIGWINCH	window size change	ignore	SB	
SIGXCPU	exceed CPU limit	abort	SB	
SIGXFSZ	exceed file size limit	abort	SB	

Availability: **O**   Original SVR2 signal   **A**   ANSI C
                  B   4.3 BSD   **S**   SVR4
                  P   POSIX.1   **J**   POSIX.1, only if job control is supported

Notes: **1**   cannot be caught, blocked, or ignored.
          2   Not reset to default, even in System V implementations.
          3   Default action is to exit in SVR4, ignore in 4.3BSD.
          4   Default action is to continue process if suspended, else to ignore. Cannot be blocked.
          5   Process can choose to allow background writes without generating this signal.
          6   Called SIGCLD in SVR3 and earlier releases.

4.2.2 Signal Generation

The kernel generates signals to processes in response to various events that may be caused by the receiving process itself, by another process, or by interrupts or external actions. The major sources of signals are as follows:

Exceptions
When an exception occurs in the process (for instance, an attempt to execute an illegal instruction), the kernel notifies the process by sending it a signal.

Other processes
A process may send a signal to another process, or set of processes, through the *kill* or *sigsend* system calls. A process may even send a signal to itself.

Terminal interrupts
Certain keyboard characters, such as control-C or control-\, send signals to the *foreground process* on that terminal. The *stty* command allows the user to bind each terminal-generated signal to a specific key.

Job control
Background processes that try to read or write to the terminal are sent job control signals. Job control shells such as *csh* and *ksh* use signals to manipulate foreground and background processes. When a process terminates or is suspended, the kernel notifies its parent via a signal.

Quotas
When a process exceeds its CPU or file size limits, the kernel sends a signal to the process.

Notifications
A process may request notification of certain events, such as a device being ready for I/O. The kernel informs the process via a signal.

Alarms
A process may set an alarm for a certain time; when it expires, the kernel notifies the process through a signal.

There are three different alarms, which use different kinds of timers. The ITIMER_REAL measures the real (clock) time, and generates the SIGALRM signal. The ITIMER_VIRTUAL measures the virtual time, that is, it runs only when the process is executing in user mode. It generates the SIGVTALRM signal. The ITIMER_PROF measures the total time used by the process, in both user and kernel modes. It generates the SIGPROF signal. There is considerable variation in how different vendors support alarms and timers.

4.2.3 Typical Scenarios

Let us consider a few examples of signal generation and delivery. Suppose a user types control-C at the terminal. This results in a terminal interrupt (as would any other character). The terminal driver recognizes this as a signal-generating character and sends the SIGINT signal to the foreground process of this terminal. (If the foreground *job* comprises more than one process, the driver sends the signal to each of them.) When this process is scheduled to run, it will see the signal upon trying to return to user mode after the context switch. Sometimes, the foreground process is the *currently running process* at the time of the interrupt. In this case, the handler interrupts the foreground process and posts the signal to it.[3] Upon return from the interrupt, the process will check for and find the signal.

Exceptions, however, result in synchronous signals. They are usually caused by a programming error (division by zero, illegal instruction, etc.) and will occur at the same point if the program is rerun in the same manner (i.e., if the same execution path is repeated). When an exception occurs in a program, it causes a *trap* to the kernel mode. The trap handler in the kernel recognizes the exception and sends the appropriate signal to the current process. When the trap handler is about to return to user mode, it calls issig(), thus receiving the signal.

It is possible for several signals to be pending to the process simultaneously. In that case, the signals are processed one at a time. A signal might also arrive while executing a signal handler; this can cause nesting of handlers. In most implementations, users can ask the kernel to selectively block certain signals before invoking a specific handler (see Section 4.4.3). This allows users to disable or control the nesting of signal handlers.

4.2.4   Sleep and Signals

What happens if a sleeping process receives a signal? Should it be awakened prematurely so that it can handle the signal, or should the signal be kept pending until the process awakens?

The answer depends on why the process has gone to sleep. If it is sleeping for an event such as disk I/O completion, that event will occur soon, and it is okay to keep any signals pending. On the other hand, if the process is waiting for the user to type a keyboard character, it may wait indefinitely. We need a provision to interrupt such processes via signals.

Therefore, UNIX has two categories of sleep—interruptible and uninterruptible. A process sleeping for a short-term event such as disk I/O is said to be in an uninterruptible sleep and cannot be disturbed by a signal. A process waiting for an event such as terminal I/O, which may not occur for a long time, sleeps in an interruptible state and will be woken up if a signal is generated for it.

If a signal is generated for a process in an uninterruptible sleep, it will be marked as pending, but no further action will be taken at that point. The process will not notice the signal even after waking up, until it is about to return to user mode or block on an interruptible event.

If a process is about to block on an interruptible event, it will check for signals just before blocking. If a signal is found, it handles the signal and aborts the system call. If a signal is generated after the process has blocked, the kernel will wake up the process. When the process wakes up and runs—either because the event it was waiting for occurred, or because its sleep was interrupted by a signal—it will first call issig() and check for signals. The call to issig() is always followed by psig () if a signal was pending, as shown in the following:

```
if (issig())
    psig();
```

---

[3]   On a multiprocessor, the target process may be running on a different processor than the one that handles the terminal interrupt. In this case, the interrupt handler must arrange a special cross-processor interrupt so that the target sees the signal.

4.3   Unreliable Signals

The original (SVR2 and earlier) implementation of signals [Bach 86] is unreliable and defective. While it adheres to the basic model described in Section 4.2, it suffers from several drawbacks.

The most important problem concerns reliable signal delivery. Signal handlers are not persistent and do not mask recurring instances of the same signal. Suppose a user installs a handler for a particular signal. When that signal occurs, the kernel will reset the signal action to default before invoking the handler. A user wishing to catch other occurrences of the signal must reinstall the handler each time, as in Example 4-1.

```
void sigint_handler (sig)
int sig;
{
    signal (SIGINT, sigint_handler);    /* reinstall the handler */
    ...                                 /* handle the signal */
}

main()
{
    signal (SIGINT, sigint_handler);    /* install the handler */
    ...
}
```

Example 4-1. Reinstalling a signal handler.

This, however, leads to a race condition. Suppose that the user types control-C twice in rapid succession. The first causes a SIGINT signal that resets the action to default and invokes the handler. If the second control-C is typed before the handler is reinstalled, the kernel will take the default action and terminate the process. This leaves a window between the time the handler is invoked and the time it is reinstalled, during which the signal cannot be caught. For this reason, the old implementation is often referred to as *unreliable signals*.

There is also a performance problem regarding sleeping processes. In the old implementation, all information regarding signal disposition is stored in a u_signal[] array in the u area, which contains one entry for each signal type. This entry contains the address of a user-defined handler, SIG_DFL to specify that the default action should be taken, or SIG_IGN to specify that the signal should be ignored.

Since the kernel can only read the u area of the current process, it has no way of knowing how another process will deal with a signal. Specifically, if the kernel has to post a signal to a process in an interruptible sleep, it cannot know if the process is ignoring the signal. It will thus post the signal and wake up the process, assuming that the process is handling the signal. If the process finds that it has awakened because of a signal that was to be ignored, it will simply go back to sleep. This spurious wakeup results in unnecessary context switches and wasteful processing. It is far better if the kernel can recognize and discard ignored signals without ever waking up the process.

Finally, the SVR2 implementation lacks a facility to block a signal temporarily, deferring its delivery until unblocked. It also lacks support for job control, where groups of processes can be suspended and resumed in order to control access to the terminal.

4.4   Reliable Signals

The above problems were first addressed in 4.2BSD, which introduced a reliable and versatile signal management framework. 4.3BSD adds a few improvements, but the basic facilities remain unchanged. Meanwhile, AT&T provided its own version of reliable signals in SVR3 [AT&T 86]. This version is incompatible with the BSD interface and is not as powerful. It retains compatibility with the original SVR2 implementation. SVR3 and 4.2BSD try to solve the same problems in different ways. Each has its own set of system calls to access their signal management functionality, and these calls differ both in name and in semantics.

The POSIX.1 standard attempts to create order from this chaos by defining a standard set of functions that POSIX-compliant systems must implement. The functions may be implemented as system calls or as library routines. Based on these requirements, SVR4 introduced a new interface that is POSIX-compliant and compatible both with BSD and with all previous versions of AT&T UNIX.

This section first examines the basic features of reliable signals. It then briefly describes the SVR3 and 4.3BSD interfaces, and finally, takes a detailed look at the SVR4 signals interface.

4.4.1   Primary Features

All reliable signal implementations provide certain common facilities. These include:

- **Persistent handlers** — Signal handlers remain installed even after the signal occurs and do not need to be explicitly reinstalled. This eliminates the window between invoking the handler and reinstalling it, during which another instance of the signal can terminate the process.
- **Masking** — A signal can be masked temporarily. (The words *masked* and *blocked* are synonymous, and are used interchangeably when referring to signals.) If a signal that is being blocked is generated, the kernel will remember it but will not post it immediately to the process. When the process unblocks the signal, the signal will be posted and handled. This allows programmers to protect critical regions of code from being interrupted by certain signals.
- **Sleeping processes** — Some of the signal disposition information of a process is visible to the kernel (kept in the proc structure instead of the u area) even when the process is not running. Consequently, if the kernel generates a signal for a process in an interruptible sleep and the process is ignoring or blocking that signal, the kernel will not need to awaken it.
- **Unblock and wait** — The *pause* system call blocks the process until a signal arrives. Reliable signals provide an additional system call—*sigpause*—that atomically unmasks a

signal and blocks the process until it receives a signal. If the unmasked signal is already pending when the system call is issued, the call returns immediately.

4.4.2   The SVR3 Implementation

SVR3 provides all the features described in the previous section. Its implementation, however, suffers from some important drawbacks. To understand this, let us consider an example that shows the use of the *sigpause* system call.

Suppose a process has declared a signal handler to catch the SIGQUIT signal and set a global flag when the signal is caught. At some time, it wants to check if the flag is set; if not, it wants to wait for it to be set. The check and the subsequent wait together constitute a *critical region* of code—if the signal arrives after the check but before waiting for the signal, it will be missed and the process will wait forever. Thus the process must mask SIGQUIT while testing the flag. If it enters the wait with the signal masked, then the signal can never be delivered. Hence we need an atomic call that will unmask the signal and block the process. The *sigpause* system call provides that function. The code in Example 4-2 works for SVR3.

```
int sig_received = 0;

void handler (int sig)
{
    sig_received++;
}

main()
{
    sigset (SIGQUIT, handler);
    ...
    /* Now wait for the signal, if it is not already pending */
    sighold (SIGQUIT);
    while (sig_received == 0)   /* signal not yet arrived */
        sigpause (SIGINT);
    /* Signal has been received, carry on */
    ...
}
```

Example 4-2. Using *sigpause* to wait for a signal.

This example illustrates some features of SVR3 signaling. The *sighold* and *sigrelse* calls allow blocking and unblocking of a signal. The *sigpause* call atomically unblocks a signal and puts the process to sleep until it receives a signal that is not ignored or blocked. The *sigset* system call specifies a persistent handler that is not reset to default when the signal occurs. The old *signal* call is retained for backward compatibility; handlers specified through *signal* are not persistent.

This interface still has several deficiencies [Stev 90]. Most important, the *sighold, sigrelse,* and *sigpause* calls deal with only one signal at a time. There is no way to atomically block or unblock multiple signals. In Example 4-2, if the handler was used by multiple signals, there is no satis-factory way to code the critical region. We could block the signals one at a time, but *sigpause* can-not atomically unblock all of them and then wait.

SVR3 also lacks support for job control and facilities such as automatic restarting of system calls. These features, and many others, are provided in the 4BSD framework.

4.4.3   BSD Signal Management

4.2BSD was the first to provide reliable signals. The facilities offered by BSD signals [Leff 89] are far more powerful than those in SVR3. Most system calls take a signal mask argument, which is a 32-bit mask of the signals on which the call operates (one bit per signal). This way a single call can operate on multiple signals. The *sigsetmask* call specifies the set of signals to be blocked. The *sig-block* call adds one or more signals to this set. Likewise, the BSD implementation of *sigpause* atomically installs a new mask of blocked signals and puts the process to sleep until a signal arrives.

The *sigvec* system call replaces *signal*. Like *signal,* it installs a handler for one signal only. In addition, it can specify a mask to be associated with the signal. When the signal is generated, the kernel will, prior to calling the handler, install a new mask of blocked signals that is a union of the current mask, the mask specified by *sigvec,* and the current signal.

Hence, a handler always runs with the current signal blocked, so that a second instance of that signal will not be delivered until the handler completes. These semantics are closer to the typi-cal scenarios involving signal handlers. Blocking additional signals while the handler runs is also frequently desirable, since signal handlers themselves are usually critical regions of code. When the handler returns, the blocked signals mask is restored to its prior value.

Another important feature is the ability to handle signals on a separate stack. Consider a process that manages its own stack. It may install a handler for the SIGSEGV signal generated when its stack overflows. Normally, this handler would run on the same (already overflowed) stack, gen-erating further SIGSEGV signals. If signal handlers could run on a separate stack, this problem could be resolved. Other applications, such as user-level threads libraries, would also benefit from a sepa-rate signal stack. The *sigstack* system call specifies a separate stack on which the handler runs. It is the user's responsibility to ensure that the stack is large enough for the handler, since the kernel does not know the stack's bounds.

BSD also introduced several additional signals, including a few devoted to *job control.*[4] A job is a group of related processes, usually forming a single pipeline. A user may run several jobs concurrently from a terminal session, but only one can be the foreground job. The foreground job is allowed to read and write to the terminal. Background jobs that try to access the terminal are sent signals that typically suspend the process. The *Korn shell (ksh)* and the *C shell (csh)* [Joy 80] use job control signals to manipulate jobs, send them to the foreground or background, and suspend or resume them. Section 4.9.1 talks more about job control.

Finally, 4BSD allows automatic restarting of slow system calls that are aborted by signals. Slow system calls include *read*s and *write*s to character devices, network connections and pipes, *wait, waitpid,* and *ioctl*. When such a call is interrupted by a signal, it is automatically restarted after

---

[4]   Job control was first supported in 4.1BSD.

the handler returns instead of being aborted with an EINTR error. 4.3BSD adds the *siginterrupt* system call, which allows selective enabling or disabling of this feature on a per-signal basis.

The BSD signal interface is powerful and flexible. Its main drawback is the lack of compatibility with the original AT&T interface (and even with the SVR3 interface, although that was released later). These incompatibilities drove third-party vendors to develop various library interfaces that tried to satisfy both camps. Ultimately, SVR4 introduced a POSIX-compliant interface that is backward compatible with previous releases of System V as well as with BSD semantics.

4.5   Signals in SVR4

SVR4 offers a set of system calls [UNIX 92] that provides a superset of the functionality of SVR3 and BSD signals, as well as support for the old unreliable signals. These include:

- *sigprocmask* (how, setp, osetp);
  Uses the setp argument to modify the mask of blocked signals. If how is SIG_BLOCK, then setp is or'ed to the existing mask. If how is SIG_UNBLOCK, the signals in setp are unblocked from the existing mask. If how is SIG_SETMASK, then the current mask is replaced by setp. Upon return, osetp contains the value of the mask prior to the modification.

- *sigaltstack* (stack, old_stack);
  Specifies a new stack to handle the signals. Handlers must specifically request the alternate stack when being installed. Other handlers use the default stack. On return, old_stack points to the previous alternate stack.

- *sigsuspend* (sigmask);
  Sets the blocked signals mask to sigmask and puts the process to sleep, until a signal that is not ignored or blocked is posted. If changing the mask unblocks such a signal, the call returns immediately.

- *sigpending* (setp);
  On return, setp contains the set of signals pending to the process. The call does not modify any signal state and is simply used to obtain information.

- *sigsendset* (procset, sig);
  Enhanced version of *kill*. Sends the signal sig to the set of processes specified by procset.

- *sigaction* (signo, act, oact);
  Specifies a handler for signal signo. Resembles the BSD *sigvec* call. The act argument points to a sigaction structure that contains the signal disposition (SIG_IGN, SIG_DFL, or handler address), the mask to be associated with the signal (similar to the mask for the BSD *sigvec* call), and one or more of the following flags:

SA_NOCLDSTOP	Do not generate SIGCHLD when a child is suspended.
SA_RESTART	Restart system call automatically if interrupted by this signal.

SA_ONSTACK   Handle this signal on the alternate stack, if one has been specified by
                 sigaltstack.

SA_NOCLDWAIT   Used only with SIGCHLD—asks the system not to create *zombie* proc-
                 esses (see Section 2.8.7) when children of calling process terminate. If
                 this process subsequently calls *wait,* it will sleep until all its children
                 terminate.

SA_SIGINFO   Provide additional information to the signal handler. Used for handling
                 hardware exceptions, etc.

SA_NODEFER   Do not automatically block this signal while its handler is running.

SA_RESETHAND   Reset the action to default before calling the handler.

SA_NODEFER and SA_RESETHAND provide backward compatibility with the original unreliable signals implementation. In all cases, oact returns the previously installed *sigaction*
data.

- *Compatibility interface*

  To provide compatibility with older releases, SVR4 also supports the *signal, sigset, sighold, sigrelse, sigignore,* and *sigpause* calls. Systems that do not require binary compatibility may implement these calls as library routines.

Except for the last set, these system calls directly correspond to the POSIX.1 functions in name,
calling syntax, and semantics.

4.6   Signals Implementation

To efficiently implement signals, the kernel must maintain some state in both the u area and the
proc structure. The SVR4 signals implementation discussed here resembles that of BSD, differing
primarily in some variable and function names. The u area contains information required to properly
invoke the signal handlers, including the following fields:

u_signal[]   Vector of signal handlers for each signal

u_sigmask[]   Signal masks associated with each handler

u_sigaltstack   Pointer to the alternate signal stack

u_sigonstack   Mask of signals to handle on the alternate stack

u_oldsig   Set of handlers that must exhibit the old, unreliable behavior

The proc structure contains fields related to generation and posting of signals, including the following:

p_cursig   The current signal being handled

p_sig   Pending signals mask

p_hold   Blocked signals mask

p_ignore   Ignored signals mask

Let us now examine at how the kernel implements various functions related to signal
delivery.

4.6.1   Signal Generation

When a signal is generated, the kernel checks the proc structure of the receiving process. If the signal is being ignored, the kernel returns without taking any action. If not, it adds the signal to the set of pending signals in p_cursig. Since p_cursig is just a bitmask with one bit per signal, the kernel cannot record multiple instances of the same signal. Hence the process will only know that at least one instance of that signal was pending.

If the process is in an interruptible sleep and the signal is not blocked, the kernel wakes up this process so it can receive the signal. Moreover, job control signals such as SIGSTOP or SIGCONT directly suspend or resume the process instead of being posted.

4.6.2   Delivery and Handling

The process checks for signals by calling issig() when about to return from kernel mode after a system call or interrupt. It also calls issig() just before entering, or after waking up from, an interruptible sleep. The issig() function looks for set bits in p_cursig. If any bit is set, issig() checks p_hold to discover if the signal is currently blocked. If not, then issig() stores the signal number in p_sig and returns TRUE.

If a signal is pending, the kernel calls psig() to handle it. psig() inspects the information in the u area pertaining to this signal. If no handler is declared, psig() takes the default action, usually process termination. If a handler is to be invoked, the p_hold mask of blocked signals is altered by adding the current signal, as well as any signal specified in the u_sigmask entry associated with this signal. The current signal is not added to this mask if the SA_NODEFER flag is specified for this handler. Likewise, if the SA_RESETHAND flag is specified, the action in the u_signal[] array is reset to SIG_DFL.

Finally, psig() calls sendsig(), which arranges for the process to return to user mode and pass control to the handler. sendsig() also ensures that when the handler completes, the process will resume the code it was executing prior to receiving the signal. If the alternate stack must be used, sendsig() invokes the handler on that stack. The implementation of sendsig() is machine-dependent, since it must know the details of stack and context manipulation.

4.7   Exceptions

An exception[5] occurs when a program encounters an unusual condition, usually an error. Examples include accessing an invalid address and attempting to divide by zero. This results in a trap to the kernel, which normally generates a signal to notify the process of the exception.

In UNIX, the kernel uses signals to notify the user of exceptions. The type of signal depends on the nature of the exception. For instance, an invalid address exception may result in a SIGSEGV signal. If the user has declared a handler for that signal, the kernel invokes the handler. If not, the default action is to terminate the process. This allows individual programs to install their own ex-

---

[5] This section describes *hardware exceptions*, which must not be confused with software exceptions supported by certain languages such as C++.

ception handlers. Some programming languages, such as Ada, have built-in exception handling mechanisms; these are implemented by the language library as signal handlers.

Exceptions are also used extensively by debuggers. Debugged (traced) programs generate exceptions at breakpoints and upon completion of the *exec* system call. The debugger must intercept these exceptions to control the program. The debugger may also wish to intercept other selected exceptions and signals generated by the debugged program. The *ptrace* system call in UNIX enables this interception; it is described further in Section 6.2.4.

There are several drawbacks to the way UNIX handles exceptions. First, *the signal handler runs in the same context as the exception*. This means that it cannot access the full register context as it was at the time of the exception. When the exception occurs, the kernel passes some of the exception context to the handler. The amount of context passed depends on the specific UNIX variant and on the hardware on which it runs. In general, a single thread must deal with two contexts—that of the handler and that of the context in which the exception occurred.

Second, *signals are designed for single-threaded processes*. UNIX variants that support multithreaded processes find it difficult to adapt signals to such an environment. Finally, due to limitations of the *ptrace* system call, *a traditional ptrace-based debugger can control only its immediate children*.

4.8   Mach Exception Handling

The limitations of UNIX exceptions prompted the development of a uniform exception handling facility in Mach [Blac 88]. Mach needed a facility that would allow binary compatibility with UNIX and also work with multithreaded applications. This facility is also part of OSF/1, which is based on Mach.

Mach abandons the idea of executing the handler in the same context as the exception. UNIX adopted that approach only because the handler needs to access and run in the same address space in which the exception occurs. Since Mach is multithreaded, it can achieve this by executing the handler in a different *thread* in the same *task*. (Mach threads and tasks are discussed in Section 6.4. In brief, a *task* holds a set of resources, including an address space, and a *thread* is an execution context, or control point, that runs in a task. The traditional UNIX process comprises a task containing a single thread.)

Mach recognizes two distinct entities—the victim (the thread that caused the exception) and the handler. Figure 4-2 describes the interaction between the two. The victim first *raises* the exception, notifying the kernel of its occurrence. It then *waits* for exception handling to complete. The handler *catches* the exception, that is, receives notification from the kernel. This notification identifies the victim and specifies the nature of the exception. It then handles the exception and *clears* it, allowing the victim to resume execution. Alternately, if it cannot handle the exception successfully, it terminates the victim.

These interactions are somewhat similar to the flow of control for a UNIX exception, except that the handler executes in a separate thread. As a result, the *raise, wait, catch,* and *clear* operations together constitute a *remote procedure call,* which Mach implements using its interprocess communication (IPC) facilities, described in Section 6.4.

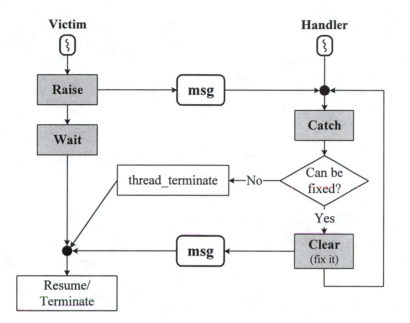

Figure 4-2. Mach exception handling.

Two messages are involved in handling a single exception. When the victim raises the exception, it sends a message to the handler and waits for the reply. The handler catches the exception when it receives the message and clears it by sending a reply message to the victim. When the victim receives the reply, it can resume execution.

4.8.1   Exception Ports

In Mach, a message is sent to a *port*, which is a protected queue of messages. Several tasks may have *send rights* (right to send messages) to a given port, but only one task may receive messages from it. Mach associates one exception port with each task and one with each thread in that task. This provides two ways of handling an exception, and these correspond to the two applications of exceptions—error handling and debugging.

Error handlers are associated with threads, since they usually only affect the victim thread. Each thread may have a different error handler. The handler's port is registered as the thread's exception port. When a new thread is created, its exception port is initialized to the NULL port, meaning that initially the thread has no error handler.

A debugger attaches to a task by registering one of its ports as that task's exception port. The debugger runs as a separate task and has the *receive rights* (right to receive messages sent to the port) to this port. Each task inherits its exception port from its parent. This allows debuggers to control all the descendants of a task that is being debugged.

Since an exception could use either the task or the thread exception port, we need a way of resolving the conflict. To do so, we observe that the thread exception port is used for error handlers that should be transparent to debuggers. For example, a handler may respond to a floating point underflow error by substituting zero as the result of the operation. Such an exception is usually of no interest to the debugger, which would normally wish to intercept unrecoverable errors only. Hence if an error handler is installed, Mach invokes it in preference to the debugger.

When an exception occurs, it is sent to the thread exception port if one exists. Thus exceptions that invoke error handlers are not seen by the debugger. If the installed error handler cannot successfully clear the exception, it forwards it to the task exception port. (Since the error handler is another thread in the same task, it has access to the victim's task exception port.) If neither handler can handle the exception, the kernel terminates the victim thread.

4.8.2   Error Handling

When the victim raises an exception, the initial message sent to the (task or thread) exception port contains the reply port, identity of the thread and task that caused the exception, and exception type. After processing the exception, the handler sends a reply message to the reply port. The task in which the exception occurred owns the receive rights to this port, and the victim thread is waiting to read the reply. When the reply arrives, the victim receives it and resumes normal execution.

Since the handler and the victim are threads in the same task, the handler shares the victim's address space. It can also access the victim's register context using the *thread_get_state* and *thread_set_state* calls.

Mach provides UNIX compatibility, and UNIX signal handlers expect to be invoked in the same context as the thread that caused the exception. This is contrary to Mach's philosophy of using a separate thread to handle the error. Mach reconciles this difference by using a system-invoked error handler. When an exception occurs for which a UNIX signal handler is installed, a message is sent to the special system-invoked handler. This handler modifies the victim thread so that the signal handler is executed when the victim resumes. It then clears the exception, causing the victim to run and process the signal. The application is responsible for unwinding the stack after the signal handler completes.

4.8.3   Debugger Interactions

A debugger controls a task by registering a port to which it has receive rights as the task's exception port. When a thread in that task has an exception that cannot be cleared by its error handler, the kernel sends a message to this port, and the debugger receives this message. The exception only stops the victim thread—all other threads in the task continue to run. A debugger may suspend the whole task using the *task_suspend* call if necessary.

Mach offers several facilities that the debugger can use to control the task. It can access the victim's address space using *vm_read* or *vm_write,* or its register context by *thread_get_state* or *thread_set_state*. It can suspend or resume the application, or terminate it by *task_terminate*.

Mach IPC is location-independent, meaning that messages can be sent to ports on the same or remote machines. The *netmsgserver*, a special user task, extends Mach IPC transparently over the network. It allocates "proxy" ports for all remote ports, receives messages intended for them, and forwards these messages across the network transparently to the sender. This allows a debugger to control a task on any node on the network, just as it would control a local task.

4.8.4   Analysis

The Mach exception handling facility addresses many of the problems faced by UNIX. It is also more robust and provides functionality not available in UNIX. Some of its important advantages are:

- A debugger is not restricted to controlling its immediate children. It can debug any task, provided it has the required permissions.
- A debugger can attach itself to a running task.[6] It does so by registering one of its ports as that task's exception port. It can also detach itself from a task, by resetting the task's exception port to its former value. This port is the only connection between the debugger and the target, and the kernel contains no special support for debugging.
- The extension of Mach IPC over the network allows the development of distributed debuggers.
- Having a separate error handler thread allows a clean separation of the handler and victim contexts and allows the handler to access the entire context of the victim.
- Multithreaded processes are handled cleanly. Only the thread that caused the exception is suspended, while others remain unaffected. If several threads cause exceptions, each generates a separate message and is handled independently.

4.9   Process Groups and Terminal Management

UNIX provides the notion of *process groups* in order to control terminal access and support login sessions. The design and implementation of these facilities vary greatly in different UNIX versions. This section begins with a review of the common concepts and then examines some important implementations.

4.9.1   Common Concepts

Process groups — Each process belongs to a process group, which is identified by its *process group ID*. The kernel uses this mechanism to take certain actions on all processes in a group. Each group may have a *group leader,* which is the process whose PID is the same as its process group ID. Normally, a process inherits the process group ID from its parent, and all other processes in the group are descendants of the leader.

---

[6] Currently, most UNIX debuggers are written using the **/proc** file system, which allows access to address spaces of unrelated processes. Hence debuggers can easily attach and detach running processes. At the time when Mach exception handling was designed, this ability was uncommon.

Controlling terminal — Each process may have a controlling terminal. This is usually the login terminal at which this process was created. All processes in the same group share the same controlling terminal.

The /dev/tty file — The special file **/dev/tty** is associated with the controlling terminal of each process. The device driver for this file simply routes all requests to the appropriate terminal. For instance, in 4.3BSD, the device number of the controlling terminal is stored in the u_ttyd field of the u area. A read to the terminal is thus implemented as

```
(*cdevsw[major(u.u_ttyd)].d_read) (u.u_ttyd, flags);
```

Thus if two processes belong to different login sessions, and they both open **/dev/tty**, they will access different terminals.

Controlling group — Each terminal is associated with a process group. This group, called the terminal's controlling group, is identified by the t_pgrp field in the tty structure for this terminal.[7] *Keyboard-generated signals, such as SIGINT and SIGQUIT, are sent to all processes in the terminal's controlling group,* that is, to all processes whose p_pgrp equals this terminal's t_pgrp.

Job control — This is a mechanism (provided in 4BSD and SVR4) that can suspend or resume a process group and control its access to the terminal. Job control shells such as *csh* and *ksh* provide control characters (typically control-Z) and commands such as *fg* and *bg* to access these features. The terminal driver provides additional control by preventing processes not in the terminal's controlling group from reading or writing the terminal.

      The original System V implementation models process groups mainly as representations of login sessions and provides no job control. 4BSD associates a new process group with every shell command line (hence, all processes connected by a shell pipeline belong to the same group), thus representing the notion of a job. SVR4 unifies these divergent and incompatible treatments by introducing the session abstraction. The following sections examine all three approaches and analyze their advantages and drawbacks.

4.9.2   The SVR3 Model

In SVR3 (and earlier AT&T releases), the process group exhibits the characteristics of a terminal login session. Figure 4-3 describes the SVR3 treatment of terminal access. The following are its important features:

Process groups — Each process inherits its parent's process group ID during *fork*. The only way to change the process group is by calling *setpgrp,* which changes the caller's group to equal its PID. The caller thus becomes the leader of the new group. Any children it subsequently *fork*s will join this group.

Controlling terminal — The terminal is owned by its controlling group. Thus when a process forms a new group, it loses its controlling terminal. Thereafter, the first terminal it opens (that is not already a controlling terminal) becomes its controlling terminal. The t_pgrp for that terminal is set to the p_pgrp of this process. All child processes inherit the controlling terminal from the group leader. No two process groups have the same controlling terminal.

---

[7] The terminal driver maintains the tty structure for each terminal.

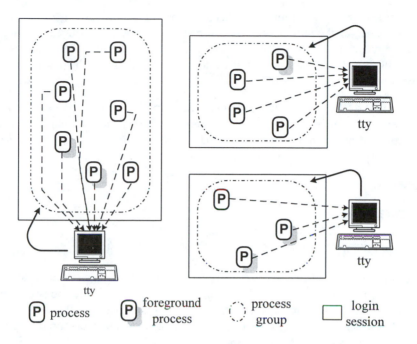

tty

$\boxed{P}$ process	$\boxed{P}$ foreground process	$\overset{\frown}{\underset{\smile}{}}$ process group	$\square$ login session

Figure 4-3. Process groups in SVR3 UNIX.

Typical scenario — The *init* process forks a child for each terminal listed in the **/etc/inittab** file. The child process calls *setpgrp,* becoming a group leader, and then *execs* the *getty* program, which displays a login prompt and waits for input. When a user types in his login name, *getty execs* the *login* program, which asks for and verifies the password, and finally, *execs* the login shell. Hence the login shell is a direct child of *init* and is also a process group leader. Usually, other processes do not create their own groups (except for system daemons started from a login session); hence all processes belonging to a login session will be in the same process group.

Terminal access — There is no support for job control. All processes that have a terminal open can access it equally, whether they are in the foreground or background. Output from such processes will be randomly intermingled on the screen. If several processes try to read the terminal concurrently, it is purely a matter of chance which process will read any particular line of input.

Terminal signals — Signals such as SIGQUIT and SIGINT that are generated at the keyboard are sent to all processes in the terminal's controlling group, thus usually to all processes in the login session. These signals are really intended for foreground processes only. Hence when the shell creates a process that will run in the background, it sets them up to ignore these signals. It also redirects the standard input of such processes to **/dev/null**, so that they may not read from the terminal through that descriptor (they may still open other descriptors to read from the terminal).

Detaching the terminal — A terminal is detached from its controlling group when its t_pgrp field is set to zero. This happens when no more processes have the terminal open or when the group leader (usually the login process) exits.

Death of group leader — The group leader becomes the controlling process of its terminal and is responsible for managing the terminal for the entire group. When it dies, its controlling terminal is disassociated from the group (its t_pgrp is set to zero). Moreover, all other processes in its group are sent a SIGHUP signal, and their p_pgrp is set to zero, so they do not belong to a process group (they become *orphaned*).

Implementation — The p_pgrp field of the proc structure contains the process group ID. The u area has two terminal-related fields—u_ttyp (pointer to tty structure of controlling terminal) and u_ttyd (device number of controlling terminal). The t_pgrp field in the tty structure contains the controlling process group of the terminal.

4.9.3   Limitations

The SVR3 process group framework has several limitations [Lenn 86]:

- There is no way for a process group to close its controlling terminal and allocate another.
- Although the process groups are modeled after login sessions, there is no way to preserve a login session after disconnecting from its controlling terminal. Ideally, we would like to have such a session persist in the system, so that it can attach to another terminal at a later time, preserving its state in the meantime.
- There is no consistent way of handling "loss of carrier" by a controlling terminal. The semantics of whether such a terminal remains allocated to the group and can be reconnected to the group differ from one implementation to another.
- The kernel does not synchronize access to the terminal by different processes in the group. Foreground and background processes can read from or write to the terminal in an unregulated manner.
- When the process group leader terminates, the kernel sends a SIGHUP signal to all processes in the group. Processes that ignore this signal can continue to access the controlling terminal, even after it is assigned to another group. This can result in a new user receiving unsolicited output from such a process, or worse, the process can read data typed by the new user, causing a possible security breach.
- If a process other than the login process invokes *setpgrp,* it will be disconnected from the controlling terminal. It can continue to access the terminal through any existing file descriptors. The process, however, is not controlled by the terminal and will not receive SIGHUP signals.
- There are no job control facilities, such as the ability to move processes between the foreground and the background.
- A program such as a terminal emulator, which opens devices other than its controlling terminal, has no way of receiving carrier loss notification from those devices.

4BSD addresses some of these problems. The next section describes the BSD approach.

4.9.4   4.3BSD Groups and Terminals

In 4.3BSD, a process group represents a *job* (also called a *task*) within a login session. A job is a set of related processes that are controlled as a single unit with regard to terminal access. The basic concepts are illustrated in Figure 4-4.

Process groups — A process inherits its group ID from its parent. A process can change its own group ID or that of any other process (subject to permissions—the caller must own the other process or be the superuser) by calling *setpgrp*. The 4.3BSD *setpgrp* call accepts two arguments—the PID of the target process, and the new group ID to assign to it. Thus a 4.3BSD process may relinquish the leadership of a group or join any arbitrary group; indeed, there can be process groups that have no leader.

Jobs — Job control shells such as *csh* typically create a new process group for each command line, whether the command is executed in the foreground or background. Therefore the job will usually consist of a single process or a set of processes connected by pipes.[8] Descendants of these processes also will be in the same group.

Login sessions — In 4.3BSD, a single login session may generate several process groups (jobs) that

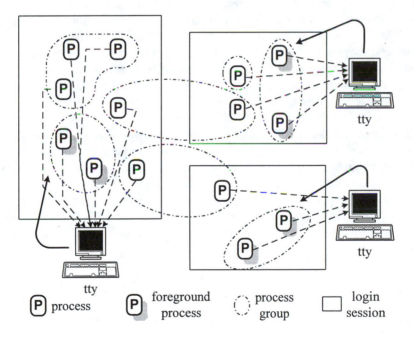

Figure 4-4. Process groups in 4.3BSD UNIX.

---

[8] It is also possible to combine two or more unconnected processes into a single process group by issuing multiple shell commands on the same line, separated by semicolons and placed within parentheses, as for example:

```
%  (cc tanman.c; cp file1 file2; echo done >newfile)
```

are active at the same time, all sharing the same controlling terminal. The t_pgrp field of the terminal's tty structure always contains the foreground job's process group.

Controlling terminals — If a process with a group ID of zero opens a terminal, the terminal becomes the controlling terminal for that process, and the process joins the terminal's current controlling group (the p_pgrp of the process is set to the t_pgrp of the terminal). If the terminal is currently not a controlling terminal for another group, then this process is first made a group leader (thus, both p_pgrp of the process and t_pgrp of the terminal are set to the process's PID). Direct descendants of *init* (thus, all login shell processes) initially have a group ID of zero. Other than that, only the superuser can reset a process's group ID to zero.

Terminal access — The foreground processes (the terminal's current controlling group, obtained from t_pgrp) always have unobstructed access to the terminal. If a background process tries to read from the terminal, the driver sends a SIGTTIN signal to all processes in its process group. SIGTTIN suspends the receiving process by default. Writes by background processes are permitted by default. 4.3BSD provides a terminal option (the LTOSTOP bit manipulated by the TIOCLSET *ioctl*) that causes a SIGTTOU signal to be sent to a background process that tries to write to the terminal. Jobs stopped by SIGTTIN or SIGTTOU can later be resumed by sending them a SIGCONT signal.

Controlling group — A process that has read access to the terminal can use the TIOCSPGRP *ioctl* call to change the terminal's controlling group (t_pgrp) to any other value. The shell uses this facility to move jobs to the foreground or background. For example, a user can resume a suspended process group and move it to the foreground by making it the controlling group and sending it a SIGCONT signal. *csh* and *ksh* provide the *fg* and *bg* commands for this purpose.

Closing the terminal — When no process has the terminal open, the terminal is disassociated from the group and its t_pgrp is set to zero. This is done by the terminal driver's *close* routine, called when the last descriptor to the terminal is closed.

Reinitializing the terminal line — 4.3BSD provides a *vhangup* system call, typically used by *init* to terminate a login session and start another. *vhangup* traverses the open file table, finds each entry that resolves to this terminal, and makes it unusable. It can do so by deleting the open mode in the file table entry or, in implementations that support the *vnode interface* (see Section 8.6), by changing the vnodeops pointer to point to a set of functions that simply return an error. *vhangup* then calls the close() routine of the terminal and, finally, sends the SIGHUP signal to the terminal's controlling group. This is the 4.3BSD solution to handling processes that continue after the login session terminates.

4.9.5 Drawbacks

While 4.3BSD job control is powerful and versatile, it has some important drawbacks:

- There is no clear representation of a login session. The original login process is not special and may not even be a group leader. SIGHUP is typically not sent when the login process terminates.
- No single process is responsible for controlling the terminal. Thus a loss of carrier condition sends a SIGHUP signal to its current controlling group, which could even be ignoring

this signal. For instance, a remote user connected via a modem would remain logged in if he or she simply disconnected the line.

- A process can change the terminal's controlling group to any value, even a nonexistent one. If a group is later created with that group ID, it will inherit the terminal and receive signals from it unintentionally.
- The programming interface is incompatible with that of System V.

Clearly, we want an approach that will preserve the concepts of login sessions and of tasks within such sessions. The next section looks at the sessions architecture of SVR4 and how it deals with these issues.

4.10   The SVR4 Sessions Architecture

The limitations of the SVR3 and 4.3BSD models can be attributed to one fundamental problem. The single abstraction of the process group cannot adequately represent both a login session and a job within such a session. SVR3 does a fair job of controlling the behavior of a login session, but cannot support job control. 4.3BSD provides powerful job control facilities, but does a poor job of isolating login sessions from one another.

Modern UNIX systems such as SVR4 and 4.4BSD have addressed these problems by representing the session and the job as separate but related abstractions. The process group identifies a single job. A new *session* object represents the login session. The following sections describe the SVR4 sessions architecture. Section 4.10.5 describes the 4.4BSD sessions implementation, which is functionally similar to SVR4 and also is POSIX-compliant.

4.10.1   Motivation

The sessions architecture addresses several deficiencies in the earlier models. Its main goals include:

- Adequately supporting both the login session and the job abstractions.
- Providing BSD-style job control.
- Retaining backward compatibility with earlier System V versions.
- Allowing a login session to attach and detach several controlling terminals during its lifetime (of course, it can have only one controlling terminal at any given time). Any such change should be propagated to all processes in the session transparently.
- Making the session leader (the process that creates the login session) responsible for maintaining the session's integrity and security.
- Allowing terminal access based solely on file access permissions. In particular, if a process successfully opens a terminal, it should be able to continue to access it as long as it is open.
- Eliminating inconsistencies of earlier implementations. For example, SVR3 exhibits an anomaly in the case where a group leader *forks* child processes before allocating the controlling terminal. Such offspring would receive signals such as SIGINT from this terminal, but would not be able to access the terminal using **/dev/tty**.

4.10.2   Sessions and Process Groups

Figure 4-5 describes the SVR4 sessions architecture [Will 89]. Each process belongs both to a session and to a process group. Likewise, each controlling terminal is associated with a session and a foreground process group (the terminal's controlling group). The session plays the role of the SVR3 process group, and the session leader is responsible for managing the login session and insulating it from other sessions. Only the session leader may allocate or deallocate a controlling terminal.

A process creates a new session by calling *setsid,* which sets both its session ID and group ID to the same value as its PID. Thus *setsid* makes the caller both a session leader and a group leader. If a process is already a group leader, it cannot become a session leader and *setsid* will fail.

The SVR4 process groups have the basic characteristics of 4.3BSD groups and typically represent a job within a login session. Thus a single login session may have several process groups active simultaneously. One of these groups is the foreground group and has unlimited access to the terminal (it is the terminal's controlling group). As in 4.3BSD, background processes that try to access the controlling terminal are sent SIGTTIN or SIGTTOU signals (SIGTTOU must be explicitly enabled, as described in Section 4.9.4).

A process inherits its process group from its parent and may change it by calling *setpgid* or *setpgrp.* The *setpgrp* call is identical to the SVR3 version and sets the caller's group to equal its PID, thus making it a group leader. The *setpgid* call is similar to the 4.3BSD *setpgrp,* but adds some

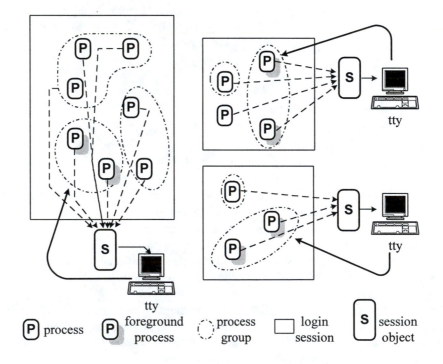

Figure 4-5. SVR4 sessions architecture.

important restrictions on the operation. Its syntax is

setpgid (pid, pgid);

Its function is to change the process group of the target process, identified by pid, to the value specified by pgid. If pgid is zero, the process group is set to the same value as the pid, thus making the process a group leader. If pid is zero, the call acts on the calling process itself. There are, however, some important restrictions. The target process must be either the caller itself or a child of the caller that has not yet called *exec*. The caller and the target processes must both belong to the same session. If pgid is not the same as the target's PID (or zero, which has the same effect), it must be equal to another existing group ID within the same session only.

Hence processes may move from one group to another within a session. The only way they can leave the session is by calling *setsid* to start a new session with themselves as the sole member. A process that is a group leader may relinquish leadership of its group by moving to another group,. Such a process, however, cannot start a new session as long as its PID is the group ID of any other process (that is, the group whose leadership the process relinquished is not empty). This prevents the confusing situation in which a process group has the same ID as a session of which it is not a part.

Likewise, a terminal's foreground (controlling) group may only be changed by a process in the session that controls the terminal, and it can only be changed to another valid group in the same session. This feature is used by job control shells to move jobs to the foreground or background.

4.10.3   Data Structures

Figure 4-6 describes the data structures used to manage sessions and process groups. The *setsid* call allocates a new session structure and resets the p_sessp and p_pgidp fields in the proc structure. The session initially has no controlling terminal.

When the session leader opens a terminal for the first time (after becoming the session leader), the terminal becomes the controlling terminal for this session, unless the caller has passed the ONOCTTY flag to the open call. The session structure is initialized to point to the vnode of this terminal, and the vnode in turn points to the stream head for the device.

Child processes of the session leader inherit the p_sessp pointer, and thus instantly see any change in the session object. Thus these processes inherit the controlling terminal, even if the terminal was opened after the child processes were created.

4.10.4   Controlling Terminals

The **/dev/tty** file again acts as an alias for the controlling terminal. Its driver resolves any calls to **/dev/tty** by looking up the session pointer in the proc structure and dereferencing it to get to the vnode of the controlling terminal. If the controlling terminal is deallocated, the kernel sets the vnode pointer in the session object to NULL, and any access to **/dev/tty** will fail. If a process had directly opened a specific terminal (as opposed to opening **/dev/tty**), it can continue to access it even after the terminal is disassociated from its current login session.

When a user logs in to the system, the login process performs the following operations:

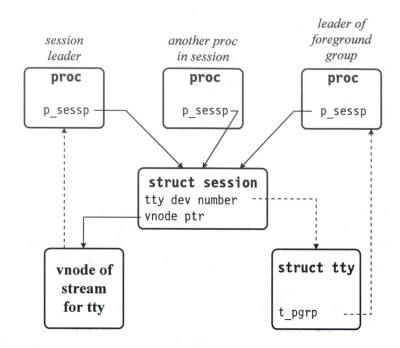

Figure 4-6. Session management data structures in SVR4 UNIX.

1. Calls *setsid* to become a session leader.
2. Closes *stdin, stdout,* and *stderr.*
3. Calls *open* to open a designated terminal. Because this is the first terminal opened by the session leader, it becomes the controlling terminal for the session. The descriptor returned by *open* refers to the real device file of the terminal.
4. Duplicates this descriptor elsewhere, so as not to use *stdin, stdout,* and *stderr* to refer to the real device file. Closes the original descriptor after duplication. The controlling terminal remains open through the duplicated descriptor.
5. Opens **/dev/tty** as *stdin,* and duplicates it into *stdout* and *stderr.* This effectively reopens the controlling terminal through the alias device. Thus the session leader and all other processes in the session (which inherit these descriptors) access the controlling terminal only through **/dev/tty** (unless another process explicitly opens the terminal's device file).
6. Finally, closes the saved descriptor, removing any direct contact with the controlling terminal.

If the terminal driver detects a broken connection (for instance, due to loss of carrier on a modem line), it sends a SIGHUP signal to the session leader only. This contrasts with the 4.3BSD treatment of sending the signal to the foreground group and the SVR3 treatment of sending it to all processes in the controlling group (session). The session leader is, in this sense, a trusted process and is expected to take the correct action when it loses the controlling terminal.

In addition, the driver sends a SIGTSTP signal to the foreground process group, if it is different from that of the session leader. This prevents foreground processes from receiving unexpected
errors when trying to access the terminal. The controlling terminal remains allocated to the session.
This gives the session leader the option of trying to reconnect to the terminal after the connection is
reestablished.

A session leader may disconnect the current controlling terminal and open a new one. The
kernel will set the session's vnode pointer to point to the vnode of the new terminal. As a result, all
processes in this login session will switch transparently to the new controlling terminal. The indirection provided by **/dev/tty** makes it easy to propagate this change of controlling terminal.

When the session leader terminates, it ends the login session. The controlling terminal is
deallocated by setting the session's vnode pointer to NULL. As a result, none of the processes in
this session can access the terminal through **/dev/tty** (they can continue to access the terminal if
they have explicitly opened its device file). Processes in the foreground group of the terminal are
sent a SIGHUP signal. All direct children of the exiting process are inherited by the *init* process.

4.10.5   The 4.4BSD Sessions Implementation

The SVR4 sessions architecture adequately represents both a login session and a job within that
session, while maintaining compatibility with the POSIX 1003.1 standard and with earlier versions
of System V. The sessions implementations in 4.4BSD and OSF/1 are essentially similar and offer

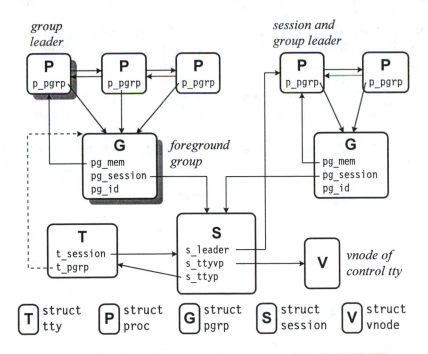

Figure 4-7. Session management data structures in 4.4BSD UNIX.

comparable facilities. They differ from SVR4 in implementation details.

For comparison, Figure 4-7 describes the data structures used in 4.4BSD [Stev 92]. One important difference is that the proc structures do not directly reference the session object. Instead, they point to the process group object (struct pgrp), which in turn points to the session structure.

4.11 Summary

The POSIX 1003.1 standard has helped bring together divergent and mutually incompatible methods of signals and controlling terminal handling. The resulting interfaces are robust and closely match the expectations of typical applications and users.

4.12 Exercises

Note — Some of the questions have different answers for each major UNIX variant. The student may answer such questions for the UNIX system with which he or she is most familiar.

1. Why are signal handlers not preserved across an *exec* system call?
2. Why is the SIGCHLD signal ignored by default?
3. What happens if a signal is generated for a process while it is in the middle of a *fork, exec,* or *exit* system call?
4. Under what circumstances will a *kill* signal not terminate a process immediately?
5. Traditional UNIX systems use the sleep priority for two purposes—to decide if a signal should wake up the sleeping process and to determine the scheduling priority of the process after waking up. What is the drawback of this approach, and how do modern systems address it?
6. What is the drawback of having signal handlers be persistent (remain installed after being invoked)? Are there any specific signals that should not have persistent handlers?
7. How does the 4.3BSD *sigpause* call differ from that of SVR3? Describe a situation in which it is more useful.
8. Why is it desirable to have the kernel restart an interrupted system call rather than have the user do so?
9. What happens if a process receives several instances of the same signal before it can handle the first instance? Would other semantics be more useful for this situation?
10. Suppose a process has two signals pending and has declared handlers for each of them. How does the kernel ensure that the process handles the second signal immediately after handling the first?
11. What if a process receives a signal while handling another? How may a process control its behavior in this case?
12. When should a process use the SA_NOCLDWAIT feature of SVR4? When should it not use it?
13. Why would an exception handler need the full context of the process that raised the exception?
14. Which process may create a new process group in (a) 4.3BSD and (b) SVR4?

15. What benefits does the SVR4 sessions architecture offer over the 4.3BSD terminal and job control facilities?

16. [Bell 88] describes a user-level session manager to support login sessions. How does this compare with the SVR4 sessions architecture?

17. What should the SVR4 kernel do when a session leader deallocates its controlling terminal?

18. How does SVR4 allow a session to reconnect to its controlling terminal? In what situations is this useful?

4.13   References

[AT&T 86]   American Telephone & Telegraph, *UNIX System V Release 3: Programmer's Reference Manual,* 1986.

[Bach 86]   Bach, M.J., *The Design of the UNIX Operating System,* Prentice-Hall, Englewood Cliffs, NJ, 1986.

[Bell 88]   Bellovin, S.M., "The Session Tty Manager," *Proceedings of the Summer 1988 USENIX Technical Conference,* Jun. 1988.

[Blac 88]   Black, D.L., Golub, D.B., Hauth, K., Tevanian, A., and Sanzi, R., "The Mach Exception Handling Facility," CMU–CS–88–129, Computer Science Department, Carnegie Mellon University, Apr. 1988.

[IEEE 90]   Institute for Electrical and Electronic Engineers, *Information Technology—Portable Operating System Interface (POSIX) Part 1: System Application Program Interface (API) [C Language],* 1003.1–1990, Dec. 1990.

[Joy 80]   Joy, W., "An Introduction to the C Shell," Computer Science Division, University of California at Berkeley, Nov. 1980.

[Leff 89]   Leffler, S.J., McKusick, M.K., Karels, M.J., and Quarterman, J.S., *The Design and Implementation of the 4.3 BSD UNIX Operating System,* Addison-Wesley, Reading, MA, 1989.

[Lenn 86]   Lenner, D.C., "A System V Compatible Implementation of 4.2 BSD Job Control," *Proceedings of the Summer 1986 USENIX Technical Conference,* Jun. 1986, pp. 459–474.

[Stev 90]   Stevens, W.R., *UNIX Network Programming,* Prentice-Hall, Englewood Cliffs, NJ, 1990.

[Stev 92]   Stevens, W.R., *Advanced Programming in the UNIX Environment,* Addison-Wesley, Reading, MA, 1992.

[UNIX 92]   UNIX Systems Laboratories, *Operating System API Reference: UNIX SVR4.2,* UNIX Press, 1992.

[Will 89]   Williams, T., "Session Management in System V Release 4," *Proceedings of the Winter 1989 USENIX Technical Conference,* Jan. 1989, pp. 365–375.

5

Process Scheduling

5.1 Introduction

Like memory and terminals, the CPU is a shared resource for which processes in the system contend. The operating system must decide how to apportion this resource among all the processes. The scheduler is the component of the operating system that determines which process to run at any given time, and how long to let it run. UNIX is essentially a time-sharing system, which means it allows several processes to run concurrently. To some extent this is an illusion (at least on a uniprocessor), because a single processor can run only one process at any given instant. The UNIX system emulates concurrency by interleaving processes on a time-share basis. The scheduler gives the CPU to each process for a brief period of time before switching to another process. This period is called a *time quantum* or *time slice*.

A description of the UNIX scheduler must focus on two aspects: The first deals with *policy*—the rules used to decide which process to run and when to switch to another. The second deals with *implementation*—the data structures and algorithms used to carry out these policies. The scheduling policy must try to meet several objectives—fast response time for interactive applications, high throughput for background jobs, avoidance of process starvation, and so forth. These goals often conflict with each other, and the scheduler must balance them the best that it can. It also must implement its policy efficiently and with minimum overhead.

At the lowest level, the scheduler arranges for the processor to switch from one process to another. This is called a *context switch*. The kernel saves the hardware execution context of the current process in its *process control block (PCB),* which is traditionally part of the u area of the proc-

112

ess. The context is a snapshot of the values of the general-purpose, memory management, and other special registers of the process. The kernel then loads the hardware registers with the context of the next process to be run. (The context is obtained from the PCB of this process.) This causes the CPU to begin executing the next process from the saved context. The primary responsibilities of the scheduler are to decide when to perform a context switch and which process to run.

Context switches are expensive operations. Besides saving a copy of the process registers, the kernel must perform many architecture-specific tasks. On some systems, it must flush the data, instruction, or address translation cache to avoid incorrect memory access (see Sections 15.9–15.13) by the new process. As a result, the new process incurs several main memory accesses when it starts running. This degrades the performance of the process, because memory access is significantly slower than cache access. Finally, on pipelined architectures such as *Reduced Instruction Set Computers* (RISC), the kernel must flush the instruction pipeline prior to switching context. These factors may influence not only the implementation, but also the scheduling policy.

This chapter first describes the handling of the clock interrupt and timer-based tasks. The clock is critical to the operation of the scheduler, because the scheduler often wants to preempt running processes when their time slice expires. The rest of this chapter examines various scheduler designs and how they affect the behavior of the system.

5.2   Clock Interrupt Handling

Every UNIX machine has a hardware clock, which interrupts the system at fixed time intervals. Some machines require the operating system to prime the clock after each interrupt; in others, the clock rearms itself. The time period between successive clock interrupts is called a *CPU tick, clock tick,* or simply, a *tick*. Most computers support a variety of tick intervals. UNIX typically sets the CPU tick at 10 milliseconds.[1] Most UNIX implementations store the clock frequency, or the number of ticks per second, in a constant called HZ, which is usually defined in the **param.h** file. For a 10-millisecond tick, HZ would be 100. Kernel functions usually measure time in number of ticks, rather than in seconds or milliseconds.

Interrupt handling is highly system-dependent. This section describes a generic implementation found in many traditional UNIX systems. The clock interrupt handler runs in response to the hardware clock interrupt, whose priority is second only to that of the power-failure interrupt. As a result, the handler must be as quick as possible and its duties kept to a minimum. It performs the following tasks:

- Rearms the hardware clock if necessary.
- Updates CPU usage statistics for the current process.
- Performs scheduler-related functions, such as priority recomputation and time-slice expiration handling.
- Sends a SIGXCPU signal to the current process if it has exceeded its CPU usage quota.

---

[1]   This is far from universal and depends on the UNIX variant. It also depends on the resolution of the system's hardware clock.

- Updates the time-of-day clock and other related clocks. For instance, SVR4 maintains a variable called lbolt to store the number of ticks that have elapsed since the system was booted.
- Handles callouts (see Section 5.2.1).
- Wakes up system processes such as the *swapper* and *pagedaemon* when appropriate.
- Handles alarms (see Section 5.2.2).

Some of these tasks do not need to be performed on every tick. Most UNIX systems define a notion of a *major tick*, which occurs once every *n* clock ticks, where *n* depends on the specific UNIX variant. The scheduler performs some of its tasks only on major clock ticks. For instance, 4.3BSD performs priority recomputation on every fourth tick, while SVR4 handles alarms and wakes up system processes once a second if necessary.

5.2.1   Callouts

A *callout* records a function that the kernel must invoke at a later time. In SVR4, for example, any kernel subsystem may register a callout by calling

```
int to_ID = timeout (void (*fn)(), caddr_t arg, long delta);
```

where fn() is the kernel function to invoke, arg is an argument to pass to fn(), and delta is the time interval in CPU ticks, after which the function must be invoked. The kernel invokes the callout function in system context. Hence the function must neither sleep nor access process context. The return value to_ID may be used to cancel the callout, using

```
void untimeout (int to_ID);
```

Callouts may be used for various periodic tasks, such as:

- Retransmission of network packets.
- Certain scheduler and memory management functions.
- Monitoring devices to avoid losing interrupts.
- Polling devices that do not support interrupts.

Callouts are considered to be normal kernel operations and must not execute at interrupt priority. Therefore, the clock interrupt handler does not directly invoke the callouts. On every tick, the clock handler checks if any callouts are due. If so, it sets a flag indicating that a *callout handler* must run. The system checks this flag when it returns to the base interrupt priority and, if set, invokes the callout handler. The handler will invoke each callout that is due. Hence, once due, the callout will run as soon as possible, but only after all pending interrupts have been serviced.[2]

The kernel maintains a list of the pending callouts. The organization of the list affects system performance as there may be several pending callouts. Since the list is checked on every CPU tick at high interrupt priority, the algorithm must optimize the checking time. The time required to

---

[2] Many implementations provide an optimization when no other interrupt is pending when the primary handler completes. In this case, the clock handler directly lowers the interrupt priority and invokes the callout handler.

insert a new callout into the list is less critical since insertions typically occur at lower priority and much less frequently than once per tick.

There are several ways to implement the callout list. One method used in 4.3BSD [Leff 89] sorts the list in order of the "time to fire". Each entry stores the difference between its time to fire and that of the previous callout. The kernel decrements the time of the first entry at each clock tick and issues the callout if the time reaches zero. Other callouts due at the same time are also issued. This is described in Figure 5-1.

Another approach uses a similarly sorted list, but stores the absolute time of expiration for each entry. This way, at each tick, the kernel compares the current absolute time with that of the first entry and issues the callout when the times are equal.

Both methods require maintaining a sorted list, which can be expensive if the list is large. An alternative solution is to use a *timing wheel*, which is a fixed-size, circular array of callout queues. At every tick, the clock interrupt handler advances a current time pointer to the next element in the array, wrapping around at the end of the array. If there are any callouts on that queue, their expiration time is checked. New callouts are inserted on the queue that is N elements away from the current queue, where N is the time to fire measured in ticks.

In effect, the timing wheel hashes the callouts based on the expiry time (time at which they are due). Within each queue, the callouts can be kept either unsorted or sorted. Sorting the callouts reduces the time required to process non-empty queues, but increases the insertion time. [Varg 87] describes further refinements to this method that use multiple hierarchical timing wheels to optimize timer performance.

5.2.2   Alarms

A process can request the kernel to send it a signal after a specific amount of time, much like an alarm clock. There are three types of *alarms*—real-time, profiling, and virtual-time. A *real-time alarm* relates to the actual elapsed time, and notifies the process via a SIGALRM signal. The *profiling alarm* measures the amount of time the process has been executing and uses the SIGPROF signal for

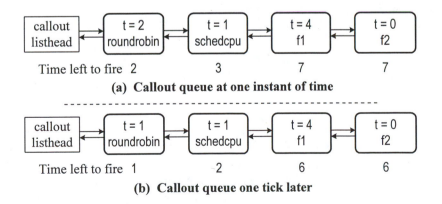

(a) Callout queue at one instant of time

(b) Callout queue one tick later

Figure 5-1. Callout implementation in BSD UNIX.

notification. The *virtual-time alarm* monitors only the time spent by the process in user mode and sends the SIGVTALRM signal.

In BSD UNIX, the *setitimer* system call allows the process to request any type of alarm and specify the time interval in microseconds. Internally, the kernel converts this interval to the appropriate number of CPU ticks, because that is the highest resolution the kernel can provide. In System V, the *alarm* system call asks for a real-time alarm. The time must be a whole number of seconds. SVR4 adds the *hrtsys* system call, which provides a high-resolution timer interface that allows time to be specified in microseconds. This allows compatibility with BSD by implementing *setitimer* (also *getitimer, gettimeofday,* and *settimeofday)* as a library routine. Likewise, BSD provides *alarm* as a library routine.

The high resolution of real-time alarms does not imply high accuracy. Suppose a user requests a real-time alarm to sound after 60 milliseconds. When that time expires, the kernel promptly delivers the SIGALRM signal to the calling process. The process, however, will not see and respond to the signal until it is next scheduled to run. This could introduce a substantial delay depending on the receiver's scheduling priority and the amount of activity in the system. High-resolution timers are helpful when used by high-priority processes, which are less likely to have scheduling delays. Even these processes can be delayed if the current process is executing in kernel mode and does not reach a preemption point. These concepts are explained further in Section 5.5.4.

The profiling and virtual alarms do not have this problem, because they are not concerned with the actual clock time. Their accuracy is affected by another factor. The clock interrupt handler charges the whole tick to the current process, even though it may have used only a part of it. Thus the time measured by these alarms reflects the number of clock interrupts that have occurred while this process was running. In the long run, this averages out and is a good indicator of the time used by the process. For any single alarm, however, it results in significant inaccuracy.

5.3   Scheduler Goals

The scheduler must judiciously apportion CPU time to all processes in the system. Naturally, as the load on the system increases, each process receives a smaller share of CPU time, and hence runs more slowly than it would on a lightly loaded system. The scheduler must ensure that the system delivers acceptable performance to each application, as long as the total workload is in the expected range.

A typical system runs several applications concurrently. These applications can be loosely categorized into the following classes, based on their scheduling requirements and performance expectations:

- **Interactive** — Applications such as shells, editors, and programs with graphical user interfaces interact constantly with their users. These applications spend a lot of time waiting for such user input as characters typed at the keyboard or mouse actions. When input is received, it must be processed quickly, otherwise the user will find the system to be unresponsive. The system needs to reduce the average time and variance between the user action and application response sufficiently, so users cannot readily detect the delay. For typing or mouse movements, the acceptable delay is about 50–150 milliseconds.

- **Batch** — Activities such as software builds and scientific computations do not require user interaction and are often submitted as background jobs. For such tasks, the measure of scheduling efficiency is the task's completion time in the presence of other activity, as compared to the time required on an otherwise inactive system.
- **Real-time** — This is a catchall class of applications that are often time-critical. Although there are many types of real-time applications, each with its own set of requirements, they share many common features. They normally need predictable scheduling behavior with guaranteed bounds on response times. For instance, a video application may want to display a fixed number of video frames per second (*fps*). It may care more about minimizing the variance than simply obtaining more CPU time. Users may prefer a constant rate of 15 *fps* to one that fluctuates noticeably between 10 and 30 *fps*, with an average of 20 *fps*.

A typical workstation may run many different types of applications simultaneously. The scheduler must try to balance the needs of each. It must also ensure that kernel functions such as paging, interrupt handling, and process management can execute promptly when required.

In a well-behaved system, all applications must continue to progress. No application should be able to prevent others from progressing, unless the user has explicitly permitted it. Moreover, the system should always be able to receive and process interactive user input; otherwise, the user would have no way to control the system.

The choice of scheduling policy has a profound effect on the system's ability to meet the requirements of different types of applications. The next section reviews the traditional (SVR3/4.3BSD) scheduler, which supports interactive and batch jobs only. The rest of this chapter examines schedulers in modern UNIX systems, which also provide some support for real-time applications.

5.4   Traditional UNIX Scheduling

We begin by describing the traditional UNIX scheduling algorithm, which is used in both SVR3 and 4.3BSD UNIX. These systems are primarily targeted at time-sharing, interactive environments with several users running several batch and foreground processes simultaneously. The scheduling policy aims to improve response times of interactive users, while ensuring that low-priority, background jobs do not starve.

Traditional UNIX scheduling is priority-based. Each process has a scheduling priority that changes with time. The scheduler always selects the highest-priority runnable process. It uses preemptive time-slicing to schedule processes of equal priority, and dynamically varies process priorities based on their CPU usage patterns. If a higher-priority process becomes ready to run, the scheduler preempts the current process even if it has not completed its *time slice* or *quantum*.

The traditional UNIX kernel is strictly nonpreemptible. If a process is executing kernel code (due to a system call or interrupt), it cannot be forced to yield the CPU to a higher-priority process. The running process may voluntarily relinquish the CPU when blocking on a resource. Otherwise, it can be preempted when it returns to user mode. Making the kernel nonpreemptible solves many synchronization problems associated with multiple processes accessing the same kernel data structures (see Section 2.5).

The following subsections describe the design and implementation of the 4.3BSD scheduler. The SVR3 implementation differs only in a few minor respects, such as some function and variable names.

5.4.1   Process Priorities

The process priority may be any integer value between 0 and 127. Numerically lower values correspond to higher priorities. Priorities between 0 and 49 are reserved for the kernel, while processes in user mode have priorities between 50 and 127. The proc structure contains the following fields that contain priority-related information:

p_pri	Current scheduling priority.
p_usrpri	User mode priority.
p_cpu	Measure of recent CPU usage.
p_nice	User-controllable nice factor.

The p_pri and p_usrpri fields are used in different ways. The scheduler uses p_pri to decide which process to schedule. When the process is in user mode, its p_pri value is identical to p_usrpri. When the process wakes up after blocking in a system call, its priority is temporarily boosted in order to give preference to kernel mode processing. Hence the scheduler uses p_usrpri to save the priority that must be assigned to the process when it returns to user mode, and p_pri to store its temporary kernel priority.

The kernel associates a *sleep priority* with of event or resource on which a process can block. The sleep priority is a kernel value, and hence is between 0 and 49. For instance, the sleep priority for terminal input is 28, whereas that for disk I/O is 20. When a process wakes up after blocking, the kernel sets its p_pri value to the sleep priority of the event or resource. Because kernel priorities are higher than user priorities, such processes are scheduled ahead of those that were executing user code. This allows system calls to complete promptly, which is desirable since processes may have locked some key kernel resources while executing a system call.

When a process completes the system call and is about to return to user mode, its scheduling priority is reset to its current user mode priority. This may lower the priority below that of another runnable process, in which case the kernel will initiate a context switch.

The user mode priority depends on two factors—the nice value and the recent CPU usage. The *nice value* is a number between 0 and 39 with a default of 20. Increasing this value decreases the priority. Background processes are automatically given higher nice values. Only a superuser can decrease the nice value of a process, thereby increasing its priority. It is called *nice* because users can be "nice" to others by increasing the nice value of less important processes.[3]

Time-sharing systems try to allocate the processor in such a way that competing applications receive approximately equal amounts of CPU time. This requires monitoring the CPU usage of different processes and using that information in scheduling decisions. The p_cpu field is a measure of the recent CPU usage of the process. It is initialized to zero when the process is created. At every

---

[3] The *nice(1)* command is normally used for this purpose. It accepts any value between −20 and 19 (only the superuser can specify negative values). This value is used as an increment to the current nice value.

tick, the clock handler increments p_cpu for the current process, to a maximum of 127. Moreover, every second, the kernel invokes a routine called schedcpu() (scheduled by a callout) that reduces the p_cpu value of each process by a *decay factor*. SVR3 uses a fixed decay factor of 1/2. 4.3BSD uses the following formula:

```
decay = (2 * load_average) / (2 * load_average + 1);
```

where load_average is the average number of runnable processes over the last second. The sched-cpu() routine also recomputes the user priorities of all processes using the formula

```
p_usrpri = PUSER + (p_cpu / 4) + (2 * p_nice);
```

where PUSER is the baseline user priority of 50.

As a result, if a process has recently accumulated a large amount of CPU time, its p_cpu factor will increase. This results in a large p_usrpri value, and hence a low priority. The longer a process waits before being scheduled, the more the decay factor lowers its p_cpu, and its priority continues to increase. This scheme prevents starvation of lower-priority processes. It also heavily favors I/O-bound processes as opposed to compute-bound ones. If a process spends most of its time waiting for I/O (e.g., an interactive shell process or a text editor), it remains at a high priority, and receives CPU time quickly when needed. Compute-bound applications such as compilers and linkers have high p_cpu values and consequently run at lower priorities.

The CPU usage factor provides fairness and parity in scheduling time-sharing processes. The basic idea is to keep the priorities of all such processes in the same approximate range over a period of time. They move up or down within this range depending on how much CPU time they have recently consumed. If priorities change too slowly, processes that begin at a lower priority will remain there for long periods of time, and starve as a result.

The effect of the decay factor is to provide an exponentially weighted average of the CPU usage of the process over its entire lifetime. The SVR3 formula yields a simple exponential average, which has the undesirable side effect of elevating priorities when the system load rises [Blac 90]. This is because in a heavily loaded system each process receives a small share of the processor. This keeps its CPU usage value low, and the decay factor reduces it further. As a result, the CPU usage does not have much impact on the priority, and processes that began with a lower priority starve disproportionately.

The 4.3BSD approach forces the decay factor to depend on the system load. When the load is high the decay is small. Consequently, processes that receive CPU cycles will have their priority lowered quickly.

5.4.2 Scheduler Implementation

The scheduler maintains an array called qs of 32 run queues (Figure 5-2). Each queue corresponds to four adjacent priorities. Thus, queue 0 is used for priorities 0–3, queue 1 for priorities 4–7, and so forth. Each queue contains the head of a doubly linked list of proc structures. A global variable whichqs contains a bitmask with one bit for each queue. The bit is set if there is a process on that queue. Only runnable processes are kept on these scheduler queues.

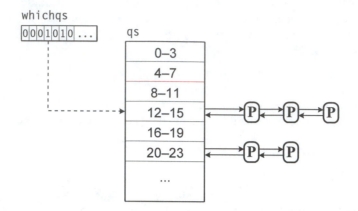

Figure 5-2. BSD scheduler data structures.

This simplifies the task of selecting a process to run. The swtch() routine, which performs the context switch, examines whichqs to find the index of the first set bit. This index identifies the scheduler queue containing the highest priority runnable process. swtch() removes a process from the head of the queue, and switches context to it. When swtch() returns, the newly scheduled process resumes execution.

The context switch involves saving the register context (general purpose registers, program counter, stack pointer, memory management registers, etc.) of the current process in its process control block (*pcb*), which is part of the u area, and then loading the registers with the saved context of the new process. The p_addr field in the proc structure points to the page table entries of the u area, and swtch() uses this to locate the new *pcb*.

Since the VAX-11 was the reference target for both 4BSD and the early System V releases, its architecture [DEC 86] has greatly influenced the scheduler implementation. The VAX has two special instructions—FFS, or *Find First Set,* and FFC, or *Find First Clear*—to manipulate 32-bit fields. This made it desirable to collapse the 128 priorities into 32 queues. It also has special instructions (INSQHI and REMQHI) to atomically insert and remove elements from doubly linked lists, and others (LDPCTX and SVPCTX) to load and save a process context. This allows the VAX to execute the entire scheduling algorithm using only a small number of machine instructions.

5.4.3   Run Queue Manipulation

The highest priority process always runs, unless the current process is executing in kernel mode. A process is assigned a fixed time quantum (100 ms in 4.3BSD). This only affects the scheduling of multiple processes on the same run queue. Every 100 milliseconds, the kernel invokes (through a callout) a routine called roundrobin() to schedule the next process from the same queue. If a higher-priority process were runnable, it would be preferentially scheduled without waiting for roundrobin(). *If all other runnable processes are on lower priority queues, the current process continues to run even though its quantum has expired.*

The `schedcpu()` routine recomputes the priority of each process once every second. Since the priority cannot change while the process is on a run queue, `schedcpu()` removes the process from the queue, changes its priority, and puts it back, perhaps on a different run queue. The clock interrupt handler recomputes the priority of the current process every four ticks.

There are three situations where a context switch is indicated:

- The current process blocks on a resource or exits. This is a voluntary context switch.
- The priority recomputation procedure results in the priority of another process becoming greater than that of the current one.
- The current process, or an interrupt handler, wakes up a higher-priority process.

The voluntary context switch is straightforward—the kernel directly calls `swtch()` from the `sleep()` or `exit()` routines. Events that cause involuntary switches occur when the system is in kernel mode, and hence cannot preempt the process immediately. The kernel sets a flag called `runrun`, which indicates that a higher priority process is waiting to be scheduled. When the process is about to return to user mode, the kernel checks the `runrun` flag. If set, it transfers control to the `swtch()` routine, which initiates a context switch.

5.4.4 Analysis

The traditional scheduling algorithm is simple and effective. It is adequate for a general time-sharing system with a mixture of interactive and batch jobs. Dynamic recomputation of the priorities prevents starvation of any process. The approach favors I/O-bound jobs that require small infrequent bursts of CPU cycles.

The scheduler has several limitations that make it unsuitable for use in a wide variety of commercial applications:

- It does not scale well—if the number of processes is very large, it is inefficient to recompute all priorities every second.
- There is no way to guarantee a portion of CPU resources to a specific process or group of processes.
- There are no guarantees of response time to applications with real-time characteristics.
- Applications have little control over their priorities. The nice value mechanism is simplistic and inadequate.
- Since the kernel is nonpreemptive, higher-priority processes may have to wait a significant amount of time even after being made runnable. This is called *priority inversion*.

Modern UNIX systems are used in many kinds of environments. In particular, there is a strong need for the scheduler to support *real-time* applications that require more predictable behavior and bounded response times. This requires a complete redesign of the scheduler. The rest of this chapter examines the new scheduling facilities in SVR4, Solaris 2.*x*, and OSF/1, as well as some non-mainstream variants.

5.5   The SVR4 Scheduler

SVR4 features a completely redesigned scheduler [AT&T 90] that tries to improve on the traditional approach. It is intended for use in many environments, and provides greater flexibility and control. The following are the major objectives of this new architecture:

- Support a diverse range of applications including those requiring real-time response.
- Separate the scheduling policy from the mechanisms that implement it.
- Provide applications with greater control over their priority and scheduling.
- Define a scheduling framework with a well-defined interface to the kernel.
- Allow new scheduling policies to be added in a modular manner, including dynamic loading of scheduler implementations.
- Limit the dispatch latency for time-critical applications.

While the effort has been driven by the desire to support real-time processes, the architecture is general and versatile enough to handle many different scheduling requirements. The fundamental abstraction is that of a *scheduling class,* which defines the scheduling policy for all processes that belong to it. The system may provide several scheduling classes. By default, SVR4 provides two classes—time-sharing and real-time.

The scheduler provides a set of class-independent routines that implement common services such as context switching, run queue manipulation, and preemption. It also defines a procedural interface for class-dependent functions such as priority computation and inheritance. Each class implements these functions differently. For instance, the real-time class uses fixed priorities, while the time-sharing class varies the process priority dynamically in response to certain events.

This object-oriented approach is similar to that used by the *vnode/vfs* system (see Section 8.6) and the memory subsystem (see Section 14.3). Section 8.6.2 provides an overview of the basic concepts of object-oriented methodology as used in modern UNIX systems. Here, the scheduler represents an *abstract base class*, and each scheduling class acts as a subclass (derived class).

5.5.1   The Class-Independent Layer

The class-independent layer is responsible for context switching, run queue management, and preemption. The highest priority process always runs, (except for nonpreemptible kernel processing). The number of priorities has been increased to 160, and there is a separate dispatch queue for each priority. Unlike the traditional implementation, numerically larger priority values correspond to higher priorities. The assignment and recomputation of process priorities, however, are performed by the class-dependent layer.

Figure 5-3 describes the data structures for run queue management. The dqactmap is a bitmap that shows which dispatch queues have at least one runnable process. Processes are placed on the queue by setfrontdq() and setbackdq(), and removed by dispdeq(). These functions may be called from the mainline kernel code, as well as from the class-dependent routines. Typically, a newly runnable process is placed at the back of its run queue, while a process that was preempted before its quantum expired is returned to the front of the queue.

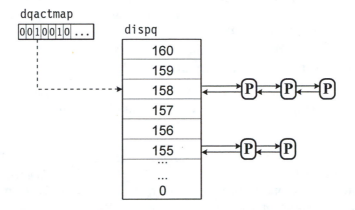

Figure 5-3. SVR4 dispatch queues.

A major limitation of UNIX for use in real-time applications is the nonpreemptive nature of the kernel. Real-time processes need to have a low *dispatch latency,* which is the delay between the time they become runnable and the time they actually begin running. If a real-time process becomes runnable while the current process is executing a system call, there may be a significant delay before the context switch can occur.

To address this problem, the SVR4 kernel defines several *preemption points*. These are places in the kernel code where all kernel data structures are in a stable state, and the kernel is about to embark on a lengthy computation. When such a preemption point is reached, the kernel checks a flag called kprunrun. If set, it indicates that a real-time process is ready to run, and the kernel preempts the current process. This bounds the amount of time a real-time process must wait before being scheduled.[4] The PREEMPT() macro checks kprunrun and calls the preempt() routine to actually preempt the process. Some examples of preemption points are:

- In the pathname parsing routine lookuppn(), before beginning to parse each individual pathname component
- In the *open* system call, before creating the file if it does not exist
- In the memory subsystem, before freeing the pages of a process

The runrun flag is used as in traditional systems, and only preempts processes that are about to return to user mode. The preempt() function invokes the CL_PREEMPT operation to perform class-dependent processing, and then calls swtch() to initiate the context switch.

swtch() calls pswtch() to perform the machine-independent part of the context switch, and then invokes lower-level assembly code to manipulate the register context, flush translation buffers, etc. pswtch() clears the runrun and kprunrun flags, selects the highest-priority runnable process,

---

[4] This code is not class-dependent, despite the explicit mention of real-time processes. The kernel merely checks kprunrun to determine if it should preempt the process. Currently, only the real-time class sets this flag, but in future there may be new classes that also require kernel preemption.

and removes it from the dispatch queue. It updates the dqactmap, and sets the state of the process to SONPROC (running on a processor). Finally, it updates the memory management registers to map the u area and virtual address translation maps of the new process.

5.5.2   Interface to the Scheduling Classes

All class-dependent functionality is provided by a generic interface whose virtual functions (see Section 8.6.2) are implemented differently by each scheduling class. The interface defines both the semantics of these functions and the linkages used to invoke the specific implementation for the class.

Figure 5-4 shows how the class-dependent interface is implemented. The classfuncs structure is a vector of pointers to the functions that implement the class-dependent interface for any class. A global class table contains one entry for each class. This entry is composed of the class name, a pointer to an initialization function, and a pointer to the classfuncs vector for that class.

When a process is first created, it inherits the priority class from its parent. Subsequently, it may be moved to a different class via the *priocntl* system call described in Section 5.5.5. The proc structure has three fields that are used by the scheduling classes:

p_cid   Class ID—this is simply an index into the global class table.

p_clfuncs   Pointer to the classfuncs vector for the class to which the process be-
                 longs. This pointer is copied from the class table entry.

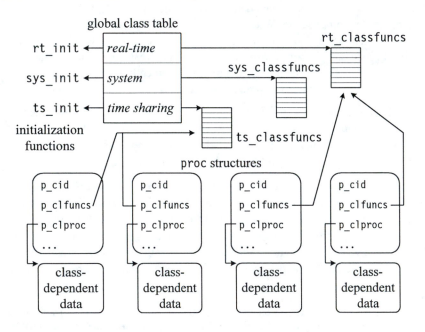

Figure 5-4. SVR4 class-dependent interface.

p_clproc   Pointer to a class-dependent private data structure.

A set of macros resolves calls to the generic interface functions and invokes the correct class-dependent functions. For instance,

```
#define CL_SLEEP(procp, clprocp, ...) \
    (*(procp)->p_clfuncs->cl_sleep)(clprocp, ...)
```

The class-dependent functions can be accessed in this manner from the class-independent code and from the *priocntl* system call.

The scheduling class decides the policies for priority computation and scheduling of the processes that belong to it. It determines the range of priorities for its processes, and if and under what conditions the process priority can change. It decides the size of the time slice each time a process runs. The time slice may be the same for all processes or may vary according to the priority. It may be anywhere from one tick to infinity. An infinite quantum is appropriate for some real-time tasks that must run to completion.

The entry points of the class-dependent interface include:

CL_TICK   Called from the clock interrupt handler—monitors the time slice, recomputes priority, handles time quantum expiration, and so forth.

CL_FORK,
CL_FORKRET   Called from *fork*—CL_FORK initializes the child's class-specific data structure. CL_FORKRET may set runrun, allowing the child process to run before the parent.

CL_ENTERCLASS,
CL_EXITCLASS   Called when a process enters or exits a scheduling class—responsible for allocating and deallocating the class-dependent data structures respectively.

CL_SLEEP   Called from sleep() — may recompute process priority.

CL_WAKEUP   Called from wakeprocs() — puts the process on the appropriate run queue; may set runrun or kprunrun.

The scheduling class decides what actions each function will take, and each class may implement these functions differently. This allows for a very versatile approach to scheduling. For instance, the clock interrupt handler of the traditional scheduler charges each tick to the current process and recomputes its priority on every fourth tick. In the new architecture, the handler simply calls the CL_TICK routine for the class to which the process belongs. This routine decides how to process the clock tick. The real-time class, for example, uses fixed priorities and does no recomputation. The class-dependent code determines when the time quantum has expired and sets runrun to initiate a context switch.

By default, the 160 priorities are divided into the following three ranges:

0–59   time-sharing class
60–99   system priorities
100–159   real-time class

The following sub-sections describe the implementation of the time-sharing and real-time classes.

5.5.3   The Time-Sharing Class

The *time-sharing class* is the default class for a process. It changes process priorities dynamically and uses *round-robin scheduling* for processes with the same priority. It uses a static *dispatcher parameter table* to control process priorities and time slices. The time slice given to a process depends on its scheduling priority. The parameter table defines the time slice for each priority. By default, the lower the priority of the process, the larger its time slice. This may seem counter-intuitive, but the reasoning is that since the lower priority process does not run often, it should be given a larger quantum when it does run.

The time-sharing class uses event-driven scheduling [Stra 86]. Instead of recomputing the priorities of all processes every second, SVR4 changes the priority of a process in response to specific events related to that process. The scheduler penalizes the process (reduces its priority) each time it uses up its time slice. On the other hand, SVR4 boosts the priority of the process if it blocks on an event or resource, or if it takes a long time to use up its quantum. Since each event usually affects a single process, the recomputation is fast. The dispatcher parameter table defines how various events change the priority of the process.

The time-sharing class uses a `struct tsproc` to store class-dependent data. Its fields include:

ts_timeleft	Time remaining in the quantum.
ts_cpupri	System part of the priority.
ts_upri	User part of the priority (*nice value*).
ts_umdpri	User mode priority (ts_cpupri + ts_upri, but no more than 59).
ts_dispwait	Number of seconds of clock time since start of quantum.

When a process resumes after sleeping in the kernel, its priority is a kernel priority and is determined by the sleep condition. When it later returns to user mode, the priority is restored from ts_umdpri. The user mode priority is the sum of ts_upri and ts_cpupri, but is restricted to a value between 0 and 59. ts_upri ranges from −20 to +19, with the default value of 0. This value can be changed by *priocntl*, but only the superuser can increase it. ts_cpupri is adjusted according to the dispatcher parameter table as described below.

The parameter table contains one entry for each priority in the class. Although every class in SVR4 has a dispatch parameter table (there is also one for the system priorities), each table has a different form. It is not a required structure for all classes, and new classes may be created that do not use such a table. For the time-sharing class, each entry in the table contains the following fields:

ts_globpri	Global priority for this entry (for the time-sharing class, this is the same as its index in the table).
ts_quantum	Time quantum for this priority.
ts_tqexp	New ts_cpupri to set when the quantum expires.
ts_slpret	New ts_cpupri to set when returning to user mode after sleeping.

ts_maxwait   Number of seconds to wait for quantum expiry before using ts_lwait.

ts_lwait   Use instead of ts_tqexp if process took longer than ts_maxwait to use up its quantum.

This table has two uses. It can be indexed by the current ts_cpupri value to access the ts_tqexp, ts_slpret, and ts_lwait fields, since these fields provide a new value of ts_cpupri based on its old value. It is indexed by ts_umdpri to access the ts_globpri, ts_quantum, and ts_maxwait fields, since these fields relate to the overall scheduling priority.

Table 5-1 shows a typical time-sharing parameter table. To see how it is used, consider a process with ts_upri = 14, and ts_cpupri = 1. Its global priority (ts_globpri) and its ts_umdpri both equal 15. When its time quantum expires, its ts_cpupri will be set to 0 (thus, ts_umdpri is set to 14). If, however, the process needs more than 5 seconds to use up its quantum, its ts_cpupri is set to 11 (thus, ts_umdpri is set to 25).

Suppose, before its quantum expires, the process makes a system call and must block on a resource. When it resumes and eventually returns to user mode, its ts_cpupri is set to 11 (from the ts_slpret column) and ts_umdpri to 25, regardless of how much time was needed to use up the quantum.

5.5.4 The Real-Time Class

The *real-time class* uses priorities in the range 100–159. These priorities are higher than any time-sharing process, even those in kernel mode, which means a real-time process will be scheduled before any kernel process. Suppose a process is already executing in kernel mode when a real-time process becomes runnable. The kernel will not preempt the current process immediately because that may leave the system in an inconsistent state. The real-time process must wait until the current process is about to return to user mode or until it reaches a kernel preemption point. Only superuser processes can enter the real-time class; they do so by calling *priocntl,* specifying the priority and time quantum.

Real-time processes are characterized by a fixed priority and time quantum. The only way they can change is if the process explicitly makes a *priocntl* call to change one or the other. The real-time dispatcher parameter table is simple—it only stores the default quantum for each priority, which is used if a process does not specify a quantum while entering the real-time class. Here too,

Table 5-1. Time-sharing dispatcher parameter table

index	globpri	quantum	tqexp	slpret	maxwait	lwait
0	0	100	0	10	5	10
1	1	100	0	11	5	11
...	...	...	...	...	...	...
15	15	80	7	25	5	25
...	...	...	...	...	...	...
40	40	20	30	50	5	50
...	...	...	...	...	...	...
59	59	10	49	59	5	59

the default parameter table assigns larger time slices for lower priorities. The class-dependent data of a real-time process is stored in a `struct rtproc`, which includes the current time quantum, time remaining in the quantum, and the current priority.

Real-time processes require bounded dispatch latency, as well as bounded response time. These concepts are explained in Figure 5-5. The dispatch latency is the time between when the process becomes runnable and when it begins to run. The response time is the time between the occurrence of an event that requires the process to respond and the response itself. Both these times need to have a well-defined upper bound that is within a reasonable limit.

The response time is the sum of the time required by the interrupt handler to process the event, the dispatch latency, and the time taken by the real-time process itself to respond to the event. The dispatch latency is of great concern to the kernel. Traditional kernels cannot provide reasonable bounds, since the kernel itself is nonpreemptible, and the process may have to wait for a long period of time if the current process is involved in some elaborate kernel processing. Measurements have shown that some code paths in the kernel can take several milliseconds, which is clearly unacceptable for most real-time applications.

SVR4 uses preemption points to divide lengthy kernel algorithms into smaller, bounded units of work. When a real-time process becomes runnable, the `rt_wakeup()` routine that handles the class-dependent wakeup processing sets the kernel flag kprunrun. When the current process (presumably executing kernel code) reaches a preemption point, it checks this flag and initiates a context switch to the waiting real-time process. Thus the wait is bounded by the maximal code path between two preemption points, which is a much more acceptable solution.

Finally, we must note that any guarantees on the latency bounds apply only when the real-time process is the highest-priority runnable process on the system. If, at any time during its wait, a

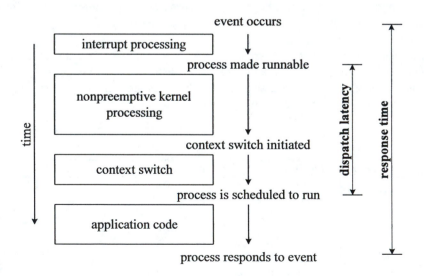

Figure 5-5. Response time and dispatch latency.

higher-priority process becomes runnable, it will be scheduled preferentially, and the latency calculation must restart from zero after that process yields the CPU.

5.5.5 The *priocntl* System Call

The *priocntl* system call provides several facilities to manipulate the priorities and scheduling behavior of the process. It accepts a set of different subcommands that can be used to perform many operations, such as

- Changing the priority class of the process.
- Setting ts_upri for time-sharing processes.
- Resetting priority and quantum for real-time processes.
- Obtaining the current value of several scheduling parameters.

Most of these operations are restricted to the superuser, and hence are unavailable to most applications. SVR4 also provides the *priocntlset* system call, which performs the same operations on a set of related processes, such as:

- All processes in the system.
- All processes in a process group or session.
- All processes in a scheduling class.
- All processes owned by a particular user.
- All processes having the same parent.

5.5.6 Analysis

SVR4 has replaced the traditional scheduler with one that is completely different in design and behavior. It provides a flexible approach that allows the addition of scheduling classes to a system. A vendor can tailor the scheduler to the needs of his applications. Dispatcher tables give much more control to the system administrator, who can alter the behavior of the system by changing the settings in the tables and rebuilding the kernel.

Traditional UNIX systems recompute the priority of each process once every second. This can take an inordinate amount of time if there are many processes. Hence the algorithm does not scale well to systems that have thousands of processes. The SVR4 time-sharing class changes process priorities based on events related to that process. Since each event usually affects only one process, the algorithm is fast and highly scalable.

Event-driven scheduling deliberately favors I/O-bound and interactive jobs over CPU-bound ones. This approach has some important drawbacks. Interactive users whose jobs also require large computations may not find the system to be responsive, since these processes may not generate enough priority-elevating events to offset the effects of CPU usage. Also, the optimal boosts and penalties to associate with different events depend on the total load on the system and the characteristics of the jobs running at any given time. Thus it may be necessary to retune these values frequently to keep the system efficient and responsive.

Adding a scheduling class does not require access to the kernel source code. The developer must take the following steps:

1. Provide an implementation of each class-dependent scheduling function.
2. Initialize a `classfuncs` vector to point to these functions.
3. Provide an initialization function to perform setup tasks such as allocating internal data structures.
4. Add an entry for this class in the class table in a *master configuration file*, typically located in the **master.d** subdirectory of the kernel build directory. This entry contains pointers to the initialization function and the `classfuncs` vector.
5. Rebuild the kernel.

An important limitation is that SVR4 provides no good way for a time-sharing class process to switch to a different class. The *priocntl* call is restricted to the superuser. A mechanism to map either specific user IDs or specific programs to a nondefault class would be very useful.

Although the real-time facilities represent a major first step, they still fall short of the desired capability. There is no provision for deadline-driven scheduling (see Section 5.9.2). The code path between preemption points is too long for many time-critical applications. In addition, true real-time systems require a fully preemptible kernel. Some of these issues have subsequently been addressed in Solaris 2.*x*, which provides several enhancements to the SVR4 scheduler. We describe this approach in the next section.

A major problem with the SVR4 scheduler is that it is extremely difficult to tune the system properly for a mixed set of applications. [Nieh 93] describes an experiment that ran three different programs—an interactive typing session, a batch job, and a video film display program—concurrently. This became a difficult proposition since both the typing and the film display required interaction with the X-server.

The authors tried several permutations of priority and scheduling class assignments to the four processes (the three applications plus the X-server). *It was very difficult to find a combination that allowed all applications to progress adequately.* For instance, the intuitive action is to place only the video in the real-time class. However, this was catastrophic, and not even the video application could progress. This was because the X-server, on which the video display depended, did not receive sufficient CPU time. Placing both video and the X-server in the real-time class gave adequate video performance (after correctly tweaking their relative priorities), but the interactive and batch jobs crawled to a halt, and the system stopped responding to mouse and keyboard events.

Through careful experimentation, it may be possible to find the right combination of priorities for a given set of applications. Such settings, however, might only work for that exact mix of programs. The load on a system varies constantly, and it is not reasonable to require careful manual tuning each time the load changes.

5.6   Solaris 2.*x* Scheduling Enhancements

Solaris 2.*x* enhances the basic scheduling architecture of SVR4 in several respects [Khan 92]. Solaris is a multithreaded, symmetric-multiprocessing operating system, and therefore its scheduler must support these features. Additionally, Solaris makes several optimizations to lower the dispatch latency for high-priority, time-critical processes. The result is a scheduler that is more suitable for real-time processing.

5.6.1 Preemptive Kernel

Kernel preemption points in SVR4 are at best a compromise solution to the bounded latency requirements of real-time processes. The Solaris 2.x kernel is fully preemptive, which allows it guarantee good response times. This is a radical change for a UNIX kernel and has far-reaching consequences. Most global kernel data structures must be protected by appropriate synchronization objects such as mutual exclusion locks (mutexes) or semaphores. Although this is a formidable task, it is also an essential requirement for a multiprocessor operating system.

Another related change is the implementation of interrupts using special kernel threads that can use the standard synchronization primitives of the kernel and block on resources if necessary (see Section 3.6.5). As a result, Solaris rarely needs to raise the interrupt level to protect critical regions, and has only a few nonpreemptible code segments. Thus a higher-priority process can be scheduled as soon as it is runnable.

Interrupt threads always run at the highest priority in the system. Solaris allows scheduling classes to be dynamically loaded. If this happens, the priorities of the interrupt threads are recomputed to ensure that they remain at the highest possible value. If an interrupt thread needs to block on a resource, it can only be restarted on the same processor.

5.6.2 Multiprocessor Support

Solaris maintains a single dispatch queue for all processors. However, some threads (such as interrupt threads) may be restricted to run on a single, specific processor. Processors can communicate with each other by sending *cross-processor interrupts*. Each processor has the following set of scheduling variables in a per-processor data structure:

cpu_thread	Thread currently running on this processor.
cpu_dispthread	Thread last selected to run on this processor.
cpu_idle	Idle thread for this processor.
cpu_runrun	Preemption flag used for time-sharing threads.
cpu_kprunrun	Kernel preemption flag set by real-time threads.
cpu_chosen_level	Priority of thread that is going to preempt the current thread on this processor.

Figure 5-6 illustrates scheduling in a multiprocessing environment. An event on processor **P1** makes thread **T6** (with priority 130) runnable. The kernel puts **T6** on the dispatch queue and calls cpu_choose() to find the processor with the lowest-priority thread running on it (in this case, **P3**). Since this priority is lower than that of **T6**, cpu_choose() marks that processor for preemption, sets its cpu_chosen_level to the priority **T6** (130), and sends it a cross-processor interrupt. Suppose at this point, before **P3** handles the interrupt and preempts thread **T3**, another processor, say **P2**, handles an event that makes thread **T7** (with priority 115) runnable. Now cpu_choose()

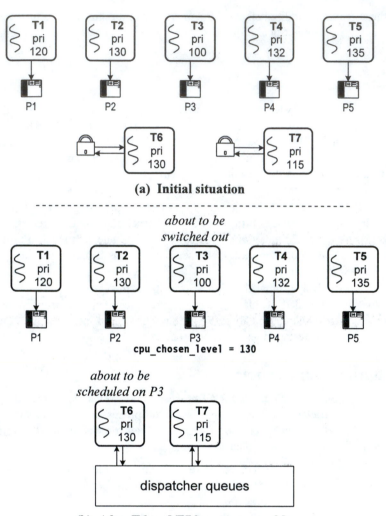

(a) **Initial situation**

(b) **After T6 and T7 become runnable**

Figure 5-6. Multiprocessor scheduling in Solaris 2.*x*.

will examine the cpu_chosen_level of **P3**, find that it is 130, and realize that a higher-priority thread is about to run on this processor. Thus, in this case, cpu_choose() will leave **T7** on the dispatch queue, avoiding the conflict.

There are certain situations where a low-priority thread can block a higher-priority thread for a long period of time. These situations are caused either by *hidden scheduling* or by *priority inversion*. Solaris eliminates many of these effects, as described in the following subsections.

5.6.3   Hidden Scheduling

The kernel often performs some work asynchronously on behalf of threads. The kernel schedules this work without considering the priority of the thread for which it is doing the work. This is called *hidden scheduling*. Two examples of this are STREAMS service routines (see Section 17.4) and callouts.

In SVR4, for example, whenever a process is about to return to user mode, the kernel calls a routine called `runqueues()` to check if there is a STREAMS *service request* pending. If so, the kernel processes the request by calling the *service* routine of the appropriate STREAMS module. This request is thus serviced by the *current process* (the one that was about to return to user mode) on behalf of some other process. If the priority of the other process is lower than that of the current process, the request is being handled at a wrong priority. As a result, the normal execution of the current process is delayed by lower-priority work.

Solaris handles this by moving STREAMS processing into kernel threads, which run at a lower priority than any real-time thread. This creates a new problem, since some STREAMS requests may be initiated by real-time threads. Because these requests are also serviced by kernel threads, they run at a lower priority than is desired. This issue cannot be resolved without drastically changing the semantics of streams processing, and remains a possible obstacle to meeting real-time requirements.

There is also a problem associated with callout processing (see Section 5.2.1). UNIX services all callouts at the lowest interrupt priority, which is still higher than any real-time priority. If the callout was issued by a low-priority thread, its servicing might delay the scheduling of a higher priority thread. Measurements on earlier releases of SunOS showed that it could take up to 5 milliseconds to process the callout queue.

To resolve this problem, Solaris handles callouts by a *callout thread* that runs at the maximum system priority, which is lower than any real-time priority. Callouts requested by real-time processes are maintained separately and invoked at the lowest interrupt level, thus ensuring prompt dispatch of time-critical callouts.

5.6.4   Priority Inversion

The *priority inversion* problem, first described in [Lamp 80], refers to a situation where a lower-priority process holds a resource needed by a higher priority process, thereby blocking that higher-priority process. There are several variations of this problem. Let us look at some examples (Figure 5-7).

The simplest case occurs when a low-priority thread **T1** holds a resource **R**, and a higher-priority thread **T2** needs it. **T2** must block until **T1** relinquishes the resource. Now consider the same scenario with the addition of thread **T3**, which has a priority between that of **T1** and **T2** (Figure 5-7(a)). Assume **T2** and **T3** are real-time threads. Because **T2** is blocked, **T3** is the highest-priority runnable thread and will preempt **T1** (Figure 5-7(b)). As a result, **T2** remains blocked until **T3** either completes or blocks, and then **T1** runs and frees the resource.

This problem can be solved using a technique called *priority inheritance* or *priority lending*. When a high-priority thread blocks on a resource, it temporarily transfers its priority to the lower-priority thread that owns the resource. Thus, in the above example, **T1** inherits the priority of **T2**,

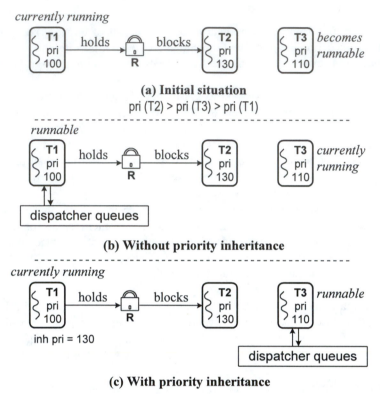

Figure 5-7. Simple priority inversion.

and hence cannot be preempted by **T3** (Figure 5-7(c)). When **T1** releases the resource, its priority returns to its original value, allowing **T2** to preempt it. **T3** will be scheduled only after **T1** has released the resource and **T2** has run and relinquished the CPU.

Priority inheritance must be transitive. In Figure 5-8, **T4** is blocked on a resource held by **T5**, which in turn is blocked on a resource held by **T6**. If the priority of **T4** is higher than that of **T5** and **T6**, then **T6** must inherit the priority of **T4** via **T5**. Otherwise, a thread **T7** whose priority is greater than that of **T5** and **T6**, but less than that of **T4**, will preempt **T6** and cause priority inversion with respect to **T4**. Thus, the inherited priority of a thread must be that of the highest-priority thread that it is directly or indirectly blocking.

The Solaris kernel must maintain extra state about locked objects to implement priority inheritance. It needs to identify which thread is the current owner of each locked object, and also the object for which each blocked thread is waiting. Since inheritance is transitive, the kernel must be able to traverse all the objects and blocked threads in the *synchronization chain* starting from any given object. The next subsection shows how Solaris implements priority inheritance.

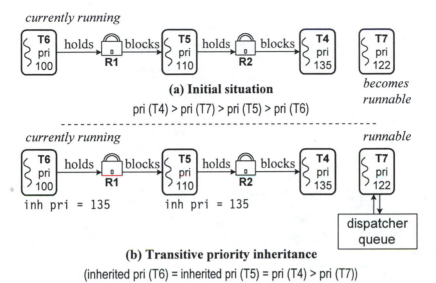

(a) Initial situation

pri (T4) > pri (T7) > pri (T5) > pri (T6)

(b) Transitive priority inheritance

(inherited pri (T6) = inherited pri (T5) = pri (T4) > pri (T7))

Figure 5-8. Transitive priority inheritance.

5.6.5   Implementation of Priority Inheritance

Each thread has two priorities—a *global priority* that is determined by its scheduling class and an *inherited priority* that depends on its interaction with synchronization objects. The inherited priority is normally zero unless the thread has benefited from priority inheritance. The scheduling priority of the thread is the higher of its inherited and global priorities.

When a thread must block on a resource, it calls the function pi_willto() to pass on, or *will*, its priority to all threads that are directly or indirectly blocking it. Since inheritance is transitive, pi_willto() passes on the inherited priority of the calling thread. The pi_willto() function traverses the synchronization chain of this thread, beginning with the object it is directly blocking on. This object contains a pointer to its *owner thread* (the one that currently holds this lock). If the scheduling priority of the owner is lower than the inherited priority of the calling thread, the owner inherits the higher value. If the owner is blocked on another resource, its thread structure contains a pointer to the corresponding synchronization object. pi_willto() follows this pointer and passes the priority onto the owner of that object, and so on. The chain ends when we reach a thread that is not blocked or an object that is not priority-inverted.[5]

---

[5]   This algorithm is known as the *computation of transitive closure*, and the chain traversed forms a *directed acyclic graph*.

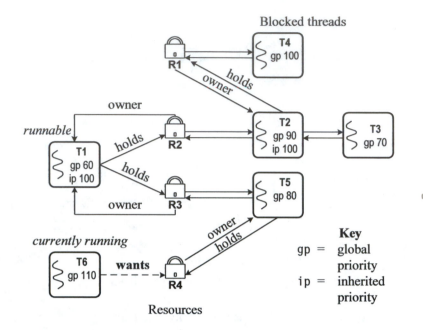

Figure 5-9. Traversing the synchronization chain.

Consider the example of Figure 5-9. Thread **T6**, which is currently running and has a global priority of 110, wants resource **R4** that is held by thread **T5**. The kernel calls `pi_willto()` which traverses the synchronization chain starting at **R4**, taking the following actions:

1. The owner of **R4** is thread **T5**, which has a global priority of 80 and no inherited priority. Since this is lower than 110, set the inherited priority of **T5** to 110.
2. **T5** is blocked on resource **R3**, which is owned by thread **T1**. **T1** has a global priority of 60 but an inherited priority of 100 (through **R2**). That is also smaller than 110, so raise the inherited priority of **T1** to 110.
3. Since **T1** is not blocked on any resource, terminate the chain traversal and return.

After `pi_willto()` returns, the kernel blocks **T6** and selects another thread to run. Since the priority of **T1** was just raised to 110, it is likely to be scheduled immediately. Figure 5-10 shows the situation after the context switch.

When a thread releases an object, it surrenders its inherited priority by calling `pi_waive()`. Sometimes, as in the previous example, a thread may have locked multiple objects. Its inherited priority is then the maximum of all priorities inherited from these objects. When this thread releases an object, its inherited priority must be recomputed based on the remaining objects it owns. This inheritance loss may reduce the thread's priority to one below that of another runnable thread, in which case the former thread will be preempted.

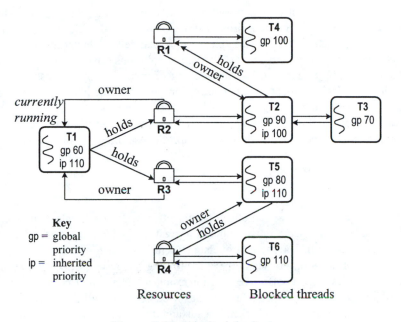

Figure 5-10. Priority inheritance.

5.6.6   Limitations of Priority Inheritance

Priority inheritance can only be implemented in situations where we know which thread is going to free the resource. This is possible when the resource is held by a single, known thread. Solaris 2.x provides four types of synchronization objects—mutexes, semaphores, condition variables, and reader/writer locks (Chapter 7 explains these primitives in detail). With mutexes, the owner is always known. For semaphores and condition variables, however, the owner is usually indeterminate, and priority inheritance is not used. This is unfortunate, because condition variables are often used in conjunction with mutexes to implement higher-level synchronization abstractions, some of which have determinable owners.

When a reader/writer lock is locked for writing, there is a single, known owner. It may, however, be held by multiple readers simultaneously. A waiting writer must block until all current readers have released the object. In this case, the object does not have a single owner, and it is not practical to have pointers to all owners in the object. Solaris addresses this case by defining an *owner-of-record,* which is the first thread that obtained the read lock. If a higher-priority writer blocks on this object, the owner-of-record thread will inherit its priority. When the owner-of-record releases its lock, there may be other unidentifiable threads that still own a lock on it, and these threads cannot inherit the writer's priority. Thus the solution is limited, but still useful, as there are many situations where a single reader holds the lock.

Priority inheritance reduces the amount of time a high-priority process must block on resources held by lower-priority processes. The worst-case delay, however, is still much greater than what is acceptable for many real-time applications. One reason is that the blocking chain can grow arbitrarily long. Another is that if a high-priority process has several critical regions in its execution path, it might block on each of them, resulting in a large total delay. This problem has received great attention in the research community. Some alternative solutions have been proposed, such as the *ceiling protocol* [Sha 90], which controls the locking of resources by processes to ensure that a high-priority process blocks at most once per activation on a resource held by a lower-priority process. Although this limits the blocking delay for high-priority processes, it causes low-priority processes to block much more often. It also requires *a priori* knowledge of all processes in the system and their resource requirements. These drawbacks limit the usefulness of this protocol to a small set of applications.

5.6.7   Turnstiles

The kernel contains hundreds of synchronization objects, one for each data structure that must be separately protected. Such objects must maintain a great deal of information, such as a queue of threads that are blocked on it. Having a large data structure for each object is wasteful, since there are hundreds of synchronization objects in the kernel, but only a few of them are in use at any given instant. Solaris provides a space-effective solution using an abstraction called a *turnstile*. A synchronization object contains a pointer to a turnstile, which contains all the data needed to manipulate the object, such as the queue of blocked threads and a pointer to the thread that currently owns the resource (Figure 5-11). Turnstiles are dynamically allocated from a pool that grows in size with the number of allocated threads in the system. The turnstile is allocated by the first thread that must block on the object. When no more threads are blocked on the object, the turnstile is released back into the pool.

In traditional UNIX systems, the kernel associates a specific *sleep channel* with each resource or event on which a process may block (see Section 7.2.3). The channel is typically an address associated with that resource or event. The kernel hashes the process onto a sleep queue based

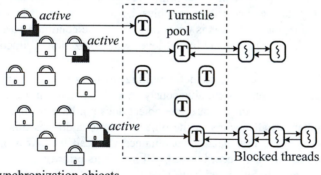

Figure 5-11. Turnstiles.

on this wait channel. Because different wait channels may map to the same sleep queue, the time taken to traverse the queue is bounded only by the total number of threads in the system. Solaris2.*x* replaces this mechanism with turnstiles. Turnstiles restrict the sleep queue to threads blocked on that very resource, thus providing a more reasonable bound on the time taken to process the queue.

Threads in a turnstile are queued in order of their priority. Synchronization objects support two kinds of unlocking behavior—*signal*,[6] which wakes up a single blocked thread, and *broadcast*, which wakes up all threads blocked on the resource. In Solaris, *signal* wakes up the highest-priority thread from the queue.

5.6.8   Analysis

Solaris 2.*x* provides a sophisticated environment for multithreaded and real-time processing for uniprocessors and multiprocessors. It addresses several shortcomings in the SVR4 scheduling implementation. Measurements on a Sparcstation 1 [Khan 92] show that the dispatch latency was under 2 milliseconds for most situations. This is largely due to the fully preemptible kernel and priority inheritance.

Although Solaris provides an environment suitable for many real-time applications, it is primarily a general-purpose operating system. A system designed purely for real-time would provide many other features such as gang scheduling of processors and deadline-driven or priority-based scheduling of I/O devices. These issues are discussed further in Section 5.9.

Let us now review some other scheduling algorithms in commercial and experimental UNIX variants.

5.7   Scheduling in Mach

Mach is a multithreaded, multiprocessor operating system. It is designed to run on all types of machines, ranging from uniprocessors to massively parallel systems containing hundreds of CPUs that share a common address space. Hence it requires a scheduler that scales well for all targets [Blac 90].

The basic programming abstractions of Mach—tasks and threads—are described in Section 3.7. The thread is the fundamental scheduling entity, and Mach schedules threads regardless of the task to which they belong. This approach sacrifices some performance, for context switches between threads of the same task are much faster than between threads belonging to different tasks (because the memory management maps need not be changed). A policy that favors intra-process switching, however, may conflict with the goals of usage and load balancing. Furthermore, the difference in performance between the two types of context switches may be insignificant, depending on the hardware and applications involved.

Each thread inherits a base scheduling priority from the task to which it belongs. This priority is combined with a CPU usage factor, which is maintained separately for each thread. Mach decays the CPU usage of each thread by a factor of 5/8 for each second that it is inactive. The decay

---

[6]   This signaling behavior is completely unrelated to the traditional UNIX signals. As UNIX inherits terminology from multiple sources, some terms are overused in this fashion.

algorithm is distributed. Each thread monitors its own CPU usage and recomputes it when it awakens after blocking. The clock interrupt handler adjusts the usage factor of the current thread. To avoid starving low-priority threads that remain on run queues without getting a chance to recompute their priorities, an internal kernel thread runs every two seconds, recomputing the priorities of all runnable threads.

The scheduled thread runs for a fixed time quantum. At the end of this quantum, it can be preempted by another thread of equal or higher priority. The current thread's priority may drop below that of other runnable threads before its initial quantum expires. In Mach, such reductions do not cause context switches. This feature reduces the number of context switches that are solely related to usage balancing. The current thread can be preempted if a higher-priority thread becomes runnable, even though its quantum has not expired.

Mach provides a feature called *handoff scheduling*, whereby a thread can directly yield the processor to another thread without searching the run queues. The interprocess communication (IPC) subsystem uses this technique for message passing—if a thread is already waiting to receive a message, the sending thread directly yields the processor to the receiver. This improves the performance of the IPC calls.

5.7.1   Multiprocessor Support

Mach supports a wide range of hardware architectures, from small uniprocessors to massively parallel machines comprising over a hundred processors. Its scheduler provides several features for efficient management of processors.

Mach does not use cross-processor interrupts for preemption. Suppose an event on one processor results in a thread becoming runnable with a priority higher than that of another thread running on a different processor. The latter thread will not be preempted until the other processor handles a clock interrupt or another scheduler-related event. The absence of cross-processor preemption does not degrade time-sharing behavior; it may, however, become necessary for efficient response to real-time applications.

Mach allows users to control processor allocation by creating *processor sets,* each of which may contain zero or more processors. Each processor belongs to a single processor set, but may be moved from one set to another. Each task or thread is assigned to a processor set, and again, the assignment may be changed at any time. Only privileged tasks are allowed to assign processors, tasks, and threads to processor sets.

A thread may run only on one of the processors in the set to which it is assigned. The assignment of the task to a processor set establishes the default set to which new threads of the task are assigned. Tasks inherit the assignment from their parent, and the *initial task* is assigned to the *default processor set*. The default set initially contains all processors of the system. It must always contain at least one processor, because internal kernel threads and daemons are assigned to this set.

Processor allocation can be handled by a user-level server program (running as a privileged task) that determines the allocation policy. Figure 5-12 describes the typical interactions between the application, the server, and the kernel. The application allocates the processor set and assigns threads to it. The server allocates processors to the set. The sequence of events is as follows:

1.   The application asks the kernel to allocate a processor set.

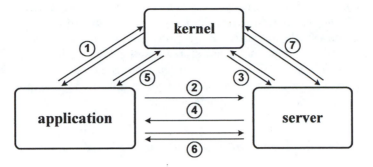

Figure 5-12. Processor allocation in Mach.

2.   The application requests the server for processors for this set.
3.   The server asks the kernel to assign processors to this set.
4.   The server replies to the application indicating that the processors have been allocated.
5.   The application asks the kernel to assign threads to this set.
6.   The application uses the processors and notifies the server when it is finished.
7.   The server reassigns the processors.

This allows tremendous flexibility in managing CPU utilization in the system, especially on a massively parallel system with a large number of processors. It is possible, for instance, to dedicate several processors to a single task or group of tasks, thereby guaranteeing a portion of the available resources to these tasks, regardless of the total load on the system. In the extreme case, an application may seek to dedicate one processor to each of its threads. This is known as *gang scheduling*.

Gang scheduling is useful for applications that require *barrier synchronization*. Such applications create several threads that operate independently for a while, then reach a synchronization point called a barrier. Each thread must wait at the barrier until the rest of the threads get there. After all threads synchronize at the barrier, the application may run some single-threaded code, then create another batch of threads and repeat the pattern of activity.

For such an application to perform optimally, the delay at the barrier must be minimized. This requires that all threads reach the barrier at about the same time. Gang scheduling allows the application to begin the threads together, and bind each to a separate processor. This helps minimize the barrier synchronization delay.

Gang scheduling is also useful for fine-grained applications whose threads interact frequently. With these applications, if a thread is preempted, it may block other threads that need to interact with it. The drawback of dedicating processors to single threads is that if the thread must block, the processor cannot be used.

All processors in the system may not be equivalent—some may be faster, some may have floating point units attached to them, and so forth. Processor sets make it easy to use the right processors for the right jobs. For example, processors with floating point units may be assigned only to threads that need to perform floating point arithmetic.

Additionally, a thread may be temporarily bound to a specific processor. This feature serves mainly to support the unparallelized (not multiprocessor-safe) portion of Mach's UNIX compatibility code, which runs on a single, designated *master processor*. Each processor has a local run queue, and each processor set has a global run queue shared by all processors in that set. Processors first examine their local run queue, thereby giving absolute preference to bound threads (even over higher-priority unbound threads). This decision was made in order to provide maximum throughput to the unparallelized UNIX code, thus avoiding a bottleneck.

5.8   The Digital UNIX Real-Time Scheduler

The Digital UNIX scheduler supports both time-sharing and real-time applications [DEC 94]. It complies with the POSIX 1003.1b interface [IEEE 93] that defines real-time programming extensions. While Digital UNIX is derived from Mach, its scheduler is completely redesigned. It supports the following three scheduling classes:

- SCHED_OTHER, or time-sharing.
- SCHED_FIFO, or first-in, first-out.
- SCHED_RR, or round-robin.

A user can call *sched_setscheduler* to set the scheduling class and priority of a process. The default class is time-sharing. It varies process priorities dynamically, based on the nice value and the CPU usage. The FIFO and round-robin classes use fixed priorities. Processes using a SCHED_FIFO policy have no time quantum and continue to run until they voluntarily yield the processor or are preempted by a higher-priority process. The time-sharing and round-robin classes impose a time quantum, which affects scheduling of processes at the same priority. When a time-sharing or round-robin process finishes its quantum, it goes to the end of the process list of its priority. Of course, if there is no runnable process at higher or equal priority, this process continues to run.

The scheduler always runs the highest-priority runnable process. Each process has a priority in the range 0–63, with smaller numbers denoting lower priorities. The scheduler maintains an ordered queue for each priority, and selects the process at the front of the highest nonempty queue. When a blocked process becomes runnable or a running process yields the processor, it is usually placed at the end of the queue for its priority. The exception is when a process is preempted before it finishes its quantum. In this case, the process is returned to the front of its queue, so that it will be allowed to finish its quantum before running other processes with the same priority.

The priority ranges for the three classes overlap, which allows a great deal of flexibility. The following rules govern the assignment of process priorities:

- Time-sharing processes have priorities between 0 and 29. Superuser privileges are required to raise the priority above 19.
- Users control time-sharing priorities by changing the nice value of the process via the nice system call. The nice value ranges from –20 to +20, with smaller numbers denoting higher priorities (for backward compatibility). Only the superuser can set negative nice values, which correspond to process priorities in the 20–29 range.

- The CPU usage factor reduces the priority of time-sharing processes according to the amount of CPU time it receives.
- System processes have fixed priorities in the range 20–31.
- Fixed-priority processes may be assigned any priority from 0 to 63. Superuser privileges are required, however, to assign priorities higher than 19. Priorities in the range 32–63 are real-time priorities, since such processes cannot be preempted by system processes.

The *sched_setparam* call changes priorities of processes in the FIFO and round-robin classes. The *sched_yield* call puts the calling process at the end of the queue for its priority, thereby yielding the processor to any runnable process at the same priority. If there is no such runnable process, the caller continues to run.

5.8.1   Multiprocessor Support

Digital UNIX allows efficient utilization of multiprocessors by tuning its scheduler to optimize context switches and cache utilization [Denh 94]. Ideally, the scheduler would like to always run the highest-priority runnable threads on all available processors. Such a policy requires the scheduler to maintain a global set of run queues shared by all processors. This can create a bottleneck, since all processors race to lock these queues. Moreover, when a thread runs, it populates the data and instruction caches on the processor. If the thread is preempted and rescheduled shortly afterward, it is advantageous to run it on the same processor if possible, since it could benefit from the earlier caching.

To reconcile these conflicting objectives, Digital UNIX uses a *soft affinity* policy for time-sharing threads. Such threads are kept on local, per-processor run queues, and hence are usually rescheduled on the same processor. This also reduces the contention on the run queues. The scheduler monitors the run queues on each processor and prevents load imbalance by moving threads from run queues of overloaded processors to run queues of lightly loaded ones.

Fixed-priority threads are scheduled from a global run queue, since they should run as soon as possible. The kernel schedules them on the processor on which they last ran whenever possible. Finally, Digital UNIX provides the *bind_to_cpu* system call, which forces a thread to run only on a specific processor. This is useful for code that is not multiprocessor-safe.

The Digital UNIX scheduler provides a POSIX-compliant real-time scheduling interface. However, it lacks many features of Mach and SVR4. It does not provide an interface for processor set allocation or handoff scheduling. Its kernel is nonpreemptive and has no provision for controlling priority inversion.

5.9   Other Scheduling Implementations

The desired scheduling behavior of the system depends on the needs of the applications that run on it. Some systems run time-critical, real-time applications, some are largely time-sharing, and some have a mix of both. Some systems have an extremely large number of running processes, for which the existing algorithms do not scale well. This has motivated several different scheduler designs, some of which have found their way into various UNIX implementations. This section examines a few interesting treatments.

5.9.1   Fair-Share Scheduling

A *fair-share scheduler* allocates a fixed share of CPU resources to each *share group* of processes. A share group may consist of a single process, all processes of a single user, all processes in a login session, and so on. The superuser may be able to choose how to apportion CPU time between the share groups. The kernel monitors the CPU usage to enforce the chosen allocation formula. If any group does not use up its allocated share, the remainder is usually divided among the other groups in the ratio of their original shares.

This approach provides each share group with a predictable amount of processing time, independent of the total load on the system. This is particularly useful in environments where computing time is a billable resource, because resources can be allocated to users at a fixed cost. It could also be used to guarantee resources to critical applications in a time-sharing system. [Henr 84] describes one implementation of a fair-share scheduler.

5.9.2   Deadline-Driven Scheduling

Many real-time applications must respond to events within certain deadlines. For instance, a multimedia server may deliver video frames to a client every 33 milliseconds. If it reads the data from a disk, it can set a deadline by which the disk read must complete. If the deadline is missed, a frame will be delayed. Deadlines may apply to I/O requests or computations. In the latter case, a thread might require a known amount of CPU time before a deadline.

Such applications benefit from *deadline-driven* scheduling algorithms. The basic principle is to vary priorities dynamically, increasing the priority as the deadline draws closer. One example of such a scheduler is in the Ferranti-Originated Real-Time Extension to UNIX (FORTUNIX), described in [Bond 88]. Its algorithm defines four different priority levels:

- Hard real-time for deadlines that must always be met.
- Soft real-time where deadlines should be met with a quantifiable probability, but occasional misses are tolerable.
- Time-sharing, with no specific deadlines, but where a reasonable response time is expected.
- Batch jobs whose deadlines are given in hours instead of milliseconds.

The system schedules processes in order of their priority level so that, for instance, a soft real-time process can only be scheduled if there is no runnable hard real-time process. Within classes 1, 2, and 4, processes are scheduled in order of their deadlines; the one with the earliest deadline is scheduled first. Processes in these classes run until they complete or block, unless a process from a higher class, or one in the same class with an earlier deadline, becomes runnable. Time-sharing processes are scheduled in the traditional UNIX manner based on a priority that depends on the nice value and the recent CPU usage.

Deadline-driven scheduling is a suitable approach for a system that primarily runs processes with known response time requirements. The same priority scheme can be applied to scheduling disk I/O requests, and so forth.

5.9.3   A Three-Level Scheduler

UNIX schedulers are unable to provide the guarantees required by real-time applications while also allowing an arbitrary, mixed workload. A major reason for this is the lack of *admission control*. There is no restriction on the number or nature of real-time and general-purpose tasks that can be started in the system. The system allows all processes to compete for resources in an uncontrolled manner. It relies on the users being sufficiently informed and cooperative to not overload the system.

[Rama 95] describes a three-level scheduler used in a real-time operating system for a multi-protocol file and media server. The scheduler provides three classes of service—isochronous, real-time, and general-purpose. The isochronous class supports periodic activities such as video frame delivery, which must be invoked at fixed intervals with minimum *jitter,* or variation. The real-time class supports aperiodic tasks that require bounded dispatch latency. Finally, the general-purpose class supports low-priority background activities. The scheduler ensures that such low-priority tasks make progress without impacting the guarantees provided to the isochronous streams.

The scheduler imposes an admission control policy. Before accepting a new video stream, it reserves all the resources the stream will require. This includes a percentage of the CPU time, disk bandwidth, and network controller bandwidth. If the server cannot reserve the resources, it does not admit the request. Each real-time service may only process a bounded number of *work units* on each activation. For instance, a network driver may process only a certain number of incoming messages before yielding the CPU. The scheduler also sets aside a fixed portion of all resources for general-purpose activities, which are not subject to admission control. This avoids starvation of general-purpose requests in a heavily loaded system.

For this to work, the system schedules not only CPU time, but also disk and network activities. It assigns priorities to I/O requests based on the task that initiates them, and handles high-priority requests before lower-priority ones. The end-to-end bandwidth reservation of all resources ensures that the system will meet the guarantees made to all admitted video streams. It also ensures that low-priority tasks make progress, even under maximal loads.

In the three-level scheduler, general-purpose tasks are fully preemptible. Real-time tasks may be preempted by isochronous tasks at well-defined preemption points, which typically occur upon completion of each single unit of work. Isochronous tasks use a *rate-monotonic* scheduling algorithm [Liu 73]. Each such task has a fixed scheduling priority, which depends on its period. The lower the period, the higher its priority. A high-priority isochronous task may preempt a lower-priority one at preemption points. [Sha 86] has shown that the rate-monotonic algorithm is optimal for scheduling fixed-priority, periodic tasks.

Another problem with traditional UNIX servers is the inability to cope with saturation due to excessive load. UNIX systems perform much of the network processing of incoming requests at the interrupt level. If the incoming traffic is very high, the system spends most of its time processing interrupts and has very few cycles remaining to service the requests. Once the incoming load exceeds a critical level, the server throughput drops rapidly. This is known as *receive livelock*. The three-level scheduler addresses this problem by moving all network processing to real-time tasks, which bound the amount of traffic they will service in a single invocation. If the incoming traffic exceeds the critical value, the server will drop excess requests, but still be able to make progress on the requests that it accepts. Hence, after peaking, the throughput remains nearly constant instead of declining.

5.10   Summary

We have examined several scheduling architectures and shown how they affect system response to different types of applications. Because computers are used in very different environments, each with its own set of requirements, no one scheduler is ideal for all systems. The Solaris 2.*x* scheduler is adequate for many applications, and provides the framework for dynamically adding other scheduling classes to suit the needs of specific environments. It lacks some features such as real-time streams I/O and user-controlled disk scheduling, but is still an improvement over the traditional UNIX scheduler. Some other solutions we have seen are targeted primarily at a specific application domain such as parallel processing or multimedia.

5.11   Exercises

1. Why are callouts not handled by the primary clock interrupt handler?
2. In which situations will timing wheels be more efficient than the 4.3BSD algorithm for managing callouts?
3. What are the advantages and disadvantages of using *delta times* as opposed to absolute times in callouts?
4. Why do UNIX systems usually favor I/O-bound processes over CPU-bound processes?
5. What are the benefits of the object-oriented interface of the SVR4 scheduler? What are the drawbacks?
6. Why are slpret and lwait given higher values than tqexp in each row of Table 5-1?
7. For what reasons are real-time processes given higher priorities than kernel processes? What are the drawbacks of doing this?
8. How does event-driven scheduling favor I/O-bound and interactive applications?
9. Regarding the [Nieh 93] experiments described on page 130, what would be the effect if the X server, the video application, and the interactive task were all assigned real-time priorities, while the batch job was given a time-sharing priority?
10. Suppose a process releases a resource for which several processes are waiting. When is it preferable to wake up all such processes, and when is it better to wake only one? If waking just one process, how should that process be chosen?
11. Gang scheduling assumes that each thread runs on a separate processor. How will an application requiring barrier synchronization behave if there are fewer processors than runnable threads? In such a situation, can the threads busy-wait at the barrier?

12.   What are the different ways in which Solaris2.*x* supports real-time applications? In what respects is this inadequate?
13.   Why is deadline-driven scheduling unsuitable for a conventional operating system?
14.   What are the characteristics of real-time processes? Give some examples of periodic and nonperiodic real-time applications.
15.   It is possible to reduce response time and dispatch latency simply by using a faster processor. What distinguishes a real-time system from a fast, high-performance system? Can a system that is slower overall be better suited for real-time applications?
16.   What is the difference between hard real-time and soft real-time requirements?
17.   Why is admission control important in a real-time system?

5.12   References

[AT&T 90]   American Telephone and Telegraph, *UNIX System V Release 4 Internals Students Guide,* 1990.

[Blac 90]   Black, D.L., "Scheduling Support for Concurrency and Parallelism in the Mach Operating System," *IEEE Computer,* May 1990, pp. 35–43.

[Bond 88]   Bond, P.G., "Priority and Deadline Scheduling on Real-Time UNIX," *Proceedings of the Autumn 1988 European UNIX Users' Group Conference,* Oct. 1988, pp. 201–207.

[DEC 86]   Digital Equipment Corporation, *VAX Architecture Handbook,* Digital Press, 1986.

[DEC 94]   Digital Equipment Corporation, *DEC OSF/1 Guide to Realtime Programming,* Part No. AA–PS33C–TE, Aug. 1994.

[Denh 94]   Denham, J.M., Long, P., and Woodward, J.A., "DEC OSF/1 Version 3.0 Symmetric Multiprocessing Implementation," *Digital Technical Journal,* Vol. 6, No. 3, Summer 1994, pp. 29–54.

[Henr 84]   Henry, G.J., "The Fair Share Scheduler," *AT&T Bell Laboratories Technical Journal,* Vol. 63, No. 8, Oct 1984, pp. 1845–1857.

[IEEE 93]   Institute for Electrical and Electronic Engineers, *POSIX P1003.4b, Real-Time Extensions for Portable Operating Systems,* 1993.

[Khan 92]   Khanna, S., Sebree, M., and Zolnowsky, J., "Realtime Scheduling in SunOS 5.0," *Proceedings of the Winter 1992 USENIX Technical Conference,* Jan. 1992.

[Lamp 80]   Lampson, B.W. and Redell, D.D., "Experiences with Processes and Monitors in Mesa," *Communications of the ACM,* vol. 23, no. 2, Feb 1980, pp. 105–117.

[Liu 73]   Liu, C.L., and Layland, J.W., "Scheduling Algorithms for Multiprogramming in a Hard Real-Time Environment:, *Journal of the ACM,* Vol. 20, no. 1, Jan. 1973, pp. 46–61.

[Leff 89]   Leffler, S.J., McKusick, M.K., Karels, M.J., and Quarterman, J.S., *The Design and Implementation of the 4.3 BSD UNIX Operating System,* Addison-Wesley, Reading, MA, 1989.

[Nieh 93]   Nieh, J., "SVR4 UNIX Scheduler Unacceptable for Multimedia Applications," *Proceedings of the Fourth International Workshop on Network and Operating Support for Digial Audio and Video*, 1993.

[Rama 95]   Ramakrishnan, K.K., Vaitzblit, L., Gray, C.G., Vahalia, U., Ting, D., Tzelnic, P., Glaser, S., and Duso, W.W.,"Operating System Support for a Video-on-Demand File Server," *Multimedia Systems,* Vol. 3, No. 2, May 1995, pp. 53–65.

[Sha 86]   Sha, L., and Lehoczky, J.P., "Performance of Real-Time Bus Scheduling Algorithms," *ACM Performance Evaluation Review,* Special Issue, Vol. 14, No. 1, May 1986.

[Sha 90]   Sha, L., Rajkumar, R., and Lehoczky, J.P., "Priority Inheritance Protocols: An Approach to Real-Time Synchronization," *IEEE Tansactions on Computers,* Vol. 39, No. 9, Sep. 1990, pp. 1175–1185.

[Stra 86]   Straathof, J.H., Thareja, A.K., and Agrawala, A.K., "UNIX Scheduling for Large Systems," *Proceedings of the Winter 1986 USENIX Technical Conference,* Jan. 1986.

[Varg 87]   Varghese, G., and Lauck, T., "Hashed and Hierarchical Timing Wheels: Data Structures for the Efficient Implementation of a Timer Facility," *Eleventh ACM Symposium on Operating Systems Principles,* Nov. 1987, pp. 25–38.

6

Interprocess Communications

6.1   Introduction

A complex programming environment often uses multiple cooperating processes to perform related operations. These processes must communicate with each other and share resources and information. The kernel must provide mechanisms that make this possible. These mechanisms are collectively referred to as *interprocess communications,* or IPC. This chapter describes the IPC facilities in major UNIX variants.

Interprocess interactions have several distinct purposes:

- **Data transfer** — One process may wish to send data to another process. The amount of data sent may vary from one byte to several megabytes.
- **Sharing data** — Multiple processes may wish to operate on shared data, such that if a process modifies the data, that change will be immediately visible to other processes sharing it.
- **Event notification** — A process may wish to notify another process or set of processes that some event has occurred. For instance, when a process terminates, it may need to inform its parent process. The receiver may be notified asynchronously, in which case its normal processing is interrupted. Alternatively, the receiver may choose to wait for the notification.
- **Resource sharing** — Although the kernel provides default semantics for resource allocation, they are not suitable for all applications. A set of cooperating processes may wish to define their own protocol for accessing specific resources. Such rules are usually imple-

mented by a locking and synchronization scheme, which must be built on top of the basic set of primitives provided by the kernel.

- **Process control** — A process such as a debugger may wish to assume complete control over the execution of another (target) process. The controlling process may wish to intercept all traps and exceptions intended for the target and be notified of any change in the target's state.

UNIX provides several different IPC mechanisms. This chapter first describes a core set of facilities found in all versions of UNIX, namely signals, pipes, and process tracing. It then examines the primitives collectively described as *System V IPC*. Finally, it looks at message-based IPC in Mach, which provides a rich set of facilities from a single, unified framework.

6.2   Universal IPC Facilities

When the UNIX system was first released externally [Thom 78], it provided three facilities that could be used for interprocess communications—signals, pipes, and process tracing.[1] These are the only IPC mechanisms common to all UNIX variants. Signals and pipes are described in greater detail elsewhere in this book; in this section, we discuss how they are used for interprocess communications.

6.2.1   Signals

Signals serve primarily to notify a process of asynchronous events. Originally intended for handling errors, they are also used as primitive IPC mechanisms. Modern UNIX versions recognize 31 or more different signals. Most have predefined meanings, but at least two, SIGUSR1 and SIGUSR2, are available for applications to use as they please. A process may explicitly send a signal to another process or processes using the *kill* or *killpg* system calls. Additionally, the kernel generates signals internally in response to various events. For instance, typing control-C at the terminal sends a SIGINT signal to the foreground process.

Each signal has a default action, which is typically to terminate the process. A process may specify an alternative response to any signal by providing a signal handler function. When the signal occurs, the kernel interrupts the process, which responds to the signal by running the handler. When the handler completes, the process may resume normal processing.

This way processes are notified of, and respond to, asynchronous events. Signals can also be used for synchronization. A process may use the *sigpause* call to wait for a signal to arrive. In early UNIX releases, many applications developed resource sharing and locking protocols based entirely on signals.

The original intent was to use signals primarily for handling errors; for example, the kernel translates hardware exceptions, such as *division by zero* or *invalid instruction*, into signals. If the process does not have an error handler for that exception, the kernel terminates the process.

---

[1] The earliest UNIX systems in Bell Telephone Laboratories did not have these features. For instance, pipes were developed by Doug McIlroy and Ken Thompson and made available in Version 3 UNIX in 1973 [Salu 94].

As an IPC mechanism, signals have several limitations: Signals are expensive. The sender must make a system call; the kernel must interrupt the receiver and extensively manipulate its stack, so as to invoke the handler and later resume the interrupted code. Moreover, they have a very limited bandwidth—because only 31 different signals exist (in SVR4 or 4.3BSD; some variants such as AIX provide more signals), a signal can convey only a limited amount of information. It is not possible to send additional information or arguments with user-generated signals.[2] Signals are useful for event notification, but are inefficient for more complicated interactions.

Signals are discussed in detail in Chapter 4.

6.2.2   Pipes

In traditional implementations, a pipe is a unidirectional, first-in first-out, unstructured data stream of fixed maximum size.[3] Writers add data to the end of the pipe; readers retrieve data from the front of the pipe. Once read, the data is removed from the pipe and is unavailable to other readers. Pipes provide a simple flow-control mechanism. A process attempting to read from an empty pipe blocks until more data is written to the pipe. Likewise, a process trying to write to a full pipe blocks until another process reads (and thus removes) data from the pipe.

The *pipe* system call creates a pipe and returns two file descriptors—one for reading and one for writing. These descriptors are inherited by child processes, which thus share access to the file. This way, each pipe can have several readers and writers (Figure 6-1). A given process may be a reader or writer, or both. Normally, however, the pipe is shared between two processes, each owning one end. I/O to the pipe is much like I/O to a file and is performed through *read* and *write* system calls to the pipe's descriptors. A process is often unaware that the file it is reading or writing is in fact a pipe.

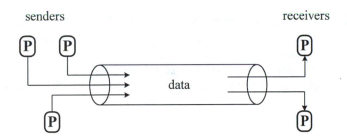

Figure 6-1. Data flow through a pipe.

---

[2] Signals generated by the kernel in response to hardware exceptions return additional information via the `siginfo` structure passed to the handler.

[3] Traditional UNIX systems such as SVR2 implement pipes in the file system and use the direct block address fields in the inode (see Section 9.2.2) to locate data blocks of the pipe. This limits the pipe size to ten blocks. Newer UNIX systems retain this limit, even though they implement pipes differently.

Typical applications such as the *shell* manipulate the descriptors so that a pipe has exactly one reader and one writer, thus using it for one-way flow of data. The most common use of pipes is to let the output of one program become the input for another. Users typically join two programs by a pipe using the shell's pipe operator ('|').

From the IPC perspective, pipes provide an efficient way of transferring data from one process to another. They have, however, some important limitations:

- Since reading data removes it from the pipe, a pipe cannot be used to broadcast data to multiple receivers.
- Data in a pipe is treated as a byte-stream and has no knowledge of message boundaries. If a writer sends several objects of different length through the pipe, the reader cannot determine how many objects have been sent, or where one object ends and the next begins.[4]
- If there are multiple readers on a pipe, a writer cannot direct data to a specific reader. Likewise, if there are multiple writers, there is no way to determine which of them sent the data.[5]

There are several ways to implement pipes. The traditional approach (in SVR2, for instance) is to use the file system mechanisms and associate an *inode* and a *file table entry* with each pipe. Many BSD-based variants use sockets to implement a pipe. SVR4 provides bidirectional, STREAMS-based pipes, described in the following section.

A related facility available in System V UNIX, and in many commercial variants, is the FIFO (first-in, first-out) file, also called a named pipe. These differ from pipes mainly in the way they are created and accessed. A user creates a FIFO file by calling *mknod,* passing it a filename and a creation mode. The mode field includes a file type of S_IFIFO and the usual access permissions. Thereafter, any process that has the appropriate permissions can open the FIFO and read or write to it. The semantics of reading and writing a FIFO are very similar to those of a pipe, and are further described in Section 8.4.2. The FIFO continues to exist until explicitly unlinked, even if no readers or writers are active.

FIFOs offer some important advantages over pipes. They may be accessed by unrelated processes. They are persistent, and hence are useful for data that must outlive the active users. They have a name in the file system name space. FIFOs also have some important drawbacks. They must be explicitly deleted when not in use. They are less secure than pipes, since any process with the right privileges can access them. Pipes are easier to set up and consume fewer resources.

6.2.3 SVR4 Pipes

SVR4 uses STREAMS (see Chapter 17) as its basic framework for networking and also to implement pipes and FIFOs. Doing so allows it to provide several new and useful features for pipes.[6] This section describes the new functionality; Section 17.9 covers the implementation details.

SVR4 pipes are bidirectional. The *pipe* system call returns two descriptors as before, but both are open for reading and writing. The syntax (same as for traditional UNIX) is

---

[4] Cooperating applications could agree on a protocol to store packet boundary information in each object.

[5] Again, cooperating applications could agree on a protocol for tagging the data source for each object.

[6] This new functionality applies only to pipes. SVR4 FIFOs behave much like traditional ones.

```
status = pipe (int fildes[2]);
```

In SVR4, this call creates two independent, first-in first-out, I/O channels that are represented by the two descriptors. Data written to `fildes[1]` can be read from `fildes[0]`, and data written to `fildes[0]` can be read from `fildes[1]`. This is very useful because many applications require two-way communication, and used two separate pipes in pre-SVR4 implementations.

SVR4 also allows a process to attach any STREAMS file descriptor to an object in the file system [Pres 90]. An application can create a pipe using *pipe*, and then bind either of its descriptors to a file name by calling

```
status = fattach (int fildes, char *path);
```

where `path` is the pathname of a file system object owned by, and writable by, the caller.[7] This object can be an ordinary file, directory, or other special file. It cannot be an active mount point (cannot have a file system mounted on it) or an object in a remote file system, and also cannot be attached to another STREAMS file descriptor. It is possible to attach a descriptor to several `path`s, thereby associating multiple names with it.

Once attached, all subsequent operations on `path` will operate on the STREAMS file until the descriptor is detached from `path` through *fdetach*. Using this facility, a process can create a pipe and then allow unrelated processes to access it.

Finally, users can push STREAMS modules onto a pipe or FIFO. These modules intercept the data flowing through the stream and process it in some way. Because the modules execute inside the kernel, they can provide functionality not possible with a user-level application. Nonprivileged users cannot add modules to the system, but can push modules onto streams they have opened.

6.2.4   Process Tracing

The *ptrace* system call provides a basic set of facilities for process tracing. It is primarily used by debuggers such as *sdb* and *dbx*. Using *ptrace*, a process can control the execution of a child process. Multiple children can be controlled with *ptrace*, though that feature is seldom used. The syntax for *ptrace* is

```
ptrace (cmd, pid, addr, data);
```

where `pid` is the process ID of the target process, `addr` refers to a location in the target's address space, and interpretation of the `data` argument depends on `cmd`. The `cmd` argument allows the parent to perform the following operations:

- Read or write a word in the child's address space.
- Read or write a word in the child's u area.
- Read or write to the child's general-purpose registers.

---

[7] Or else the caller must be a privileged process.

- Intercept specific signals. When an intercepted signal is generated for the child, the kernel will suspend the child and notify the parent of the event.
- Set or delete *watchpoints* in the child's address space.
- Resume the execution of a stopped child.
- Single-step the child—resume its execution, but arrange for it to stop again after executing one instruction.
- Terminate the child.

One command (cmd == 0) is reserved for the child. The child uses this command to inform the kernel that it (the child) will be traced by its parent. The kernel sets the child's *traced* flag (in its proc structure), which affects how the child responds to signals. If a signal is generated to a traced process, the kernel suspends the process and notifies its parent via a SIGCHLD signal, instead of invoking the signal handler. This allows the parent to intercept the signal and act appropriately. The *traced* flag also changes the behavior of the *exec* system call. When the child invokes a new program, *exec* generates a SIGTRAP signal to the child before returning to user mode. Again, this allows the parent to gain control of the child before the child begins to run.

The parent typically creates the child, which invokes *ptrace* to allow the parent to control it. The parent then uses the *wait* system call to wait for an event that changes the child's state. When the event occurs, the kernel wakes up the parent. The return value of *wait* indicates that the child has stopped rather than terminated and supplies information about the event that caused the child to stop. The parent then controls the child by one or more *ptrace* commands.

Although *ptrace* has allowed the development of many debuggers, it has several important drawbacks and limitations:

- A process can only control the execution of its direct children. If the traced process *forks*, the debugger cannot control the new process or its descendants.
- *ptrace* is extremely inefficient, requiring several context switches to transfer a single word from the child to the parent. These context switches are necessary because the debugger does not have direct access to the child's address space.
- A debugger cannot trace a process that is already running, because the child first needs to call *ptrace* to inform the kernel that it is willing to be traced.
- Tracing a *setuid* program raises a security problem if such a program subsequently calls *exec*. A crafty user could use the debugger to modify the target's address space, so that *exec* invokes the shell instead of the program it was asked to run. As a result, the user obtains a shell with superuser privileges. To avoid this problem, UNIX either disables tracing of *setuid* programs or inhibits the *setuid* and *setgid* actions on subsequent *exec* calls.

For a long time, *ptrace* was the only tool for debugging programs. Modern UNIX systems such as SVR4 and Solaris provide much more efficient debugging facilities using the **/proc** file system [Faul 91], described in Section 9.11.2. It is free from the limitations of *ptrace* and provides additional capabilities such as allowing a process to debug unrelated processes, or allowing a debugger to attach to a running process. Many debuggers have been rewritten to use **/proc** instead of *ptrace*.

6.3   System V IPC

The facilities described in the previous section do not satisfy the IPC requirements of many applications. A major advancement came with System V UNIX, which provided three mechanisms—*semaphores*, *message queues*, and *shared memory*—that have collectively come to be known as System V IPC [Bach 86]. They were originally designed to support the needs of transaction-processing applications. Subsequently, they have been implemented by most UNIX vendors, including those making BSD-based systems. This section describes the functionality provided by these mechanisms and how they are implemented in UNIX.

6.3.1   Common Elements

The three mechanisms are very similar in their interface to the programmer, as well as their implementation. In describing these common features, we use the term *IPC resource* (or simply, a resource) to refer to a single semaphore set, message queue, or shared memory region. Each instance of an IPC resource has the following attributes:

- **Key** — a user-supplied integer that identifies this instance of the resource.
- **Creator** — user and group IDs of the process that created the resource.
- **Owner** — user and group IDs of the owner of the resource. When the resource is created, the creator of the resource is also its owner. Subsequently, a process that has permission to change the owner may specify a new owner. The creator, current owner, and superuser processes have this permission.
- **Permissions** — file system-type read/write/execute permissions for owner, group, and others.

A process acquires a resource by making a *shmget, semget,* or *msgget* system call, passing to it the key, certain flags, and other arguments that depend on the specific mechanism. The permitted flags are IPC_CREAT and IPC_EXCL. IPC_CREAT asks the kernel to create the resource if it does not exist. IPC_EXCL is used in conjunction with IPC_CREAT and asks the kernel to return an error if the resource already exists. If no flags are specified, the kernel searches for an existing resource with the same key.[8] If found, and if the caller has permission to access it, the kernel returns a *resource ID* that may be used to locate the resource quickly for further operations.

Each mechanism has a control system call (*shmctl, semctl,* or *msgctl*) that provides several commands. The commands include IPC_STAT and IPC_SET to obtain and set status information (the specifics depend on the mechanism), and IPC_RMID to deallocate the resource. Semaphores provide additional control commands to obtain and set values of individual semaphores in the set.

Each IPC resource must be explicitly deallocated by the IPC_RMID command. Otherwise, the kernel considers it to be active even if all processes that were using it have terminated. This property can be quite useful. For instance, a process may write data to a shared memory region or message

---

[8] If the key is the special value IPC_PRIVATE, the kernel creates a new resource. This resource cannot be accessed through other *get* calls (since the kernel will generate a new resource each time), and hence the caller has exclusive ownership of it. The owner can share the resource with its children, who inherit it through the *fork* system call.

queue and then exit; at a later time, another process can retrieve this data. The IPC resource can persist and be usable beyond the lifetime of the processes accessing it.

The drawback, however, is that the kernel cannot determine if a resource has deliberately been left active for use by future processes, or if it has been abandoned accidentally, perhaps because the process that would have freed it terminated abnormally before doing so. As a result, the kernel must retain the resource indefinitely. If this happens often, the system could run out of that resource. At the very least, the resource ties up memory that could be better used.

Only the creator, current owner, or a superuser process can issue the IPC_RMID command. Removing a resource affects all processes that are currently accessing it, and the kernel must ensure that these processes handle this event gracefully and consistently. The specifics of this issue differ for each IPC mechanism and are discussed in the following sections.

To implement this interface, each type of resource has its own fixed-size resource table. The size of this table is configurable and limits the total number of instances of that IPC mechanism that can simultaneously be active in the system. The resource table entry comprises a common ipc_perm structure and a part specific to the type of resource. The ipc_perm structure contains the common attributes of the resources (the key, creator and owner IDs, and permissions), as well as a sequence number, which is a counter that is increased each time the entry is reused.

When a user allocates an IPC resource, the kernel returns the resource ID, which it computes by the formula

```
id = seq * table_size + index;
```

where seq is the sequence number of this resource, table_size is the size of the resource table, and index is the index of the resource in the table. This ensures that a new id is generated if a table element is reused, since seq is incremented. This prevents processes from accessing a resource using a stale id.

> **Note:** To **increment** a variable means to increase its value by one; to **decrement** it means to decrease its value by one. These terms are derived from the increment (++) and decrement (--) operators of C.

The user passes the id as an argument to subsequent system calls on that resource. The kernel translates the id to locate the resource in the table using the formula

```
index = id % table_size;
```

6.3.2 Semaphores

Semaphores [Dijk 65] are integer-valued objects that support two atomic operations—P() and V().[9] The P() operation decrements the value of the semaphore and blocks if its new value is less than

---

[9] The names P() and V() are derived from the Dutch words for these operations.

zero. The V() operation increments its value; if the resulting value becomes greater than or equal to zero, V() wakes up a waiting thread or process (if any). The operations are atomic in nature.

Semaphores may be used to implement several synchronization protocols. For example, consider the problem of managing a counted resource, that is, a resource with a fixed number of instances. Processes try to acquire an instance of the resource, and release it when they finish using it. This resource can be represented by a semaphore that is initialized to the number of instances. The P() operation is used while trying to acquire the resource; it will decrement the semaphore each time it succeeds. When the value reaches zero (no free resources), further P() operations will block. Releasing a resource results in a V() operation, which increments the value of the semaphore, causing blocked processes to awaken.

In many UNIX systems, the kernel uses semaphores internally to synchronize its operations. It is also desirable to provide the same facility for applications. System V provides a generalized version of semaphores. The *semget* system call creates or obtains an array of semaphores (there is a configurable upper bound on the array size). Its syntax is

```
semid = semget (key, count, flag);
```

where key is a 32-bit value supplied by the caller. *semget* returns an array of count semaphores associated with key. If no semaphore set is associated with key, the call fails unless the caller has supplied the IPC_CREAT flag, which creates a new semaphore set. If the IPC_EXCL flag was also provided, *semget* returns an error if a semaphore set already exists for that key. The semid value is used in subsequent semaphore operations to identify this semaphore array.

The *semop* system call is used to perform operations on the individual semaphores in this array. Its syntax is

```
status = semop (semid, sops, nsops);
```

where sops is a pointer to an nsops-element array of sembuf structures. Each sembuf, as described below, represents one operation on a single semaphore in the set:

```
struct sembuf    {
    unsigned short sem_num;
    short sem_op;
    short sem_flg;
};
```

sem_num identifies one semaphore from the array and sem_op specifies the action to perform on it. The value of sem_op is interpreted as follows:

sem_op > 0   Add sem_op to the semaphore's current value. This may result in waking up processes that are waiting for the value to increase.

sem_op = 0   Block until the semaphore's value becomes zero.

sem_op < 0   Block until the semaphore's value becomes greater than or equal to the ab-
                         solute value of sem_op, then subtract sem_op from that value. If the sema-
                         phore's value is already greater than the absolute value of sem_op, the
                         caller does not block.

Thus, a single *semop* call can specify several individual operations, and the kernel guarantees that either all or none of the operations will complete. Moreover, the kernel guarantees that no
other *semop* call on this array will begin until this one completes or blocks. If a *semop* call must
block after completing some of its component operations, the kernel *rewinds* the operation to the
beginning (undoes all modifications) to ensure atomicity of the entire call.

The sem_flg argument can supply two flags to the call. The IPC_NOWAIT flag asks the kernel to return an error instead of blocking. Also, a deadlock may occur if a process holding a semaphore exits prematurely without releasing it. Other processes waiting to acquire it may block forever
in the P() operation. To avoid this, a SEM_UNDO flag can be passed to *semop*. If so, the kernel re-
members the operation, and automatically rolls it back if the process exits.

Finally, semaphores must be explicitly removed by the IPC_RMID command of the *semctl*
call. Otherwise, the kernel retains them even they are no longer being used by any process. This allows semaphores to be used in situations that span process lifetimes, but can tie up resources if applications exit without destroying the semaphores.

When a process issues the IPC_RMID command, the kernel frees up the semaphore in the resource table. The kernel also wakes up any processes that have blocked on some semaphore operation; these processes return an EIDRM status from the *semop* call. Once the semaphore is removed,
processes can no longer access it (whether using the key or the semid).

Implementation Details

The kernel translates the semid to obtain the semaphore resource table entry, which is described by
the following data structure:

```
struct semid_ds {
    struct ipc_perm sem_perm;      /* see Section 6.3.1 */
    struct sem* sem_base;          /* pointer to array of semaphores in set */
    ushort sem_nsems;              /* number of semaphores in set */
    time_t sem_otime;              /* last operation time */
    time_t sem_ctime;              /* last change time */
    ...
};
```

For each semaphore in the set, the kernel maintains its value and synchronization information in the
following structure:

```
struct sem {
    ushort semval;    /* current value */
    pid_t sempid;     /* pid of process that invoked the last operation */
    ushort semncnt;   /* num of procs waiting for semval to increase */
    ushort semzcnt;   /* num of procs waiting for semval to equal 0 */
};
```

Finally, the kernel maintains an *undo list* for each process that has invoked semaphore operations with the SEM_UNDO flag. This list contains a record of each operation that must be rolled back. When a process exits, the kernel checks if it has an undo list; if so, the kernel traverses the list and reverses all the operations.

Discussion

Semaphores allow the development of complex synchronization facilities for use by cooperating processes. On early UNIX systems that did not support semaphores, applications requiring synchronization sought and used other atomic operations in UNIX. One alternative is the *link* system call, which fails if the new link already exists. If two processes try the same *link* operation at the same time, only one of them will succeed. It is, however, expensive and senseless to use file system operations such as *link* merely for interprocess synchronization, and semaphores fill a major need of application programmers.

The major problems with semaphores involve race conditions and deadlock avoidance. Simple semaphores (as opposed to semaphore arrays) can easily cause a deadlock if processes must acquire multiple semaphores. For example, in Figure 6-2, process **A** holds semaphore **S1** and tries to acquire semaphore **S2**, while process **B** holds **S2** and tries to acquire **S1**. Neither process can progress. Although this simple case is easy to detect and avoid, a deadlock can occur in an arbitrarily complex scenario involving several semaphores and processes.

It is impractical to have deadlock detection and avoidance code in the kernel. Moreover, there are no general, bounded algorithms that apply to all possible situations. The kernel thus leaves all deadlock detection to the applications. By providing semaphore sets with compound atomic operations, the kernel supplies mechanisms to handle multiple semaphores intelligently. Applications can choose from several well-known deadlock avoidance techniques, some of which are discussed in Section 7.10.1.

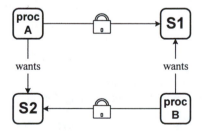

Figure 6-2. Semaphores can cause deadlocks.

One major problem in the System V semaphore implementation is that the allocation and initialization of the semaphores are not atomic. The user calls *semget* to allocate a semaphore set, followed by *semctl* to initialize it. This can lead to race conditions that must be prevented at the application level [Stev 90].

Finally, the need to explicitly delete the resource through IPC_RMID is a common problem with all IPC mechanisms. Although it allows the lifetime of the resource to exceed that of its creator, it creates a garbage collection problem if processes exit without destroying their resources.

6.3.3   Message Queues

A message queue is a header pointing at a linked list of messages. Each message contains a 32-bit *type* value, followed by a *data* area. A process creates or obtains a message queue using the *msgget* system call, which has the syntax

```
msgqid = msgget (key, flag);
```

The semantics of the call are similar to those of *semget*. The key is a user-chosen integer. The IPC_CREAT flag is required to create a new message queue, and IPC_EXCL causes the call to fail if a queue already exists for that key. The msgqid value is used in further calls to access the queue.

The user places messages on the queue by calling

```
msgsnd (msgqid, msgp, count, flag);
```

where msgp points to the message buffer (containing a *type* field followed by data area), and count is the total number of bytes in the message (including the *type* field). The IPC_NOWAIT flag can be used to return an error if the message cannot be sent without blocking (if the queue is full, for example—the queue has a configurable limit on the total amount of data it can hold).

Figure 6-3 describes the operation of a message queue. Each queue has an entry in the message queue resource table, and is represented by the following structure:

```
struct msqid_ds {
    struct ipc_perm msg_perm;      /* described in Section 6.3.1 */
    struct msg* msg_first;         /* first message on queue */
    struct msg* msg_last;          /* last message on queue */
    ushort msg_cbytes;             /* current byte count on queue */
    ushort msg_qbytes;             /* max bytes allowed on queue */
    ushort msg_qnum;               /* number of messages currently on queue */
    ...
};
```

Messages are maintained in the queue in order of arrival. They are removed from the queue (in first-in, first-out order) when read by a process, using the call

```
count = msgrcv (msgqid, msgp, maxcnt, msgtype, flag);
```

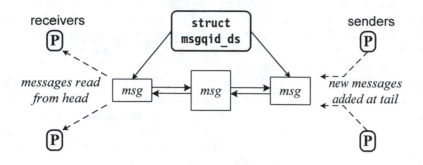

Figure 6-3. Using a message queue.

Here `msgp` points to a buffer into which the incoming message will be placed, and `maxcnt` limits the amount of data that can be read. If the incoming message is larger than `maxcnt` bytes, it will be truncated. The user must ensure that the buffer pointed to by `msgp` is large enough to hold `maxcnt` bytes. The return value specifies the number of bytes successfully read.

If `msgtype` equals zero, *msgrcv* returns the first message on the queue. If `msgtype` is greater than zero, *msgrcv* returns the first message of type `msgtype`. If `msgtype` is less than zero, *msgrcv* returns the first message of the lowest type that is less than or equal to the absolute value of `msgtyp`. Again, the `IPC_NOWAIT` flag causes the call to return immediately if an appropriate message is not on the queue.

Once read, the message is removed from the queue and cannot be read by other processes. Likewise, if a message is truncated because the receiving buffer is too small, the truncated part is lost forever, and no indication is given to the receiver.

A process must explicitly delete a message queue by calling *msgctl* with the `IPC_RMID` command. When this happens, the kernel frees the message queue and deletes all messages on it. If any processes are blocked waiting to read or write to the queue, the kernel awakens them, and they return from the call with an `EIDRM` (message ID has been removed) status.

Discussion

Message queues and pipes provide similar services, but message queues are more versatile and address several limitations of pipes. Message queues transmit data as discrete messages rather than as an unformatted byte-stream. This allows data to be processed more intelligently. The message *type* field can be used in various ways. For instance, it can associate priorities with messages, so that a receiver can check for urgent messages before reading nonurgent ones. In situations where a message queue is shared by multiple processes, the *type* field can be used to designate a recipient.

Message queues are effective for transferring small amounts of data, but become very expensive for large transfers. When one process sends a message, the kernel copies the message into an internal buffer. When another process retrieves this message, the kernel copies the data to the receiver's address space. Thus each message transfer involves two data copy operations, resulting in poor performance. Later in this chapter, we describe how Mach IPC allows efficient transfer of large amounts of data.

Another limitation of message queues is that they cannot specify a receiver. Any process with the appropriate permissions can retrieve messages from the queue. Although, as mentioned earlier, cooperating processes can agree on a protocol to specify recipients, the kernel does not assist with this. Finally, message queues do not supply a *broadcast* mechanism, whereby a process can send a single message to several receivers.

The STREAMS framework, available in most modern UNIX systems, provides a rich set of facilities for message passing. It provides more functionality than, and is more efficient than, message queues, rendering the latter almost obsolete. One feature that is available in message queues but not in STREAMS is the ability to retrieve messages selectively, based on their types. This may be useful for certain applications. Most applications, however, find STREAMS more useful, and message queues have been retained in modern UNIX variants primarily for backward compatibility. Chapter 17 describes STREAMS in detail.

6.3.4   Shared Memory

A shared memory region is a portion of physical memory that is shared by multiple processes. Processes may attach this region to any suitable virtual address range in their address space. This address range may differ for each process (Figure 6-4). Once attached, the region may be accessed like any other memory location without requiring system calls to read or write data to it. *Hence, shared memory provides the fastest mechanism for processes to share data.* If a process writes to a shared memory location, the new contents of that location are immediately visible to all processes sharing the region.[10]

A process initially obtains or creates a shared memory region by calling

```
shmid = shmget (key, size, flag);
```

where size is the size of this region, and the other parameters and flags are the same as for *semget*

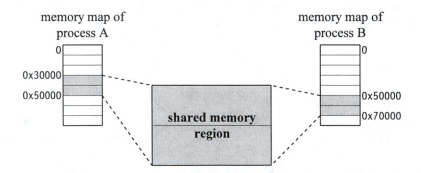

Figure 6-4. Attaching a shared memory region.

---

[10] On a multiprocessor, additional operations are required to ensure cache consistency. Section 15.13 discusses some of these issues.

or *msgget*. The process then attaches the region to a virtual address, using

```
addr = shmat (shmid, shmaddr, shmflag);
```

The shmaddr argument suggests an address to which the region may be attached. The shmflag argument can specify the SHM_RND flag, which asks the kernel to round shmaddr down by an appropriate alignment factor. If shmaddr is zero, the kernel is free to choose any address. The SHM_RDONLY flag specifies that the region should be attached as read-only. The *shmat* call returns the actual address to which the region was attached.

A process can detach a shared memory region from its address space by calling

```
shmdt (shmaddr);
```

To destroy the region completely, a process must use the IPC_RMID command of the *shmctl* system call. This marks the region for deletion, and the region will be destroyed when all processes detach it from their address space. The kernel maintains a count of processes attached to each region. Once a region has been marked for deletion, new processes cannot attach to it. If the region is not explicitly deleted, the kernel will retain it even if no process is attached to it. This may be desirable for some applications: a process could leave some data in a shared memory region and terminate; at a later time, another cooperating process could attach to this region using the same key and retrieve the data.

The implementation of shared memory depends heavily on the virtual memory architecture of the operating system. Some variants use a single *page table* to map the shared memory region and share the table with all processes attached to it. Others have separate, per-process address translation maps for the region. In such a model, if one process performs an action that changes the address mapping of a shared page, the change must be applied to all mappings for that page. SVR4, whose memory management is described in Chapter 14, uses an anon_map structure to locate the pages of the shared memory region. Its shared memory resource table contains entries represented by the following structure:

```
struct shmid_ds {
    struct ipc_perm shm_perm;    /* described in Section 6.3.1 */
    int shm_segsz;               /* segment size in bytes */
    struct anon_map *shm_amp;    /* pointer to memory mgmt info */
    ushort shm_nattch;           /* number of current attaches */
    ...
};
```

Shared memory provides a very fast and versatile mechanism that allows a large amount of data to be shared without copying or using system calls. Its main limitation is that it does not provide synchronization. If two processes attempt to modify the same shared memory region, the kernel will not serialize the operations, and the data written may be arbitrarily intermingled. Processes sharing a shared memory region must devise their own synchronization protocol, and they usually do so using primitives such as semaphores. These primitives involve one or more system calls that impose an overhead on shared memory performance.

Most modern UNIX variants (including SVR4) also provide the *mmap* system call, which maps a file (or part of a file) into the address space of the caller. Processes can use *mmap* for IPC by mapping the same file into their address space (in the `MAP_SHARED` mode). The effect is similar to a shared memory region that is initialized to the contents of the file. If a process modifies a mapped file, the change is immediately visible to all processes that have mapped that file; the kernel will also update the file on disk. One advantage of *mmap* is that it uses the file system name space instead of keys. Unlike shared memory, whose pages are backed by swap space (see Section 14.7.6), *mmap*'ed pages are backed by the file to which they are mapped. Section 14.2 describes *mmap* in detail.

6.3.5   Discussion

There are several similarities between the IPC mechanisms and the file system. The resource ID is like a file descriptor. The *get* calls resemble *open*, IPC_RMID resembles *unlink*, and the *send* and *receive* calls resemble *read* and *write*. The *shmdt* call provides *close*-like functionality for shared memory. For message queues and semaphores, however, there is no equivalent of the *close* system call, which might be desirable for removing resources cleanly. As a result, processes using a message queue or semaphore may suddenly find that the resource no longer exists.

In contrast, the keys associated with a resource form a name space that is distinct from the file system name space.[11] Each mechanism has its own name space, and the key uniquely identifies a resource within it. Because the key is a simple, user-chosen integer, it is useful only on a single machine and is unsuitable for a distributed environment. Also, it is difficult for unrelated processes to choose and agree upon an integer-valued key and avoid conflicts with keys used by other applications. Hence, UNIX provides a library routine called *ftok* (described in the *stdipc(3C)* manual page) to generate a key that is based on a file name and an integer. Its syntax is

```
key = ftok (char *pathname, int ndx);
```

The *ftok* routine generates a key value, usually based on ndx and the inode number of the file. An application can choose a unique file name more easily than a unique integer value (for instance, it can use the pathname of its own executable file), and hence reduce the likelihood of key conflicts. The ndx parameter allows greater flexibility and can be used, for example, to specify a project ID known to all cooperating processes.

Security is a problem, because the resource IDs are actually indexes into a global resource table. An unauthorized process can access a resource simply by guessing the ID. It can thus read or write messages or shared memory, or tamper with semaphores used by other processes. The permissions associated with each resource offer some protection, but many applications must share the resources with processes belonging to different users, and hence cannot use very restrictive permissions. Using the sequence number as a component of the resource ID provides a little more protection, since there are more IDs to guess from, but still poses a serious problem for applications that are concerned about security.

---

[11] Several operating systems, such as Windows/NT and OS/2, use pathnames to name shared memory objects.

Much of the functionality provided by System V IPC can be duplicated by other file system facilities such as file locking or pipes. However, the IPC facilities are much more versatile and flexible, and offer better performance than their file system counterparts.

6.4   Mach IPC

The remainder of this chapter discusses Mach's message-based IPC facility. In Mach, IPC is the central and most important kernel component. Instead of the operating system supporting IPC mechanisms, Mach provides an IPC facility that supports much of the operating system. There were several important goals in the design of Mach IPC:

- Message passing must be the fundamental communication mechanism.
- The amount of data in a single message may range from a few bytes to an entire address space (typically up to four gigabytes). The kernel should enable large transfers without unnecessary data copying.
- The kernel should provide secure communications and allow only authorized threads to send and receive messages.
- Communication and memory management are tightly coupled. The IPC subsystem uses the copy-on-write mechanisms of the memory subsystem to efficiently transfer large amounts of data. Conversely, the memory subsystem uses IPC to communicate with user-level memory managers (known as "external pagers").
- Mach IPC must support communication between user tasks, and also between the user and the kernel. In Mach, a thread makes a system call by sending a message to the kernel, and the kernel returns the result in a reply message.
- The IPC mechanism should be suitable for applications based on the client-server model. Mach uses user-level server programs to perform many services (such as file system and memory management) that are traditionally handled by the operating system kernel. These servers use Mach IPC to handle requests for service.
- The interface should be transparently extensible to a distributed environment. The user should not need to know whether he is sending a message to a local receiver or to a remote node.

Mach IPC has evolved steadily over various releases. Sections 6.4 to 6.9 discuss the IPC facility in Mach 2.5, which is the most popular Mach release and the basis for operating systems such as OSF/1 and Digital UNIX. Mach 3.0 enhances the IPC mechanisms in several respects; these features are discussed in Section 6.10.

This chapter makes several references to Mach tasks and threads. Section 3.7.1 discusses these abstractions in detail. In brief, a *task* is a collection of resources, including an address space in which one or more threads execute. A *thread* is a dynamic entity that represents an independent program counter and stack—thus a logical control sequence—in a program. A UNIX process is equivalent to a task containing a single thread. All threads in a task share the resources of that task.

6.4.1   Basic Concepts

The two fundamental IPC abstractions in Mach are messages and ports [Rash 86]. A *message* is a collection of typed data. A *port* is a protected queue of messages. A message can be sent only to a port, not to a task or thread. Mach associates *send rights* and *receive rights* with each port. These rights are owned by tasks. A send right allows a task to send messages to the port; a receive right allows it to receive messages sent to the port. Several tasks may own send rights to a single port, but only one task, the *owner* of the port, holds the receive rights.[12] Thus a port allows many-to-one communication, as illustrated in Figure 6-5.

A message may be simple or complex. A simple message contains ordinary data that is not interpreted by the kernel. A complex message may contain ordinary data, out-of-line memory (data that is passed by reference, using copy-on-write semantics), and send or receive rights to various ports. The kernel interprets the information in a complex message and transforms it to a form meaningful to the receiver.

Each port has a reference count that monitors the number of rights to it. Each such right (also known as a *capability*) represents one name of that port. The names are integers, and the name space is local to each task. Thus two tasks may have different names for the same port (Figure 6-6). Conversely, the same port name may refer to different ports in different tasks.

Ports also represent kernel objects. Hence each object, such as a task, thread, or processor, is represented by a port. Rights to these ports represent object references and allow the holder to perform operations on that object. The kernel holds the receive rights to such ports.

Each port has a finite-size message queue. The size of this queue provides a simple flow-control mechanism. Senders are blocked when the queue is full, and receivers when the queue is empty.

Each task and thread has a default set of ports. For instance, each task has send rights to a *task_self* port that represents itself (the kernel has receive rights to this port) and receive rights to a *task_notify* port (to which the kernel has send rights). Tasks also have send rights to a *bootstrap* port that provides access to a name server. Each thread has send rights to a *thread_self* port, and receive

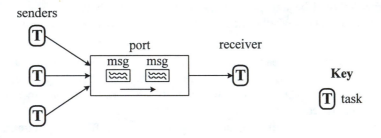

Figure 6-5. Communicating via a Mach port.

---

[12] Earlier versions of Mach had separate ownership and receive rights. Mach 2.5 and newer releases replace the ownership rights with the *backup port* facility, which is described in Section 6.8.2.

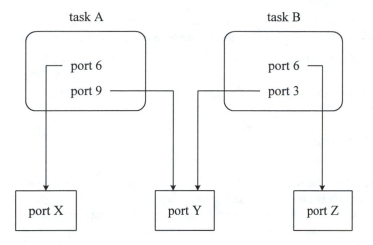

Figure 6-6. Local names for ports.

rights to a *reply* port, used to receive replies from system calls and remote procedure calls to other tasks. There is also an *exception* port associated with each task and each thread. The rights to the per-thread ports are owned by the task in which the thread runs; hence these ports can be accessed by all threads within the task.

Tasks also inherit other port rights from their parent. Each task has a list of *registered ports*. These allow the task to access various system-wide services. These ports are inherited by new tasks during task creation.

6.5 Messages

Mach is a message-passing kernel, and most system services are accessed by exchanging messages. Mach IPC provides communication between user tasks, between users and the kernel, and between different kernel subsystems. A user-level program called the *netmsgserver* transparently extends Mach IPC across the network, so that tasks can exchange messages with remote tasks as easily as with local ones. The fundamental abstractions of Mach IPC are the message and the port. This section describes the data structures and functions that implement these abstractions.

6.5.1 Message Data Structures

A message is a collection of typed data. It can contain three basic types of data:

- Ordinary data that is not interpreted by the kernel and is passed on to the receiver by physically copying it.
- Out-of-line memory, used to transfer large chunks of data using *copy-on-write* techniques, as described in Section 6.7.2.

- Send or receive rights to ports.

The message is composed of a fixed-size header, immediately followed by a variable-size set of data components (Figure 6-7). The message header includes the following information:

- **type** — simple (ordinary data only) or complex (may have out-of-line memory or port rights).
- **size** of the entire message (including the header).
- **destination port**.
- **reply port** — send right to a port to which the receiver can send a reply; this field is set only when the sender wants a reply.
- **message ID** — may be used by applications as they desire.

The message is constructed in the sending task's address space before it is sent. At that time, the destination and reply ports are the task's local names for these ports. Before delivering the message, the kernel must transform these port names into values that are meaningful to the receiver. This is described in Section 0.

Each data component consists of a type descriptor, followed by the data itself. The descriptor contains the following information:

- **name** — identifies the type of data. Mach 2.5 recognizes 16 different name values, including *internal memory*, *port send* or *receive rights*, and scalars such as *byte*, *16-bit integer*,

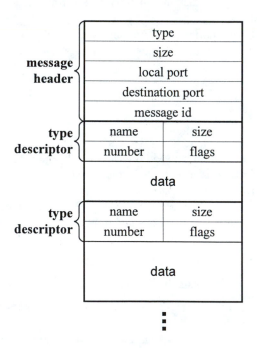

Figure 6-7. A Mach message.

32-bit integer, *string*, or *real*.

- **size** — size of each data item in this component.
- **number** — number of data items in this component.
- **flags** — specify if the data is in-line or out-of-line and if the memory or port rights must be deallocated from the sender task.

6.5.2 Message Passing Interface

Applications may use message passing in several different ways:

- To send a message, but not expect a reply.
- To wait for unsolicited messages and process them when they arrive.
- To send a message and expect a reply, but not wait for it. The application receives the reply asynchronously and processes it at a later, more convenient time.
- To send a message and wait for a reply.

The programming interface [Baro 90] to message passing consists of three functions that jointly allow all these forms of communication:

```
msg_send (msg_header_t* hdr,
          msg_option_t option,
          msg_timeout_t timeout);

msg_rcv  (msg_header_t* hdr,
          msg_option_t option,
          msg_timeout_t timeout);

msg_rpc  (msg_header_t* hdr,
          msg_size_t rcv_size,
          msg_option_t option,
          msg_timeout_t send_timeout,
          msg_timeout_t receive_timeout);
```

The *msg_send* call sends a message but does not expect a reply. The call may block if the destination port's message queue is full. Likewise, *msg_rcv* blocks until a message is received. Each call accepts a SEND_TIMEOUT or RCV_TIMEOUT option; if specified, the call blocks for a maximum of timeout milliseconds. After the timeout period expires, the call returns with a *timed out* status instead of remaining blocked. The RCV_NO_SENDERS option causes *msg_rcv* to return if no one else has a send right to the port.

The *msg_rpc* call sends an outgoing message, then waits for a reply to arrive. It is merely an optimized way of performing a *msg_send* followed by a *msg_rcv*. The reply reuses the message buffer used by the outgoing message. The options for *msg_rpc* include all the options of *msg_send* and *msg_rcv*.

The header contains the size of the message. When calling *msg_rcv*, the header contains the maximum size of the incoming message that the caller can accept; upon return, the header contains the actual size received. In the *msg_rpc* call, rcv_size must be specified separately, because the header contains the size of the outgoing message.

6.6   Ports

Ports are protected queues of messages. Tasks can acquire send or receive rights or capabilities to a port. Ports can only be accessed by holders of the appropriate rights. Although many tasks may have send rights to a port, only one task can hold a receive right. The holder of a receive right automatically has a send right to that port.

Ports are also used to represent Mach objects such as tasks, threads, and processors. The kernel holds the receive rights to such ports. Ports are reference-counted, and each send right constitutes a reference to the object represented by the port. Such a reference allows the holder to manipulate the underlying object. For instance, the *task_self* port of a task represents that task. The task can send messages to that port to request kernel services that affect the task. If another task, perhaps a debugger, also has send rights to this port, it can perform operations on this task, such as suspending it, by sending messages to the port. The specific operations that are permitted depend on the object and the interface it wishes to export.

This section describes the port name space and the data structures used to represent a port.

6.6.1   The Port Name Space

Each capability or port right represents a name of that port. The names are simple integers, and the name space is local to each task. Thus different tasks may have different names for the same port; conversely, the same name may represent different ports in different tasks. In that sense, port names are similar to UNIX file descriptors.

Each task can have at most one name for any port. Port rights can be relayed through messages, and thus a task may acquire a right to the same port several times. The kernel ensures that the same name is reused each time. As a result, a task may compare two port names—if they do not match, they cannot refer to the same port.

Each port is also represented by a global kernel data structure. The kernel must translate the local port name to a global name (address of the global data structure for that port), and vice-versa. In the case of file descriptors, each UNIX process maintains a descriptor table in its u area that stores pointers to the corresponding open file objects. Mach uses a different translation method, described in Section 6.6.3.

6.6.2   The Port Data Structure

The kernel maintains a kern_port_t data structure for each port. It contains the following information:

- Reference count of all names (rights) to this port.
- Pointer to the task that holds the receive rights.
- Local name for the port in the receiver task.

- Pointer to a backup port. If this port is deallocated, the backup port receives all messages sent to it.
- Doubly linked list of messages.
- Queue of blocked senders.
- Queue of blocked receivers. Although a single task has receive rights, many threads in the task may be waiting to receive a message.
- Linked list of all translations for this object.
- Pointer to the *port set,* and pointers to next and previous ports in this set, if the port belongs to a port set (Section 6.8.3).
- Count of messages currently in the queue.
- Maximum number of messages (backlog) allowed in the queue.

6.6.3 Port Translations

Mach maintains one translation entry for each port right. The translation entries must manage a set of *<task, port, local_name, type>* tuples, where *task* is the task that owns the right, *port* is a pointer to the kernel data structure for the port, *local_name* is the name of the port within the task, and *type* is send or receive. Mach uses the translations in several different ways:

- *msg_send* must convert a *<task, local_name>* to *port.*
- *msg_rcv* must convert a *<task, port>* to *local_name.*
- When a task deallocates a port, it must find all rights for that port.
- When a task is destroyed, the kernel must find all port translations for that task and release the corresponding references.
- When a port is destroyed, the kernel must find all translations for that port, and notify tasks that hold rights to it.

This requires a translation scheme that can efficiently support all the above operations. Figure 6-8 describes the Mach 2.5 port translation data structures. Mach uses two global hash tables to find the entries quickly—TP_table hashes the entries based on *<task, port>*, and TL_table hashes them based on *<task, local_name>*. The kernel_port_t and task data structures hold the heads of the linked lists of translations for that port or task respectively.

Hence in Figure 6-8, the entries *a*, *b*, and *c* describe translations of different ports in the same task, while entries *c*, *d*, and *e* are translations of the same port in different tasks. Entries *b*, *d*, and *f* hash to the same index in the TP_table, while entries *e* and *g* hash to the same index in the TL_table. Each translation entry is described by a port_hash_t structure, which contains the following information:

- task — the task that owns this right.
- local_name — name for the right in this task.
- type — send or receive.
- obj — pointer to port object in kernel.

Additionally, each translation entry is on each of the following doubly linked lists:

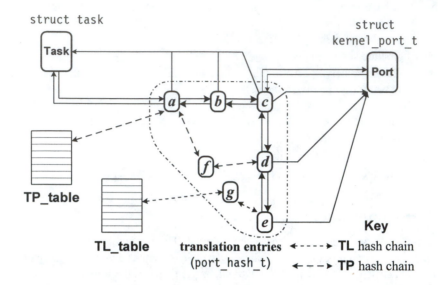

Figure 6-8. Port translation in Mach.

- `TP_chain` — hash chain based on <`task, port`>.
- `TL_chain` — hash chain based on <`task, local_name`>.
- `task_chain` — list of all translations owned by the same task.
- `obj_chain` — list of all translations for this port.

6.7   Message Passing

A single message transfer requires several operations:

1. The sender creates the message in its own address space.
2. The sender issues the *msg_send* system call to send the message. The message header contains the destination port.
3. The kernel copies the message into an internal data structure (`kern_msg_t`) using the `msg_copyin()` routine. In this process, port rights are converted to pointers to the ports' kernel objects, and out-of-line memory is copied into a holding map.
4. (a) If a thread is waiting to receive the message (the thread is on the blocked receivers queue of this port), it is awakened and the message is given to it directly.
   (b) Otherwise, if the port's message queue is full, the sender blocks until a message is removed from the queue.
   (c) Otherwise, the message is queued at the port, where it remains until a thread in the receiver task performs a *msg_rcv*.

5. The kernel returns from *msg_send* once the message has been queued or given to the receiver.

6. When the receiver calls *msg_rcv,* the kernel calls `msg_dequeue()` to remove a message from the queue. If the queue is empty, the receiver blocks until a message arrives.

7. The kernel copies the message into the receiver's address space using the `msg_copyout()` function, which performs further translations on out-of-line memory and port rights.

8. Often the sender expects a reply. For this to happen, the receiver must have a send right to a port owned by the sender. The sender sends this right to the receiver using the *reply port* field in the message header. In such a case, the sender would normally use the *mach_rpc* call to optimize this exchange. This call is semantically equivalent to a *msg_send* followed by a *msg_rcv.*

Figure 6-9 describes the transformations on the different components of a message during the transfer process. Let us now take a closer look at some important issues of message passing.

6.7.1 Transferring Port Rights

There are several reasons for transferring port rights in messages. The most frequent case is that of a reply port (Figure 6-10). A thread in task **T1** sends a message to port **P2**, which is owned by task **T2**. In this message, **T1** passes the send right to port **P1**, to which **T1** has the receive rights. As a result, **T2** can send the reply message to **P1**, and the sending thread will wait for it. This situation is so common that the message header itself contains a field to hold the reply port right.

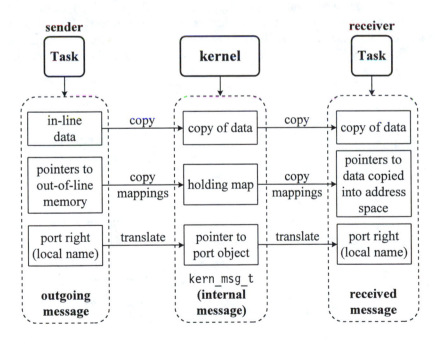

Figure 6-9. Two stages of a message transfer.

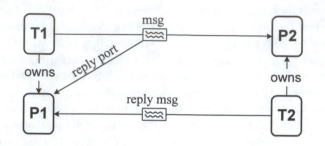

Figure 6-10. Messages can contain the send rights to a reply port.

Another common situation involves the interactions between a server program, a client, and a name server (Figure 6-11). The name server holds send rights to several server programs in the system. Typically, the servers register themselves with the name server when they begin executing (a). All tasks inherit a send right to a name server during task creation (this value is stored in the bootstrap port field in the task structure).

When a client wishes to access a server program, it must first acquire send rights to a port owned by the server. To do so, it queries the name server (b), which returns a send right to that server (c). The client uses that right to send a request to the server (d). The request contains a reply port that the server can use to reply to the client (e). Further interactions between this server-client pair need not involve the name server.

The sender sends a port right using its local name for the port. The type descriptor for that component of the message informs the kernel that the item is a port right. The local name means nothing to the receiver, and hence the kernel must translate it. To do this, the kernel searches the translation entries by hashing on <*task, local_name*> and identifies the kernel object (global name) for that port.

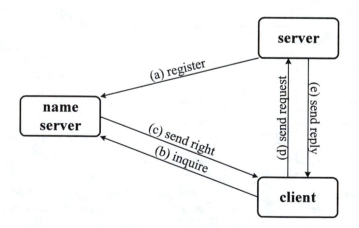

Figure 6-11. Using a name server to initiate contact between a client and a server.

When the message is retrieved, the kernel must translate this global name to a local name in the receiving task. It first checks if the receiver already has a right for this port (by hashing on <*task, port*>). If so, the kernel translates it to the same name. Otherwise, the kernel allocates a new port name in the receiver and creates a translation entry that maps the name to the port. Port names are usually small integers, and the kernel uses the lowest available integer for the new name.

Because the kernel creates an extra reference for this port, it must increment the reference count in the port object. The kernel does so when it copies the message into system space, since the new reference is created at that point. Alternately, the sender could have specified the deallocate flag in the type descriptor. In that case, the kernel deallocates the right in the sender task and does not need to increment the port reference count.

6.7.2 Out-of-Line Memory

If a message contains a small amount of data, it can be transferred by physically copying the data, first into a kernel buffer, and later (when retrieved) into the receiving task's address space. This approach, however, is expensive for large data transfers. Because Mach allows a message to contain as much as an entire address space (up to four gigabytes on 32-bit architectures), it must provide a more efficient way of transferring such data.

Typically, with large transfers, most of the data may never be modified by either the sender or the receiver. In such a case there is no need to make another copy of the data. A page must be copied only if and when one of the two tasks attempts to modify it. Until then, both tasks share a single physical copy of the page. Mach implements this method by using the copy-on-write sharing mechanisms of Mach's virtual memory subsystem. Chapter 15 describes Mach memory management in detail. Here, we restrict the discussion to IPC-related issues.

Figure 6-12 describes the transfer of out-of-line memory. The sender specifies out-of-line memory using a flag in the *type descriptor*. The msg_copyin() routine (called from *msg_send*) modifies the sender task's mappings for these pages to be read-only and copy-on-write. It then creates a temporary "holding map" for these pages in the kernel, and also marks those entries as read-only and copy-on-write (Figure 6-12(a)). When the receiver calls *msg_rcv*, the msg_copyout() function allocates an address range in the receiving task and copies the entries from the holding map to the receiver's address map. It marks the new entries as read-only and copy-on-write, and deallocates the holding map (Figure 6-12(b)).

At this point, the sender and receiver share the pages as copy-on-write. When either task attempts to modify such a page, it incurs a page fault. The fault handler recognizes the situation, and resolves the fault by making a new copy of the page and changing the faulting task's mappings to point to it. It also changes protections so that both tasks can now write to their copy of the page (Figure 6-12(c)).

Note that out-of-line memory transfer involves two phases—first, the message is placed on the queue and the pages are in transit; later, when the message is retrieved, the pages are shared by both sender and receiver. The holding map handles the transition phase. It ensures that if the sender modifies the page before the receiver retrieves it, the kernel will create a new copy for the sender, and the receiver will continue to access the original copy.

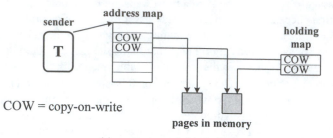

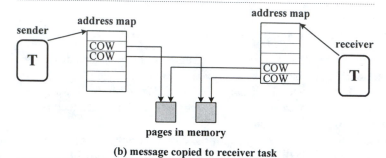

(a) message copied to holding map

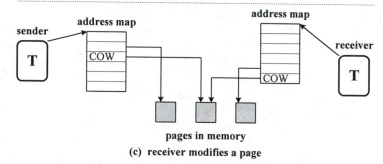

(b) message copied to receiver task

(c) receiver modifies a page

Figure 6-12. Transferring out-of-line memory.

This approach works best when neither the sender nor the receiver modifies the shared pages. This is true of many applications. Even if the pages are modified, this approach saves a copy operation. *In-line memory is copied twice—once from sender to kernel, then again from kernel to receiver. Out-of-line memory is copied at most once, the first time either task tries to modify it.*

The sender may set the deallocate flag in the type descriptor. In this case, the kernel does not use copy-on-write sharing. It simply copies the address map entries to the holding map during msg_copyin() and deallocates them from the sender's address map. When the message is retrieved, msg_copyout() copies the entries to the receiver's address map and deletes the holding map. As a result, the pages move from the sender's address space to that of the receiver without any data copying.

6.7.3 Control Flow

The message transfer proceeds along one of two paths—fast or slow. The slow path applies if a receiver is not waiting when a message is sent. In this case, the sender queues the message at the port and returns. When a receiver does a *msg_rcv*, the kernel dequeues the message and copies it into the receiver's address space.

Each port has a configurable limit, called its *backlog*, on the maximum number of messages that may be queued to it. When that limit is reached, the port is full and new senders will block until some messages are retrieved from the queue. Each time a message is retrieved from a port that has blocked senders, one sender will be awakened. When the last message is dequeued from the port, all blocked senders are awakened.

The fast path scenario occurs when a receiver is already waiting for the message. In this case, *msg_send* does not queue the message to the port. Instead, it wakes up the receiver and directly hands the message to it. Mach provides a facility called *handoff scheduling* [Drav 91], where one thread directly yields the processor to another specific thread. The fast path code uses this facility to switch to the receiver thread, which completes its *msg_rcv* call, using msg_copyout() to copy the message to its address space routine. This eliminates the overhead of queuing and dequeuing the message, and also speeds up the context switch, because the new thread to run is directly selected.

6.7.4 Notifications

A notification is an asynchronous message sent by the kernel to inform a task of certain events. The kernel sends the message to the task's *notify port*. Mach IPC uses three types of notifications:

NOTIFY_PORT_DESTROYED	When a port is destroyed, this message is sent to the owner of its backup port (if any). Port destruction and backup ports are discussed in the next section.
NOTIFY_PORT_DELETED	When a port is destroyed, this message is sent to all tasks that hold send rights to the port.
NOTIFY_MSG_ACCEPTED	When sending a message to a port whose queue is full, the sender can request this notification (using a SEND_NOTIFY option) when a message is removed from the queue.

The last case requires some elaboration. When the SEND_NOTIFY option is used, the message is transferred even if the queue is full. The kernel returns a SEND_WILL_NOTIFY status, which asks the sender not to send more messages to the queue until it receives the NOTIFY_MSG_ACCEPTED notification. This allows senders to send messages without blocking.

6.8 Port Operations

This section describes several operations on ports.

6.8.1   Destroying a Port

A port is destroyed when its receive right is released, typically when its owner task terminates. When that happens, a NOTIFY_PORT_DELETED notification is sent to all tasks that have a send right to it. Any messages waiting in the port's queue are destroyed. Blocked senders and receivers are awakened, and receive a SEND_INVALID_PORT or RCV_INVALID_PORT error respectively.

    The destruction can become complex because the queued messages may contain rights to other ports. If any of these are receive rights, the corresponding ports must also be destroyed. In fact, a malicious user can send the receive right to a port in a message to that very port. Such situations are rare, but when they do occur, they cause some deadlock and unbounded recursion problems that Mach 2.5 cannot adequately resolve.

6.8.2   Backup Ports

The *port_set_backup* call assigns a *backup port* to a port. If a port having a backup is destroyed, the kernel does not deallocate the port; instead, it transfers the receive rights to the backup port.

    Figure 6-13 illustrates this process. Port **P1** has previously assigned port **P2** as its backup. When **P1** is destroyed (perhaps due to termination of its owner task **T1**), the kernel sends a

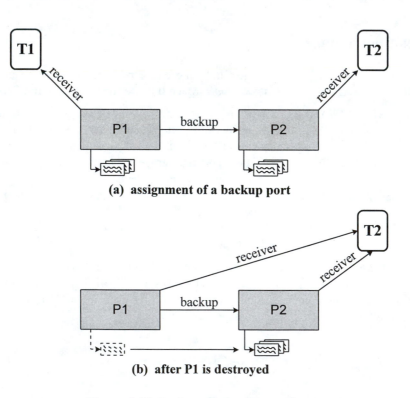

(a) assignment of a backup port

(b) after P1 is destroyed

Figure 6-13. Backup port implementation.

NOTIFY_PORT_DESTROYED message to **P2**'s owner. **P1** is not deallocated, but holds send rights to **P2**. All messages sent to **P1** are automatically routed to **P2**, and can be retrieved by **P2**'s owner.

6.8.3   Port Sets

A port set (Figure 6-14) consists of a group of ports whose receive rights are replaced by a single set-wide receive right. Thus a single task can receive from the set. Moreover, it cannot receive selectively from individual ports in the set. In contrast, messages are sent to the constituent ports and not to the port set. Tasks have send rights to specific ports in the set, and when a message is received, it contains information about the port to which it was sent.

Port sets are useful when a server manages several objects. It may associate a port with each of them and place them all in a single port set. The server can then receive messages sent to any port in that set. Each message requests an operation on the port's underlying object. Because the message identifies the port it was sent to, the server knows which object to manipulate.

The port set functionality is comparable to that of the UNIX *select* system call, which allows a process to check for input on several descriptors. *An important difference is that the time taken to retrieve a message from a port set, or to send a message to a port in the set, is independent of the number of ports in the set.*

The port's kernel object contains a pointer to the set to which it belongs, as well as pointers to maintain a doubly linked list of all ports in a set. If the port is not a member of a port set, these pointers are NULL. The port set object contains a single message queue. The queues of the component ports are not used. Each port, however, retains its own count and limit (backlog) on the number of messages queued to it and also its own queue of blocked senders.

When a thread sends a message to a port that is a member of a set, the kernel checks that the port's backlog has not been exceeded (if so, it adds the sender to the port's blocked senders queue) and increments the count of messages queued to that port. It records the identity of the port in the message and places the message in the port set's queue. When a thread in the receiver task invokes a

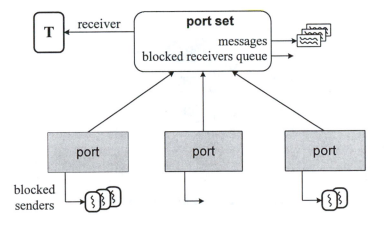

Figure 6-14. Port set implementation.

msg_rcv on a port set, the kernel retrieves the first message in the set's queue, regardless of the component port to which the message was queued.

Port sets are created and destroyed by the *port_set_allocate* and *port_set_deallocate* calls. Individual ports in the set are inserted and removed by the *port_set_insert* and *port_set_remove* calls.

6.8.4   Port Interpolation

Port interpolation allows a task to replace a right belonging to another task with a right to a different port, or to acquire a right from another task. This facility gives debuggers and emulators fine control over target tasks.

Figure 6-15 illustrates a possible scenario between a debugger task and a target task. The debugger first removes the target's send right to its *task_self* port using the *task_extract_send* call and obtains it for itself. It then calls *task_insert_send* to insert a send right to a port **P1**, owned by the debugger, in place of the target's *task_self* right. Similarly, the debugger uses the *task_extract_receive* and *task_insert_receive* calls to consume the target's receive right to its *task_notify* port, and substitute the receive right to another port **P2** to which the debugger has send rights.

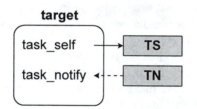

(a) target task before interpolation

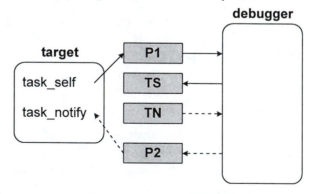

(b) after port interpolation

Figure 6-15. Port interpolation by a debugger.

Once this is accomplished, the debugger intercepts any messages sent by the target to its *task_notify* port (Mach system calls). The debugger processes the call and ensures that a reply is eventually sent to the reply port specified in the message. The debugger can choose to emulate the call and send the reply itself. Alternatively, it can forward the message to the kernel using the target's original *task_notify* port (to which the debugger now has send rights). When sending the message to the kernel, it can direct the reply to the target's reply port or specify its own reply port, thus intercepting the kernel's reply.

Likewise, the debugger intercepts any notifications sent to this task and decides whether to handle them on the target's behalf or forward them to the target. Hence a debugger (or other task) can control any port of a target task, provided it has send rights to the task's *task_self* port.

6.9   Extensibility

Mach IPC is designed to be transparently extensible to a distributed environment. A user-level program called the *netmsgserver* extends Mach IPC across a network, so that users can communicate with tasks on remote machines as easily as with local tasks. Applications are unaware of the remote connection and continue to use the same interface and system calls used for local communications. An application is typically unaware if it is communicating with a local or remote task.

There are two important reasons why Mach is able to provide such transparent extensibility. First, the port rights provide a location-independent name space. The sender simply sends the message using a local name of the port (the send right). It does not have to know if the port represents a local or remote object. The kernel maintains the mappings between the task's local name of the port and the port's kernel object.

Second, senders are anonymous. Messages do not identify the senders. The sender may pass the send right to a reply port in the message. The kernel translates this so that the receiver sees only a local name for this right, and cannot determine who the sender is. Moreover, the sender need not own the reply port; it only needs to own a send right to it. By specifying a reply port that is owned by another task, the sender can direct the reply to a different task. This is also useful for debugging, emulation, and so forth.

The *netmsgserver* operation is simple. Figure 6-16 shows a typical scenario. Each machine on the network runs a *netmsgserver* program. If a client on node **A** wishes to communicate with a server on node **B**, the *netmsgserver* on **A** sets up a proxy port to which the client sends the message. It then retrieves messages sent to that port and forwards them to the *netmsgserver* on machine **B**, which in turn forwards them to the server's port.

If the client expects a reply, it specifies a reply port in the message. The *netmsgserver* on **A** retains the send right to the reply port. The *netmsgserver* on **B** creates a proxy port for the reply port and sends the right to the proxy port to the server. The server replies to the proxy port, and the reply is routed via the two *netmsgservers* to the client's reply port.

Servers register themselves with the local *netmsgserver* and pass it the send right to a port to which the server listens. The *netmsgservers* maintain a distributed database of such registered network ports and provide them the same services (protection, notifications, etc.) that the kernel provides to local ports. Thus the *netmsgservers* query each other to provide a global name lookup

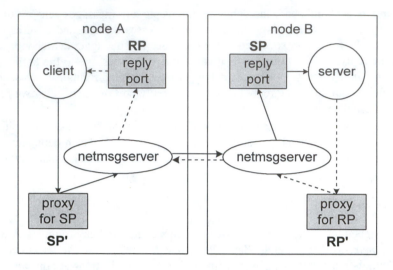

Figure 6-16. Remote communications using *netmsgservers*.

service. Tasks use this service to acquire send rights to ports registered with remote *netmsgservers*. In the absence of a network, this degenerates into a simple local name service.

The *netmsgservers* communicate with each other using low-level network protocols, not through IPC messages.

6.10   Mach 3.0 Enhancements

Mach 3.0 introduced several enhancements to the IPC subsystem [Drav 90], and addressed some important problems in the 2.5 implementation. The changes affect both the interface and the internal data structures and algorithms. This section explores some of the important changes.

A major problem in Mach 2.5 involves send rights. IPC is used heavily in client-server interactions. The client typically sends a message containing the send right to a reply port owned by the client. Once the server has sent the reply, it no longer needs to retain this right. It cannot, however, afford to deallocate the right. This is because another thread in the server application may have received, and may still be using, a send right to the same port, as the result of a separate message. The kernel translates the second right to the same local name, so that the server has a single send right to this port. If the first thread deallocates this right, the second thread will be unable to send its reply.

Servers work around this by never deallocating such send rights. This creates other problems. It is a security risk—the client may not want the server to hold this right indefinitely. It also unnecessarily uses up translation table entries, which impacts the entire system. Finally, it causes unnecessary notifications to be generated to servers when the client destroys this port. The kernel must send such notifications to all servers who have retained a send right to the port, and the servers must receive and process them, even though they have no real interest in this port.

Mach 3.0 has three separate enhancements that address this general problem—send-once rights, notification requests, and user-references for send rights.

6.10.1 Send-Once Rights

A *send-once right* to a port is, as its name implies, a send right that may only be used once. It is generated by the task that holds the port's receive right, but can then be transferred from task to task. It guarantees that a message will result from it. Normally, the send-once right is consumed by using it as a destination port in a (reply) message; it is destroyed when the message is received. If the right is destroyed in any other way, such as when the task that holds the right terminates abruptly, the kernel sends a send-once notification to the port instead.

The kernel maintains send-once rights separately from send rights. Thus if a task acquires a send right and a send-once right to the same port, it will have separate local names for the two rights. A task may acquire multiple send-once rights to the same port. Unlike send rights, each send-once right is given its own unique name. The reference count in the port's kernel object only reflects the outstanding send rights, and is not affected by send-once rights.

Mach 3.0 uses send-once rights to specify reply ports. This right is destroyed once the reply is received, so the server does not retain it indefinitely. This eliminates the unnecessary notifications when the client destroys the port.

6.10.2 Mach 3.0 Notifications

Mach 2.5 sends notifications asynchronously to the tasks in response to various system events. The tasks have no control over which notifications they receive. Usually, they have no interest in the event and simply discard the notification. Such unnecessary notifications degrade overall system performance.

Furthermore, a single task-wide notification port is too limiting. A thread could intercept and destroy a notification that another thread in the task may be awaiting. User-level libraries increase the likelihood of this scenario, because the main programs and the libraries each use notifications differently and independently.

Mach 3.0 sends notifications only to tasks that request them by explicitly calling *mach_port_request_notification*. This request specifies a send-once right for the notification port. Mach 3.0 thus allows several notification ports in a task. Each program component or thread can allocate its own notification port, and avoid contention with others.

6.10.3 User-Reference Counting of Send Rights

If a task acquires multiple send rights to a port, the kernel maps them all to a single local name in the task's port name space, thus combining them into a single send right. If a thread deallocates this right, no other thread will be able to use it, even if the other thread had acquired the right independently.

While send-once rights eliminate one source of this problem, they do not resolve it completely. Send-once rights are primarily used to provide reply ports to servers. Send rights may be acquired in various ways. If a client wants to communicate with a server, the client acquires (through the name server) a send right to it. If multiple threads in the client independently initiate contact with the server, they will each receive a send right, which will be combined into a single name. If one of these threads deallocates the name, it will have an impact on all other threads.

Mach 3.0 addresses this problem by associating a user-reference with each send right. Thus in the previous example, the kernel increments the reference count each time the task obtains the same send right, and decrements it each time a thread deallocates the right. When the last reference is released, the kernel can remove the right safely.

6.11   Discussion

Mach uses IPC not only for communication between processes, but also as a fundamental kernel structuring primitive. The virtual memory subsystem uses IPC to implement copy-on-write [Youn 87], and the kernel uses IPC to control tasks and threads. The basic abstractions of Mach, such as *tasks*, *threads*, and *ports*, interact with one another through message passing.

This architecture provides some interesting functionality. For instance, the *netmsgserver* transparently extends the IPC mechanisms to a distributed system, so that a task may control and interact with objects on remote nodes. This allows Mach to provide facilities such as remote debugging, distributed shared memory, and other client-server programs.

In contrast, the extensive use of message passing results in poor performance. For a while there was a great interest in building microkernel operating systems, where most of the facilities are provided by user-level server tasks that communicate with one another using IPC. While many vendors are still working on such solutions, the performance concerns have driven these efforts away from the mainstream.

The proponents of Mach have argued that IPC performance is not an important factor in designing microkernel operating systems [Bers 92] because of the following reasons:

- Improvements in IPC performance have been far greater than in other areas of the operating system.
- With the increasing reliance on hardware caches, the cost of operating system services will be dominated by cache hit patterns. Since the IPC code is well localized, it can be easily tuned to use the cache optimally.
- Some data transfer can be achieved through other mechanisms such as shared memory.
- Migrating some of the kernel functionality into user-level servers reduces the number of mode switches and protection boundary crossings, which are expensive.

Researchers have devoted considerable attention to improving IPC performance [Bers 90, Barr 91]. So far, however, Mach IPC has had a limited impact in the commercial world. Even Digital UNIX, which is based on Mach, does not use Mach IPC in many of its kernel subsystems.

6.12 Summary

This chapter described several IPC mechanisms. Signals, pipes, and ptrace are universal facilities, available in all but the earliest UNIX systems. The System V IPC suite, comprising shared memory, semaphores, and message queues, is also available in most modern variants. In the Mach kernel, all objects use IPC to interact with each other. Mach IPC is extensible through the netmsgserver, allowing the development of distributed, client-server applications.

Some other IPC mechanisms are covered elsewhere in the book—file locking in Chapter 8, memory-mapped files in Chapter 14, and STREAMS pipes in Chapter 17.

6.13 Exercises

1. What are the limitations of *ptrace* as a tool for writing debuggers?
2. The `pid` argument of *ptrace* must specify the process ID of a child of the caller. What are the implications of relaxing this requirement? Why should processes not be able to use ptrace to interact with arbitrary processes?
3. Compare the IPC functionality provided by pipes and message queues. What are the advantages and drawbacks of each? When is one more suitable than the other?
4. Most UNIX systems allow a process to attach the same shared memory region to more than one location in its address space. Is this a bug or a feature? When would this be useful? What problems could it cause?
5. What issues must a programmer be concerned with in choosing an address to attach a shared memory region to? What errors would the operating system protect against?
6. How can the `IPC_NOWAIT` flag be used to prevent deadlocks when using semaphores?
7. Write programs to allow cooperating processes to lock a resource for exclusive use, using (a) FIFO files, (b) semaphores, (c) the *mkdir* system call, and (d) *flock* or *lockf* system calls. Compare and explain their performance.
8. What side effects, if any, must the programmer be concerned with in each of the above cases?
9. Is it possible to implement resource locking through (a) signals alone or (b) shared memory and signals? What would be the performance of such a facility?
10. Write programs to transfer a large amount of data between two processes, using (a) a pipe, (b) a FIFO, (c) a message queue, and (d) shared memory with semaphores for synchronization. Compare and explain their performance.
11. What are the security problems associated with System V IPC? How can a malicious program eavesdrop on, or interfere with, communications between other processes?
12. Semaphores are created with *semget* but initialized with *semctl*. Hence creation and initialization cannot be accomplished in a single atomic operation. Describe a situation where this might lead to a race condition and suggest a solution to the problem.
13. Can System V message queues be implemented on top of Mach IPC? What problems must such an implementation solve?

14.   Why are send-once rights useful?

15.   How do port sets help in developing a client-server application for Mach?

6.14   References

[Bach 86]   Bach, M.J., *The Design of the UNIX Operating System,* Prentice-Hall, Englewood Cliffs, NJ, 1986.

[Baro 90]   Baron, R.V., Black, D., Bolosky, W., Chew, J., Draves, R.P., Golub, D.B., Rashid, R.F., Tevanian, A., Jr., and Young, M.W., *Mach Kernel Interface Manual,* Department of Computer Science, Carnegie-Mellon University, Jan. 1990.

[Barr 91]   Barrera, J.S.,III, "A Fast Mach Network IPC Implementation," *Proceedings of the USENIX Mach Symposium,* Nov. 1991, pp. 1–12.

[Bers 90]   Bershad, B.N., Anderson, T.E., Lazowska, E.D., and Levy, H.M., "Lightweight Remote Procedure Call," *ACM Transactions on Computer Systems,* Vol. 8, No. 1, Feb. 1990, pp. 37–55.

[Bers 92]   Bershad, B.N., "The Increasing Irrelevance of IPC Performance for Microkernel-Based Operating Systems," *USENIX Workshop on Micro-Kernels and Other Kernel Architectures,* Apr. 1992, pp. 205–212.

[Dijk 65]   Dijkstra, E.W., "Solution of a Problem in Concurrent Programming Control," *Communications of the ACM,* Vol. 8, Sep. 1965, pp. 569–578.

[Drav 90]   Draves, R.P., "A Revised IPC Interface," *Proceedings of the First Mach USENIX Workshop,* Oct. 1990, pp. 101–121.

[Drav 91]   Draves, R.P., Bershad, B.N., Rashid, R.F., and Dean, R.W., "Using Continuations to Implement Thread Management and Communication in Operating Systems," Technical Report CMU–CS–91–115R, School of Computer Science, Carnegie-Mellon University, Oct. 1991.

[Faul 91]   Faulkner, R. and Gomes, R., "The Process File System and Process Model in UNIX System V," *Proceedings of the 1991 Winter USENIX Conference,* Jan. 1991, pp. 243–252.

[Pres 90]   Presotto, D.L., and Ritchie, D.M., "Interprocess Communications in the Ninth Edition UNIX System," *UNIX Research System Papers,* Tenth Edition, Vol. II, Saunders College Publishing, 1990, pp. 523–530.

[Rash 86]   Rashid, R.F., "Threads of a New System," *UNIX Review,* Aug. 1986, pp. 37–49.

[Salu 94]   Salus, P.H., *A Quarter Century of UNIX,* Addison-Wesley, Reading, MA, 1994.

[Stev 90]   Stevens, R.W., *UNIX Network Programming,* Prentice-Hall, Englewood Cliffs, NJ, 1990.

[Thom 78]   Thompson, K., "UNIX Implementation," *The Bell System Technical Journal,* Vol. 57, No. 6, Part 2, Jul.-Aug. 1978, pp. 1931–1946.

[Youn 87]   Young, M., Tevanian, A., Rashid, R.F., Golub, D., Eppinger, J., Chew, J., Bolosky, W., Black, D., and Baron, R., "The Duality of Memory and Communication in the Implementation of a Multiprocessor Operating System," *Proceedings of the Eleventh ACM Symposium on Operating Systems Principles,* Nov. 1987, pp. 63–76.

7

Synchronization and Multiprocessors

7.1 Introduction

The desire for more processing power has led to several advances in hardware architectures. One of the major steps in this direction has been the development of multiprocessor systems. These systems consist of two or more processors sharing the main memory and other resources. Such configurations offer several advantages. They provide a flexible growth path for a project, which may start with a single processor and, as its computing needs grow, expand seamlessly by adding extra processors to the machine. Systems used for compute-intensive applications are often CPU-bound. The CPU is the main bottleneck, and other system resources such as the I/O bus and memory are underutilized. Multiprocessors add processing power without duplicating other resources, and hence provide a cost-effective solution for CPU-bound workloads.

Multiprocessors also provide an extra measure of reliability; if one of the processors should fail, the system could still continue to run without interruption. This, however, is a double-edged sword, since there are more potential points of failure. To ensure a high *mean time before failure* (MTBF), multiprocessor systems must be equipped with fault-tolerant hardware and software. In particular, the system should recover from the failure of one processor without crashing.

Several variants of UNIX have evolved to take advantage of such systems. One of the earliest multiprocessing UNIX implementations ran on the AT&T 3B20A and the IBM 370 architectures [Bach 84]. Currently, most major UNIX implementations are either native multiprocessing systems (DECUNIX, Solaris 2.*x*) or have multiprocessing variants (SVR4/MP, SCO/MPX).

Ideally, we would like to see the system performance scale linearly with the number of processors. Real systems fall short of this goal for several reasons. Since the other components of the system are not duplicated, they can become bottlenecks. The need to synchronize when accessing shared data structures, and the extra functionality to support multiple processors, adds CPU overhead and reduces the overall performance gains. The operating system must try to minimize this overhead and allow optimal CPU utilization.

The traditional UNIX kernel assumes a uniprocessor architecture and needs major modifications to run on multiprocessor systems. The three main areas of change are synchronization, parallelization, and scheduling policies. Synchronization involves the basic primitives used to control access to shared data and resources. The traditional primitives of sleep/wakeup combined with interrupt blocking are inadequate in a multiprocessing environment and must be replaced with more powerful facilities.

Parallelization concerns the efficient use of the synchronization primitives to control access to shared resources. This involves decisions regarding lock granularity, lock placement, deadlock avoidance, and so forth. Section 7.10 discusses some of these issues. The scheduling policy also needs to be changed to allow the optimal utilization of all processors. Section 7.4 analyzes some issues related to multiprocessor scheduling.

This chapter first describes the synchronization mechanisms in traditional UNIX systems and analyzes their limitations. It follows with an overview of multiprocessor architectures. Finally the chapter describes synchronization in modern UNIX systems. The methods describe work well on both uniprocessor and multiprocessor platforms.

In traditional UNIX systems, the process is the basic scheduling unit, and it has a single thread of control. As described in Chapter 3, many modern UNIX variants allow multiple threads of control in each process, with full kernel support for these threads. Such multithreaded systems are available both on uniprocessor and multiprocessor architectures. In these systems, individual threads contend for and lock the shared resources. In the rest of this chapter, we refer to a thread as the basic scheduling unit since it is the more general abstraction. For a single-threaded system, a thread is synonymous with a process.

7.2   Synchronization in Traditional UNIX Kernels

The UNIX kernel is reentrant—several processes may be executing in the kernel at the same time, perhaps even in the same routine. On a uniprocessor only one process can actually execute at a time. However, the system rapidly switches from one process to another, providing the illusion that they are all executing concurrently. This feature is usually called *multiprogramming*. Since these processes share the kernel, the kernel must synchronize access to its data structures in order to avoid corrupting them. Section 2.5 provides a detailed discussion of traditional UNIX synchronization techniques. In this section, we summarize the important principles.

The first safeguard is that the traditional UNIX kernel is nonpreemptive. Any thread executing in kernel mode will continue to run, even though its time quantum may expire, until it is ready to leave the kernel or needs to block for some resource. This allows kernel code to manipulate several data structures without any locking, knowing that no other thread can access them until the current thread is done with them and is ready to relinquish the kernel in a consistent state.

7.2.1   Interrupt Masking

The no-preemption rule provides a powerful and wide-ranging synchronization tool, but it has certain limitations. Although the current thread may not be preempted, it may be interrupted. Interrupts are an integral part of system activity and usually need to be serviced urgently. The interrupt handler may manipulate the same data structures with which the current thread was working, resulting in corruption of that data. Hence the kernel must synchronize access to data that is used both by normal kernel code and by interrupt handlers.

UNIX solves this problem by providing a mechanism for blocking (masking) interrupts. Associated with each interrupt is an *interrupt priority level* (*ipl*). The system maintains a *current ipl* value and checks it whenever an interrupt occurs. If the interrupt has a higher priority than the *current ipl*, it is handled immediately (preempting the lower-priority interrupt currently being handled). Otherwise, the kernel blocks the interrupt until the *ipl* falls sufficiently. Prior to invoking the handler, the system raises the *ipl* to that of the interrupt; when the handler completes, the system restores the *ipl* to the previous value (which it saves). The kernel can also explicitly set the *ipl* to any value to mask interrupts during certain critical processing.

For example, a kernel routine may want to remove a disk block buffer from a buffer queue it is on; this queue may also be accessed by the disk interrupt handler. The code to manipulate the queue is a *critical region*. Before entering the critical region, the routine will raise the *ipl* high enough to block disk interrupts. After completing the queue manipulation, the routine will set the *ipl* back to its previous value, thus allowing the disk interrupts to be serviced. The *ipl* thus allows effective synchronization of resources shared by the kernel and interrupt handlers.

7.2.2   Sleep and Wakeup

Often a thread wants to guarantee exclusive use of a resource even if it needs to block for some reason. For instance, a thread wants to read a disk block into a block buffer. It allocates a buffer to hold the block and then initiates disk activity. This thread needs to wait for the I/O to complete, which means it must relinquish the processor to some other thread. If the other thread acquires the same buffer and uses it for some different purpose, the contents of the buffer may become indeterminate or corrupted. This means that threads need a way of locking the resource while they are blocked.

UNIX implements this by associating *locked* and *wanted* flags with shared resources. When a thread wants to access a sharable resource, such as a block buffer, it first checks its *locked* flag. If the flag is clear, the thread sets the flag and proceeds to use the resource. If a second thread tries to access the same resource, it finds the *locked* flag set and must block (go to sleep) until the resource becomes available. Before doing so, it sets the associated *wanted* flag. Going to sleep involves linking the thread onto a queue of sleeping threads, changing its state information to show that it is sleeping on this resource, and relinquishing the processor to another thread.

When the first thread is done with the resource, it will clear the *locked* flag and check the *wanted* flag. If the *wanted* flag is set, it means that at least one other thread is waiting for (blocked on) this resource. In that case, the thread examines the *sleep queue* and wakes up all such threads. Waking a thread involves unlinking it from the sleep queue, changing its state to *runnable*, and putting it on the scheduler queue. When one of these threads is eventually scheduled, it again checks the *locked* flag, finds that it is clear, sets it, and proceeds to use the resource.

7.2.3   Limitations of Traditional Approach

The traditional synchronization model works correctly for a uniprocessor, but has some important performance problems that are described in this section. In a multiprocessor environment, the model breaks down completely, as will be shown in Section 7.4.

Mapping Resources to Sleep Queues

The organization of the sleep queues leads to poor performance in some situations. In UNIX, a thread blocks when waiting for a resource lock or an event. Each resource or event is associated with a *sleep channel*, which is a 32-bit value usually set to the address of the resource. There is a set of sleep queues, and a hash function maps the channel (hence, maps the resource) to one of these queues as shown in Figure 7-1. A thread goes to sleep by enqueuing itself onto the appropriate sleep queue and storing the sleep channel in its proc structure.

This approach has two consequences. First, more than one event may map to the same channel. For instance, one thread locks a buffer, initiates I/O activity to it, and sleeps until the I/O completes. Another thread tries to access the same buffer, finds it locked, and must block until it becomes available. Both events map to the same channel, namely the address of that buffer. When the I/O completes, the interrupt handler will wake up both threads, even though the event the second thread was waiting for has not yet occurred.

Second, the number of hash queues is much smaller than the number of different sleep channels (resources or events); hence, multiple channels map to the same hash queue. A queue thus contains threads waiting on several different channels. The wakeup() routine must examine each of them and only wake up threads blocked on the correct channel. As a result, the total time taken by wakeup() depends not on the number of processes sleeping on that channel, but on the total number

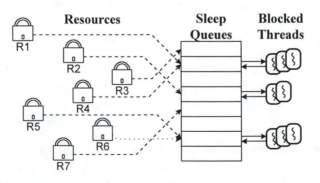

Figure 7-1. Mapping resources to global sleep queues.

of processes sleeping on that queue. This sort of unpredictable delay is usually undesirable and may be unacceptable for kernels that support real-time applications requiring bounded dispatch latency (see Section 5.5.4).

One alternative is to associate a separate sleep queue for each resource or event (Figure 7-2). This approach would optimize the latency of the wakeup algorithm, at the expense of memory overhead for all the extra queues. The typical queue header contains two pointers (forward and backward) as well as other information. The total number of synchronization objects in the system may be quite large and putting a sleep queue on each of them may be wasteful.

Solaris 2.x provides a more space-efficient solution [Eykh 92]. Each synchronization object has a two-byte field that locates a *turnstile* structure that contains the sleep queue and some other information (Figure 7-3). The kernel allocates turnstiles only to those resources that have threads blocked on them. To speed up allocation, the kernel maintains a pool of turnstiles, and the size of this pool is greater than the number of active threads. This approach provides more predictable real-time behavior with minimal storage overhead. Section 5.6.7 describes turnstiles in greater detail.

Shared and Exclusive Access

The sleep/wakeup mechanism is adequate when only one thread should use the resource at a time. It does not, however, readily allow for more complex protocols such as readers-writers synchronization. It may be desirable to allow multiple threads to share a resource for reading, but require exclusive access before modifying it. File and directory blocks, for example, can be shared efficiently using such a facility.

7.3   Multiprocessor Systems

There are three important characteristics of a multiprocessor system. The first is its memory model, which defines the way in which the processors share the memory. Second is the hardware support for synchronization. Finally, the software architecture determines the relationships between the processors, kernel subsystems, and user processes.

7.3.1   Memory Model

From a hardware perspective, multiprocessor systems can be divided into three categories (see Figure 7-4), depending on their coupling and memory access semantics:

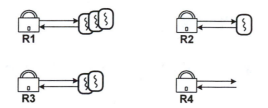

Figure 7-2. Per-resource blocked-thread queues.

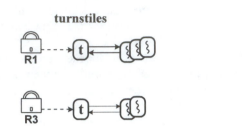

turnstiles

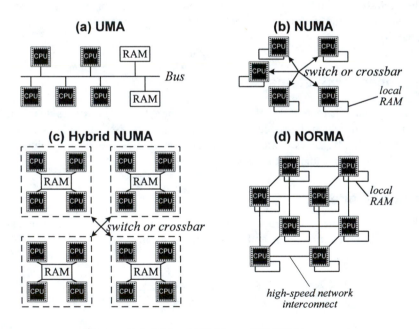

Figure 7-3. Queuing blocked threads on turnstiles.

- *Uniform Memory Access* (UMA)
- *Non-Uniform Memory Access* (NUMA)
- *No Remote Memory Access* (NORMA)

The most common system is the UMA, or shared memory, multiprocessor (Figure 7-4(a)). Such a system allows all CPUs equal access to main memory[1] and to I/O devices, usually by having

Figure 7-4. UMA, NUMA, and NORMA systems.

---

[1] However, the data, instruction, and address translation caches are local to each processor.

everything on a single system bus. This is a simple model from the operating system perspective. Its main drawback is scalability. UMA architectures can support only a small number of processors. As the number of processors increases, so does the contention on the bus. One of the largest UMA systems is the SGI Challenge, which supports up to 36 processors on a single bus.

In a NUMA system (Figure 7-4(b)), each CPU has some local memory, but can also access memory local to another processor. The remote access is slower, usually by an order of magnitude, than local access. There are also hybrid systems (Figure 7-4(c)), where a group of processors shares uniform access to its local memory, and has slower access to memory local to another group. The NUMA model is hard to program without exposing the details of the hardware architecture to the applications.

In a NORMA system (Figure 7-4(d)), each CPU has direct access only to its own local memory and may access remote memory only through explicit message passing. The hardware provides a high-speed interconnect that increases the bandwidth for remote memory access. Building a successful system for such an architecture requires cache management and scheduling support in the operating system, as well as compilers that can optimize the code for such hardware.

This chapter restricts itself to UMA systems.

7.3.2 Synchronization Support

Synchronization on a multiprocessor is fundamentally dependent on hardware support. Consider the basic operation of locking a resource for exclusive use by setting a *locked* flag maintained in a shared memory location. This may be accomplished by the following sequence of operations:

1. Read the flag.
2. If the flag is 0 (hence, the resource is unlocked), lock the resource by setting the flag to 1.
3. Return TRUE if the lock was obtained, or else return FALSE.

On a multiprocessor, two threads on two different processors may simultaneously attempt to carry out this sequence of operations. As Figure 7-5 shows, both threads may think they have exclusive access to the resource. To avoid such a disaster, the hardware has to provide a more powerful primitive that can combine the three subtasks into a single indivisible operation. Many architectures solve this problem by providing either an atomic test-and-set or a conditional store instruction.

Atomic Test-and-Set

An atomic test-and-set operation usually acts on a single bit in memory. It tests the bit, sets it to one, and returns its old value. Thus at the completion of the operation the value of the bit is one (locked), and the return value indicates whether it was already set to one prior to this operation. The operation is guaranteed to be atomic, so if two threads on two processors both issue the same instruction on the same bit, one operation will complete before the other starts. Further, the operation is also atomic with respect to interrupts, so that an interrupt can occur only after the operation completes.

Such a primitive is ideally suited for simple locks. If the test-and-set returns one, the calling thread owns the resource. If it returns zero, the resource is locked by another thread. Unlocking the resource is done by simply setting the bit to zero. Some examples of test-and-set instructions are

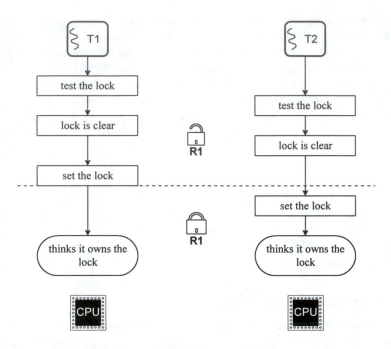

Figure 7-5. Race condition if test-and-set is not atomic.

BBSSI (**B**ranch on **B**it **S**et and **S**et **I**nterlocked) on the VAX-11 [Digi 87] and LDSTUB (**L**oa**D** and **ST**ore Unsigned **B**yte) on the SPARC.

Load-Linked and Store-Conditional Instructions

Some processors such as the MIPS R4000 and Digital's Alpha AXP use a pair of special load and store instructions to provide an atomic read-modify-write operation. The *load-linked* instruction (also called the *load-locked* instruction) loads a value from memory into a register and sets a flag that causes the hardware to monitor the location. If any processor writes to such a monitored location, the hardware will clear the flag. The *store-conditional* instruction stores a new value into the location provided the flag is still set. In addition, it sets the value of another register to indicate if the store occurred.

Such a primitive may be used to generate an atomic increment operation. The variable is read using load-linked, and its new value is set using store-conditional. This sequence is repeated until it succeeds. Event counters in DG/UX [Kell 89] are based on this facility.

Some systems such as the Motorola MC88100 use a third approach based on a *swap-atomic* instruction. This method is explored further in the exercises at the end of this chapter. Any of these hardware mechanisms becomes the first building block for a powerful and comprehensive synchronization facility. The high-level software abstractions described in the following sections are all built on top of the hardware primitives.

7.3.3   Software Architecture

From a software perspective, again there are three types of multiprocessing systems—master-slave, functionally asymmetric, and symmetric. A *master-slave system* [Gobl 81] is asymmetric: one processor plays the role of a *master processor*, and the rest are *slaves*. The master processor may be the only one allowed to do I/O and receive device interrupts. In some cases, only the master processor runs kernel code, and the slaves run only user-level code. Such constraints may simplify the system design, but reduce the advantage of multiple processors. Benchmark results [Bach 84] have shown that a UNIX system typically spends more than 40% of its time running in kernel mode, and it is desirable to spread this kernel activity among all processors.

Functionally asymmetric multiprocessors run different subsystems on different processors. For instance, one processor may run the networking layer, while another manages I/O. Such an approach is more suitable for a special-purpose system rather than a general-purpose operating system like UNIX. The Auspex NS5000 file server [Hitz 90] is a successful implementation of this model.

Symmetric multiprocessing (SMP) is by far the more popular approach. In an SMP system, all CPUs are equal, share a single copy of the kernel text and data, and compete for system resources such as devices and memory. Each CPU may run the kernel code, and any user process may be scheduled on any processor. This chapter describes SMP systems only, except where explicitly stated otherwise.

The rest of this chapter describes modern synchronization mechanisms, used for uniprocessor and multiprocessor systems.

7.4   Multiprocessor Synchronization Issues

One of the basic assumptions in the traditional synchronization model is that a thread retains exclusive use of the kernel (except for interrupts) until it is ready to leave the kernel or block on a resource. This is no longer valid on a multiprocessor, since each processor could be executing kernel code at the same time. *We now need to protect all kinds of data that did not need protection on a uniprocessor.* Consider for example, access to an *IPC resource table* (see Section 6.3.1). This data structure is not accessed by interrupt handlers and does not support any operations that might block the process. Hence on a uniprocessor, the kernel can manipulate the table without locking it. In the multiprocessor case, two threads on different processors can access the table simultaneously, and hence must lock it in some manner before use.

The locking primitives must be changed as well. In a traditional system, the kernel simply checks the *locked* flag and sets it to lock the object. On a multiprocessor, two threads on different processors can concurrently examine the *locked* flag for the same resource. Both will find it clear and assume that the resource is available. Both threads will then set the flag and proceed to access the resource, with unpredictable results. The system must therefore provide some kind of an atomic *test-and-set* operation to ensure that only one thread can lock the resource.

Another example involves blocking of interrupts. On a multiprocessor, a thread can typically block interrupts only on the processor on which it is running. It is usually not possible to block interrupts across all processors—in fact, some other processor may have already received a conflicting interrupt. The handler running on another processor may corrupt a data structure that the thread is accessing. This is compounded by the fact that the handler cannot use the sleep/wakeup synchronization model, since most implementations do not permit interrupt handlers to block. The system should provide some mechanism for blocking interrupts on other processors. One possible solution is a global *ipl* managed in software.

7.4.1   The Lost Wakeup Problem

The sleep/wakeup mechanism does not function correctly on a multiprocessor. Figure 7-6 illustrates a potential race condition. Thread **T1** has locked a resource **R1**. Thread **T2**, running on another processor, tries to acquire the resource, and finds it locked. **T2** calls `sleep()` to wait for the resource. Between the time **T2** finds the resource locked and the time it calls `sleep()`, **T1** frees the resource and proceeds to wake up all threads blocked on it. Since **T2** has not yet been put on the sleep queue, it will miss the wakeup. The end result is that the resource is not locked, but **T2** is blocked waiting for it to be unlocked. If no one else tries to access the resource, **T2** could block indefinitely. This is known as the lost wakeup problem, and requires some mechanism to combine the test for the resource and the call to `sleep()` into a single atomic operation.

It is clear then, that we need a whole new set of primitives that will work correctly on a multiprocessor. This gives us a good opportunity to examine other problems with the traditional model and devise better solutions. Most of these issues are performance related.

7.4.2   The Thundering Herd Problem

When a thread releases a resource, it wakes up all threads waiting for it. One of them may now be able to lock the resource; the others will find the resource still locked and will have to go back to sleep. This may lead to extra overhead in wakeups and context switches.

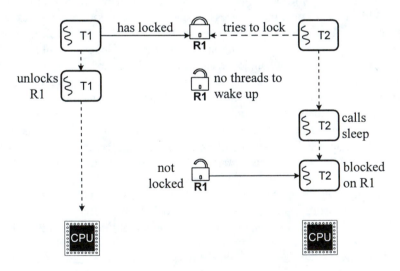

Figure 7-6. The lost wakeup problem.

This problem is not as acute on a uniprocessor, since by the time a thread runs, whoever had locked the resource is likely to have released it. On a multiprocessor, however, if several threads were blocked on a resource, waking them all may cause them to be simultaneously scheduled on different processors, and they would all fight for the same resource again. This is frequently referred to as the *thundering herd* problem.

Even if only one thread was blocked on the resource, there is still a time delay between its waking up and actually running. In this interval, an unrelated thread may grab the resource, causing the awakened thread to block again. If this happens frequently, it could lead to starvation of this thread.

We have examined several problems with the traditional synchronization model that affect correct operation and performance. The rest of this chapter describes several synchronization mechanisms that function well on both uniprocessors and multiprocessors.

7.5 Semaphores

The early implementations of UNIX on multiprocessors relied almost exclusively on *Dijkstra's semaphores* [Dijk 65] (also called *counted semaphores*) for synchronization. A semaphore is an integer-valued variable that supports two basic operations—P() and V(). P() decrements the semaphore and blocks if its new value is less than zero. V() increments the semaphore; if the resulting value is less than or equal to zero, it wakes up a thread blocked on it (if any). Example 7-1 describes these functions, plus an initialization function initsem() and a CP() function, which is a nonblocking version of P():

```
void initsem (semaphore *sem, int val)
{
    *sem = val;
}

void P(semaphore *sem)    /* acquire the semaphore */
{
    *sem -= 1;
    while (*sem < 0)
        sleep;
}

void V(semaphore *sem)    /* release the semaphore */
{
    *sem += 1;
    if (*sem <= 0)
        wakeup a thread blocked on sem;
}
```

```
boolean_t CP(semaphore *sem)      /*    try to acquire semaphore without blocking */
{
    if (*sem > 0)    {
        *sem -= 1;
        return TRUE;
    } else
        return FALSE;
}
```

Example 7-1. Semaphore operations.

The kernel guarantees that the semaphore operations will be atomic, even on a multiprocessor system. Thus if two threads try to operate on the same semaphore, one operation will complete or block before the other starts. The P() and V() operations are comparable to sleep and wakeup, but with somewhat different semantics. The CP() operation allows a way to poll the semaphore without blocking and is used in interrupt handlers and other functions that cannot afford to block. It is also used in deadlock avoidance cases, where a P() operation risks a deadlock.

7.5.1   Semaphores to Provide Mutual Exclusion

Example 7-2 shows how a semaphore can provide mutual exclusion on a resource. A semaphore can be associated with a shared resource such as a linked list, and initialized to one. Each thread does a P() operation to lock a resource and a V() operations to release it. The first P() sets the value to zero, causing subsequent P() operations to block. When a V() is done, the value is incremented and one of the blocked threads is awakened.

```
/* During initialization */
semaphore sem;
initsem (&sem, 1);

/* On each use */
P (&sem);
Use resource;
V (&sem);
```

Example 7-2. Semaphore used to lock resource for exclusive use.

7.5.2   Event-Wait Using Semaphores

Example 7-3 shows how a semaphore can be used to wait for an event by initializing it to zero. Threads doing a P() will block. When the event occurs, a V() needs to be done for each blocked thread. This can be achieved by calling a single V() when the event occurs and having each thread do another V() upon waking up, as is shown in Example 7-3.

```
/* During initialization */
semaphore event;
initsem (&event, 0);      /* probably at boot time */

/* Code executed by thread that must wait on event */
P (&event);               /* Blocks if event has not occurred */
/* Event has occurred */
V (&event);               /* So that another thread may wake up */
/* Continue processing */

/* Code executed when event occurs */
V (&event);               /* Wake up one thread */
```

Example 7-3. Semaphores used to wait for an event.

7.5.3   Semaphores to Control Countable Resources

Semaphores are also useful for allocating countable resources, such as message block headers in a STREAMS implementation. As shown in Example 7-4, the semaphore is initialized to the number of available instances of that resource. Threads call P() while acquiring an instance of the resource and V() while releasing it. Thus the value of the semaphore indicates the number of instances currently available. If the value is negative, then its absolute value is the number of pending requests (blocked threads) for that resource. This is a natural solution to the classic producers-consumers problem.

```
/* During initialization */
semaphore counter;
initsem (&counter, resourceCount);

/* Code executed to use the resource */
P (&counter);    /* Blocks until resource is available */
Use resource;    /* Guaranteed to be available now */
V (&counter);    /* Release the resource */
```

Example 7-4. Semaphore used to count available instances of a resource.

7.5.4   Drawbacks of Semaphores

Although semaphores provide a single abstraction flexible enough to handle several different types of synchronization problems, they suffer from a number of drawbacks that make them unsuitable in several situations. To begin with, a semaphore is a high-level abstraction based on lower-level primitives that provide atomicity and a blocking mechanism. For the P() and V() operations to be atomic on a multiprocessor system, there must be a lower-level atomic operation to guarantee exclusive access to the semaphore variable itself. Blocking and unblocking require context switches and manipulation of sleep and scheduler queues, all of which make the operations slow. This expense may be tolerable for some resources that need to be held for a long time, but is unacceptable for locks held for a short time.

The semaphore abstraction also hides information about whether the thread actually had to block in the P() operation. This is often unimportant, but in some cases it may be crucial. The UNIX buffer cache, for instance, uses a function called getblk() to look for a particular disk block in the buffer cache. If the desired block is found in the cache, getblk() attempts to lock it by calling P(). If P() were to sleep because the buffer was locked, there is no guarantee that, when awakened, the buffer would contain the same block that it originally had. The thread that had locked the buffer may have reassigned it to some other block. Thus after P() returns, the thread may have locked the wrong buffer. This problem can be solved within the framework of semaphores, but the solution is cumbersome and inefficient, and indicates that other abstractions might be more suitable [Ruan 90].

7.5.5   Convoys

Compared to the traditional sleep/wakeup mechanism, semaphores offer the advantage that processes do not wake up unnecessarily. When a thread wakes up within a P(), it is guaranteed to have the resource. The semantics ensure that the ownership of the semaphore is transferred to the woken up thread before that thread actually runs. If another thread tries to acquire the semaphore in the meantime, it will not be able to do so. This very fact, however, leads to a performance problem called semaphore *convoys* [Lee 87]. A convoy is created when there is frequent contention on a semaphore. Although this can degrade the performance of any locking mechanism, the peculiar semantics of semaphores compound the problem.

Figure 7-7 shows the formation of a convoy. **R1** is a critical region protected by a semaphore. At instant **(a)**, thread **T2** holds the semaphore, while **T3** is waiting to acquire it. **T1** is run-

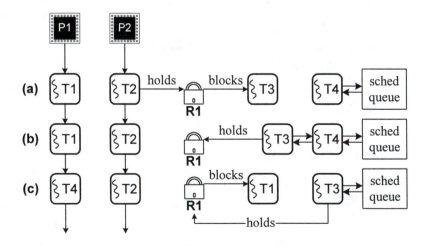

Figure 7-7. Convoy formation.

ning on another processor, and **T4** is waiting to be scheduled. Now suppose **T2** exits the critical region and releases the semaphore. It wakes up **T3** and puts it on the scheduler queue. **T3** now holds the semaphore, as shown in **(b)**.

Now suppose **T1** needs to enter the critical region. Since the semaphore is held by **T3**, **T1** will block, freeing up processor **P1**. The system will schedule thread **T4** to run on **P1**. Hence in **(c)**, **T3** holds the semaphore and **T1** is blocked on it; neither thread can run until **T2** or **T4** yields its processor.

The problem lies in step **(c)**. Although the semaphore has been assigned to **T3**, **T3** is not running and hence is not in the critical region. As a result, **T1** must block on the semaphore even though no thread is in the critical region. The semaphore semantics force allocation in a first-come, first-served order.[2] This forces a number of unnecessary context switches. Suppose the semaphore was replaced by an *exclusive lock,* or *mutex.* Then, in step **(b)**, **T2** would release the lock and wake up **T3**, but **T3** would not own the lock at this point. Consequently, in step **(c)**, **T1** would acquire the lock, eliminating the context switch.

> Note: *Mutex, short for mutual exclusion lock, is a general term that refers to any primitive that enforces exclusive access semantics.*

In general, it is desirable to have a set of inexpensive lower-level primitives instead of a single monolithic higher-level abstraction. This is the trend in the modern multiprocessing kernels, and the following sections examine the low-level mechanisms that together provide a versatile synchronization facility.

7.6   Spin Locks

The simplest locking primitive is a *spin lock*, also called a *simple lock* or a *simple mutex*. If a resource is protected by a spin lock, a thread trying to acquire the resource will *busy-wait* (loop, or spin) until the resource is unlocked. It is usually a scalar variable that is zero if available and one if locked. The variable is manipulated using a busy-wait loop around an atomic test-and-set or similar instruction available on the machine. Example 7-5 shows an implementation of a spin lock. It assumes that `test_and_set()` returns the old value of the object.

```
void spin_lock (spinlock_t *s)  {
    while (test_and_set (s) != 0)      /* already locked */
        ;                              /* loop until successful */
}

void spin_unlock (spinlock_t *s)    { *s = 0; }
```

Example 7-5. Spin lock implementation.

---

[2] Some implementation may choose the thread to wake up based on priority. The effect in this example would be the same.

Even this simple algorithm is flawed. On many processors, `test_and_set()` works by locking the memory bus, so this loop could monopolize the bus and severely degrade system performance. A better approach is to use two loops—if the test fails, the inner loop simply waits for the variable to become zero. The simple test in the inner loop does not require locking the bus. Example 7-6 shows the improved implementation:

```
void spin_lock (spinlock_t *s)
{
    while (test_and_set (s) != 0)    /* already locked */
        while (*s != 0)
            ;                        /* wait until unlocked */
}

void spin_unlock (spinlock_t *s)    { *s = 0; }
```

Example 7-6. Revised spin lock implementation.

7.6.1   Use of Spin Locks

The most important characteristic of spin locks is that a thread ties up a CPU while waiting for the lock to be released. It is essential, then, to hold spin locks only for extremely short durations. In particular, they must not be held across blocking operations. It may also be desirable to block interrupts on the current processor prior to acquiring a spin lock, so as to guarantee low holding time on the lock.

The basic premise of a spin lock is that a thread busy-waits on a resource on one processor while another thread is using the resource on a different processor. This is only possible on a multiprocessor. On a uniprocessor, if a thread tries to acquire a spin lock that is already held, it will loop forever. Multiprocessor algorithms, however, must operate correctly regardless of the number of processors, which means that they should handle the uniprocessor case as well. This requires strict adherence to the rule that threads not relinquish control of the CPU while holding a spin lock. On a uniprocessor, this ensures that a thread will never have to busy-wait on a spin lock.

The major advantage of spin locks is that they are inexpensive. When there is no contention on the lock, both the *lock* and the *unlock* operations typically require only a single instruction each. They are ideal for locking data structures that need to be accessed briefly, such as while removing an item from a doubly linked list or while performing a *load-modify-store* type of operation on a variable. Hence they are used to protect those data structures that do not need protection in a uniprocessor system. They are also used extensively to protect more complex locks, as shown in the following sections. Semaphores, for instance, use a spin lock to guarantee atomicity of their operations, as shown in Example 7-7.

```
spinlock_t list;
spin_lock (&list);
item->forw->back = item->back;
item->back->forw = item->forw;
spin_unlock (&list);
```

Example 7-7. Using a spin lock to access a doubly linked list.

7.7   Condition Variables

A *condition variable* is a more complex mechanism associated with a *predicate* (a logical expression that evaluates to TRUE or FALSE) based on some shared data. It allows threads to block on it and provides facilities to wakeup one or all blocked threads when the result of the predicate changes. It is more useful for waiting on events than for resource locking.

Consider, for example, one or more server threads waiting for client requests. Incoming requests are to be passed to waiting threads or put on a queue if no one is ready to service them. When a server thread is ready to process the next request, it first checks the queue. If there is a pending message, the thread removes it from the queue and services it. If the queue is empty, the thread blocks until a request arrives. This can be implemented by associating a condition variable with this queue. The shared data is the message queue itself, and the predicate is that the queue be nonempty.

The condition variable is similar to a sleep channel in that server threads block on the condition and incoming messages awaken them. On a multiprocessor, however, we need to guard against some race conditions, such as the lost wakeup problem. Suppose a message arrives after a thread checks the queue but before the thread blocks. The thread will block even though a message is available. We therefore need an atomic operation to test the predicate and block the thread if necessary.

Condition variables provide this atomicity by using an additional mutex, usually a spin lock. The mutex protects the shared data, and avoids the lost wakeup problem. The server thread acquires the mutex on the message queue, then checks if the queue is empty. If so, it calls the wait() function of the condition with the spin lock held. The wait() function takes the mutex as an argument and atomically blocks the thread and releases the mutex. When the message arrives on the queue and the thread is woken up, the wait() call reacquires the spin lock before returning. Example 7-8 provides a sample implementation of condition variables:

```
struct condition  {
    proc *next;             /* doubly linked list */
    proc *prev;             /* of blocked threads */
    spinlock_t listLock;    /* protects this list */
};
```

```
void wait (condition *c, spinlock_t *s)
{
    spin_lock (&c->listLock);
    add self to the linked list;
    spin_unlock (&c->listLock);
    spin_unlock (s);          /* release spinlock before blocking */
    swtch();                  /* perform context switch */
    /* When we return from swtch, the event has occurred */
    spin_lock (s);            /* acquire the spin lock again */
    return;
}

void do_signal (condition *c)
/* Wake up one thread waiting on this condition */
{
    spin_lock (&c->listLock);
    remove one thread from linked list, if it is nonempty;
    spin_unlock (&c->listLock);
    if a thread was removed from the list, make it runnable;
    return;
}

void do_broadcast (condition *c)
/* Wake up all threads waiting on this condition */
{
    spin_lock (&c->listLock);
    while (linked list is nonempty)  {
        remove a thread from linked list;
        make it runnable;
    }
    spin_unlock (&c->listLock);
}
```

Example 7-8. Implementation of condition variables.

7.7.1   Implementation Issues

There are a few important points to note. The predicate itself is not part of the condition variable. It must be tested by the calling routine before calling wait(). Further, note that the implementation uses two separate mutexes. One is listLock, which protects the doubly linked list of threads blocked on the condition. The second mutex protects the tested data itself. It is not a part of the condition variable, but is passed as an argument to the wait() function. The swtch() function and the code to make blocked threads runnable may use a third mutex to protect the scheduler queues.

We thus have a situation where a thread tries to acquire one spin lock while holding another. This is not disastrous since the restriction on spin locks is only that threads are not allowed to block while holding one. Deadlocks are avoided by maintaining a strict locking order—the lock on the predicate must be acquired before listLock.

It is not necessary for the queue of blocked threads to be a part of the condition structure itself. Instead, we may have a global set of sleep queues as in traditional UNIX. In that case, the listLock in the condition is replaced by a mutex protecting the appropriate sleep queue. Both methods have their own advantages, as discussed earlier.

One of the major advantages of a condition variable is that it provides two ways to handle event completion. When an event occurs, there is the option of waking up just one thread with do_signal() or all threads with do_broadcast(). Each may be appropriate in different circumstances. In the case of the server application, waking one thread is sufficient, since each request is handled by a single thread. However, consider several threads running the same program, thus sharing a single copy of the program text. More than one of these threads may try to access the same nonresident page of the text, resulting in page faults in each of them. The first thread to fault initiates a disk access for that page. The other threads notice that the read has already been issued and block waiting for the I/O to complete. When the page is read into memory, it is desirable to call do_broadcast() and wake up all the blocked threads, since they can all access the page without conflict.

7.7.2   Events

Frequently, the predicate of the condition is simple. Threads need to wait for a particular task to complete. The completion may be flagged by setting a global variable. This situation may be better expressed by a higher-level abstraction called an *event* that combines a *done* flag, the spin lock protecting it, and the condition variable into a single object. The event object presents a simple interface, allowing two basic operations—awaitDone() and setDone(). awaitDone() blocks until the event occurs, while setDone() marks the event as having occurred and wakes up all threads blocked on it. In addition, the interface may support a nonblocking testDone() function and a reset() function, which once again marks the event as not done. In some cases, the boolean *done* flag may be replaced by a variable that returns more descriptive completion information when the event occurs.

7.7.3   Blocking Locks

Often, a resource must be locked for a long period of time and the thread holding this lock must be permitted to block on other events. Thus a thread that needs the resource cannot afford to spin until the resource becomes available, and must block instead. This requires a *blocking lock* primitive that offers two basic operations—lock() and unlock()—and optionally, a tryLock(). Again there are two objects to synchronize—the *locked* flag on the resource and the sleep queue—which means that we need a spin lock to guarantee atomicity of the operations. Such locks may be trivially implemented using condition variables, with the predicate being the clearing of the locked flag. For performance reasons, blocking locks might be provided as fundamental primitives. In particular, if each resource has its own sleep queue, a single spin lock might protect both the flag and the queue.

7.8   Read-Write Locks

Although modification of a resource requires exclusive access, it is usually acceptable to allow several threads to simultaneously read the shared data, as long as no one is trying to write to it at that time. This requires a complex lock that permits both shared and exclusive modes of access. Such a facility may be built on top of simple locks and conditions [Birr 89]. Before we look at an implementation, let us examine the desired semantics. A read-write lock may permit either a single writer or multiple readers. The basic operations are lockShared(), lockExclusive(), unlockShared() and unlockExclusive(). In addition, there might be tryLockShared() and tryLockExclusive(), which return FALSE instead of blocking, and also upgrade() and downgrade(), which convert a shared lock to exclusive and vice versa. A lockShared() operation must block if there is an exclusive lock present, whereas lockExclusive() must block if there is either an exclusive or shared lock on the resource.

7.8.1   Design Considerations

What should a thread do when releasing a lock? The traditional UNIX solution is to wake up all threads waiting for the resource. This is clearly inefficient—if a writer acquires the lock next, other readers and writers will have to go back to sleep; if a reader acquires the lock, other writers will have to go back to sleep. It is preferable to find a protocol that avoids needless wakeups.

If a reader releases a resource, it takes no action if other readers are still active. When the last active reader releases its shared lock, it must wake up a single waiting writer.

When a writer releases its lock, it must choose whether to wake up another writer or the other readers (assuming both readers and writers are waiting). If writers are given preference, the readers could starve indefinitely under heavy contention. The preferred solution is to wake up all waiting readers when releasing an exclusive lock. If there are no waiting readers, we wake up a single waiting writer.

This scheme can lead to writer starvation. If there is a constant stream of readers, they will keep the resource read-locked, and the writer will never acquire the lock. To avoid this situation, a lockShared() request must block if there is any waiting writer, even though the resource is currently only read-locked. Such a solution, under heavy contention, will alternate access between individual writers and batches of readers.

The upgrade() function must be careful to avoid deadlocks. A deadlock can occur unless the implementation takes care to give preference to upgrade requests over waiting writers. If two threads try to upgrade a lock, each would block since the other holds a shared lock. One way to avoid that is for upgrade() to release the shared lock before blocking if it cannot get the exclusive lock immediately. This results in additional problems for the user, since another thread could have modified the object before upgrade() returns. Another solution is for upgrade() to fail and release the shared lock if there is another pending upgrade.

7.8.2   Implementation

Example 7-9 implements a read-write lock facility:

```
struct rwlock    {
    int nActive;        /* num of active readers, or -1 if a writer is active */
    int nPendingReads;
    int nPendingWrites;
    spinlock_t sl;
    condition canRead;
    condition canWrite;
};

void lockShared (struct rwlock *r)
{
    spin_lock (&r->sl);
    r->nPendingReads++;
    if (r->nPendingWrites > 0)
        wait (&r->canRead, &r->sl); /* don't starve writers */
    while (r->nActive < 0)          /* someone has exclusive lock */
        wait (&r->canRead, &r->sl);
    r->nActive++;
    r->nPendingReads--;
    spin_unlock (&r->sl);
}

void unlockShared (struct rwlock *r)
{
    spin_lock (&r->sl);
    r->nActive--;
    if (r->nActive == 0)     {         /* no other readers */
        spin_unlock (&r->sl);
        do_signal (&r->canWrite);
    } else
        spin_unlock (&r->sl);
}

void lockExclusive (struct rwlock *r)
{
    spin_lock (&r->sl);
    r->nPendingWrites++;
    while (r->nActive)
        wait (&r->canWrite, &r->sl);
    r->nPendingWrites--;
```

```
    r->nActive = -1;
    spin_unlock (&r->sl);
}

void unlockExclusive (struct rwlock *r)
{
    boolean_t wakeReaders;
    spin_lock (&r->sl);
    r->nActive = 0;
    wakeReaders = (r->nPendingReads != 0);
    spin_unlock (&r->sl);
    if (wakeReaders)
        do_broadcast (&r->canRead); /* wake all readers */
    else
        do_signal (&r->canWrite);   /* wake a single writer */
}

void downgrade (struct rwlock *r)
{
    boolean_t wakeReaders;
    spin_lock (&r->sl);
    r->nActive = 1;
    wakeReaders = (r->nPendingReads != 0);
    spin_unlock (&r->sl);
    if (wakeReaders)
        do_broadcast (&r->canRead); /* wake all readers */
}

void upgrade (struct rwlock *r)
{
    spin_lock (&r->sl);
    if (r->nActive == 1) {            /* no other reader */
        r->nActive = -1;
    } else {
        r->nPendingWrites++;
        r->nActive--;                 /* release shared lock */
        while (r->nActive)
            wait (&r->canWrite, &r->sl);
        r->nPendingWrites--;
        r->nActive = -1;
    }
    spin_unlock (&r->sl);
}
```

Example 7-9. Implementation of read-write locks.

7.9 Reference Counts

Although a lock may protect the data inside an object, we frequently need another mechanism to protect the object itself. Many kernel objects are dynamically allocated and deallocated. If a thread deallocates such an object, other threads have no way of knowing it and may try to access the object using a direct pointer (which they earlier acquired) to it. In the meantime, the kernel could have reallocated the memory to a different object, leading to severe system corruption.

If a thread has a pointer to an object, it expects the pointer to be valid until the thread relinquishes it. The kernel can guarantee it by associating a reference count with each such object. The kernel sets the count to one when it first allocates the object (thus generating the first pointer). It increments the count each time it generates a new pointer to the object.

This way, when a thread gets a pointer to an object, it really acquires a reference to it. It is the thread's responsibility to release the reference when no longer needed, at which time the kernel decrements the object's reference count. When the count reaches zero, no thread has a valid reference to the object, and the kernel may deallocate the object.

For example, the file system maintains reference counts for *vnodes*, which hold information about active files (see Section 8.7). When a user opens a file, the kernel returns a file descriptor, which constitutes a reference to the vnode. The user passes the descriptor to subsequent *read* and *write* system calls, allowing the kernel to access the file quickly without repeated name translations. When the user closes the file, the reference is released. If several users have the same file open, they reference the same vnode. When the last user closes the file, the kernel can deallocate the vnode.

The previous example shows that reference counts are useful in a uniprocessor system as well. They are even more essential for multiprocessors, since without proper reference counting, a thread may deallocate an object while a thread on another processor is actively accessing it.

7.10 Other Considerations

There are several other factors to consider in the design of a complex locking facility and the way in which the locks are used. This section examines some important issues.

7.10.1 Deadlock Avoidance

It is often necessary for a thread to hold locks on multiple resources. For instance, the implementation of condition variables described in Section 7.7 uses two mutexes: one protects the data and predicate of the condition, while the other protects the linked list of threads blocked on the condition. Trying to acquire multiple locks lead to a deadlock, as illustrated in Figure 7-8. Thread **T1** holds resource **R1** and tries to acquire resource **R2**. At the same time, thread **T2** may be holding **R2** and trying to acquire **R1**. Neither thread can make progress.

The two common deadlock avoidance techniques are *hierarchical locking* and *stochastic locking*. Hierarchical locking imposes an order on related locks and requires that all threads take locks in the same order. In the case of condition variables, for instance, a thread must lock the condition's predicate before locking the linked list. As long as the ordering is strictly followed, deadlock cannot occur.

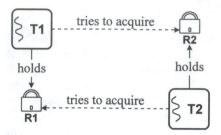

Figure 7-8. Possible deadlock when using spin locks.

There are situations in which the ordering must be violated. Consider a buffer cache implementation that maintains disk block buffers on a doubly linked list, sorted in *least recently used (LRU)* order. All buffers that are not actively in use are on the LRU list. A single spin lock protects both the queue header and the forward and backward pointers in the buffers on that queue. Each buffer also has a spin lock to protect the other information in the buffer. This lock must be held while the buffer is actively in use.

When a thread wants a particular disk block, it locates the buffer (using hash queues or other pointers not relevant to this discussion) and locks it. It then locks the LRU list in order to remove the buffer from it. Thus the normal locking order is *"first the buffer, then the list."*

Sometimes a thread simply wants any free buffer and tries to get it from the head of the LRU list. It first locks the list, then locks the first buffer on the list and removes it from the list. This, however, reverses the locking order, since it locks the list before the buffer.

It is easy to see how a deadlock can occur. One thread locks the buffer at the head of the list and tries to lock the list. At the same time, another thread that has locked the list tries to lock the buffer at the head. Each will block waiting for the other to release the lock.

The kernel uses stochastic locking to handle this situation. When a thread attempts to acquire a lock that would violate the hierarchy, it uses a `try_lock()` operation instead of `lock()`. This function attempts to acquire the lock, but returns failure instead of blocking if the lock is already held. In this example, the thread that wants to get any free buffer will lock the list and then go down the list, using `try_lock()` until it finds a buffer it can lock. Example 7-10 describes an implementation of `try_lock()` for spin locks:

```
int try_lock (spinlock_t *s)
{
    if (test_and_set (s) != 0)    /* already locked */
        return FAILURE;
    else
        return SUCCESS;
}
```

Example 7-10. Implementation of `try_lock()`.

7.10.2   Recursive Locks

A lock is recursive if an attempt by a thread to acquire a lock it already owns would succeed without blocking. Why is this a desirable feature? Why should a thread attempt to lock something it has already locked? The typical scenario has a thread locking a resource, then calling a lower-level routine to perform some operation on it. This lower-level routine may also be used by other higher-level routines that do not lock the resource prior to calling it. Thus the lower-level routine does not know if the resource is already locked. If it tries to lock the resource, a single process deadlock may occur.

Such a situation can, of course, be avoided by explicitly informing the lower-level routine about the lock via an extra argument. This, however, breaks many existing interfaces and is awkward, since sometimes the lower routine may be several function calls down. The resulting interfaces would be extremely nonmodular. An alternative is to allow the locks to be recursive. This adds some overhead, since the lock must now store some sort of owner ID and check it any time it would normally block or deny a request. More important, it allows functions to deal only with their own locking requirements, without worrying about which locks its callers hold, resulting in clean, modular interfaces.

One example when such a lock is used is directory writes in the BSD file system (ufs). The routine `ufs_write()` handles writes to both files and directories. Requests for file writes usually access the file through the file table entry, which directly gives a pointer to the file's *vnode*. Thus the vnode is passed on directly to `ufs_write()`, which is responsible for locking it. For a directory write, however, the directory vnode is acquired by the pathname traversal routine, which returns the vnode in a locked state. When `ufs_write()` is called for this node, it will deadlock if the lock is not recursive.

7.10.3   To Block or to Spin

Most complex locks can be implemented as blocking locks or as complex spin locks, without impacting their functionality or interface. Consider an object that is protected by a complex lock (such as a semaphore or a read-write lock). In most of the implementations described in this chapter, if a thread tries to acquire the object and finds it locked, the thread blocks until the object is released. The thread could just as easily busy-wait and still preserve the semantics of the lock.

The choice between blocking and busy-waiting is often dictated by performance considerations. Since busy-waiting ties up a processor, it is generally frowned upon. However, certain situations mandate busy-waiting. If the thread already holds a simple mutex, it is not allowed to block. If the thread tries to acquire another simple mutex, it will busy-wait; if it tries to acquire a complex lock, it will release the mutex it already holds (such as with conditions).

Sleep and wakeup, however, are expensive operations themselves, involving one context switch at each end and manipulating sleep and scheduler queues. Just as it is preposterous to do a busy-wait on a lock for an extended period of time, it is inefficient to sleep on a resource that is likely to be available soon.

Moreover, some resources may be subject to short-term or long-term locking, depending on the situation. For instance, the kernel may keep a partial list of free disk blocks in memory. When this list becomes empty, it must be replenished from disk. In most instances, the list needs to be locked briefly while adding or removing entries to it in memory. When disk I/O is required, the list must be locked for a long time. Thus neither a spin lock nor a blocking lock is by itself a good solution. One alternative is to provide two locks, with the blocking lock being used only when the list is being replenished. It is preferable, however, to have a more flexible locking primitive.

These issues can be effectively addressed by storing a hint in the lock that suggests whether contending threads should spin or block. The hint is set by the owner of the lock and examined whenever an attempt to acquire the lock does not immediately succeed. The hint may be either advisory or mandatory.

An alternative solution is provided by the *adaptive locks* of Solaris 2.*x* [Eykh 92]. When a thread **T1** tries to acquire an adaptive lock held by another thread **T2**, it checks to see if **T2** is currently active on any processor. As long as **T2** is active, **T1** executes a busy-wait. If **T2** is blocked, **T1** blocks as well.

7.10.4   What to Lock

A lock can protect several things—data, predicates, invariants, or operations. Reader-writer locks, for example, protect data. Condition variables are associated with predicates. An invariant is similar to a predicate but has slightly different semantics. When a lock protects an invariant, it means that the invariant is TRUE except when the lock is held. For instance, a linked list might use a single lock while adding or removing elements. The invariant protected by this lock is that the list is in a consistent state.

Finally, a lock can control access to an operation or function. This restricts the execution of that code to at most one processor at a time, even if different data structures are involved. The *monitors* model of synchronization [Hoar 74] is based on this approach. Many UNIX variants use a master processor for unparallelized (not multiprocessor-safe) portions of the kernel, thus serializing access to such code. This approach usually leads to severe bottlenecks and should be avoided if possible.

7.10.5   Granularity and Duration

System performance depends greatly on the locking granularity. At one extreme, some asymmetric multiprocessing systems run all kernel code on the master processor, thus having a single lock for the whole kernel.[3] At the other extreme, a system could use extremely fine-grained locking with a separate lock for each data variable. Clearly, that is not the ideal solution either. The locks would consume a large amount of memory, performance would suffer due to the overhead of constantly acquiring and releasing locks, and the chances of deadlock would increase because it is difficult to enforce a locking order for such a large number of objects.

The ideal solution, as usual, lies somewhere in between, and there is no consensus on what it is. Proponents of coarse-granularity locking [Sink 88] suggest starting with a small number of locks to protect major subsystems and adding finer granularity locks only where the system exhibits a

---

[3] Sometimes, even SMP systems use a master processor to run code that is not multiprocessor-safe. This is known as *funneling*.

bottleneck. Systems such as Mach, however, use a fine-grained locking structure and associate locks with individual data objects.

Locking duration, too, must be carefully examined. It is best to hold the lock for as short a time as possible, so as to minimize contention on it. Sometimes, however, this may result in extra locking and unlocking. Suppose a thread needs to perform two operations on an object, both requiring a lock on it. In between the two operations, the thread needs to do some unrelated work. It could unlock the object after the first operation and lock it again for the second one. It might be better, instead, to keep the object locked the whole time, provided that the unrelated work is fairly short. Such decisions must be made on a case-by-case basis.

7.11 Case Studies

The primitives described in Sections 7.5–7.8 constitute a kind of grab bag from which an operating system can mix and match to provide a comprehensive synchronization interface. This section examines the synchronization facilities in the major multiprocessing variants of UNIX.

7.11.1 SVR4.2/MP

SVR4.2/MP is the multiprocessor version of SVR4.2. It provides four types of locks—basic locks, sleep locks, read-write locks, and synchronization variables [UNIX 92]. Each lock must be explicitly allocated and deallocated through *xxx*_ALLOC and *xxx*_DEALLOC operations, where *xxx*_ is the type-specific prefix. The allocation operation takes arguments that are used for debugging.

Basic Locks

The basic lock is a nonrecursive mutex lock that allows short-term locking of resources. It may not be held across a blocking operation. It is implemented as a variable of type lock_t. It is locked and unlocked by the following operations:

```
pl_t LOCK (lock_t *lockp, pl_t new_ipl);
UNLOCK (lock_t *lockp, pl_t old_ipl);
```

The LOCK call raises the interrupt priority level to new_ipl before acquiring the lock and returns the previous priority level. This value must be passed to the UNLOCK operation, so that it may restore the *ipl* to the old level.

Read-Write Locks

A *read-write lock* is a nonrecursive lock that allows short-term locking with single-writer, multiple-reader semantics. It may not be held across a blocking operation. It is implemented as a variable of type rwlock_t and provides the following operations:

```
pl_t RW_RDLOCK (rwlock_t *lockp, pl_t new_ipl);
pl_t RW_WRLOCK (rwlock_t *lockp, pl_t new_ipl);
void RW_UNLOCK (rwlock_t *lockp, pl_t old_ipl);
```

The treatment of interrupt priorities is identical to that for basic locks. The locking operations raise the *ipl* to the specified level and return the previous *ipl*. RW_UNLOCK restores the *ipl* to the old level. The lock also provides nonblocking operations RW_TRYRDLOCK and RW_TRYWRLOCK.

Sleep Locks

A *sleep lock* is a nonrecursive mutex lock that permits long-term locking of resources. It may be held across a blocking operation. It is implemented as a variable of type sleep_t, and provides the following operations:

```
void SLEEP_LOCK (sleep_t *lockp, int pri);
bool_t SLEEP_LOCK_SIG (sleep_t *lockp, int pri);
void SLEEP_UNLOCK (sleep_t *lockp);
```

The pri parameter specifies the scheduling priority to assign to the process after it awakens. If a process blocks on a call to SLEEP_LOCK, it will not be interrupted by a signal. If it blocks on a call to SLEEP_LOCK_SIG, a signal will interrupt the process; the call returns TRUE if the lock is acquired, and FALSE if the sleep was interrupted. The lock also provides other operations, such as SLEEP_LOCK_AVAIL (checks if lock is available), SLEEP_LOCKOWNED (checks if caller owns the lock), and SLEEP_TRYLOCK (returns failure instead of blocking if lock cannot be acquired).

Synchronization Variables

A *synchronization variable* is identical to the *condition variables* discussed in Section 7.7. It is implemented as a variable of type sv_t, and its predicate, which is managed separately by users of the lock, must be protected by a basic lock. It supports the following operations:

```
void SV_WAIT (sv_t *svp, int pri, lock_t *lockp);
bool_t SV_WAIT_SIG (sv_t *svp, int pri, lock_t *lockp);
void SV_SIGNAL (sv_t *svp, int flags);
void SV_BROADCAST (sv_t *svp, int flags);
```

As in sleep locks, the pri argument specifies the scheduling priority to assign to the process after it wakes up, and SV_WAIT_SIG allows interruption by a signal. The lockp argument is used to pass a pointer to the basic lock protecting the predicate of the condition. The caller must hold lockp before calling SV_WAIT or SV_WAIT_SIG. The kernel atomically blocks the caller and releases lockp. When the caller returns from SV_WAIT or SV_WAIT_SIG, lockp is not held. The predicate is not guaranteed to be true when the caller runs after blocking. Hence the call to SV_WAIT or SV_WAIT_SIG should be enclosed in a while loop that checks the predicate each time.

7.11.2 Digital UNIX

The Digital UNIX synchronization primitives are derived from those of Mach. There are two types of locks—simple and complex [Denh 94]. A simple lock is a basic spin lock, implemented using the atomic test-and-set instruction of the machine. It must be declared and initialized before being used.

It is initialized to the unlocked state and cannot be held across blocking operations or context switches.

The complex lock is a single high-level abstraction supporting a number of features, such as shared and exclusive access, blocking, and recursive locking. It is a reader-writer lock and provides two options—*sleep* and *recursive*. The sleep option can be enabled or disabled while initializing the lock or at any later time. If set, the kernel will block requesters if the lock cannot be granted immediately. Further, the sleep option must be set if a thread wishes to block while holding the lock. The recursive option can be set only by a thread that has acquired the lock for exclusive use; it can be cleared only by the same thread that set the option.

The interface provides nonblocking versions of various routines, which return failure if the lock cannot be acquired immediately. There are also functions to upgrade (shared to exclusive) or downgrade (exclusive to shared). The upgrade routine will release the shared lock and return failure if there is another pending upgrade request. The nonblocking version of upgrade returns failure but does not drop the shared lock in this situation.

Sleep and Wakeup

Since a lot of code was ported from 4BSD, it was desirable to retain the basic functions of `sleep()` and `wakeup()`. Thus blocked threads were put on global sleep queues rather than per-lock queues. The algorithms needed modification to work correctly on multiprocessors, and the chief issue here was the lost wakeup problem. To fix this while retaining the framework of thread states, the `sleep()` function was rewritten using two lower-level primitives—`assert_wait()` and `thread_block()`, as shown in Figure 7-9.

Suppose a thread needs to wait for an event that is described by a predicate and a spin lock that protects it. The thread acquires the spin lock and then tests the predicate. If the thread needs to

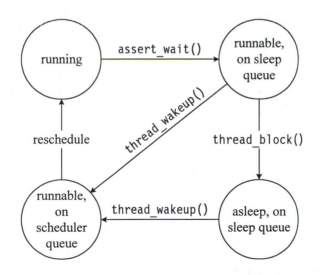

Figure 7-9. Sleep implementation in Digital UNIX.

block, it calls `assert_wait()`, which puts it on the appropriate sleep queue. It then releases the spin lock and calls `thread_block()` to initiate a context switch. If the event occurs between the release of the spin lock and the context switch, the kernel will remove the thread from the sleep queue and put it on the scheduler queue. Thus the thread does not lose the wakeup.

7.11.3   Other Implementations

The initial multiprocessing version of SVR4 was developed at NCR [Camp 91]. This version introduced the concept of *advisory processor locks* (APLs), which are recursive locks containing a *hint* for contending threads. The hint specifies if contending threads should spin or sleep, and whether the hint is advisory or mandatory. The thread owning the lock may change the hint from sleep to spin or vice versa. Such APLs may not be held across calls to sleep and are used mainly to single-thread the access to longer-term locks. The distinctive feature of APLs is that they are automatically released and reacquired across a context switch. This means that the traditional sleep/wakeup interface can be used without change. Further, locks of the same class can avoid deadlock by sleeping, since the sleep releases all previously held locks. The implementation also provided nonrecursive spin locks and read-write APLs.

The NCR version was modified by the Intel Multiprocessor Consortium, formed by a group of companies to develop the official multiprocessing release of SVR4 [Peac 92]. One important change involved the function that acquires an APL lock. This function now also takes an interrupt priority level as an argument. This allows raising of the processor priority around the holding of the lock. If the lock cannot be granted immediately, the busy-wait occurs at the original (lower) priority. The function returns the original priority, which can be passed to the unlocking function.

The lowest-level primitives are a set of atomic arithmetic and logical operations. The arithmetic operations allow atomic incrementing and decrementing of reference counts. The logical functions are used for fine-grained multithreading of bit manipulations of flag fields. They all return the original value of the variable on which they operate. At the next higher level are simple spin locks that are not released automatically on context switches. These are used for simple operations like queue insertion or removal. The highest-level locks are *resource locks*. Resource locks are long-term locks with single-writer, multiple-reader semantics, which may be held across blocking operations. The implementation also provides synchronous and asynchronous *cross-processor interrupts*, which are used for operations such as *clock tick distribution* and *address translation cache coherency* (see Section 15.9).

Solaris 2.*x* uses adaptive locks (see Section 7.10.3) and turnstiles (see Section 7.2.3) for better performance. It provides semaphores, reader-writer locks, and condition variables as high-level synchronization objects. It also uses kernel threads to handle interrupts, so that interrupt handlers use the same synchronization primitives as the rest of the kernel and block if necessary. Section 3.6.5 discusses this feature in greater detail.

Every known multiprocessor implementation uses some form of spin locks for low-level short-term synchronization. The sleep/wakeup mechanism is usually retained, perhaps with some changes, to avoid rewriting a lot of code. The major differences are in the choice of the higher-level abstractions. The early implementations on the IBM/370 and the AT&T 3B20A [Bach 84] relied exclusively on semaphores. Ultrix [Sink 88] uses blocking exclusive locks. Amdahl's UTS kernel

[Ruan 90] is based on conditions. DG/UX [Kell 89] uses *indivisible event counters* to implement *sequenced locks*, which provide a somewhat different way of waking one process at a time.

7.12   Summary

Synchronization problems on a multiprocessor are intrinsically different from and more complex than those on a uniprocessor. There are a number of different solutions, such as sleep/wakeup, conditions, events, read-write locks, and semaphores. These primitives are more similar than different, and it is possible, for example, to implement semaphores on top of conditions and vice-versa. Many of these solutions are not limited to multiprocessors and may also be applied to synchronization problems on uniprocessors or on loosely coupled distributed systems. Many multiprocessing UNIX systems are based on existing uniprocessing variants and, for these, porting considerations strongly influence the decision of which abstraction to use. Mach and Mach-based systems are mainly free of these considerations, which is reflected in their choice of primitives.

7.13   Exercises

1. Many systems have a swap-atomic instruction that swaps the value of a register with that of a memory location. Show how such an instruction may be used to implement an atomic test-and-set.

2. How can an atomic test-and-set be implemented on a machine using load-linked and store-conditional?

3. Suppose a convoy forms due to heavy contention on a critical region that is protected by a semaphore. If the region could be divided into two critical regions, each protected by a separate semaphore, would it reduce the convoy problem?

4. One way to eliminate a convoy is to replace the semaphore with another locking mechanism. Could this risk starvation of threads?

5. How is a reference count different from a shared lock?

6. Implement a blocking lock on a resource, using a spin lock and a condition variable, with a locked flag as the predicate (see Section 7.7.3).

7. In exercise 6, is it necessary to hold the spin lock protecting the predicate while clearing the flag? [Ruan 90] discusses a `waitlock()` operation that can improve this algorithm.

8. How do condition variables avoid the lost wakeup problem?

9. Implement an *event* abstraction that returns a status value to waiting threads upon event completion.

10. Suppose an object is accessed frequently for reading or writing. In what situations is it better to protect it with a simple mutex, rather than with a read-write lock?

11. Does a read-write lock have to be blocking? Implement a read-write lock that causes threads to busy-wait if the resoure is locked.

12. Describe a situation in which a deadlock may be avoided by making the locking granularity *finer*.

13. Describe a situation in which a deadlock may be avoided by making the locking granularity *coarser*.

14. Is it necessary for a multiprocessor kernel to lock each variable or resource before accessing it? Enumerate the kinds of situations where a thread may access or modify an object without locking it.

15. Monitors [Hoar 74] are language-supported constructs providing mutual exclusion to a region of code. For what sort of situations do they form a natural solution?

16. Implement `upgrade()` and `downgrade()` functions to the read-write lock implementation in Section 7.8.2.

7.14   References

[Bach 84]   Bach, M., and Buroff, S., "Multiprocessor UNIX Operating Systems," *AT&T Bell Laboratories Technical Journal,* Vol. 63, Oct. 1984, pp. 1733–1749.

[Birr 89]   Birrell, A.D., "An Introduction to Programming with Threads," Digital Equipment Corporation Systems Research Center, 1989.

[Camp 91]   Campbell, M., Barton, R., Browning, J., Cervenka, D., Curry, B., Davis, T., Edmonds, T., Holt, R., Slice, R., Smith, T., and Wescott, R., "The Parallelization of UNIX System V Release 4.0," *Proceedings of the Winter 1991 USENIX Conference,* Jan. 1991, pp. 307–323.

[Denh 94]   Denham, J.M., Long, P., and Woodward, J.A., "DEC OSF/1 Version 3.0 Symmetric Multiprocessing Implementation," *Digital Technical Journal,* Vol. 6, No. 3, Summer 1994, pp. 29–54.

[Digi 87]   Digital Equipment Corporation, *VAX Architecture Reference Manual,* 1984.

[Dijk 65]   Dijkstra, E.W., "Solution of a Problem in Concurrent Programming Control," *Communications of the ACM,* Vol. 8, Sep. 1965, pp. 569–578.

[Eykh 92]   Eykholt, J.R., Kleinman, S.R., Barton, S., Faulkner, R., Shivalingiah, A., Smith, M., Stein, D., Voll, J., Weeks, M., and Williams, D., "Beyond Multiprocessing: Multithreading the SunOS Kernel," *Proceedings of the Summer 1992 USENIX Conference,* Jun. 1992, pp. 11–18.

[Gobl 81]   Goble, G.H., "A Dual-Processor VAX 11/780," *USENIX Association Conference Proceedings,* Sep. 1981.

[Hoar 74]   Hoare, C. A.R., "Monitors: An Operating System Structuring Concept," *Communications of the ACM,* Vol. 17, Oct. 1974, pp.549–557.

[Hitz 90]   Hitz, D., Harris, G., Lau, J.K., and Schwartz, A.M., "Using UNIX as One Component of a Lightweight Distributed Kernel for Multiprocessor File Servers," *Proceedings of the Winter 1990 USENIX Technical Conference,* Jan. 1990, pp. 285–295.

[Kell 89]   Kelley, M.H., "Multiprocessor Aspects of the DG/UX Kernel," *Proceedings of the Winter 1989 USENIX Conference,* Jan. 1989, pp. 85–99.

[Lee 87]   Lee, T.P., and Luppi, M.W., "Solving Performance Problems on a Multiprocessor UNIX System," *Proceedings of the Summer 1987 USENIX Conference,* Jun. 1987, pp. 399–405.

[Nati 84]   National Semiconductor Corporation, *Series 32000 Instruction Set Reference Manual,* 1984.

[Peac 92]   Peacock, J.K., Saxena, S., Thomas, D., Yang, F., and Yu, F., "Experiences from Multithreading System V Release 4," *The Third USENIX Symposium of Experiences with Distributed and Multiprocessor Systems (SEDMS III),* Mar. 1992, pp. 77–91.

[Ruan 90]   Ruane, L.M., "Process Synchronization in the UTS Kernel," *Computing Systems,* Vol. 3, Summer 1990, pp. 387–421.

[Sink 88]   Sinkewicz, U., "A Strategy for SMP ULTRIX," *Proceedings of the Summer 1988 USENIX Technical Conference,* Jun. 1988, pp. 203–212.

[UNIX 92]   UNIX System Laboratories, *Device Driver Reference—UNIX SVR4.2,* UNIX Press, Prentice-Hall, Englewood Cliffs, NJ, 1992.

8

File System Interface and Framework

8.1 Introduction

The operating system must provide facilities for persistent storage and management of data. In UNIX, the *file* abstraction acts as a container for data, and the *file system* allows users to organize, manipulate, and access different files. This chapter describes the interface between the file system and user applications, as well as the framework used by the kernel to support different kinds of file systems. Chapters 9, 10, and 11 describe several different file system implementations that allow users to access data on local and remote machines.

The file system interface comprises the system calls and utilities that allow user programs to operate on files. This interface has remained fairly stable over the years, changing incrementally and in compatible ways. The file system framework, however, has been overhauled completely. The initial framework supported only one type of file system. All files were local to the machine and were stored on one or more disks physically connected to the system. This has been replaced by the *vnode/vfs interface,* which allows multiple file system types, both local and remote, to coexist on the same machine.

The early commercially released versions of UNIX contained a simple file system now known as the System V file system *(s5fs)* [Thom 78]. All versions of System V UNIX, as well as Berkeley UNIX versions earlier than 4.2BSD, support this file system. 4.2BSD introduced a new, Fast File System (FFS) [McKu 84], which provides much better performance and greater functionality than *s5fs*. FFS has since gained wide acceptance, culminating in its inclusion in SVR4. Chapter 9 describes both *s5fs* and FFS, as well as some special-purpose file systems based on the vnode/vfs interface.

> **Note:** The terms **FFS** and **ufs** (UNIX file system) are often used inter-changeably. To be specific, FFS refers to the original implementation of the Berkeley Fast File System. The term ufs refers to the implementation of FFS within the vnode/vfs framework. In this book, we use the two terms in this manner.

As it became easy to connect computers through a network, developers began to find ways to access files on remote nodes. The mid-1980s saw the emergence of several competing technologies that provided transparent file sharing among interconnected computers. Chapter 10 describes the three most important alternatives—the Network File System (NFS), Remote File Sharing (RFS), and the Andrew File System (AFS).

In recent years, several new file systems have been developed that improve upon FFS or address the needs of specific applications. Most use sophisticated techniques such as journaling, snapshots, and volume management to provide better performance, reliability, and availability. Chapter 11 describes some of these modern file systems.

8.2 The User Interface to Files

The UNIX kernel allows user processes to interact with the file system through a well-defined, procedural interface. This interface encapsulates the user's view of the file system and specifies the behavior and semantics of all relevant system calls. The interface exports a small number of abstractions to the user: *files, directories, file descriptors,* and *file systems*.

As mentioned earlier, there are several different types of file systems, such as *s5fs* and FFS. Each implements the same interface, thus providing applications with a consistent view of all files. Each file system may impose its own limitations on certain aspects of the interface. For instance, the *s5fs* file system allows at most 14 characters in a file name, whereas FFS allows as many as 255 characters.

8.2.1 Files and Directories

A *file* is logically a container for data. Users may create a file and store data by writing it to the file. A file permits both sequential and random access to its data. The kernel provides several control operations to name, organize, and control access to files. The kernel does not interpret the content or structure of a file. It regards the file simply as a collection of bytes and provides byte-stream access to its contents. Some applications require more complex semantics such as record-based or indexed access. They are free to devise their own mechanisms on top of the kernel's primitives.

From a user's perspective, UNIX organizes files in a hierarchical, tree-structured name space (Figure 8-1). The tree consists of files and directories, with the files at the leaf nodes.[1] A directory contains name information about files and other directories that reside in it. Each file or directory name may contain any ASCII characters except for '/' and the NULL character. The file system may impose a limit on the length of a filename. The root directory is called "/". Filenames only need to be unique within a directory. In Figure 8-1, both the **bin** and **etc** directories have a file called **passwd**. To uniquely identify a file, it is necessary to specify its complete *pathname*. The pathname is composed of all the components in the path from the root directory to the node, separated by '/' characters. Hence the two **passwd** files have the same filename, but different pathnames—**/bin/passwd** and **/etc/passwd**. The '/' character in UNIX serves both as the name of the root directory and as a pathname component separator.

UNIX supports the notion of a *current working directory* for each process, maintained as part of the process state. This allows users to refer to files by their *relative pathnames,* which are interpreted relative to the current directory. There are two special pathname components: the first is ".", which refers to the directory itself; the second is "..", which refers to the parent directory. The root directory has no parent, and its ".." component refers to the root directory itself. In Figure 8-1, a user whose current directory is **/usr/local** may refer to the **lib** directory either as **/usr/lib** *(absolute pathname)* or as **../lib** (relative pathname). A process may change its current directory by making the *chdir* system call.

A directory entry for a file is called a *hard link,* or simply a *link,* to that file. Any file may have one or more links to it, either in the same or in different directories. Thus a file is not bound to a single directory and does not have a unique name. The name is not an attribute of the file. The file continues to exist as long as its link count is greater than zero. The file links are equal in all ways and are simply different names for the same file. The file may be accessed through any of its links, and there is no way to tell which is the original link. Modern UNIX file systems also provide another type of link called a *symbolic link,* described in Section 8.4.1.

Each different type of file system has its own internal directory format. Since application programmers want to read the contents of directories in a portable way, the POSIX.1 standard

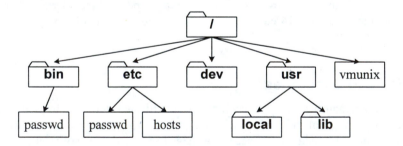

Figure 8-1. Files are organized in a directory tree.

---

[1] The existence of hard links means the correct abstraction is a *directed acyclic graph* (ignoring the ".." entries that refer back to the parent directory), but for most practical purposes the tree abstraction is simpler and just as adequate.

specifies the following standard library routines to operate on directories:

```
dirp = opendir (const char *filename);
direntp = readdir (dirp);
rewinddir (dirp);
status = closedir (dirp);
```

These routines were first introduced in 4BSD and are now supported by SVR4 and most commercial variants. When the user calls *opendir,* the library associates a directory stream with it and returns a stream handle to the user. The stream object maintains an offset to the next entry to be read. Each *readdir* call returns a single directory entry and advances the offset. The entries are returned in file-system-independent format, defined by the following structure:

```
struct dirent   {
    ino_t d_ino;                  /* inode number (see Section 8.2.2) */
    char  d_name[NAME_MAX + 1]; /* null-terminated filename */
};
```

The value of NAME_MAX depends on the file system type. SVR4 also provides a *getdents* system call to read directory entries in file-system-independent format. The format of entries returned by *getdents* is different from that of struct dirent. Hence users should use the more portable POSIX functions wherever possible.

8.2.2   File Attributes

Apart from the file name, the file system maintains a set of attributes for each file. These attributes are stored not in the directory entry, but in an on-disk structure typically called an *inode*. The word *inode* is derived from *index node*. The exact format and contents of the inode are not the same for all file systems. The *stat* and *fstat* system calls return the file's attributes in a filesystem-independent format. The commonly supported attributes of a file include the following:

- File type — Besides regular files, UNIX recognizes several special types of files including directories, FIFOs (first-in, first-out files), symbolic links, and special files that represent block or character devices.
- Number of hard links to the file.
- File size in bytes.
- Device ID — Identifies the device on which the file is located.
- Inode number — There is a single inode associated with each file or directory regardless of how many links it has. Each inode on a given disk partition (logical disk, see Section 8.3.1) has a unique *inode number*. Hence a file is uniquely identified by specifying its device ID and inode number. These identifiers are not stored in the inode itself. The device ID is a property of the file system—all files of a single file system have the same device ID. Directory entries store the inode number along with the filename.
- User and group IDs of the owner of the file.

- Timestamps — There are three timestamps for each file: the time the file was last accessed, the time it was last modified, and the time its attributes (excluding the other timestamps) were last changed.
- Permissions and mode flags, described below.

There are three types of permissions associated with each file—*read, write,* and *execute.* The users trying to access a file are also divided into three categories—the owner of the file,[2] people in the same group as the owner, and everybody else (that is, *owner, group,* and *others*). This means that all permissions associated with a file can be specified by nine bits. Directory permissions are handled differently. Write access to a directory allows you to create and delete files in that directory. Execute access allows you to access files in that directory. A user may never directly write to a directory, even if the permissions allow it. The contents of a directory are modified only by file creations and deletions.

The permissions mechanism is simple but primitive. Today, most UNIX vendors offer enhanced security features, either in their default implementations or in special *secure* versions.[3] These normally involve some form of an *access-control list,* which allows a more detailed specification of who may access a file and in what manner [Fern 88].

There are three *mode flags—suid, sgid,* and *sticky.* The *suid* and *sgid* flags apply to executable files. When a user executes the file, if the *suid* flag is set, the kernel sets the user's effective UID to that of the owner of the file. The *sgid* flag affects the effective GID in the same way. (Section 2.3.3 defines UIDs and GIDs.) Since the *sgid* flag serves no purpose if the file is not executable, it is overloaded for another purpose. If the file does not have *group-execute* permission and the *sgid* flag is set, then *mandatory file/record locking* [UNIX 92] has been enabled on the file.

The *sticky* flag also is used for executable files and requests the kernel to retain the program image in the *swap area* (see Section 13.2.4) after execution terminates. System administrators often set the *sticky* flag for frequently executed files in order to improve performance. Most modern UNIX systems leave all images on swap as long as possible (using some form of a *least recently used* replacement algorithm), and hence do not use the *sticky* flag.

The *sgid* and *sticky* flags are used differently for directories. If the *sticky* flag is set and the directory is writable, then a process may remove or rename a file in that directory only if its effective UID is that of the owner of the file or directory, or if the process has write permissions for the file. If the *sticky* flag is clear, then any process that has write access to the directory may remove or rename files in it.

When a file is created, it inherits the effective UID of the creating process. Its owner GID may take one of two values. In SVR3, the file inherits the effective GID of the creator. In 4.3BSD, it inherits the GID of the directory in which it is created. SVR4 uses the *sgid* flag of the parent directory to select the behavior. If the *sgid* flag is set for a directory, then new files created in the direc-

---

[2] Also known as the *user,* for the sake of the *chmod* command, which uses the abbreviations *u, g,* and *o* to refer to *user (owner), group,* and *others.*

[3] Most secure UNIX versions base their requirements on a set of criteria published by the Department of Defense for evaluating trusted computer systems. This document, informally known as the Orange Book [DoD 85], defines various levels of security that a system may provide.

tory inherit the GID from the parent directory. If the *sgid* flag is clear, then new files inherit the GID of the creator.

UNIX provides a set of system calls to manipulate file attributes. These calls take the pathname of the file as an argument. The *link* and *unlink* calls create and delete hard links respectively. The kernel deletes the file only after all its hard links have been removed, and no one is actively using the file. The *utimes* system call changes the *access* and *modify* timestamps of the file. The *chown* call changes the owner UID and GID. The *chmod* system call changes the permissions and mode flags of the file.

8.2.3   File Descriptors

A process must first open a file in order to read or write to it. The *open* system call has the following syntax:

```
fd = open (path, oflag, mode);
```

where `path` is the absolute or relative pathname of the file and `mode` specifies the permissions to associate with the file if it must be created. The flags passed in `oflag` specify if the file is to be opened for *read, write, read-write,* or *append,* if it must be created, and so forth. The *creat* system call also creates a file. It is functionally equivalent to an open call with the `O_WRONLY`, `O_CREAT`, and `O_TRUNC` flags (see Section 8.10.4).

Each process has a default *file creation mask,* which is a bitmask of permissions that should *not* be granted to newly created files. When the user specifies a `mode` to *open* or *creat,* the kernel clears the bits specified in the default mask. The *umask* system call changes the value of the default mask. The user can override the mask by calling *chmod* after the file is created.

When the user calls *open,* the kernel creates an *open file object* to represent the *open instance* of the file. It also allocates a *file descriptor,* which acts as a handle, or reference, to the open file object. The *open* system call returns the file descriptor *(fd)* to the caller. A user may open the same file several times; also, multiple users may open the same file. In each case, the kernel generates a new open file object and a new file descriptor.

The file descriptor is a per-process object. The same descriptor number in two different processes may, and usually does, refer to different files. The process passes the file descriptor to I/O-related system calls such as *read* and *write.* The kernel uses the descriptor to quickly locate the open file object and other data structures associated with the open file. This way, the kernel can perform tasks such as pathname parsing and access control once during the *open,* rather than on each I/O operation. Open files may be closed by the *close* system call and also are closed automatically when the process terminates.

Each file descriptor represents an independent session with the file. The associated open file object holds the context for that session. This includes the mode in which the file was opened and the *offset pointer* at which the next read or write must start. In UNIX, files are accessed sequentially by default. When the user opens the file, the kernel initializes the offset pointer to zero. Subsequently, each read or write advances the pointer by the amount of data transferred.

Keeping the offset pointer in the open file object allows the kernel to insulate different sessions to the file from one another (Figure 8-2). If two processes open the same file,[4] a read or write by one process advances only its own offset pointer and does not affect that of the other. This allows multiple processes to share the file transparently. This functionality must be used with care. In many cases, multiple processes accessing the same file should synchronize access to it using the file locking facilities described in Section 8.2.6.

A process may duplicate a descriptor through the *dup* or *dup2* system calls. These calls create a new descriptor that references the same open file object and hence shares the same session (Figure 8-3). Similarly, the *fork* system call duplicates all the descriptors in the parent and passes them on to the child. Upon return from *fork*, the parent and child share the set of open files. This form of sharing is fundamentally different from having multiple open instances. Since the two descriptors share the same session to the file, they both see the same view of the file and use the same offset pointer. If an operation on one descriptor changes the offset pointer, the change will be visible to the other as well.

A process may pass a file descriptor to another unrelated process. This has the effect of passing a reference to the open file object. The kernel copies the descriptor into the first free slot in the receiver's descriptor table. The two descriptors share the same open file object and hence the same offset pointer. Usually, the sending process closes its descriptor after sending it. This does not close the open file, even if the other process has not yet received the descriptor, since the kernel holds on to the second descriptor while it is in transit.

The interface for descriptor passing depends on the UNIX variant. SVR4 passes the descriptor over a *STREAMS pipe* (see Section 17.9), using the *ioctl* call with the I_SENDFD command. The other process receives it through the I_RECVFD ioctl call. 4.3BSD uses *sendmsg* and *recvmsg* calls to a socket connection (see Section 17.10.3) between the two processes. Descriptor passing is useful for implementing some types of network applications. One process, the *connection server*, can set up a network connection on behalf of a client process, then pass the descriptor representing the con-

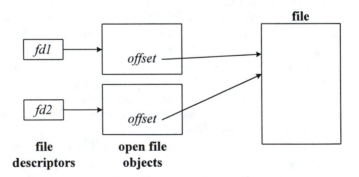

Figure 8-2. A file is opened twice.

---

4 Or if a process opens the same file twice.

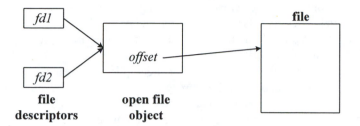

Figure 8-3. Descriptor cloned through *dup, dup2,* or *fork.*

nection back to the client. Section 11.10 describes the *portal* file system in 4.4BSD, which takes this concept one step further.

8.2.4 File I/O

UNIX allows both random and sequential access to files. The default access pattern is sequential. The kernel maintains an offset pointer into the file, which is initialized to zero when a process first opens the file. This marks the current position in the file, at which the next I/O operation will begin. Each time the process reads or writes data, the kernel advances the pointer by the amount of data transferred. The *lseek* call permits random access by setting the offset pointer to a specified value. The next *read* or *write* call will transfer data starting at that offset.

　　The *read* and *write* calls have similar semantics, and we use *read* as an example.[5] Its syntax is

```
nread = read (fd, buf, count);
```

where fd is the file descriptor, buf is a pointer to a buffer in the user address space into which the data must be read, and count is the number of bytes to read.

　　The kernel reads data from the file associated with fd, starting at the offset stored in the open file object. It may read fewer than count bytes if it reaches the end of the file or, in case of FIFOs or device files, if there is not enough data available. For instance, a *read* issued to a terminal in *canonical* mode returns when the user types a carriage return, even if the line contains fewer bytes than requested. Under no circumstances will the kernel transfer more than count bytes. It is the user's responsibility to ensure that buf is large enough to hold count bytes of data. The *read* call returns the actual number of bytes transferred (nread). *read* also advances the offset pointer by nread bytes so that the next *read* or *write* will begin where this one finished.

　　While the kernel allows multiple processes to open and share the file at the same time, it serializes I/O operations to it. For instance, if two processes issue writes to the file at (almost) the same time, the kernel will complete one write before beginning the other. This allows each operation to have a consistent view of the file.

---

[5] Most programmers do not use the *read* and *write* system calls directly. Instead, they use the standard library functions *fread* and *fwrite*, which provide additional functionality such as data buffering.

A file may be opened in *append mode* by passing the O_APPEND flag to the open system call. This causes the kernel to set the offset pointer to the end of the file prior to each write system call through that descriptor. Again, if one user opens a file in append mode, it has no effect on operations on the file through other descriptors.

Multithreaded systems must handle additional complications resulting from sharing descriptors between threads. For instance, one thread may do an lseek just before another thread issues a read, causing the second thread to read from a different offset than intended. Some systems, such as Solaris, provide *pread/pwrite* system calls to perform an atomic seek and read/write. Section 3.6.6 discusses this issue in more detail.

8.2.5   Scatter-Gather I/O

The *read* and *write* system calls transfer a number of bytes between a logically contiguous portion of the file and a contiguous range of locations in the process address space. Many applications want to atomically read (or write) data from a file into a number of noncontiguous buffers in their address space. The *read* system call is inefficient for this purpose, because the process would have to first read the data into a single buffer and then copy it to the desired locations. UNIX provides two additional calls—*readv* and *writev*—that perform *scatter-gather I/O,* moving data from the file into multiple buffers in user space.

As an example, consider a network file transfer protocol that receives a file from a remote node and must write it out to a local disk. Data arrives in a series of network packets, each containing a part of the file. Without scatter-gather I/O, the protocol would have to assemble all the packets into a single buffer, then write it to disk. Using *writev,* however, the protocol simply composes a single request that collects the data from all the packets. The syntax for *writev* (*readv* is analogous) is

```
nbytes = writev (fd, iov, iovcnt);
```

where fd is the file descriptor, iov is a pointer to an array of *<base, length>* pairs (struct iovec) that describe the set of source buffers, and iovcnt is the number of elements in the array. As with *write,* the return value nbytes specifies the number of bytes actually transferred. The offset pointer determines the location of the start of the data in the file, and the kernel advances it by nbytes bytes upon completion of the call.

Figure 8-4 illustrates the effect of a scatter-gather write. The kernel creates a struct uio to manage the operation and initializes it with information from the system call arguments and the open file object. It then passes a pointer to the uio structure to lower-level functions that perform the I/O. The operation atomically transfers data from all the specified user buffers to the file.

8.2.6   File Locking

By default, UNIX allows multiple processes to concurrently access the file for reading or writing. Each *read* or *write* call is atomic, but there is no synchronization across system call boundaries. As a result, if a process reads a file through multiple *read* calls, another process may change the file between two *read*s.

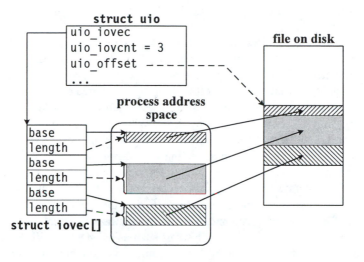

Figure 8-4. Scatter-gather I/O.

This behavior is unsuitable for many applications that need to protect a file across multiple accesses. Hence UNIX provides facilities to lock files. File locking may be advisory or mandatory. *Advisory locks* are not enforced by the kernel and only protect the file from cooperating processes that explicitly check for the lock. *Mandatory locks* are enforced by the kernel, which will reject operations conflicting with the lock. Locking requests may be blocking or nonblocking; the latter return an error code of EWOULDBLOCK if the lock cannot be granted.

4BSD provides the *flock* system call, which only supports advisory locking of open files, but allows both shared and exclusive locks. File locking in System V UNIX varies with the release. SVR2 supports only advisory locking, for both files and *records* (byte ranges within files). SVR3 adds mandatory locking, but requires that the file first be enabled for mandatory locking through a *chmod* call as described in Section 8.2.2. This feature is an artifact of XENIX binary compatibility. SVR4 adds BSD compatibility and supports single-writer, multiple-reader locks. The *fcntl* call provides the locking functions, but most applications use a simpler programming interface offered by the C library function *lockf*.

8.3   File Systems

Although the UNIX file hierarchy appears monolithic, it is actually composed of one or more independent subtrees, each of which contains a complete, self-contained *file system*. One file system is configured to be the *root file system,* and its root directory becomes the *system root directory*. The other file systems are attached to the existing structure by *mounting* each new file system onto a directory in the existing tree. Once mounted, the root directory of the mounted file system *covers* or hides the directory on which it is mounted, and any access to the *"mounted-on" directory* is translated to an access to the root directory of the mounted file system. The mounted file system remains visible until it is unmounted.

Figure 8-5 shows a file hierarchy composed of two file systems. In this example, **fs0** is installed as the root file system of the machine, and the file system **fs1** is mounted on the **/usr** directory of **fs0**. **/usr** is called the "mounted-on" directory or the *mount point,* and any attempts to access **/usr** results in accessing the root directory of the file system mounted on it.

If the **/usr** directory of **fs0** contains any files, they are hidden, or covered, when **fs1** is mounted on it, and may no longer accessed by users. When **fs1** is unmounted, these files become visible and are accessible once again. Pathname parsing routines in the kernel must understand mount points and behave correctly when traversing mount points in either direction. The original *s5fs* and FFS implementations used a *mount table* to track mounted file systems. Modern UNIX systems use some form of a *vfs list* (virtual file system list), as is described in Section 8.9.

The notion of mountable subsystems serves to hide the details of the storage organization from the user. The file name space is homogeneous, and the user does not need to specify the disk drive as part of the file name (as required in systems such as MS-DOS or VMS). File systems may be taken off-line individually to perform backups, compaction, or repair. The system administrator may vary the protections on each file system, perhaps making some of them read-only.

Mountable file systems impose some restrictions on the file hierarchy. A file cannot span file systems and hence may grow only as much as the free space on the file system to which it belongs. Rename and hard link operations cannot span file systems. Each file system must reside on a single *logical disk* and is limited by the size of that disk.

8.3.1 Logical Disks

A *logical disk* is a storage abstraction that the kernel sees as a linear sequence of fixed sized, randomly accessible, blocks. The disk device driver (see Section 16.6) maps these blocks to the underlying physical storage. The *newfs* or *mkfs* utilities create a UNIX file system on the disk. Each file

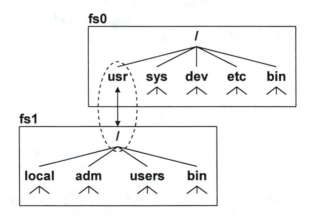

Figure 8-5. Mounting one file system onto another.

system is fully contained in a single logical disk, and one logical disk may contain only one file system. Some logical disks may not contain file systems, but are used by the memory subsystem for swapping.

Logical disks allow physical storage to be mapped in a variety of useful ways. In the simplest case, each logical disk is mapped to a single, entire, physical disk. The most common feature is to divide a disk into a number of physically contiguous *partitions,* each a logical device. Older UNIX systems provided only this feature. As a result, the word *partition* is often used to describe the physical storage of a file system.

Modern UNIX systems support many other useful storage configurations. Several disks may be combined into a single logical disk or *volume,* thus supporting files larger than the size of a single disk. *Disk mirroring* allows a redundant copy of all data, increasing the reliability of the file system. *Stripe sets* provide increased throughput from a file system by *striping* the data across a set of disks. Several types of *RAID* (Redundant Arrays of Inexpensive Disks) configurations provide a mix of reliability and performance enhancements to suit the requirements of different types of installations [Patt 88].

8.4 Special Files

One of the distinctive features of the UNIX file system is the generalization of the *file* abstraction to include all kinds of I/O-related objects, such as directories, symbolic links, hardware devices like disks, terminals and printers, pseudodevices such as the system memory, and communication abstractions such as pipes and sockets. Each of these is accessed through file descriptors, and the same set of system calls that operate on ordinary files also manipulate these special files. For instance, a user can send data to a line printer simply by opening the special file associated with it and writing to it.

On the other hand, UNIX imposes a simple byte-stream model on files. Many real-world applications require much richer data abstractions such as record-based or indexed-sequential access. Such applications find the UNIX model inadequate and end up layering their own access methods on top of it. Some I/O objects do not support all file operations. Terminals and printers, for instance, have no notion of random access or seeks. Applications often need to verify (typically through *fstat*) what kind of file they are accessing.

8.4.1 Symbolic Links

Early UNIX systems such as SVR3 and 4.1BSD supported hard links only. Although extremely useful, hard links have several limitations. A hard link may not span file systems. Creating hard links to directories is barred except to the superuser, who also is discouraged from doing so. This is because such links may create cycles in the directory tree, wreaking havoc on a number of utilities such as *du* or *find* that recursively traverse the tree.

The only reason UNIX allows (privileged) users to create hard links to directories is the absence of the *mkdir* system call in early versions (SVR2 and earlier) of UNIX. To create a directory, the user had to call *mknod* to create the directory special file, followed by two calls to *link* to add the entries for ".". and "..". This led to several problems and race conditions since the three operations were not executed atomically [Bach 86]. SVR3 added the *mkdir* and *rmdir* system calls, but continued to allow linking to directories to maintain backward compatibility with older applications.

Hard links also create control problems. Suppose user *X* owns a file named **/usr/X/file1**. Another user *Y* may create a hard link to this file and call it **/usr/Y/link1** (Figure 8-6). To do so, *Y* only needs execute permission for the directories in the path and write permission to the **/usr/Y** directory. Subsequently, user *X* may unlink **file1** and believe that the file has been deleted (typically, users do not often check the link counts on their own files). The file, however, continues to exist through the other link.

Of course, **/usr/Y/link1** is still owned by user *X,* even though the link was created by user *Y.* If *X* had write-protected the file, then *Y* will not be able to modify it. Nevertheless, *X* may not wish to allow the file to persist. In systems that impose disk-usage *quotas, X* will continue to be charged for it. Moreover, there is no way *X* can discover the location of the link, particularly if *Y* has read-protected the **/usr/Y** directory (or if *X* no longer knows the inode number of the file).

4.2BSD introduced *symbolic links* to address many of the limitations of hard links. They were soon adapted by most vendors and incorporated into *s5fs* in SVR4. The *symlink* system call creates a symbolic link. It is a special file that points to another file (the *linked-to* file). The file type attribute identifies it as a symbolic link. The data portion of the file contains the pathname of the linked-to file. Many systems allow small pathnames to be stored in the inode of the symbolic link. This optimization was first introduced in ULTRIX.

The pathname contained in the symbolic link may be absolute or relative. The pathname traversal routines recognize symbolic links and translate them to obtain the name of the linked-to file. If the name is relative, it is interpreted relative to the directory containing the link. While symbolic link handling is transparent to most programs, some utilities need to detect and handle symbolic links. This is enabled by the *lstat* system call, which suppresses translation of the final symbolic link in a pathname. Hence if file **mylink** is a symbolic link to the file **myfile**, then *lstat* (`mylink`, `...`) returns the attributes of **mylink**, while *stat* (`mylink`, `...`) returns the attributes of **myfile**. Having detected a symbolic link through *lstat,* the user may call *readlink* to retrieve the contents of the link.

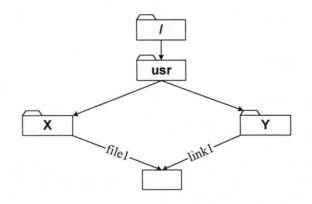

Figure 8-6. Hard links to a file.

8.4.2   Pipes and FIFOs

Pipes and FIFOs are file abstractions that provide a first-in, first-out data stream. They differ mainly in how they are created. A FIFO is created by the *mknod* system call and may then be opened and accessed by any process that knows the name and has the permissions. It continues to exist until explicitly deleted. A pipe is created by the *pipe* system call, which returns a read and a write descriptor to it. The process that creates the pipe may pass these descriptors to its descendants through *fork,* thus sharing the pipe with them.[6] A pipe may have multiple readers and writers. When no more readers or writers remain, the kernel automatically deletes the pipe.

I/O operations on FIFOs and pipes are quite similar. Writes append data to the end, while reads remove data from the head. Once data has been read, it is removed from the pipe and is unavailable even to other readers. The kernel defines a parameter called PIPE_BUF (5120 bytes by default), which limits the amount of data a pipe may hold. If a write would cause the pipe or FIFO to overflow, the writer would block until enough data is removed from it (through reads). If a process tries to write more than PIPE_BUF bytes in a single *write* call, the kernel cannot guarantee atomicity of the write. The data may become interleaved on arbitrary boundaries with writes by other processes.

The treatment of reads is a little different. If the size requested is greater than the amount of data currently in the pipe or FIFO, the kernel reads whatever data is available and returns the byte count to the caller. If no data is available, the reader will block until another process writes to the pipe. The O_NDELAY option (set through *open* for FIFOs or *fcntl* for either) puts the pipe or FIFO in nonblocking mode: reads and writes will complete without blocking, transferring as much data as possible.

Pipes maintain counts of active readers and writers. When the last active writer closes the pipe, the kernel wakes up all waiting readers. They may read the data still in the pipe. Once the pipe is empty, the readers will get a return value of 0 from the next *read* and interpret it as the end of file. If the last reader closes the pipe, the kernel sends a SIGPIPE signal to blocked writers. Subsequent writes will return with an EPIPE error.

The initial implementations of pipes used the file system and assigned an inode and a block list for each pipe. Many BSD-based variants used *sockets* (see Section 17.10.3) to implement a pipe. SVR4 builds pipes and FIFOs using STREAMS. Section 17.9 describes this implementation in detail. SVR4 pipes are bidirectional and maintain a separate data stream for each direction. This better addresses the needs of most applications, which desire a full-duplex, interprocess communication mechanism.

8.5   File System Framework

The traditional UNIX kernel had a monolithic file system organization. It could only support one file system type—*s5fs*. The introduction of FFS in 4.2BSD gave vendors an alternative to *s5fs*, but the basic framework precluded the two file systems from coexisting. Although many vendors pre-

---

[6]   Only those descendants that are created after the pipe can share access to it.

ferred FFS for its performance and features, others chose to retain *s5fs* for backward compatibility. Either way, it was not a happy solution.

Moreover, while both *s5fs* and FFS were adequate for general time-sharing applications, many applications found neither suitable to their needs. Database applications, for example, need better support for transaction processing. Applications that use large, read-mostly or read-only files would prefer extent-based allocation, which improves the performance of sequential reads. The early UNIX systems had no way for vendors to add a custom file system without extensively over-hauling the kernel. This was too restrictive for UNIX to become the operating system of choice for a wider variety of environments.

There also was a growing need for supporting non-UNIX file systems. This would permit a UNIX system running on a personal computer to access files on DOS partitions on the same machine or, for that matter, floppy disks written by DOS.

Most important, the proliferation of computer networks led to an increased demand for sharing files between computers. The mid-1980s saw the emergence of a number of distributed file systems—such as AT&T's *Remote File Sharing (RFS)* and Sun Microsystem's *Network File System (NFS)*—that provided transparent access to files on remote nodes.

These developments necessitated fundamental changes in the UNIX file system framework to support multiple file system types. Here again there were several alternative approaches, such as AT&T's *file system switch* [Rifk 86], Sun Microsystem's *vnode/vfs* architecture [Klei 86], and Digital Equipment Corporation's *gnode* architecture [Rodr 86]. For a while, these rival technologies battled for acceptance and dominance. Eventually, AT&T integrated Sun's vnode/vfs and NFS technologies into SVR4, enabling them to become *de facto* industry standards.

The vnode/vfs interface has evolved substantially from its original implementation. While all major variants have embraced its fundamental approach, each provides a different interface and implementation. This chapter concentrates on the SVR4 version of this interface. Section 8.11 summarizes other important implementations.

8.6   The Vnode/Vfs Architecture

Sun Microsystems introduced the *vnode/vfs interface* as a framework for supporting multiple file system types. It has since gained widespread acceptance and became part of System V UNIX in SVR4.

8.6.1   Objectives

The vnode/vfs architecture has several important objectives:

- The system should support several file system types simultaneously. These include UNIX (*s5fs* or *ufs*) and non-UNIX (DOS, A/UX, etc.) file systems.
- Different disk partitions may contain different types of file systems. Once they are mounted on each other, however, they must present the traditional picture of a single homogenous file system. The user is presented with a consistent view of the entire file tree and need not be aware of the differences in the on-disk representations of the subtrees.

- There should be complete support for sharing files over a network. A file system on a remote machine should be accessible just like a local file system.
- Vendors should be able to create their own file system types and add them to the kernel in a modular manner.

The main goal was to provide a framework in the kernel for file access and manipulation, and a well-defined interface between the kernel and the modules that implemented specific file systems.

8.6.2   Lessons from Device I/O

Even though the early UNIX versions had just one type of file system, there were many types of files. Besides ordinary files, UNIX supported a variety of devices, which were accessed through special device files. Although each device driver had its own implementation of the low-level I/O routines, they all provided a uniform interface to the user, who accessed them with the same system calls as those for ordinary files.

The framework for device I/O thus provides an insight into the requirements for multiple file system support. Section 16.3 describes the device driver framework in detail. Here, we summarize the part of the interface relevant to our discussion. UNIX divides devices into two broad categories—block and character. Their interfaces to the kernel are different in some respects, but the basic framework is the same. We shall use the example of character devices.

UNIX requires each character device to support a standard set of operations. These operations are encapsulated in a `struct cdevsw`, which is a vector of function pointers, as shown below.

```
struct cdevsw   {
    int (*d_open)();
    int (*d_close)();
    int (*d_read)();
    int (*d_write)();
    ...
} cdevsw[];
```

Hence cdevsw[] is a global array of `struct cdevsw`'s and is called the *character device switch*. The fields of the structure define the interface to an abstract character device. Each different type of device provides its own set of functions that implements this interface. For example, the line printer may provide the functions `lpopen()`, `lpclose()`, and so forth. Each device type has a different *major device number* associated with it. This number forms an index into the global cdevsw[] array, giving each device its own entry in the switch. The fields of the entry are initialized to point to the functions provided by that device.

Suppose a user issues a *read* system call to a character device file. In a traditional UNIX system, the kernel will:

1. Use the file descriptor to get to the open file object.
2. Check the entry to see if the file is open for read.

3. Get the pointer to the *in-core inode* from this entry. In-core inodes (also called *in-memory inodes*) are file system data structures that keep attributes of active files in memory. They are described in detail in Section 9.3.1.

4. Lock the inode so as to serialize access to the file.

5. Check the inode mode field and find that the file is a character device file.

6. Use the major device number (stored in the inode) to index into a table of character devices and obtain the cdevsw entry for this device. This entry is an array of pointers to functions that implement specific operations for this device.

7. From the cdevsw, obtain the pointer to the d_read routine for this device.

8. Invoke the d_read operation to perform the device-specific processing of the read request. The code looks like the following:

```
result = (*(cdevsw[major].d_read))(...);
```

where major is the major device number of that device.

9. Unlock the inode and return to the user.

As we can see, much of this processing is independent of the specific device. Steps 1 through 4 and Step 9 apply to ordinary files as well as to device files and are thus independent of file type. Steps 5 through 7 represent the interface between the kernel and devices, which is encapsulated in the cdevsw table. All the device-specific processing is localized in Step 8.

Note that the cdevsw fields such as d_read define an abstract interface. Each device implements it through specific functions, for instance, lpread() for a line printer or ttread() for a terminal. The major device number works as a key, translating the generic d_read operation to the device-specific function.

The same general principles can be extended to the problem of multiple file system support. We need to separate the file subsystem code into file-system-independent and file-system-dependent parts. The interface between these two portions is defined by a set of generic functions that are called by the file-system-independent code to perform various file manipulation and access operations. The file-system-dependent code, which is different for each file system type, provides specific implementations of these functions. The framework provides mechanisms for adding new file systems and for translating the abstract operations to the specific functions for the files being accessed.

Object-Oriented Design — A Digression

The vnode/vfs interface was designed using object-oriented programming concepts. These concepts have since been applied to other areas of the UNIX kernel, such as memory management, message-based communications, and process scheduling. It is useful to briefly review the fundamentals of object-oriented programming as they apply to UNIX kernel development. Although such techniques are naturally suited to object-oriented languages such as *C*++ [Elli 90], UNIX developers have chosen to implement them in *C* to be consistent with the rest of the kernel.

The object-oriented approach is based on the notion of classes and objects. A class is a complex data type, made up of data member fields and a set of member functions. An object is an instance of a class and has storage associated with it. The member functions of a class operate on individual objects of that class. Each member (data field or function) of a class may be either *public* or *private*. Only the public members are visible externally to users of the class. Private data and functions may only be accessed internally by other functions of that class.

From any given class, we may generate one or more derived classes, called subclasses (see Figure 8-7). A *subclass* may itself be a base for further derived classes, thus forming a class hierarchy. A subclass inherits all the attributes (data and functions) of the base class. It may also add its own data fields and extra functions. Moreover, it may override some of the functions of the base class and provide its own implementation of these.

Because a subclass contains all the attributes of the base class, an object of the subclass type is also an object of the base class type. For instance, the class *directory* may be a derived class of the base class *file*. This means that every directory is also a file. Of course, the reverse is not true—every file is not a directory. Likewise, a pointer to a directory object is also a pointer to a file object. The attributes added by the derived class are not visible to the base class. Therefore a pointer to a base object may not be used to access the data and functions specific to a derived class.

Frequently, we would like to use a base class simply to represent an abstraction and define an interface, with derived classes providing specific implementations of the member functions. Thus the file class may define a function called `create()`, but when a user calls this function for an arbitrary file, we would like to invoke a different routine depending on whether the file is actually a regular file, directory, symbolic link, device file, and so on. Indeed, we may have no generic implementation of `create()` that creates an arbitrary file. Such a function is called a *pure virtual function*.

Object-oriented languages provide such facilities. In C++, for instance, we can define an *abstract base class* as one that contains at least one *pure virtual function*. Since the base class has no implementation for this function, it cannot be instantiated. It may only be

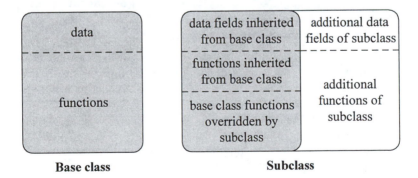

Figure 8-7. Relationship between a base class and its subclass.

used for deriving subclasses, which provide specific implementations of the virtual functions. All objects are instances of one subclass or another, but the user may manipulate them using a pointer to a base class, without knowing which subclass they belong to. When a virtual function is invoked for such an object, the implementation automatically determines which specific function to call, depending on the actual subtype of the object.

As mentioned earlier, languages such as C++ and SmallTalk have built-in constructs to describe the notions like classes and virtual functions. In C, these concepts are supported with some smoke and mirrors. In the next section, we see how the vnode/vfs layer is implemented in an object-oriented manner.

8.6.3   Overview of the Vnode/Vfs Interface

The *vnode* (virtual node) abstraction represents a file in the UNIX kernel; the *vfs* (virtual file system) represents a file system. Both can be regarded as abstract base classes, from which we can derive subclasses that provide specific implementations for different file system types such as *s5fs, ufs*, NFS, and FAT (the MS-DOS file system).

Figure 8-8 shows the vnode class in SVR4. The data fields in the base vnode contain information that does not depend on the file system type. The member functions may be divided into two categories. The first is a set of virtual functions that define the file-system-dependent interface. Each different file system must provide its own implementation of these functions. The second is a set of high-level *utility routines* that may be used by other kernel subsystems to manipulate files. These functions in turn call the file-system-dependent routines to perform the low-level tasks.

The base vnode has two fields that implement subclassing. The first is v_data, which is a

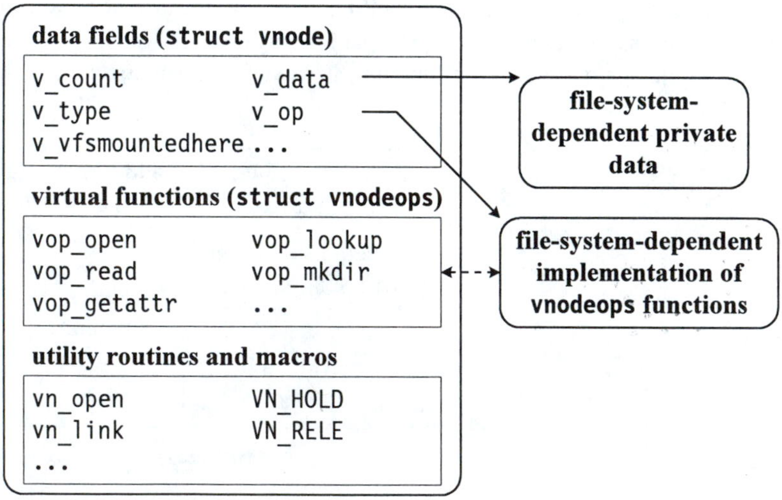

Figure 8-8. The vnode abstraction.

pointer (of type caddr_t) to a private data structure that holds the file-system-specific data of the vnode. For *s5fs* and *ufs* files, this structure is simply the traditional (*s5fs* and *ufs*, respectively) inode structure. NFS uses an rnode structure, *tmpfs* (see Section 9.10.2) uses a tmpnode, and so forth. Since this structure is accessed indirectly through v_data, it is opaque to the base vnode class, and its fields are only visible to functions internal to the specific file system.

The v_op field points to a struct vnodeops, which consists of a set of pointers to functions that implement the virtual interface of the vnode. Both the v_data and v_op fields are filled in when the vnode is initialized, typically during an *open* or *create* system call. When the file-system-independent code calls a virtual function for an arbitrary vnode, the kernel dereferences the v_op pointer and calls the corresponding function of the appropriate file system implementation. For example, the VOP_CLOSE operation allows the caller to close the file associated with the vnode. This is accessed by a macro such as

```
#define VOP_CLOSE(vp, ...)    (*((vp)->v_op->vop_close))(vp, ...)
```

where the ellipsis represent the other arguments to the close routine. Once vnodes have been properly initialized, this macro ensures that invoking the VOP_CLOSE operation would call the ufs_close() routine for a *ufs* file, the nfs_close() routine for an NFS file, and so forth.

Similarly, the base class *vfs* has two fields—vfs_data and vfs_op—that allow proper linkage to data and functions that implement specific file systems. Figure 8-9 shows the components of the vfs abstraction.

In C, a base class is implemented simply as a struct, plus a set of global kernel functions (and macros) that define the public nonvirtual functions. The base class contains a pointer to another structure that consists of a set of function pointers, one for each virtual function. The v_op and v_data pointers (vfs_op and vfs_data for the vfs class) allow the linkage to the subclass and hence provide run time access to the file-system-dependent functions and data.

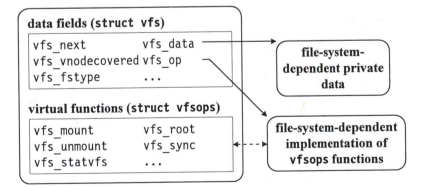

Figure 8-9. The vfs abstraction.

8.7   Implementation Overview

The following sections examine the vnode/vfs interface in more detail and show how it implements various file operations.

8.7.1   Objectives

A set of implementation goals evolved to allow the development of a flexible interface that can be used efficiently by a large variety of diverse file systems:

- Each operation must be carried out on behalf of the current process, which may be put to sleep if a function must block on a resource or event.
- Certain operations may need to serialize access to the file. These may lock data structures in the file-system-dependent layer and must unlock them before the operation completes.
- The interface must be stateless. There must be no implicit use of global variables such as u area fields to pass state information between operations.
- The interface must be reentrant. This requirement disallows use of global variables such as u_error and u_rval1 to store error codes or return values. In fact, all operations return error codes as return values.
- File system implementations should be allowed, but not forced, to use global resources such as the buffer cache.
- The interface must be usable by the server side of a remote file system to satisfy client requests.
- The use of fixed-size static tables must be avoided. Dynamic storage allocation should be used wherever possible.

8.7.2   Vnodes and Open Files

The *vnode* is the fundamental abstraction that represents an active file in the kernel. It defines the interface to the file and channels all operations on the file to the appropriate file-system-specific functions. There are two ways in which the kernel accesses a vnode. First, the I/O-related system calls locate vnodes through file descriptors, as described in this section. Second, the pathname traversal routines use file-system-dependent data structures to locate the vnode. Section 8.10.1 talks more about pathname traversal.

A process must open a file before reading or writing to it. The *open* system call returns a file descriptor to the caller. This descriptor, which is typically a small integer, acts as a handle to the file and represents an independent session, or stream, to that file. The process must pass that descriptor to subsequent *read* and *write* calls.

Figure 8-10 shows the relevant data structures. The file descriptor is a per-process object that contains a pointer to an *open file object* (struct file), as well as a set of per-descriptor flags. Currently, the flags supported are FCLOSEXEC, which asks the kernel to close the descriptor when the process calls *exec*, and U_FDLOCK, which is used for file locking.

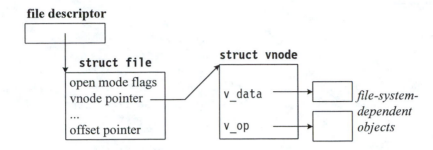

Figure 8-10. File-system-independent data structures.

The open file object holds the context that manages a session with that file. If multiple users have the file open (or the same user has it open multiple times), each has its own open file object. Its fields include:

- Offset in the file at which the next read or write should start.
- Reference count of the number of file descriptors that point to it. This is normally 1, but could be greater if descriptors are cloned through *dup* or *fork*.
- Pointer to the vnode of the file.
- Mode with which the file was opened. The kernel checks this mode on each I/O operation. Hence if a user has opened a file for read only, he cannot write to the file using that descriptor even if he has the necessary privileges.

Traditional UNIX systems use a static, fixed-size file descriptor table in the u area. The descriptor returned to the user is an index into this table. The size of the table (typically 64 elements) limits the number of files the user could keep open at a time. In modern UNIX systems, the descriptor table is not limited in size, but may grow arbitrarily large.[7]

Some implementations, such as SVR4 and SunOS, allocate descriptors in chunks of (usually) 32 entries and keep the chunks in a linked list, with the first chunk in the u area of the process. This complicates the task of dereferencing the descriptor. Instead of simply using the descriptor as an index into the table, the kernel must first locate the appropriate chunk, then index into that chunk. This scheme removes the restrictions on the number of files a process may have open, at the cost of some increased code complexity and performance.

Some newer SVR4-based systems allocate the descriptor table dynamically and extend it when necessary by calling kmem_realloc(), which either extends the table in-place or copies it into a new location where it has room to grow. This allows dynamic growth of the descriptor table and quick translation of descriptors, at the cost of copying the table over when allocating it.

8.7.3   The Vnode

The vnode is represented by the following data structure:

---

[7]   It is still bounded by the resource limit RLIMIT_NOFILE.

```
struct vnode    {
    u_short v_flag;                /* V_ROOT, etc. */
    u_short v_count;               /* reference count */
    struct vfs *vfsmountedhere;    /* for mount points */
    struct vnodeops *v_op;         /* vnode operations vector */
    struct vfs *vfsp;              /* file system to which it belongs */
    struct stdata *v_stream;       /* pointer to associated stream, if any */
    struct page *v_page;           /* resident page list */
    enum vtype v_type;             /* file type */
    dev_t v_rdev;                  /* device ID for device files */
    caddr_t v_data;                /* pointer to private data structure */
    ...
};
```

The fields are described in greater detail in other sections.

8.7.4   Vnode Reference Count

The v_count field of the vnode maintains a *reference count* that determines how long the vnode must remain in the kernel. A vnode is allocated and assigned to a file when the file is first accessed. Thereafter, other objects may maintain pointers, or references, to this vnode and expect to access the vnode using that pointer. This means that as long as such references exist, the kernel must retain the vnode and not reassign it to another file.

This reference count is one of the generic properties of the vnode and is manipulated by the file-system-independent code. Two macros, VN_HOLD and VN_RELE, increment and decrement the reference count, respectively. When the reference count reaches zero, the file is inactive and the vnode may be released or reassigned.

It is important to distinguish a reference, or hold, from a lock. Locking an object prevents others from accessing it in some way, depending on whether the locking is exclusive or read-write. Holding a reference to an object merely ensures the persistence of the object. The file-system-dependent code locks vnodes for short times, typically for the duration of a single vnode operation. A reference is typically held for a long time, not only across multiple vnode operations but also across multiple system calls. The following are some of the operations that acquire a vnode reference:

- Opening a file acquires a reference (increments the reference count) to the vnode. Closing the file releases the reference (decrements the count).
- A process holds a reference to its current working directory. When the process changes the working directory, it acquires a reference to the new directory and releases the reference to the old one.
- When a new file system is mounted, it acquires a reference to the mount point directory. Unmounting the file system releases the reference.

- The pathname traversal routine acquires a reference to each intermediate directory it encounters. It holds the reference while searching the directory and releases it after acquiring a reference to the next pathname component.

Reference counts ensure persistence of the vnode and also of the underlying file. When a process deletes a file that another process (or perhaps the same process) still has open, the file is not physically deleted. The directory entry for that file is removed so no one else may open it. The file itself continues to exist since the vnode has a nonzero reference count. The processes that currently have the file open may continue to access it until they close the file. This is equivalent to *marking the file for deletion*. When the last reference to the file is released, the file-system-independent code invokes the VOP_INACTIVE operation to complete the deletion of the file. For a *ufs* or *s5fs* file, for example, the inode and the data blocks are freed at this point.

This feature is very useful in creating temporary files. An application like a compiler uses several temporary files to store results of intermediate phases. These files should be cleaned up if the application were to terminate abnormally. The application ensures this by opening the file and then immediately unlinking it. The link count becomes zero and the kernel removes the directory entry. This prevents other users from seeing or accessing the file. Since the file is open, the in-core reference count is 1. Hence the file continues to exist, and the application may read and write to it. When the application closes the file, either explicitly or implicitly when the process terminates, the reference count becomes zero. The kernel completes the file deletion and frees its data blocks and inode. Many UNIX systems have a standard library function called *tmpfile,* which creates a temporary file.

8.7.5 The Vfs Object

The *vfs* object (struct vfs) represents a file system. The kernel allocates one vfs object for each active file system. It is described by the following data structure:

```
struct vfs  {
    struct vfs *vfs_next;           /* next VFS in list */
    struct vfsops *vfs_op;          /* operations vector */
    struct vnode *vfs_vnodecovered; /* vnode mounted on */
    int vfs_fstype;                 /* file system type index */
    caddr_t vfs_data;               /* private data */
    dev_t vfs_dev;                  /* device ID */
    ...
};
```

Figure 8-11 shows the relationships between the vnode and vfs objects in a system containing two file systems. The second file system is mounted on the **/usr** directory of the root file system. The global variable rootvfs points to the head of a linked list of all vfs objects. The vfs for the root file system is at the head of the list. The vfs_vnodecovered field points to the vnode on which the file system is mounted.

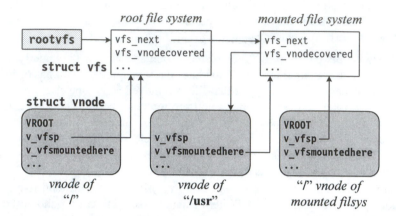

Figure 8-11. Relationships between vnode and vfs objects.

The `v_vfsp` field of each vnode points to the vfs to which it belongs. The root vnodes of each file system have the `VROOT` flag set. If a vnode is a *mount point*, its `v_vfsmountedhere` field points to the vfs object of the file system mounted on it. Note that the root file system is not mounted anywhere and does not cover any vnode.

8.8   File-System-Dependent Objects

In this section, we describe the file-system-dependent objects of the vnode/vfs interface and how the file-system-independent layer accesses them.

8.8.1   The Per-File Private Data

The vnode is an abstract object. It cannot exist in isolation and is always instantiated in the context of a specific file. The file system to which the file belongs provides its own implementation of the abstract vnode interface. The `v_op` and `v_data` fields of the vnode tie it to its file-system-dependent part. `v_data` points to a private data structure that holds file-system-dependent information about the file. The data structure used depends on the file system the file belongs to—*s5fs* and *ufs* files use `inode` structures,[8] NFS uses `rnodes`, and so forth.

`v_data` is an opaque pointer, meaning that the file-system-independent code cannot directly access the file-system-dependent object. The file-system-dependent code, however, can and does access the base vnode object. We therefore need a way to locate the vnode through the private data object. Since the two objects are always allocated together, it is efficient to combine them into one. In the reference implementations of the vnode layer, the vnode is simply a part of the file-system-dependent object. Note that this is merely a prevalent method in existing implementations. It would

---

[8] The two inode structures are different in many respects.

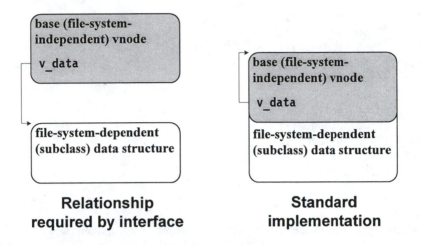

Figure 8-12. File-system-dependent vnode.

be perfectly acceptable to have separate data structures for the vnode and the file-system-dependent portion, as long as the v_data field is initialized appropriately. Figure 8-12 illustrates both relationships.

8.8.2   The vnodeops Vector

The vnode interface defines a set of operations on a generic file. The file-system-independent code manipulates the file using these operations only. It cannot access the file-system-dependent objects directly. The struct vnodeops, which defines this interface, is described as follows:

```
struct vnodeops {
    int   (*vop_open)();
    int   (*vop_close)();
    int   (*vop_read)();
    int   (*vop_write)();
    int   (*vop_ioctl)();
    int   (*vop_getattr)();
    int   (*vop_setattr)();
    int   (*vop_access)();
    int   (*vop_lookup)();
    int   (*vop_create)();
    int   (*vop_remove)();
    int   (*vop_link)();
    int   (*vop_rename)();
    int   (*vop_mkdir)();
    int   (*vop_rmdir)();
```

```
       int    (*vop_readdir)();
       int    (*vop_symlink)();
       int    (*vop_readlink)();
       void   (*vop_inactive)();
       void   (*vop_rwlock)();
       void   (*vop_rwunlock)();
       int    (*vop_realvp)();
       int    (*vop_getpage)();
       int    (*vop_putpage)();
       int    (*vop_map)();
       int    (*vop_poll)();
       ...
};
```

Each file system implements this interface in its own way, and provides a set of functions to do so. For instance, *ufs* implements the VOP_READ operation by reading the file from the local disk, while NFS sends a request to the remote file server to get the data. Hence each file system provides an instance of the struct vnodeops—*ufs,* for example, defines the object:

```
struct vnodeops ufs_vnodeops = {
    ufs_open,
    ufs_close,
    ...
};
```

The v_op field of the vnode points to the vnodeops structure for the associated file system type. As Figure 8-13 shows, all files of the same file system type share a single instance of this structure and access the same set of functions.

8.8.3   File-System-Dependent Parts of the Vfs Layer

Like the vnode, the vfs object has pointers to its private data and its operations vector. The vfs_data field points to an opaque, per-file-system data structure. Unlike vnodes, the vfs object and its private data structure are usually allocated separately. The vfs_op field points to a struct vfsops, described as follows:

```
struct vfsops {
    int (*vfs_mount)();
    int (*vfs_unmount)();
    int (*vfs_root)();
    int (*vfs_statvfs)();
    int (*vfs_sync)();
    ...
};
```

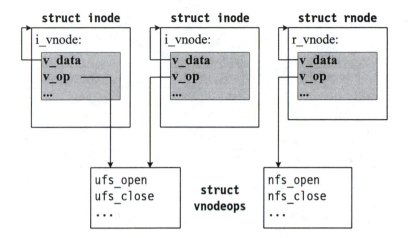

Figure 8-13. File-system-dependent vnode objects.

Each file system type provides its own implementation of these operations. Hence there is one instance of `struct vfsops` for each file system type—ufs_vfsops for *ufs*, nfs_vfsops for NFS, and so forth. Figure 8-14 shows the vfs layer data structures for a system containing two *ufs* and one NFS file system.

8.9   Mounting a File System

The implementors of the vfs interface had to modify the *mount* system call to support the existence of multiple file system types. The syntax for *mount* in SVR4 is

```
mount (spec, dir, flags, type, dataptr, datalen)
```

where `spec` is the name of the device file representing the file system, `dir` is the pathname of the mount point directory, `type` is a string that specifies which kind of file system it is, `dataptr` is a pointer to additional file-system-dependent arguments, and `datalen` is the total size of these extra parameters. In this section, we describe how the kernel implements the *mount* system call.

8.9.1   The Virtual File System Switch

In order to properly route vnode and vfs operations to the appropriate file-system-specific implementations, the different file system types must be properly configured into the system. The kernel needs a mechanism that tells it how to access the interface functions of each file system.

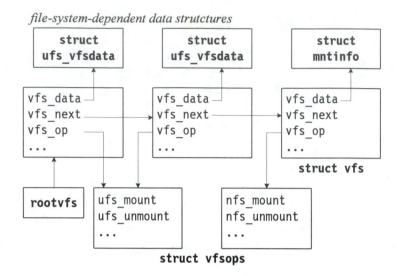

Figure 8-14. vfs layer data structures.

SVR4 uses a mechanism called the *virtual file system switch*, which is a global table containing one entry for each file system type. Its elements are described by

```
struct vfssw {
    char *vsw_name;             /* file system type name */
    int (*vsw_init)();          /* address of initialization routine */
    struct vfsops *vsw_vfsops;  /* vfs operations vector for this fs */
    ...
} vfssw[];
```

8.9.2 *mount* Implementation

The *mount* system call obtains the vnode of the *mount point* directory by calling lookuppn(). It checks that the vnode represents a directory and that no other file system is mounted on it. (Note that lookuppn() acquires a hold on this directory, which remains until the file system is unmounted.) It then searches the vfssw[] table to find the entry matching the *type* name.

Having located the switch entry, the kernel invokes its vsw_init operation. This calls a file-system-specific initialization routine that allocates data structures and resources needed to operate the file system. The kernel then allocates a new vfs structure and initializes it as follows:

1. Adds the structure to the linked list headed by rootvfs.
2. Sets the vfs_op field to point to the vfsops vector specified in the switch entry.
3. Sets the vfs_vnodecovered field to point to the vnode of the mount point directory.

The kernel then stores a pointer to the vfs structure in the v_vfsmountedhere field of the covered directory's vnode. Finally, it invokes the VFS_MOUNT operation of the vfs to perform the file-system-dependent processing of the *mount* call.

8.9.3   VFS_MOUNT Processing

Each file system provides its own function to implement the VFS_MOUNT operation. This function must perform the following operations:

1. Verify permissions for the operation.
2. Allocate and initialize the private data object of the file system.
3. Store a pointer to it in the vfs_data field of the vfs object.
4. Access the root directory of the file system and initialize its vnode in memory. The only way the kernel accesses the root of a mounted file system is through the VFS_ROOT operation. The file-system-dependent part of the vfs must maintain information necessary to locate the root directory.

Typically, local file systems may implement VFS_MOUNT by reading in the file system metadata (such as the *superblock* for *s5fs*) from disk, while distributed file systems may send a remote mount request to the file server.

8.10   Operations on Files

In this section, we examine how several important file operations are handled in the vnode/vfs design. Specifically, we look at pathname traversal and the *open* and *read* system calls.

8.10.1   Pathname Traversal

The file-system-independent function lookuppn() translates a pathname and returns a pointer to the vnode of the desired file. It also acquires a hold on that vnode. The starting point of the search depends on whether the pathname is relative or absolute. For relative pathnames, lookuppn() starts at the current directory, obtaining its vnode pointer from the u_cdir field of the u area. For absolute pathnames, it starts at the root directory. Its vnode pointer is in global variable rootdir.[9]

lookuppn() acquires a hold (increments the reference count) on the starting vnode and then executes a loop, parsing one component of the pathname at a time. Each iteration of the loop must perform the following tasks:

1. Make sure the vnode is that of a directory (unless the last component has been reached). The v_type field in the vnode contains this information.

---

[9] A process can call *chroot* to change its notion of the root directory to something other than the system root. This affects how the kernel interprets absolute pathnames for this process. Usually, certain login shells call *chroot* on behalf of the process. System administrators may use this facility to restrict some users to a part of the global file tree. To allow for this case, lookuppn() first examines the u.u_rdir field in the u area and, if that is NULL, checks the rootdir variable.

2. If the component is "..," and the current directory is the system root, move on to the next component. The system root directory acts as its own parent.

3. If the component is "..," and the current directory is the root of a mounted file system, access the *mount point* directory. All root directories have the VROOT flag set. The v_vfsp field points to the vfs structure for that file system, which contains a pointer to the *mount point* in the field vfs_vnodecovered.

4. Invoke the VOP_LOOKUP operation on this vnode. This results in a call to the *lookup* function of this specific file system (s5lookup(), ufs_lookup(), etc.). This function searches the directory for the component and, if found, returns a pointer to the vnode of that file (allocating it if not already in the kernel). It also acquires a hold on that vnode.

5. If the component was not found, check to see if this is the last component. If so, return success (the caller may have intended to create the file) and also pass back a pointer to the parent directory without releasing the hold on it. Otherwise, return with an ENOENT error.

6. If the new component is a mount point (v_vfsmountedhere != NULL), follow the pointer to the vfs object of the mounted file system and invoke its vfs_root operation to return the *root vnode* of that file system.

7. If the new component is a symbolic link (v_type == VLNK), invoke its VOP_SYMLINK operation to translate the symbolic link. Append the rest of the pathname to the contents of the link and restart the iteration. If the link contains an absolute pathname, the parsing must resume from the system root.

    The caller of lookuppn() may pass a flag that suppresses symbolic link evaluation for the last component of the pathname. This is to accommodate certain system calls such as *lstat* that do not want to traverse symbolic links at the end of pathnames. Also, a global parameter called MAXSYMLINKS (usually set to 20) limits the maximum number of symbolic links that may be traversed during a single call to lookuppn(). This prevents the function from going into a possibly infinite loop due to badly conceived symbolic links— for example, if **/x/y** were a symbolic link to **/x**.

8. Release the directory it just finished searching. The hold was acquired by the VOP_LOOKUP operation. For the starting point, it was explicitly obtained by lookuppn().

9. Finally, go back to the top of the loop and search for the next component in the directory represented by the new vnode.

10. When no components are left, or if a component is not found, terminate the search. If the search was successful, do not release the hold on the final vnode and return a pointer to this vnode to the caller.

8.10.2   Directory Lookup Cache

The *directory name lookup cache* is a central resource available to any file system implementations wishing to use it. It consists of an LRU (*least recently used* order) cache of objects that contain a directory vnode pointer, the name of a file in that directory, and a pointer to the vnode of that file. The cache locates its entries rapidly by organizing them in hash buckets based on the parent directory and filename.

If a file system wishes to use the name cache, its *lookup* function (the one that implements the VOP_LOOKUP operation) first searches the cache for the desired file name. If found, it simply increments the reference count of the vnode and returns it to the caller. This avoids the directory search, thus saving several disk reads. Cache hits are likely since programmers typically make several requests on a few frequently used files and directories. In event of a cache miss, the lookup function searches the directory. If the component is found, it adds a new cache entry for future use.

Since the file system can access vnodes without going through pathname traversal, it may perform operations that invalidate a cache entry. For instance, a user may unlink a file, and the kernel may later reassign the vnode to another file. Without proper precautions, a subsequent search for the old file may result in an incorrect cache hit, fetching a vnode that does not belong to that file. The cache must therefore provide a way of ensuring or checking the validity of its entries. Both 4.3BSD and SVR4 implement a directory lookup cache, and each uses a different technique to resolve this issue.

4.3BSD does not use the vnode/vfs interface, and its name lookup cache directly locates the in-memory inode of the file. The inode has a *generation number,* also called a *capability,* which is incremented each time the inode is reassigned to a new file. The name lookup cache is hint-based. When adding a new entry to the cache, the file system copies the inode generation number of the file into the entry. The cache lookup function checks this number against the current generation number of the inode. If the numbers are unequal, the entry is invalid and results in a cache miss.

In SVR4, the cache entry holds a reference to the vnode of the cached file and releases it when the entry is flushed or reassigned. Although this method ensures that cache entries are always valid, it has certain drawbacks. For example, the kernel must retain some inactive vnodes simply because there is a name cache entry that references them. Also, it prevents other parts of the kernel from ensuring exclusive use of a file or device.

8.10.3 The VOP_LOOKUP Operation

VOP_LOOKUP is the interface to the file-system-specific function that looks up a filename component in a directory. It is invoked through a macro as follows:

```
error = VOP_LOOKUP(vp, compname, &tvp, ...);
```

where vp is a pointer to the parent directory vnode and compname is the component name. On successful return, tvp must point to the vnode of compname and its reference count must be incremented.

Like other operations in this interface, this results in a call to a file-system-specific *lookup* function. Usually, this function first searches the name lookup cache. If there is a cache hit, it increments the reference count and returns the vnode pointer. In case of a cache miss, it searches the parent directory for the name. Local file systems perform the search by iterating through the directory entries block by block. Distributed file systems send a search request to the server node.

If the directory contains a valid match for the component, the lookup function checks if the vnode of the file is already in memory. Each file system has its own method of keeping track of its in-memory objects. In *ufs,* for instance, the directory search results in an inode number, which *ufs* uses to index into a hash table and search for the inode. The in-memory inode contains the vnode. If the vnode is found in memory, the lookup function increments its reference count and returns it to the caller.

Often the directory search produces a match for the component, but the vnode is not in memory. The lookup function must allocate and initialize a vnode, as well as the file-system-dependent private data structure. Usually, the vnode is part of the private data structure, and hence both are allocated as one unit. The two objects are initialized by reading in the attributes of the file. The v_op field of the vnode is set to point to the vnodeops vector for this file system, and a hold is added to the vnode. Finally, the lookup function adds an entry to the directory name lookup cache and places it at the end of the LRU list of the cache.

8.10.4   Opening a File

The arguments to the *open* system call include a pathname, a set of flags, and permissions to assign to the file should it need to be created. The flags include O_READ, O_WRITE, O_APPEND, O_TRUNC (truncate to zero length), O_CREAT (create the file if it does not exist), and O_EXCL (used in conjunction with O_CREAT to return an error if file already exists). The implementation of *open* is handled almost entirely in the file-system-independent layer. The algorithm is as follows:

1. Allocate a file descriptor (see Section 8.2.3). If *open* returns successfully, its return value is an index that identifies the descriptor in the chunk list.
2. Allocate an open file object (struct file) and store a pointer to it in the file descriptor. SVR4 allocates this object dynamically. Earlier implementations use a static, fixed-size table.
3. Call lookuppn() to traverse the pathname and return the vnode of the file to be opened. lookuppn() also returns a pointer to the parent directory vnode.
4. Check the vnode (by invoking its VOP_ACCESS operation) to ensure that the caller has the permissions necessary for the type of access desired.
5. Check for, and reject, certain illegal operations, such as opening a directory or an active executable file for writing (otherwise, the user executing the program will get unexpected results).
6. If the file does not exist, check if the O_CREAT option is specified. If so, invoke VOP_CREATE on the parent directory to create the file. Otherwise, return the ENOENT error code.
7. Invoke the VOP_OPEN operation of that vnode for the system-dependent processing. Typically, this routine does nothing, but some file systems may wish to perform additional tasks at this point. For instance, the *specfs* file system, which handles all device files, might want to call the *open* routine of the device driver.
8. If the O_TRUNC option has been specified, invoke VOP_SETATTR to set the file size to zero. The file-system-dependent code will perform the necessary cleanup, such as releasing the file's data blocks.
9. Initialize the open file object. Store the vnode pointer and the open mode flags in it, set its reference count to one and its offset pointer to zero.
10. Finally, return the index of the file descriptor to the user.

Note that `lookuppn()` increments the reference count on the vnode and also initializes its `v_op` pointer. This ensures that subsequent system calls can access the file using the file descriptor (the vnode will remain in memory) and that the file-system-dependent functions will be correctly routed.

8.10.5 File I/O

To perform I/O to a file, a user first opens it and then calls *read* or *write* (*readv* or *writev* for scatter-gather I/O) on the descriptor returned by the *open* call. The file-system-independent code packages the parameters of the request into a `uio` structure as described in Section 8.2.5. In case of the *read* and *write* calls, the `uio` will point to a single-element `iovec[]` array. The kernel uses the file descriptor to locate the open file object and checks that the file is opened for the type of access desired. If so, it dereferences the vnode pointer in the open file object to locate the vnode.

UNIX semantics demand that I/O system calls to a file be serialized. If two users simultaneously call *read* or *write* to the same file, the kernel must complete one operation before starting the other. Hence the kernel locks the vnode before starting the *read* or *write* and unlocks it after the I/O completes. SVR4 does so using the new `VOP_RWLOCK` and `VOP_RWUNLOCK` operations. Finally, it calls the `VOP_READ` or `VOP_WRITE` function for the file-system-dependent processing of the operation. Most of the processing of the *read* and *write* system calls takes place in the file-system-dependent layer. This is described further in Section 9.3.3 for *s5fs* and Section 10.6.3 for NFS. In SVR4, file I/O is closely related to the virtual memory subsystem. This relationship is discussed in Section 14.8.

8.10.6 File Attributes

Several system calls either modify or inquire about specific attributes of a file such as owner ID or permissions (see Section 8.2.2). In earlier UNIX versions, these calls directly read or wrote fields in the in-core inode and, if necessary, copied them to the on-disk inode, all in a very implementation-dependent manner. Since the vnode interface can deal with quite arbitrary file system types, which may have very different on-disk and in-memory structures for metadata storage, it provides a generalized interface.

The operations `VOP_GETATTR` and `VOP_SETATTR` read and write file attributes, respectively, using a file-system-independent object called a `struct vattr`. Although this structure contains the information found in a typical *s5fs* or *ufs* inode, the format is quite generic and not tied to any particular file system types. It is up to the specific implementations to translate between the information in this structure and its own metadata structures.

8.10.7 User Credentials

Several file system operations must check if the caller has the permissions for the type of file access desired. Such access control is governed by the user ID and group IDs of the caller, which traditionally were stored in the u area of the calling process. In modern UNIX systems, this information is encapsulated in a *credentials* object (struct cred), which is explicitly passed (through a pointer) to most file operations.

Each process has a statically allocated credentials object, typically in the u area or proc structure. For operations on local files, we pass a pointer to this object, which seems no different from the earlier treatment of obtaining the information directly from the u area. The benefit of the new method is in the handling of remote file operations, which are executed by a server process on behalf of remote clients. Here, the permissions are determined by the credentials of the client, not by those of the server process. Thus the server can dynamically allocate a credentials structure for each client request and initialize it with the UID and GIDs of the client.

Since these credentials are passed from one operation to another, and must be retained until the operations complete, the kernel associates a reference count with each object and frees the structure when the count drops to zero.

8.11   Analysis

The vnode/vfs interface provides a powerful programming paradigm. It allows multiple file system types to coexist. Vendors may add file systems to the kernel in a modular fashion. The object-oriented framework effectively separates the file system from the rest of the kernel. This has led to the development of several interesting file system implementations. The file system types found in a typical SVR4 installation include:

s5fs	Original System V file system
ufs	Berkeley Fast File System, adapted to the vnode/vfs interface
vxfs	Veritas journaling file system, which has several advanced features
specfs	A file system for device special files
NFS	Network File System
RFS	Remote File Sharing file system
fifofs	A file system for first-in, first-out files
/proc	A file system that represents each process as a file
bfs	Boot file system

Many variants, such as Solaris, also support the MS-DOS FAT file system. This is particularly useful for moving files to and from DOS machines through *floppy disks*. The next few chapters describe a number of file systems in greater detail.

The SunOS vnode/vfs design, now incorporated into SVR4, has gained wide acceptance. It is important, however, to examine some of its drawbacks and to see how some other UNIX variants have addressed these issues. Its shortcomings are mainly the result of the way it implements path-name lookup. The remainder of this section examines these drawbacks and looks at some recent variants that address them.

8.11.1   Drawbacks of the SVR4 Implementation

One of the major performance problems is that `lookuppn()` translates the pathname one component at a time, calling the file-system-dependent `VOP_LOOKUP` function for each component. Not only does this cause excessive function call overhead but, for remote file systems, it also requires a large number of interactions between the client and the server. Such an approach was chosen since the primary concern was the support of Sun's Network File system (NFS), which restricts lookup operations to one component at a time. Since that is not necessarily true of all remote file systems, it would be preferable if the individual file system could decide what part of the file name to parse in one operation.

The second problem arises from the statelessness of the pathname lookup operation, again motivated by the stateless nature of the NFS protocol. Since the lookup operation does not lock the parent directory, it does not guarantee the validity of its results for any length of time. The following example illustrates the problems this causes.

Let us suppose a user requests the creation of the file **/a/b**. This is implemented in two steps. The kernel first performs a lookup to determine whether the file already exists. If it does not, the kernel creates the file, using the `VOP_CREAT` entry point of the vnode of **/a**. The problem is that between the time the lookup returned (with an `ENOENT` result) and the creation call, the **/a** directory was not locked, and another process may have created that very file. Therefore, to guarantee correctness, the `VOP_CREAT` operation has to rescan the directory, causing unnecessary overhead.

One way to avoid this overhead is for the lookup function to not translate the final component whenever the lookup is to be followed by a *create* or *delete* operation. This compromises the modularity of the interface, since the operations are not independent of each other.

There have been several alternative approaches to providing multiple file system support in UNIX. Each of them is based on the concept of having a generic interface implemented by individual file systems. The differences can be traced to variations in design goals, differences in the base operating systems, and from the specific file systems primarily targeted by the designs. Two of the early alternatives were the *file system switch* in AT&T's SVR3 UNIX [Rifk 86] and the *generic file system (GFS)* in Ultrix [Rodr 86]. Both retained the concept of the inode as the principal object representing a file, but split the inode into file-system-dependent and file-system-independent parts. Among the modern UNIX variants, both 4.4BSD and OSF/1 provide alternative models of the vnode interface. The following sections describe these interfaces.

There are other, more fundamental, problems with the vnode/vfs interface. Although it is designed to allow modular file system development, it does not meet this goal well. It is impossible to write any but the most trivial file systems without having the operating system source code. There are many intricate dependencies between the file system and the memory management subsystem, some of which are explained in Section 14.8. Moreover, the interface is not consistent across different UNIX variants, nor across different releases of the same operating system. As a result, while a small number of new, full-function file systems have been developed using this interface (such as Episode and BSD-LFS, described in Chapter 11), file system development is still a difficult process. Section 11.11 analyzes these issues in greater detail and describes new work based on a *stackable vnode* interface that provides better facilities for building file systems.

8.11.2   The 4.4BSD Model

The 4.4BSD vnode interface [Kare 86] tries to rectify the shortcomings of the SunOS/SVR4 approach by using a stateful model and an enhanced lookup operation that incorporates features of the 4.3BSD (and GFS) namei interface. It permits locking of vnodes across multiple operations and passes state information between related operations of a multistage system call.

Pathname traversal is driven by the namei() routine, which first calls the lookup routine for the current directory vnode, passing it the entire pathname to be translated. The file-system-dependent *lookup* routine may translate one or more components in a single call, but will not cross a mount point. An implementation such as NFS may translate just one component in one call, whereas *s5fs* or *ufs* lookup routines may translate the whole pathname (unless there is a mount point in the path). namei() passes the remainder of the pathname to the next lookup operation, after performing mount point processing if applicable.

The arguments to the lookup function are encapsulated in a nameidata structure. This structure contains several additional fields for passing state information and for returning extra information. It may then be passed on to other operations such as *create* and *symlink,* allowing related operations to share a lot of state without passing several variables on the stack.

One of the fields in nameidata states the reason for the pathname traversal. If the search is for creation or deletion, then the final lookup operation locks the vnode of the parent directory. It also returns additional information in nameidata, such as the location of the file in that directory (if found) and the first empty slot in the directory (for subsequent creation). This nameidata structure is then passed on to the *create* or *delete* operation. Since the parent directory was locked by the lookup, its contents are unchanged and the *create* or *delete* does not have to repeat the final directory search. Upon completion, this operation will unlock the parent directory.

Sometimes, after lookup completes, the kernel might decide not to proceed with the creation or deletion (perhaps because the caller does not have adequate permissions). In that case, it must invoke an abortop operation to release the lock on the parent directory.

Even though the interface is stateful, in that locks may be held across multiple operations, the locking and unlocking are performed in the file-system-dependent layer. The interface can thus accommodate both stateless and stateful file systems, while avoiding redundant operations where possible. For instance, stateless file systems such as NFS may perform no locking of the parent directory and, in fact, may choose to defer the search for the final component to the *create* or *delete* operation that follows.

The major problem with this approach is that it serializes all operations on a directory, since the lock is held for the entire duration of the operation, even if the caller must block for I/O. The implementation uses an exclusive lock, which prevents even two read-only operations from executing in parallel. In particular, for time-sharing systems, this would cause great delays while accessing highly shared directories such as "/" or "/**etc**". For multiprocessor implementations, such serialization is particularly unacceptable.

Another optimization involved the maintenance of a per-process cache of the directory and offset of the last successful name lookup. This helps the performance of operations that iteratively act on all files of a directory. namei() uses this cache while searching for the final component of a pathname. If the parent directory is the same as in the previous call to namei(), the search begins at this cached offset instead of at the start of the directory (wrapping around the end if necessary).

The 4.4BSD file system interface provides many other interesting features, such as *stackable* vnodes and *union mounts*. These are described in Section 11.12.

8.11.3   The OSF/1 Approach

OSF/1 sought to eliminate the performance problems associated with redundant directory operations while retaining the stateless nature of the vnode interface. Moreover, the approach had to work correctly and efficiently both on uniprocessor and multiprocessor systems. This was implemented [LoVe 91] by considering all state information passed between related operations as simply a hint. This hint was associated with a timestamp, which could be checked for validity by subsequent operations. The file system could use these hints at its discretion to avoid redundant checking when the information had not changed between operations.

The file metadata is protected by a multiprocessor-safe, mutual-exclusion *(mutex)* lock. This mutex is implemented as a simple spin lock, and held for brief periods of time. In particular, this lock is held only by the file-system-dependent code, and never across multiple operations, which means that metadata might change between operations. Such changes are monitored by associating a timestamp with each such synchronization object. This timestamp consists of a simple, monotonically increasing counter incremented each time the associated object is modified. The hint-based directory lookup cache in 4BSD, described in Section 8.10.2, uses a similar scheme.

As an example, consider the operation of creating a file. While searching for the last component, the *lookup* operation locks the parent directory and scans it to check if the file already exists. If not, it determines the offset in the directory where the new entry can be placed. It then unlocks the parent directory and returns this information to the caller, along with the current timestamp of the parent directory. Subsequently, the kernel calls direnter() to make the new entry in the parent directory, and passes it the suggested offset along with the saved timestamp. direnter() compares this timestamp with the current timestamp of the directory. If the two are equal, the directory is unchanged since the lookup, and the name can be inserted at the suggested offset without rechecking the directory. If the timestamps are different, the directory has been modified in the meantime and the search must be repeated.

These changes were motivated by performance considerations for multiprocessor platforms, but their advantages are also apparent for the uniprocessor case. The changes cause some new race conditions, but those that have been identified have been fixed by methods described in [LoVe 91]. The OSF/1 model combines the advantages of the stateless and stateful models and supports several file systems such as AFS (see Section 10.15) and Episode (see Section 11.8).

8.12   Summary

The vnode/vfs interface provides a powerful mechanism for modular development and addition of file systems to the UNIX kernel. It allows the kernel to deal simply with abstract representations of files called vnodes and relegates the file-system-dependent code to a separate layer accessed through a well-defined interface. Vendors may build file systems that implement this interface. The process is similar to writing a device driver.

It is important, however, to note the great variation in the different incarnations of this interface. While various implementations such as SVR4, BSD, and OSF/1 are all based on similar general principles, they differ substantially both in the specifics of the interface (such as the set of operations and their arguments, as well as the format of the vnode and vfs structures), and in their policies regarding state, synchronization, etc. This means that file system developers would have to make major modifications to make their file system compatible with the different vfs interfaces.

8.13   Exercises

1. What are the advantages of having a byte-stream representation of files? In what ways is this model inadequate?
2. Suppose a program makes repeated calls to *readdir* to list the contents of a directory. What would happen if other users were to create and delete files in the directory in between?
3. Why are users never allowed to directly write to a directory?
4. Why are file attributes not stored in the directory entry itself?
5. Why does each process have a default creation mask? Where is this mask stored? Why does the kernel not use the mode supplied to *open* or *creat* directly?
6. Why should a user not be allowed to write to a file opened in read-only mode, if he or she has privileges to do so?
7. Consider the following shell script called `myscript`:
    ```
    date
    cat /etc/motd
    ```
    What is the effect of executing the following command? How are the file descriptors shared?
    ```
    myscript > result.log
    ```
8. What is the advantage of having *lseek* be a separate system call, instead of passing the starting offset to every *read* or *write?* What are the drawbacks?
9. When would a *read* return fewer bytes than requested?
10. What are the benefits of scatter-gather I/O? What applications are most likely to use it?
11. What is the difference between advisory and mandatory locks? What kind of applications are likely to use byte-range locks?
12. Suppose a user's current working directory is **/usr/mnt/kaumu**. If the administrator mounts a new file system on the **/usr/mnt** directory, how will it affect this user? Would the user be able to continue to see the files in **kaumu**? What would be the result of a *pwd* command? What other commands would behave unexpectedly?
13. What are the drawbacks of using a symbolic link instead of a hard link?
14. Why are hard links not allowed to span file systems?
15. What problems could arise from incorrect use of hard links to directories?
16. What should the kernel do when the reference count on a vnode drops to zero?

17.   Discuss the relative merits and drawbacks of hint-based and reference-based directory name lookup caches.

18.   [Bark 90] and [John 95] describe two implementations that dynamically allocate and deallocate vnodes. Can such a system use a hint-based name lookup cache?

19.   Give an example of an infinite loop caused by symbolic links. How does `lookuppn()` handle this?

20.   Why does the `VOP_LOOKUP` operation parse only one component at a time?

21.   4.4BSD allows a process to lock a vnode across multiple vnode operations in a single system call. What would happen if the process was killed by a signal while holding the lock? How can the kernel handle this situation?

8.14   References

[Bach 86]   Bach, M.J., *The Design of the UNIX Operating System,* Prentice-Hall, Englewood Cliffs, NJ, 1986.

[Bark 90]   Barkley, R.E., and Lee, T.P., "A Dynamic File System Inode Allocation and Reallocation Policy," *Proceedings of the Winter 1990 USENIX Technical Conference,* Jan. 1990, pp. 1–9.

[DoD 85]   Department of Defense, *Trusted Computer System Evaluation Criteria,* DOD 5200.28–STD, Dec. 1985.

[Elli 90]   Ellis, M.A., and Stroustrup, B., *The Annotated C++ Reference Manual,* Addison-Wesley, Reading, MA, 1990.

[Fern 88]   Fernandez, G., and Allen, L., "Extending the UNIX Protection Model with Access Control Lists," *Proceedings of the Summer 1988 USENIX Technical Conference,* Jun. 1988, pp. 119–132.

[John 95]   John, A., "Dynamic Vnodes—Design and Implementation," *Proceedings of the Winter 1995 USENIX Technical Conference,* Jan. 1995, pp. 11–23.

[Kare 86]   Karels, M.J. and McKusick, M.K., "Toward a Compatible Filesystem Interface," *Proceedings of the Autumn 1986 European UNIX Users' Group Conference,* Oct. 1986, pp. 481–496.

[Klei 86]   Kleiman, S.R., "Vnodes: An Architecture for Multiple File System Types in Sun UNIX," *Proceedings of the Summer 1986 USENIX Technical Conference,* Jun. 1986, pp. 238–247.

[LoVe 91]   LoVerso, S., Paciorek, N., Langerman, A., and Feinberg, G., "The OSF/1 UNIX Filesystem (UFS)," *Proceedings of the Winter 1991 USENIX Conference,* Jan. 1991, pp. 207–218.

[McKu 84]   McKusick, M.K., Joy, W.N., Leffler, S.J., and Fabry, R.S., "A Fast File System for UNIX," *ACM Transactions on Computer Systems,* vol. 2, (Aug. 1984), pp. 181–197.

[Patt 88]   Patterson, D.A., Gibson, G.A., and Katz, R.H., "A Case for Redundant Arrays of Inexpensive Disks (RAID)," *Proceedings of the 1988 ACM SIGMOD Conference of Management of Data,* Jun. 1988.

[Rifk 86]   Rifkin, A.P., Forbes, M.P., Hamilton, R.L., Sabrio, M., Shah, S., and Yueh, K., "RFS Architectural Overview," *Proceedings of the Summer 1986 USENIX Technical Conference,* Jun. 1986, pp. 248–259.

[Rodr 86]   Rodriguez, R., Koehler, M., and Hyde, R., "The Generic File System," *Proceedings of the Summer 1986 USENIX Technical Conference,* Jun. 1986, pp. 260–269.

[Thom 78]   Thompson, K., "UNIX Implementation," *The Bell System Technical Journal,* Jul.-Aug. 1978, Vol. 57, No. 6, Part 2, pp. 1931–1946.

[UNIX 92]   UNIX System Laboratories, *Operating System API Reference, UNIX SVR4.2,* UNIX Press, Prentice-Hall, Englewood Cliffs, NJ, 1992.

9

File System Implementations

9.1 Introduction

The previous chapter described the *vnode/vfs interface,* which provides a framework for supporting multiple file system types and defines the interface between the file system and the rest of the kernel. Today's UNIX systems support many different types of file systems. These can be classified as local or distributed. Local file systems store and manage their data on devices directly connected to the system. Distributed file systems allow a user to access files residing on remote machines. This chapter describes many local file systems. Chapter 10 discusses distributed file systems, and Chapter 11 describes some newer file systems that provide advanced features such as journaling, volume management, and high availability.

The two local, general-purpose file systems found in most modern UNIX systems are the System V file system *(s5fs)* and the Berkeley Fast File System (FFS). *s5fs* [Thom 78] is the original UNIX file system. All versions of System V, as well as several commercial UNIX systems, support *s5fs*. FFS, introduced by Berkeley UNIX in release 4.2BSD, provides more performance, robustness, and functionality than *s5fs*. It gained wide commercial acceptance, culminating in its inclusion in SVR4. (SVR4 supports three general-purpose file systems: *s5fs,* FFS, and V*x*FS, the Veritas journaling file system.)

When FFS was first introduced, the UNIX file system framework could support only one type of file system. This forced vendors to choose between *s5fs* and FFS. The vnode/vfs interface, introduced by Sun Microsystems [Klei 86] allowed multiple file system types to coexist on a single machine. The file system implementations also required modifications to integrate with the vnode/vfs framework. The integrated version of FFS is now known as the UNIX file system *(ufs)*.[1] [Bach 86] provides a comprehensive discussion of *s5fs,* and [Leff 89] does so for FFS. This chapter summarizes and compares the two implementations, both for completeness and to provide the background for understanding the advanced file systems described in the following chapters.

In UNIX, the file abstraction includes various I/O objects, including network connections through sockets or STREAMS, interprocess communication mechanisms such as pipes and FIFOs, and block and character devices. The vnode/vfs architecture builds on this philosophy by representing both files and file systems as abstractions that present a modular interface to the rest of the kernel. This motivated the development of several special-purpose file systems. Many of these have little to do with files or I/O and merely exploit the abstract nature of this interface to provide special functionality. This chapter examines some of the interesting implementations.

Finally, this chapter describes the UNIX *block buffer cache*. In earlier UNIX versions such as SVR3 and 4.3BSD, all file I/O used this cache. Modern releases such as SVR4 integrate file I/O and memory management, accessing files by mapping them into the kernel's address space. Although this chapter provides some details about this approach, most of the discussion must be deferred to Chapter 14, which describes the SVR4 virtual memory implementation. The traditional buffer cache mechanism is still used for *metadata* blocks. The term *metadata* refers to the attributes and ancillary information about a file or file system. Rather than being part of a specific file system implementation, the buffer cache is a global resource shared by all file systems.

We begin with *s5fs,* and describe its on-disk layout and kernel organization. Although FFS differs from *s5fs* in many important respects, it also has many similarities, and the basic operations are implemented in the same way. Our discussion of FFS will focus on the differences. Except where noted, the general algorithms of *s5fs,* described in Section 9.3, also apply to FFS.

9.2   The System V File System *(s5fs)*

The file system resides on a single logical disk or partition (see Section 8.3.1), and each logical disk may hold one file system at the most. Each file system is self-contained, complete with its own root directory, subdirectories, files, and all associated data and metadata. The user-visible file tree is formed by joining one or more such file systems.

Figure 9-1 shows the layout of an *s5fs* disk partition. A partition can be logically viewed as a linear array of blocks. The size of a disk block is 512 bytes multiplied by some power of two (different releases have used block sizes of 512, 1024, or 2048 bytes). It represents the granularity of space allocation for a file, and that of an I/O operation. The *physical block number* (or simply, the block number) is an index into this array, and uniquely identifies a block on a given disk partition. This number must be translated by the disk driver into cylinder, track, and sector numbers. The translation depends on the physical characteristics of the disk (number of cylinders and tracks, sectors per track, etc.) and the location of the partition on the disk.

---

[1] Initially, the term *ufs* differed in meaning for different variants. System V-based releases used it to refer to their native file system, which is now known as *s5fs*. BSD-based systems used the terms *ufs* and *s5fs* as we use them in this book. The confusion was resolved when SVR4 also adopted this convention.

Figure 9-1. *s5fs* on-disk layout.

At the beginning of the partition is the *boot area,* which may contain code required to *boot-strap* (load and initialize) the operating system. Although only one partition needs to contain this information, each partition contains a possibly empty boot area. The boot area is followed by the *superblock,* which contains attributes and metadata of the file system itself.

Following the superblock is the *inode list,* which is a linear array of *inodes.* There is one inode for each file. Inodes are described in Section 9.2.2. Each inode can be identified by its *inode number,* which equals its index in the inode list. The size of an inode is 64 bytes. Several inodes fit into a single disk block. The starting offsets of the superblock and the inode list are the same for all partitions on a system. Consequently, an inode number can be easily translated to a block number and the offset of the inode from the start of that block. *The inode list has a fixed size (configured while creating the file system on that partition), which limits the maximum number of files the partition can contain.* The space after the inode list is the *data area.* It holds data blocks for files and directories, as well as *indirect blocks,* which hold pointers to file data blocks and are described in Section 9.2.2.

9.2.1   Directories

An *s5fs directory* is a special file containing a list of files and subdirectories. It contains fixed-size records of 16 bytes each. The first two bytes contain the inode number, and the next fourteen the file name. This places a limit of 65535 files per disk partition (since 0 is not a valid inode number) and 14 characters per file name. If the filename has fewer than fourteen characters, it is terminated by a NULL character. Because the directory is a file, it also has an inode, which contains a field identifying the file as a directory. The first two entries in the directory are ".", which represents the directory itself, and "..", which denotes the parent directory. If the inode number of an entry is zero, it indicates that the corresponding file no longer exists. The root directory of a partition, as well as its ".." entry, always has an inode number of 2. This is how the file system can identify its root directory. Figure 9-2 shows a typical directory.

9.2.2   Inodes

Each file has an inode associated with it. The word *inode* derives from *index node.* The inode contains administrative information, or metadata, of the file. It is stored on disk within the inode list. When a file is open, or a directory is active, the kernel stores the data from the disk copy of the inode into an in-memory data structure, also called an inode. This structure has many additional fields that are not saved on disk. Whenever it is ambiguous, we use the term *on-disk inode* to refer

73	.
38	..
9	file1
0	deletedfile
110	subdirectory_1
65	archana

Figure 9-2. *s5fs* directory structure.

to the on-disk data structure (struct dinode) and *in-core inode* to refer to the in-memory structure
(struct inode). Table 9-1 describes the fields of the on-disk inode.

The di_mode field is subdivided into several bit-fields (Figure 9-3). The first four bits specify the *file type,* which may be IFREG (regular file), IFDIR (directory), IFBLK (block device), IFCHR
(character device), etc. The nine low-order bits specify read, write, and execute permissions for the
owner, members of the owner's group, and others, respectively.

The di_addr field requires elaboration. UNIX files are not contiguous on disk. As a file
grows, the kernel allocates new blocks from any convenient location on the disk. This has the advantage that it is easy to grow and shrink files without the disk fragmentation inherent in contiguous
allocation schemes. Obviously, fragmentation is not completely eliminated, because the last block
of each file may contain unused space. On average, each file wastes half a block of space.

This approach requires the file system to maintain a map of the disk location of every block
of the file. Such a list is organized as an array of physical block addresses. The logical block number
within a file forms an index into this array. The size of this array depends on the size of the file. A
very large file may require several disk blocks to store this array. Most files, however, are quite
small [Saty 81], and a large array would only waste space. Moreover, storing the disk block array on
a separate block would incur an extra read when the file is accessed, resulting in poor performance.

Table 9-1. Fields of struct dinode

Field	Size (bytes)	Description
di_mode	2	file type, permissions, etc.
di_nlinks	2	number of hard links to file
di_uid	2	owner UID
di_gid	2	owner GID
di_size	4	size in bytes
di_addr	39	array of block addresses
di_gen	1	generation number (incremented each time inode is re-used for a new file)
di_atime	4	time of last access
di_mtime	4	time file was last modified
di_ctime	4	time inode was last changed (except changes to di_atime or di_mtime)

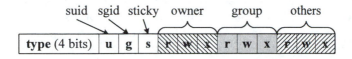

Figure 9-3. Bit-fields of di_mode.

The UNIX solution is to store a small list in the inode itself and use extra blocks for large files. This is very efficient for small files, yet flexible enough to handle very large files. Figure 9-4 illustrates this scheme. The 39-byte di_addr field comprises a thirteen-element array, with each element storing a 3-byte physical block number. Elements 0 through 9 in this array contain the block numbers of blocks 0 through 9 of the file. Thus, for a file containing 10 blocks or fewer, all the block addresses are in the inode itself. Element 10 is the block number of an indirect block, that is, a block that contains an array of block numbers. Element 11 points to a *double-indirect block,* which contains block numbers of other indirect blocks. Finally, element 12 points to a *triple-indirect block,* which contains block numbers of double-indirect blocks.

Such a scheme, for a 1024-byte block size, allows addressing of 10 blocks directly, 256 more blocks through the single indirect block, 65536 (256×256) more blocks through the double indirect block, and 16,777,216 ($256 \times 256 \times 256$) more blocks through the triple indirect block.

UNIX files may contain *holes.* A user may create a file, seek (set the *offset pointer* in the open file object by calling *lseek*—see Section 8.2.4) to a large offset, and write data to it. The space before this offset contains no data and is a hole in the file. If a process tries to read that part of the file, it will see NULL (zero-valued) bytes.

Such holes can sometimes be large, spanning entire blocks. It is wasteful to allocate disk space for such blocks. Instead, the kernel sets the corresponding elements of the di_addr array, or

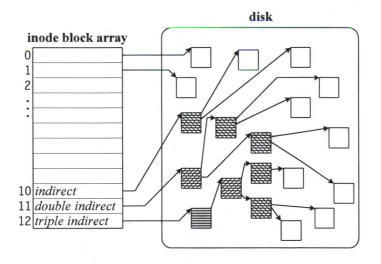

Figure 9-4. disk block array in *s5fs* inode.

of the indirect block, to zero. When a user tries to read such a block, the kernel returns a zero-filled block. Disk space is allocated only when someone tries to write data to the block.

Refusing to allocate disk space for holes has some important consequences. A process may unexpectedly run out of disk space while trying to write data to the hole. If a file containing a hole is copied, the new file will have zero-filled pages on the disk instead of the hole. This happens because copying involves reading the file's contents and writing them to the destination file. When the kernel reads a hole, it creates zero-filled pages, which are then copied without further interpretation. *This can cause problems for backup and archiving utilities such as **tar** or **cpio** that operate at the file level rather than the raw disk level. A system administrator may back up a file system, and discover that the same disk does not have enough room to restore its contents.*

9.2.3   The Superblock

The *superblock* contains metadata about the file system itself. There is one superblock for each file system, and it resides at the beginning of the file system on disk. The kernel reads the superblock when mounting the file system and stores it in memory until the file system is unmounted. The superblock contains the following information:

- Size in blocks of the file system.
- Size in blocks of the inode list.
- Number of free blocks and inodes.
- Free block list.
- Free inode list.

Because the file system may have many of free inodes or disk blocks, it is impractical to keep either free list completely in the superblock. In the case of inodes, the superblock maintains a partial list. When the list becomes empty, the kernel scans the disk to find free inodes (di_mode == 0) to replenish the list.

This approach is not possible for the free block list, since there is no way to determine if a block is free by examining its contents. Hence, at all times, the file system must maintain a complete list of all free blocks in the disk. As shown in Figure 9-5, this list spans several disk blocks.

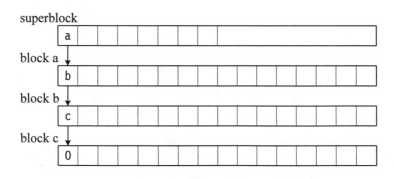

Figure 9-5. free block list in *s5fs*.

The superblock contains the first part of the list and adds and removes blocks from its tail. The first element in this list points to the block containing the next part of the list, and so forth.

At some point, the block allocation routine discovers that the free block list in the super-block contains only a single element. The value stored in that element is the number of the block containing the next part of the free list (block *a* in Figure 9-5) . It copies the list from that block into the superblock, and that block now becomes free. This has the advantage that the space required to store the free block list depends directly on the amount of free space on the partition. For a nearly full disk, no space needs to be wasted to store the free block list.

9.3   *S5fs* Kernel Organization

The inode is the fundamental file-system-dependent object of *s5fs*. It is the private data structure associated with an *s5fs* vnode. As mentioned earlier, in-core inodes are different from on-disk inodes. This section discusses in-core inodes, and how *s5fs* manipulates them to implement various file system operations.

9.3.1   In-Core Inodes

The `struct inode` represents an in-core inode. It contains all the fields of the on-disk inode, and some additional fields, such as:

- The *vnode*—the i_vnode field of the inode contains the vnode of the file.
- *Device ID* of the partition containing the file.
- *Inode number* of the file.
- *Flags* for synchronization and cache management.
- Pointers to keep the inode on a *free list*.
- Pointers to keep the inode on a *hash queue*. The kernel hashes inodes by their inode numbers, so as to locate them quickly when needed.
- Block number of *last block read.*

Figure 9-6 uses a simple example with four hash queues to show how inodes are organized by *s5fs*.

The disk block array is handled differently. While the `di_addr[]` array in the on-disk inode used three bytes for each block number, the in-core inode uses four-byte elements. This is a trade-off between space and performance. Space saving is more critical for the on-disk inode; perform-ance is more important for the in-core inode.

9.3.2   Inode Lookup

The `lookuppn()` function in the file-system-independent layer performs pathname parsing. As de-scribed in Section 8.10.1, it parses one component at a time, invoking the `VOP_LOOKUP` operation. When searching an *s5fs* directory, this translates to a call to the `s5lookup()` function. `s5lookup()` first checks the *directory name lookup cache* (see Section 8.10.2). In case of a cache miss, it reads the directory one block at a time, searching the entries for the specified file name.

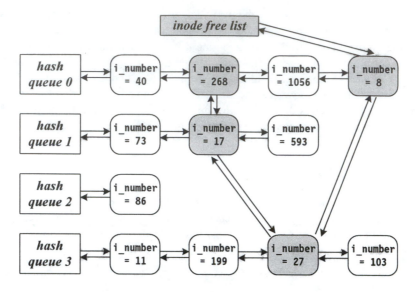

Figure 9-6. Organization of in-core inodes.

If the directory contains a valid entry for the file, s5lookup() obtains the inode number from the entry. It then calls iget() to locate that inode. iget() hashes on the inode number and searches the appropriate hash queue for the inode. If the inode is not in the table, iget() allocates an inode (this is described in Section 9.3.4), and initializes it by reading in the on-disk inode. While copying the on-disk inode fields to the in-core inode , it expands the di_addr[] elements to four bytes each. It then puts the inode on the appropriate hash queue. It also initializes the vnode, setting its v_op field to point to the s5vnodeops vector, v_data to point to the inode itself, and v_vfsp to point to the vfs to which the file belongs. Finally, it returns a pointer to the inode to s5lookup(). s5lookup(), in turn, returns a pointer to the vnode to lookuppn().

Note that iget() is the only function in *s5fs* that allocates and initializes inodes and vnodes. For instance, when creating a new file, s5create() allocates an unused inode number (from the free inode list in the superblock) and calls iget() to bring that inode into memory.

9.3.3   File I/O

The *read* and *write* system calls both accept a file descriptor (the index returned by open), a user buffer address that is the destination (for *read*) or source (for *write*) of the data, and a count specifying the number of bytes to be transferred. The offset in the file is obtained from the open file object associated with the descriptor. At the end of the I/O operation, this offset is advanced by the number of bytes transferred, which means the next *read* or *write* will begin where the previous one completed. For random I/O, the user must first call *lseek* to set the file offset to the desired location.

The file-system-independent code (see Section 8.6) uses the descriptor as an index into the descriptor table to obtain the pointer to the open file object (struct file) and verifies that the file is opened in the correct mode. If it is, the kernel obtains the vnode pointer from the `file` structure. Before starting I/O, the kernel invokes VOP_RWLOCK operation to serialize access to the file. *s5fs* implements this by acquiring an exclusive lock on the inode.[2] This ensures that all data read or written in a single system call is consistent and all *write* calls to the file are single-threaded. The kernel then invokes the vnode's VOP_READ or VOP_WRITE operation. This results in a call to `s5read()` or `s5write()`, respectively.

In earlier implementations, the file I/O routines used the *block buffer cache,* an area of memory reserved for file system blocks. SVR4 unifies file I/O with virtual memory and uses the buffer cache only for metadata blocks. Section 9.12 describes the old buffer cache. This section summarizes the SVR4 operations. They are further detailed in the discussion of virtual memory in Section 14.8.

Let us use the *read* operation as an example. `s5read()` translates the starting offset for the I/O operation to the logical block number in the file and the offset from the beginning of the block. It then reads the data one page[3] at a time, by mapping the block into the kernel virtual address space and calling `uiomove()` to copy the data into user space. `uiomove()` calls the `copyout()` routine to perform the actual data transfer. If the page is not in physical memory, or if the kernel does not have a valid address translation for it, `copyout()` will generate a page fault. The fault handler will identify the file to which the page belongs and invoke the VOP_GETPAGE operation on its vnode.

In *s5fs,* this operation is implemented by `s5getpage()`, which first calls a function called `bmap()` to convert the logical block number to a physical block number on the disk. It then searches the vnode's page list (pointed to by `v_page`) to see if the page is already in memory. If it is not, `s5getpage()` allocates a free page and calls the disk driver to read the data from disk.

The calling process sleeps until the I/O completes. When the block is read, the disk driver wakes up the process, which resumes the data copy in `copyout()`. Before copying the data to user space, `copyout()` verifies that the user has write access to the buffer into which it must copy the data. Otherwise, the user may inadvertently or maliciously specify a bad address, causing many problems. For instance, if the user specifies a kernel address, the kernel will overwrite its own text or data structures.

`s5read()` returns when all data has been read or an error has occurred. The system-independent code unlocks the vnode (using VOP_RWUNLOCK), advances the offset pointer in the `file` structure by the number of bytes read, and returns to the user. The return value of *read* is the total number of bytes read. This usually equals the number requested, unless the end of file is reached or some other error occurs.

The *write* system call proceeds similarly, with a few differences. The modified blocks are not written immediately to disk, but remain in memory, to be written out later according to the cache heuristics. Besides, the *write* may increase the file size and may require the allocation of data blocks, and perhaps indirect blocks, for disk addresses. Finally, if only part of a block is being written, the kernel must first read the entire block from disk, modify the relevant part, and then write it back to the disk.

---

[2]   Many UNIX variants use a single-writer, multiple-readers lock, which allows better concurrency.

[3]   A *page* is a memory abstraction. It may contain one block, many blocks, or part of a block.

9.3.4   Allocating and Reclaiming Inodes

An inode remains active as long as its vnode has a non-zero reference count. When the count drops to zero, the file-system-independent code invokes the VOP_INACTIVE operation, which frees the inode. In SVR2, free inodes are marked invalid, so they have to be read back from disk if needed. This is inefficient, and hence newer UNIX systems cache the inodes for as long as possible. When an inode becomes inactive, the kernel puts it on the free list, but does not invalidate it. The iget() function can find the inode if needed, because it remains on the correct hash queue until it is reused.

Each file system has a fixed-size *inode table* that limits the number of active inodes in the kernel. In SVR3, the inode caching mechanism simply uses a *least recently used* replacement algorithm. The kernel releases inodes to the back of this list and allocates them from the front of the list. Although this is a common cache heuristic, it is suboptimal for the inode cache. This is because certain inactive inodes are likely to be more useful than others.

When a file is actively used, its inode is *pinned* (see the following note) in the table. As the file is accessed, its pages are cached in memory. When the file becomes inactive, some of its pages may still be in memory. These pages can be located through the vnode's *page list,* accessed through its v_page field. The paging system also hashes them based on the *vnode pointer* and the *offset* of the page in the file. If the kernel reuses the inode (and vnode), these pages lose their identity. If a process needs the page, the kernel must read it back from disk, even though the page is still in memory.

> **Note:** *An object is said to be **pinned** in memory if it is ineligible for freeing or deletion. Reference-counted objects are pinned until the last reference is released. As another example, a process can pin part of its address space in memory using the **mlock** system call.*

It is therefore better to reuse those inodes that have no pages cached in memory. When the vnode reference count reaches zero, the kernel invokes its VOP_INACTIVE operation to release the vnode and its private data object (in this case, the inode). When releasing the inode, the kernel checks the vnode's page list. It releases the inode to the front of the free list if the page list is empty and to the back of the free list if any pages of the file are still in memory. In time, if the inode remains inactive, the paging system frees its pages.

[Bark 90] describes a new inode allocation and reclaim policy, which allows the number of in-core inodes to adjust to the load on the system. Instead of using a fixed-size inode table, the file systems allocate inodes dynamically using the kernel memory allocator. This allows the number of inodes in the system to rise and fall as needed. The system administrator no longer needs to guess the appropriate number of inodes to pre-configure into the system.

When iget() cannot locate an inode on its hash queue, it removes the first inode from the free list. If this inode still has pages in memory, iget() returns it to the back of the free list and calls the kernel memory allocator to allocate a new inode structure. It is possible to generalize the algorithm to scan the free list for an inode with no in-memory pages, but the implementation described here is simple and efficient. Its only drawback is that it may allocate a few more inodes in memory than are absolutely necessary.

Experiments using a multiuser, time-sharing workload benchmark [Gaed 82] show that the new algorithm reduces *system time* (amount of CPU time spent in kernel mode) usage by 12% to 16%. Although initially implemented for *s5fs,* the optimization is general enough to be applied to other file systems such as FFS.

9.4 Analysis of *s5fs*

s5fs is distinguished by its simple design. This very simplicity, however, creates problems in the areas of reliability, performance, and functionality. In this section we examine some of these problems, which have motivated the design of the BSD fast file system.

The major reliability concern is the superblock. The superblock contains vital information about the entire file system, such as the free block list and the size of the free inode list. Each file system contains a single copy of its superblock. If that copy is corrupted, the entire file system becomes unusable.

Performance suffers for several reasons. *s5fs* groups all inodes together at the beginning of the file system, and the remaining disk space contains the file data blocks. Accessing a file requires reading the inode and then the file data, so this segregation causes a long seek on the disk between the two operations and hence increases I/O times. Inodes are allocated randomly, with no attempt to group related inodes such as those of files in the same directory. Hence an operation that accesses all files in a directory (*ls -l,* for example) also causes a random disk access pattern.

Disk block allocation is also suboptimal. When the file system is first created (by a program called *mkfs*), *s5fs* configures the free block list optimally so that blocks are allocated in a rotationally consecutive order. However, as files are created and deleted, blocks are returned to the list in random order. After the file system has been used for a while, the order of blocks in the list becomes completely random. This slows down sequential access operations on files, because logically consecutive blocks may be very far apart on the disk.

Disk block size is another concern that affects performance. SVR2 used a block size of 512 bytes, and SVR3 raised it to 1024 bytes. Increasing the block size allows more data to be read in a single disk access, thus improving performance. At the same time, it wastes more disk space, since, on average, each file wastes half a block. This indicates the need for a more flexible approach to allocating space to files.

Finally, there are some major functionality limitations. Restricting of file names to 14 characters may not have mattered much in the pioneer days of UNIX, but for a powerful, commercially viable operating system, such a restriction is unacceptable. Several applications automatically generate file names, often by adding further extensions to existing file names, and they struggle to do this efficiently within 14 characters. The limit of 65535 inodes per file system is also too restrictive.

These concerns led to the development of a new file system in Berkeley UNIX. Known as the Fast File System (FFS), it was first released in 4.2BSD.[4] The following sections describe its important features.

---

[4] FFS first appeared in 4.1bBSD, which was a test release internal to Berkeley. It was also part of 4.1cBSD, another test release that was sent to about 100 sites [Salu 94].

9.5   The Berkeley Fast File System

The Fast File System [McKu 84] addresses many limitations of *s5fs*. The following sections describe its design and show how it improves reliability, performance, and functionality. FFS provides all the functionality of *s5fs,* and most of the system call handling algorithms and the kernel data structures remain unchanged. The major differences lie in the disk layout, on-disk structures, and free block allocation methods. FFS also provides new system calls to support these added features.

9.6   Hard Disk Structure

To understand the factors that influence the disk performance, it is important to examine the way data is laid out on a disk. Figure 9-7 shows the format of a typical hard disk manufactured in the early- and mid-1980s. This disk is composed of several *platters,* each associated with a *disk head.*[5] Each platter contains several *tracks* that form concentric circles; the outermost track is track 0, and so forth. Each track is further divided into *sectors,* and the sectors are also numbered sequentially. The sector size, typically 512 bytes, defines the granularity of a disk I/O operation. The term cylinder refers to the set of tracks, one per platter, at the same distance from the disk axis. Thus, cylinder zero comprises track zero of each platter, and so forth. On many disks, all disk heads move together. Hence at any given time, all the heads are on the same track number and same sector number of each platter.

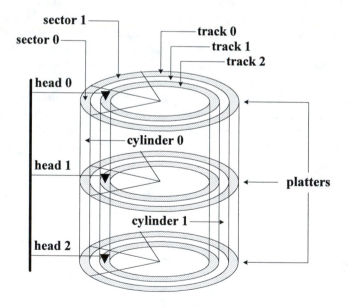

Figure 9-7. Conceptual view of a hard disk.

---

5   Actually, both sides of the platter are used, and there is a separate disk head for each side.

UNIX views the disk as a linear array of blocks. The number of sectors in a block is a small power of two; for this section, let us assume there is exactly one sector per block. When a UNIX process wants to read a particular block number, the device driver translates that into a logical sector number, and from it, computes the physical track, head, and sector number. In this scheme, the sector numbers increase first, then the head number, and finally the cylinder (track) number. Each cylinder thus contains a sequential set of block numbers. After computing the location of the desired block, the driver must move the disk heads to the appropriate cylinder. This *head seek* is the most time-consuming component of the disk I/O operation, and the seek latency depends directly on how far the heads must move. Once the heads move into position, we must wait while the disk spins until the correct sector passes under the heads. This delay is called the *rotational latency*. Once the correct sector is under the disk head, the transfer may begin. The actual transfer time is usually just the time for one sector to move across the head. Optimizing I/O bandwidth thus requires minimizing the number and size of the head seeks, and reducing rotational latency by proper placement of the blocks on the disk.

9.7   On-Disk Organization

A disk partition comprises of a set of consecutive cylinders on the disk, and a formatted partition holds a self-contained file system. FFS further divides the partition into one or more *cylinder groups,* each containing a small set of consecutive cylinders. This allows UNIX to store related data in the same cylinder group, thus minimizing disk head movements. Section 9.7.2 discusses this in greater detail.

The information in the traditional superblock is divided into two structures. The FFS superblock contains information about the entire file system—the number, sizes and locations of cylinder groups, block size, total number of blocks and inodes, and so forth. The data in the superblock does not change unless the file system is rebuilt. Furthermore, each cylinder group has a data structure describing summary information about that group, including the free inode and free block lists. The superblock is kept at the beginning of the partition (after the boot block area), but that is not enough. The data in the superblock is critical, and must be protected from disk errors. Each cylinder group therefore contains a duplicate copy of the superblock. FFS maintains these duplicates at different offsets in each cylinder group in such a way that no single track, cylinder, or platter contains all copies of the superblock. The space between the beginning of the cylinder group and the superblock copy is used for data blocks, except for the first cylinder group.

9.7.1   Blocks and Fragments

As discussed earlier, larger block sizes improve performance by allowing more data to be transferred in a single I/O operation, but waste more space (on average, each file wastes half a block). FFS tries to have the best of both worlds by dividing the blocks into *fragments*. In FFS, although all blocks in a single file system must be of same size, different file systems on the same machine may have different block sizes. The block size is a power of two greater than or equal to a minimum of 4096. Most implementations add an upper limit of 8192 bytes. This is much larger than the 512- or 1024-byte blocks in *s5fs* and, in addition to increased throughput, allows files as large as 2^{32} bytes

(4 gigabytes) to be addressed with only two levels of indirection. FFS does not use the triple indirect block, although some variants use it to support file sizes greater than 4 gigabytes.

Typical UNIX systems have numerous small files that need to be stored efficiently [Saty 81]. The 4K block size wastes too much space for such files. FFS solves this problem by allowing each block to be divided into one or more fragments. The fragment size is also fixed for each file system and is set when the file system is created. The number of fragments per block may be set to 1, 2, 4, or 8, allowing a lower bound of 512 bytes, the same as the disk sector size. Each fragment is individually addressable and allocable. This requires replacing the free block list with a bitmap that tracks each fragment.

An FFS file is composed entirely of complete disk blocks, except for the last block, which may contain one or more consecutive fragments. The file block must be completely contained within a single disk block. Even if two adjacent disk blocks have enough consecutive free fragments to hold a file block, they may not be combined. Furthermore, if the last block of a file contains more than one fragment, these fragments must be contiguous and part of the same block.

This scheme reduces space wastage, but requires occasional recopying of file data. Consider a file whose last block occupies a single fragment. The remaining fragments in that block may be allocated to other files. If that file grows by one more fragment, we need to find another block with two consecutive free fragments. The first fragment must be copied from the original position, and the second fragment filled with the new data. If the file usually grows in small increments, its fragments may have to be copied several times, thus impacting performance. FFS controls this by allowing only direct blocks to contain fragments.

Hence for best performance, applications should write a full block at a time to the files whenever possible. Different file systems on the same machine may have different block sizes. Applications can use the *stat* system call to obtain the attributes of a file in a file-system-independent format. One attribute returned by *stat* is a hint as to the best unit size for I/O operations, which, in the case of FFS, is the block size. This information is used by the Standard I/O library, as well as other applications that manage their own I/O.

9.7.2 Allocation Policies

In *s5fs* the superblock contains one list of free blocks and another of free inodes; elements are simply added to or removed from the end of the list. The only time any order is imposed on these lists is while creating the file system—the free block list is created in a rotationally optimal order, and the free inode list is sequential. After some amount of use, the lists become effectively random, and there is no control over where a block or inode is allocated on the disk.

In contrast, FFS aims to colocate related information on the disk and optimize sequential access. It provides a greater degree of control on the allocation of disk blocks and inodes, as well as directories,. These allocation policies use the cylinder group concept, and require the file system to know various parameters associated with the disk. The following rules summarize these policies:

- Attempt to place the inodes of all files of a single directory in the same cylinder group. Many commands (*ls -l* being the best example) access all inodes of a directory in rapid succession. Users also tend to exhibit locality of access, working on many files in the same directory (their current working directory) before moving to another.

- Create each new directory in a different cylinder group from its parent, so as to distribute data uniformly over the disk. The allocation routine chooses the new cylinder group from groups with an above-average free inode count; from these, it selects the one with the fewest directories.

- Try to place the data blocks of the file in the same cylinder group as the inode, because typically the inode and data will be accessed together.

- To avoid filling an entire cylinder group with one large file, change the cylinder group when the file size reaches 48 kilobytes and again at every megabyte. The 48-kilobyte mark was chosen because, for a 4096-byte block size, the inode's direct block entries describe the first 48 kilobytes.[6] The selection of the new cylinder group is based on its free block count.

- Allocate sequential blocks of a file at rotationally optimal positions, if possible. When a file is being read sequentially, there is a time lag between when a block read completes and when the kernel processes the I/O completion and initiates the next read. Because the disk is spinning during this time, one or more sectors may have passed under the disk head. Rotational optimization tries to determine the number of sectors to skip so that the desired sector is under the disk head when the read is initiated. This number is called the *rotdelay* factor, or the disk's *interleave*.

The implementation must balance the localization efforts with the need to distribute the data throughout the disk. Too much localization causes all data to be crammed into the same cylinder group; in the extreme case, we have a single large cylinder group, as in *s5fs*. The rules that begin subdirectories in different groups and that break large files prevent such a scenario.

This implementation is highly effective when the disk has plenty of free space, but deteriorates rapidly once the disk is about 90% full. When there are very few free blocks, it becomes difficult to find free blocks in optimal locations. Thus the file system maintains a *free space reserve* parameter, usually set at 10%. Only the superuser can allocate space from this reserve.

9.8 FFS Functionality Enhancements

Because FFS has a different on-disk organization than *s5fs*, migrating to FFS requires dumping and restoring all disks. Since the two file systems are fundamentally incompatible, the designers of FFS introduced other functional changes that were not compatible with *s5fs*.

Long file names

FFS changed the directory structure to allow file names to be greater than 14 characters. FFS directory entries, shown in Figure 9-8, vary in length. The fixed part of the entry consists of the inode number, the allocation size, and the size of the filename in the entry. This is followed by a null-terminated filename, padded to a 4-byte boundary. The maximum size of the filename is currently 255 characters. When deleting a filename, FFS merges the released space with the previous entry (Figure 9-8b). Hence the allocation size field records the total space consumed by the variable part

---

6   The number of direct blocks in the disk address array was increased from 10 to 12 in FFS.

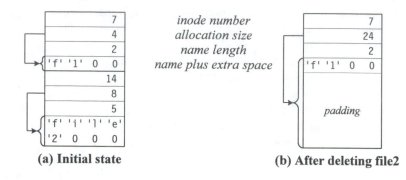

(a) Initial state   **(b) After deleting file2**

Figure 9-8. FFS directory.

of the entry. The directory itself is allocated in 512-byte chunks, and no entry may span multiple chunks. Finally, to facilitate writing of portable code, the standard library adds a set of directory access routines that allow file-system-independent access to directory information (see Section 8.2.1).

Symbolic links

Symbolic links (see Section 8.4.1) address many limitations of hard links. A symbolic link is a file that points to another file, called the *target* of the link. The *type* field in the inode identifies the file as a symbolic link, and the file data is simply the pathname of the target file. The pathname may be absolute or relative. The pathname traversal routine recognizes and interprets symbolic links. If the name is relative, it is interpreted relative to the directory containing the link. Although symbolic link handling is transparent to most programs, some utilities need to detect and handle symbolic links. They can use the *lstat* system call, which does not translate the final symbolic link in the pathname, and the *readlink* call, which returns the contents (target) of the link. Symbolic links are created by the *symlink* system call.

Other enhancements

4.2BSD added a *rename* system call to allow atomic renames of files and directories, which previously required a *link* followed by an *unlink*. It added a *quota* mechanism to limit the file system resources available to any user. Quotas apply to both inodes and disk blocks and have a *soft limit* that triggers a warning, along with a *hard limit* that the kernel enforces.

Some of these features have been subsequently incorporated into *s5fs*. In SVR4, *s5fs allows symbolic links and supports atomic renaming. It does not, however, support long filenames or disk quotas.*

9.9   Analysis

The performance gains of FFS are substantial. Measurements on a VAX/750 with a UNIBUS adapter [Krid 83] show that read throughput increases from 29 kilobytes/sec in *s5fs* (with 1-kilobyte blocks) to 221 kilobytes/sec in FFS (4-kilobyte blocks, 1-kilobyte fragments), and CPU utilization increases from 11% to 43%. With the same configurations, write throughput increased from 48 to 142 kilobytes/sec, and CPU utilization from 29% to 43%.

It is also important to examine disk space wastage. The average wastage in the data blocks is half a block per file in *s5fs,* and half a fragment per file in FFS. If the fragment size in FFS equals the block size in *s5fs,* this factor will even out. The advantage of having large blocks is that less space is required to map all the blocks of a large file. Thus the file system requires few indirect blocks. In contrast, more space is required to monitor the free blocks and fragments. These two factors also tend to cancel out, and the net result of disk utilization is about the same when the new fragment size equals the old block size.

The free space reserve, however, must be counted as wasted space, because it is not available to user files. When this is factored in, the percentage of waste in an *s5fs* with 1K blocks approximately equals that in an FFS with 4K blocks, 512-byte fragments, and the free space reserve set at 5%.

The disk layout described in Figure 9-7 is obsolete for many newer disks. Modern SCSI (Small Computer Systems Interface) disks [ANSI 92] do not have fixed-size cylinders. They take advantage of the fact that outer tracks can hold more data than inner ones and divide the disk into several zones. Within each zone, each track has the same number of sectors.

FFS is oblivious to this, and hence users are forced to use completely fictional cylinder sizes. To support the FFS notion of equal-sized tracks, vendors usually take the total number of 512-byte sectors on the disk and factor it into a number of tracks and sectors per track. This factoring is performed in a convenient way that does not particularly resemble the physical characteristics of the drive. As a result, the careful rotational placement optimizations of FFS accomplish very little, and may hurt performance in many cases. Grouping the cylinders is still useful, because blocks on nearby cylinders, as seen by FFS, are still located on nearby tracks on the disks.

Overall, FFS provides great benefits, which are responsible for its wide acceptance. System V UNIX also added FFS as a supported file system type in SVR4. Moreover, SVR4 incorporated many features of FFS into *s5fs*. Hence, in SVR4, *s5fs* also supports symbolic links, shared and exclusive file locking, and the *rename* system call.

Although FFS is a substantial improvement over *s5fs,* it is far from being the last word in file systems. There are several ways to improve performance further. One way is by chaining kernel buffers together, so that several buffers can be read or written in a single disk operation. This would require modifying all disk drivers. Another possibility is to pre-allocate several blocks to rapidly growing files, releasing the unused ones when closing the file. Other important approaches, including log-structured and extent-based file systems, are described in Chapter 11.

FFS itself has had several enhancements since it was first introduced. 4.3BSD added two types of caching to speed up name lookups [McKu 85]. First, it uses a hint-based directory name lookup cache. This cache shows a hit rate of about 70% of all name translations. When FFS was ported to SVR4, the implementors moved this cache out of the file-system-dependent code and made it a global resource available to all file systems. They also changed its implementation so that it held references (instead of hints) to the cached files. Section 8.10.2 discusses the directory name lookup cache in greater detail.

Second, each process caches the directory offset of the last component of the most recently translated pathname. If the next translation is for a file in the same directory, the search begins at this point instead of at the top of the directory. This is helpful in cases where a process is scanning a directory sequentially, which accounts for about 10–15% of name lookups. The SVR4 implementation moved this cached offset into the in-core inode. This allows FFS to cache an offset for each directory, instead of one directory per process. On the other hand, if multiple processes are concurrently using the same directory, its cached offset is unlikely to be useful.

9.10   Temporary File Systems

Many utilities and applications, notably compilers and window managers, extensively use temporary files to store results of intermediate phases of execution. Such files are deleted when the application exits. This means they are short-lived and need not be persistent (need not survive a system crash). The kernel uses the block buffer cache to defer data writes, and the temporary files are usually deleted before the data needs to be flushed to disk. As a result, I/O to such files is fast and does not involve disk activity. However, the creation and deletion of temporary files remain slow, because these tasks involve multiple synchronous disk accesses to update directory and metadata blocks. The synchronous updates are really unnecessary for temporary files, because they are not meant to be persistent. It is therefore desirable to have a special file system that allows high speed creation and access of transient files.

This problem has long been addressed by using RAM disks, which provide file systems that reside entirely in physical memory. RAM disks are implemented by a device driver that emulates a disk, except that the data is stored in physical memory itself and can be accessed in a fraction of the time needed for disk access. This does not require creation of a special file system type. Once a RAM disk is installed (by allocating a contiguous range of physical memory), a local file system such as *s5fs* or FFS can be built in it using conventional tools like *newfs*. The difference between a RAM disk and an ordinary disk is visible only at the device driver level.

The main disadvantage of this approach is that dedicating a large amount of memory to exclusively support a RAM disk was a poor use of system resources. The amount of memory actively needed to support temporary files varies continually as system usage patterns change. Furthermore, because RAM disk memory is maintained separately from kernel memory, the metadata updates require additional memory-to-memory copies. Clearly, it is desirable to have a special file system implementation that efficiently uses memory to support temporary files. The following subsections describe two such implementations.

9.10.1   The Memory File System

The Memory File System *(mfs)* was developed at the University of California at Berkeley [McKu 90]. The entire file system is built in the virtual address space of the process that handled the *mount* operation. This process does not return from the *mount* call, but remains in the kernel, waiting for I/O requests to the file system. Each `mfsnode`, which is the file-system-dependent part of the vnode, contains the PID of the *mount process,* which now functions as an I/O server. To perform I/O, the calling process places a request on a queue that is maintained in the `mfsdata` structure (per-file-system private data), wakes up the mount process, and sleeps while the request is serviced. The mount process satisfies the request by copying the data from or to the appropriate portion of its address space, and awakens the caller.

Since the file system is in the virtual memory of the mount process, it can be paged out like any other data, by the standard memory management mechanisms. The pages of the *mfs* files compete with all the other processes for physical memory. Pages that are not actively referenced are written to the swap area, and must be faulted in if needed later. This allows the system to support a temporary file system that may be much larger than the physical memory.

Although this file system is substantially faster than an on-disk system, it has several drawbacks, largely due to the limitations of the BSD memory architecture. Using a separate process to handle all I/O requires two context switches for each operation. The file system still resides in a separate (albeit virtual) address space, which means we still need extra in-memory copy operations. The format of the file system is the same as that of FFS, even though concepts such as cylinder groups are meaningless for a memory-based system.

9.10.2   The *tmpfs* File System

The *tmpfs* file system, developed by Sun Microsystems [Snyd 90], combined the powerful facilities of the vnode/vfs interface and the new VM (virtual memory) architecture [Ging 87] to provide an efficient mechanism for temporary files. The VM facilities mentioned here are described in detail in Chapter 14.

tmpfs is implemented entirely in the kernel, without requiring a separate server process. All file metadata is stored in non-paged memory, dynamically allocated from the kernel heap. The data blocks are in paged memory and are represented using the *anonymous page* facility in the VM subsystem. Each such page is mapped by an *anonymous object* (struct anon), which contains the location of the page in physical memory or on the swap device. The tmpnode, which is the file-system-dependent object for each file, has a pointer to the *anonymous map* (struct anon_map) for the file. This map is an array of pointers to the anonymous object for each page of the file. The linkages are shown in Figure 9-9. Because the pages themselves are in paged memory, they can be swapped out by the paging subsystem and compete for physical memory with other processes, just as in *mfs*.

These anonymous objects and maps are also used by the VM subsystem to describe pages of a process's address space. This allows a process to directly map a *tmpfs* file into its address space, using the *mmap* system call interface. Such a mapping is implemented by sharing the anon_map of the file with that process. The process can thus directly access the pages of that file without copying them into its address space.

The *tmpfs* implementation addresses several shortcomings of the *mfs* approach. It does not use a separate I/O server and thus avoids wasteful context switches. Holding the meta-data in unpaged kernel memory eliminates the memory-to-memory copies and some disk I/O. The support for memory mapping allows fast, direct access to file data.

A third approach to temporary file systems is explored in [Ohta 90]. It provides an additional *delay* option to the *mount* system call, which sets a corresponding flag in the private vfs_data object for *ufs*. Many *ufs* routines that normally update the disk synchronously (typically while updat-

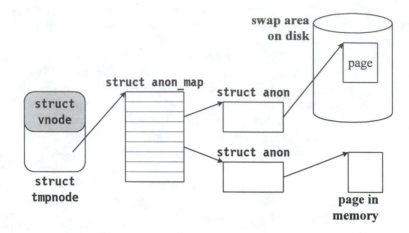

Figure 9-9. Locating *tmpfs* pages.

ing metadata) are modified to first check this flag. If the flag is set, these routines defer the write by simply marking the buffer as *dirty*. This approach has several advantages. It does not use a separate RAM disk, and hence avoids the overhead in space and time to maintain two in-memory copies of the blocks. Its performance measurements are impressive. The main drawback is that it requires changes to several *ufs* routines, so it cannot be added easily to an existing kernel without access to the *ufs* source code. On a system that supports multiple file system types, each implementation would have to be modified to use the delay mount option.

9.11   Special-Purpose File Systems

The initial application of the vnode/vfs interface was to allow local file systems such as *s5fs* and FFS, and remote file systems such as RFS and NFS (see Chapter 10) to coexist in one system. Shortly after this interface became accepted, several special-purpose file systems were developed that took advantage of its power and versatility. Some of these have become part of the standard SVR4 release, while others are provided as vendor-added components. The following sections describe some of the more interesting file systems.

9.11.1   The *Specfs* File System

The *specfs* file system provides a uniform interface to device files. It is invisible to users and cannot be mounted. It exports a common interface that may be used by any file system that supports special files. The primary purpose of *specfs* is to intercept I/O calls to device files and translate them to calls to the appropriate device driver routines. On the surface, this is a straightforward task—the v_type field of the vnode identifies the file as a device file, and the v_rdev field provides the major and minor device numbers. The file-system-independent code should be able to call the device driver directly using the block and character device switches.

We run into problems, however, when multiple device files refer to the same underlying device. When different users access a device using different file names, the kernel must synchronize access to the device. For block devices, it must also ensure consistency of copies of its blocks in the buffer cache. Clearly, the kernel needs to be aware of which different vnodes actually represent the same device.

The *specfs* layer creates a *shadow vnode* for each device file. Its file-system-dependent data structure is called an *snode*. Lookup operations to the device file return a pointer to the shadow vnode instead of the *real vnode*. The real vnode can be obtained, if necessary, by the vop_realvp operation. The *snode* has a field called s_commonvp, which points to a *common vnode* (associated with another snode) for that device. There is only one common vnode for each device (identified by the device number and type), and multiple snodes may point to it. All operations that require synchronization, as well as block device reads and writes, are routed through this common vnode. Section 16.4 describes the implementation in greater detail.

9.11.2   The /proc File System

The **/proc** file system [Faul 91] provides an elegant and powerful interface to the address space of any process. It was initially designed as a facility to support debugging, intended to replace *ptrace,* but it has evolved into a general interface to the process model. It allows a user to read and modify the address space of another process and to perform several control operations on it, using the standard file system interface and system calls. Consequently, access control is arbitrated through the familiar read-write-execute permissions. By default, **/proc** files may be read or written only by their owner.

In the early implementations, each process was represented by a file in the **/proc** directory. The name of the file was the decimal value of the process ID, and its size equaled the size of the process's user address space. Any address in a process was accessed by opening the corresponding **/proc** file and using the *lseek, read,* and *write* system calls. A set of *ioctl* commands to this file allowed various control operations on the process.

The implementation of **/proc** has changed considerably since its introduction, and this section describes the SVR4.2 interface. In SVR4.2, each process is represented by a *directory* under **/proc**, and the directory name is the decimal representation of the process ID. Each directory contains the following files and subdirectories:

status	This read-only file contains information about the process state. Its format is defined by struct pstatus, which includes the process ID, process group and session IDs, sizes and locations of the stack and heap, and other information.
psinfo	This read-only file contains information needed by the *ps(1)* command. Its format is defined by struct psinfo, which includes some of the fields of the status file, and other information such as the image size and the device ID of the controlling terminal.
ctl	This write-only file allows users to perform control operations on the target process by writing formatted messages to this file. Some control operations are described later in this section.

map	This read-only file describes the virtual address map of the process. It contains an array of prmap structures, each element of which describes a single contiguous address range in the process. Process address maps are explained in Section 14.4.3.
as	This read-write file maps the virtual address space of the process. Any address in the process may be accessed by *lseek*ing to that offset in this file, and then performing a *read* or *write*.
sigact	This read-only file contains signal handling information. The file contains an array of sigaction structures (see Section 4.5), one for each signal.
cred	This read-only file contains the user credentials of the process. Its format is defined by struct prcred.
object	This directory contains one file for each object mapped into the address space of the process (see Section 14.2). A user can get a file descriptor for the object by opening the corresponding file.
lwp	This directory contains one subdirectory for each LWP (see Chapter 3) of the process. Each subdirectory contains three files—**lwpstatus**, **lwpsinfo**, and **lwpctl**—which provide per-LWP status and control operations, similar to the **status**, **psinfo**, and **ctl** files, respectively.

It is important to note that these are not physical files with real storage. They merely provide an interface to the process. Operations on these files are translated by the **/proc** file system to appropriate actions on the target process or its address space. Several users may open a **/proc** file concurrently. The O_EXCL flag provides advisory locking when opening an **as, ctl**, or **lwpctl** file for writing. The **ctl** and **lwpctl** files provide several control and status operations, including the following:

PCSTOP	Stops all LWPs of the process.
PCWSTOP	Waits for all LWPs of the process to stop.
PCRUN	Resumes a stopped LWP. Additional actions may be specified by optional flags, such as PRCSIG to clear the current signal, or PRSTEP to single-step the process.
PCKILL	Sends a specified signal to the process.
PCSENTRY	Instructs the LWP to stop on entry to specified system calls.
PCSEXIT	Instructs the LWP to stop on exit from specified system calls.

There is no explicit support for breakpoints. They may be implemented simply by using the *write* system call to deposit a breakpoint instruction at any point in the text segment. Most systems designate an approved breakpoint instruction. Alternatively, we could use any illegal instruction that causes a trap to the kernel.

The **/proc** interface provides mechanisms to handle children of a target process. The debugger can set an *inherit-on-fork* flag in the target process and monitor exits from *fork* and *vfork* calls. This causes both parent and child to stop on return from *fork*. When the parent stops, the debugger can examine the return value from *fork* to determine the child PID and open the **/proc** files of the child. Since the child stops before it returns from *fork*, the debugger has complete control over it from that point.

This interface has allowed the development of several sophisticated debuggers and profilers. For instance, **/proc** allows *dbx* to attach to and detach from running programs. The implementation works correctly with **/proc** files on remote machines accessed via RFS [Rifk 86]. This allows applications to debug and control remote and local processes in identical manner. The *ptrace* system call has become obsolete and unnecessary. Several other commands, notably *ps*, have been reimplemented to use **/proc**. A generalized data watchpoint facility has evolved based on the VM system's ability to dynamically change protections on memory pages.

9.11.3 The Processor File System

The *processor* file system [Nadk 92] provides an interface to the individual processors on a multiprocessor machine. It is mounted on the **/system/processor** directory and has one file for each processor on the system. The filename is the decimal representation of the processor number. The file is of fixed size, is read-only, and its data fields contain the following information:

- Processor status — online or offline.
- CPU type.
- CPU speed in MHz.
- Cache size in kilobytes.
- Whether it has a floating point unit.
- Drivers bound to it.
- The time at which the processor state was last changed.

Additionally, the file system contains a write-only file called *ctl*, accessible only to the superuser. Writing to this file triggers operations on individual processors, such as setting a processor on-line or off-line.

The processor file system is part of the multiprocessor version of SVR4.2. In the future, it may be extended to support notions such as processor sets and light-weight processes by associating such entities with additional files in its name space.

9.11.4 The Translucent File System

The *Translucent File System (TFS)* [Hend 90] was developed at Sun Microsystems to address the needs of large software development efforts. It aims to provide mechanisms for advanced version and build control, and also to support Sun's configuration management tool, the Network Software Environment (NSE). It is shipped as a standard component of SunOS.

There are some typical demands on a large software build environment. Users often maintain a private hierarchy of the build tree, because they may want to modify certain files. They do not need private copies of unchanged files, but they do want to be insulated from changes made by other developers. Furthermore, the environment needs to provide version control facilities, so that a user can choose which version of the build tree he wants to access.

TFS provides these facilities using *copy-on-write* semantics for the file system. Files from the shared hierarchy are copied to the user's private hierarchy as they are modified. To achieve this, a TFS directory is composed of several layers, where each layer is a physical directory. The layers are joined by hidden files called *searchlinks,* which contain the directory name of the next layer. Each layer is like a revision of the directory, and the front layer is the newest revision.

The files seen in a TFS directory are the union of the files in all the layers. The latest revision of a file is accessed by default (layers are searched front to back). If an earlier version is desired, it is necessary to explicitly follow the searchlinks chain. This can be done at the user level, since each layer is merely a directory. Copy-on-write is implemented by making all layers except the front layer read-only; a file in another layer must be copied to the front layer before it can be modified.

TFS performance suffers because each lookup may have to search several layers (the number of layers can become quite large in a typical environment). TFS addresses this problem by aggressively using name lookup caches. It also provides facilities for variant layers corresponding to different machine architectures, because object files are different for each variant. User programs do not need to be changed to access TFS files. The system administrator must perform some initial setup to take advantage of TFS. Although TFS was initially designed to run as an NFS server, it has since been changed to directly use the vnode/vfs interface.

Section 11.12.1 describes the *union mount* file system in 4.4BSD, which provides similar functionality but is based on the 4.4BSD stackable vnode interface.

9.12   The Old Buffer Cache

Disk I/O is a major bottleneck in any system. The time required to read a 512-byte block from disk is of the order of a few milliseconds. The time needed to copy the same amount of data from one memory location to another is of the order of a few microseconds. The two differ by a factor of about a thousand. If every file I/O operation requires disk access, the system will be unacceptably slow. It is essential to make every effort to minimize disk I/O operations, and UNIX achieves this by caching recently accessed disk blocks in memory.

Traditional UNIX systems use a dedicated area in memory called the *block buffer cache* to cache blocks accessed through the file system. The virtual memory system caches process text and data pages separately. Modern UNIX systems such as SVR4 and SunOS (version 4 and above) integrate the buffer cache with the paging system. In this section, we describe the old buffer cache. Section 14.8 describes the new, integrated approach.

The buffer cache is composed of data buffers, each large enough to hold one disk block. BSD-based systems have variable-size buffers, since different file systems on the same machine may have different block and fragment sizes. The cache associates a header with each buffer, to hold naming, synchronization, and cache management information. The size of the cache is typically 10% of physical memory.

The *backing store* of a cache is the persistent location of the data. A cache can manage data from several different backing stores. For the block buffer cache, the backing store is the file systems on disk. If the machine is networked, the backing store includes files on remote nodes.

Generally, a cache can be write-through or write-behind. A write-through cache writes out modified data to the backing store immediately. This has several advantages. The data on the backing store is always current (except perhaps for the last write operation), and there is no problem of data loss or file system corruption in event of a system crash. Also, cache management is simple, making this approach a good choice for hardware-implemented caches, such as track buffers on certain hard disks.

The write-through approach is unsuitable for the block buffer cache, since it imposes a major performance penalty. About a third of file I/O operations are writes, and many of them are very transient—the data is overwritten, or the file deleted, within minutes of the write. This would cause many unnecessary writes, slowing the system tremendously.

For this reason, the UNIX buffer cache is primarily write-behind.[7] Modified blocks are simply marked as *dirty,* and written to the disk at a later time. This allows UNIX to eliminate many writes and also to reorder the writes in a way that optimizes disk performance. Delaying the writes, however, can potentially corrupt the file system in event of a crash. This issue is discussed in Section 9.12.5.

9.12.1   Basic Operation

Whenever a process must read or write a block, it first searches for the block in the buffer cache. To make this search efficient, the cache maintains a set of hash queues based on the device and block number of the block. If the block is not in the cache, it must be read from disk (except when the entire block is being overwritten). The kernel allocates a buffer from the cache, associates it with this block, and initiates a disk read if needed. If the block is modified, the kernel applies the modifications to the buffer cache copy and marks it as dirty by setting a flag in the buffer header. When a dirty block must be freed for reuse, it is first written back to the disk.

When a buffer is being actively used, it must first be locked. This happens before initiating disk I/O or when a process wants to read or write that buffer. If the buffer is already locked, the process trying to access it must sleep until it is unlocked. Because the disk interrupt handler may also try to access the buffer, the kernel disables disk interrupts while trying to acquire the buffer.

When the buffer is not locked, it is kept on a free list. The free list is maintained in *least recently used (LRU)* order. Whenever the kernel needs a free buffer, it chooses the buffer that has not been accessed for the longest time. This rule is based on the fact that typical system usage demonstrates a strong *locality of reference*: recently accessed data is more likely to be accessed before data that has not been accessed in a long time. When a buffer is accessed and then released, it is placed at the end of the free list (it is at this point most recently used). As time passes, it advances towards the list head. If at any time it is accessed again, it returns to the end of the list. When it reaches the head of the list, it is the least recently used buffer and will be allocated to any process that needs a free buffer.

There are some exceptions to this scenario. The first involves buffers that become invalid, either due to an I/O error or because the file they belong to is deleted or truncated. Such buffers will be placed immediately at the head of the queue, since they are guaranteed not to be accessed again.

---

[7] Certain metadata updates are written back synchronously, as described in Section 9.12.5.

The second involves a dirty buffer that reaches the head of the list, at which time it is removed from the list and put on the disk driver's write queue. When the write completes, the buffer is marked as clean and can be returned to the free list. Because it had already reached the list head without being accessed again, it is returned to the head of the list instead of the end.

9.12.2 Buffer Headers

Each buffer is represented by a buffer header. The kernel uses the header to identify and locate the buffer, synchronize access to it, and to perform cache management. The header also serves as the interface to the disk driver. When the kernel wants to read or write the buffer from or to the disk, it loads the parameters of the I/O operation in the header and passes the header to the disk driver. The header contains all the information required for the disk operation. Table 9-2 lists the important fields of the `struct buf`, which represents the buffer header.

The `b_flags` field is a bitmask of several flags. The kernel uses the B_BUSY and B_WANTED to synchronize access to the buffer. B_DELWRI marks a buffer as dirty. The flags used by the disk driver include B_READ, B_WRITE, B_ASYNC, B_DONE, and B_ERROR. The B_AGE flag indicates an aged buffer that is a good candidate for reuse.

9.12.3 Advantages

The primary motivation for the buffer cache is to reduce disk traffic and eliminate unnecessary disk I/O, and it achieves this effectively. Well-tuned caches report hit rates of up to 90% [Oust 85]. There are also several other advantages. The buffer cache synchronizes access to disk blocks through the locked and wanted flags. If two processes try to access the same block, only one will be able to lock it. The buffer cache offers a modular interface between the disk driver and the rest of the kernel. No other part of the kernel can access the disk driver, and the entire interface is encapsulated in the fields of the buffer header. Moreover, the buffer cache insulates the rest of the kernel from the alignment requirements of disk I/O, since the buffers themselves are page aligned. There are no problems of arbitrary disk I/O requests to possibly unaligned kernel addresses.

Table 9-2. Fields of `struct buf`

Fields	Description
`int b_flags`	status flags
`struct buf *b_forw, *b_back`	pointers to keep buf in hash queue
`struct buf *av_forw, *av_back`	pointers to keep buf on free list
`caddr_t b_addr`	pointer to the data itself
`dev_t b_edev`	device number
`daddr_t b_blkno`	block number on device
`int b_error`	I/O error status
`unsigned b_resid`	number of bytes left to transfer

9.12.4 Disadvantages

Despite the tremendous advantages, there are some important drawbacks of the buffer cache. First, the write-behind nature of the cache means that data may be lost if the system crashes. This could also leave the disk in an inconsistent state. This issue is further explored in Section 9.12.5. Second, although reducing disk access greatly improves performance, the data must be copied twice—first from the disk to the buffer, then from the buffer to the user address space. The second copy is orders of magnitude faster than the first, and normally the savings in disk access more than compensate for the expense of the additional memory-to-memory copy. It can become an important factor, however, when sequentially reading or writing a very large file. In fact, such an operation creates a related problem called *cache wiping*. If a large file is read end-to-end and then not accessed again, it has the effect of flushing the cache. Since all blocks of this file are read in a short period of time, they consume all the buffers in the cache, flushing out the data that was in them. This causes a large number of cache misses for a while, slowing down the system until the cache is again populated with a more useful set of blocks. Cache wiping can be avoided if the user can predict it. The Veritas File System (VxFS), for example, allows users to provide hints as to how a file will be accessed. Using this feature, a user can disable caching of large files and ask the file system to transfer the data directly from the disk to user address space.

9.12.5 Ensuring File System Consistency

The major problem with the buffer cache is that data on the disk may not always be current. This is not a problem when the system is up and running, since the kernel uses the cached copy of the disk block, which is always up-to-date. The problem occurs if the system crashes, because several modifications may be lost. The loss of data may affect file data blocks or metadata. UNIX handles both cases differently.

From the perspective of the operating system, if some file data writes do not reach the disk, the loss is not catastrophic, although it may seem that way to the user. This is because it does not compromise file system consistency. Requiring all writes to be synchronous is prohibitively expensive, and thus the default for file data writes is write-behind. There are, however, a few ways to force the kernel to write the data to the disk. The *sync* system call initiates disk writes for all dirty buffers. It does not, however, wait for these writes to complete, so there is no guarantee that a block has actually been written to disk after the *sync* call completes. A user can open a file in synchronous mode, forcing all writes to this file to be synchronous. Finally, several implementations have an *update daemon* (called the *fsflush* process in SVR4) which calls *sync* periodically (typically, once every 30 seconds) to clean the cache.

If some metadata changes are lost, the file system can become inconsistent. Many file operations modify more than one metadata object, and if only some of these changes reach the disk, the file system may become corrupted. For instance, adding a *link* to a file involves writing an entry for the new name in the appropriate directory and incrementing the *link count* in the inode. Suppose the system were to crash after the directory change was saved but before the inode was updated to disk. When the system reboots, it will have two directory entries referencing a file that has a link count of one. If someone deletes the file using either of the names, the inode and disk blocks will be freed, since the link count will drop to zero. The second directory entry will then point to an unallocated inode (or one that is reassigned to another file). Such damage to the file system must be avoided.

There are two ways in which UNIX tries to prevent such corruption. First, the kernel chooses an order of metadata writes that minimizes the impact of a system crash. In the previous example, consider the effect of reversing the order of the writes. Now suppose the system were to crash with the inode updated but not the directory. When it reboots, this file has an extra link, but the original directory entry is valid and the file can be accessed without any problems. If someone were to delete the file, the directory entry would go away, but the inode and data blocks would not be freed because the link count is still one. Although this does not prevent corruption, it causes less severe damage than the earlier order.

Thus the order of metadata writes must be carefully chosen. The problem of enforcing the order still remains, since the disk driver does not service the requests in the order that they are received. The only way the kernel can order the writes is to make them synchronous. Hence in the above case, the kernel will write the inode to the disk, wait until the write completes, and then issue the directory write. The kernel uses such synchronous metadata writes in many operations that require modifying more than one related object [Bach 86].

The second way of combating file system corruption is the *fsck* (file system check) utility [Kowa 78, Bina 89]. This program examines a file system, looks for inconsistencies, and repairs them if possible. When the correction is not obvious, it prompts the user for instructions. By default, the system administrator runs *fsck* each time the system reboots and may also run it manually at any time. *fsck* uses the raw interface to the disk driver to access the file system. It is further described in Section 11.2.4.

9.13   Summary

The vnode/vfs interface allows multiple file systems to coexist on a machine. In this chapter, we have described the implementation of several file systems. We began with the two most popular local file systems—*s5fs* and FFS. We then described several special-purpose file systems that took advantage of the special properties of the vnode/vfs interface to provide useful functionality. Finally, we discussed the buffer cache, which is a global resource shared by all file systems.

In the following chapters, we describe many other file systems. The next chapter discusses distributed file systems—in particular, NFS, RFS, AFS, and DFS. Chapter 11 deals with advanced and experimental file systems that use techniques such as logging to provide better functionality and performance.

9.14   Exercises

1.   Why do *s5fs* and FFS have a fixed number of on-disk inodes in each file system?
2.   Why is the inode separate from the directory entry of the file?
3.   What are the advantages and drawbacks of having each file allocated contiguously on disk? Which applications are likely to desire such a file system?

4.   What happens if a disk error destroys the *s5fs* superblock?

5.   What are the benefits of allocating and deallocating inodes dynamically?

6.   A system using a reference-based directory name lookup cache may run out of free inodes simply because the lookup cache references many inodes that would otherwise be free. How should the file system handle this situation?

7.   A name lookup in a very large directory can be extremely inefficient for conventional file systems like *s5fs* and FFS. Explore the possibility of organizing the directory as a hash table. Should the hash table be only in memory, or should it be part of the persistent storage? Does this duplicate the functionality of the name lookup cache?

8.   In 4.4BSD, the name lookup cache also maintains entries for unsuccessful lookups. What is the advantage of caching this information? What problems will the implementation need to address?

9.   Why must the *write* system call sometimes read the data block from disk first?

10. Why does FFS allocate each new directory in a different cylinder group from its parent?

11. In what situations does the rotdelay factor actually worsen the file system performance?

12. Why would the rotational layout algorithms of FFS hurt performance when using modern SCSI disks?

13. What is the purpose of the free space reserve in FFS?

14. Suppose a file system decides to store the data portion of small files in the inode itself, rather than in a separate data block. What would be the benefits and problems of this approach?

15. What are the advantages of using a special file system for temporary files?

16. What can an operating system do to reduce cache wiping?

17. What are the benefits of separating the buffer cache from the virtual memory subsystem? What are the drawbacks?

9.15   References

[ANSI 92]   American National Standard for Information Systems, *Small Computer Systems Interface–2 (SCSI-2)*, X3.131–199X, Feb. 1992.

[Bach 86]   Bach, M.J., *The Design of the UNIX Operating System*, Prentice-Hall, Englewood Cliffs, NJ, 1986.

[Bark 90]   Barkley, R.E., and Lee, T.P., "A Dynamic File System Inode Allocation and Reclaim Policy," *Proceedings of the Winter 1990 USENIX Technical Conference*, Jan. 1990, pp. 1–9.

[Bina 89]   Bina, E.J., and Emrath, P.A., "A Faster *fsck* for BSD UNIX," *Proceedings of the Winter 1989 USENIX Technical Conference, Jan. 1989*, pp. 173–185.

[Faul 91]   Faulkner, R. and Gomes, R., "The Process File System and Process Model in UNIX System V," *Proceedings of the 1991 Winter USENIX Conference*, Jan. 1991, pp. 243–252.

[Gaed 82]   Gaede, S., "A Scaling Technique for Comparing Interactive System Capacities," *Conference Proceedings of CMG XIII*, Dec. 1982, pp. 62–67.

[Ging 87]   Gingell, R.A., Moran, J.P., and Shannon, W.A., "Virtual Memory Architecture in SunOS," *Proceedings of the Summer 1987 USENIX Technical Conference,* Jun. 1987, pp. 81–94.

[Hend 90]   Hendricks, D., "A FileSystem for Software Development," *Proceedings of the Summer 1990 USENIX Technical Conference,* Jun. 1990, pp. 333-340.

[Klei 86]   Kleiman, S.R., "Vnodes: An Architecture for Multiple File System Types in Sun UNIX," *Proceedings of the Summer 1986 USENIX Technical Conference,* Jun. 1986, pp. 238–247.

[Kowa 78]   Kowalski, T., "FSCK—The UNIX System Check Program," Bell Laboratory, Murray Hill, N.J. 07974, Mar. 1978.

[Krid 83]   Kridle, R., and McKusick, M., "Performance Effects of Disk Subsystem Choices for VAX Systems Running 4.2BSD UNIX," Technical Report No. 8, Computer Systems Research Group, Dept. of EECS, University of California at Berkeley, CA, 1983.

[Leff 89]   Leffler, S.J., McKusick, M.K., Karels, M.J., and Quarterman, J.S., *The Design and Implementation of the 4.3BSD UNIX Operating System,* Addison-Wesley, Reading, MA, 1989.

[McKu 84]   McKusick, M.K., Joy, W.N., Leffler, S.J., and Fabry, R.S., "A Fast File System for UNIX," *ACM Transactions on Computer Systems,* vol. 2, (Aug. 1984), pp. 181–197.

[McKu 85]   McKusick, M.K., Karels, M., and Leffler, S.J., "Performance Improvements and Functional Enhancements in 4.3BSD," *Proceedings of the Summer 1985 USENIX Conference,* Jun. 1985, pp. 519–531.

[McKu 90]   McKusick, M.K., Karels, M.K., and Bostic, K., "A Pageable Memory Based Filesystem," *Proceedings of the Summer 1990 USENIX Technical Conference,* Jun. 1990.

[Nadk 92]   Nadkarni, A.V., "The Processor File System in UNIX SVR4.2," *Proceedings of the 1992 USENIX Workshop on File Systems,* May 1992, pp. 131–132.

[Ohta 90]   Ohta, M. and Tezuka, H., "A Fast /tmp File System by Delay Mount Option," *Proceedings of the Summer 1990 USENIX Conference,* Jun. 1990, pp. 145–149.

[Oust 85]   Ousterhout, J.K., Da Costa, H., Harrison, D., Kunze, J.A., Kupfer, M. and Thompson, J.G., "A Trace-Driven Analysis of the UNIX 4.2 BSD File System," *Proceedings of the Tenth Symposium on Operating System Principles,* Dec. 1985, pp. 15–24.

[Rifk 86]   Rifkin, A.P., Forbes, M.P., Hamilton, R.L., Sabrio, M., Shah, S., and Yueh, K., "RFS Architectural Overview," *Proceedings of the Summer 1986 USENIX Technical Conference,* Jun. 1986, pp. 248–259.

[Salu 94]   Salus, P.H., *A Quarter Century of UNIX,* Addison-Wesley, Reading, MA, 1994.

[Saty 81]   Satyanarayan, M., "A Study of File Sizes and Functional Lifetimes," *Proceedings of the Eighth Symposium on Operating Systems Principles,* 1981, pp. 96–108.

[Snyd 90]   Snyder, P., "tmpfs: A Virtual Memory File System," *Proceedings of the Autumn 1990 European UNIX Users' Group Conference,* Oct. 1990, pp. 241–248.

[Thom 78]   Thompson, K., "UNIX Implementation," *The Bell System Technical Journal,* Jul.-Aug. 1978, Vol. 57, No. 6, Part 2, pp. 1931–1946.

10

Distributed File Systems

10.1 Introduction

Since the 1970s, the ability to connect computers to each other on a network has revolutionized the computer industry. The increase in network connectivity has fueled a desire to share files between different computers. The early efforts in this direction were restricted to copying entire files from one machine to another, such as the *UNIX-to-UNIX copy (uucp)* program [Nowi 90] and *File Transfer Protocol (ftp)* [Post 85]. Such solutions, however, do not come close to fulfilling the vision of being able to access files on remote machines as though they were on local disks.

The mid-1980s saw the emergence of several distributed file systems that allow transparent access to remote files over a network. These include the *Network File System (NFS)* from Sun Microsystems [Sand 85a], the *Remote File Sharing system (RFS)* from AT&T [Rifk 86], and the *Andrew File System (AFS)* from Carnegie-Mellon University [Saty 85]. All three are sharply different in their design goals, architecture, and semantics, even though they try to solve the same fundamental problem. Today, RFS is available on many System V-based systems. NFS has gained much wider acceptance and is available on numerous UNIX and non-UNIX systems. AFS development has passed on to Transarc Corporation, where it has evolved into the *Distributed File System (DFS)* component of Open Software Foundation's *Distributed Computing Environment (DCE)*.

This chapter begins by discussing the characteristics of distributed file systems. It then describes the design and implementation of each of the above-mentioned file systems and examines their strengths and weaknesses.

10.2   General Characteristics of Distributed File Systems

A conventional, centralized file system allows multiple users on a single system to share access to files stored locally on the machine. A distributed file system extends the sharing to users on different machines interconnected by a communication network. Distributed file systems are implemented using a client-server model. The client is a machine that accesses a file, while a server is one that stores the file and allows clients to access it. Some systems may require clients and servers to be distinct machines, while others may allow a single machine to act as both client and server.

It is important to note the distinction between distributed file systems and distributed operating systems [Tann 85]. A distributed operating system, such as *V* [Cher 88] or *Amoeba* [Tann 90], is one that looks to its users like a centralized operating system, but runs simultaneously on multiple machines. It may provide a file system that is shared by all its host machines. A distributed file system, however, is a software layer that manages communication between conventional operating systems and file systems. It is integrated with the operating systems of the host machines and provides a distributed file access service to systems with centralized kernels.

There are several important properties of distributed file systems [Levy 90]. Each file system may have some or all of these properties. This gives us a basis to evaluate and compare different architectures.

- **Network transparency**—Clients should be able to access remote files using the same operations that apply to local files.
- **Location transparency**—The name of a file should not reveal its location in the network.
- **Location independence**—The name of the file should not change when its physical location changes.
- **User mobility**—Users should be able to access shared files from any node in the network.
- **Fault tolerance**—The system should continue to function after failure of a single component (a server or a network segment). It may, however, degrade in performance or make part of the file system unavailable.
- **Scalability**—The system should scale well as its load increases. Also, it should be possible to grow the system incrementally by adding components.
- **File mobility**—It should be possible to move files from one physical location to another in a running system.

10.2.1   Design Considerations

There are several important issues to consider in designing a distributed file system. These involve tradeoffs in functionality, semantics, and performance. We can compare different file systems according to how they deal with these issues:

- **Name space** — Some distributed file systems provide a uniform name space, such that each client uses the same pathname to access a given file. Others allow each client to customize its name space by mounting shared subtrees to arbitrary directories in the file hierarchy. Both methods have some appeal.

- **Stateful or stateless operation** — A stateful server is one that retains information about client operations between requests and uses this state information to service subsequent requests correctly. Requests such as *open* and *seek* are inherently stateful, since someone must remember which files a client has opened, as well as the seek offset in each open file. In a stateless system, each request is self-contained, and the server maintains no persistent state about the clients. For instance, instead of maintaining a seek offset, the server may require the client to specify the offset for each read or write. Stateful servers are faster, since the server can take advantage of its knowledge of client state to eliminate a lot of network traffic. However, they have complex consistency and crash recovery mechanisms. Stateless servers are simpler to design and implement, but do not yield as good performance.

- **Semantics of sharing** — The distributed file system must define the semantics that apply when multiple clients access a file concurrently. *UNIX semantics* require that changes made by one client be visible to all other clients when they issue the next read or write system call. Some file systems provide *session semantics,* where the changes are propagated to other clients at the open and close system call granularity. Some provide even weaker guarantees, such as a time interval that must elapse before the changes are certain to have propagated to other clients.

- **Remote access methods** — A pure client-server model uses the *remote service method* of file access, wherein each action is initiated by the client, and the server is simply an agent that does the client's bidding. In many distributed systems, particularly stateful ones, the server plays a much more active role. It not only services client requests, but also participates in cache coherency mechanisms, notifying clients whenever their cached data is invalid.

We now look at the distributed file systems that are popular in the UNIX world, and see how they deal with these issues.

10.3 Network File System (NFS)

Sun Microsystems introduced NFS in 1985 as a means of providing transparent access to remote file systems. Besides publishing the protocol, Sun also licensed a reference implementation, which was used by vendors to port NFS to several operating systems. NFS has since become a *de facto* industry standard, supported by virtually every UNIX variant and several non-UNIX systems such as VMS and MS-DOS.

The NFS architecture is based on a *client-server* model. A file server is a machine that exports a set of files. Clients are machines that access such files. A single machine can act as both a server and a client for different file systems. The NFS code, however, is split into client and server portions, allowing client-only or server-only systems.

Clients and servers communicate via *remote procedure calls,* which operate as synchronous requests. When an application on the client tries to access a remote file, the kernel sends a request to the server, and the client process blocks until it receives a reply. The server waits for incoming client requests, processes them, and sends replies back to the clients.

10.3.1   User Perspective

An NFS server *exports* one or more file systems. Each exported file system could be either an entire disk partition or a subtree thereof.[1] The server can specify, typically through entries in the **/etc/exports** file, which clients may access each exported file system and whether the access permitted is read-only or read-write.

Client machines can then mount such a file system, or a subtree of it, onto any directory in their existing file hierarchy, just as they would mount a local file system. The client may mount the directory as read-only, even though the server has exported it as read-write. NFS supports two types of mounts—*hard* and *soft*. This influences client behavior if the server does not respond to a request. If the file system is hard-mounted, the client keeps retrying the request until a reply is received. For a soft-mounted file system, the client gives up after a while and returns an error. Once the *mount* succeeds, the client can access files in the remote file system using the same operations that apply to local files. Some systems also support *spongy mounts,* which behave as hard mounts for mount retries but as soft mounts for subsequent I/O operations.

NFS mounts are less restrictive than those of local file systems. The protocol does not require the caller of mount to be a privileged user, although most clients impose this requirement.[2] The client may mount the same file system at multiple locations in the directory tree, even onto a subdirectory of itself. The server can export only its local file systems and may not cross its own mount points during pathname traversal. Thus, for a client to see the all the files on a server, it must mount all of the server's file systems.

This is illustrated in Figure 10-1. The server system **nfssrv** has two disks. It has mounted **dsk1** on the **/usr/local** directory of **dsk0** and has exported the directories **/usr** and **/usr/local**. Suppose a client executes the following four *mount* operations:

```
mount -t nfs    nfssrv:/usr         /usr
mount -t nfs    nfssrv:/usr/u1      /u1
mount -t nfs    nfssrv:/usr         /users
mount -t nfs    nfssrv:/usr/local   /usr/local
```

All four mounts will succeed. On the client, the **/usr** subtree reflects the entire **/usr** subtree of **nfssrv**, since the client has also mounted **/usr/local**. The **/u1** subtree on the client maps the **/usr/u1** subtree on **nfssrv**. This illustrates that it is legal to mount a subdirectory of an exported file system.[3] Finally, the **/users** subtree on the client only maps that part of the **/usr** subtree of **nfssrv** that resides on **dsk0**; the file system on **dsk1** is not visible under **/users/local** on the client.

10.3.2   Design Goals

The original NFS design had the following objectives:

---

[1] Different UNIX variants have their own rules governing the granularity of the exports. Some may only allow an entire file system to be exported, whereas some may permit only one subtree per file system.

[2] Digital's ULTRIX, for instance, allows any user to mount an NFS file system so long as the user has write permission to the mount point directory.

[3] Not all implementations allow this.

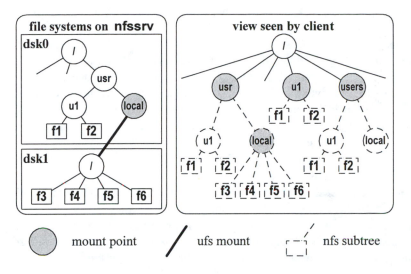

Figure 10-1. Mounting NFS file systems.

- NFS should not be restricted to UNIX. Any operating system should be able to implement an NFS server or client.
- The protocol should not be dependent on any particular hardware.
- There should be simple recovery mechanisms from server or client crashes.
- Applications should be able to access remote files transparently, without using special pathnames or libraries and without recompiling.
- UNIX file system semantics must be maintained for UNIX clients.
- NFS performance must be comparable to that of a local disk.
- The implementation must be transport-independent.

10.3.3 NFS Components

An NFS implementation is composed of several components. Some of these are localized either to the server or to the client, whereas some are shared by both. A few components are not required for the core functionality, but form part of the extended NFS interface:

- The *NFS protocol* defines the set of requests that may be made by the client to the server and the arguments and return values for each. Version 1 of the protocol existed only within Sun Microsystems and was never released. All NFS implementations support *NFS version 2 (NFSv2),*[4] which was first released in SunOS 2.0 in 1985 [Sand 85b]; hence this chapter deals mainly with this version. Section 10.10 discusses *version 3* of the protocol,

---

4 This includes those that support NFSv3.

which was published in 1993 and has been implemented by a number of vendors. Table 10-1 enumerates the complete set of NFSv2 requests.

- The *Remote Procedure Call (RPC) protocol* defines the format of all interactions between the client and the server. Each NFS request is sent as an RPC packet.

- The *Extended Data Representation (XDR)* provides a machine-independent method of encoding data to send over the network. All RPC requests use XDR encoding to pass data. Note that XDR and RPC are used for many other services besides NFS.

- The *NFS server code* is responsible for processing all client requests and providing access to the exported file systems.

- The *NFS client code* implements all client system calls on remote files by sending one or more RPC requests to the server.

- The *Mount protocol* defines the semantics for mounting and unmounting NFS file systems. Table 10-2 contains a brief description of the protocol.

- Several *daemon processes* are used by NFS. On the server, a set of *nfsd* daemons listen for and respond to client NFS requests, and the *mountd* daemon handles mount requests. On the client, a set of *biod* daemons handles asynchronous I/O for blocks of NFS files.

- The *Network Lock Manager (NLM)* and the *Network Status Monitor (NSM)* together provide the facilities for locking files over a network. These facilities, while not formally tied to NFS, are found on most NFS implementations and provide services not possible in the base protocol. NLM and NSM implement the server functionality via the *lockd* and *statd* daemons, respectively.

Table 10-1. NFSv2 operations

Proc	Input args	Results
NULL	void	void
GETATTR	fhandle	status, fattr
SETATTR	fhandle, sattr	status, fattr
LOOKUP	dirfh, name	status, fhandle, fattr
READLINK	fhandle	status, link_value
READ	fhandle, offset, count, totcount	status, fattr, data
WRITE	fhandle, offset, count, totcount, data	status, fattr
CREATE	dirfh, name, sattr	status, fhandle, fattr
REMOVE	dirfh, name	status
RENAME	dirfh1, name1, dirfh2, name2	status
LINK	fhandle, dirfh, name	status
SYMLINK	dirfh, name, linkname, sattr	status
MKDIR	dirfh, name, sattr	status, fhandle, fattr
RMDIR	dirfh, name	status
READDIR	fhandle, cookie, count	status, dir_entries
STATFS	fhandle	status, file_stats

Key: fattr = file attributes; sattr = attributes to set; cookie = opaque object returned by previous READDIR; fhandle = file handle; dirfh = file handle of directory.

Table 10-2. Mount protocol (version 1)

Procedure	Input args	Results
NULL	void	void
MNT	pathname	status, fhandle
DUMP	void	mount list
UMNT	pathname	void
UMNTALL	void	void
EXPORT	void	export list

Key: fhandle = handle of top-level directory of mounted subtree.

10.3.4 Statelessness

The single most important characteristic of the NFS protocol is that the server is stateless and does not need to maintain any information about its clients to operate correctly. Each request is completely independent of others and contains all the information required to process it. The server need not maintain any record of past requests from clients, except optionally for caching or statistics gathering purposes.

For example, the NFS protocol does not provide requests to open or close a file, since that would constitute state information that the server must remember. For the same reason, the READ and WRITE requests pass the starting offset as a parameter, unlike *read* and *write* operations on local files, which obtain the offset from the *open file object* (see Section 8.2.3).[5]

A stateless protocol makes crash recovery simple. No recovery is required when a client crashes, since the server maintains no persistent information about the client. When the client reboots, it may remount the file systems and start up applications that access the remote files. The server neither needs to know nor cares about the client crashing.

When a server crashes, the client finds that its requests are not receiving a response. It then continues to resend the requests until the server reboots.[6] At that time, the server will receive the requests and can process them since the requests did not depend on any prior state information. When the server finally replies to the requests, the client stops retransmitting them. The client has no way to determine if the server crashed and rebooted or was simply slow.

Stateful protocols, however, require complex crash-recovery mechanisms. The server must detect client crashes and discard any state maintained for that client. When a server crashes and reboots, it must notify the clients so that they can rebuild their state on the server.

A major problem with statelessness is that the server must commit all modifications to stable storage before replying to a request. This means that not only file data, but also any metadata such as inodes or indirect blocks must be flushed to disk before returning results. Otherwise, a server crash might lose data that the client believes has been successfully written out to disk. (A system

---

[5] Some systems provide *pread* and *pwrite* calls, which accept the offset as an argument. This is particularly useful for multithreaded systems (see Section 3.3.2).

[6] This is true only for *hard mounts* (which are usually the default). For *soft mounts,* the client gives up after a while and returns an error to the application.

crash can lose data even on a local file system, but in that case the users are aware of the crash and of the possibility of data loss.) Statelessness also has other drawbacks. It requires a separate protocol (NLM) to provide file locking. Also, to address the performance problems of synchronous writes, most clients cache data and metadata locally. This compromises the consistency guarantees of the protocol, as discussed in detail in Section 10.7.2.

10.4   The Protocol Suite

The primary protocols in the NFS suite are RPC, NFS, and Mount. They all use XDR for data encoding. Other related protocols are the NLM, NSM, and the *portmapper*. This section describes XDR and RPC.

10.4.1   Extended Data Representation (XDR)

Programs that deal with network-based communications between computers have to worry about several issues regarding the interpretation of data transferred over the network. Since the computers at each end might have very different hardware architectures and operating systems, they may have different notions about the internal representation of data elements. These differences include byte ordering, sizes of data types such as integers, and the format of strings and arrays. Such issues are irrelevant for communication with the same machine or even between two like machines, but must be resolved for heterogeneous environments.

Data transmitted between computers can be divided into two categories—opaque and typed. Opaque, or byte-stream, transfers may occur, for example, in file transfers or modem communications. The receiver simply treats the data as a stream of bytes and makes no attempt to interpret it. Typed data, however, is interpreted by the receiver, and this requires that the sender and receiver agree on its format. For instance, a *little-endian* machine may send out a two-byte integer with a value of 0x0103 (259 in decimal). If this is received by a *big-endian* machine, it would (in absence of prior conventions) be interpreted as 0x0301 (decimal 769). Obviously, these two machines will not be able to understand each other.

The XDR standard [Sun 87] defines a machine-independent representation for data transmission over a network. It defines several basic data types and rules for constructing complex data types. Since it was introduced by Sun Microsystems, it has been influenced by the Motorola 680x0 architecture (the Sun-2 and Sun-3 workstations were based on the 680x0 hardware) in issues such as byte ordering. Some of the basic definitions of XDR are as follows:

- **Integers** are 32-bit entities, with byte 0 (numbering the bytes from left to right) representing the most significant byte. Signed integers are represented in two's complement notation.
- **Variable-length opaque data** is described by a *length* field (which is a four-byte integer), followed by the data itself. The data is NULL-padded to a four-byte boundary. The *length* field is omitted for fixed-length opaque data.

- **Strings** are represented by a *length* field followed by the ASCII bytes of the string, NULL-padded to a four-byte boundary. If the string length is an exact multiple of four, there is no (UNIX-style) trailing NULL byte.
- **Arrays** of homogeneous elements are encoded by a *size* field followed by the array elements in their natural order. The size field is a four-byte integer and is omitted for fixed-size arrays. Each element's size must be a multiple of four bytes. While the elements must be of the same type, they may have different sizes, for instance, in an array of strings.
- **Structures** are represented by encoding their components in their natural order. Each component is padded to a four-byte boundary.

Figure 10-2 illustrates some examples of XDR encoding. In addition to this set of definitions, XDR also provides a formal language specification to describe data. The RPC specification language, described in the next section, simply extends the XDR language. Likewise, the *rpcgen* compiler understands the XDR specification and generates routines that encode and decode data in XDR form.

XDR forms a universal language for communication between arbitrary computers. Its major drawback is the performance penalty paid by computers whose natural data representation semantics do not match well with that of XDR. Such computers must perform expensive conversion operations for each data element transmitted. This is most wasteful when the two computers themselves are of like type and do not need data encoding when communicating with each other.

For instance, consider two VAX-11 machines using a protocol that relies on XDR encoding. Since the VAX is little-endian (byte 0 is least significant byte), the sender would have to convert each integer to big-endian form (mandated by XDR), and the receiver would have to convert it back to little-endian form. This wasteful exercise could be prevented if the representation provided some

Value	**XDR Representation**
0x203040	00 | 20 | 30 | 40
Array of 3 integers {0x30, 0x40, 0x50}	00 | 00 | 00 | 30 00 | 00 | 00 | 40 00 | 00 | 00 | 50
Variable length array of strings { "Monday", "Tuesday" }	00 | 00 | 00 | 02 00 | 00 | 00 | 06 'M' | 'o' | 'n' | 'd' 'a' | 'y' | 00 | 00 00 | 00 | 00 | 07 'T' | 'u' | 'e' | 's' 'd' | 'a' | 'y' | 00

Figure 10-2. Examples of XDR encoding.

means of communicating the machine characteristics, so that conversions were required only for unlike machines. DCE RPC [OSF 92] uses such an encoding scheme in place of XDR.

10.4.2   Remote Procedure Calls (RPC)

The *Remote Procedure Call (RPC) protocol* specifies the format of communications between the client and the server. The client sends RPC requests to the server, which processes them and returns the results in an RPC reply. The protocol addresses issues such as message format, transmission, and authentication, which do not depend on the specific application or service. Several services have been built on top of RPC, such as NFS, Mount, NLM, NSM, *portmapper,* and Network Information Service (NIS).

> *There are several different RPC implementations. NFS uses the RPC protocol introduced by Sun Microsystems [Sun 88], which is known as Sun RPC or ONC-RPC. (ONC stands for Open Network Computing.) Throughout this book, the term RPC refers to Sun RPC, except when explicitly stated otherwise. The only other RPC facility mentioned in the book is that of OSF's Distributed Computing Environment, which is referred to as DCE RPC.*

Unlike DCE RPC, which provides synchronous and asynchronous operations, Sun RPC uses synchronous requests only. When a client makes an RPC request, the calling process blocks until it receives a response. This makes the behavior of the RPC similar to that of a local procedure call.

The RPC protocol provides reliable transmission of requests, meaning it must ensure that a request gets to its destination and that a reply is received. Although RPC is fundamentally transport-independent, it is often implemented on top of UDP/IP (User Datagram Protocol/Internet Protocol), which is inherently unreliable. The RPC layer implements a reliable datagram service by keeping track of unanswered requests and retransmitting them periodically until a response is received.

Figure 10-3 describes a typical RPC request and (successful) reply. The xid is a transmission ID, which tags a request. The client generates a unique xid for each request, and the server returns the same xid in the reply. This allows the client to identify the request for which the response has arrived and the server to detect duplicate requests (caused by retransmissions from the client). The direction field identifies the message as a request or a reply. The rpc_vers field identifies the version number of the RPC protocol (current version = 2). prog and vers are the program and version number of the specific RPC service. An RPC service may register multiple protocol versions. The NFS protocol, for instance, has a program number of 100003 and supports version numbers 2 and 3. proc identifies the specific procedure to call within that service program. In the reply, the reply_stat and accept_stat fields contain status information.

RPC uses five authentication mechanisms to identify the caller to the server—AUTH_NULL, AUTH_UNIX, AUTH_SHORT, AUTH_DES, and AUTH_KERB. AUTH_NULL means no authentication. AUTH_UNIX is composed of UNIX-style credentials, including the client machine name, a UID, and one or more GIDs. The server may generate an AUTH_SHORT upon receipt of an AUTH_UNIX creden-

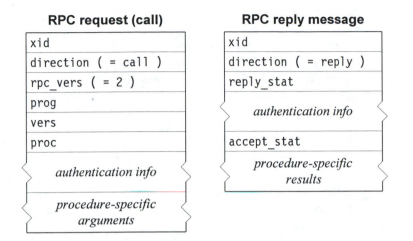

Figure 10-3. RPC message formats.

tial, and return it to the caller for use in subsequent requests. The idea is that the server can decipher AUTH_SHORT credentials very quickly to identify known clients, thus providing faster authentication. This is an optional feature and not many services support it. AUTH_DES is a secure authentication facility using a mechanism called *private keys* [Sun 89]. AUTH_KERB is another secure facility based on the *Kerberos* authentication mechanism [Stei 88]. Each service decides which authentication mechanisms to accept. NFS allows all five, except that it allows AUTH_NULL only for the NULL procedure. Most NFS implementations, however, use AUTH_UNIX exclusively.

Sun also provides an RPC programming language, along with an *RPC compiler* called *rpcgen*. An RPC-based service can be fully specified in this language, resulting in a formal interface definition. When *rpcgen* processes this specification, it generates a set of C source files containing XDR conversion routines and stub versions of the client and server routines, and a header file containing definitions used by both client and server.

10.5   NFS Implementation

We now examine how typical UNIX systems implement the NFS protocol. NFS has been ported to several non-UNIX systems such as MS-DOS and VMS. Some of these are client-only or server-only implementations, while others provide both pieces. Moreover, there are several dedicated NFS server implementations from vendors like Auspex, Network Appliance Corporation, and Novell, which do not run on general-purpose operating systems. Finally, there are a number of user-level implementations of NFS for various operating systems, many available as shareware or freeware. The implementation details on such systems are, of course, fundamentally different, and Section 10.8 describes some interesting variations. In this section, we restrict our discussion to kernel implementations of NFS in conventional UNIX systems that also support the vnode/vfs interface.

10.5.1   Control Flow

In Figure 10-4, the server has exported a *ufs* file system, mounted by the client. When a process on the client makes a system call that operates on an NFS file, the file-system-independent code identifies the vnode of the file and invokes the relevant vnode operation. For NFS files, the file-system-dependent data structure associated with the vnode is the *rnode* (for remote node). The v_op field in the vnode points to the vector of NFS client routines (struct vnodeops) that implement the various vnode operations. These routines act by constructing RPC requests and sending them to the server. The calling process on the client blocks until the server responds (see footnote 6). The server processes the requests by identifying the vnode for the corresponding local file and invoking the appropriate vnodeops calls, which are implemented by the local file system (*ufs* in this example).

Finally, the server completes processing the request, bundles the results into an RPC reply message and sends it back to the client. The RPC layer on the client receives the reply and wakes up the sleeping process. This process completes execution of the client vnode operation and the rest of the system call, and returns control to the user.

This implies the client must maintain a local vnode for each active NFS file. This provides the proper linkages to route the vnode operations to the NFS client functions. It also allows the client to cache attributes of remote files, so that it can perform some operations without accessing the server. The issues related to client caching are discussed in Section 10.7.2.

10.5.2   File Handles

When a client makes an NFS request to the server, it must identify the file it wants to access. Passing the pathname on each access would be unacceptably slow. The NFS protocol associates an ob-

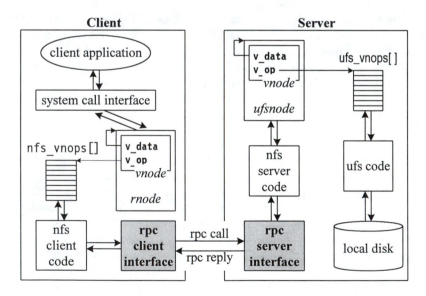

Figure 10-4. Control flow in NFS.

ject called a *file handle* with each file or directory. The server generates this handle when the client first accesses or creates the file through a LOOKUP, CREATE, or MKDIR request. The server returns the handle to the client in the reply to the request, and the client can subsequently use it in other operations on this file.

The client sees the file handle as an opaque, 32-byte object and makes no attempt to interpret the contents. The server can implement the file handle as it pleases, as long as it provides a unique one-to-one mapping between files and handles. Typically, the file handle contains a *file system ID,* which uniquely identifies the local file system, the *inode number* of the file, and the *generation number* of that inode. It may also contain the inode number and generation number of the exported directory through which the file was accessed.

The generation number was added to the inode to solve problems peculiar to NFS. It is possible that, between the client's initial access of the file (typically through LOOKUP, which returns the file handle) and when the client makes an I/O request on the file, the server deletes the file and reuses its inode. Hence the server needs a way of determining that the file handle sent by the client is obsolete. It does this by incrementing the generation number of the inode each time the inode is freed (the associated file is deleted). The server can now recognize requests that refer to the old file and respond to them with an ESTALE *(stale file handle)* error status.

10.5.3 The Mount Operation

When a client mounts an NFS file system, the kernel allocates a new vfs structure and invokes the nfs_mount() function. nfs_mount() sends an RPC request to the server, using the Mount protocol. The argument to this request is the pathname of the directory to be mounted. The *mountd* daemon on the server receives this request and translates the pathname. It checks whether the pathname is that of a directory and whether that directory is exported to the client. If so, *mountd* returns a successful completion reply, in which it sends the file handle of that directory.

The client receives the successful reply and completes the initialization of the vfs structure. It records the name and network address of the server in the private data object of the *vfs.* It then allocates the rnode and vnode for the root directory. If the server crashes and reboots, the clients still have the file systems mounted, but the server has lost that information. Since the clients are sending valid file handles in NFS requests, the server can assume that a successful *mount* had taken place previously and rebuild its internal records.

The server does, however, need to check access rights to the file system on *each* NFS request. It must ensure that the files being operated on are exported to that client (if the request will modify the file, it must be exported read-write). To make this check efficient, the file handle contains the <*inode, generation number*> of the exported directory. The server maintains an in-memory list of all exported directories, so it can perform this check quickly.

10.5.4 Pathname Lookup

The client gets the file handle of the top-level directory as a result of the *mount* operation. It obtains other handles during pathname lookup or as a result of CREATE or MKDIR. The client initiates *lookup* operations during system calls such as *open, creat,* and *stat.*

On the client, *lookup* begins at the current or root directory (depending on whether the path-name is relative or absolute) and proceeds one component at a time. If the current directory is an NFS directory or if we cross a mount point and get to an NFS directory, the lookup operation calls the NFS-specific VOP_LOOKUP function. This function sends a LOOKUP request to the server, passing it the file handle of the parent directory (which the client had saved in the rnode) and the name of the component to be searched.

The server extracts the file system ID from the handle and uses it to locate the vfs structure for the file system. It then invokes the VFS_VGET operation on this file system, which translates the file handle and returns a pointer to the vnode of the parent directory (allocating a new one if it is not already in memory). The server then invokes the VOP_LOOKUP operation on that vnode, which calls the corresponding function of the local file system. This function searches the directory for the file and, if found, brings its vnode into memory (unless it is already there, of course) and returns a pointer to it.

The server next invokes the VOP_GETATTR operation on the vnode of the target file, followed by VOP_FID, which generates the file handle for the file. Finally, it generates the reply message, which contains the status, the file handle of the component, and its file attributes.

When the client receives the reply, it allocates a new rnode and vnode for the file (if this file had been looked up previously, the client may already have a vnode for it). It copies the file handle and attributes into the rnode and proceeds to search for the next component.

Searching for one component at a time is slow and requires several RPCs for a single path-name. The client may avoid some RPCs by caching directory information (see Section 10.7.2.). Al-though it would seem more efficient to send the entire pathname to the server in a single LOOKUP call, that approach has some important drawbacks. First, since the client may have mounted a file system on an intermediate directory in the path, the server needs to know about all the client's mount points to parse the name correctly. Second, parsing an entire pathname requires the server to understand UNIX pathname semantics. This conflicts with the design goals of statelessness and op-erating system independence. NFS servers have been ported to diverse systems such as VMS and Novell NetWare, which have very different pathname conventions. Complete pathnames are used only in the *mount* operation, which uses a different protocol altogether.

10.6   UNIX Semantics

Since NFS was primarily intended for UNIX clients, it was important that UNIX semantics be pre-served for remote file access. The NFS protocol, however, is stateless, which means that clients cannot maintain open files on the server. This leads to a few incompatibilities with UNIX, which we describe in the following paragraphs.

10.6.1   Open File Permissions

UNIX systems check access permissions when a process first opens the file, not on every read or write. Suppose, after a user opens a file for writing, the owner of the file changes its permissions to read-only. On a UNIX system, the user can continue to write to the file until he closes it. NFS, lacking the concept of open files, checks the permissions on each read or write. It would therefore return an error in such a case, which the client would not expect to happen.

Although there is no way to fully reconcile this issue, NFS provides a work-around. *The server always allows the owner of the file to read or write the file, regardless of the permissions.* On the face of it, this seems a further violation of UNIX semantics, since it appears to allow owners to modify their own write-protected files. The NFS client code, however, prevents that from happening. When the client opens the file, the LOOKUP operation returns the file attributes along with the handle. The attributes contain the file permissions at the time of the *open*. If the file is write-protected, the client code returns an EACCESS *(access denied)* error from the *open* call. It is important to note that the server's security mechanisms rely on proper behavior of the client. In this instance, the problem is not serious, since it only affects the owner's lack of write access. Section 10.9 discusses the major problems with NFS security.

10.6.2 Deletion of Open Files

If a UNIX process deletes a file that another process (or that process itself) still has open, the kernel simply marks the file for deletion and removes its entry from the parent directory. Although no new processes can now open this file, those that have it open can continue to access it. When the last process that has the file open closes it, the kernel physically deletes the file. This feature is used by several utilities to implement temporary files.

Once again, this is a problem for NFS, since the server does not know about open files. The work-around this time involves modifying the NFS client code, since the client *does* know about open files. When the client detects an attempt to delete an open file, it changes the operation to a RENAME, giving the file a new location and name. The client usually chooses some unusual and long name that is unlikely conflict with existing files. When the file is last closed, the client issues a REMOVE request to delete the file.

This works well when the process that has the file open is on the same machine as the one deleting the file. There is no protection, however, against the file being deleted by a process on another client (or on the server). If that happens, the user will get an unexpected error *(stale file handle)* when he next tries to read or write that file. Another problem with this work-around is that if the client crashes between the RENAME and REMOVE operations, a garbage file is left behind on the server.

10.6.3 Reads and Writes

In UNIX, a *read* or *write* system call locks the vnode of the file at the start of the I/O. This makes file I/O operations atomic at the system call granularity. If two *writes* are issued to the same file at roughly the same time, the kernel serializes them and completes one before starting the other. Likewise, it ensures that the file cannot change while a *read* is in progress. The local file-system-dependent code handles the locking, within the context of a single vop_rdwr operation.

For an NFS file, the client code serializes concurrent access to a file by two processes on the same client. If, however, the two processes are on different machines, they access the server independently. A *read* or *write* operation may span several RPC requests (the maximum size of an RPC message is 8192 bytes), and the server, being stateless, maintains no locks between requests. NFS offers no protection against such overlapping I/O requests.

Cooperating processes can use the Network Lock Manager (NLM) protocol to lock either entire files or portions thereof. This protocol only offers advisory locking, which means that another process can always bypass the locks and access the file if it so chooses.

10.7   NFS Performance

One of the design goals of NFS was that its performance be comparable to that of a small local disk. The metric of interest is not raw throughput, but the time required to do normal work. There are several benchmarks that try to simulate a normal workload on an NFS file system, the most popular being *LADDIS* [Witt 93] and *nhfsstone* [Mora 90]. This section discusses the major performance problems of NFS and how they have been addressed.

10.7.1   Performance Bottlenecks

NFS servers are usually powerful machines with large caches and fast disks, which compensate for the time taken for RPC requests going back and forth. There are several areas, however, where the NFS design directly leads to poor performance.

Being a stateless protocol, NFS requires that all writes be committed to stable storage before replying to them. This includes not only modifications to the file metadata (inodes and indirect blocks), but also to the body of the file. As a result, any NFS request that modifies the file system in any way (such as WRITE, SETATTR, or CREATE) is extremely slow.

Fetching of file attributes requires one RPC call per file. As a result, a command such as *ls -l* on a directory results in a large number of RPC requests. In the local case, such an operation is fast, since the inodes end up in the buffer cache, so the *stat* calls need only a memory reference.

If the server does not reply to a request fast enough, the client retransmits it to account for the server crashing or the request being lost on the network. Processing the retransmitted request further adds to the load on the server and may aggravate the problem. This has a cascading effect, resulting in an overloaded server bogged down by the incoming traffic.

Let us look at some ways of addressing NFS performance problems and the repercussions of these solutions.

10.7.2   Client-Side Caching

If every operation on a remote file required network access, NFS performance would be intolerably slow. Hence most NFS clients resort to caching both file blocks and file attributes. They cache file blocks in the buffer cache and attributes in the rnodes. This caching is dangerous, since the client has no way of knowing if the contents of the cache are still valid, short of querying the server each time they must be used.

Clients take certain precautions to reduce the dangers of using stale data. The kernel maintains an expiry time in the rnode, which monitors how long the attributes have been cached. Typically, the client caches the attributes for 60 seconds or less after fetching them from the server. If they are accessed after the quantum expires, the client fetches them from the server again. Likewise, for file data blocks, the client checks cache consistency by verifying that the file's *modify time* has not changed since the cached data was read from the server. The client may use the cached value of this timestamp or issue a GETATTR if it has expired.

Client-side caching is essential for acceptable performance. The precautions described here reduce, but do not eliminate, the consistency problems. In fact, they introduce some new race conditions, as described in [Mack 91] and [Jusz 89].

10.7.3   Deferral of Writes

The NFS requirement of synchronous writes applies only to the server. The client is free to defer writes, since if data is lost due to a client crash, the users know about it. The client policy, therefore, is to use asynchronous writes for full blocks (issue the WRITE request but do not wait for the reply) and delayed writes for partial blocks (issue the WRITE sometime later). Most UNIX implementations flush delayed writes to the server when the file is closed and also every 30 seconds. The *biod* daemons on the client handle these writes.

Although the server must commit writes to stable storage before replying, it does not have to write them to disk. It may use some special hardware to make sure that the data will not be lost in the event of a crash. For instance, some servers use a special, battery backed, *nonvolatile memory (NVRAM)*. The WRITE operation simply transfers the data to an NVRAM buffer (provided one was free). The server flushes the NVRAM buffers to disk at a later time. This allows the server to respond quickly to write requests, since the transfer to NVRAM is much faster than a disk write. The disk driver can optimize the order of the NVRAM-to-disk writes, so as to minimize disk head movements. Moreover, multiple updates to the same buffer could be written to disk in a single operation. [Mora 90] and [Hitz 94] describe NFS server implementations that use NVRAM.

[Jusz 94] shows a technique called write-gathering that reduces the synchronous write bottleneck without using special hardware. It relies on the fact that typical NFS clients use a number of *biod* daemons to handle write operations. When a client process opens a file and writes to it, the kernel simply caches the changes and marks them for delayed write. When the client closes the file, the kernel flushes its blocks to the server. If there are sufficient *biod*s available on the client, they can all issue the writes in parallel. As a result, servers often receive a number of writes requests for the same file bunched together.

Using write-gathering, the server does not process WRITE requests immediately. Rather, it delays them for a little while, in the hope that it receives other WRITEs for the same file in the meantime. It then gathers all requests for the same file and processes them together. After completing them all, the server replies to each of them. This technique is effective when the clients use *biod*s and is optimal when they use a large number of *biod*s. Although it appears to increase the latency of individual requests, it improves performance tremendously by reducing the total number of disk operations on the server. For instance, if the server gathers n writes to a file, it may be able to commit them to disk using a single data write and a single inode write (as opposed to n of each). Write-gathering improves the server throughput, and reduces the load on its disks. These gains more than offset the latency increase caused by the delay, and the overall effect is to reduce the average time of the writes.

Some servers rely on an *uninterruptible power supply (UPS)* to flush blocks to disk in case of a crash. Some simply ignore the NFS requirement of synchronous writes, expecting crashes to be rare occurrences. The plethora of solutions and work-arounds to this problem simply highlights its severity. NFSv3, described in Section 10.10, provides a protocol change that allows clients and servers to use asynchronous writes safely.

10.7.4   The Retransmissions Cache

In order to provide reliable transmission, RPC clients repeatedly retransmit requests until they receive a response. Typically, the waiting period is quite short (configurable, typically 1–3 seconds) for the first retransmission and increases exponentially for each subsequent retry. If, after a certain number of retries, the client still does not receive a response, it may (in some implementations) send a new request identical to the old, but with a different transmission ID *(xid)*.

Retransmissions occur due to packet loss (original request or the reply) on the network or because the server could not reply promptly enough. Very often the reply to the original request is on the way when the client sends a second copy. Multiple retransmissions usually happen when the server crashes or when the network is extremely congested.

The server needs to handle such duplicate requests correctly and efficiently. NFS requests can be divided into two types—*idempotent* and *nonidempotent* [Jusz 89]. Idempotent requests, such as READ or GETATTR, can be executed twice without any ill effects. Nonidempotent requests may result in incorrect behavior if repeated. Requests that modify the file system in any way are nonidempotent.

For example, consider the following sequence of events caused by a duplicate REMOVE operation:

1. Client sends a REMOVE request for a file.
2. Server removes the file successfully.
3. Server sends a success reply to the client. This reply is lost on the network.
4. Client sends a duplicate REMOVE request.
5. Server processes the second REMOVE, which fails because the file has already been deleted.
6. Server sends an error message to the client. This message reaches the client.

As a result, the client gets an error message, even though the REMOVE operation succeeded.

Reprocessing of duplicate requests also hurts server performance, because the server spends a lot of time doing work it should never do. This aggravates a situation that was bad to start with, since the retransmission probably occurred because the server was overloaded and therefore slow.

It is therefore necessary to detect and handle retransmissions correctly. To do so, the server keeps a cache of recent requests. A request can be identified as a duplicate if its xid, procedure number, and client ID match those of another request in the cache. (This is not always foolproof, because some clients may generate the same xid for requests from two different users.) This cache is normally called the *retransmissions cache* or the *xid cache*.

The original Sun reference port maintained such a cache only for the CREATE, REMOVE, LINK, MKDIR, and RMDIR requests. It checked the cache only after a request failed, to determine if the failure was due to the request being a retransmission. If so, it sent a success reply to the client. This was inadequate—it covered only some of the loopholes and opened up new consistency problems. Moreover, it does not address the performance problems, since the server does not check the cache until after it has processed the request.

[Jusz 89] provides a detailed analysis of the problems in handling retransmissions. Based on that, Digital revamped the xid cache in Ultrix. The new implementation caches *all* requests and checks the cache before processing new requests. Each cache entry contains request identification (client ID, xid, and procedure number), a *state* field, and a *timestamp*. If the server finds the request in the cache, and the state of the request is *in progress,* it simply discards the duplicate. If the state is *done,* the server discards the duplicate if the timestamp indicates that the request has completed recently (within a *throwaway window* set at 3–6 seconds). Beyond the throwaway window, the server processes the request if idempotent. For nonidempotent requests, the server checks to see if the file has been modified since the original timestamp. If not, it sends a success response to the client; otherwise, it retries the request. Cache entries are recycled on a *least recently used* basis so that if the client continues to retransmit, the server will eventually process the request again.

The xid cache helps eliminate several duplicate operations, improving both the performance and the correctness of the server. It is possible to take this one step further. If the server caches the reply message along with the xid information, then it can handle a duplicate request by retransmitting the cached reply. Duplicates that arrive within the throwaway window may still be discarded altogether. This will further reduce wasteful reprocessing, even for idempotent requests. This approach requires a large cache capable of saving entire reply messages. Some replies, such as those for READ or READDIR requests, can be very large. It is better to exclude these requests from the xid cache and process them again if necessary.

10.8   Dedicated NFS Servers

Most UNIX vendors design file servers by repackaging workstations in a rack and adding more disks, network adapters, and memory. These systems run the vendor's UNIX variant, which is designed primarily for use in a multiprogramming environment and is not necessarily appropriate for high-throughput NFS service. Some vendors have designed systems specifically for use as dedicated NFS servers. These systems either add to the functionality of UNIX or completely replace the operating system. This section describes two such architectures.

10.8.1   The Auspex Functional Multiprocessor Architecture

Auspex Systems entered the high-end NFS server market with a functional multiprocessing (FMP) system called the NS5000. The FMP architecture [Hitz 90] recognizes that NFS service comprises two major subsystems—network and file system.[7] It uses a number of Motorola 680*x*0 processors sharing a common backplane, each dedicated to one of these subsystems. These processors run a small *functional multiprocessing kernel (FMK)* and communicate with each other via high-speed

---

[7] The original design separated the storage functionality into a third subsystem. The recent line of products do not feature separate storage processors.

message passing. One processor (also a 68020) runs a modified version of SunOS4.1 (with FMK support added to it) and provides management functionality. Figure 10-5 shows the basic design.

The UNIX front end can communicate directly to each of the functional processors. It talks to network processors through the standard network *if* driver and to file system processors through a special *local file system,* which implements the *vfs* interface. The UNIX processor also has direct access to the storage through a special device driver that represents an *Auspex disk* and converts disk I/O requests into FMK messages. This allows utilities such as *fsck* and *newfs* to work without change.

Normal NFS requests bypass the UNIX processor altogether. The request comes in at a network processor, which implements the IP, UDP, RPC, and NFS layers. It then passes the request to the file system processor, which may issue I/O requests to the storage processor. Eventually, the network processor sends back the reply message to the client.

The FMK kernel supports a small set of primitives including light-weight processes, message passing, and memory allocation. By eliminating a lot of the baggage associated with the traditional UNIX kernel, FMK provides extremely fast context switching and message passing. For instance, FMK has no memory management and its processes never terminate.

This architecture provided the basis for a high-throughput NFS server that established Auspex Systems as a leader in the high-end NFS market. Recently, its position has been challenged by cluster-based NFS servers from vendors such as Sun Microsystems and Digital Equipment Corporation.

10.8.2   IBM's HA-NFS Server

[Bhid 91] describes a prototype implementation of HA-NFS, a highly available NFS server designed at IBM. HA-NFS separates the problem of high availability NFS service into three compo-

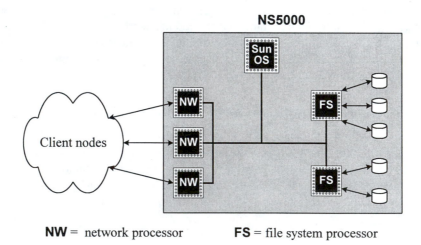

NW = network processor   **FS** = file system processor

Figure 10-5. Auspex NS5000 architecture.

nents—network reliability, disk reliability, and server reliability. It uses disk mirroring and optional network replication to address the first two problems and uses a pair of cooperating servers to provide server reliability.

Figure 10-6 illustrates the HA-NFS design. Each server has two network interfaces and, correspondingly, two IP addresses. A server designates one of its network interfaces as the primary interface and uses it for normal operation. It uses the secondary interface only when the other server fails.

HA-NFS also uses dual-ported disks, which are connected to both servers through a shared SCSI bus. Each disk has a primary server, which alone accesses it during normal operation. The secondary server takes over the disk when the primary server fails. Thus the disks are divided into two groups, one for each server.

The two servers communicate with each other through periodic heartbeat messages. When a server does not receive a heartbeat from the other, it initiates a series of probes to make sure the other server has actually failed. If so, it initiates a failover procedure. It takes control of the failed server's disks and sets the IP address of its secondary network interface to that of the failed server's primary interface. This allows it to receive and service messages intended for the other server.

The takeover is transparent to clients, who only see reduced performance. The server seems to be unresponsive while the failover is in progress. Once failover completes, the surviving server may be slow, since it now handles the load normally meant for two servers. There is, however, no loss in service.

Each server runs IBM's AIX operating system, which uses a metadata logging file system. HA-NFS adds information about the RPC request to log entries for NFS operations. When a server takes over a disk during failover, it replays the log to restore the file system to a consistent state and recovers its retransmission cache from the RPC information in the log. This prevents inconsistencies due to retransmissions during failover. The two servers also exchange information about clients that

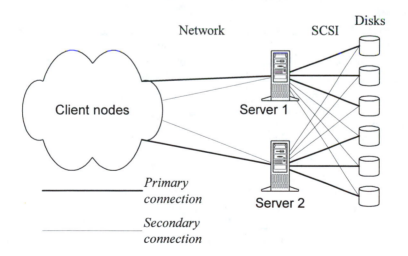

Figure 10-6. HA-NFS configuration.

have made file locking requests using NSM and NLM [Bhid 92]. This allows recovery of the lock manager state after failure of one of the servers.

There are two ways to make the IP address takeover transparent to clients. One is to use special network interface cards that allow their hardware addresses to be changed. During failover, the server changes both the IP address and the hardware address of the secondary interface to those of the failed server's primary interface. In absence of such hardware, the server can take advantage of some side effects of certain *address resolution protocol (ARP)* requests [Plum 82] to update the new *<hardware address, IP address>* mapping in the clients.

10.9   NFS Security

It is difficult for any network application to provide the same level of security as a local system. While NFS seeks to provide UNIX semantics, its security mechanisms are woefully inadequate. This section examines the major loopholes in NFS security and some possible solutions.

10.9.1   NFS Access Control

NFS performs access control at two points—when the file system is mounted and also on every NFS request. Servers maintain an *exports list* that specifies which client machines can access each exported file system and whether the access permitted is read-only or read-write. When a client tries to mount a file system, the server *mountd* checks this list and denies access to ineligible clients. There are no restrictions on specific users, meaning that any user on an eligible client can mount the file system.[8]

On each NFS request, the client sends authentication information, usually in AUTH_UNIX form. This information contains the user and group IDs of the owner of the process making the request. The NFS server uses this information to initialize a credentials structure, which is used by the local file systems for access control.

For this to work, the server and all the clients must share a flat *<UID, GID>* space. This means that any given UID must belong to the same person on all machines sharing NFS file systems. If user **u1** on machine **m1** has the same UID as user **u2** on machine **m2**, the NFS server will not be able to distinguish the two and will allow each user complete access to the other's files.

This is a major problem in today's typical workgroups, where each user has his or her own private workstation, and a central NFS server maintains common files (including, in many cases, login directories). Since each user typically has root privileges to his own workstation, he can create accounts with any *<UID, GIDs>*, thereby impersonating anyone else. Such an impostor can freely access the victim's files on the server, without the victim ever learning about it. The impostor can do this without writing sophisticated programs or modifying the kernel or the network. The only line of defense is to restrict NFS access to known clients that can be trusted or monitored. This is the strongest demonstration of the fact that NFS security is nonexistent.

There are other ways of breaking into NFS. Since NFS relies on data that is being sent over unsecured networks, it is easy to write programs that imitate NFS clients and send packets contain-

---

[8]   Many client implementations allow only privileged users to mount NFS file systems.

ing fake authentication data, perhaps even appearing to come from a different machine. This would allow break-ins even by users who do not have root permission on a machine or by users on machines that do not have NFS access to a server.

10.9.2 UID Remapping

There are some ways to prevent such intrusions. The first line of defense involves *UID remapping*. This means that instead of a flat *<UID, GIDs>* space on the server and all clients, the server maintains a translation map for each client. This map defines the translation from credentials received over the network to an identity to be used on the server. This identity is also described by a *<UID, GIDs>* set, but the set may be different from that sent by the client.

For instance, the translation map may specify that UID 17 from client **c1** translates to UID 33 on the server, whereas UID 17 from client **c2** translates to UID 17 on the server, and so forth. It may also define translations for the GIDs. The map may contain several default translations or *wildcards* (e.g., *"no translation required for credentials from a set of trusted clients"*). Typically, it would also specify that if a particular incoming credential does not match any map entry or default rule, then that credential is mapped to user *nobody,* which is a special user that can only access files that have world permissions.

Such UID remapping can be implemented at the RPC level. This means that the translations would apply to any RPC-based service and take place before the request was interpreted by NFS. Since such translations require additional processing, this would degrade the performance of all RPC-based services, even if a particular service did not need that level of security.

An alternative approach is to implement UID remapping at the NFS level, perhaps by merging the map with the **/etc/exports** file. This would enable the server to apply different mappings for different file systems. For instance, if the server exports its **/bin** directory as read-only and the **/usr** directory as read-write, it may want to apply UID maps only to the **/usr** directory, which might contain sensitive files that users wish to protect. The drawback of this approach is that each RPC service would have to implement its own UID maps (or other security mechanisms), perhaps duplicating effort and code.

Very few mainstream NFS implementations provide any form of UID remapping at all. Secure versions of NFS prefer to use secure RPC with AUTH_DES or AUTH_KERB authentication, described in Section 10.4.2.

10.9.3 Root Remapping

A related problem involves root access from client machines. It is not a good idea for superusers on all clients to have root access to files on the server. The usual approach is for servers to map the superuser from any client to the user *nobody.* Alternatively, many implementations allow the **/etc/exports** file to specify an alternative UID to which root should be mapped.

Although this takes care of the obvious problems with superuser access, it has some strange effects on users logged in as root (or who are executing a privileged program installed in *setuid* mode). These users have fewer privileges to NFS files than ordinary users. They may not, for instance, be able to access their own files on the server.

Many of the above problems are not restricted to NFS. The traditional UNIX security framework is designed for an isolated (no network), multiuser environment and is barely adequate even in that domain. The introduction of a network where nodes trust each other severely compromises the security and opens several loopholes. This has led to the development of several network security and authentication services, the most notable in the UNIX world being Kerberos [Stei 88]. A more detailed discussion of network security is beyond the scope of this book.

10.10   NFS Version 3

NFSv2 became enormously popular and was ported to many different hardware platforms and operating systems. This also helped highlight its shortcomings. While some of the problems could be addressed by clever implementations, many problems were inherent to the protocol itself. In 1992, engineers from several companies gathered for a series of meetings in Boston, Massachusetts, to develop version 3 of the NFS protocol [Pawl 94, Sun 95]. NFSv3 is beginning to appear in commercial releases. Digital Equipment Corporation was the first to support NFSv3 in DEC OSF release 3,[9] and Silicon Graphics, Inc. and a few others have also followed suit. Rick Macklem of the University of Guelph has made available a public domain implementation for 4.4BSD, which may be obtained by *anonymous ftp* from **snowhite.cis.uoguelph.ca:/pub/nfs**.

NFSv3 addresses several important limitations of NFSv2. The main problem with NFSv2 performance is the requirement that the server must commit all modifications to stable storage before replying. This is due to the stateless nature of the protocol, since the client has no other way of knowing that the data has been safely transferred. NFSv3 allows asynchronous writes by adding a new COMMIT request, which works as follows: When a client process writes to an NFS file, the kernel sends asynchronous WRITE requests to the server. The server may save the data in its local cache and reply to the client immediately. The client kernel holds on to its copy of the data, until the process closes the file. At that time, the kernel sends a COMMIT request to the server, which flushes the data to disk and returns successfully. When the client receives the reply to the COMMIT request, it can discard its local copy of the data.

Asynchronous writes are optional in NFSv3, and specific clients or servers may not support them. For instance, clients that do not have adequate data caching facilities may continue to use old-style writes, which the server must write to stable storage immediately. Servers may choose to use synchronous writes even for asynchronous requests, in which case, they must indicate this in the reply.

Another major problem in NFSv2 is its use of 32-bit fields for specifying file sizes and read and write offsets. This limits the protocol to supporting files smaller than 4 gigabytes. Many applications need to deal with larger files and find this constraint unacceptable. NFSv3 widens these fields to 64 bits, thus allowing files up to 1.6×10^{19} bytes (16 billion terabytes) in size.

The NFSv2 protocol causes far too many LOOKUP and GETATTR requests. For instance, when a user reads a directory through *ls -l,* the client sends a READDIR request to the server, which returns

---

[9]   DEC OSF/1 is now known as Digital UNIX.

a list of the filenames in the directory. The client then issues a LOOKUP and a GETATTR for each file in the list. For a large directory, this can cause excessive network traffic.

NFSv3 provides a READDIRPLUS operation, which returns the names, file handles, and attributes of the files in the directory. This allows a single NFSv3 request to replace the entire sequence of NFSv2 requests. The READDIRPLUS request must be used with care, since it returns a large amount of data. If the client wants information about one file only, it may be cheaper to use the old sequence of calls.

Implementations that support NFSv3 must also support NFSv2. The client and server normally use the highest version of the protocol that both of them support. When it first contacts the server, the client uses its highest protocol version; if the server does not understand the request, the client tries the next lowest version and so on, until they find a commonly supported version.

Only time will tell how effective and successful NFSv3 will be. The changes described above are very welcome improvements to the NFS protocol, and should result in great performance improvement. NFSv3 also cleans up a few minor problems with NFSv2. Some of the smaller changes reduce the performance of NFSv3, but the benefits of asynchronous writes and READDIR-PLUS are expected to more than compensate for that.

10.11   Remote File Sharing (RFS)

AT&T introduced the Remote File Sharing (RFS) file system in SVR3 UNIX to provide access to remote files over a network. While its basic objective is similar to that of NFS, RFS has a fundamentally different architecture and design.

The major design goal of RFS is to provide completely transparent access to remote files and devices, in a way that preserves all UNIX semantics. This implies support for all file types, including device files and named pipes (FIFO files), as well as for file and record locking. Other important goals include binary compatibility, so that existing applications do not need to be modified to use RFS (except to deal with some new error codes), and network independence, so that RFS can be used over both local- and wide-area networks (LANs and WANs).

The initial implementation was portable only to other SVR3 UNIX systems on different hardware. This limitation was due to RFS's use of the *file system switch* mechanism of SVR3. SVR4 integrated RFS with the vnode/vfs interface, which made it portable to many other UNIX variants. This redesign was based on an earlier port of RFS to SunOS [Char 87]. We shall concentrate on this vnode-based implementation of RFS.

10.12   RFS Architecture

Similar to NFS, RFS is based on a client-server model. The server advertises (exports) directories, and the client mounts them. Any machine may be a client, or a server, or both. The similarities end there. *RFS is a completely stateful architecture, which is necessary to correctly provide UNIX open file semantics.* This has a far-reaching impact both on its implementation and its functionality.

RFS uses a reliable, virtual-circuit transport service such as TCP/IP. Each client-server pair uses a single virtual circuit, established during the first *mount* operation. If the client mounts any other directories of the server, all the mounts are multiplexed on the same circuit. The circuit is kept open for the duration of the mounts. If either the client or server crashes, the circuit breaks, and the other becomes aware of the crash and can take appropriate action.

Network independence is achieved by implementing RFS on top of the STREAMS framework (see Chapter 17) and using AT&T's transport provider interface (TPI). RFS can communicate over multiple streams and thus use several different transport providers on the same machine. Figure 10-7 illustrates the communication setup between the client and the server.

RFS associates a symbolic *resource name* with each directory advertised (exported) by any server. A centralized *name server* maps resource names to their network location. This allows the resources (exported file trees) to be moved around in the network; clients can access the resource without having to know its current location.[10]

Since RFS is intended to work over large networks, resource management can become complex. Therefore, RFS provides the concept of a *domain,* which is a logical grouping of a set of machines in the network. Resources are identified by the domain name and the resource name, which now must be unique only within the domain. If the domain name is not specified, the current domain is assumed. The name server may only store the information about resources in its own domain and forward other requests to name servers of the respective domains.

10.12.1   Remote Message Protocol

The initial design of RFS used a *remote system call* model, which provides an RFS operation for each system call that operates on a remote file. For each such operation, the client packages the arguments to the system call, as well as information about the client process's environment, into an

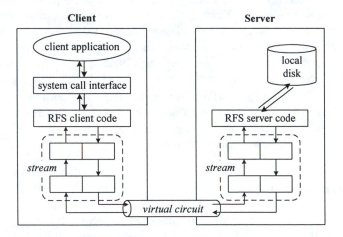

Figure 10-7. Communications in RFS.

---

[10] Of course, the resource cannot be moved while any client has it mounted.

RFS request. The server recreates the client's environment and executes the system call. The client process blocks until the server processes the request and sends back a response message, containing the results of the system call. The client then interprets the results and completes the system call, returning control to the user. This implementation was called the RFS1.0 protocol.

When RFS was integrated with the vnode/vfs interface, it was necessary for RFS to implement each vnode operation. In the port to SunOS [Char 87], each vnode operation was implemented in terms of one or more RFS1.0 requests. For instance, `vn_open` could simply use the `RFS_OPEN` request, whereas `vn_setattr` required an `RFS_OPEN`, followed by one or more of `RFS_CHMOD`, `RFS_CHOWN`, and `RFS_UTIME`.

SVR4 introduced a new version of the RFS protocol, called RFS2.0. It provided a set of requests that directly mapped vnode and vfs operations, thus providing a cleaner integration with the vnode/vfs interface. This did, however, bring up the problem of backward compatibility, since different machines on the network may be running different UNIX releases and, thus, different versions of RFS.

To address this, SVR4 clients and servers understand both RFS protocols. When the connection is made (during the first *mount* operation), the client and the server exchange information about which protocols each of them can handle and agree on the protocol they both understand. Thus RFS2.0 is only used when both machines support it. If one of the machines is running SVR4 and the other SVR3, they will use the RFS1.0 protocol.

This requires SVR4 to implement each vnode and vfs operation in two ways—one when speaking to another SVR4 machine and the other when talking to an older system.

10.12.2 Stateful Operation

RFS is an inherently stateful file system, which means the server maintains state about the clients. In particular, the server records which files have been opened by the client, and increments the reference counts on their vnodes. In addition, the server keeps track of file/record locks held by each client and reader/writer counts for named pipes. The server also maintains a table of all clients that have mounted its file systems. This table stores the client internet address, the mounted file system, and parameters of the virtual circuit connection.

The stateful nature requires that the server and the client are informed when the other crashes and that they perform appropriate recovery actions. This is discussed in detail in Section 10.13.3.

10.13 RFS Implementation

The RFS protocol allows a clean separation of the client and server functionality. Mount operations are handled separately by the *remote mount* facility, in conjunction with the name server. Let us examine each of these components separately.

10.13.1 Remote Mount

An RFS server can advertise a directory using the *advfs* system call. The arguments to *advfs* include the pathname of the exported directory, the resource name associated with the directory, and a list of client machines authorized to access the resource. In addition, the server may require a password check to be performed during virtual circuit establishment.

The server calls *advfs* to advertise a directory. *advfs* creates an entry for the directory in a resource list in the kernel (Figure 10-8). This entry contains the resource name, a pointer to the vnode of the exported directory, and a list of authorized clients. It also contains the head of a list of mount entries for each of the clients that mount this resource. In SVR4, the *advfs* system call has been replaced by the *rfsys* call, which exports several subfunctions, including one to advertise a file system.

Figure 10-9 describes the interactions between the RFS server, the name server, and the client. The server invokes the *adv(1)* command to register its advertised resource with the name server. Some time later, a client mounts an RFS resource by a command such as

```
mount -d <RNAME> /mnt
```

where *<RNAME>* is the name of the resource. The *mount* command queries the name server to obtain the network location for this resource and sets up a virtual circuit if necessary. It then invokes the *mount* system call with the pathname of the local mount point and a flag specifying an RFS type mount. The RFS-specific arguments to the system call include the virtual circuit pointer and the resource name.

The *mount* system call sends a MOUNT request to the server, passing it the symbolic resource name. The server locates the resource table entry, verifies that the client is authorized to mount the resource, and adds an entry for the client in the mount list for that resource. It increments the reference count of the exported directory to account for the remote mount and sends a successful reply back to the client. This response contains a *mount ID*, which the client can send back in future requests to this file system. The server uses the mount ID to quickly locate the corresponding resource.

When the client receives the MOUNT response, it completes its part of the processing. It sets up the *vfs* entry, storing the mount ID in the file system-specific data structure. It also sets up the

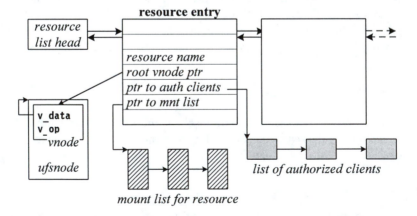

Figure 10-8. RFS resource list.

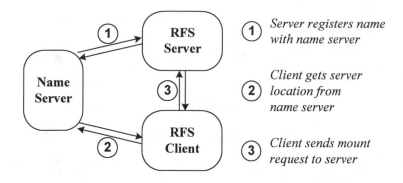

Figure 10-9. Mounting an RFS file system.

vnode for the root directory of the resource. The v_data field of an RFS vnode points to a data structure called a *send descriptor,* which contains information about the virtual circuit (such as a pointer to the stream), as well as a file handle that the server can use to locate the corresponding local vnode.

The first mount operation between a client and a server establishes the virtual circuit. All subsequent mounts (and RFS operations) are multiplexed over this circuit, which is maintained until the last resource is unmounted. The mount operation initiates a connection to a daemon process on the server, using the transport interface. Once the connection is established, the client and the server negotiate the run-time parameters, including the protocol version number, and the hardware architecture type. If the two machines have different architectures, they use XDR for data encoding.

The initial virtual circuit establishment occurs in user mode, using the standard network programming interface in the system. Once established, the user calls the FWFD function of the *rfsys* system call, to pass the virtual circuit into the kernel.

10.13.2   RFS Clients and Servers

The client can access an RFS file either through its pathname or through a file descriptor. The kernel may encounter an RFS mount point while traversing a pathname. In RFS1.0, this results in sending the remainder of the pathname to the RFS server, which will parse it in a single operation and return a handle to the vnode. RFS2.0 allows the client to mount other file systems on RFS directories, and therefore checks to see if this is the case. If so, the client must translate the pathname one component at a time, so as to process the mount point correctly. If not, it sends the entire pathname to the server. The server returns a handle, which the client stores in the private data of the vnode. Figure 10-10 shows the data structures on the client and server.

Subsequent operations on the file access it through the file descriptor, which the kernel uses to locate the vnode. The vnode operations invoke RFS client functions, which extract the file handle from the vnode and pass it in RFS requests to the server. The handle is opaque to the client. Usually, it simply contains a pointer to the vnode on the server.

The RFS server runs as one or more independent daemon processes. They execute entirely in the kernel, in order to avoid context switches between user and kernel mode. Each daemon listens

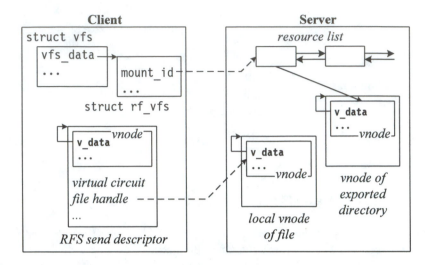

Figure 10-10. RFS data structures.

for incoming requests and services each request to completion before attending to the next one. While servicing a request, the daemon assumes the identity of the client process, using the credentials, resource limits, and other attributes passed in the message. The RFS daemons may sleep if they need to wait for resources and are scheduled just like normal processes.

10.13.3   Crash Recovery

Stateful systems need elaborate crash recovery mechanisms. Both the client and the server need to detect and handle the other's failure. When either machine crashes, the virtual circuit between them breaks, causing the underlying transport mechanism to notify RFS of the event. The circuit may also be broken by a network failure, which is treated just like a crash by RFS. The recovery mechanisms are different for the server and the client.

When a client crashes, the server must *undo* all state related to that client. To do so, the server maintains per-client state information for each inode and uses it to perform the following actions:

1. Decrements the inode's reference count by the number of references held by the crashed client.
2. Releases any reader/writer locks on named pipes in use by the client.
3. Releases any file/record locks held by the client.

In the event of a server crash, all client processes waiting for responses from the server are woken up, and the system calls return an ENOLINK error message. All RFS inodes referring to files on that server are flagged such that subsequent operations on them return an error. A user-level daemon (*rfudaemon (1M)*) is awakened to handle any additional recovery tasks.

10.13.4   Other Issues

Process pool — Since RFS allows transparent access to remote devices and named pipes, server processes may block for a long time waiting for device or pipe I/O.[11] Thus the server needs to maintain a dynamic pool of processes. Whenever a client request arrives and all server processes are busy, it creates a new process. This pool has a (tunable) upper bound, and the last process is not allowed to sleep.

Remote signals — UNIX allows a signal to abort a system call, and this facility must be extended to RFS environments. Suppose a client process is blocked because it is waiting for the server to respond to a request. If this process receives a signal, the client kernel sends a *signal* request to the server. This request identifies the process using a *system ID* along with the PID. The server uses this information to locate the daemon process sleeping on behalf of this client and posts the signal to it.

Data transfer — For a local *read* or *write* system call, the copyin() and copyout() routines move data between the buffer cache and the user address space. RFS operations must move data to or from the request messages. A special flag in the process table entry identifies the process as being an RFS server, and the copyin() and copyout() routines check this flag and handle the transfer appropriately.

10.14   Client-Side Caching

If every I/O operation required remote access, RFS performance would suffer terribly. Some form of caching is essential for reasonable throughput. The problem with any distributed cache is maintaining consistency of data that may reside in multiple client caches, as well as on the server. NFSv2, as we saw in Section 10.7.2, takes a very cavalier attitude to this problem, which is acceptable for a stateless system not too particular about preserving full UNIX semantics. RFS, however, needs to be much more circumspect and must establish a workable consistency protocol.

Client caching was introduced in RFS in SVR3.1 [Bach 87]. It is activated at mount time, allowing the user to disable the cache if desired (this makes sense for some applications who do their own caching). The RFS cache has been designed to provide a strong degree of consistency, meaning that there can be no situations where users can get obsolete data from the cache.

The cache is strictly write-through. Clients send all writes to the server immediately, after updating the local cached copy. This does not improve the write performance, but is important for consistency. A *read* system call returns cached data if and only if all the data requested is available in the cache (reads may span multiple buffers). If any part of the data is not in the local cache, the client fetches all the data from the server in a single operation. If only the missing blocks were read from the server, we could not guarantee the atomicity of the *read,* since the blocks from the cache and those from the server could reflect different states of the file.

The RFS cache shares the resources of the local block buffer cache. Some of the buffers are reserved for RFS use, some for local files, and the rest are available to both. This prevents local files from monopolizing the buffer pool. Buffers are reused in *least recently used* order.

---

[11] In practice, using RFS to share devices is problem-prone, except in completely homogeneous environments. Small differences in system call semantics may make device sharing impossible.

10.14.1   Cache Consistency

The strong cache consistency model guarantees that a read always returns data that is identical to the server's image of the file at the time of access. The server's image reflects the disk copy of the file, as well as any more recent blocks in the server's buffer cache.

Any modification to a file, either by a user on the server, or by one of the clients, invalidates the cached copies on all other clients. One way to achieve this is to notify all affected clients upon each write operation, but this leads to extensive network traffic and is prohibitively expensive. RFS provides consistency in a more efficient manner, by distinguishing between clients that have the file open and those who have already closed it.

Consistency protocols are only required for files that are shared by multiple clients. If a remote file is shared by different processes on the same machine, the cache consistency can be provided by the client itself, without involving the server.

Figure 10-11 shows how RFS maintains cache consistency. When the server receives the first *write* request for a file open on more than one client, it suspends the *write* operation and sends an *invalidate* message to all other clients who have the file open. These clients invalidate any cached data for this file and temporarily disable caching for it. Subsequent reads for that file will bypass the cache and fetch data from the server. The caching is reenabled when the writer process closes the file or when a certain (tunable) time interval has elapsed since the last modification. Once all clients invalidate the cache and acknowledge the message, the write request is allowed to resume.

There may be some clients who have closed the file, but still retain some of its blocks in

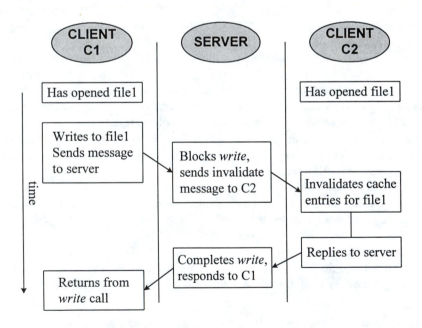

Figure 10-11. RFS cache consistency algorithm.

their cache. It is important to prevent them from using stale cached blocks if they reopen the file. This is achieved by associating a *version number* with each file, which is incremented each time the file is modified. The server returns the version number in the response to each open request, and the client stores it in its cache. If a file has been modified since the client closed it, the client will get back a different version number when it tries to reopen the file. When that happens, the client can flush all the blocks associated with that file, ensuring that it will not access stale cached data.

Under normal circumstances, the RFS consistency mechanisms provide strong consistency guarantees at a reasonable cost. Problems may arise if one of the client crashes or becomes unresponsive. It may then take a long time to respond to cache invalidation requests, preventing other nodes from completing their operations. In this way, a single errant client can cause problems for the whole network. Overall, the benefits of caching are far greater than the cost of maintaining consistency, and the RFS cache has demonstrated a performance improvement of about a factor of two (over the old implementation) on benchmarks with one to five clients.

10.15   The Andrew File System

Both NFS and RFS are targeted at small LANs with a limited number of clients. Neither scales well to a large network spanning several buildings and hundreds or thousands of clients, such as those found in typical university campuses. In 1982, Carnegie-Mellon University (CMU) and IBM jointly formed the Information Technology Center (ITC) to develop the computing infrastructure for educational computing. One of its main projects was the *Andrew File System (AFS),* a distributed file system capable of scaling to thousands of users [Morr 86].

The ITC released several versions of the AFS, culminating in AFS 3.0. Thereafter, work on AFS moved to Transarc Corporation, formed by many of its original developers. At Transarc, AFS evolved into the *Distributed File System (DFS)* component of OSF's Distributed Computing Environment (DCE). The following sections describe the design and implementation of AFS. Section 10.18 talks about DCE DFS.

Besides scalability, the designers of AFS specified several important objectives [Saty 85]. AFS must be UNIX-compatible, so UNIX binaries can run unmodified on AFS clients. It must provide a uniform, location-independent name space for shared files. Users can access their files from any client node in the network, and files can be moved to a new location without quiescing the system. It must be fault-tolerant, so that failure of a single server or network component does not make the entire system unavailable. Faults must be isolated close to the point of failure. It should provide security without trusting client workstations or the network. Finally, the performance should be comparable to a time-sharing system.

10.15.1   Scalable Architecture

There are three important problems in making a distributed file system scalable. If a single server handles a large number of clients, we get both server congestion and network overload. Inadequate client-side caching causes excessive network traffic. Finally, if the server performs the bulk of the processing of all operations, it will become overloaded sooner. A scalable system must address all these issues correctly.

AFS controls network congestion and server overload by segmenting the network into a number of independent clusters. Unlike NFS and RFS, AFS uses dedicated servers. Each machine is either a client or a server, but not both. Figure 10-12 shows the organization of an AFS network. Each cluster contains a number of clients, plus a server that holds the files of interest to those clients, such as the user directories of the owners of the client workstations.

This configuration provides fastest access to files residing on the server on the same network segment. Users can access files on any other server, but the performance will be slower. The network can be dynamically reconfigured to balance loads on servers and network segments.

AFS uses aggressive caching of files, coupled with a stateful protocol, to minimize network traffic. Clients cache recently accessed files on their local disks. The original implementation cached entire files. Since that was not practical for very large files, AFS3.0 divides the file into 64-kilobyte chunks, and caches individual chunks separately. The AFS servers participate actively in client cache management, by notifying clients whenever the cached data becomes invalid. Section 10.16.1 describes this protocol further.

AFS also reduces server load by moving the burden of name lookups from the server to the clients. Clients cache entire directories and parse the filenames themselves. Section 10.16.2 describes this in detail.

10.15.2   Storage and Name Space Organization

The collection of AFS servers (called *Vice,* which has been rumored to stand for *Vast Integrated Computing Environment*) together holds the shared files. AFS organizes files in logical units called *volumes*. A volume [Side 86] is a collection of related files and directories and forms a subtree in the shared file hierarchy. For instance, a volume may contain all files belonging to a single user. Typically, one disk partition may hold several small volumes. A large volume, however, may span multiple disks.

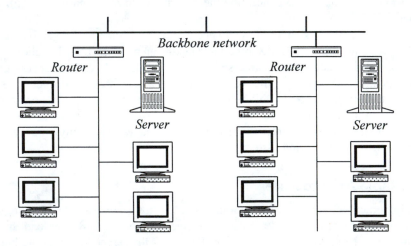

Figure 10-12. AFS network organization.

The volume provides a unit of file system storage that is distinct from partitions, which provide units of physical storage. This separation has several advantages. Volumes may be moved freely from one location to another, without affecting active users. This may be done for load balancing, or to adjust for permanent moves of users. If a user moves his or her home workstation to a different part of the network, the system administrator can move the user's volume to the local server. Volumes also allow files that are much larger than a single disk. Read-only volumes can be replicated on several servers to increase availability and performance. Finally, each volume can be individually backed up and restored.

AFS provides a single, uniform name space that is independent of the storage location. Each file is identified by an *fid*, which consists of a *volume ID*, a *vnode number*, and a *vnode uniquifier*. Historically, AFS uses the term *vnode* to mean a *Vice inode;* hence, the vnode number is an index into the inode list of the volume. The uniquifier is a generation number, incremented each time the vnode is reused.

The volume location database provides location independence and transparency. It provides a mapping between a volume ID and the physical location of the volume. The database is replicated on each server, so that it does not become a bottleneck resource. If a volume is moved to another location, the original server retains its forwarding information, so that the databases on the other servers need not be updated immediately. While the volume is being transferred, the original server may still handle updates, which are later migrated to the new server. At some point, the volume is temporarily quiesced to transfer the recent changes.

Each client workstation must have a local disk. This disk contains a few local files, plus a directory on which it mounts the shared file hierarchy. Conventionally, each workstation mounts the shared tree on the same directory. The local files include the system files essential for minimal operation, plus some files the user may want to keep local for reasons of security or performance. Hence each client sees the same shared name space, plus its own, unique, local files. The local disk also acts as a cache for recently accessed shared files.

10.15.3   Session Semantics

In a centralized UNIX system, if a process modifies a file, other processes see the new data on the next *read* system call. Enforcing UNIX semantics in a distributed file system causes excessive network traffic and performance degradation. AFS 2.0 uses a less restrictive consistency protocol, called *session semantics,* which performs cache consistency operations only at file *open* or *close*. Clients flush modified data to the server only when the file is closed. When that happens, the server notifies other clients that their cached copies have become invalid. Clients do not check data validity on every read or write access to the file, but continue to use stale data until they open the file again. Hence users on different machines see changes to a shared file at the *open* and *close* system call granularity, rather than at the *read* and *write* system call granularity as in UNIX.

AFS provides stronger guarantees for metadata operations, which are updated to the server (and from the server, to other clients) immediately. For instance, if a *rename* system call completes on one client, no other machine on the network can open the file under the old name, and all can open it under its new name.

The consistency guarantees of session semantics are much weaker than those of UNIX semantics. AFS 3.0 checks the data validity on every read or write, thus providing better consistency.
It still falls short of UNIX semantics, since the client does not flush changes to the server until the
file is closed. DFS, the new incarnation of AFS, enforces UNIX semantics through a token passing
mechanism, which is described in Section 10.18.2.

10.16   AFS Implementation

AFS has distinct servers and clients. The collection of servers is referred to as Vice, and the client
workstations are called Virtue. Both servers and clients run some flavor of UNIX as the underlying
operating system. Initial AFS implementations used simple, user-level processes to implement the
client and server functionality. The client kernel was modified slightly to detect references to shared
files and forward them to the AFS client process, known as *Venus*. In AFS 3.0, the client kernel
contains the *AFS cache manager,* which provides AFS functionality through the vnode/vfs interface. The server runs as a single, multithreaded, user process (using user-level threads libraries on
traditional systems). In recent versions, most of the server functionality has migrated to the kernel,
and runs in the context of daemon processes.

10.16.1   Caching and Consistency

The cache manager [Spec 89] implements the vnode operations for AFS files on the client. When a
client first opens an AFS file, the cache manager reads in the whole file (or a 64K chunk, for files
larger than 64 kilobytes) and caches it as a file in the client's local file system. The cache manager
redirects all *read* and *write* calls to the cached copy. When the client closes the file, the cache manager flushes the changes to the server.

When the cache manager fetches the file from the server, the server also supplies a callback
associated with the data. The callback is a promise that the data is valid. If another client modifies
the file and writes the changes back to the server, the server notifies all clients holding callbacks for
the file. This is called *breaking the callback*. The client responds by discarding the stale data, and
fetching it again from the server if needed.[12]

The client caches file attributes separately from file data. Attributes are cached in memory,
unlike file data, which is cached on the local disk. The client and server use the same callback
mechanism for attributes. The client notifies the server when it changes any file attributes, and the
server immediately breaks all associated callbacks.

Certain race conditions can cause problems with the callback-breaking mechanism
[Kaza 88]. Suppose the client fetches a file from the server, just as the server sends a message
breaking the callback to that very file. If the file data arrives later, the client does not know if the
broken callback notification applies to the current data or to a previous callback for the file and,
therefore, cannot tell if the callback is valid. AFS solves this by simply discarding the data and

---

[12] Prior to AFS 3.0, clients discarded the stale data only on the next open. This, along with the large chunk size, made
those implementations unsuitable for transaction processing and database systems.

fetching it from the server again. This may cause some extra network traffic and slow down the operation. Such a situation requires an unlikely combination of events and, in practice, does not happen very often.

A more severe problem is when a temporary network failure prevents the delivery of a callback-breaking message. In AFS, the client may run for a long time without contacting the server. During this time, it will incorrectly assume that its cached data is correct. To bound this time, the client regularly probes each file server from which it has callback promises (once every ten minutes, by default).

The callback mechanism implies a stateful server. The server keeps track of all callbacks it has issued for each file. When a client modifies the file, the server must break all outstanding callbacks for that file. If the volume of this information becomes unmanageable, the server can break some existing callbacks and reclaim storage. The client must maintain validation information for cached files.

10.16.2   Pathname Lookup

A scalable system must prevent server overload. One way to do so is to shift certain operations from the server to clients. In particular, *pathname lookup* is a CPU-intensive operation, and AFS handles it directly on clients.

The client caches both symbolic links and directories. It also caches entries from the volume location database. It traverses the pathname one component at a time. If it does not have the directory in the local cache, it fetches the entire directory from the server. It then searches the directory for the component. The directory entry maps the component name to its *fid,* which contains the volume ID, vnode number and vnode uniquifier.

If the client knows the volume location, it contacts the corresponding server to get the next component (unless the component is already in the local cache). If not, it queries the volume location database on the nearest server and caches the reply. The client treats the cached database entries as hints. If the information has changed, the server will reject the request, and the client must query a server database for the correct location. It is also possible that the volume has migrated, and the nearest server does not know about it yet. In this case, the client will first try the old location of the volume; that server will have the forwarding address and react appropriately.

10.16.3   Security

AFS considers Vice (the collection of servers) as the boundary of security. It considers both user workstations and the network as inherently insecure (with good reason). It avoids passing unencrypted passwords over the network, since it is too easy to catch them through computers that can snoop on the network.

AFS uses the Kerberos authentication system [Stei 88], developed at the Massachusetts Institute of Technology. Kerberos clients authenticate themselves not by transmitting a password known to the client and the server, but by answering encrypted challenges from the server. The server encrypts the challenge with the key known to both the server and the client. The client decrypts the challenge, encrypts the answer with the same key, and sends the encrypted answer to the server. Since the server uses a different challenge each time, the client cannot reuse the same response.

[Hone 92] identifies several loopholes in the way in which AFS 3.0 uses Kerberos. The client keeps several important data structures unencrypted in its address space, making it vulnerable to users who can acquire root privilege on their own workstations. Such users can traverse the kernel data structures to obtain authenticated Kerberos tickets of other users. Moreover, the challenge-response protocol in AFS 3.0 is susceptible to attack from another node on the network that sends out fake challenges to the client. Transarc subsequently fixed these loopholes in AFS 3.1.

AFS also provides *access-control lists (ACLs)* for directories (but not for individual files). Each ACL is an array of pairs. The first item in each pair is a user or group name, and the second defines rights granted to that user or group. The ACLs support four types of permissions on a directory—**l**ookup, **i**nsert, **d**elete, and **a**dminister (modify the ACL for this directory). In addition, they allow three types of permissions for files in that directory—**r**ead, **w**rite, and lo**c**k. AFS also retains the standard UNIX permission bits, and a user must pass both tests (ACL and UNIX permissions) to operate on a file.

10.17   AFS Shortcomings

AFS is a highly scalable architecture. At CMU, AFS became operational in mid-1985, and by January 1989, it supported 9000 user accounts, 30 file servers, 1000 client machines, and about 45 gigabytes of storage. It is also suitable for wide-area file sharing. By the spring of 1992, there were 67 AFS cells available worldwide for public mounting [Gerb 92]. Users could access files from dispersed locations such as the OSF Research Institute in Grenoble, France; the Keio University in Japan, and the National Institute of Health in Washington, DC, using regular UNIX commands such as *cd, ls,* and *cat*. [Howa 88] describes a through series of performance tests, which confirm that AFS reduces server CPU utilization, network traffic, and overall time for remote operation.

Client performance, however, is far from satisfactory [Stol 93]. The AFS client uses the local file system to cache recently accessed file chunks. When accessing that data, it must perform a series of additional, time-consuming operations. Besides accessing the local file, the cache manager must validate the cached data (check for broken callbacks) and perform the mapping from the AFS file or chunk to the local file. Moreover, if the request spans multiple chunks, the cache manager must break it up into several smaller requests, each operating on a single chunk. As a result, even for data that is already in the cache, accessing an AFS file takes up to twice as long as accessing a local file. By careful tuning, the AFS overhead in the *fast path* (the case where data is valid and the request is isolated to one chunk) can be reduced to about 10–15%.

The stateful model is difficult to implement. The cache consistency algorithms must deal with several race conditions and potential deadlocks. As implemented, the model falls far short of UNIX semantics. Its consistency guarantees are much weaker, since clients write back changes only when a process closes the file. This can lead to many unpredictable results. The client may be unable to flush the file due to server crashes, network failures, or real errors such as the disk becoming full. This has two important consequences. First, the *close* system call fails much more often for AFS files than for other file systems. Many applications do not check the return value of *close* or take any corrective action. In many cases, the application closes files implicitly when it terminates.

Second, the *write* system call often succeeds when it should not (e.g., when the write extends the file but the disk is full). Both situations have unexpected results on the client.

Finally, shifting the pathname lookup to the client decreases the server load, but requires the client to understand the directory format of the server. Contrast this with NFS, which provides directory information in a hardware and operating system independent format.

Some of the drawbacks of AFS are addressed by DFS, which we describe in the next section.

10.18   The DCE Distributed File System (DCE DFS)

In 1989, Transarc Corporation took over the development and productization of AFS. With their efforts, the Open Software Foundation accepted the AFS technology as the basis for the distributed file system of OSF's *Distributed Computing Environment (DCE)*. This new incarnation is often referred to as DCE DFS, or simply as DFS. In the rest of this chapter, we call it DFS.

DFS has evolved from AFS and is similar to it in several respects. It improves upon AFS in the following ways:

1.   It allows a single machine to be both a client and a server.
2.   It provides stronger, UNIX-like sharing semantics and consistency guarantees.
3.   It allows greater interoperability with other file systems.

Transarc developed the Episode file system [Chut 92] as the local file system for DFS servers. Episode, described in detail in Section 11.8, provides high availability (through the use of logging), as well as support for logical volumes (what are *Volumes* in AFS are called *filesets* in Episode) and POSIX-compatible access-control lists. In this chapter, we concentrate on the distributed components of DFS.

10.18.1   DFS Architecture

The DFS architecture [Kaza 90] is similar to that of AFS in many regards. It uses a stateful client-server model with an active server that initiates cache invalidation messages. It caches entire files (64-kilobyte chunks for large files) in the client's local file system. It uses a volume location database to provide name transparency.

DFS improves upon AFS in many respects. It uses the vnode/vfs interface both on the client and on the server, to allow interoperability with other file systems and access protocols. It allows local users on the server node to access the DFS file system as well. DFS clients and servers communicate using DCE RPC [OSF 92], which offers several useful features such as synchronous and asynchronous modes, Kerberos authentication, and support for long-haul operation and connection-oriented transport.

Figure 10-13 shows the overall architecture of DFS. The client is fairly similar to the AFS client, the main difference being in their handling of directories. Both AFS and DFS clients cache directory information. DFS, however, allows the server to export many different file system types (but Episode is preferred, since it is designed specifically for DFS), so the client may not understand

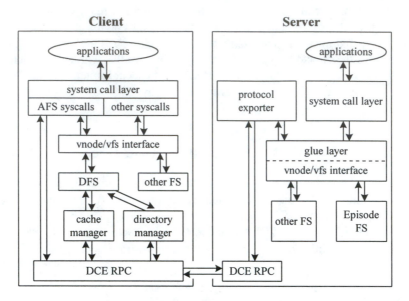

Figure 10-13. DFS architecture.

the format of the server's directories. Hence DFS clients cache the results of individual lookups, rather than entire directories.

The DFS server design is very different from AFS. In AFS, the access protocol and the file system are a single, integrated entity. In DFS, the two are separated and interact through the vnode/vfs interface. This allows DFS to export the server's native file system. It also allows local applications on the server to access the exported file system. The DFS server uses an extended vfs interface (called VFS+), which has additional functions to support volumes and access-control lists. Episode supports all VFS+ operations, and hence provides full DFS functionality. Other local file systems may not support the extensions and may provide only a subset of the DFS functionality.

The *protocol exporter* services requests from DFS clients. It maintains state information for each client and informs the client whenever some of its cached data becomes invalid. The *glue layer* in the vfs interface maintains consistency between the protocol exporter and other file access methods (local access and other distributed protocols supported by the server), as explained in Section 10.18.2.

10.18.2   Cache Consistency

DFS exports strict UNIX single-system semantics for access to shared files. If one client writes data to a file, any client reading the file should see the new data. DFS guarantees cache consistency at the *read* and *write* system call granularity, unlike AFS, which does so at the *open* and *close* system call level.

To implement these semantics, the DFS server includes a *token manager,* which keeps track of all active client references to files. On each reference, the server gives the client one or more *tokens,* which guarantee the validity of file data or attributes. The server may cancel the guarantee at any time by revoking the token. The client must then treat the corresponding cached data as invalid, and fetch it again from the server if needed.

DFS supports four types of tokens, each dealing with a different set of file operations:

Data tokens   There are two types of data tokens—*read* and *write.* Each applies to a range of bytes within a file. If the client holds a read token, its cached copy of that part of the file is valid. If it holds a write token, it may modify its cached data without flushing it to the server. When the server revokes a read token, the client must discard its cached data. When the server revokes a write token, the client must write any modifications back to the server and then discard the data.

Status tokens   These tokens provide guarantees about cached file attributes. Again there are two types—*status read* and *status write.* Their semantics are similar to those of data read and write tokens. If a client holds the status write token to a file, the server will block other clients that try to even read the file's attributes.

Lock tokens   These allow the holder to set different types of file locks on byte ranges in the file. As long as the client holds a lock token, it does not need to contact the server to lock the file, since it is guaranteed that the server will not grant a conflicting lock to another client.

Open tokens   Allow the holder to open a file. There are different types of open tokens, corresponding to different open modes—*read, write, execute,* and *exclusive write.* For instance, a client holding an *open for execute* token is assured that no other client will be able to modify the file. This particular guarantee is difficult for other distributed file systems to support. It is necessary because most UNIX systems access executable files one page at a time (demand paging, see Section 13.2). If a file were modified while being executed, the client would get part of the old program and part of the new one, leading to strange and unpredictable results.

DFS defines a set of compatibility rules when different clients want tokens for the same file. Tokens of different types are mutually compatible, since they relate to separate components of a file. For tokens of the same type, the rules vary by token type. For data and lock tokens, the read and write tokens are incompatible if their byte ranges overlap. Status read and write tokens are always incompatible. For open tokens, exclusive writes are incompatible with any other subtype, and execute tokens are incompatible with normal writes as well. The rest of the combinations are mutually compatible.

Tokens are similar to the AFS callbacks—both provide cache consistency guarantees that the server may revoke at any time. Unlike callbacks, tokens are typed objects. AFS defines a single type of callback for file data and one for file attributes. DFS provides several token types, as previously described. This allows a greater degree of concurrency in the file system, and enables UNIX-style single-user semantics for access to shared files.

10.18.3   The Token Manager

Each server has a *token manager,* which resides in the glue layer of the vnode interface. The glue layer contains a wrapper routine for each vnode operation. This routine acquires all tokens required to complete the operation and then calls the file-system-dependent vnode routine.

In many cases, a vnode operation requires multiple tokens. Some operations also require directory lookups to identify the set of vnodes whose tokens must be obtained before performing the operation. For instance, a *rename* operation requires *status write* tokens for the source and destination directories, if the two are different. The operation must also search the destination directory to check if it already has a file with the new name. If so, *rename* must obtain additional tokens for deleting that file. The token manager must take care to avoid deadlock, using mechanisms similar to those used by physical file systems.

Often a client request conflicts with a token already granted to another client. The token manager must block the request and revoke the conflicting tokens by notifying the other client (current owner of the token). If the token was for reading, its owner simply returns the token to the server and marks its cached data as invalid. If the token was for writing, its owner flushes any modified data to the server before returning the token. If the token is for locking or opening, the owner may not return the token until it unlocks or closes the file. When the token manager gets the token back, it completes the request and gives the token to the caller.

The token manager needs to be in the vnode layer, since DFS may coexist with other access methods, such as local access through system calls and other distributed protocols such as NFS. The token manager acquires tokens regardless of the access method, so as to ensure DFS guarantees during mixed-mode access. For instance, suppose two clients access the same file concurrently, one using DFS and another using NFS. If the NFS access did not acquire or check for tokens, it would violate the guarantees made to the DFS client. By placing the token manager in the glue layer, the server synchronizes all operations on the file.

10.18.4   Other DFS Services

DFS requires more than just the protocol exporter and the client cache manager. It provides a number of ancillary services that cooperate with file service operations. These include:

Fileset location database *(fldb)*   This is a global, replicated database that contains the location of each volume. It stores information about the location of the fileset and its replicas, and it is similar to the AFS volume location database.

Fileset server *(ftserver)*   Implements per-fileset operations such as fileset migration.

Authentication server   Provides Kerberos-based authentication.

Replication server *(rpserver)*   DFS supports fileset replication for increasing availability of important data. Replication protects
against network and server outages, and also reduces
bottlenecks by distributing the load for heavily used
filesets across several machines. The replicas are
read-only, but the original may be read-write. DFS
allows two forms of replication—release and
scheduled. With release replication, clients must issue explicit *fts release* commands to update the replicas from the original. Scheduled replication automatically updates replicas at fixed intervals.

10.18.5   Analysis

DFS provides a comprehensive set of facilities for distributed file access. Its Episode file system
uses logging to reduce crash recovery time, thereby increasing file system availability. It uses two
separate abstractions—aggregates and filesets—to organize the file system. Aggregates are units of
physical storage, while filesets are logical divisions of the file system. In this way, it decouples the
logical and physical organization of data.

Episode uses POSIX-compliant access-control lists for finer granularity file protection. Although this allows for a more flexible and robust security scheme than that of UNIX, it is unfamiliar
to system administrators and users. Similarly, Kerberos provides a secure authentication framework
for DFS, but requires modification to several programs such as *login, ftp,* and various batch and
mail utilities.

DFS uses fileset replication to increase the availability of data and to reduce access times by
distributing the load among different servers. Replication also allows online backup of individual
filesets, since a replica is a frozen, consistent snapshot of the fileset. The fileset location database
provides location independence and transparency.

The DFS architecture is based on client-side caching with server-initiated cache invalidation.
This approach is suitable for large-scale networks, since it reduces network congestion under normal
usage patterns. By implementing both server and client on top of the vnode/vfs interface, DFS
achieves interoperability with other physical file systems and with other local and remote file access
protocols.

However, the DCE DFS architecture is complex and difficult to implement. It requires not
only DCE RPC but also a variety of related services, such as the X.500 global directory service
[OSF 93]. In particular, it is not easy to support DFS on small machines and simple operating systems (MS-DOS readily comes to mind). This will be a barrier to its acceptance in truly heterogeneous environments.

The cache consistency and deadlock avoidance mechanisms are highly complex as well. The
algorithms must also recover correctly from failure of individual clients, servers, or network segments. This is a problem with any distributed file system that provides fine-granularity concurrent
access semantics.

10.19   Summary

This chapter describes the architecture and implementation of four important distributed file systems—NFS, RFS, AFS, and DFS. NFS is the simplest to implement and is the most portable architecture. It has been ported to a large variety of platforms and operating systems, making it the protocol of choice for truly heterogeneous environments. However, it does not scale well, falls far short of UNIX semantics, and suffers from poor write performance. RFS provides UNIX semantics and also sharing of devices, but only works with System V UNIX and variants derived from it. AFS and DFS are highly scalable architectures. DFS provides UNIX semantics, and is interoperable with other access protocols. It is, however, complex and unwieldy, and difficult to implement. It is an emerging technology, and only time will tell how successful it will become.

There are few published measurements of relative performance of these file systems. [Howa 88] compares the performance of NFS and AFS using identical hardware configurations. The results show that for a single server, NFS is faster at low loads (less than 15 clients), but deteriorates rapidly for higher loads. Both systems have evolved substantially since then, but the factors affecting scalability have not changed significantly.

10.20   Exercises

1.   Why is network transparency important in a distributed file system?
2.   What is the difference between location transparency and location independence?
3.   What are the benefits of a stateless file system? What are the drawbacks?
4.   Which distributed file system provides UNIX semantics for shared access to files? Which provides session semantics?
5.   Why is the mount protocol separate from the NFS protocol?
6.   How would an asynchronous RPC request operate? Suggest a client interface to send an asynchronous request and receive a reply.
7.   Write an RPC program that allows the client to send a text string to be printed on the server. Suggest a use for such a service.
8.   Suppose an NFS server crashes and reboots. How does it know what file systems its clients have mounted? Does it care?
9.   Consider the following shell command, executed from an NFS-mounted directory:
         echo hello > krishna.txt
     What sequence of NFS requests will this cause? Assume the file **krishna.txt** does not already exist.
10. In Exercise 9, what would be the sequence of requests if **hello.txt** already existed?
11. NFS clients fake the deletion of open files by renaming the file on the server and deleting it when the file is closed. If the client crashes before deleting the file, what happens to the file? Suggest a possible solution.
12. The write system call is asynchronous and does not wait for the data to be committed to stable storage. Why should the NFS write operation be synchronous? How do server or client crashes affect outstanding writes?

13. Why is NFS not suitable for wide-area operation?

14. Why is RFS only usable in homogeneous environments?

15. How well does RFS meet the goals of network transparency, location independence, and location transparency?

16. In what ways does DFS improve upon AFS?

17. What is the function of the DFS protocol exporter?

18. How do DFS tokens differ from AFS callbacks?

19. Which of the distributed file systems discussed in this chapter provides user or file mobility?

20. Compare the name space seen by users in NFS, RFS, AFS, and DFS environments.

21. Compare the consistency semantics of client-side caching in NFS, RFS, AFS, and DFS.

10.21 References

[Bach 87]   Bach, M.J., Luppi, M.W., Melamed, A.S., and Yueh, K., "A Remote-File Cache for RFS," *Proceedings of the Summer 1987 USENIX Technical Conference,* Jun. 1987, pp. 273–279.

[Bhid 91]   Bhide, A., Elnozahy, E., and Morgan, S., "A Highly Available Network File Server," *Proceedings of the Winter 1991 USENIX Technical Conference,* Jan. 1991, pp. 199–205.

[Bhid 92]   Bhide, A., and Shepler, S., "A Highly Available Lock Manager for HA–NFS," *Proceedings of the Summer 1992 USENIX Technical Conference,* Jun. 1992, pp. 177–184.

[Char 87]   Chartok, H., "RFS in SunOS," *Proceedings of the Summer 1987 USENIX Technical Conference,* Jun. 1987, pp. 281–290.

[Cher 88]   Cheriton, D.R., "The V Distributed System," *Communications of the ACM,* Vol. 31, No. 3, Mar. 1988, pp. 314–333.

[Chut 92]   Chutani, S., Anderson, O.T., Kazar, M.L., Leverett, B.W., Mason, W.A., and idebotham, R.N., "The Episode File System," *Proceedings of the Winter 1992 USENIX Technical Conference,* Jan. 1992, pp. 43–59.

[Gerb 92]   Gerber, B., "AFS: A Distributed File System that Supports Worldwide Networks," *Network Computing,* May 1992, pp. 142–148.

[Hitz 90]   Hitz, D., Harris, G., Lau, J.K., and Schwartz, A.M., "Using UNIX as One Component of a Lightweight Distributed Kernel for Multiprocessor File Servers," *Proceedings of the Winter 1990 USENIX Technical Conference,* Jan. 1990, pp. 285–295.

[Hitz 94]   Hitz, D., Lau, J., and Malcolm, M., "File System Design for an NFS File Server Appliance," *Proceedings of the Winter 1994 USENIX Technical Conference,* Jan. 1994, pp. 235–245.

[Hone 92]   Honeyman, P., Huston, L.B., and Stolarchuk, M.T., "Hijacking AFS," *Proceedings of the Winter 1992 USENIX Technical Conference,* Jan. 1992, pp. 175–181.

[Howa 88]   Howard, J.H., Kazar, M.L., Menees, S.G., Nichols, D.A., Satyanarayanan, M., and
             Sidebotham, R.N., "Scale and Performance in a Distributed File System," *ACM
             Transactions on Computer Systems,* Vol. 6, No. 1, Feb. 1988, pp. 55–81.

[Jusz 89]   Juszczak, C., "Improving the Performance and Correctness of an NFS Server,"
             Procedings of the Winter 1989 USENIX Technical Conference, Jan. 1989, pp. 53–63.

[Jusz 94]   Juszczak, C., "Improving the Write Performance of an NFS Server," *Proceedings of
             the Winter 1994 USENIX Technical Conference,* Jan. 1994, pp. 247–259.

[Kaza 88]   Kazar, M.L., "Synchronization and Caching Issues in the Andrew File System,"
             Proceedings of the Winter 1988 USENIX Technical Conference, Feb. 1988, pp. 27–
             36.

[Kaza 90]   Kazar, M.L., Leverett, B.W., Anderson, O.T., Apostolides, V., Bottos, B.A., Chutani,
             S., Everhart, C.F., Mason, W.A., Tu, S.-T., and Zayas, E.R., "Decorum File System
             Architectural Overview," *Proceedings of the Summer 1990 USENIX Technical
             Conference,* Jun. 1990.

[Levy 90]   Levy, E., and Silberschatz, A., "Distributed File Systems: Concepts and Examples,"
             ACM Computing Surveys, Vol. 22, No. 4, Dec. 1990, pp. 321–374.

[Mack 91]   Macklem, R., "Lessons Learned Tuning the 4.3BSD Reno Implementation of the
             NFS Protocol," *Proceedings of the Winter 1991 USENIX Technical Conference,* Jan.
             1991, pp. 53–64.

[Mora 90]   Moran, J., Sandberg, R., Coleman, D., Kepecs, J. and Lyon, B., "Breaking Through
             the NFS Performance Barrier," *Proceedings of the Spring 1990 European UNIX
             Users' Group Conference,* Apr. 1990, pp. 199–206.

[Morr 86]   Morris, J.H., Satyanarayanan, M., Conner, M.H., Howard, J.H., Rosenthal, D.S.H.,
             and Smith, F.D., "Andrew: A Distributed Personal Computing Environment,"
             Communications of the ACM, Vol. 29, No. 3, Mar. 1986, pp. 184–201.

[Nowi 90]   Nowitz, D.A., "UUCP Administration," *UNIX Research System Papers, Tenth
             Edition,* Vol. II, Saunders College Publishing, 1990, pp. 563–580.

[OSF 92]   Open Software Foundation, *OSF DCE Application Environment Specification,*
             Prentice-Hall, Englewood Cliffs, NJ, 1992.

[OSF 93]   Open Software Foundation, *OSF DCE Administration Guide—Extended Services,*
             Prentice-Hall, Englewood Cliffs, NJ, 1993.

[Pawl 94]   Pawlowski, B., Juszczak, C., Staubach, P., Smith, C., Lebel, D., and Hitz, D., "NFS
             Version 3 Design and Implementation," *Proceedings of the Summer 1994 USENIX
             Technical Conference,* Jun. 1994, pp. 137–151.

[Post 85]   Postel, J., and Reynolds, J., "The File Transfer Protocol," RFC 959, Oct. 1985.

[Plum 82]   Plummer, D.C., "An Ethernet Address Resolution Protocol," RFC 826, Nov. 1982.

[Rifk 86]   Rifkin, A.P., Forbes, M.P., Hamilton, R.L., Sabrio, M., Shah, S., and Yueh, K., "RFS
             Architectural Overview," *Proceedings of the Summer 1986 USENIX Technical
             Conference,* Jun. 1986, pp. 248–259.

[Sand 85a]   Sandberg, R., Goldberg, D., Kleiman, S.R., Walsh, D., and Lyon, B., "Design and
             Implementation of the Sun Network Filesystem," *Proceedings of the Summer 1985
             USENIX Technical Conference,* Jun. 1985, pp. 119–130.

[Sand 85b]   Sandberg, R., "Sun Network Filesystem Protocol Specification," Sun Microsystems, Inc., Technical Report, 1985.

[Saty 85]   Satyanarayanan, M., Howard, J.H., Nichols, D.A., Sidebotham, R.N., Spector, A.Z., and West, M.J., "The ITC Distributed File System: Principles and Design," *Tenth ACM Symposium on Operating Systems Principles,* Dec. 1985, pp. 35–50.

[Side 86]   Sidebotham, R.N., "VOLUMES—The Andrew File System Data Structuring Primitive," *Proceedings of the Autumn 1986 European UNIX Users' Group Conference,* Oct. 1986, pp. 473–480.

[Spec 89]   Spector, A.Z., and Kazar, M.L., "Uniting File Systems," *Unix Review,* Vol. 7, No. 3, Mar. 1989, pp. 61–70.

[Stei 88]   Steiner, J.G., Neuman, C., and Schiller, J.I., "Kerberos: An Authentication Service for Open Network Systems," *Proceedings of the Winter 1988 USENIX Technical Conference,* Jan. 1988, pp. 191–202.

[Stol 93]   Stolarchuk, M.T., "Faster AFS," *Proceedings of the Winter 1993 USENIX Technical Conference,* Jan. 1993, pp. 67–75.

[Sun 87]   Sun Microsystems, Inc., "XDR: External Data Representation Standard," RFC 1014, DDN Network Information Center, SRI International, Jun. 1989.

[Sun 88]   Sun Microsystems, Inc., "RPC: Remote Procedure Call, Protocol Specification, Version 2," RFC 1057, DDN Network Information Center, SRI International, Jun. 1989.

[Sun 89]   Sun Microsystems, Inc., "Network File System Protocol Specification," RFC 1094, DDN Network Information Center, SRI International, Mar. 1989.

[Sun 95]   Sun Microsystems, Inc., "NFS Version 3 Protocol Specification," RFC 1813, DDN Network Information Center, SRI International, Jun. 1995.

[Tann 85]   Tannenbaum, A.S., and Van Renesse, R., "Distributed Operating Systems," *ACM Computing Surveys,* Vol. 17, No. 4, Dec. 1985, pp. 419–470.

[Tann 90]   Tannenbaum, A.S., Van Renesse, R., Van Staveren, H., Sharp, G.J., Mullender, S.J., Jansen, J., and Van Rossum, G., "Experiences with the Amoeba Distributed Operating System," *Communications of the ACM,* Vol. 33, No. 12, Dec. 1990, pp. 46–63.

[Witt 93]   Wittle, M., and Keith, B., "LADDIS: The Next Generation in NFS File Server Benchmarking," *Proceedings of the Summer 1993 USENIX Technical Conference,* Jun. 1993, pp. 111–128.

11

Advanced File Systems

11.1   Introduction

Operating systems need to adapt to changes in computer hardware and architecture. As newer and faster machines are designed, the operating system must change to take advantage of them. Often developments in some components of the computer outpace those in other parts of the system. This changes the balance of the resource utilization characteristics, and the operating system must reevaluate its policies accordingly.

Since the early 1980s, the computer industry has made very rapid strides in the areas of CPU speed and memory size and speed [Mash 87]. In 1982, UNIX was typically run on a VAX 11/780, which had a 1-mips (million instructions per second) CPU and 4–8 megabytes of RAM, and was shared by several users. By 1995, machines with a 100-mips CPU and 32 megabytes or more of RAM have become commonplace on individual desktops. Unfortunately, hard disk technology has not kept pace, and although disks have become larger and cheaper, disk speeds have not increased by more than a factor of two. The UNIX operating system, designed to function with moderately fast disks but small memories and slow processors, has had to adapt to these changes.

Using traditional file systems on today's computers results in severely I/O-bound systems, unable to take advantage of the faster CPUs and memories. As described in [Stae 91], if the time taken for an application on a system is c seconds for CPU processing and i seconds for I/O, then the performance improvement seen by making the CPU infinitely fast is restricted to the factor **$(1 + c/i)$.** If i is large compared to c, then reducing c yields little benefit. It is essential to find ways to reduce the time the system spends doing disk I/O, and one obvious target for performance improvements is the file system.

Throughout the mid- and late 1980s, an overwhelming majority of UNIX systems had either *s5fs* or FFS (see Chapter 9) on their local disks. Both are adequate for general time-sharing applications, but their deficiencies are exposed when used in diverse commercial environments. The vnode/vfs interface made it easier to add new file system implementations into UNIX. Its initial use, however, was restricted to small, special-purpose file systems, which did not seek to replace *s5fs* or FFS. Eventually, the limitations of *s5fs* and FFS motivated the development of several advanced file systems that provide better performance or functionality. By the early 1990s, many of these had gained acceptance in mainstream UNIX versions. In this chapter, we discuss the drawbacks of traditional file systems, consider various ways of addressing them, and examine some of the major file systems that have emerged as alternatives to *s5fs* and FFS.

11.2   Limitations of Traditional File Systems

The *s5fs* file system was popular due to its simple design and structure. It was, however, very slow and inefficient, which motivated the development of FFS. Both these file systems, however, have several limitations, which can be broadly divided into the following categories:

- **Performance** — Although FFS performance is significantly better than that of *s5fs,* it is still inadequate for a commercial file system. Its on-disk layout restricts FFS to using only a fraction of the total disk bandwidth. Furthermore, the kernel algorithms force a large number of synchronous I/O operations, resulting in extremely long completion times for many system calls.
- **Crash recovery** — The buffer cache semantics mean that data and metadata may be lost in the event of a crash, leaving the file system in an inconsistent state. Crash recovery is performed by a program called *fsck,* which traverses the entire file system, finding and fixing problems as best as it can. For large disks, this program takes a long time, since the whole disk must be examined and rebuilt. This results in unacceptable delays *(downtime)* before the machine can reboot and become available.
- **Security** — Access to a file is controlled by permissions associated with user and group IDs. The owner may allow access to the file to him- or herself only, to all users in a certain group, or to the whole world. In a large computing environment, this mechanism is not flexible enough, and a finer granularity access-control mechanism is desirable. This usually involves some type of an *access-control list (ACL),* which allows the file owner to explicitly allow or restrict different types of access to specific users and groups. The UNIX inode is not designed to hold such a list, so the file system must find other ways of implementing ACLs. This may require changing the on-disk data structures and file system layout.
- **Size** — There are many unnecessary restrictions on the size of the file system and of individual files. Each file and file system must fit in its entirety on a single disk partition. We could devote the entire disk to a single partition; even so, typical disks are only one gigabyte or smaller in size. Although that may seem large enough for most purposes, sev-

eral applications (for example, in the database and multimedia domains) use much larger files. In fact, the constraint that the file size be less than 4 gigabytes (since the size field in the inode is 32 bits long) is also considered too restrictive.

Let us now examine the performance and crash recovery issues in greater detail, identify their underlying causes, and explore ways in which they may be addressed.

11.2.1   FFS Disk Layout

Unlike *s5fs,* FFS tries to optimize the allocation of blocks for a file, so as to increase the speed of sequential access. It tries to allocate blocks of a file contiguously on disk whenever possible. Its ability to do so depends on how full and fragmented the disk has become. Empirical evidence [McVo 91, McKu 84] shows that it can do an effective job until the disk approaches about 90% of its capacity.

The major problem, however, is due to the rotational delay it introduces between contiguous blocks. FFS is designed to read or write a single block in each I/O request. For an application reading a file sequentially, the kernel will perform a series of single-block reads. Between two consecutive reads, the kernel must check for the next block in the cache and issue the I/O request if necessary. As a result, if the two blocks are on consecutive sectors on the disk, the disk would rotate past the beginning of the second block before the kernel issues the next read. The second read would have to wait for a full disk rotation before it can start, resulting in very poor performance.

To avoid this, FFS estimates the time it would take for the kernel to issue the next read and computes the number of sectors the disk head would pass over in that time. This number is called the rotational delay, or *rotdelay*. The blocks are interleaved on disk such that consecutive logical blocks are separated by *rotdelay* blocks on the track, as shown in Figure 11-1. For a typical disk, a complete rotation takes about 15 milliseconds, and the kernel needs about 4 milliseconds between requests. If the block size is 4 kilobytes and each track has 8 such blocks, the *rotdelay* must be 2.

Although this avoids the problem of waiting for a full disk rotation, it still restricts throughput (in this example) to one-third the disk bandwidth at most. Increasing the block size to 8 kilobytes will reduce the *rotdelay* to 1 and increase throughput to one-half the disk bandwidth. This is still way short of the maximum throughput supported by the disk, and the restriction is caused solely by the file system design. If the file system reads and writes entire tracks (or more) in each operation, rather than one block at a time, it can achieve I/O rates close to the actual disk bandwidth.

On many disks, this problem disappears for *read* operations. This is because the disk maintains a high-speed cache, and any disk read stores an entire track in the cache. If the next operation needs a block from the same track, the disk can service the request directly from its cache at the speed of the I/O bus, without losing time in rotational waits. Disk caches are usually write-through, so each write is propagated to the appropriate place on disk before returning. [1] If the cache were not write-through, a disk crash would lose some data that the user was told had been successfully written to disk. Hence, although an on-disk cache improves read performance, write operations continue to suffer from the rotational delay problems and do not utilize the full disk bandwidth.

---

[1] Some modern SCSI disks cache writes on a per-track basis, using the rotational energy of the drive to write cached data in case of a power failure.

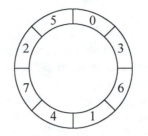

8 sectors / track
`rotdelay` = 2

Figure 11-1. Layout of blocks in a track in FFS.

11.2.2   Predominance of Writes

Several studies on file system usage and access patterns [Oust 85] have shown that read requests for file data or metadata outnumber write requests by about two to one. The reverse, however, is true for disk I/O requests, which are predominantly writes. This unusual behavior is caused by the UNIX buffer cache. Since applications exhibit a strong locality of reference in their file access, the buffer cache has a high hit rate (80–90%) and satisfies most read requests without disk I/O.

Write operations, too, are normally completed by modifying the cached copy, without resorting to disk I/O. If, however, the disk is not updated periodically, we run the risk of losing a large amount of data in the event of a crash. Therefore, most UNIX implementations run an *update* daemon process, which periodically flushes dirty blocks to disk. Moreover, several operations require synchronous updates to inodes, indirect blocks, and directory blocks to ensure that the file system is in a recoverable state following a crash. (This is explained in detail in the next section.) These two factors result in the dominance of write requests to the disk. As increasing memory sizes result in larger buffer caches, reads account for a very small fraction of disk traffic.

Many of the synchronous writes turn out to be quite unnecessary. Typical usage patterns exhibit a strong locality of reference, which means the same block is very likely to be modified again soon. Moreover, many files have a very short lifetime—they are created, accessed, and deleted in a matter of seconds, causing several synchronous writes that serve no real purpose.

The problem is worse if the file system is exported through NFS. Since NFS requires that all writes be committed to stable storage, the write traffic is much higher, since all data writes and most metadata writes must be synchronous.

Finally, *disk head seeks* (moving the disk head to the correct track) add substantially to the cost of an I/O operation. Although sequential access to a file should cause almost no seeks on a well-tuned FFS, a time-sharing environment (or a system that also acts as a file server) sees a very mixed load, resulting in a more random disk access pattern. Average seek times tend to be several times the rotational delay for contiguous FFS blocks.

As described in Section 11.2.1, on-disk caches eliminate rotational delays for most sequential reads, but not for writes. Since writes account for most of the disk activity, the operating system needs to find other ways to solve this problem.

11.2.3   Metadata Updates

Certain system calls require several metadata changes. In order to prevent file system corruption due to a system crash, these modifications may need to be written in a precise order. For instance, when a file is deleted (its last link is unlinked), the kernel must remove the directory entry, free the inode, and free the disk blocks used by the file. These operations must be done in this exact order, to ensure consistency across a system crash.

Suppose the file system frees the inode before removing the directory entry, and the system crashes in between. Upon reboot, the directory will have a reference to an unallocated inode. By first removing the directory entry, we limit the damage to having an unreferenced inode with a nonzero link count, which simply means it cannot be reused. This is a less severe problem, and should easily be fixed by *fsck*. In the former case, if the inode had been reallocated to another file, *fsck* would not know which is the valid directory entry.

Similarly, suppose while truncating a file, the file system frees the disk blocks before writing the modified inode to disk. It is possible for these blocks to be allocated to another file, whose inode may be written out to disk before that of the truncated file. If the system were to crash at this point, both inodes would reference the same blocks, resulting in user-visible corruption. This cannot be fixed by *fsck,* since it would have no way of knowing which inode is the rightful owner of these blocks.

In traditional file systems, such ordering is achieved through synchronous writes. This results in poor performance, especially since these writes are not contiguous on disk and thus require time-consuming seeks. Worse yet, NFS operations require synchronous writes for all data blocks as well. Clearly, we need some way to reduce the number of synchronous writes in the system, as well as to localize the writes so as to reduce seeks.

11.2.4   Crash Recovery

Ordering the metadata writes helps control the damage caused by a system crash, but does not eliminate it. In most cases, the effect is to ensure that the file system is recoverable. In cases where some disk sectors are damaged due to hardware failures, a complete recovery may not be possible. The *fsck* utility rebuilds a file system after a crash. It is a user-level program that accesses the file system through the raw device interface. It performs the following sequence of operations:

1.   Read and check all inodes and build a bitmap of used data blocks.
2.   Record inode numbers and block addresses of all directories.
3.   Validate the structure of the directory tree, making sure that all links are accounted for.
4.   Validate directory contents to account for all the files.
5.   If any directories could not be attached to the tree in phase 2, put them in the **lost+found** directory.
6.   If any file could not be attached to a directory, put it in the **lost+found** directory.
7.   Check the bitmaps and summary counts for each cylinder group.

As we can see, *fsck* has a lot of work to do, and machines with several large file systems may experience a long delay before they can restart after a crash. In many environments, such delays are unacceptable, and we need to find alternatives that allow rapid crash recovery.

Finally, *fsck* provides a limited form of crash recovery—it returns the file system to a consistent state. A reliable file system should deliver more than that. The ideal, of course, would be full recovery, which requires each operation to be committed to stable storage before returning control to the user. While that policy is followed by NFS and some non-UNIX file systems such as that of MS-DOS, it suffers from poor performance. A more reasonable objective is to limit the damage caused by the crash, without sacrificing performance. As we shall see (Section 11.7), such a goal can indeed be attained.

11.3   File System Clustering (Sun-FFS)

A simple way to achieve higher performance is through clustering of file I/O operations. Most file accesses in UNIX involve reading or writing a file sequentially in its entirety, even though that may span multiple system calls. It seems wasteful, then, to restrict individual disk I/Os to one block (typically 8 kilobytes) at a time. Many non-UNIX file systems allocate files in one or more *extents,* which are large, physically contiguous areas on the disk. This allows the system to read or write large chunks of the file in a single disk operation. While the UNIX *one-block-at-a-time* allocation policy offers several advantages, such as easy dynamic growth of files, it seems to preclude efficient sequential access.

These considerations prompted the development of *file clustering* enhancements to FFS in SunOS [McVo 91], which were later incorporated into SVR4 and 4.4BSD. In this chapter, we refer to this improved implementation as *Sun-FFS*. Its goal is to achieve higher performance by having larger granularity I/O operations, without changing the on-disk structure of the file system. Its implementation requires only a small number of localized changes to the internal kernel routines.

The FFS disk block allocator does an excellent job of allocating contiguous blocks to a file, using a smart algorithm that anticipates further allocation requests. Hence Sun-FFS makes no changes to the allocator and retains the block-at-a-time allocation policy.

Sun-FFS sets the *rotdelay* factor to zero, since the goal is to avoid paying the penalty inherent in rotational interleaving. The `maxcontig` field in the superblock contains the number of contiguous blocks to store before applying the *rotdelay* spacing. This field is usually set to one, but is meaningless whenever *rotdelay* is zero. Therefore, Sun-FFS uses this field to store the desired *cluster size*. This allows the superblock to store this extra parameter without changing its data structure.

Whenever a read request requires a disk access, it is desirable to read in an entire cluster. This is achieved by modifying the interface to the `bmap()` routine. In the traditional FFS implementation, `bmap()` takes a single logical block number and returns the physical block number for that block. Sun-FFS changes this interface to have `bmap()` return an additional *contigsize* value, which specifies the size of the physically contiguous extent of the file starting at the specified block. The *contigsize* value is at most `maxcontig`, even though the file may have a greater amount of contiguous data.

Sun-FFS uses *contigsize* to read in an entire cluster at a time. It performs read-aheads in the usual way, except that they are on a per-cluster basis. In some cases, the allocator cannot find a complete cluster, and the *contigsize* value returned by `bmap()` is smaller than `maxcontig`. The read-ahead logic is based on the *contigsize* returned by `bmap()` and not on the ideal cluster size.

Write clustering requires a change to the `ufs_putpage()` routine, which flushes a page to disk. In Sun-FFS, this routine simply leaves the pages in the cache and returns successfully to the caller, until a full cluster is in the cache or the sequential write pattern is broken. When that happens, it calls `bmap()` to find the physical location of these pages and writes them out in a single operation. If the allocator has not been able to place the pages contiguously on disk, `bmap()` returns a smaller length, and `ufs_putpage()` spreads the write over two or more operations.

While Sun-FFS adds a few refinements to address issues such as cache wiping, the above changes describe the bulk of the clustering enhancements. Performance studies have shown that sequential reads and writes are improved by about a factor of two, whereas random access occurs at about the same or slightly better speed than traditional FFS. The clustering approach does not enhance NFS write performance, since NFS requires all changes to be committed to disk synchronously. To extend the benefits of clustering to NFS writes, it is necessary to incorporate the NFS write-gathering optimizations to NFS described in Section 10.7.3.

11.4   The Journaling Approach

Many modern file systems use a technique called *logging* or *journaling* to address many of the drawbacks of traditional file systems, which were discussed in Section 11.2. The basic concept is to record all file system changes in an append-only log file. The log is written sequentially, in large chunks at a time, which results in efficient disk utilization and high performance. After a crash, only the tail of the log needs to be examined, which means quicker recovery and higher reliability.

This, of course, is an oversimplification. Although the advantages seem attractive, there are several complex issues to deal with and tradeoffs to consider. There have been numerous implementations of logging file systems, both in research and in industry, and each of these has a fundamentally different architecture. Let us start by identifying the principal characteristics that distinguish these file systems from each other and then examine some of the more important designs in detail.

11.4.1   Basic Characteristics

There are several decisions to be made while designing a logging file system:

- **What to log** — Journaling file systems fall into two main camps: those that log all modifications and those that log only metadata changes. Metadata logs may further restrict logging to selected operations. For instance, they may choose not to log changes to file timestamps, ownership, or permissions, and log only those changes that affect file system consistency.
- **Operations or values** — A log may record either the individual operations or the results of the operations. The former is useful, for instance, when logging changes to the disk block allocation bitmap. Since each change affects just a few bits, the log of the operation could fit in a compact record. However, when logging data writes, it is preferable to write the entire contents of the modified block to the log.
- **Supplement or substitute** — *Log-enhanced file systems* retain the traditional on-disk structures, such as inodes and superblocks, and use the log as a supplemental record. In a

log-structured file system, the log is the only representation of the file system on disk. Such an approach, of course, requires full logging (data as well as metadata).

- **Redo and undo logs** — There are two types of logs: *redo-only* and *undo-redo*. A redo-only log records only the modified data. An undo-redo log records both old and new values of the data. The redo-only log simplifies crash recovery, but places greater constraints on the ordering of writes to the log and of in-place metadata updates (see Section 11.7.2 for details). The undo-redo log is larger and has more complex recovery mechanisms, but allows greater concurrency during normal use.

- **Garbage collection** — Although a small number of implementations expand the log end-lessly, moving old portions of the log onto tertiary storage, the popular approach is to have a finite-sized log. This requires garbage collection of obsolete portions of the log, which is treated as a logically circular file. This can be done on a running system or may require stand-alone operation.

- **Group commit** — In order to meet the performance goals, the file system must write the log in large chunks, bundling together several small writes if necessary. In deciding the frequency and granularity of these writes, we need to make a tradeoff between perform-ance and reliability, since the unwritten chunk is vulnerable to a crash.

- **Retrieval** — In a log-structured file system, we need an efficient way of retrieving data from the log. Although the normal expectation is that a large cache will satisfy most reads, making disk access a rarity, we still need to make sure that cache misses can be handled in a reasonable time. This requires an efficient indexing mechanism to locate arbitrary file blocks in the log.

11.5   Log-Structured File Systems

Log-structured file systems use a sequential, append-only log as their only on-disk structure. The idea is to gather a number of file system changes into a large log entry and write it to disk in a single operation. This, of course, requires a major overhaul of the on-disk structure of the file system, as well as of the kernel routines that access it.

The advantages seem impressive. Since writes are always to the tail of the log, they are all sequential, and disk seeks are eliminated. Each log write transfers a large amount of data, typically a full disk track. This eliminates the need for rotational interleaving and allows the file system to use the full disk bandwidth. All components of an operation—data and metadata—can be bundled into a single atomic write, thus providing a high degree of reliability comparable to that of transaction-based systems. Crash recovery is very fast—the file system locates the last consistent log entry and uses it to reconstruct the system state. Any partially committed operations following that entry are simply discarded.

All this is fine as long as we only keep writing to the log, but what happens when we wish to retrieve data from it? The traditional mechanisms of locating data on the disk (fixed locations of su-perblocks, cylinder groups, and inodes) are no longer available, and we need to search the log for the data we need. This problem is largely addressed by having a huge in-memory cache (remember our assumption that modern systems have large, inexpensive memories and high-speed processors, but slow disks). On a system in steady state (one that has been running for a while), a large cache could easily have a hit rate of more than 90%. Nevertheless, for those blocks that must be accessed from disk (and there will be many of these when the system is initially booted), we need a way to locate the data in the log in a reasonable time. Hence a fully log-structured file system must provide an efficient way of addressing its contents.

The 4.4BSD log-structured file system, known as BSD-LFS [Selt 93], is based on similar work in the Sprite operating system [Rose 90a]. In the rest of this section, we describe its structure and implementation, and see how it achieves its objectives of reliability and performance.

11.6   The 4.4BSD Log-Structured File System

BSD-LFS dedicates the entire disk to the log, which is the only persistent representation of the file system. All writes go to the tail of the log, and garbage collection is done by a *cleaner* process, allowing the log to wrap around. The log is divided into fixed-size segments (typically, half a megabyte). Each segment has a pointer to the next, resulting in a logically contiguous log, without requiring consecutive segments to be physically adjacent to each other (thus disk seeks may be required when crossing segment boundaries).

BSD-LFS retains the familiar directory and inode structures, as well as the indirect block scheme for addressing logical blocks of large files. Hence, once the inode of a file is located, its data blocks can be accessed in the usual manner. The important issue is how to find the inode. The original FFS configures inodes statically on disk, in fixed locations in the different cylinder groups. Consequently, it can simply compute the disk address of the inode from its inode number.

In BSD-LFS, inodes are written to disk as part of the log and hence do not have fixed addresses. Each time the inode is modified, it is written to a new location in the log. This requires an additional data structure called an *inode map,* which stores the current disk address of each inode. BSD-LFS maintains this map in physical memory, but writes it to the log at periodic checkpoints.

Although BSD-LFS tries to write a complete segment at a time, this is often not possible. A partial segment may have to be written due to memory shortages (cache being full), *fsync* requests, or NFS operations. Thus a *segment,* which describes a physical partitioning of the disk, is made up of one or more *partial segments,* which comprise a single atomic write to the log (Figure 11-2).

Each partial segment has a segment header, which contains the following information, used during crash recovery and garbage collection:

- Checksums, which are used to detect media errors and incomplete writes
- Disk address of each inode in the partial segment
- For each file that has data blocks located in the segment, the inode number and inode version number, as well as the logical block numbers
- Creation time, flags, and so on.

The system also maintains a *segment usage table,* which stores the number of live bytes (data that is not obsolete) in each segment, and the time that the segment was last modified. The cleaner process uses this information to choose the segments to clean.

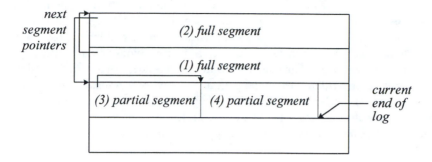

Figure 11-2. BSD-LFS log structure.

11.6.1   Writing the Log

BSD-LFS gathers dirty blocks until it has enough to fill a complete segment. A partial segment may have to be written due to an NFS request, *fsync* call, or due to memory shortfalls. If the disk controller supports scatter-gather I/O (fetching the data from noncontiguous memory locations), the blocks are written out directly from the buffer cache. Otherwise, the kernel may allocate temporary, 64K staging buffers for the transfer.

In preparing for the transfer, the disk blocks are sorted by logical block number within the files. Disk addresses are assigned to each block at this time, and the inodes (and indirect blocks if needed) must be modified to reflect these addresses. These inodes are bundled into the same segment, along with any other dirty metadata blocks.

Since the log is append-only, each time a disk block is modified, it is written to a new location in the log. This means that older copies of the block in the log have become obsolete and may be reclaimed by the cleaner process. Figure 11-3 illustrates an operation that modifies both the data and the inode of a file.

Each write operation flushes all the dirty data from the cache, which means that the log contains all the information required for a complete recovery. The inode map and segment usage table represent redundant information, which can be derived from the log, albeit slowly. These two structures are contained in a regular, read-only file called the *ifile*. The ifile can be accessed by users like any other file, but it is special in the sense that ifile modifications are not written out in each segment. Instead, the system defines periodic *checkpoints,* at which it flushes the ifile to disk. Keeping the ifile as an ordinary file allows the number of inodes in the system to vary dynamically.

11.6.2   Data Retrieval

Efficient file system operation requires a large cache, so that most requests can be satisfied without disk access. It is important to treat the cache misses efficiently, and the BSD-LFS data structures make this easy. Files are located by traversing directories one component at a time and obtaining the inode number of the next component, just as in FFS. The only difference is in the way BSD-LFS locates the inode on disk. Instead of computing the disk address directly from the inode number, it looks up the address in the inode map, using the inode number as an index.

In the cache, data blocks are identified and hashed by vnode and logical block number. The indirect blocks do not easily fit into this scheme. In FFS, indirect blocks are identified by the vnode of the disk device and the physical block number. Because LFS does not assign disk addresses until the segment is ready to be written, there is no convenient way to map these blocks. To get around this problem, LFS uses negative logical block numbers to refer to indirect blocks. Each indirect block number is the negative of that of the first block it references. Each double indirect block has a number equal to one less than that of the first indirect block it points to, and so on.

11.6.3   Crash Recovery

Crash recovery in BSD-LFS is fast and easy. The first step is to locate the latest checkpoint and initialize the in-memory inode map and segment usage table from it. Any changes to these structures since the checkpoint are recovered by replaying the portion of the log following the checkpoint. Before replaying each partial segment, the timestamps must be compared to ensure that the segment was written after the checkpoint, and the recovery is complete when we hit an older segment. The checksum in the segment summary makes sure that the partial segment is complete and consistent. If not, that segment (presumably the last one written) is discarded from the log, and recovery is complete. The only data lost is that in the last partial segment if it was not completely written, or the modifications that have occurred since the last write.

This recovery procedure is quick, the time taken being proportional to the time elapsed since the last checkpoint. It cannot, however, detect hard errors that damage one or more disk sectors. A complete file system verification is done by a task similar to *fsck*, which can continue to run in the background after the system has been brought up quickly by the replaying the log.

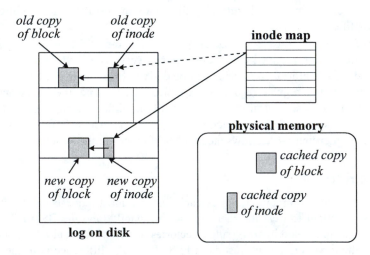

Figure 11-3. Writing to a file in BSD-LFS.

11.6.4   The *Cleaner* Process

The log wraps around when it reaches the end of the disk. When that happens, the file system must ensure that it does not overwrite useful data. This requires a garbage collection mechanism, which collects active data from a segment and moves it to a new location, making the segment reusable.

Garbage collection may be performed in parallel with other system activity. It involves reading a segment of the log and finding its valid entries. Log entries become invalid either when they are followed by newer entries for the same object (due to subsequent operations on the same file or directory) or when the corresponding object is removed (for example, when a file is deleted). If the segment contains any valid entries, these are simply gathered and written out to the tail of the log (Figure 11-4). The entire segment may then be reused.

In BSD-LFS, a user process called the cleaner performs garbage collection, using the *ifile* and a set of special system calls. It first selects a segment to clean by examining the segment usage table, and reads the segment into its address space. For each partial segment, the cleaner loops through the blocks to determine which ones are still live. Likewise, it checks each inode by comparing its version number with that in the inode map. Live inodes and blocks must be written back to the file system in such a way that the inode modify and access times are not changed. LFS writes them in the next partial segment, to new locations. Finally, it discards obsolete inodes and blocks, and marks the segment as reusable.

Four new system calls were added to allow the cleaner to accomplish its tasks:

lfs_bmapv	Computes the disk addresses for a set of <*inode, logical block*> pairs. If the address of a block is the same as that in the segment being cleaned, the block is live.
lfs_markv	Appends a set of blocks to the log, without updating the inode's modify and access times.
lfs_segwait	Sleeps until a timeout expires or another segment is written.
lfs_segclean	Marks a segment as clean, so it may be reused.

11.6.5   Analysis

There are three areas that create awkward problems for BSD-LFS. First, when a directory operation involves more than one metadata object, these modifications may not all make it to the same partial segment. This requires additional code to detect such cases and recover correctly if only a part of the operation survives the crash.

Second, disk block allocation occurs when the segment is being written, not when the block is first created in memory. Careful accounting of free space is necessary, or else a user may see a successful return from a *write* system call, but the kernel may later find that there is no room on the disk.

Finally, efficient operation of BSD-LFS requires a large physical memory, not only for the buffer cache, but also for the large data structures and staging buffers required for logging and garbage collection.

[Selt 93] and [Selt 95] describe detailed experiments comparing the performance of BSD-LFS with traditional FFS and with Sun-FFS. The results show that BSD-LFS provides superior per-

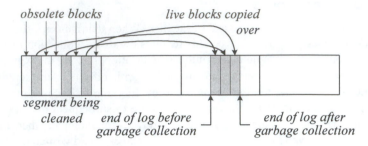

Figure 11-4. Garbage collection in a metadata log.

formance to traditional FFS in most circumstances (the exception being under high degrees of multiprogramming, where its performance is slightly worse). In comparison with Sun-FFS, BSD-LFS is clearly superior in metadata-intensive tests (which focus on operations such as *create, remove, mkdir,* and *rmdir*). In measurements of *read* and *write* performance and general multiuser benchmarks, the results are less clear. Sun-FFS is faster in most I/O-intensive benchmarks, especially when the BSD-LFS cleaner is turned on. The two are comparable for general, multiuser simulations such as the Andrew benchmark [Howa 88].

The performance gains of BSD-LFS are questionable at best, since Sun-FFS provides equal or better gains at a mere fraction of the implementation cost. LFS requires rewriting not only the file system, but also a host of utilities, such as *newfs* and *fsck,* that understand the on-disk structures. The real advantages of BSD-LFS are that it provides fast crash recovery and improves the performance of metadata operations. Section 11.7 shows how metadata logging can provide the same benefits with a lot less effort.

Another log-structured file system worthy of note is the *Write-Anywhere File Layout (WAFL)* system used by *Network Appliance Corporation* in their FAServer family of dedicated NFS servers [Hitz 94]. WAFL integrates a log-structured file system with nonvolatile memory (NV-RAM) and a RAID-4 disk array to achieve extremely fast response times for NFS access. WAFL adds a useful facility called *snapshots*. A snapshot is a frozen, read-only copy of an active file system. The file system can maintain a number of snapshots of itself, taken at different times, subject to space constraints. Users can access the snapshots to retrieve older versions of files or to *undelete* accidentally removed files. System administrators can use a snapshot to backup the file system, since it provides a consistent picture of the file system at a single instance of time.

11.7   Metadata Logging

In metadata logging systems, the log supplements the normal representation of the file system. This simplifies the implementation considerably, since no modification is necessary to *nonmutative* operations (those that do not modify the file system). The on-disk structure of the file system is left undisturbed, and data and metadata can be accessed from disk (upon a cache miss) in exactly the same way as in a traditional file system. The log is read only during crash recovery and perhaps for garbage collection. The rest of the file system code uses the log in append-only mode.

This approach provides the primary benefits of logging—rapid crash recovery and faster metadata operations—without the drawbacks of a log-structured file system (complex, requires rewriting of utilities, garbage collection degrades performance). Metadata logging has minimal impact on normal I/O operations, but needs careful implementation to prevent the logging overhead from reducing overall system performance.

The metadata log typically records changes to inodes, directory blocks and indirect blocks. It may also include changes to superblocks, cylinder group summaries, and disk allocation bitmaps, or the system may opt to reconstruct this information during crash recovery.

The log may reside either inside the file system itself or externally as an independent object. The choice is governed by considerations regarding efficient disk usage and performance. The Cedar file system [Hagm 87], for instance, implements the log as a fixed-size, circular file, using preallocated blocks near the middle cylinders of the disk (so that it can be accessed quickly). The log file is just like any other file: It has a name and an inode, and it may be accessed without special mechanisms. In the Calaveras file system [Vaha 95], all file systems on a machine share a single log, which resides on a separate disk. The Veritas file system [Yage 95] keeps the log separate from the file system, but allows the system administrator to decide whether to dedicate a separate disk.

11.7.1   Normal Operation

As a first example, let us consider a redo-only, new-value (the log records the new values of the changed objects) logging scheme, such as the one in the Cedar file system [Hagm 87]. The log does not deal with file data writes, which continue to be handled in the usual way. Figure 11-5 describes an operation such as *setattr,* which modifies a single inode. The kernel executes the following sequence of actions:

1. Updates the cached copy and marks it dirty.
2. Builds a log entry, which consists of a header identifying the modified object, followed by the new contents of the object.
3. Writes the entry to the tail of the log. When the write completes, the operation has been committed to disk.
4. Writes the inode back to its real disk location at some later time. This is called the *in-place update*.

This simple example illustrates how logging can impact system performance. On one hand, each metadata update is written to disk twice—once in the log entry and once during the in-place update. On the other hand, since the in-place updates are delayed, they are often eliminated or batched. For instance, the same inode may be modified several times before it is flushed to disk, and multiple inodes in the same disk block are written back in a single I/O operation. For a metadata logging implementation to perform reasonably, the reduction in the in-place updates should compensate for the logging overhead.

Batching can be applied to log writes as well. Many file operations modify multiple metadata objects. For instance, a *mkdir* modifies the parent directory and its inode, and also allocates and initializes a new directory and inode. Some file system combine all changes caused by a

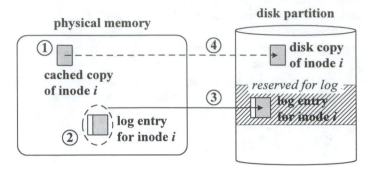

Figure 11-5. Metadata logging implementation.

single operation into one log entry. Some go further and collect changes from a number of operations into a single entry.

This decision affects not only the performance, but also the reliability and consistency guarantees of the file system. If the file system crashes, it will lose any changes that were not written out to the log. If the file system is used for NFS access, it cannot reply to the client requests until the changes have been committed to the log. If multiple operations modify the same object, the changes must be serialized to avoid inconsistency. This is discussed in detail in Section 11.7.2.

Since the log is fixed in size, it wraps around when it reaches its end. The file system must prevent it from overwriting useful data. A log entry is considered active until all its objects have been flushed to their on-disk locations (the in-place updates). There are two ways to deal with the wraparound condition. One is to perform explicit garbage collection, as in BSD-LFS. The cleaner must constantly stay one step ahead of the log and free up space by moving active entries to the tail of the log [Hagm 87]. A simpler approach is to be more proactive with in-place updates. If the log is large enough for in-place updates to keep it clean at peak loads, garbage collection can be avoided altogether. This does not require a very large log—a few megabytes are sufficient for small servers or time-sharing systems.

11.7.2   Log Consistency

A logging file system must worry about consistency when an operation modifies multiple objects (see Section 11.2.3). It must also ensure consistency between multiple concurrent operations on the same set of objects. In this section, we describe consistency issues in a redo-only log; Section 11.8.3 talks about consistency in an undo-redo log.

A redo-only log performs crash recovery by replaying the log, writing each entry out to its actual disk location. This assumes that the log has the latest copy of any metadata object. Hence during normal operation, the file system must never perform an in-place update until the object is written out to the log. Such a log is often called an *intent log* [Yage 95], since each entry contains objects that the file system intends to write to disk.

Suppose an operation modifies two metadata objects—**A** and **B**, in that order. A robust file system may provide either an ordering or a transactional guarantee for multiple updates. An *ordering guarantee* promises that after recovering from a crash, the disk would have the new contents of object **B** only if it also had the new contents of object **A**. A *transactional guarantee* is stronger, promising that either both modifications would survive the crash, or neither would.

A redo log can satisfy the ordering guarantee by delaying the in-place update of any metadata object until after its log entry is committed to disk. It writes objects to the log in the order in which they are modified or created. In the previous example, it writes the log entry for object **A** before that of **B** (it may also write them out in a single log entry). This preserves the ordering of the changes even if the in-place update of **B** precedes that of **A**.

Transactional guarantee in a redo-only log requires that neither object may be flushed to disk until the log entries for both blocks are written out successfully. This may be trivial if the two blocks have been bundled into a single log entry, but this cannot always be guaranteed. Suppose the in-place update of **A** occurred before writing the log entry for **B**, and the system were to crash in between. There is no way of recovering the old copy of **A** or the new copy of **B**. Hence we need to force both log entries to disk before writing back either cached entry. The log also needs to add information that identifies the two updates as belonging to the same transaction, so that we do not replay partial transactions during recovery.

There is, in fact, a stronger requirement, which applies to concurrent operations on the same object. *It is incorrect to even read a modified object until it has been written to the log.* Figure 11-6 shows a potential race condition. Process **p1** modifies object **A** and is about to write it out, first to the log and then to disk. Before it can do so, process **p2** reads object **A** and, based on its contents, modifies object **B**. It then writes **B** to the log, and is about to write it to the disk. If the system were to crash at this instant, the log contains the new value of **B**, but the new value of **A** is neither in the log nor on disk. Since the change to **B** depends on the change to **A**, this situation is potentially inconsistent.

To take a concrete example, suppose **p1** is deleting a file from a directory, while **p2** is creating a file with the same name in the same directory. **p1** deletes the file name from block **A** of the directory. **p2** finds that the directory does not have a file with this name and proceeds to make a directory entry in block **B** of the directory. When the system recovers from the crash, it has the old block **A** and the new block **B**, both of which have a directory entry for the same file name.

11.7.3 Recovery

If the system crashes, the file system recovers by replaying the log, and using its entries to update metadata objects on disk. This section describes recovery in a redo-only log. Section 11.8.3 discusses the issues related to undo-redo logs. The main problem is to determine the beginning and end of the log, since it wraps around continuously. [Vaha 95] describes one solution. During normal operation, the file system assigns an entry number to each entry. This number is monotonically increasing and corresponds to the location of the entry in the log. When the log wraps around, the entry number continues to increase. Hence at any time, the relationship between the entry number and its location in the log (its offset from the start of the log, measured in 512-byte units) is given by

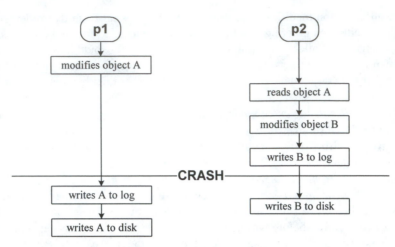

Figure 11-6. Race condition in a redo-only log.

```
entry location = entry number % size of log;
```

The file system constantly monitors the entry numbers of the first and last active entry in the log and writes these values in the header of each log entry. To replay the log, the system must locate the highest numbered entry. This marks the tail of the log; its header also contains the entry number of the current head of the log.

Having identified the head and tail of the log, the system recovers by writing out the metadata objects from each entry to their actual locations on disk. The entry header contains the identity and physical location of each object in the entry. This approach restricts the metadata loss to the few entries that were not written out to the log. An incomplete log entry can be identified easily, since each entry has either a checksum or a trailer record. Such a partial entry is discarded during crash recovery.

The recovery time does not depend on the size of the file system, but is proportional to the active size of the log at the time of the crash. This depends on the load on the system, and the frequency of the in-place updates. Metadata logging systems usually recover in a matter of seconds, as composed to systems using *fsck,* which require several minutes or even hours. It may still be necessary to run some disk-checking utility, since the log does not protect against corruption caused by hard disk errors. Such a utility can run in the background, after the system has recovered and is operational.

11.7.4 Analysis

Metadata logging provides the important benefits of logging, namely rapid crash recovery and faster metadata operations, without the complexity and implementation effort of log-structured file systems. The system recovers from a crash by replaying the log, writing its metadata objects to their on-disk locations. This usually takes a fraction of the time required by disk-checking utilities such as *fsck*.

Metadata logging also speeds up operations that modify multiple metadata objects, such as *mkdir* and *rmdir,* by collecting all changes made by the operation into a single log entry, thus reducing the number of synchronous writes. In this way, it also provides ordering or transactional guarantees (depending on the implementation) for related metadata changes. This makes the file system more robust than traditional architectures.

The overall impact on performance is unclear. Logging has no impact on operations that do not modify the file system and little impact on data writes. Overall, logging is meant to reduce the number of in-place metadata writes by deferring them. To obtain adequate performance, this reduction should compensate for the logging overhead.

[Vaha 95] shows that the log may become a performance bottleneck and describes several optimizations to prevent this. It also describes a number of experiments comparing two file systems whose sole difference is that one uses logging and the other does not. The logging file system is much faster in metadata-intensive benchmarks, but is only marginally better in a LADDIS benchmark [Witt 93], which simulates multiuser NFS access.

Metadata logging has some important drawbacks and limitations. Although it minimizes the metadata changes lost in a crash, it does not limit the loss of ordinary file data (other than by running the *update* daemon). This also means that we cannot assure transactional consistency for all operations—if an operation modifies both a file and its inode, the two are not updated atomically. Hence a crash may result in just one of the two components of the transaction being recovered.

Overall, metadata logging offers increased robustness and rapid recovery, as well as modest performance gains, without changing the on-disk structure of the file system. It is also relatively easy to implement, since only the part of the file system that deals with writing metadata to disk needs to be modified.

The debate between metadata logging and log-structured file systems has raged for some time in the UNIX community. *Metadata logging is winning the argument* and has been the basis of several successful commercial implementations, including the *Veritas File System (VxFS)* from Veritas Corporation, IBM's *Journaling File System (JFS)*, and Transarc's *Episode File System* (see Section 11.8). Moreover, since metadata logging does not affect the data transfer code, it is possible to combine it with other enhancements such as file-system clustering (Section 11.3) or NFS write-gathering (Section 10.7.3), resulting in a file system that performs well for both data and metadata operations.

11.8   The Episode File System

In 1989, Transarc Corporation took over the development of the Andrew File System (AFS, described in Section 10.15) from Carnegie-Mellon University. AFS evolved into the Episode file system [Chut 92], which since became the local file system component of OSF's *Distributed Computing Environment (DCE)*. Episode provides several advanced features not found in traditional UNIX file systems, such as enhanced security, large files, logging, and the separation of storage abstractions from the logical file system structure. Section 10.18 described DCE's Distributed File System (DCE DFS). In this section, we discuss the structure and features of Episode.

11.8.1   Basic Abstractions

Episode introduces several new file system abstractions, namely *aggregates, containers, filesets,* and *anodes.* An *aggregate* is the generalization of a partition, and refers to a logically contiguous array of disk blocks. It hides the details of the physical partitioning of the disks from the rest of the file system. An aggregate may be composed of one or more physical disk partitions.[2] It can transparently provide powerful functionality such as disk mirroring and striping. It enables a single file to span more than one physical disk, thus allowing the creation of very large files.

A *fileset* is a logical file system, consisting of a directory tree headed by the fileset root directory. Each fileset can be independently mounted and exported.[3] An aggregate may contain one or more filesets, and filesets can be moved from one aggregate to another even while the system is up and these filesets are being used for normal file operations. Figure 11-7 shows the relationship between aggregates, filesets, and physical disks.

A *container* is an object that can store data. It it is composed of several blocks. Each fileset resides in a container, which stores all the file data and metadata of that fileset. Each aggregate has three additional containers, for the bitmap, log, and aggregate fileset table, as explained below.

An *anode* is analogous to the UNIX inode. Episode has one anode for each file, as well as one for each container.

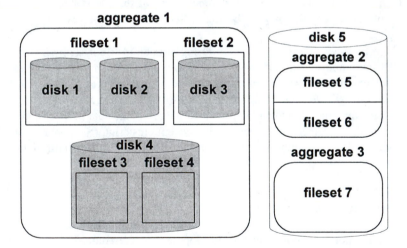

Figure 11-7. Storage organization in Episode.

---

[2] IBM's Journaling File System (JFS) was among the first UNIX file systems to allow logical volumes to span disk partitions.

[3] Current DCE tools only allow all the filesets in an aggregate to be exported together.

11.8.2   Structure

The aggregate comprises several containers. The *fileset container* stores all its files and anodes. The anodes reside in the *fileset anode table* at the head of the container and are followed by the data and indirect blocks. A container does not occupy contiguous storage within the aggregate, so it can shrink and grow dynamically with ease. Thus the file block addresses refer to block numbers within the aggregate and not within the container.

The *bitmap container* allows aggregate wide block allocation. For each fragment in the aggregate, it stores whether the fragment is allocated and whether it is used for logged or unlogged data. This last information is used for special functions that must be performed when reusing a logged fragment for unlogged data, and vice versa.

The *log container* contains an undo-redo, metadata-only log of the aggregate. The advantages of undo-redo logs are discussed in Section 11.8.3. The log is fixed in size and is used in a circular fashion. Although current implementations place the log in the same aggregate as the one it represents, that is not a strict requirement.

The *aggregate fileset table* (Figure 11-8) contains the superblock and the anode for each container in the aggregate. Directory entries reference files by the fileset ID and the anode number within the fileset. A file is located by first searching the aggregate fileset table for the anode of the fileset and then indexing into the fileset's anode table for the desired file. Of course, appropriate use of caching speeds up most of these operations.

Containers allow three modes of storage—*inline, fragmented,* and *blocked.* Each anode has some extra space, and the inline mode stores small amounts of data in that. This is useful for symbolic links, access-control lists, and small files. In the fragmented mode, several small containers may share a single disk block. The blocked mode allows large containers and supports four levels of indirection. This allows a maximum file size of 2^{31} disk blocks.[4]

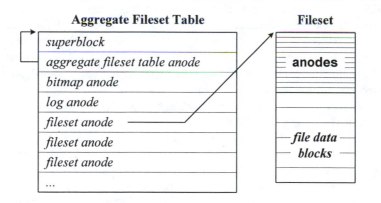

Figure 11-8. The aggregate fileset table and the fileset.

---

[4]   The file size is further bounded by $(2^{32} \times$ fragment size).

11.8.3   Logging

Episode uses a redo-undo metadata log, which provides the strong transactional guarantees described in Section 11.7.2. The redo-undo log offers greater flexibility, since each entry stores both the old and the new value of the object. During crash recovery, the file system has the option of replaying an entry by writing its new value to the on-disk object, or rolling it back by writing the old value.

Transactional guarantees in redo-only logs require a *two-phase locking* protocol, which locks all objects involved in a transaction until the entire transaction is committed to disk, so that no other transaction will even read any uncommitted data. This reduces the concurrency of the system, and incurs a substantial penalty in performance. Episode avoids this by using a mechanism called an *equivalence class,* which contains all active transactions that involve the same metadata objects. The equivalence class has the property that either all its transactions commit or none do.

In the event of a crash, the recovery procedure replays all complete equivalent classes, but rolls back all transactions of an incomplete equivalent class. This allows a high degree of concurrency during normal operation. However, it doubles the size of each log entry, increases the I/O traffic to the log disk, and complicates log recovery.

In Episode, the buffer cache is tightly integrated with the logging facility. Higher-level functions do not modify buffers directly, but call the logging functions. The logger correlates the buffers with log entries and ensures that a buffer is not flushed to disk until its log entry has been written successfully.

11.8.4   Other Features

Cloning — Filesets may be replicated, or moved from one aggregate to another, by a process known as fileset cloning. Each anode in the fileset is individually cloned, and the clones share the data blocks with the original anodes through copy-on-write techniques. The cloned fileset is read-only and resides in the same aggregate as the original. Clones can be created very quickly, without disturbing access to the original fileset. They are used widely by administrative tools, such as backup programs, which operate on the clone instead of the original. If any block in the original fileset is modified, a new copy must be made, so that the version seen by the clone is unchanged.

Security — Episode provides POSIX-style access-control lists (ACLs), which are far more versatile than the owner-group-other permission sets of UNIX. Any file or directory may have an ACL associated with it. The ACL is a list of entries. Each entry consists of a user or group ID and a set of rights granted to that user or group. There are six types of rights to any object—*read, write, execute, control, insert,* and *delete* [OSF 93]. A user having the control right to an object may modify its ACL. Insert and delete rights apply only to directories and allow creation and removal, respectively, of files in that directory. A standard set of wildcard characters allows a single ACL entry to refer to multiple users or groups. For example, the following entry grants the user *rohan* permission to read, write, execute, and insert entries in the directory with which the entry is associated:

```
user:rohan:rwx-i-
```

Each *dash* indicates a permission that is not granted. In this example, *rohan* does not have control and delete permissions.

11.9 Watchdogs

A file system implementation defines its policies on several issues such as naming, access control, and storage. These semantics are applied uniformly to all its files. Often, it is desirable to override the default policies for some files that might benefit from special treatment, such as in the following examples:

- Allow users to implement different access control mechanisms.
- Monitor and log all access to a particular file.
- Take some automatic actions upon receipt of mail.
- Store the file in compressed form and automatically decompress it when read.

Such functionality was provided in an extension to FFS developed at the University of Washington [Bers 88]. The basic idea was to associate a user-level process called a *watchdog* with a file or directory. This process intercepts selected operations on the file and can provide its own implementation of those functions. Watchdog processes have no special privileges, are completely transparent to applications accessing the files, and incur additional processing expense only for the operations they override.

A *wdlink* system call was added to associate a watchdog process with a file, thus making it a *guarded file*. The arguments to *wdlink* specified the filename and the name of the watchdog program. The program name was stored in a 20-byte area in the inode that was reserved for "future use" in BSD UNIX. To circumvent the 20-character limit, the names referred to entries in a public directory called **/wdogs**, which contained symbolic links to the real watchdog programs.

When a process tries to open a guarded file, the kernel sends a message to the watchdog process (starting it up if not already running). The watchdog may use its own policies to permit or deny access, or it may pass the decision back to the kernel. If the open is permitted, the watchdog informs the kernel of the set of operations on the file that it is interested in guarding. This set of guarded operations may be different for different open instances of the file, thus providing multiple views of the same file.

Once opened, whenever a user tries to invoke a guarded operation, the kernel relays it to the watchdog (Figure 11-9). The watchdog must do one of three things:

- Perform the operation. This may involve passing additional data between the kernel and the watchdog (such as for read or write operations). To avoid loops, the watchdog is allowed direct access to the file it is guarding.
- Deny the operation, passing back an error code.
- Simply acknowledge the operation, and ask the kernel to perform it in the usual manner. The watchdog may perform some additional processing, such as accounting, before deferring the operation to the kernel.

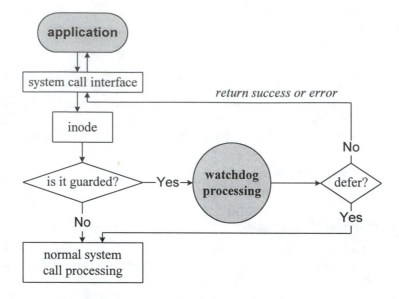

Figure 11-9. Watchdog operation.

11.9.1   Directory Watchdogs

A watchdog may also be associated with a directory. It would then guard operations on the directory and could be used to control access to all its files (since access control is performed on each directory in a pathname). A directory watchdog is given some special powers. It guards, by default, all files within that directory that do not have watchdogs directly associated with them.

This allows some interesting applications. Users may access nonexistent files in a guarded directory, provided the associated watchdog is capable of maintaining the illusion. In such a case, none of the operations on that file may be deferred back to the kernel.

11.9.2   Message Channels

The communication between the kernel and the watchdog is handled by message passing. Each watchdog is associated with a unique Watchdog Message Channel (WMC), created by a new *createwmc* system call. This call returns a file descriptor, which the watchdog can use to receive and send messages to the kernel.

Each message contains a type field, a session identifier and the message contents. Each open instance of the file constitutes a unique session with the watchdog. Figure 11-10 describes the data structures maintained by the kernel. The open file table entry for a guarded file points to an entry in a global session table. This in turn points to the kernel's end of the WMC, which contains a queue of unread messages. The WMC also points to the watchdog process.

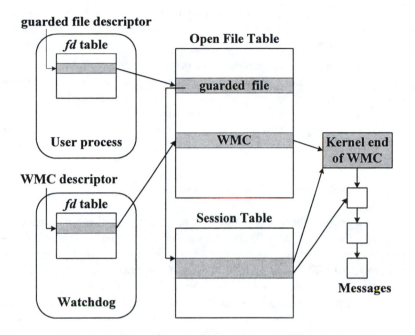

Figure 11-10. Watchdog data structures.

The watchdog reads the messages and sends its replies using the file descriptor returned by *createwmc*. This maps to an entry for the WMC in the open file table, which points back to the kernel end of the WMC. Thus both the watchdog and the kernel can access the message queue, and put and get messages from it.

A master watchdog process manages all watchdog processes. It controls their creation (when the guarded file is opened) and termination (usually upon the last close of the file). It may choose to keep some frequently used watchdogs active even when no one has the associated file open, to avoid the cost of starting up new processes each time.

11.9.3   Applications

The original implementation described several interesting applications:

wdacl	Associates an access-control list with a file. A single watchdog may control access to many files.
wdcompact	Provides on-line compression and decompression.
wdbiff	Watches a user's mailbox and notifies the user when new mail arrives. This may be extended to provide auto-answering or auto-forwarding capabilities.
wdview	Presents different views of a directory to different users.

wddate   Allows users to read the current date and time from a file. The file itself
                    contains no data; the watchdog reads the system clock whenever the file is
                    accessed.

User interfaces that provide graphical views of the file tree can also benefit from watchdogs.
Whenever a user creates or deletes a file, the watchdog can ask the user interface to redraw itself to
reflect the new state of the directory. As these examples show, watchdogs provide a versatile
mechanism to extend the file system in several ways, limited only by the imagination. The ability to
redefine individual operating system functions at the user level is extremely useful and merits consideration in modern operating systems.

11.10   The 4.4BSD Portal File System

Watchdogs allow a user-level process to intercept operations by other processes on a watched file.
The 4.4BSD *portal file system* [Stev 95] provides a similar function. It defines a name space of files
that processes can open. When a process opens a file in this file system, the kernel passes a message
to a *portal daemon,* which processes the open request and returns a descriptor to the process. The
portal daemon, not the file system itself, defines the set of valid filenames and their interpretation.

The portal daemon creates a UNIX socket [Leff 89] and invokes the *listen* system call to allow incoming connection requests to the socket. It then mounts the portal file system, usually on the
/p directory. It then enters a loop, where it calls *accept* to wait for a connection request and processes requests as they arrive.

Suppose a user opens a file in the portal file system. This causes the following chain of
events (see Figure 11-11):

1. The kernel first calls `namei()` to parse the filename. When `namei()` crosses the mount
   point of the portal file system, it calls `portal_lookup()` to parse the rest of the pathname.
2. `portal_lookup()` allocates a new vnode and saves the pathname in the vnode's private
   data object.
3. The kernel then invokes the `VOP_OPEN` operation on the vnode, which results in a call to
   `portal_open()`.

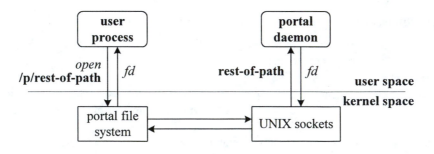

Figure 11-11. Opening a file in the portal file system.

4. portal_open() passes the pathname to the portal daemon, which returns from the accept system call.
5. The portal daemon processes the name as it sees fit and generates a file descriptor.
6. The daemon sends the descriptor back to the caller over a socket-pair connection set up by the kernel.
7. The kernel copies the descriptor into the first unused slot in the caller's descriptor table.
8. The portal daemon dismantles the connection and calls *accept* to await further connection requests.

Usually, the daemon creates a new child process to handle each request. The child executes steps 5 through 7 and exits, thus dismantling the connection. The parent calls *accept* immediately after creating the child.

11.10.1   Using Portals

The portal file system can be used in a number of ways. The portal daemon determines the functionality it provides and also how it interprets the name space. One important application is the connection server, mentioned earlier in Section 8.2.4. This server opens network connections on behalf of other processes. Using portals, a process can create a TCP (Transmission Control Protocol) connection simply by opening a file called

/p/tcp/*node*/*service*

where **node** is the name of the remote machine to connect to, and **service** is the TCP service (such as *ftp* or *rlogin*) that the caller wishes to access. For instance, opening the file **/p/tcp/archana/ftp** opens a connection to the ftp server on node **archana**.

The daemon performs all the work required to set up the connection. It determines the network address of the remote machine, contacts the portmapper on that node to determine the port number for the service, creates a TCP socket, and connects to the server. It passes the file descriptor for the connection back to the calling process, which can use the descriptor to communicate to the server.

This makes TCP connections available to *naive applications*. A naive application is one that only uses stdin, stdout, and stderr, and does not use special knowledge about other devices. For instance, a user can redirect the output of a *shell* or *awk* script to a remote node by opening the appropriate portal file.

Similar to watchdogs, the portal file system allows a user process to intercept file operations by other processes, and implement them on their behalf. There are a few important differences. The portal daemon only intercepts the *open* system call, whereas a watchdog may intercept a number of operations of its choosing. Watchdogs may also intercept an operation, perform some work, and then ask the kernel to complete the operation. Finally, the portal daemon defines its name space. This is possible because, in 4.4BSD, namei() passes the rest of the pathname to portal_lookup() when it crosses the mount point. Watchdogs usually operate on the existing file hierarchy, although directory watchdogs can extend the name space in a limited way.

11.11   Stackable File System Layers

The vnode/vfs interface was an important step toward a flexible framework for developing UNIX file systems. It has led to many new file systems, described in Chapters 9–11. It has, however, some important limitations:

- The interface is not uniform across UNIX variants. As described in Section 8.11, there are substantial differences between the set of operations defined by the interface in SVR4, 4.4BSD, and OSF/1, as well as in their detailed semantics. For instance, the VOP_LOOKUP operation parses one component at a time in SVR4, but may parse several components in 4.4BSD.
- Even for a single vendor, the interface has evolved considerably from one release to another. For instance, SunOS4.0 replaced buffer cache operations such as VOP_BMAP and VOP_BREAD with paging operations such as VOP_GETPAGE and VOP_PUTPAGE. SVR4 added new operations, such as VOP_RWLOCK and VOP_RWUNLOCK, which were incorporated into later SunOS releases.
- The file system and the memory management subsystem are highly interdependent. As a result, it is impossible to write a general-purpose file system without a full understanding of the memory management architecture.
- The interface is not as opaque as originally intended. The kernel accesses many fields of the vnode directly, instead of through a procedural interface. As a result, it is difficult to change the structure of vnodes while providing binary compatibility with previous versions.
- The interface does not support *inheritance*. A new file system cannot inherit some of the functionality of an existing file system.
- The interface is not extensible. A file system cannot add new functions or alter the semantics of existing operations.

These factors inhibit advances in file system technology. Developing a new general-purpose file system, such as Transarc's Episode File System or Veritas Corporation's Veritas File System, is a major undertaking. Large teams are required to port the file system to different UNIX variants and to newer releases of the operating system from each vendor. Moreover, many vendors do not wish to develop entire file systems. Rather, they want to add some functionality to existing implementations, such as replication, encryption and decryption, or access-control lists.

Independent research efforts at the University of California at Los Angeles [Heid 94] and at SunSoft [Rose 90b, Skin 93] resulted in frameworks using stackable file system layers, which provide better support for modular file system development. The UCLA implementation has been incorporated in 4.4BSD, while the SunSoft effort is in the prototype stage. In this section, we describe the important features of stackable file systems and describe some applications of this approach.

11.11.1   Framework and Interface

The vfs interface allows different file systems to coexist on a single machine. It defines a set of operations, which are implemented differently by each file system. Whenever a user invokes an opera-

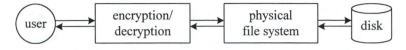

Figure 11-12. An encryption-decryption layer.

tion on a file, the kernel dynamically routes it to the file system to which the file belongs. This file system is responsible for complete implementation of the operation.

The stackable layers framework allows multiple file systems to be mounted on top of each other. Each file is represented by a vnode stack, with one vnode for each file system in the stack. When the user invokes a file operation, the kernel passes it to the topmost vnode. This vnode may do one of two things: It may execute the operation completely and pass the results back to the caller. Alternatively, it may perform some processing, and pass the operation down to the next vnode in the stack. This way, the operation can pass through all the layers. On return, the results again go up through all the layers, giving each vnode the chance to do some additional processing.

This allows incremental file system development. For instance, a vendor may provide an encryption-decryption module, which sits on top of any physical file system (Figure 11-12). This module intercepts all I/O operations, encrypting data while writing and decrypting it while reading. All other operations are passed directly to the lower layer.

The stacking may allow fan-in or fan-out configurations. A fan-in stack allows multiple higher layers to use the same lower layer. For example, a compression layer may compress data while writing and decompress it while reading. A backup program may want to read the compressed data directly while copying it to a tape. This results in the fan-in configuration shown in Figure 11-13.

A fan-out stack allows a higher layer to control multiple lower layers. This could be used for a hierarchical storage manager (HSM) layer, which keeps recently accessed files on local disks, and migrates rarely used files onto optical disks or tape jukeboxes (Figure 11-14). The HSM layer intercepts each file access, both to track file usage and to download files from tertiary storage when needed. [Webb 93] describes an HSM implementation using a framework that combines features of stackable layers and watchdogs.

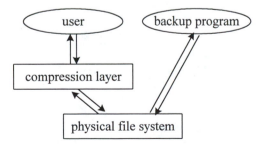

Figure 11-13. A fan-in configuration.

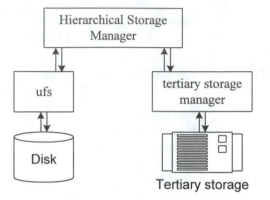

Figure 11-14. A hierarchical storage manager.

11.11.2   The SunSoft Prototype

[Rose 90b] describes the initial work on stackable vnodes at Sun Microsystems. This work was passed on to the UNIX International Stackable Files Working Group [Rose 92] and later resumed at SunSoft. The SunSoft prototype [Skin 93] resolves many problems and limitations of the [Rose 90b] interface.

In this implementation, a vnode contains nothing more than a pointer to a linked list of *pvnodes,* one for each file system layered on that node (Figure 11-15). The pvnode contains pointers to the vfs, the vnodeops vector, and its private data. Each operation is first passed to the topmost pvnode, which may pass it down to the lower layers if necessary.

The development of the prototype identified several important issues:

- In the current interface, the vnode has several data fields that are accessed directly by the kernel. These must be moved into the private data object, and read and written through a procedural interface.

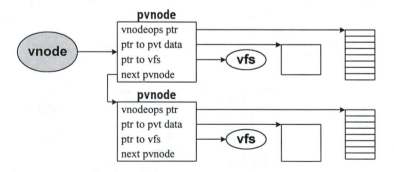

Figure 11-15. The SunSoft prototype.

- A vnode may hold a reference to another vnode as part of its private data. For example, the root directory vnode of a file system keeps a reference to the mount point.
- The vfs operations must also be passed on to lower layers. To achieve this, many vfs operations were converted to vnode operations that can be invoked on any vnode of the file system.
- Many operations in the current interface operate on multiple vnodes. To function correctly, these must be broken up into separate suboperations on each vnode. For instance, VOP_LINK must be divided into two operations: one on the file vnode to fetch its file ID and increment its link count, and another on the directory vnode to add the entry for the file.
- A transaction facility is needed to ensure atomic execution of suboperations invoked by the same high-level operation.
- The *<vnode, offset>* name space for the page cache does not map well to the stacked vnode interface, since the page now belongs to multiple vnodes. The interface with the virtual memory system must be redesigned to handle this.

11.12 The 4.4BSD File System Interface

The virtual file system interface in 4.4BSD is based on the work on stackable layers in the Ficus file system at UCLA [Heid 94]. Sections 8.11.2 and 11.10 described other features of the 4.4BSD file system. This section describes the part of the interface that deals with stacking, and some interesting file system implementations based on it.

In 4.4BSD, the *mount* system call pushes a new file system layer onto the vnode stack, and *unmount* pops off the topmost layer. As in the SunSoft model, each operation is first passed to the topmost layer. Each layer can either complete the operation and return the results, or pass the operation (with or without additional processing) to the next lower layer.

4.4BSD allows a file system layer to be attached to multiple locations in the file system name space. This allows the same file to be accessed through multiple paths (without using separate links). Moreover, other layers in the stack may be different for each mount point, resulting in different semantics of the same operation. This allows the fan-in configurations described in Section 11.11.1. For example, a file system may be mounted at **/direct** and **/compress**, and a compression layer pushed onto **/compress**. This allows users to perform on-the-fly compression-decompression by accessing the files through **/compress**. The *backup* program can access the file system through **/direct** and bypass the decompression.

File systems can add new operations to the interface. When the system boots, the kernel dynamically builds the vnodeops vector as a union of the operations supported by each file system. To implement this, all file systems use a standard *bypass* function to handle unknown operations. The bypass function passes the operation and its arguments to the next lower layer. Since it cannot know the number and types of the arguments, 4.4BSD packages all arguments to a vnode operation in an argument structure. It then passes a pointer to this structure as a single parameter to all operations. When a layer does not recognize the operation, it simply passes the argument pointer to the next layer. If a layer does recognize the operation, it also knows how to interpret the structure.

The following section describes two interesting applications of the stackable file system interface.

11.12.1   The Nullfs and Union Mount File Systems

The *nullfs* file system [McKu 95] is a largely pass-through file system that allows arbitrary subtrees of the file hierarchy to be mounted anywhere else in the file system. The effect is to provide a second pathname for each file in the subtree. It passes most operations on to the original file system. This facility can be used in some interesting ways. For example, a user who has subtrees on many different physical file systems can attach them under a common directory, thus seeing a single subtree containing all her files.

The *union mount* file system [Pend 95] provides functionality similar to the Translucent File System (TFS) described in Section 9.11.4. It provides a union, or merger, of the file systems mounted below it. The topmost layer is logically the most recent, and it is the only writable layer. When a user looks up a file, the kernel goes down the layers until it finds a layer containing the file. If a user tries to modify a file, the kernel first copies it to the topmost layer. As in TFS, if a user deletes a file, the kernel creates a *whiteout* entry in the topmost layer, which prevents it from searching the lower layers for this file on subsequent lookups. Special operations are provided to bypass and remove whiteout entries, allowing accidentally erased files from being recovered.

11.13   Summary

We have seen several advanced file systems in this chapter. Some of them replace existing implementations such as FFS and *s5fs*, whereas some extend the traditional file systems in different ways. These file systems offer higher performance, quicker crash recovery, increased reliability, or enhanced functionality. Some of these systems have already gained commercial acceptance; most recent UNIX releases feature an enhanced file system that uses some form of logging.

The vnode/vfs interface has been an important enabling technology, allowing these new implementations to be integrated into the UNIX kernel. The stackable layers framework addresses many limitations of the vnode interface and promotes incremental file system development. 4.4BSD has already adopted this approach, and commercial vendors are exploring it.

11.14   Exercises

1. Why does FFS use a *rotdelay* factor to interleave disk blocks? What does it assumme about usage patterns and buffer cache sizes?
2. How would file system clustering affect the performance of an NFS server?
3. What is the difference between file system clustering and write-gathering (described in Section 10.7.3)? What situation is each one useful in? When is it beneficial to combine the two?
4. Would file system clustering reduce the benefit of nonvolatile memory? What is a good way of using NV-RAM in a system that supports clustering?

5. What is the benefit of delaying disk writes?

6. Suppose a file system writes all metadata synchronously, but delays data writes until the update daemon runs. To what security problems could this lead? Which data blocks must be written synchronously to avoid this?

7. Can a log-structured file system improve performance by scheduling garbage collection during off-peak times? What restrictions does this place on the use of the system?

8. A file system can use an in-memory bitmap to track the active and obsolete parts of the log. Discuss the suitability of this approach for a log-structured file system and for a metadata logging file system.

9. Suppose a metadata logging system records changes to inodes and directory blocks in its log, but writes out indirect blocks synchronously. Describe a scenario where this might lead to an inconsistent file system after a crash.

10. In a metadata logging file system, can a single log hold the updates for all file systems? What are the benefits and drawbacks of this approach?

11. Is it advantageous to keep a metadata log on the same physical disk as the file system itself?

12. Why does Episode use a two-phase locking protocol? Why does the Cedar file system not need this?

13. Suppose a user wanted to record all access to his files by other users. Can he do so using either watchdogs or portals? Would it have any other effect on system behavior?

14. Consider a disk containing union-mounted directories. What would happen if the disk becomes full and a user tries to free space by deleting a set of files that live in a lower layer?

11.15 References

[Bers 88]   Bershad, B.N., and Pinkerton, C.B., "Watchdogs—Extending the UNIX File System," *Computing Systems,* Vol. 1, No. 2, Spring 1988, pp. 169–188.

[Chut 92]   Chutani, S., Anderson, O.T., Kazar, M.L., Mason, W.A., and Sidebotham, R.N., "The Episode File System," *Proceedings of the Winter 1992 USENIX Technical Conference,* Jan. 1992, pp. 43–59.

[Hagm 87]   Hagmann, R., "Reimplementing the Cedar File System Using Logging and Group Commit," *Proceedings of the 11th Symposium on Operating Systems Principles,* Nov. 1987, pp. 155–162.

[Heid 94]   Heidemann, J.S., and Popek, G.J., "File-System Development with Stackable Layers," *ACM Transactions on Computer Systems,* Vol. 12, No. 1, Feb. 1994, pp. 58–89.

[Hitz 94]   Hitz, D., Lau, J., and Malcolm, M., "File System Design for an NFS File Server Appliance," *Proceedings of the Winter 1994 USENIX Technical Conference,* Jan. 1994, pp. 235–245.

[Howa 88]   Howard, J.H., Kazar, M.L., Menees, S.G., Nichols, D.A., Satyanarayanan, M., and Sidebotham, R.N., "Scale and Performance in a Distributed File System," *ACM Transactions on Computer Systems,* Vol. 6, No. 1, Feb. 1988, pp. 55–81.

[Leff 89]   Leffler, S.J., McKusick, M.K., Karels, M.J., and Quarterman, J.S., *The Design and Implementation of the 4.3 BSD UNIX Operating System,* Addison-Wesley, Reading, MA, 1989.

[Mash 87]   Mashey, J.R., "UNIX Leverage—Past, Present, Future," *Proceedings of the Winter 1987 USENIX Technical Conference,* Jan. 1987, pp. 1–8.

[McKu 84]   McKusick, M.K., Joy, W.N., Leffler, S.J., and Fabry, R.S., "A Fast File System for UNIX," *ACM Transactions on Computer Systems,* Vol. 2, No. 3, Aug 1984, pp. 181–197.

[McKu 95]   McKusick, M.K., "The Virtual Filesystem Interface in 4.4BSD," *Computing Systems,* Vol. 8, No. 1, Winter 1995, pp. 3–25.

[McVo 91]   McVoy, L.W., and Kleiman, S.R., "Extent-like Performance from a UNIX File System," *Proceedings of the 1991 Winter USENIX Conference,* Jan. 1991, pp. 33–43.

[OSF 93]   Open Software Foundation, *OSF DCE Administration Guide—Extended Services,* Prentice-Hall, Englewood Cliffs, NJ, 1993.

[Oust 85]   Ousterhout, J.K., Da Costa, H., Harrison, D., Kunze, J.A., Kupfer, M., and Thompson, J.G., "A Trace-Driven Analysis of the UNIX 4.2 BSD File System," *Proceedings of the 10th Symposium on Operating System Principles,* Dec. 1985, pp. 15–24.

[Pend 95]   Pendry, J.-S., and McKusick, M.K., "Union Mounts in 4.4BSD-Lite," *Proceedings of the Winter 1995 USENIX Technical Conference,* Jan. 1995, pp. 25–33.

[Rose 90a]   Rosenblum, M., and Ousterhout, J.K., "The LFS Storage Manager," *Proceedings of the Summer 1990 USENIX Technical Conference,* Jun. 1990, pp. 315–324.

[Rose 90b]   Rosenthal, D.S.H., "Evolving the Vnode Interface," *Proceedings of the Summer 1990 USENIX Technical Conference,* Jun. 1990, pp. 107–118.

[Rose 92]   Rosenthal, D.S.H., "Requirements for a "Stacking" Vnode/VFS Interface," UNIX International Document SF–01–92–N014, Parsippany, NJ, 1992.

[Selt 93]   Seltzer, M., Bostic, K., McKusick, M.K., and Staelin, C., "An Implementation of a Log-Structured File System for UNIX," *Proceedings of the Winter 1993 USENIX Technical Conference,* Jan. 1993, pp. 307–326.

[Selt 95]   Seltzer, M., and Smith, K.A., "File System Logging Versus Clustering: A Performance Comparison," *Proceedings of the Winter 1995 USENIX Technical Conference,* Jan. 1995, pp. 249–264.

[Skin 93]   Skinner, G.C., and Wong, T.K., "Stacking Vnodes: A Progress Report," *Proceedings of the Summer 1993 USENIX Technical Conference,* Jun. 1993, pp. 161–174.

[Stae 91]   Staelin, C., "Smart Filesystems," *Proceedings of the Winter 1991 USENIX Conference,* Jan. 1991, pp. 45–51.

[Stev 95]   Stevens, W.R., and Pendry, J.-S., "Portals in 4.4BSD," *Proceedings of the Winter 1995 USENIX Technical Conference,* Jan. 1995, pp. 1–10.

[Vaha 95]   Vahalia, U., Gray, C., and Ting, D., "Metadata Logging in an NFS Server," *Proceedings of the Winter 1995 USENIX Technical Conference,* Jan. 1995, pp. 265–276.

[Webb 93]   Webber, N., "Operating System Support for Portable Filesystem Extensions," *Proceedings of the Winter 1993 USENIX Technical Conference,* Jan. 1993, pp. 219–228.

[Witt 93]   Wittle, M., and Keith, B., "LADDID: The Next Generation in NFS File Server Benchmarking." *Proceedings of the Summer 1993 USENIX Technical Conference, Jun. 1993,* pp. 111–128.

[Yage 95]   Yager, T., "The Great Little File System," *Byte,* Feb. 1995, pp. 155–158.

12

Kernel Memory Allocation

12.1   Introduction

The operating system must manage all the physical memory and allocate it both to other kernel subsystems and to user processes. When the system boots, the kernel reserves part of physical memory for its own text and static data structures. This portion is never released and hence is unavailable for any other purpose.[1] The rest of the memory is managed dynamically—the kernel allocates portions of it to various clients (processes and kernel subsystems), which release it when it is no longer needed.

UNIX divides memory into fixed-size frames or *pages*. The page size is a power of two, with 4 kilobytes being a fairly typical value.[2] Because UNIX is a *virtual memory* system, pages that are logically contiguous in a process address space need not be physically adjacent in memory. The next three chapters describe virtual memory. The memory management subsystem maintains mappings between the logical *(virtual)* pages of a process and the actual location of the data in physical memory. As a result, it can satisfy a request for a block of logically contiguous memory by allocating several physically non-contiguous pages.

This simplifies the task of page allocation. The kernel maintains a linked list of free pages. When a process needs some pages, the kernel removes them from the free list; when the pages are released, the kernel returns them to the free list. The physical location of the pages is unimportant.

---

[1]   Many modern UNIX systems (AIX, for instance) allow part of the kernel to be pageable.

[2]   This is a software-defined page size and need not equal the hardware page size, which is the granularity for protection and address translation imposed by the memory management unit.

The memall() and memfree() routines in 4.3BSD and the get_page() and freepage() routines in SVR4 implement this *page-level allocator*.

The page-level allocator has two principal clients (Figure 12-1). One is the *paging system,* which is part of the virtual memory system. It allocates pages to user processes to hold portions of their address space. In many UNIX systems, the paging system also provides pages for disk block buffers. The other client is the *kernel memory allocator,* which provides odd-sized buffers of memory to various kernel subsystems. The kernel frequently needs chunks of memory of various sizes, usually for short periods of time.

The following are some common users of the kernel memory allocator:

- The pathname translation routine may allocate a buffer (usually 1024 bytes) to copy a pathname from user space.
- The allocb() routine allocates STREAMS buffers of arbitrary size.
- Many UNIX implementations allocate zombie structures to retain exit status and resource usage information about deceased processes.
- In SVR4, the kernel allocates many objects (such as proc structures, vnodes, and file descriptor blocks) dynamically when needed.

Most of these requests are much smaller than a page, and hence the page-level allocator is inappropriate for this task. A separate mechanism is required to allocate memory at a finer granularity. One simple solution is to avoid dynamic memory allocation altogether. Early UNIX implementations [Bach 86] used fixed-size tables for vnodes, proc structures, and so forth. When memory was required for holding temporary pathnames or network messages, they borrowed buffers from the block buffer cache. Additionally, a few *ad hoc* allocation schemes were devised for special situations, such as the *clists* used by the terminal drivers.

This approach has several problems. It is highly inflexible, because the sizes of all tables and caches are fixed at boot time (often at compile time) and can not adjust to the changing demands on

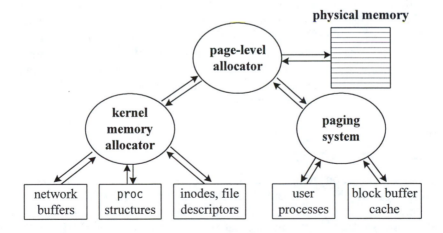

Figure 12-1. Memory allocators in the kernel.

the system. The default sizes of these tables are selected by the system developers based on the usage patterns expected with typical workloads. Although system administrators can usually tune these sizes, they have little guidance for doing so. If any table size is set too low, the table could overflow and perhaps crash the system without warning. If the system is configured conservatively, with large sizes of all tables, it wastes too much memory, leaving little for the applications. This causes the overall performance to suffer.

Clearly, the kernel needs a general-purpose memory allocator that can handle requests for large and small chunks of data efficiently. In the following section, we describe the requirements for this allocator and the criteria by which we can judge different implementations. We then describe and analyze various memory allocators used by modern UNIX systems.

12.2   Functional Requirements

The kernel memory allocator (KMA) services requests for dynamic memory allocation from several clients such as the pathname parser, STREAMS, and the interprocess communication facility. It does not handle requests for user process pages, which are the responsibility of the paging system.

When the system boots, the kernel first reserves space for its own text and static data structures, as well as some pre-defined pools such as the block buffer cache. The page-level allocator manages the remaining physical memory, which is contended for both by the kernel's own dynamic allocation requests and by user processes.

The page-level allocator pre-allocates part of this space to the KMA, which must use this memory *pool* efficiently. Some implementations allow no change in the total memory given to the KMA. Others allow the KMA to steal more memory from the paging system. Some even permit a two-way exchange, so the paging system can steal back excess free memory held by the KMA.

If the KMA runs out of memory, it blocks the caller until more memory is free. The caller may send a flag in the request, asking the KMA to return a failure status (usually a NULL pointer) instead of blocking. This option is most used by interrupt handlers, which must take some corrective action if the request fails. For example, if a network interrupt cannot allocate memory to hold an incoming packet, it may simply drop the packet, hoping the sender will retransmit it later.

The KMA must monitor which parts of its pool are allocated and which are free. Once a piece of memory is freed, it should be available to other requests. Ideally, a request for memory should fail only when memory is really full, that is, when the total free memory available to the allocator is less than the amount requested. In reality, the allocator fails sooner than that because of *fragmentation*—even if there is enough memory available to satisfy the request, it may not be available as one contiguous chunk.

12.2.1   Evaluation Criteria

An important criterion for evaluating a memory allocator is its ability to minimize wastage. Physical memory is limited, so the allocator must be space-efficient. One measure of efficiency is the *utilization factor*, which is the ratio of the total memory requested to that required to satisfy the requests. An ideal allocator would have 100% utilization; in practice, 50% is acceptable [Korn 85]. The major cause of wasted memory is fragmentation—the free memory is broken into chunks that are too small to be useful. The allocator reduces fragmentation by coalescing adjacent chunks of free memory into a single large chunk.

A KMA must be fast, because it is used extensively by various kernel subsystems, including interrupt handlers, whose performance is usually critical. Both the average and the worst-case latency are important. Because kernel stacks are small, the kernel uses dynamic allocation in many situations where a user process would simply allocate the object on its stack. This makes allocation speed all the more important. A slow allocator degrades the performance of the entire system.

The allocator must have a simple programming interface that is suitable for a wide variety of clients. One possibility is to have an interface similar to the malloc() and free() functions of the user-level memory allocator provided by the standard library:

```
void* malloc (size_t nbytes);
void free (void* ptr);
```

An important advantage of this interface is that the free() routine does not need to know the size of the region being freed. Often, one kernel function allocates a chunk of memory and passes it to another subsystem, which eventually frees it. For example, a network driver may allocate a buffer for an incoming message and send it to a higher-level module to process the data and free the buffer. The module releasing the memory may not know the size of the allocated object. If the KMA can monitor this information, it will simplify the work of its clients.

Another desirable interface feature is that the client not be forced to release the entire allocated area all at once. If a client wants to release only part of the memory, the allocator should handle it correctly. The malloc()/free() interface does not permit this. The free() routine will release the entire region and will fail if called with a different address from that returned by malloc(). Allowing clients to grow a buffer (for instance by a realloc() function) would also be useful.

Allocated memory should be properly aligned for faster access. On many RISC architectures, this is a requirement. For most systems, longword alignment is sufficient, but 64-bit machines such as DEC's Alpha AXP [DEC 92] may require alignment on an eight-byte boundary. A related issue is the minimum allocation size, which is usually eight or sixteen bytes.

Many commercial environments have a cyclical usage pattern. For example, a machine may be used for database queries and transaction processing during the day and for backups and database reorganization at night. These activities may have different memory requirements. Transaction processing might consume several small chunks of kernel memory to implement database locking, while backups may require that most of the memory be dedicated to user processes.

Many allocators partition the pool into separate regions, or *buckets,* for requests of different sizes. For instance, one bucket may contain all 16-byte chunks, while another may contain all 64-byte chunks. Such allocators must guard against a bursty or cyclical usage pattern as described above. In some allocators, once memory has been assigned to a particular bucket, it cannot be reused for requests of another size. This may result in a large amount of unused memory in some buckets, and hence not enough in others. A good allocator provides a way to dynamically recover excess memory from one bucket for use by another.

Finally, the interaction with the paging system is an important criterion. The KMA must be able to borrow memory from the paging system when it uses up its initial quota. The paging system must be able to recover unused memory from the KMA. This exchange should be properly controlled to ensure fairness and avoid starvation of either system.

We now look at several allocation methods, and analyze them using the above criteria.

12.3   Resource Map Allocator

The *resource map* is a set of *<base, size>* pairs that monitor areas of free memory (see Figure 12-2). Initially, the pool is described by a single map entry, whose *base* equals the starting address of the pool and *size* equals the total memory in the pool (Figure 12-2(a)). As clients allocate and free chunks of memory, the pool becomes fragmented, and the kernel creates one map entry for each contiguous free region. The entries are sorted in order of increasing base address, making it easy to coalesce adjacent free regions.

Using a resource map, the kernel can satisfy new allocation requests using one of three policies:

- **First fit** — Allocates memory from the first free region that has enough space. This is the fastest algorithm, but may not be optimal for reducing fragmentation.
- **Best fit** — Allocates memory from the smallest region that is large enough to satisfy the request. This has the drawback that it might leave several free regions that are too small to be useful.
- **Worst fit** — Allocates memory from the largest available region, unless a perfect fit is found. This may seem counter-intuitive, but its usefulness is based on the expectation that the region left behind after the allocation will be large enough to be used for a future request.

No one algorithm is ideal for all usage patterns. [Knut 73] provides a detailed analysis of these and other approaches. UNIX chooses the first-fit method.

Figure 12-2 describes a simple resource map that manages a 1024-byte region of memory. It supports two operations:

```
offset_t rmalloc (size);    /* returns offset of allocated region */
void rmfree (base, size);
```

Initially (Figure 12-2(a)), the entire region is free and is described by a single map entry. We then have two allocation requests, for 256 and 320 bytes respectively. This is followed by the release of 128 bytes starting at offset 256. Figure 12-2(b) shows the state of the map after these operations. We now have two free regions, and hence two map entries to describe them.

Next, another 128 bytes are released starting at offset 128. The allocator discovers that this region is contiguous with the free region that starts at offset 256. It combines them into a single, 256-byte, free region, resulting in the map shown in Figure 12-2(c). Finally, Figure 12-2(d) shows the map at a later time, after many more operations have occurred. Note that while the total free space is 256 bytes, the allocator cannot satisfy any request greater than 128 bytes.

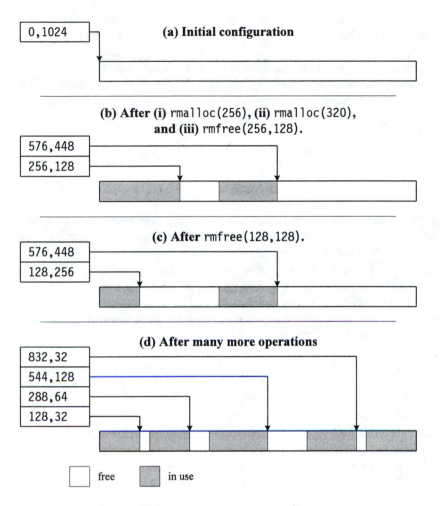

Figure 12-2. Using a resource map allocator.

12.3.1   Analysis

The resource map provides a simple allocator. The following are its main advantages:

- The algorithm is easy to implement.
- The resource map is not restricted to memory allocation. It can manage collections of arbitrary objects that are sequentially ordered and require allocation and freeing in contiguous chunks (such as page table entries and semaphores, as described below).

- It can allocate the exact number of bytes requested without wasting space. In practice, it will usually round up requests to four- or eight-byte multiples for simplicity and alignment.

- A client is not constrained to release the exact region it has allocated. As the previous example shows, the client can release any part of the region, and the allocator will handle it correctly. This is because the arguments to rmfree() provide the size of the region being freed, and the bookkeeping information (the map) is maintained separately from the allocated memory.

- The allocator coalesces adjacent free regions, allowing memory to be reused for different sized requests.

However, the resource map allocator also has some major drawbacks:

- After the allocator has been running for a while, the map becomes highly fragmented, creating many small free regions. This results in low utilization. In particular, the resource map allocator does poorly in servicing large requests.

- As the fragmentation increases, so does the size of the resource map, since it needs one entry for each free region. If the map is preconfigured with a fixed number of entries, it might overflow, and the allocator may lose track of some free regions.

- If the map grows dynamically, it needs an allocator for its own entries. This is a recursive problem, to which we offer one solution below.

- To coalesce adjacent free regions, the allocator must keep the map sorted in order of increasing base offsets. Sorting is expensive, even more so if it must be performed in-place, such as when the map is implemented as a fixed array. The sorting overhead is significant, even if the map is dynamically allocated and organized as a linked list.

- The allocator must perform a linear search of the map to find a free region that is large enough. This is extremely time consuming and becomes slower as fragmentation increases.

- Although it is possible to return free memory at the tail of the pool to the paging system, the algorithm is really not designed for this. In practice, the allocator never shrinks its pool.

The poor performance of the resource map is the main reason why it is unsuitable as a general-purpose kernel memory allocator. It is, however, used by some kernel subsystems. The System V interprocess communication facility uses resource maps to allocate semaphore sets and data areas for messages. The virtual memory subsystem in 4.3BSD uses this algorithm to manage system page table entries that map user page tables (see Section 13.4.2).

The map management can be improved in some circumstances. It is often possible to store the map entry in the first few bytes of the free region. This requires no extra memory for the map and no dynamic allocation for map entries. A single global variable can point to the first free region, and each free region stores its size and a pointer to the next free entry. This requires free regions to be at least two words long (one for the size, one for the pointer), which can be enforced by requiring allocation and freeing words in multiples of two. The Berkeley Fast File System (FFS), described in Section 9.5, uses a variation of this approach to manage free space within directory blocks.

While this optimization is suitable for the general memory allocator, it cannot be applied to other uses of the resource map, such as for semaphore sets or page table entries, where the managed objects have no room for map entry information.

12.4   Simple Power-of-Two Free Lists

The power-of-two free lists method is used frequently to implement `malloc()` and `free()` in the user-level C library. This approach uses a set of free lists. Each list stores buffers of a particular size, and all the sizes are powers of two. For example, in Figure 12-3, there are six free lists, storing buffers of sizes 32, 64, 128, 256, 512, and 1024 bytes.

Each buffer has a one-word header, which reduces its usable area by this amount. When the buffer is free, its header stores a pointer to the next free buffer. When the buffer is allocated, its header points to the free list to which it should be returned. In some implementations, it contains the size of the allocated area instead. This helps detect certain bugs, but requires the `free()` routine to compute the free list location from the size.

To allocate memory, the client calls `malloc()`, passing the required size as an argument. The allocator computes the size of the smallest buffer that is large enough to satisfy the request. This involves adding space for the header to the requested size and rounding the resulting value to the next power of two. The 32-byte buffers satisfy requests for 0–28 bytes, the 64-byte buffers satisfy requests for 29–60 bytes, and so on. The allocator then removes a buffer from the appropriate free list and writes a pointer to the free list in the header. It returns to the caller a pointer to the byte immediately following the header in the buffer.

When the client releases the buffer, it calls the `free()` routine, passing the pointer returned by `malloc()` as an argument. The user does not have to specify the size of the buffer being freed. It is essential, however, to free the entire buffer obtained from `malloc()`; there is no provision for freeing only part of the allocated buffer. The `free()` routine moves the pointer back four bytes to access the header. It obtains the free list pointer from the header and puts the buffer on that list.

The allocator can be initialized either by preallocating a number of buffers to each list or by leaving the lists empty at first and calling the page-level allocator to populate them as required. Sub-

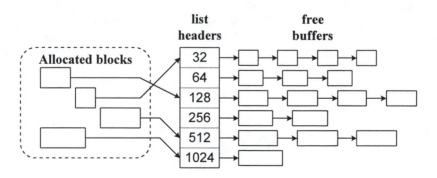

Figure 12-3. The power-of-two free list allocator.

sequently, if a list becomes empty, the allocator may handle a new `malloc()` request for that size in one of three ways:

- Block the request until a buffer of the appropriate size is released.
- Satisfy the request with a larger buffer, beginning with the next list and continuing the search until it finds a nonempty list.
- Obtain additional memory from the page-level allocator to create more buffers of that size.

Each method has its benefits and drawbacks, and the proper choice depends on the situation. For example, a kernel implementation of this algorithm may use an additional priority argument for allocation requests. In this case, the allocator may block low-priority requests that cannot be satisfied from the correct free list, but complete high-priority requests by one of the other two methods.

12.4.1   Analysis

The above algorithm is simple and reasonably fast. Its main appeal is that it avoids the lengthy linear searches of the resource map method and eliminates the fragmentation problem entirely. In situations where a buffer is available, its worst-case performance is well bounded. The allocator also presents a familiar programming interface, with the important advantage that the `free()` routine need not be given the buffer size as an argument. As a result, an allocated buffer can be passed to other functions and subsystems and eventually freed using only the pointer to the buffer. On the other hand, the interface does not allow a client to release only part of the allocated buffer.

There are many important drawbacks of this algorithm. The rounding of requests to the next power of two often leaves a lot of unused space in the buffer, resulting in poor memory utilization. The problem becomes worse due to the need to store the header in the allocated buffers. Many memory requests are for an exact power-of-two bytes. For such requests, the wastage is almost 100%, since the request must be rounded to the next power of two to allow for the header. For example, a 512-byte request would consume a 1024-byte buffer.

There is no provision for coalescing adjacent free buffers to satisfy larger requests. Generally, the size of each buffer remains fixed for its lifetime. The only flexibility is that large buffers may sometimes be used for small requests. Although some implementations allow the allocator to steal memory from the paging system, there is no provision to return surplus free buffers to the page-level allocator.

While the algorithm is much faster than the resource map method, it can be further improved. In particular, the round-up loop, shown in Example 12-1, is slow and inefficient:

```
void*malloc (size)
{
    int ndx = 0;                    /* free list index */
    int bufsize = 1 << MINPOWER;    /* size of smallest buffer */
    size += 4;                      /* account for header */
    assert (size <= MAXBUFSIZE);
```

```
    while (bufsize < size)  {
        ndx++;
        bufsize <<= 1;
    }
... /* at this point, ndx is the index of the appropriate free list */
}
```

Example 12-1. Crude implementation of `malloc()`.

The next section describes an improved algorithm that addresses many of these problems.

12.5 The McKusick-Karels Allocator

Kirk McKusick and Michael Karels introduced an improved power-of-two allocator [McKu 88], which is now used in several UNIX variants including 4.4BSD and Digital UNIX. In particular, it eliminates space wastage in the common case where the size of the requested memory was exactly a power of two. It also optimizes the round-up computation and eliminates it if the allocation size is known at the time of compilation.

The McKusick-Karels algorithm requires the memory managed by the allocator to comprise a set of contiguous pages and all buffers belonging to the same page to be the same size (a power of two). It uses an additional page usage array (kmemsizes[]) to manage its pages. Each page may be in one of three states:

- Free—the corresponding element of kmemsizes[] contains a pointer to the element for the next free page.
- Divided into buffers of a particular size—the kmemsizes[] element contains the size.
- Part of a buffer that spanned multiple pages—the kmemsizes[] element corresponding to the first page of the buffer contains the buffer size.

Figure 12-4 shows a simple example for a 1024-byte page size. freelistarr[] is the usual array of free list headers for all buffer sizes smaller than one page.

Since all buffers on the same page are of the same size, allocated buffers do not need a header to store a free list pointer. The free() routine locates the page by masking off the low-order bits of the buffer address and finding the size of the buffer in the corresponding element of the kmemsizes[] array. Eliminating the header in allocated buffers yields the greatest savings for memory requests whose sizes are an exact power of two.

The call to malloc() is replaced by a macro that rounds the request to the next power of two (allocated buffers have no header information) and removes a buffer from the appropriate free list. The macro calls the malloc() function for requests of one or more pages or if the appropriate free list is empty. In the latter case, malloc() calls a routine that consumes a free page and divides it into buffers of the required size. In the macro, the round-up loop is replaced by a set of conditional expressions. Example 12-2 provides an implementation for the pool shown in Figure 12-4:

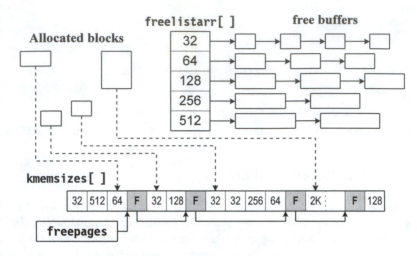

Figure 12-4. The McKusick - Karels allocator.

```
#define NDX(size)    \
    (size) > 128    \
        ? (size) > 256 ? 4 : 3  \
        : (size) > 64   \
            ? 2 \
            : (size) > 32 ? 1 : 0


#define MALLOC(space, cast, size, flags)    \
    {   \
        register struct freelisthdr* flh;   \
        if (size <= 512 &&  \
        (flh = freelistarr [NDX(size)]) != NULL)    {   \
            space = (cast)flh->next;    \
            flh->next = *(caddr_t *)space;  \
        } else  \
            space = (cast)malloc (size, flags); \
    }
```

Example 12-2. Using macros to speed up malloc.

The main advantage of using a macro is that when the allocation size is known at the time of compilation, the NDX() macro reduces to a compile-time constant, saving a substantial number of instructions. Another macro handles the simple cases of buffer release, calling the free() function in only a few cases, such as when freeing large buffers.

12.5.1   Analysis

The McKusick-Karels algorithm is a significant improvement over the simple power-of-two allocator described in Section 12.4. It is faster, wastes less memory, and can handle large and small requests efficiently. However, the algorithm suffers from some of the drawbacks inherent in the power-of-two approach. There is no provision for moving memory from one list to another. This makes the allocator vulnerable to a bursty usage pattern that consumes a large number of buffers of one particular size for a short period. Also, there is no way to return memory to the paging system.

12.6   The Buddy System

The *buddy system* [Pete 77] is an allocation scheme that combines free buffer coalescing with a power-of-two allocator.[3] Its basic approach is to create small buffers by repeatedly halving a large buffer and coalescing adjacent free buffers whenever possible. When a buffer is split, each half is called the *buddy* of the other.

　　To explain this method, let us consider a simple example (Figure 12-5), where a buddy algorithm is used to manage a 1024-byte block with a minimum allocation size of 32 bytes. The allocator uses a bitmap to monitor each 32-byte chunk of the block; if a bit is set, the corresponding chunk is in use. It also maintains free lists for each possible buffer size (powers of two between 32 and 512). Initially, the entire block is a single buffer. Let us consider the effect of the following sequence of requests and allocator actions:

1. *allocate (256):* Splits the block into two buddies—**A** and **A'**—and puts **A'** on the 512-byte free list. It then splits **A** into **B** and **B'**, puts **B'** on the 256-byte free list, and returns **B** to the client.

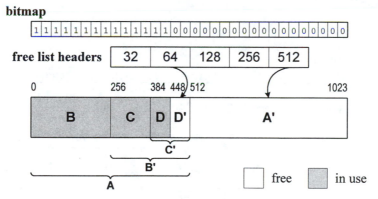

Figure 12-5. The buddy system.

---

[3] This is the binary buddy system, which is the simplest and most popular buddy system. We can implement other buddy algorithms by splitting buffers into four, eight, or more pieces.

2. *allocate (128):*   Finds the 128-byte free list empty. It checks the 256-byte list, re-moves **B′** from it, and splits it into **C** and **C′**. Then, it puts **C′** on the 128-byte free list and returns **C** to the client.

3. *allocate (64):*   Finds the 64-byte list empty, and hence removes **C′** from 128-byte free list. It splits **C′** into **D** and **D′**, puts **D′** on the 64-byte list, and re-turns **D** to the client. Figure 12-5 shows the situation at this point.

4. *allocate (128):*   Finds the 128-byte and 256-byte lists empty. It then checks the 512-byte free list and removes **A′** from it. Next, it splits **A′** into **E** and **E′**, and further splits **E** into **F** and **F′**. Finally, it puts **E′** onto the 256-byte list, puts **F′** on the 128-byte list, and returns **F** to the client.

5. *release (C, 128):*   Returns **C** to the 128-byte free list. This leads to the situation shown in Figure 12-6.

So far, there has been no coalescing. Suppose the next operation is

6. *release (D, 64):*   The allocator will note that **D′** is also free and will coalesce **D** with **D′** to obtain **C′**. It will further note that **C** is also free and will coalesce it with **C′** to get back **B′**. Finally, it will return **B′** to the 256-byte list, resulting in the situation in Figure 12-7.

A few points of interest need to be clarified:

- There is the usual rounding of the request to the next power of two.
- For each request in this example, the corresponding free list is empty. Often, this is not the case. If there is a buffer available on the appropriate free list, the allocator uses it, and no splitting is required.

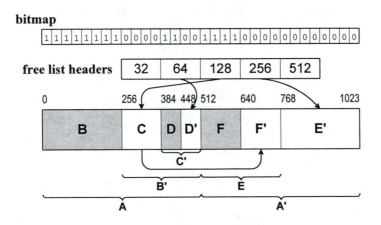

Figure 12-6. The buddy system, stage 2.

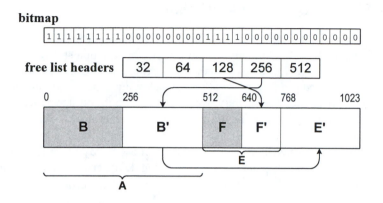

Figure 12-7. The buddy system, stage 3.

- The address and size of a buffer provide all the information required to locate its buddy. This is because the algorithm automatically gives each buffer an alignment factor equal to its size. Thus, for example, a 128-byte buffer at offset 256 has its buddy at offset 384, while a 256-byte buffer at the same offset has its buddy at offset 0.
- Each request also updates the bitmap to reflect the new state of the buffer. While coalescing, the allocator examines the bitmap to determine whether a buffer's buddy is free.
- While the above example uses a single, 1024-byte page, the allocator can manage several disjoint pages simultaneously. The single set of free list headers can hold free buffers from all pages. The coalescing will work as before, since the buddy is determined from the buffer's offset in the page. The allocator will, however, maintain a separate bitmap for each page.

12.6.1 Analysis

The buddy system does a good job of coalescing adjacent free buffers. That provides flexibility, allowing memory to be reused for buffers of a different size. It also allows easy exchange of memory between the allocator and the paging system. Whenever the allocator needs more memory it can obtain a new page from the paging system and split it as necessary. Whenever the release routine coalesces an entire page, the page can be returned to the paging system.

The main disadvantage of this algorithm is its performance. Every time a buffer is released, the allocator tries to coalesce as much as possible. When allocate and release requests alternate, the algorithm may coalesce buffers, only to split them again immediately. The coalescing is recursive, resulting in extremely poor worst-case behavior. In the next section, we examine how SVR4 modifies this algorithm to overcome this performance bottleneck.

Another drawback is the programming interface. The release routine needs both the address and size of the buffer. Moreover, the allocator requires that an entire buffer be released. Partial release is insufficient, since a partial buffer has no buddy.

12.7   The SVR4 Lazy Buddy Algorithm

The major problem with the simple buddy algorithm is the poor performance due to repetitive coalescing and splitting of buffers. Normally, memory allocators are in a steady state, where the number of in-use buffers of each size remains in a fairly narrow range. Under such conditions, coalescing offers no advantage and is only a waste of time. Coalescing is necessary only to deal with bursty conditions, where there are large, temporary, variations in the buffer usage pattern.

We define a *coalescing delay* as the time taken to either coalesce a single buffer with its buddy or determine that its buddy is not free. The coalescing results in a buffer of the next larger size, and the process is recursive until we find a buffer whose buddy is not free. In the buddy algorithm, each release operation incurs at least one coalescing delay, and often more than one.

A straightforward solution is to defer coalescing until it becomes necessary, and then to coalesce as many buffers as possible. Although this reduces the average time for allocation and release, the few requests that invoke the coalescing routine are slow. Because the allocator may be called from time-critical functions such as interrupt handlers, it is essential to control this worst-case behavior. We need an intermediate approach that defers coalescing, but does not wait until the situation is critical, and amortizes the cost of coalescing over several requests. [Lee 89] suggests a solution based on low- and high-watermarks on each buffer class. The SVR4 approach [Bark 89] described below is based on the same idea, but is more efficient.

12.7.1   Lazy Coalescing

Buffer release involves two steps. First, the buffer is put on the free list, making it available for other allocation requests. Second, the buffer is marked as free in the bitmap and coalesced with adjacent buffers if possible; this is the coalescing operation. The normal buddy system performs both steps on each release operation.

The lazy buddy system always performs the first step, which makes the buffer *locally free* (available for allocation within the class, but not for coalescing). Whether it performs the second step depends on the state of the buffer class. At any time, a class has N buffers, of which A buffers are active, L are locally free, and G are *globally free* (marked free in the bitmap, available for coalescing). Hence,

```
N = A + L + G
```

Depending on the values of these parameters, a buffer class is said to be in one of three states:

- **lazy** — buffer consumption is in a steady state (allocation and release requests are about equal) and coalescing is not necessary.
- **reclaiming** — consumption is borderline; coalescing is needed.
- **accelerated** — consumption is not in a steady state, and the allocator must coalesce faster.

The critical parameter that determines the state is called the *slack*, defined as

```
slack = N − 2L − G
```

The system is in the lazy state when *slack* is 2 or more, in the reclaiming state when *slack* equals 1, and in the accelerated state when *slack* is zero. The algorithm ensures that *slack* is never negative. [Bark 89] provides comprehensive proof of why the *slack* is an effective measure of the buffer class state.

When a buffer is released, the SVR4 allocator puts it on the free list and examines the resulting state of the class. If the list is in the lazy state, the allocator does no more. The buffer is not marked as free in the bitmap. Such a buffer is called a *delayed* buffer and is identified as such by a flag in the buffer header (the header is present only on buffers on the free list). Although it is available for other same-size requests, it cannot be coalesced with adjacent buffers.

If the list is in the reclaiming state, the allocator marks the buffer as free in the bitmap and coalesces it if possible. If the list is in accelerated state, the allocator coalesces two buffers—the one just released and an additional delayed buffer, if there is one. When it releases the coalesced buffer to the next higher-sized list, the allocator checks the state of that class to decide whether to coalesce further. Each of these operations changes the *slack* value, which must be recomputed.

To implement this algorithm efficiently, the buffers are doubly linked on the free lists. Delayed buffers are released to the head of the list, and non-delayed buffers to the tail. This way, delayed buffers are reallocated first; this is desirable because they are the least expensive to allocate (no bitmap update is required). Moreover, in the accelerated stage, the additional delayed buffer can be quickly checked for and retrieved from the head of the list. If the first buffer is non-delayed, there are no delayed buffers on the list.

This is a substantial improvement over the basic buddy system. In steady state, all lists are in the lazy state, and no time is wasted in coalescing and splitting. Even when a list is in the accelerated state, the allocator coalesces at most two buffers on each request. Hence, in the worst-case situation, there are at most two coalescing delays per class, which is at most twice as bad as the simple buddy system.

[Bark 89] analyzes the performance of the buddy and lazy buddy algorithms under various simulated workloads. It shows that the average latency of the lazy buddy method is 10% to 32% better than that of the simple buddy system. As expected, however, the lazy buddy system has greater variance and poorer worst-case behavior for the release routine.

12.7.2   SVR4 Implementation Details

SVR4 uses two types of memory pools—large and small. Each small pool begins with a 4096-byte block, divided into 256-byte buffers. The first two buffers are used to maintain the data structures (such as the bitmap) for this pool, while the rest are available for allocation and splitting. This pool allocates buffers whose sizes are powers of two ranging from 8 to 256 bytes. A large pool begins with a 16-kilobyte block and allocates buffers of size 512 to 16K bytes. In steady state, there are numerous active pools of both types.

The allocator exchanges memory with the paging system in pool-sized units. When it needs more memory, it acquires a large or small pool from the page-level allocator. When all memory in a pool is coalesced, the allocator returns the pool to the paging system.

A large pool is coalesced by the lazy buddy algorithm alone, because the pool size equals that of the largest buffer class. For a small pool, the buddy algorithm only coalesces up to 256 bytes, and we need a separate function to gather the 256-byte buffers of a pool. This is time-consuming, and should be performed in the background. A system process called the *kmdaemon* runs periodically to coalesce the pools and return free pools to the page-level allocator.

12.8   The Mach-OSF/1 Zone Allocator

The *zone* allocator used in Mach and OSF/1 [Sciv 90] provides fast memory allocation and performs garbage collection in the background. Each class of dynamically allocated objects (such as proc structures, credentials, or message headers) is assigned its own *zone,* which is simply a pool of free objects of that class. Even if objects of two classes have the same size, they have their own zone. For example, both *port translations* and *port sets* (see Chapter 6) are 104 bytes in size [DEC 93], but each has its own zone. There is also a set of power-of-two-sized zones used by miscellaneous clients that do not require a private pool of objects.

Zones are initially populated by allocating memory from the page-level allocator, which also provides additional memory when required. Any single page is only used for one zone; hence, all objects on the same physical page belong to the same class. The free objects of each zone are maintained on a linked list, headed by a struct zone. These themselves are dynamically allocated from a *zone of zones,* each element of which is a struct zone.

Each kernel subsystem initializes the zones it will need, using the function

```
zinit (size, max, alloc, name);
```

where size is the size of each object, max is the maximum size in bytes the zone may reach, alloc is the amount of memory to add to the zone each time the free list becomes empty (the kernel rounds it to a whole number of pages), and name is a string that describes the objects in the zone. zinit() allocates a zone structure from the *zone of zones* and records the size, max, and alloc values in it. zinit() then allocates an initial alloc-byte region of memory from the page-level allocator and divides it into size-byte objects, which it puts on the free list. All active zone structures are maintained on a linked list, described by the global variables first_zone and last_zone (Figure 12-8). The first element on this list is the *zone of zones,* from which all other elements are allocated.

Thereafter, allocation and release are extremely fast, and involve nothing more than removing objects from and returning objects to the free list. If an allocation request finds the free list empty, it asks the page-level allocator for alloc more bytes. If the size of the pool reaches max bytes, further allocations will fail.

12.8.1   Garbage Collection

Obviously, a scheme like this requires garbage collection, otherwise a bursty usage pattern will leave a lot of memory unusable. This happens in the background, so that it does not lead to deviant worst-case behavior of a few operations. The allocator maintains an array called the *zone page map,* with one element for each page that is assigned to a zone. Each map entry contains two counts:

- in_free_list is the number of objects from that page on the free list.

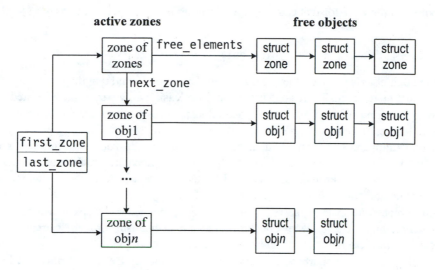

Figure 12-8. The zone allocator.

- alloc_count is the total number of objects from that page assigned to the zone.

The alloc_count is set whenever the page is acquired by the zone from the page-level allocator. Since the page size may not be an exact multiple of the object size, an object may occasionally span two pages. In this case, it is included in the alloc_count of both pages. The in_free_list count is not updated with each allocation and release operation, but is recomputed each time the garbage collector runs. This minimizes the latency of individual allocator requests.

The garbage collector routine, zone_gc(), is invoked by the swapper task each time it runs. It walks through the list of zones and, for each zone, makes two passes through its free list. In the first pass, it scans each free element and increments the in_free_count of the page to which it belongs. At the end of this scan, if the in_free_list and alloc_count of any page are equal, all objects on that page are free, and the page can be recaptured.[4] Hence, in the second pass, zone_gc() removes all such objects from the free list. Finally, it calls kmem_free() to return each free page to the page-level allocator.

12.8.2 Analysis

The zone allocator is fast and efficient. It has a simple programming interface. Objects are allocated by

```
obj = void* zalloc (struct zone* z);
```

---

[4] If the page being recaptured has objects at its top or bottom that span two pages, such objects must be removed from the free list, and the alloc_count of the other page must be decremented to reflect this.

where z points to the zone for that class of objects, set up by an earlier call to `zinit()`. The objects are released by

```
void zfree(struct zone* z, void* obj);
```

This requires that clients release allocated objects in their entirety and that they know to which zone the objects must be released. There is no provision for releasing only part of the allocated object.

One interesting property is that the zone allocator uses itself to allocate zone structures for newly created zones (using the *zone of zones*). This leads to a "chicken-and-egg problem" when the system is bootstrapped. The memory management system needs zones to allocate its own data structures, while the zones subsystem needs the page-level allocator, which is part of the memory management system. This problem is addressed by using a small, statically configured, region of memory to create and populate the *zone of zones*.

Zone objects are exactly the required size and do not incur the space wastage inherent in power-of-two methods. The garbage collector provides a mechanism for memory reuse—free pages can be returned to the paging system and later recovered for other zones.

The efficiency of the garbage collector is a major concern. Because it runs as a background task, it does not directly impact the performance of individual allocation or release requests. The garbage collection algorithm is slow, as it involves a linear traversal, first of all free objects and then of all pages in the zone. This affects the system responsiveness, for the garbage collector ties up the CPU until it completes.

[Sciv 90] claims that the addition of garbage collection did not significantly change the performance of a parallel compilation benchmark. There are, however, no definitive published measurements of garbage collection overhead, and it is difficult to estimate its impact on the overall system performance. The garbage collection algorithm, however, is complex and inefficient. Compare this with the slab allocator (Section 12.10), which has a simple and fast garbage collection mechanism and also exhibits better worst-case behavior.

12.9   A Hierarchical Allocator for Multiprocessors

Memory allocation for a shared-memory multiprocessor raises some additional concerns. Data structures such as free lists and allocation bitmaps used by traditional systems are not multiprocessor-safe and must be protected by locks. In large, parallel systems, this results in heavy contention for these locks, and CPUs frequently stall while waiting for the locks to be released.

One solution to this problem is implemented in Dynix, a multiprocessor UNIX variant for the Sequent S2000 machines [McKe 93]. It uses a hierarchical allocation scheme that supports the System V programming interface. The Sequent multiprocessors are used in large on-line transaction-processing environments, and the allocator performs well under that load.

Figure 12-9 describes the design of the allocator. The lowest *(per-CPU)* layer allows the fastest operations, while the highest *(coalesce-to-page)* layer is for the time-consuming coalescing process. There is also (not shown) a *coalesce-to-vmblock* layer, which manages page allocation within large (4MB-sized) chunks of memory.

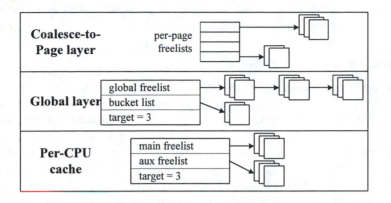

Figure 12-9. A hierarchical allocator for a multiprocessor.

The *per-CPU* layer manages one set of power-of-two pools for each processor. These pools are insulated from the other processors, and hence can be accessed without acquiring global locks. Allocation and release are fast in most cases, as only the local free list is involved.

Whenever the per-CPU free list becomes empty, it can be replenished from the *global layer*, which maintains its own power-of-two pools. Likewise, excess buffers in the per-CPU cache can be returned to the global free list. As an optimization, buffers are moved between these two layers in *target*-sized groups (three buffers per move in the case shown in Figure 12-9), preventing unnecessary linked-list operations.

To accomplish this, the per-CPU layer maintains two free lists—*main* and *aux*. Allocation and release primarily use the main free list. When this becomes empty, the buffers on *aux* are moved to *main,* and the *aux* list is replenished from the global layer. Likewise, when the *main* list overflows (size exceeds *target*), it is moved to *aux,* and the buffers on *aux* are returned to the global layer. This way, the global layer is accessed at most once per *target*-number of accesses. The value of target is a tunable parameter. Increasing *target* reduces the number of global accesses, but ties up more buffers in per-CPU caches.

The global layer maintains global power-of-two free lists, and each list is subdivided into groups of *target* buffers. Occasionally, it is necessary to transfer odd-sized groups of blocks to the global layer, due to low-memory operations or per-CPU cache flushes. Such blocks are added to a separate bucket list, which serves as a staging area for the global free list.

When a global list exceeds a global target value, excess buffers are returned to the *coalesce-to-page layer*. This layer maintains per-page free lists (all buffers from the page are the same size). This layer places the buffers on the free list to which they belong, and increases the free count for that page. When all buffers on a page are returned to this list, the page can be given back to the paging system. Conversely, the coalesce-to-page layer can borrow memory from the paging system to create new buffers.

The coalesce-to-page layer sorts its lists based on the number of free blocks on each page. This way, it allocates buffers from pages having the fewest free blocks. Pages with many free blocks get more time to recover other free blocks, increasing the probability of returning them to the paging system. This results in a high coalescing efficiency.

12.9.1 Analysis

The Dynix algorithm provides efficient memory allocation for shared memory multiprocessors. It supports the standard System V interface, and allows memory to be exchanged between the allocator and the paging system. The per-CPU caches reduce the contention on the global lock, and the dual free lists provide a fast exchange of buffers between the per-CPU and global layers.

It is interesting to contrast the Dynix coalescing approach with that of the Mach zone-based allocator. The Mach algorithm employs a mark-and-sweep method, linearly scanning the entire pool each time. This is computationally expensive, and hence is relegated to a separate background task. In Dynix, each time blocks are released to the coalesce-to-page layer, the per-page data structures are updated to account for them. When all the buffers in a page are freed, the page can be returned to the paging system. This happens in the foreground, as part of the processing of release operations. The incremental cost for each release operation is small; hence it does not lead to unbounded worst-case performance.

Benchmark results [McKe 93] show that for a single CPU, the Dynix algorithm is faster than the McKusick-Karels algorithm by a factor of three to five. The improvement is even greater for multiprocessors (a hundred to a thousand-fold for 25 processors). These comparisons, however, are for the best-case scenario, where allocations occur from the per-CPU cache. This study does not describe more general measurements.

12.10   The Solaris 2.4 *Slab* Allocator

The slab allocator [Bonw 94], introduced in Solaris 2.4, addresses many performance problems that are ignored by the other allocators described in this chapter. As a result, the slab allocator delivers better performance and memory utilization than other implementations. Its design focuses on three main issues—object reuse, hardware cache utilization, and allocator footprint.

12.10.1 Object Reuse

The kernel uses the allocator to create various kinds of temporary objects, such as inodes, proc structures, and network buffers. The allocator must execute the following sequence of operations on an object:

1. Allocate memory.
2. Construct (initialize) the object.
3. Use the object.
4. Deconstruct it.
5. Free the memory.

Kernel objects are usually complex, and contain sub-objects such as reference counts, linked list headers, mutexes, and condition variables. Object construction involves setting these fields to a fixed, *initial* state. The deconstruction phase deals with the same fields, and in many cases, leaves them in their initial state before deallocating the memory.

For instance, a vnode contains the header of a linked list of its resident pages. When the vnode is initialized, this list is empty. In many UNIX implementations [Bark 90], the kernel deallocates the vnode only after all its pages have been flushed from memory. Hence, just before freeing the vnode (the deconstruction stage), its linked list is empty again.

If the kernel reuses the same object for another vnode, it does not need to reinitialize the linked list header, for the deconstruction took care of that. The same principle applies to other initialized fields. For instance, the kernel allocates objects with an initial reference count of one, and deallocates them when the last reference is released (hence, the reference count is one, and is about to become zero). Mutexes are initialized to an *unlocked* state, and must be unlocked before releasing the object.

This shows the advantage of caching and reusing the same object, rather than allocating and initializing arbitrary chunks of memory. Object caches are also space-efficient, as we avoid the typical rounding to the next power of two. The zone allocator (Section 12.8) is also based on object caching and gives efficient memory utilization. However, because it is not concerned with the object state, it does not eliminate the reinitialization overhead.

12.10.2   Hardware Cache Utilization

Traditional memory allocators create a subtle but significant problem with hardware cache utilization. Many processors have a small, simple, level-1 data cache whose size is a power of two. (Section 15.13 explains hardware caches in detail.) The MMU maps addresses to cache locations by

```
cache location = address % cache size;
```

When the hardware references an address, it first checks the cache location to see if the data is in the cache. If it is not, the hardware fetches the data from main memory into the cache, overwriting the previous contents of that cache location.

Typical memory allocators such as the McKusick-Karels and the buddy algorithms round memory requests to the next power of two and return objects aligned to that size. Moreover, most kernel objects have their important, frequently accessed fields at the beginning of the object.

The combined effect of these two factors is dramatic. For instance, consider an implementation where the in-core inode is about 300 bytes, the first 48 bytes of which are frequently accessed. The kernel allocates a 512-byte buffer aligned at a 512-byte boundary. Of these 512 bytes, only 48 bytes (9%) are frequently used.

As a result, parts of the hardware cache that are close to the 512-byte boundary suffer serious contention, whereas the rest of the cache is underutilized. In this case, inodes can utilize only 9% of the cache. Other objects exhibit similar behavior. This anomaly in buffer address distribution results in inefficient use of the hardware cache and, hence, poor memory performance.

The problem is worse for machines that interleave memory access across multiple main buses. For instance, the SPARCcenter 2000 [Cekl 92] interleaves data in 256-byte stripes across two buses. For the above example of inode use, most of the accesses involve bus 0, resulting in unbalanced bus use.

12.10.3   Allocator Footprint

The footprint of an allocator is the portion of the hardware cache and the *translation lookaside buffer (TLB)* that is overwritten by the allocation itself. (Section 13.3.1 explains TLBs in detail.) Memory allocators using resource maps or buddy algorithms must examine several objects to find a suitable buffer. These objects are distributed in many different parts of memory, often far from each other. This causes many cache and TLB misses, reducing the performance of the allocator. The impact is even greater, because the allocator's memory accesses overwrite *hot* (active) cache and TLB entries, requiring them to be fetched from main memory again.

Allocators such as McKusick-Karels and zone have a small footprint, since the allocator determines the correct pool by a simple computation and merely removes a buffer from the appropriate free list. The slab allocator uses the same principles to control its footprint.

12.10.4   Design and Interfaces

The slab allocator is a variant of the zone method and is organized as a collection of object caches. Each cache contains objects of a single type; hence, there is one cache of vnodes, one of proc structures, and so on. Normally, the kernel allocates objects from, and releases them to, their respective caches. The allocator also provides mechanisms to give more memory to a cache, or recover excess memory from it.

Conceptually, each cache is divided into two parts—a front end and a back end (Figure 12-10). The front end interacts with the memory client. The client obtains constructed objects from the cache and returns deconstructed objects to it. The back end interacts with the page-level allocator, exchanging slabs of unconstructed memory with it as the system usage patterns change.

A kernel subsystem initializes a cache to manage objects of a particular type, by calling

```
cachep = kmem_cache_create (name, size, align, ctor, dtor);
```

where name is a character string describing the object, size is the size of the object in bytes, align is the alignment required by the objects, and ctor and dtor are pointers to functions that construct and deconstruct the object respectively. The function returns a pointer to the cache for that object.

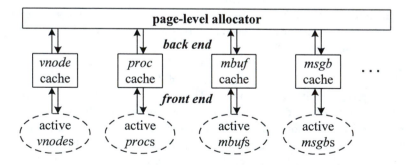

Figure 12-10. Slab allocator design.

Thereafter, the kernel allocates an object from the cache by calling

```
objp = kmem_cache_alloc (cachep, flags);
```

and releases it with

```
kmem_cache_free (cachep, objp);
```

This interface does not construct or deconstruct objects when reusing them. Hence the kernel must restore the object to its *initial* state before releasing it. As explained in Section 12.10.1, this usually happens automatically and does not require additional actions.

When the cache is empty, it calls kmem_cache_grow() to acquire a *slab* of memory from the page-level allocator and create objects from it. The slab is composed of several contiguous pages managed as a monolithic chunk by the cache. It contains enough memory for several instances of the object. The cache uses a small part of the slab to manage the memory in the slab and divides the rest of the slab into buffers that are the same size as the object. Finally, it initializes the objects by calling their constructor (specified in the ctor argument to kmem_cache_create()), and adds them to the cache.

When the page-level allocator needs to recover memory, it calls kmem_cache_reap() on a cache. This function finds a slab whose objects are all free, deconstructs these objects (calling the function specified in the dtor argument to kmem_cache_create()), and removes the slab from the cache.

12.10.5   Implementation

The slab allocator uses different techniques for large and small objects. We first discuss small objects, many of which can fit into a one-page slab. The allocator divides the slab into three parts—the kmem_slab structure, the set of objects, and some unused space (Figure 12-11). The kmem_slab structure occupies 32 bytes and resides at the end of the slab. Each object uses an extra four bytes to store a free list pointer. The unused space is the amount left over after creating the maximum possible number of objects from the slab. For instance, if the inode size is 300 bytes, a 4096-byte slab will hold 13 inodes, leaving 104 bytes unused (accounting for the kmem_slab structure and the free list pointers). This space is split into two parts, for reasons explained below.

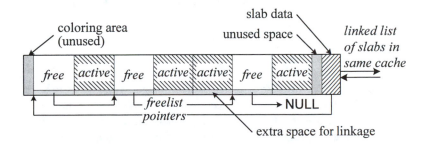

Figure 12-11. Slab organization for small objects.

The `kmem_slab` structure contains a count of its in-use objects. It also contains pointers to chain it in a doubly linked list of slabs of the same cache, as well as a pointer to the first free object in the slab. Each slab maintains its own, singly linked, free buffer list, storing the linkage information in a four-byte field immediately following the object. This field is needed only for free objects. It must be distinct from the object itself, since we do not want to overwrite the constructed state of the object.

The unused space is split into two parts: a *slab coloring area* at the head of the slab and the rest just before the `kmem_slab` structure. The cache tries to use a different-sized coloring area in each of its slabs, subject to alignment restrictions. In our inode cache example, if the inodes require an 8-byte alignment, the slabs can have 14 different coloring sizes (0 through 104 in 8-byte increments). This allows a better distribution of the starting offsets of the objects of this class, resulting in more balanced and efficient use of the hardware cache and memory buses.

The kernel allocates an object from a slab by removing the first element from the free list and incrementing the slab's in-use count. When freeing the object, it identifies the slab by a simple computation:

```
slab address = object address % slab size;
```

It then returns the object to the slab's free list, and decrements the in-use count.

When its in-use count becomes zero, the slab is free, or eligible for reclaiming. The cache chains all its slabs on a partly sorted, doubly linked list. It stores fully active slabs (all objects in use) at the beginning, partially active slabs in the middle, and free slabs at the tail. It also maintains a pointer to the first slab that has a free object and satisfies allocations from that slab. Hence the cache does not allocate objects from a completely free slab until all partly active slabs are exhausted. If the page-level allocator must reclaim memory, it checks the slab at the tail of the list and removes the slab if free.

Large Object Slabs

The above implementation is not space-efficient for large objects, which are usually multiples of a page in size. For such objects, the cache allocates slab management data structures from a separate pool of memory (another object cache, of course). In addition to the `kmem_slab` structure, the cache uses a `kmem_bufctl` structure for each object in the cache. This structure contains the free list linkage, a pointer to the `kmem_slab`, and a pointer to the object itself. The slab also maintains a hash table to provide a reverse translation from the object to the `kmem_bufctl` structure.

12.10.6 Analysis

The slab allocator is a well-designed, powerful facility. It is space-efficient, because its space overhead is limited to the `kmem_slab` structure, the per-object linkage field, and an unused area no larger than one object per slab. Most requests are serviced extremely quickly by removing an object from the free list and updating the in-use count. Its coloring scheme results in better hardware cache and memory bus utilization, thus improving overall system performance. It also has a small footprint, as it accesses only one slab for most requests.

The garbage collection algorithm is much simpler than that of the zone allocator, which is based on similar principles. The cost of garbage collection is spread over all requests, since each operation changes the in-use count. The actual reclaim operation involves some additional overhead, for it must scan the different caches to find a free slab. The worst-case performance is proportional to the total number of caches, not the number of slabs.

One drawback of the slab allocator is the management overhead inherent in having a separate cache for each type of object. For common classes of objects, where the cache is large and often used, the overhead is insignificant. For small, infrequently used caches, the overhead is often unacceptable. This problem is shared by the Mach zone allocator and is solved by having a set of power-of-two buffers for objects that do not merit a cache of their own.

The slab allocator would benefit from the addition of per-processor caches such as those of Dynix. [Bonw 94] acknowledges this and mentions it as a possible future enhancement.

12.11 Summary

The design of a general-purpose kernel memory allocator raises many important issues. It must be fast, easy to use, and use memory efficiently. We have examined several allocators and analyzed their advantages and drawbacks. The resource map allocator is the only one that permits release of part of the allocated object. Its linear search methods yield unacceptable performance for most applications. The McKusick-Karels allocator has the simplest interface, using the standard malloc() and free() syntax. It has no provision for coalescing buffers or returning excess memory to the page-level allocator. The buddy system constantly coalesces and breaks buffers to adjust to shifting memory demands. Its performance is usually poor, particularly when there is frequent coalescing. The zone allocator is normally fast, but has inefficient garbage collection mechanisms.

The Dynix and slab allocators offer significant improvements over these methods. Dynix uses a power-of-two method, but adds per-processor caches and fast garbage collection (the coalesce-to-page layer). The slab allocator is a modified zone algorithm. It improves performance through object reuse and balanced address distribution. It also uses a simple garbage collection algorithm that bounds the worst-case performance. As was previously noted, adding per-CPU caches to the slab algorithm would provide an excellent allocator.

Table 12-1 summarizes the results of a set of experiments [Bonw 94] comparing the slab allocator with the SVR4 and McKusick-Karels allocators. The experiments also show that object reuse reduces the time required for allocation plus initialization by a factor of 1.3 to 5.1, depending on the object. This benefit is in addition to the improved allocation time noted in the table.

Table 12-1. Performance measurements of popular allocators

	SVR4	McKusick-Karels	slab
Average time for alloc + free (microseconds)	9.4	4.1	3.8
Total fragmentation (waste)	46%	45%	14%
Kenbus benchmark performance (number of scripts executed per minute)	199	205	233

Many of these techniques can also be applied to user-level memory allocators. However, the requirements of user-level allocators are quite different; hence, a good kernel allocator may not work as well at the user level, and vice versa. User-level allocators deal with a very large amount of (virtual) memory, practically limitless for all but the most memory-intensive applications. Hence, coalescing and adjusting to shifting demands are less critical than rapid allocation and deallocation. A simple, standard interface is also extremely important, since they are used by many diverse, independently written applications. [Korn 85] describes several different user-level allocators.

12.12 Exercises

1. In what ways do the requirements for a kernel memory allocator differ from those for a user-level allocator?
2. What is the maximum number of resource map entries required to manage a resource with n items?
3. Write a program that evaluates the memory utilization and performance of a resource map allocator, using a simulated sequence of requests. Use this to compare the first-fit, best-fit, and worst-fit approaches.
4. Implement the free() function for the McKusick-Karels allocator.
5. Write a scavenge() routine that coalesces free pages in the McKusick-Karels allocator and releases them to the page-level allocator.
6. Implement a simple buddy algorithm that manages a 1024-byte area of memory with a minimum allocation size of 16 bytes.
7. Determine a sequence of requests that would cause the worst-case behavior for the simple buddy algorithm.
8. In the SVR4 lazy buddy algorithm described in Section 12.7, how would each of following events change the values of N, A, L, G, and *slack?*
    (a) A buffer is released when *slack* is greater than 2.
    (b) A delayed buffer is reallocated.
    (c) A non-delayed buffer is allocated (there are no delayed buffers).
    (d) A buffer is released when *slack* equals 1, but none of the free buffers can be coalesced because their buddies are not free.
    (e) A buffer is coalesced with its buddy.
9. Which of the other memory allocators can be modified to have a Dynix-style per-CPU free list in case of multiprocessors? Which algorithms cannot adopt this technique? Why?
10. Why does the slab allocator use different implementations for large and small objects?
11. Which of the allocators described in this chapter have simple programming interfaces?
12. Which of the allocators allow a client to release part of an allocated block?
13. Which of the allocators can reject an allocation request even if the kernel has a block of memory large enough to satisfy the request?

12.13   References

[Bach 86]   Bach, M.J., *The Design of the UNIX Operating System,* Prentice-Hall, Englewood Cliffs, NJ, 1986.

[Bark 89]   Barkley, R.E., and Lee, T.P., "A Lazy Buddy System Bound By Two Coalescing Delays per Class," *Proceedings of the Twelfth ACM Symposium on Operating Systems Principles,* Dec. 1989, pp. 167–176.

[Bark 90]   Barkley, R.E., and Lee, T.P., "A Dynamic File System Inode Allocation and Reclaim Policy," *Proceedings of the Winter 1990 USENIX Technical Conference,* Jan. 1990, pp. 1–9.

[Bonw 94]   Bonwick, J., "The Slab Allocator: An Object-Caching Kernel Memory Allocator," *Proceedings of the Summer 1994 USENIX Technical Conference,* Jun. 1994, pp. 87–98.

[Cekl 92]   Cekleov, M., Frailong, J.-M., and Sindhu, P., *Sun–4D Architecture,* Revision 1.4, Sun Microsystems, 1992.

[DEC 92]   Digital Equipment Corporation, *Alpha Architecture Handbook,* Digital Press, 1992.

[DEC 93]   Digital Equipment Corporation, *DEC OSF/1 Internals Overview—Student Workbook,* 1993.

[Knut 73]   Knuth, D., *The Art of Computer Programming, Vol. 1, Fundamental Algorithms,* Addison-Wesley, Reading, MA, 1973.

[Korn 85]   Korn, D.G., and Vo, K.-P., "In Search of a Better Malloc," *Proceedings of the Summer 1985 USENIX Technical Conference,* Jun. 1985, pp. 489–505.

[Lee 89]   Lee, T.P., and Barkley, R.E., "A Watermark-Based Lazy Buddy System for Kernel Memory Allocation," *Proceedings of the Summer 1989 USENIX Technical Conference,* Jun. 1989, pp. 1–13.

[McKe 93]   McKenney, P.E., and Slingwine, J., "Efficient Kernel Memory Allocation on Shared-Memory Multiprocessors," *Proceedings of the Winter 1993 USENIX Technical Conference,* Jan. 1993, pp. 295–305.

[McKu 88]   McKusick, M.K., and Karels, M.J., "Design of a General-Purpose Memory Allocator for the 4.3BSD UNIX Kernel," *Proceedings of the Summer 1988 USENIX Technical Conference,* Jun. 1988, pp. 295–303.

[Pete 77]   Peterson, J.L., and Norman, T.A., "Buddy Systems," *Communications of the ACM,* Vol. 20, No. 6, Jun. 1977, pp. 421–431.

[Sciv 90]   Sciver, J.V., and Rashid, R.F., "Zone Garbage Collection," *Proceedings of the USENIX Mach Workshop,* Oct. 1990, pp. 1–15.

[Step 83]   Stephenson, C.J., "Fast Fits: New Methods for Dynamic Storage Allocation," *Proceedings of the Ninth ACM Symposium on Operating Systems Principles,* Vol. 17, no. 5, 1983, pp. 30–32.

13

Virtual Memory

13.1 Introduction

One of the primary functions of the operating system is to manage the memory resources of the system efficiently. Each system has a high-speed, randomly accessible primary memory, also known as main memory, physical memory, or simply, as memory or core. Its access time is of the order of a few CPU cycles.[1] A program may directly reference code or data that is resident in main memory. Such memory is relatively expensive and therefore limited. The system uses a number of secondary storage devices (usually disks or other server machines on a network) to store information that does not fit in main memory. Access to such devices is several orders of magnitudes slower than to primary memory and requires explicit action on part of the operating system. The memory management subsystem in the kernel is responsible for distributing information between main memory and secondary storage. It interacts closely with a hardware component called the *memory management unit (MMU)*, which is responsible for getting data to and from main memory.

Life would be very simple for the operating system in the absence of memory management. The system would keep only one program in memory at a time, loaded contiguously at a known, fixed address. This would simplify the task of linking and loading, and absolve the hardware of any address translation chores. All addressing would be directly to physical addresses, and the program would have the entire machine to itself (shared, of course, with the operating system). This would be the fastest, most efficient way of running any single program.

---

[1] For instance, in 1995, a typical desktop system has a 75 Mhz processor and a 70-nanosecond memory access time, which equals 5.25 CPU cycles.

Such a scenario is often found on real-time, embedded, and small microprocessor-based systems. For general-purpose systems, the drawbacks are obvious. First, program size is bounded by memory size, and there is no way to run large programs. Second, with just one program loaded in memory, the entire system is idle when the program must wait for I/O. While the system is optimized for the single, small program case, it is hopelessly inadequate for providing a multiprogramming environment.

Accepting the need for some form of memory management, let us draw up a wish list of things we would like to be able to do:

- Run programs larger than physical memory. Ideally, we should be able to run programs of arbitrary size.
- Run partially loaded programs, thus reducing program startup time.
- Allow more than one program to reside in memory at one time, thereby increasing CPU utilization.
- Allow relocatable programs, which may be placed anywhere in memory and moved around during execution.
- Write machine-independent code—there should be no *a priori* correspondence between the program and the physical memory configuration.
- Relieve programmers of the burden of allocating and managing memory resources.
- Allow sharing—for example, if two processes are running the same program, they should be able to share a single copy of the program code.

These goals are realized through the use of *virtual memory* [Denn 70]. The application is given the illusion that it has a large main memory at its disposal, although the computer may have a relatively small memory. This requires the notion of an *address space* as distinct from memory locations. The program generates references to code and data in its address space, and these addresses must be translated to locations in main memory. The hardware and software must cooperate to bring information into main memory when it is needed for processing by the program and to perform the address translations for each access.

Virtual memory does not come without cost. The translation tables and other data structures used for memory management reduce the physical memory available to programs. The cost of address translation is added to the execution time for each instruction and is particularly severe when it involves extra memory accesses. When a process attempts to access a page that is not resident in memory, the system generates a fault. It handles the fault by bringing the page into memory, which may require time-consuming disk I/O operations. In all, memory management activities take up a significant amount of CPU time (about 10% on a busy system). The usable memory is further reduced by *fragmentation*—for instance, in a page-based system, if only a part of a page contains useful data, the rest is wasted. All these factors underscore the importance of an efficient design that emphasizes performance as well as functionality.

13.1.1   Memory Management in the Stone Age

Early implementations of UNIX (Version 7 and before) ran on the PDP-11, which had a 16-bit architecture with an address space of 64 kilobytes. Some models supported separate instruction and data spaces, but that still restricted the process size to 128 kilobytes. This limitation led to the development of various *software overlay* schemes for both user programs and the kernel [Coll 91]. Such methods reuse memory by overwriting a part of the address space that is no longer useful with another part of the program. For example, once the system is up and running, it no longer needs the system initialization code and can reclaim that space for use by other parts of the program. Such overlay schemes require explicit actions by the application developer, who needs to be familiar with the details of the program and the machine on which it runs. Programs using overlays are inherently unportable, since the overlay scheme depends on the physical memory configuration. Even adding more memory to the machine requires modifying these programs.

The memory management mechanisms were restricted to *swapping* (Figure 13-1). Processes were loaded in physical memory contiguously and in their entirety. A small number of processes could fit into physical memory at the same time, and the system would time-share between them. If another process wanted to run, one of the existing processes needed to be swapped out. Such a process would be copied to a predefined *swap partition* on a disk. *Swap space* was allocated on this

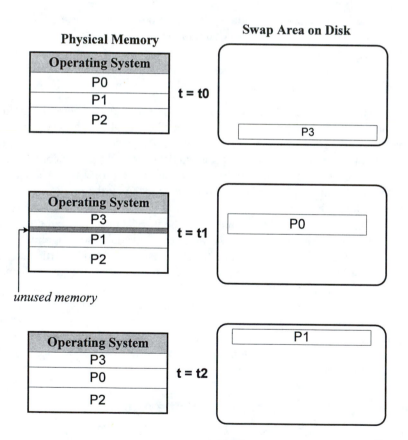

Figure 13-1. Swapping based memory management.

partition for each process at process creation time, so as to guarantee its availability when needed.

Demand paging made its appearance in UNIX with the introduction of the VAX-11/780 in 1978, with its 32-bit architecture, 4-gigabyte address space, and hardware support for demand paging [DEC 80]. 3BSD was the first major UNIX release to support demand paging [Baba 79, Baba 81]. By the mid-1980s, all versions of UNIX used demand paging as the primary memory management technique, with swapping relegated to a secondary role.

In a demand-paged system, both memory and process address space are divided into fixed-size pages, and these pages are brought into and out of memory as required. A page of physical memory is often called a *page frame* (or a physical page). Several processes may be active at any time, and physical memory may contain just some of the pages of each process (Figure 13-2). Each program runs as though it is the only program on the system. Program addresses are *virtual* and are divided by the hardware into a page number and an offset in the page. The hardware, in conjunction with the operating system, translates the virtual page number in the program address space to a physical *page frame number* and accesses the appropriate location. If the required page is not in memory, it must be brought into memory. In pure demand paging, no page is brought into memory until needed (referenced). Most modern UNIX systems do some amount of *anticipatory paging*, bringing in pages the system predicts will be needed soon.

A demand paging scheme may be used along with or instead of swapping. There are several benefits:

- Program size is limited only by virtual memory, which, for 32-bit machines, can be up to 4 gigabytes.
- Program startup is fast since the whole program does not need to be in memory in order to run.
- More programs may be loaded at the same time, since only a few pages of each program

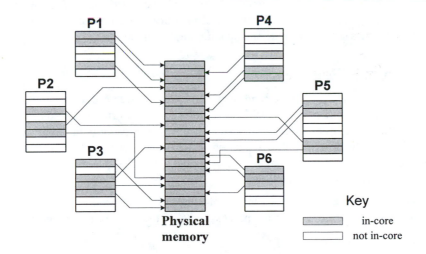

Figure 13-2. Physical memory holds a few pages of each process.

need to be in memory at any given time.

*   Moving individual pages into and out of memory is a lot cheaper than swapping entire processes or segments.

No discussion of memory management is complete without a mention of *segmentation*. This technique divides a process's address space into several segments. Each address in the program consists of a segment ID and an offset from the base of the segment. Each segment may have individual protections (read/write/execute) associated with it. Segments are loaded contiguously in physical memory, and each segment is described by a descriptor containing the physical address at which it is loaded (its base address), its limit or size, and protections. The hardware checks segment boundaries on each memory access, preventing the process from corrupting an adjacent segment. Program loading and swapping may be done on segment granularity instead of the whole program.

Segmentation may also be combined with paging [Bach 86] to provide a flexible, hybrid memory management mechanism. In such a system, segments need not be physically contiguous in memory. Each segment has its own address translation map, which translates segment offsets to physical memory locations. The Intel 80x86[2] architecture, for instance, supports this model.

Programmers typically think of the process address space as consisting of text, data, and stack regions, and the notion of segments maps well to this view. Although many versions of UNIX explicitly define these three regions, they are usually supported as a high-level abstraction composed of a set of virtually contiguous pages and not as hardware-recognized segments. Segmentation has not been popular in mainstream UNIX variants, and we do not discuss it in further detail.

13.2   Demand Paging

The paging system is responsible for allocating and managing the address spaces of all processes. It tries to optimize the use of the physical resources, including the main memory and secondary storage devices, to provide the desired functionality with minimum overhead. This chapter, as well as Chapters 14 and 15, examine several different virtual memory architectures. We begin by exploring some fundamental issues shared by all demand paging implementations.

13.2.1   Functional Requirements

Having accepted the desirability of a demand-paged architecture, we need to think about what functionality it must provide. The primary goal is to allow a process to run in a *virtual address space* and to perform translations from virtual to physical addresses transparently to the process. This goal must be achieved with the least possible impact on system resources. Nearly all other requirements can be derived directly or indirectly from this primary goal. From that perspective, we can develop a more detailed set of requirements, as follows:

*   **Address space management** — The kernel allocates the address space to the process during *fork* and releases it when the process *exit*s. If the process makes an *exec* system

---

[2]   This book uses the term 80x86 (or more simply, x86) to refer to properties generic to the Intel 80386, 80486, and Pentium architectures.

call, the kernel releases the old address space and allocates a new one that corresponds to the new program. Other major operations on the address space include changing the size of the data region or the stack, and adding a new region (such as shared memory).

- **Address translation** — For each instruction that accesses memory, the MMU needs to translate virtual addresses generated by the process to physical addresses in main memory. In a demand-paged system, a page is the unit of memory allocation, protection, and address translation. The virtual address is converted into a virtual page number and an offset within that page. The virtual page number is converted to a physical page number using some kind of *address translation map*s. If an instruction accesses a page that is not in physical memory (not resident), it will cause a *page fault* exception. The fault handler in the kernel must resolve the fault by bringing the page into memory.

- **Physical memory management** — Physical memory is the most important resource controlled by the memory management subsystem. Both the kernel and the user processes contend for memory, and these requests must be satisfied quickly. The total size of all active processes is usually much larger than that of physical memory, which can hold only a limited subset of this data. Hence the system uses physical memory as a cache of useful data. The kernel must optimize the utilization of this cache and ensure consistency and currency of the data.

- **Memory protection** — Processes must not access or modify pages in an unauthorized manner. The kernel must protect its own code and data against modification by user processes. Otherwise, a program may accidentally (or maliciously) corrupt the kernel. For security reasons, the kernel must also prevent processes from reading its code or data. Processes should not be able to access pages belonging to other processes. A part of the process's address space may even be protected from the process itself. For example, the text region of a process is usually write-protected, so that the process cannot accidentally corrupt it. The kernel implements the system's memory protection policies using the available hardware mechanisms. If the kernel detects an attempt to access an illegal location, it notifies the offending process by sending it a segmentation violation (SIGSEGV) signal.[3]

- **Memory sharing** — The characteristics of UNIX processes and their interactions naturally suggest sharing of certain portions of their address spaces. For instance, all processes running the same program can share a single copy of the text region of the program. Processes may explicitly ask to share a region of memory with other cooperating processes. The text regions of standard libraries may be shared in the same manner. These are examples of high-level sharing. There is also potential for low-level sharing of individual pages. For instance, after a *fork,* the parent and child may share a single copy of data and stack pages as long as neither tries to modify them.

These and other forms of sharing improve performance by reducing the contention on physical memory and by eliminating the in-memory copying and disk I/O needed to maintain multiple copies of the same data. The memory management subsystem must decide what forms of sharing it supports and how to implement such sharing.

---

[3] In some cases, the kernel sends the SIGBUS (bus error) signal instead.

- **Monitoring system load** — Usually, the paging system is able to cope with the demands of the active processes. Sometimes, however, the system may become overloaded. When that happens, processes do not get enough memory for their active pages and hence are unable to make progress. The load on the paging system depends on the number and size of the active processes, as well as their memory reference patterns. The operating system needs to monitor the paging system to detect such a situation and to take corrective action when required. This may involve controlling the system load by preventing new processes from starting up or by deactivating some existing processes.
- **Other facilities** — Some of the other functions provided by the memory management system include support for memory-mapped files, dynamically linked shared libraries, and execution of programs residing on remote nodes.

The memory management architecture has a great impact on overall system performance, and therefore the design must be sensitive to performance and scalability. Portability is important as well, to allow the system to run on different types of machines. Finally, the memory subsystem should be transparent to the user, who should be able to write code without worrying about the underlying memory architecture.

13.2.2 The Virtual Address Space

The address space of a process comprises all (virtual) memory locations that the program may reference or access. At any instant, the address space, along with the process's register context, reflects the current state of the program. When the process invokes a new program via *exec,* the kernel builds an address space that corresponds to the new image. Demand-paged architectures divide this space into fixed-size pages. The pages of a program may hold several types of information:

- text
- initialized data
- uninitialized data
- modified data
- stack
- heap
- shared memory
- shared libraries

These page types differ in the protections, method of initialization, and how they are shared by processes. Text pages are usually read-only, while data, stack, and heap pages are read-write. Protections on shared memory pages are usually set when the region is first allocated.

Text pages are normally shared by all processes running the same program. Pages in a shared memory region are shared by all processes that attach the region to their address space. A shared library may contain both text and data pages. The text pages are shared by all processes accessing the library. Library data pages are not shared, and each process gets its own private copy of these pages. (Some implementations may allow them to be shared until they are modified.)

13.2.3   Initial Access to a Page

A process can start running a program with none of its pages in physical memory. As it accesses each nonresident page, it generates a page fault, which the kernel handles by allocating a free page and initializing it with the appropriate data.

The method of initialization is different for the first access to a page and for subsequent accesses. In this section, we describe the first access. Text and initialized data pages are read in from the executable file. Uninitialized data pages are filled with zeroes, so that global uninitialized variables are automatically initialized to zero. Shared library pages are initialized from the library file. The u area and kernel stack are set up during process creation by copying the pages from the parent.

If a process executes a program that another process is already executing or has recently executed, then some or all of its text pages may be in physical memory or on fast devices such as the swap area (discussed in Section 13.2.4). In this case, the system can avoid the expense of retrieving these pages from the executable file. This issue is discussed in detail later in Sections 13.4.4 and 14.6.

13.2.4   The Swap Area

The total size of all active programs is often much greater than the physical memory, which consequently holds only some of the pages of each process. If a process needs a page that is not resident, the kernel makes room for it by appropriating another page and discarding its old contents.

Ideally, we would like to only replace those pages that will never be needed again, such as pages belonging to terminated processes. Often this is not possible, and the kernel must steal a page that may be required in the future. Thus, the kernel must save a copy of the page on secondary storage. UNIX uses a *swap area,* comprising one or more disk partitions, to hold such temporary pages. When the system is initially configured, certain disk partitions are left unformatted and are reserved for swapping. They may not be used by the file system.

Figure 13-3 describes how a page moves between physical memory and various secondary storage locations. If a page that has been saved on swap is accessed again, the kernel handles the page fault by reading it in from the swap area. To do so, it must maintain some type of *swap map* that describes the location of all outswapped pages. If this page must be removed from memory again, it must be saved only if its contents are different from the saved copy. This happens if the page is *dirty,* that is, if it was modified since it was last read in from the swap area. The kernel thus needs some way to recognize if a page is dirty. This can be easy for some systems where the page table entries have a hardware-supported dirty bit. Without such hardware support, the kernel must obtain this information in other ways, as we shall see in Section 13.5.3.

Text pages do not need to be saved in the swap area, since they can be recovered from the executable file itself. Some implementations swap out text pages as well, for performance reasons. Swap maps are usually very efficient, and the kernel can look up the swap location of a page simply by indexing into an in-memory table. To locate the page in the executable file, the kernel must go through the file system, which involves examining the inode and perhaps some indirect blocks (see Section 9.2.2). This is a much slower method, particularly if additional disk accesses are required to read the indirect blocks. However, swapping out the text pages requires extra disk I/O, which may

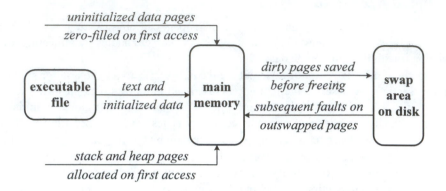

Figure 13-3. Pages move into and out of main memory.

offset the faster swap-ins. Most modern implementations do not swap out the text pages, but read them back from the file if needed.

13.2.5   Translation Maps

The paging system may use four different types of translation maps to implement virtual memory, as shown in Figure 13-4:

Hardware address translations — For each instruction that accesses memory, the hardware has to translate the virtual address in the program to a location in physical memory. Each machine pro-

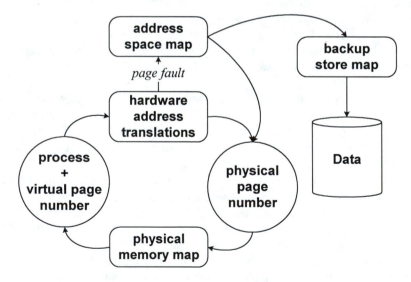

Figure 13-4. Address translations.

vides some *hardware address translation* mechanism, so that the operating system does not need to be involved in each translation. Section 13.3 examines three examples of memory architectures, all of which involve some form of *translation lookaside buffers (TLBs)* and *page tables*. Although the hardware dictates the form of these data structures, the operating system is responsible for their setup and maintenance.

The hardware address translation maps are the only data structures known to the MMU hardware. The other maps described in this section are known only to the operating system.

Address space map — When the hardware is unable to translate an address, it generates a *page fault*. This might happen because the page is not in physical memory or because the hardware does not have a valid translation for it. The fault handler in the kernel must resolve the fault by bringing the page into memory if necessary and loading a valid hardware translation entry.

The hardware-recognized maps may not provide complete information about the address space of a process. For example, on the MIPS R3000, the hardware uses only a small TLB. The operating system may maintain additional maps that fully describe the address space.

Physical memory map — Frequently, the kernel also needs to perform the reverse mapping and determine the owning process and the virtual page number for a given physical page. For instance, when the kernel removes an active page from physical memory, it must invalidate any translation for that page. To do so, it must locate the page table entry and/or TLB entry for the page; otherwise, the hardware will continue to expect the page to be at this physical location. Thus the kernel maintains a physical memory map that keeps track of what data is stored in each physical page.

Backing store map — When the fault handler cannot find a page in physical memory, it allocates a new page and initializes it in one of two ways—by filling it with zeroes or by reading it in from secondary storage. In the latter case, the page could be obtained from the executable file, from a shared library object file, or from its saved copy in the swap area. These objects comprise the *backing store* for the pages of a process. The kernel must maintain maps to locate pages on the backing store.

13.2.6   Page Replacement Policies

To make room for a new page, the kernel must reclaim a page that is currently in memory. The page replacement policy deals with how the kernel decides which page to reclaim [Bela 66]. The ideal candidate is a dead page, that is, one that will never be required again (for example, a page belonging to a terminated process). If there are no dead pages (or not enough of them), the kernel may choose a *local* or *global* replacement policy. A local policy allocates a certain number of pages to each process or group of related processes. If a process needs a new page, it must replace one of its own pages. If the kernel uses a global policy, it can steal a page from any process, using global selection criteria such as usage patterns.

Local policies are necessary when it is important to guarantee resources to certain processes. For example, the system administrator may allocate a larger set of pages to a more important process. Global policies, on the other hand, are simpler to implement and more suitable for a general time-sharing system. Most UNIX variants implement a global replacement policy, but reserve a minimum number of resident pages for each active process.

For a global replacement policy, the kernel must choose criteria for deciding which pages should be kept in memory. Ideally, we want to keep those pages that are going to be needed in the near future. We call this set of pages the *working set* of a process. If the page reference behavior of the processes were known in advance, the working set could be determined exactly, at least in theory. In practice, we have little advance knowledge of the access pattern of processes, and we must rely on empirical studies of typical processes to guide our implementation.

Such studies have shown that processes tend to exhibit *locality of reference,* that is, a process tends to localize its references to a small subset of its pages, and this subset changes slowly. For instance, when executing a function, all instructions are on the page (or pages) containing that function, and after a while, the process may move to a different function, thus changing its working set. Similarly for data references, loops that operate on arrays and functions that perform several operations on a structure are examples of code that exhibits locality of reference.

The practical inference is that recently accessed pages are more likely to be accessed again in the near future. Thus, a good approximation to the working set is the set of pages most recently accessed. This leads to a *least recently used (LRU)* policy for page replacement—discard those pages that have not been accessed for the longest time. Such an LRU policy is also adopted by the filesystem buffer cache, since file access patterns exhibit similar trends. For memory management, however, the LRU policy must be modified due to practical considerations, as seen in Section 13.5.3.

Finally, the kernel must decide when to free active pages. One option is to look for a page to reclaim only when a process actually needs to bring a page into memory. This is inefficient and degrades system performance. The better solution is to maintain a pool of free pages and periodically add pages to this pool, so that the load on the paging system is more evenly distributed over time.

13.3   Hardware Requirements

The memory management subsystem relies on the hardware to perform several tasks. These tasks are carried out by a hardware component called the Memory Management Unit (MMU), which functionally sits between the CPU and the primary memory. The architecture of the MMU has far-reaching impact on the design of the memory management system in the kernel. With that in mind, we first discuss the MMU functionality in abstraction and then look at three specific examples— Intel *x*86, IBM RS/6000, and MIPS R3000—to see how the architectural characteristics influence the kernel design.

The primary task of the MMU is the translation of virtual addresses. Most systems implement address translation maps using page tables, TLBs, or both. We describe page tables in this section and TLBs in the next. Typically, there is one page table for kernel addresses and one or more page tables to describe the user address space of each process. A page table is an array of entries, one per virtual page of the process. The index of the *page table entry (PTE)* in the table defines the page it describes. For example, PTE 3 of the text region page table describes virtual page 3 of the text region.

A page table entry is usually 32 bits in size and is divided into several fields. These fields contain the physical page frame number, protection information, a *valid* bit, a *modified* bit, and optionally, a *referenced* bit. The page table format is hardware-prescribed; other than that, page tables are simply data structures located in main memory. Several page tables reside in memory at any time. The MMU uses only the *active* tables, whose locations are loaded in hardware page table registers. Typically, on a uniprocessor, there are two active page tables—one for the kernel and one for the currently running process.

The MMU breaks a virtual address into the virtual page number and the offset within the page. It then locates the page table entry for this page, extracts the physical page number, and combines that with the offset to compute the physical address.

Address translation may fail for three reasons:

- **Bounds error** — The address does not lie in the range of valid addresses for the process. There is no page table entry for that page.
- **Validation error** — The page table entry is marked invalid. This usually means the page is not resident in memory. There are some situations where the valid bit is clear even if the page is valid and resident; they are covered in Section 13.5.3.
- **Protection error** — The page does not permit the type of access desired (e.g., write access to a read-only page or user access to a kernel page).

In all such cases, the MMU raises an exception and passes control to a handler in the kernel.[4] Such an exception is called a *page fault*, and the fault handler is passed the offending virtual address as well as the type of fault (validation or protection—bounds errors result in a validation fault). The handler may try to service the fault by bringing the page into memory or to notify the process by sending it a signal (usually SIGSEGV).

If the fault can be successfully handled, the process (when it eventually runs again) must restart the instruction that caused the fault. This requires the hardware to save the correct information required to restart the offending instruction prior to generating the page fault.

Every time a page is written to, the hardware sets the *modified* bit in its PTE. If the operating system finds this bit set, it saves the page on stable storage before recycling it. If the hardware supports a *referenced* bit in its PTEs, it sets this bit on each reference to a page. This allows the operating system to monitor the usage of resident pages and recycle those that do not seem useful.

If a process has a large virtual address space, its page table may become extremely large. For instance, if a process has an address space of 2 gigabytes and the page size is 1024 bytes, then the page table must have 2 million entries, and thus be 8 megabytes in size. It is impractical to keep such a large table in physical memory. Moreover, most of this address space is probably not really being used—a typical process address space comprises a number of regions (text, data, stack, etc.) scattered in different parts of this space. Thus the system needs a more compact way of describing the address space.

This problem is addressed by having segmented page tables or by paging the page table itself. The first approach works best when the system explicitly supports segmentation. Each segment of the process has its own page table, which is just large enough to hold the valid address range for

---

4 Some architectures do not support protection faults. On such systems, the kernel must force validation faults by unmapping the page, then determine the appropriate action based on whether the page is in memory and the type of access attempted.

that segment. In the second approach, the page table itself is paged, which means an additional higher-level page table is used to map the lower-level page table. With such a multitiered page table hierarchy, we need to allocate only those pages of the lower-level table that map valid addresses of the process. The two-level approach is more common, but some architectures such as the SPARC Reference MMU [SPARC 91] allow three levels of page tables.

The page table thus forms a link between the MMU and the kernel, both of which can access, use, and modify the PTEs. The hardware also has a set of MMU registers, which point to the page tables. The MMU is responsible for using the PTE to translate virtual addresses, checking the *valid* and protection bits in the process, and for setting *referenced* and *modified* bits as appropriate. The kernel must set up the page tables, fill in the PTEs with the correct data, and set the MMU registers to point to them. These registers usually need to be reset on each *context switch*.

13.3.1 MMU Caches

Page tables alone cannot provide efficient address translation. Each instruction would require several memory accesses—one to translate the virtual address of the program counter, one to fetch the instruction, and similarly, two accesses for each memory operand involved. If the page tables themselves are paged or tiered, the number of accesses increases further. Since each memory access requires at least one CPU cycle, so many accesses will saturate the memory bandwidth and increase the instruction execution time to unacceptable limits.

This problem is addressed in two ways. The first is by adding a high-speed cache that is searched before each memory access. Machines may support separate data and instruction caches or a single cache for both. Getting data from the cache is much faster than accessing main memory. On many machines (especially older ones), the cache is addressed by physical memory. It is completely managed by the hardware and is transparent to the software. Cache access takes place after the address translation, so that the benefits are modest. Many newer architectures such as Hewlett-Packard's PA-RISC [Lee 89] use a virtually addressed cache, which allows the cache search to proceed in parallel with address translation. This approach greatly improves performance, but has a number of cache consistency problems, which must be dealt with by the kernel (see Section 15.13).

The second approach to reducing memory accesses is an on-chip translation cache, called a *translation lookaside buffer (TLB)*. The TLB is an *associative* cache of recent address translations. TLB entries are similar to page table entries and contain address translation and protection information. They may also have a *tag* that identifies the process to which the address belongs. The cache is associative in the sense that the lookup is content-based rather than index-based—the virtual page number is searched for simultaneously in all the TLB entries.

The MMU usually controls most TLB operations. When it cannot find a translation in the TLB, it looks it up in the software address maps (such as the page tables) and loads it into a TLB entry. The operating system also needs to cooperate in some situations. If the kernel changes a page table entry, the change is not automatically propagated to the TLB's cached copy of the entry. The kernel must explicitly purge any TLB entry that it invalidates, so that the MMU will reload it from memory when the page is next accessed. For example, the kernel may write-protect a page in response to an explicit user request (through the *mprotect* system call). It must purge any old TLB entry that maps to this page, or else the process would still be able to write to the page (since the old mapping allowed writes).

The hardware defines the way in which the kernel can operate on the TLB. It may either provide explicit instructions for loading or invalidating TLB entries, or such functions may occur as a byproduct of certain instructions. On some systems (such as the MIPS R3000), the hardware uses only the TLBs, and any page tables or other maps are managed solely by the kernel. On such systems, the operating system is involved on each TLB miss and must load the correct translation into the TLB.

Although all MMUs must provide the same basic functionality, the way in which they do so may vary a lot. The MMU architecture dictates the virtual and physical page size, the types of protection available, and the format of the address translation entries. On machines with hardware-supported page tables, the MMU defines the page table hierarchy and the registers that map the page tables. It also defines the division of labor between itself and the kernel, and the extent of the kernel's role in manipulating the address and translation caches. With that in mind, we now look at three different architectures, with an emphasis on their impact on UNIX memory management implementation.

13.3.2   The Intel 80x86

The Intel 80x86 has been one of the major platforms for System V-based UNIX versions. It has a 4-gigabyte address space (hence, 32-bit addresses), with a page size of 4096 bytes, and support for both segmentation and paging [Intel 86]. Figure 13-5 describes the steps in address translation. Each virtual address consists of a 16-bit segment selector and a 32-bit offset. The segmentation layer converts this to a 32-bit *linear address,* which is further translated to a physical address by the paging layer. Paging may be disabled by clearing the high-order bit of a control register called **CR0**. In that case, the linear address *is* the physical address.

The process address space may contain up to 8192 segments. Each segment is described by a segment descriptor, which holds base, size, and protection information. Each process has its own *local descriptor table (LDT),* with one entry for each of its segments. There is also a systemwide

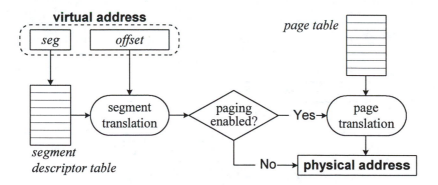

Figure 13-5. Address translation on the Intel 80x86.

global descriptor table (GDT), which has entries for the kernel code, data, and stack segments, plus some special objects including the per-process LDTs. When translating a virtual address, the MMU uses the segment selector to identify the correct segment descriptor, either from the GDT or from the current LDT (depending on a bit in the selector). It makes sure the offset is less than the segment size and adds it to the segment base address to obtain the linear address.

UNIX implementations on the *x86* use segmentation only for memory protection, kernel entry, and context switching [Robb 87]. It hides the notion of segmentation from user processes, who see a flat address space. To achieve this, the kernel sets up all user segments with base address 0 and a large size that excludes only the high end of virtual memory, which is reserved for kernel code and data. Code segments are protected as read-only and data as read-write, but both refer to the same locations. Each LDT also refers to some special segments—a *call gate segment* for system call entry and a *task state segment (TSS)* to save the register context across a context switch.

The *x86* uses a two-level page table scheme (Figure 13-6). The 4-kilobyte page size implies that a process may have up to one million pages. Rather than having one huge page table, the *x86* uses a number of small page tables for each process. Each page table is one page in size, and thus holds 1024 PTEs. It maps a contiguous region 4 megabytes in size, aligned at a 4-megabyte boundary. Hence a process may have up to 1024 page tables. Most processes, however, have sparse address spaces and use only a few page tables.

Each process also has a *page directory,* which contains PTEs that map the page tables themselves. The directory is one page in size and holds 1024 PTEs, one for each page table. The page

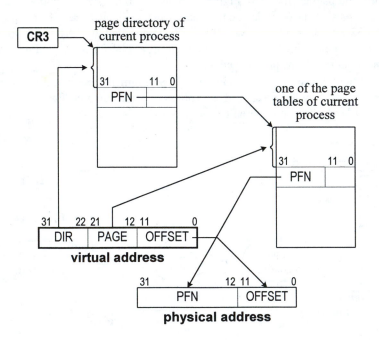

Figure 13-6. Address translation on Intel *x86*.

directory is the level-1 page table, and the page tables themselves are the level-2 tables. The rest of this discussion uses the terms *page directory* and *page table* instead of level-1 and level-2 tables.

The control register **CR3** stores the physical page number of the current page directory in its 20 high-order bits. Hence it is also known as the **PDBR** (Page Directory Base Register). Virtual addresses on the 80x86 can be broken into 3 parts. The top 10 bits contain the DIR field, which becomes the index into the page directory. This is combined with the page number from **CR3** to give the physical address of the page directory entry for the appropriate page table. The next 10 bits contain the PAGE field, which stores the virtual page number relative to the start of that region. This is used as an index in the page table to get the desired PTE, which in turn contains the physical page number of the desired page. This in turn is combined with the low-order 12 bits of the virtual address, which contain the byte offset in the page, to yield the physical address.

Each page table entry contains the physical page number, protection field, and *valid, referenced,* and *modified* bits (Figure 13-7). The protection field has two bits—one to specify read-only (bit clear) or read-write (bit set) access and another to specify if the page is a user page (bit clear) or supervisor (bit set). When the process is running in kernel mode, all pages are accessible read-write (write protection is ignored). In user mode, supervisor pages are inaccessible regardless of the read-write bit setting, which only applies to user pages. Since both page directory entries as well as page table entries have protection fields, access must be permitted by both entries.

The support for the *referenced* bit simplifies the kernel's task of monitoring page usage. The **CR3** register needs to be reset on each *context switch* so that it points to the page directory of the new process.

The TLB in the *x86* architecture is never directly accessed by the kernel. The entire TLB, however, is flushed automatically whenever the **PDBR** is written to, either explicitly by a move instruction or as an indirect result of a *context switch*. The UNIX kernel flushes the TLB whenever it invalidates a page table entry (for example, when reusing a page).

The *x86* supports four privilege levels or *protection rings,* of which UNIX uses only two. The kernel runs in the innermost ring, which is the most privileged. This allows it to execute privileged instructions (such as those that modify MMU registers) and to access all segments and all pages (user and supervisor). User code runs in the outermost, least privileged ring. It may execute only nonprivileged instructions and access only the user pages in its own segments. The *call gate*

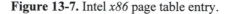

31		12	6 5	2 1 0
PFN			D|A	U|W|P

PFN   Page Frame Number
D   Dirty
A   Accessed (Referenced)
U   User (0) / Supervisor (1)
W   Read (0) / Write (1)
P   Present (valid)

Figure 13-7. Intel *x86* page table entry.

segment allows the user to make system calls. It puts the system into the inner ring and transfers control to a location specified in the call gate, which is under control of the kernel.

13.3.3   The IBM RS/6000

The IBM RS/6000 [Bako 90] is a *reduced instruction set computer* (RISC) machine that runs AIX, IBM's System V-based operating system. Its memory architecture has two interesting features—it uses a single, flat, system address space, and it uses an *inverted page table* for address translation. Hewlett-Packard's PA-RISC [Lee 89] is another system with these features.

The problem with a regular page table, which is indexed by virtual address, is that its size is proportional to that of the virtual address space, which may be extremely large for some processes. Many modern systems allow 64-bit addresses, resulting in even larger address spaces. Consequently, the page tables can become too large for the available physical memory. One solution, adopted by systems such as the Intel *x86*, is to have hierarchical page tables. Even so, for large processes the kernel must support paging of the page tables themselves.

The inverted page table provides another way of bounding the total physical memory required to maintain address translation information. Such a table has one entry for each page in physical memory and maps physical page numbers to virtual addresses. Since physical memory is much smaller than the total virtual memory of all processes in the system, the inverted page table is very compact. The MMU, however, needs to translate virtual addresses, which an inverted table cannot do directly. Hence the system must provide other data structures for virtual to physical address translation, as described in the following paragraphs.

The RS/6000 uses two types of virtual addresses. There is a single, flat, system virtual address space with 52-bit addresses. The total size of this space is 2^{52}, or approximately $4 * 10^{15}$, bytes. Each process uses 32-bit addresses, and the per-process address space maps into parts of the system address space, as shown in Figure 13-8. The virtual and physical page size is 4096 bytes, which is the same as the default disk block size. The 32-bit process virtual address is divided into 3 parts—a 4-bit segment ID, a 16-bit page index, and a 12-bit offset in the page. Thus the address space comprises 16 segments, and each segment is 256 megabytes in size.

The RS/6000 has 16 segment registers, which are loaded with the segment descriptors of the current process. Each segment is assigned a specific role. Segment 1 holds user program text. Segment 2 is the private data segment of the process. It holds the user data, heap, and stack, and the kernel stack and u area of the process. Segments 3–10 are shared segments, used for shared memory and mappings to files (see Section 14.2). Segment 13 holds shared text, such as that loaded from shared memory. The rest of the segments are for kernel use only. They are shared by all processes, but can be accessed only in kernel mode. Segment 0 holds the kernel text, 11 and 12 hold memory management structures, and 14 holds kernel data structures. Segment 15 is reserved for I/O addresses.

Figure 13-9 shows the translation from process to system virtual address. The segment ID identifies the segment register, which is 32 bits in size. It contains a 24-bit segment index, which forms the 24 high-order bits of the system virtual address. This is combined with the 16-bit virtual page index from the process virtual address to form the virtual page number in the system address space. This must be further translated to obtain the physical page number.

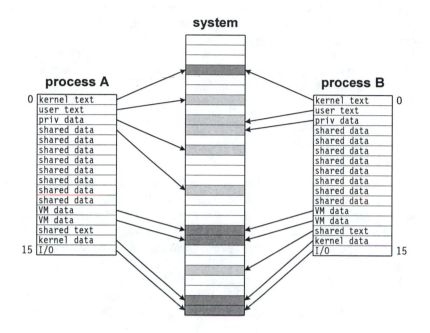

Figure 13-8. RS/6000 address spaces.

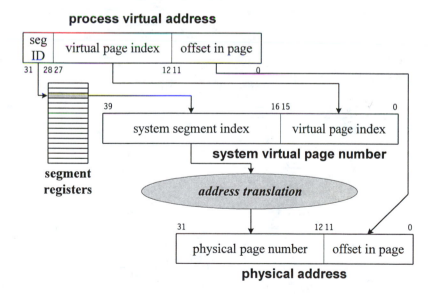

Figure 13-9. RS/6000 address translation—part 1.

As explained earlier, the RS/6000 does not maintain a direct virtual to physical address translation map. Instead, it maintains an inverted page table called the *page frame table (PFT),* with one entry for each physical page. The system uses a hashing technique to translate virtual addresses, as shown in Figure 13-10. A data structure called the *hash anchor table (HAT)* contains information used to convert a system virtual page number to a hash value, which points to a linked list of PFT entries. Each PFT entry contains the following fields:

- The virtual page number to which it maps.
- A pointer to the next entry in the hash chain.
- Flags such as valid, referenced, and modified.
- Protection and locking information.

The RS/6000 uses the HAT to locate the hash chain and traverses the chain till it finds an entry for the desired virtual page number. The index of the entry in the PFT equals the physical page number, which is 20 bits in size. This is combined with the 12-bit page offset from the process virtual address to obtain the physical address.

This translation process is slow and expensive and should not be required for each memory access. The RS/6000 maintains two separate TLBs—a 32-entry instruction TLB and a 128-entry data TLB. In normal operation, these buffers should take care of most address translation, and the hashed lookup is required only when there is a TLB miss. In addition, the RS/6000 has separate data and instruction caches. The data cache is 32 or 64 kilobytes in size, and the instruction cache is 8 or 32 kilobytes, depending on the individual system model [Chak 94]. These caches are virtually ad-

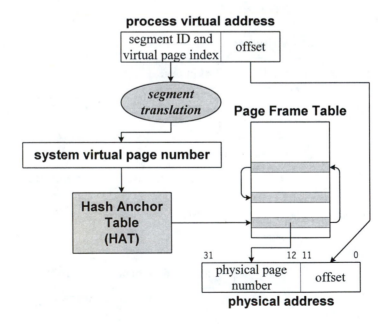

Figure 13-10. RS/6000 address translation—part 2.

dressed; therefore, address translation is not required when there is a cache hit. Virtually addressed caches require kernel involvement to address some consistency problems. These issues are described in Section 15.13.

13.3.4 The MIPS R3000

The MIPS R3000 is a RISC system and has been a platform for SVR4 UNIX as well as Digital Equipment Corporation's ULTRIX (a 4.2BSD-based system). It has an unusual MMU architecture [Kane 88] in that there is no hardware support for page tables. The only address translations performed by the hardware are those defined by the on-chip TLB.

This has far-reaching implications on the division of memory management tasks and the interface between the hardware and the kernel. In the Intel *x86* architecture, for instance, the structure of the TLB entry is opaque to the kernel. The only operations allowed are invalidation of single entries keyed by virtual address or of the entire TLB. In contrast, the MIPS architecture makes the format and contents of the TLB entry public to the kernel and allows operations to read, modify, and load specific entries.

The virtual address space itself is divided into four segments, as shown in Figure 13-11. The *kuseg,* spanning the first two gigabytes, contains the user address space. The other three segments are accessible only in kernel mode. *kseg0* and *kseg1* each map directly to the first 512 megabytes of physical memory, thus requiring no TLB mapping. Of these, *kseg0* uses the data/instruction caches, but *kseg1* does not. The top gigabyte is devoted to *kseg2,* which is the mapped, cacheable kernel segment. Addresses in *kseg2* can be mapped to any physical memory location.

Figure 13-12 describes the MMU registers and the format of the TLB entry. The MIPS page size is fixed at 4 kilobytes; thus the virtual address is divided into a 20-bit virtual page number and a 12-bit offset. The TLB contains 64 entries, and each entry is 64 bits in size. The **entryhi** and **entrylo** registers have the same format as the high and low 32 bits of the TLB entry, respectively, and are used to read and write a TLB entry. The VPN (virtual page number) and PFN (physical frame number) fields allow translation of virtual to physical page numbers. The PID field acts as a tag, associating each TLB entry with a process. This PID, which is 6 bits in size, can take the values 0

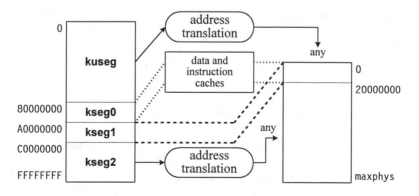

Figure 13-11. MIPS R3000 virtual address space.

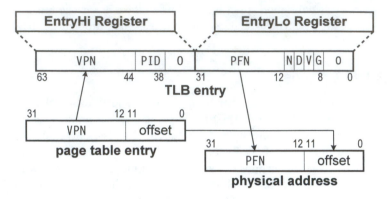

Figure 13-12. MIPS R3000 address translation.

through 63, and is not the same as the traditional process ID. Each process that may have active TLB entries will be assigned a *tlbpid* between 0 and 63. The kernel sets the PID field in the **entryhi** register to the *tlbpid* of the current process. The hardware compares it to the corresponding field in the TLB entries, and rejects translations that do not match. This allows the TLB to contain entries for the same virtual page number belonging to different processes without conflict.

The N *(no-cache)* bit, if set, says that the page should not go through the data or instruction caches. The G *(global)* bit specifies that the PID should be ignored for this page. If the V *(valid)* bit is clear, the entry is invalid, and if the D *(dirty)* bit is clear, the entry is write-protected. Note that there is neither a *referenced* bit nor a *modified* bit.

In translating *kuseg* or *kseg2* addresses, the virtual page number is compared with all TLB entries simultaneously. If a match is found and the G bit is clear, the PID of the entry is compared with the current *tlbpid*, stored in the **entryhi** register. If they are equal (or if the G bit is set) and the V bit is set, the PFN field yields the valid physical page number. If not, a **TLBmiss** exception is raised. For write (store) operations, the D bit must be set, or else a **TLBmod** exception will be raised.

Since the hardware provides no further facilities (such as page table support), these exceptions must be handled by the kernel. The kernel will look at its own mappings, and either locate a valid translation or send a signal to the process. In the former case, it must load a valid TLB entry and restart the faulting instruction. The hardware imposes no requirements on whether the kernel mappings should be page table-based and what the page table entries should look like. In practice, however, UNIX implementations on MIPS use page tables so as to retain the basic memory management design. The format of the **entrylo** register is the natural form of the PTEs, and the eight low-order bits, which are unused by hardware, may be used by the kernel in any way.

The lack of *referenced* and *modified* bits places further demands on the kernel. The kernel must know which pages are modified, since they must be saved before reuse. This is achieved by write-protecting all clean pages (clearing the D bit in their TLBs), so as to force a **TLBmod** exception on the first write to them. The exception handler can then set the D bit in the TLB and set appropriate bits in the software PTE to mark the page as dirty. Reference information must also be collected indirectly, as shown in Section 13.5.3.

This architecture leads to a larger number of page faults, since every TLB miss must be handled by the software. The need to track page modifications and references causes even more page faults. This is offset by the speed gained by a simpler memory architecture, which allows very fast address translation when there is a TLB cache hit. Further, the faster CPU speed helps keep down the cost of the page fault handling. Finally, the unmapped region *kseg0* is used to store the static text and data of the kernel. This increases the speed of execution of kernel code, since address translations are not required. It also reduces contention on the TLB, which is needed only for user addresses and for some dynamically allocated kernel data structures.

13.4   4.3BSD — A Case Study

So far we have described the basic concepts of demand paging, and how hardware characteristics can influence the design. To understand the issues involved more clearly, we use 4.3BSD memory management as a case study. The first UNIX system to support virtual memory was 3BSD. Its memory architecture evolved incrementally over the subsequent releases. 4.3BSD was the last Berkeley release based on this memory model. 4.4BSD adopted a new memory architecture based on Mach; this is described in Section 15.8. [Leff 89] provides a more complete treatment of 4.3BSD memory management. In this chapter, we summarize its important features, evaluate its strengths and drawbacks, and develop the motivation for the more sophisticated approaches described in the following chapters.

Although the target platform for the BSD releases was the VAX-11, it has been successfully ported to several other platforms. The hardware characteristics impact many kernel algorithms, in particular the lower-level functions that manipulate page tables and the translation buffer. Porting BSD memory management has not been easy, since the hardware dependencies permeate through all parts of the system. *As a result, several BSD-based implementations emulate the VAX memory architecture in software, including its address space layout and its page table entry format.* We avoid a detailed description of the VAX memory architecture, since the machine is now obsolete. Instead, we describe some of its important features as part of the BSD description.

4.3BSD uses a small number of fundamental data structures—the *core map* describes physical memory, the *page tables* describe virtual memory, and the *disk maps* describe the swap areas. There are also resource maps to manage allocation of resources such as page tables and swap space. Finally, some important information is stored in the proc structure and u area of each process.

13.4.1   Physical Memory

Physical memory can be viewed as a linear array of bytes ranging from 0 to *n*, where *n* is the total amount of memory on the system. It is logically divided into pages, with the page size dependent on the machine architecture. This memory can be divided into three sections, as shown in Figure 13-13. At the low end is the *nonpaged pool,* which contains the kernel code and the portion of the kernel data that can be allocated either statically or at boot time. Since a kernel page fault can block a process in the kernel at an inconvenient point, most UNIX implementations require all kernel pages to

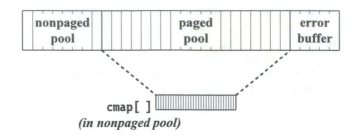

Figure 13-13. Layout of physical memory.

be nonpageable. The very high end of physical memory is reserved for error messages generated during a system crash. In between these two regions is the *paged pool,* which occupies the bulk of physical memory. It contains all the pages belonging to user processes, as well as dynamically allocated kernel pages. The latter are marked nonpageable, even though they are part of the paged pool.

These physical pages are called page frames, and the frame holds the contents of a process page. The page stored in the frame can be replaced at any time by a different page, and thus we need to maintain information about the contents of each frame. This is done using a *core map,* which is an array of struct cmap entries, one entry for each frame in the paged pool.[5] The core map itself is a kernel data structure, allocated at boot time and resident in the nonpaged pool. The core map entry contains the following information about the frame:

- **Name** — The *name* or identity of the page stored in the frame. The name space for a process page is described by the owner process ID, the type (data or stack), and the virtual page number of the page in that region. Text pages may be shared by several processes, and thus their owner is the text structure for that program. The core map entry stores the index into the process table or the text table. The name *<type, owner, virtual page number>* allows the kernel to perform reverse address translation, that is, to locate the PTE corresponding to the page frame, as seen in Figure 13-14.

- **Free list** — Forward and backward pointers to link free pages onto a free list. This list is maintained in *approximate least recently used* order (Section 13.5.3) and is used by the memory allocation routines to allocate and free physical memory.

- **Text page cache** — The name of a page is meaningful only as long as the owner process is alive. This is okay for data and stack pages, because such pages are garbage once the process exits. In case of a text page, however, there is a chance that another process may soon try to rerun the same program. If this happens and some of the text pages are still resident in memory, it makes sense to reuse them instead of reading them afresh from disk. To identify such pages even after their owner(s) have terminated, the core map entry stores the disk locations (device and block number) of text pages. Such pages are also

---

[5] Actually, there is one cmap entry for each cluster of frames. Clusters provide the notion of a logical page composed of a (fixed) number of physical pages. This enhances performance by increasing the granularity of several operations and reducing the size of data structures such as the core map.

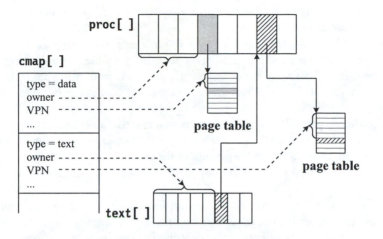

Figure 13-14. Physical to virtual address translation.

hashed onto a set of hash queues (based on device and block number) for quick retrieval. The disk location may either identify the page in the executable file or on the swap device.

- **Synchronization** — A set of flags synchronizes access to the page. The page is locked while moving it to or from the disk.

13.4.2   The Address Space

BSD virtual memory uses the VAX-11 address space model. The VAX-11 is a 32-bit machine with a 512-byte page size. Its 4-gigabyte address space is divided into four regions of equal size. The first gigabyte is the **P0** (program) region, which contains the text and data sections of the process. This is followed by the **P1** (control) region, which contains the user stack, the u area, and the kernel stack. Next is the **S0** (system) region, which contains the kernel text and data. The fourth region is reserved and not supported by current VAX hardware. This scheme allows for easy growth of each region, without arbitrary gaps in the address space.

The VAX hardware supports page tables and uses them directly for virtual address translation. The page tables serve multiple purposes. The kernel uses them to describe the address space of a process (the proc structure holds a summary description, including the location and size of the page tables), as well as to store information about how the pages must be initialized (see Section 13.4.3). To do so, the kernel manipulates those bits in the PTE that are not used by the hardware.

There is a single *system page table* that maps the kernel text and data, and each process has two page tables to map its **P0** (text and data) and **P1** (user stack, u area, etc.) regions. The system page table is contiguous in physical memory. Each user page table is contiguous in system virtual memory and is mapped by a set of contiguous PTEs in the *Userptmap* section of the system page table. The kernel uses a resource map, composed of a set of *<base, size>* pairs, to describe the free portions of *Userptmap*. Allocation from this map is done on a first-fit basis. Under heavy load, this map may become too fragmented, and a process may not find enough contiguous PTEs to map its page tables. In such a case, the kernel invokes the *swapper* to swap out a process in an attempt to free up space in *Userptmap* (see Section 0).

Can page tables be shared? In particular, if two processes are running the same program, can they share the page table for the text region? This is generally possible, and many variants of UNIX allow such sharing. BSD UNIX, however, has subtle problems with this approach. Each process must have a single page table for the **P0** region, which must be contiguous in system virtual address space and, hence, be described by a contiguous set of *system PTEs* in *Userptmap*. Since the data region is not shared, only a part of the **P0** page table is sharable. Because each process has its own set of *Userptmap* entries, the PTEs for the page table pages for the text region must point to the same set of pages. This in turn means that the beginning of the data region page table must start on a new page and be described by a new PTE in *Userptmap*. This requires the data region to be aligned on a 64K boundary.

Such a requirement would have resulted in an incompatible, user-visible change. To avoid that, BSD requires each process to have its own text page table. If multiple processes share a text region, their text page table entries need to be kept in sync. For example, if one of the processes brings a page into memory, that change must be propagated to the PTE for that page in all processes sharing that region. Figure 13-15 shows how the kernel locates all the page tables mapping a particular text region.

13.4.3   Where Is the Page?

At any time, a particular page of a process may be in one of the following states:

- **Resident** — The page is in physical memory, and the page table entry contains its physical page frame number.
- **Fill-on-demand** — The page has not yet been referenced by the process and must be brought into memory when first accessed. There are two types of fill-on-demand pages:

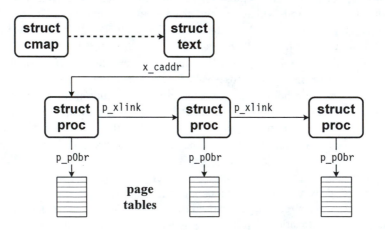

Figure 13-15. Multiple mappings for a text page.

- ■ **Fill-from-text** — Text and initialized data pages are read in from the executable file upon first access.
- ■ **Zero-fill** — Uninitialized data, heap, and stack pages are created and filled with zeros when required.

- • **Outswapped** — These are pages that have once been read into memory and subsequently paged out to make room for other pages. These pages may be recovered from their swap area locations.

The kernel must maintain sufficient information about all nonresident pages, so that it can bring them in when needed. For swapped out pages, it must store their locations on the swap device. For zero-fill pages, the kernel only needs to recognize them as such. For fill-from-text pages, it must determine their location in the filesystem. This can be done by the file system routines that read the disk block array in the inode. That, however, is inefficient, since it frequently requires accessing other disk blocks (indirect blocks) to locate the page.

A better approach is to store all such translations in memory management data structures when the program is initially invoked. This allows a single pass through the block array in the inode and the indirect blocks to locate all the text and initialized data pages. This could be done using a second table that maps all the nonresident pages. The *disk block descriptor table* in SVR3 UNIX provides this functionality. This solution, however, involves significant memory overhead, requiring an additional table essentially the same size as the page table.

The 4.3BSD solution relies on the fact that, except for the *protection* and *valid* bits, the rest of the fields in the page table entry are not examined by the hardware unless the *valid* bit is set. Since all nonresident pages have the *valid* bit clear, those fields can be replaced by other information that tracks these pages. Figure 13-16(a) shows the hardware-defined format of the VAX-11

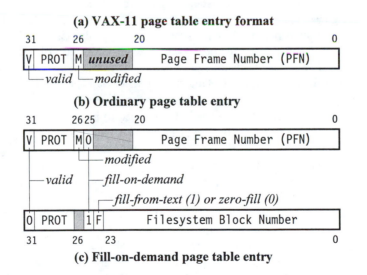

Figure 13-16. 4.3BSD page table entry format.

page table entry. 4.3BSD uses bit 25, which is not used by the hardware, to define fill-on-demand entries, described as follows.

For ordinary page table entries (Figure 13-16(b)), the fill-on-demand bit is clear. When the bit is set, it indicates that the page is a fill-on-demand page (*valid* bit must be clear) and that the page table entry is a special, fill-on-demand entry with a different set of fields (Figure 13-16(c)). Instead of the *page frame number* and the *modified* bit, such an entry stores a *filesystem block number* and a bit specifying if the page is fill-from-text (bit set) or zero-fill (bit clear). For a fill-from-text page, the device number is obtained from the text structure for that program.

The treatment of outswapped pages is different. The PTEs for such pages have the *valid* and *fill-on-demand* bits clear and the *page frame number* set to zero. The kernel maintains separate *swap maps* to locate these pages on the swap device, as explained in Section 13.4.4.

13.4.4   Swap Space

Swap space is required for two reasons. First, if we need to swap out an entire process, all its pages must be saved to disk. Second, individual pages of a process may need to be removed from main memory, and we need a place to save them. One or more logical disks, or partitions, are reserved for this use. These partitions are *raw,* that is, they do not contain a filesystem. 4BSD allows swap partitions on multiple disks, in order to improve paging performance. These partitions are logically interleaved to act as a single swap partition. This balances the swapping load evenly on all partitions. The location of a page in swap space is specified by a pseudodevice number representing the logical swap partition and the offset on that device. This is converted internally to the appropriate physical partition and the offset in that partition.

Strictly speaking, swap space needs to be allocated only for pages that need to be paged out. Such an aggressive policy can result in *memory overcommit,* causing a process to run out of swap space at an arbitrary point in time. If, for instance, that were to happen during normal program execution, it might hang or terminate the program unexpectedly. To avoid that, 4.3BSD enforces a very conservative swap allocation policy. When a process starts up, the kernel allocates all the swap space necessary for its data and stack regions. Swap space is allocated in large chunks, so there is room for some expansion, but if the regions grow larger than that, more swap space must be allocated before allowing the region to grow. This ensures that swap space exhaustion only occurs at well-defined points, when a region is being created or expanded.

Text pages (and unmodified data pages) do not need to be swapped out, since they can be retrieved from the executable file. This is a problem in the BSD implementation, since the location of the block in the file is stored in the *fill-on-demand PTE*. Once the page is brought into memory, that information is overwritten by the *page frame number*. As a result, retrieving the page from the file involves recomputing its location and, perhaps, accessing one or more indirect blocks. This is prohibitively expensive, and to avoid that, such pages are saved on swap as well. If multiple processes are running the same program, only a single copy of the text region needs to be on swap. Since the text region is fixed in size, swap space for it can be allocated in one contiguous chunk. This allows several adjacent pages to be read together in a single disk operation.

The kernel records swap space allocation in per-region dmap structures. The first chunk allocated to a region is of size dmmin (typically 16 kilobytes). Each subsequent chunk is twice the size

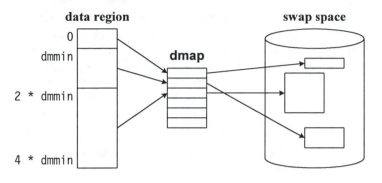

Figure 13-17. Recording swap space in a `dmap`.

of the previous one, until the size reaches dmmax (typically 0.5 to 2 megabytes). Thereafter, all chunks are of size dmmax. The dmap structure (Figure 13-17) is an array of fixed size, with each element of the array containing the start address of that chunk on the swap device. The index of that element (along with dmmin and dmmax) translates into the size of the chunk. The (fixed) size of the dmap array places a hard limit on the maximum permissible size of the data or stack region. The u area holds the maps for the data and stack regions. The text region is mapped differently, since its size is fixed. Regardless of the number of processes sharing it, only one copy of the text needs to be saved on disk, and hence the swap map is part of the text structure. Allocation is done in chunks of fixed size dmtext (usually 512 kilobytes); the last chunk may be only partially full.

13.5   4.3BSD Memory Management Operations

Let us now examine the algorithms for some of the important memory management operations in 4.3BSD—process creation, page fault handling, page replacement, and swapping.

13.5.1   Process Creation

The *fork* system call creates a new (child) process, whose address space is a duplicate of that of the parent. This involves several memory management operations:

- **Swap space** — The first step is to allocate swap space for the data and stack regions of the child. The amount of swap space given to the child equals that held by the parent at this time. If swap allocation fails, *fork* returns an error.
- **Page tables** — The kernel must first allocate contiguous PTEs in *Userptmap* to map the page tables for this process. If this fails, the system resorts to swapping another process out in order to free up room in *Userptmap*. The system PTEs are initialized by allocating physical pages from the memory free list.
- **U area** — A new u area is allocated and initialized by copying the u area of the parent. In order to directly access fields in the child's u area, the kernel maps it to a special map in system space called Forkmap.

- **Text region** — The child is added to the list of processes sharing the text structure used by the parent, and the page table entries for the text region are copied from the parent.
- **Data and stack** — Data and stack must be copied one page at a time. For pages that are still fill-on-demand, only the PTEs need to be copied. The rest of the pages are duplicated by allocating physical memory for them and copying the pages from the parent. If the page in the parent's space has been swapped out, it must be read in from swap and then copied. The child's PTEs are set to point to the new copies of these pages. All newly copied pages are marked modified, so that they will be saved to swap before reuse.

The *fork* operation is expensive, largely due to all the copying involved in the last step. Copying all the entire data and stack regions seems wasteful, considering that most processes will either exit or call *exec* to invoke a new program soon after *fork*ing, thus discarding the whole address space.

There have been two major approaches to reduce this overhead. The first is called *copy-on-write,* which was adopted by System V UNIX. Here, the child and parent refer to a single copy of the data and stack pages, whose protections are changed to read-only. If either tries to modify any of the pages, we get a protection fault. The fault handler recognizes the situation and makes a new copy of that page, changes the protections back to read-write, and updates the PTEs in the parent and the child. This way, only those pages modified by either the parent or child need to be copied, reducing the cost of process creation.

Implementing copy-on-write requires reference counts maintained on a per-page basis, which was one of the reasons it was not adopted by BSD UNIX. Instead, BSD provides an alternate system call named *vfork* (virtual fork), which addresses the problem in a different way.

vfork is used when the *fork* is expected to be soon followed by an *exit* or *exec*. Instead of duplicating the address space, the parent passes its own space to the child and then sleeps until the child *execs* or *exits*. When that happens, the kernel wakes up the parent, who recaptures the space from the child. The only resources created for the child are the u area and the proc structure. The passing of the address space is accomplished by simply copying the page table registers from the parent to the child. Not even the page tables need to be copied. Only the PTEs mapping the u area need to be changed.

vfork is extremely lightweight and a lot faster than copy-on-write. Its drawback is that it allows the child to modify the contents or size of the parent's address space. The burden lies on the programmer to ensure that *vfork* is properly used.

13.5.2   Page Fault Handling

There are two types of page faults—validation and protection. Validation faults occur either if there is no PTE for that page *(bounds error)* or if the PTE is marked invalid. Protection faults occur if the type of access desired is not permitted by the protections on the page. If a user tries to access a page for which the PTE is both invalid and protected, a protection fault will occur. (It makes no sense to service the validation fault if the attempted access was to be disallowed anyway.)

For both faults, the system saves enough state required to restart the instruction and then passes control to a fault handling routine in the kernel. For a bounds error, the process is usually terminated by a signal, unless the error was due to user stack overflow. In that case, the kernel calls a routine to grow the stack automatically. Protection errors likewise result in a signal to the process; systems implementing copy-on-write must check for that scenario, and handle such protection faults by making a new writable copy of that page. For all other cases, a routine called `pagein()` is called to handle the fault.

    `pagein()` is passed the faulting virtual address, from which it obtains the PTE. If the page is resident (the PTE is not fill-on-demand, and the page frame number is not zero), the `cmap` entry for that page is also obtained. Together, these contain information about the state of the page and govern the actions of `pagein()`. Figure 13-18 shows the basic `pagein()` algorithm. There are seven different scenarios:

1.   The PTE may have simply been marked invalid for *referenced* bit simulation, as explained in Section 13.5.3. This is the case when the page is resident, and the `cmap` entry is not marked free. `pagein()` simply sets the *valid* bit and returns.

2.   The page is resident and on the free list. This is similar to case 1, except that the `cmap` entry is marked free. `pagein()` resets the *valid* bit and removes the `cmap` entry from the free list.

3.   For a text page, another process could have started a read on the page. This happens if two processes sharing a text region fault on the same page around the same time. The second process finds that the page frame number is nonzero, but the core map entry is marked *locked* and *in-transit*. `pagein()` will set the *wanted* flag and block the second process, which will sleep on the address (see Section 7.2.3) of the text structure for this page. When the first process unlocks the page after it has been read in, it will wake up the second process. Because the second process may not run immediately after being awakened, it cannot assume the page is still in memory and must begin the search all over again.

4.   Text pages could be in memory even though the PTE does not have a page frame number for them. This would happen if they were left behind by another process that terminated a short while back. Such pages can be located by searching the appropriate hash queue using the *<device, block number>* pair as a key. If found, the page can be removed from the free list and reused.

In the remaining cases, the page is not in memory. After determining its location, `pagein()` must first allocate a page from the free page list and then read in the page as follows:

5.   The page is on the swap device. The *fill-on-demand* bit is clear, the page frame number is zero, and case 4 does not apply. The swap maps are consulted to locate the page on swap, and the page is read in from the swap device.

6.   Zero-fill pages are handled by filling the newly allocated page with zeroes.

7.   The page is fill-from-text and was not found on the hash queue (case 4). It is read in from the executable file. This read occurs directly from the file to the physical page, bypassing the buffer cache. This may cause a consistency problem if the disk copy of the page is obsolete. Hence the kernel searches the buffer cache for this page, and if found, flushes the cache copy to disk before reading it in to the process page. This solution requires two disk copy operations and is inefficient, but was retained for historical reasons. It would be better to copy directly from the buffer cache if the page was found there.

    In cases 5 and 6, the new page is marked as modified, so it will be saved on swap before reuse.

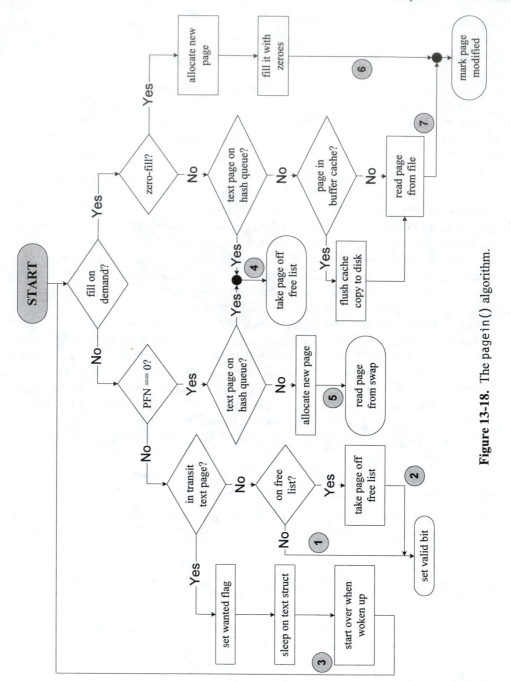

Figure 13-18. The pagein() algorithm.

13.5.3   The Free Page List

Frequently, the kernel must bring a new page into memory. Once memory is full, this requires displacing a page that is currently in memory. 4.3BSD uses a global replacement policy to choose the pages to remove.

Obviously, the best candidates for reuse are pages that will never be needed again, such as data and stack pages of terminated processes. Such pages should always be used ahead of potentially useful pages. If no such pages can be found, the principle of locality suggests that pages should be reclaimed in LRU order. Recently used pages are more likely to be needed soon, compared to those that have not been used for a while.

Given these criteria, it is impractical to search for a proper candidate at the time we need the page. It is far better to maintain a list of reusable pages and take pages from this list whenever needed. The list should be kept well populated at all times and should be ordered in such a way that the head of the list contains the best candidates. Ideally, we want to keep all garbage pages at the head of this free list, followed by some useful pages in LRU order. The BSD kernel maintains such a list, and the system parameters minfree and maxfree determine the minimum and maximum desired size of this list. The current size of this list is described by the variable freemem.

There is a practical problem with maintaining strict LRU ordering. It requires the list to be reordered on each reference to a page, which could happen on each instruction that accesses a user address. This would be prohibitively expensive, and 4.3BSD chooses an effective compromise. It replaces the *least recently used* policy by a *not recently used* policy [Baba 81]. A page is eligible to be freed if it has not been recently referenced.

Such a policy can be implemented by making two passes over each page, a certain time apart. The first pass turns off the *referenced* bit for the PTE of that page. The second pass checks the *referenced* bit, and if it is still off, the page is eligible to be freed, since it has not been referenced in the time between the two passes. The algorithm used is called the *two-handed clock*. The cmap table is treated as a circular (wraparound) table and two pointers (hands) are maintained a fixed distance (number of cmap entries) apart (see Figure 13-19). These pointers advance together. The front hand turns off the *referenced* bit, and the back hand checks this bit. If the bit is still off, the page has not been referenced since the front hand set the bit and hence is eligible to be freed. If this page is dirty, it must be saved on swap before freeing.

Some architectures, such as the VAX-11 and the MIPS R3000, do not support a *referenced* bit in the hardware. This can be overcome by simulating the *referenced* bit in software. To do this, the front hand turns off the *valid* bit in the PTE, forcing a page fault if the page is referenced. The page fault handler recognizes the situation (case 1 in the previous section) and simply sets the *valid* bit back. Thus, if the back hand finds the *valid* bit is off, it means that the page has not been referenced in the interim and is a candidate to be freed. This does have an overhead in that extra page faults are generated simply to track this reference information.

A separate process called the *pagedaemon* (always process 2) is responsible for page replacement. This allows pages to be written out to swap without blocking an innocent process. Further, since the *pagedaemon* is writing out pages belonging to other processes, it must first map those pages into its own address space. Pages are written directly to swap, without going through the buffer cache, using a special set of swap buffer headers. The writes are performed asynchronously,

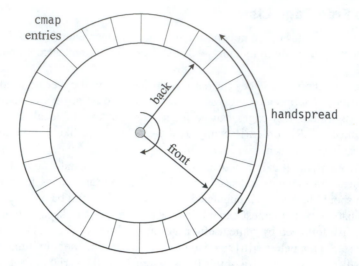

Figure 13-19. The two-handed clock.

so the *pagedaemon* can continue to examine other pages in the meantime. When the writes complete, the completion routine puts these pages onto a cleaned list, from which they are returned to the free memory list by a routine called cleanup().

13.5.4 Swapping

Although the paging system works admirably most of the time, it can break down under heavy load. The major problem, called *thrashing*, occurs when there is not enough memory to contain the working sets of the active processes. This may happen because there are too many active processes or because their access patterns are too random (and hence their working sets are too large). This results in a sharp increase in the page fault rate. When the pages are faulted in, they replace other pages that were part of the working set of an active process, which escalates the problem further. The situation can worsen until the system is spending most of its time in page fault handling, and the processes can make little progress.

This problem may be addressed by reducing the number of active processes, thus controlling the system load. Processes that are "deactivated" may not be scheduled to run. It then makes sense to free up as much of the memory used by such processes as possible, if necessary, by copying data to the swap space. This operation is known as swapping the process out. When the load on the system reduces, the process may be swapped back in.

A special process called the *swapper* monitors the system load, and swaps processes in and out when needed. During system initialization, the kernel creates a process with PID 0, which finally calls sched(), the central function of the *swapper*. Process 0 thus becomes the *swapper*. It sleeps most of the time, but wakes up periodically to check the system state and takes further action if required. The *swapper* will swap out a process in the following cases:

- **Userptmap fragmentation** — A process may be unable to allocate contiguous PTEs in *Userptmap* to map its page tables, if the *Userptmap* is too full or too fragmented. This may occur during *fork, exec,* or region growth. In such a case, the *swapper* will swap out an existing process to try to make room in *Userptmap*.

- **Memory shortfall** — The variable freemem stores the number of clusters on the free list. When freemem remains below desired limits for a period of time, it is an indication of paging system overload, and the *swapper* is invoked.

- **Inactive processes** — If a process has been inactive for a long time (more than 20 seconds), it is likely to remain inactive and may be swapped out. For example, a user may have gone home without logging off, leaving an inactive shell process. Although its resident pages will eventually be swapped out anyway, swapping the whole process out frees up other important resources, such as *Userptmap* entries.

How does the *swapper* choose the process to swap out? The ideal candidate is a process that has been sleeping for more than 20 seconds. Otherwise, the *swapper* selects the four largest processes, and of these, swaps out the one that has been resident in memory the longest. The other three will be swapped out in turn if we still need more memory.

The *swapper* must perform the following tasks when swapping out a process:

1. Allocate swap space for the u area, kernel stack, and page tables.
2. Detach the process from its text region. If no other process is sharing this region, the text must be swapped out as well.
3. Save the resident data and stack pages on swap, then the page tables, and finally the u area and kernel stack.
4. Release the system PTEs in *Userptmap* that map the page tables for this process.
5. Record the swap location of the u area in the proc structure.

When one or more processes are swapped out, the *swapper* periodically checks if it is possible to bring them back in. This depends on there being enough free memory and enough room in *Userptmap*. If several processes have been swapped out, the *swapper* assigns them a *swapin priority* based on their size, *nice value* (see Section 5.4.1), how long they have been swapped out, and for how long they had been asleep. The process with the highest *swapin priority* is chosen to be swapped in.

The swapin procedure is basically the reverse of swapout. The process is attached to the text region and PTEs are allocated in *Userptmap* to map its page tables. Physical memory is allocated for the u area, kernel stack, and page tables, which are then read in from swap. The swap allocation for these regions is released. The process is then marked runnable and put on the scheduler queue. The data and stack pages will be paged in as required when the process runs.

13.6   Analysis

The BSD memory management design provides powerful functionality using a small number of primitives. The only hardware requirement is demand-paging support (since segmentation is not used). There are, however, several important shortcomings and drawbacks to keep in mind:

- There is no support for execution of remote programs (across a network). This is because there is no support in the vanilla BSD file system for accessing remote files. If the file system provides this facility, the extensions to the memory subsystem are simple.
- There is no support for sharing of memory, other than read-only sharing of the text region. In particular, there is no equivalent of the System V shared memory facility.
- *vfork* is not a true substitute for *fork,* and the lack of copy-on-write hurts the performance of applications that rely extensively on *fork.* In particular, *daemons* and other server applications that *fork* a child process for each incoming request are heavily impacted.
- Each process must have its own copy of the page table for a shared text region. This not only wastes space, but also requires keeping these page tables synchronous by migrating changes made by one process to the corresponding PTEs of other processes sharing the text.
- There is no support for memory-mapped files. Section 14.2 discusses this facility in detail.
- There is no support for shared libraries.
- There is a problem with debugging a program that is being run by multiple processes. If the debugger deposits a breakpoint in the program, it modifies the corresponding text page. This modification is seen by all processes running this program, which can have unexpected results. To avoid that, the system disallows putting breakpoints in a shared text and disallows new processes from running a program that is being debugged. These solutions are obviously unsatisfactory.
- The BSD implementation reserves enough swap space in advance to page out every single page in the process address space. Such a policy ensures that a process can run out of swap space only when it tries to grow (or in *fork* or *exec*) and not arbitrarily in the middle of execution. This conservative approach requires a large amount of swap space on the system. From another perspective, the swap space on the system limits the size of the programs you can run.
- There is no support for using swap space on remote nodes, which is required for facilities such as diskless operation.
- The design is heavily influenced by and optimized for the VAX architecture. This makes it less suitable for the wide range of machines to which UNIX has been ported. Further, the machine dependencies are scattered all over the code, making the porting effort even greater.
- The code is not modular, so it is difficult to add features and change individual components or policies. For example, storing the filesystem block number in invalid (fill-on-demand) PTEs prevents a clean separation of the address translation and the page fetch tasks.

Despite these shortcomings, the 4.3BSD design provides a sound foundation for the modern memory architectures—such as those of SVR4, 4.4BSD, and Mach—described in the following chapters. These architectures have retained many of the BSD methods, but they have changed the underlying design in order to provide more functionality and address many of the limitations of the BSD approach.

The 4.3BSD architecture was sensible for the systems available in the 1980s, which typically had slow CPUs and small memories, but relatively large disks. Hence the algorithms were optimized to reduce memory consumption at the cost of doing extra I/O. In the 1990s, typical desktop systems have large memories and fast processors, but relatively small disks. Most user files reside on dedicated file servers. The 4.3BSD memory management model is not suitable for such systems. 4.4BSD introduced a new memory architecture based on that of Mach. This is described in Section 15.8.

13.7   Exercises

1. Which of the objectives listed in Section 13.2.1 can be met by a system that used swapping as the only memory management mechanism?
2. What are the advantages of demand paging compared with segmentation?
3. Why do UNIX systems use anticipatory paging? What are its drawbacks?
4. What are the benefits and drawbacks of copying text pages to the swap area?
5. Suppose an executable program resides on a remote node. Would it be better to copy the entire image to the local swap area before executing it?
6. The hardware and the operating system cooperate to translate virtual addresses. How is the responsibility divided? Explore how the answer to this question varies for the three architectures described in Section 13.3.
7. What are the benefits and drawbacks of a global page replacement policy as compared with a local policy?
8. What steps can a programmer take to minimize the working set of an application?
9. What are the advantages of inverted page tables?
10. Why does the MIPS 3000 cause a large number of spurious page faults? What are the advantages of this architecture that offset the cost of processing these additional faults?
11. Suppose a 4.3BSD process faults on a page that is both nonresident and protected (does not permit the type of access desired). Which case should the fault handler check for first? What should the handler do?
12. Why does the core map manage only the pages in the paged pool?
13. What do we mean by the *name* of a page? Does a page have just one name? What are the different name spaces for pages in 4.3BSD?
14. What is the minimum amount of swap space a 4.3BSD system must have? What is the advantage of having an extremely large swap area?
15. What are the factors that limit the maximum amount of virtual address space a process may have? Why, if at all, is it important for a process to be thrifty in its use of virtual memory?
16. Is it better to distribute the swap space over multiple physical disks? Why or why not?
17. Why is a pure LRU policy unsuitable for page replacement?
18. Early BSD releases [Baba 81, Leff 89] used a one-handed clock algorithm, which turned off *referenced* bits in the first pass, and swapped out pages whose *referenced* bits were still off in the second pass. Why is this algorithm inferior to the two-handed clock?

13.8   References

[Baba 79]   Babaoglu, O., Joy, W.N., and Porcar, J., "Design and Implementation of the
               Berkeley Virtual Memory Extensions to the UNIX Operating System," *Technical
               Report,* CS Division, EECS Department, University of California, Berkeley, CA,
               Dec. 1979.

[Baba 81]   Babaoglu, O., and Joy, W.N., "Converting a Swap-Based System to Do Paging in an
               Architecture Lacking Page-Referenced Bits," *Proceedings of the Eighth ACM
               Symposium on Operating Systems Principles,* Dec. 1981, pp. 78–86.

[Bach 86]   Bach, M.J., *The Design of the UNIX Operating System,* Prentice-Hall, Englewood
               Cliffs, NJ, 1986.

[Bako 90]   Bakoglu, H.B., Grohoski, G.F., and Montoye, R.K., "The IBM RISC System/6000
               Processor: Hardware Overview," *IBM Journal of Research and Development,* Vol.
               34, Jan. 1990.

[Bela 66]   Belady, L.A., "A Study of Replacement Algorithms for Virtual Storage Systems,"
               IBM Systems Journal, Vol. 5, No. 2, 1966, pp. 78–101.

[Chak 94]   Chakravarty, D., *Power RISC System/6000—Concepts, Facilities, and Architecture,*
               McGraw-Hill, 1994.

[Coll 91]   Collinson, P., "Virtual Memory," *SunExpert Magazine,* Apr. 1991, pp. 28–34.

[DEC 80]   Digital Equipment Corporation, *VAX Architecture Handbook,* Digital Press, 1980.

[Denn 70]   Denning, P.J., "Virtual Memory," *Computing Surveys,* Vol. 2, No. 3, Sep. 1970, pp.
               153–189.

[Intel 86]   Intel Corporation, *80386 Programmer's Reference Manual,* 1986.

[Kane 88]   Kane, G., *Mips RISC Architecture,* Prentice-Hall, Englewood Cliffs, NJ, 1988.

[Lee 89]   Lee, R.B., "Precision Architecture," *IEEE Computer,* Vol. 21, No. 1, Jan. 1989, pp.
               78–91.

[Leff 89]   Leffler, S.J., McKusick, M.K., Karels, M.J., and Quarterman, J.S., *The Design and
               Implementation of the 4.3 BSD UNIX Operating System,* Addison-Wesley, Reading,
               MA, 1989.

[Robb 87]   Robboy, D., "A UNIX Port to the 80386," *UNIX Papers for UNIX Developers and
               Power Users,* The Waite Group, 1987, pp. 400–426.

[SPARC 91]   SPARC International, *SPARC Architecture Manual Version 8,* 1991.

14

The SVR4 VM Architecture

14.1 Motivation

In SunOS 4.0, Sun Microsystems introduced a memory management architecture called *VM* (for Virtual Memory). The previous versions of SunOS were based on the BSD memory management model, which had all the limitations described in the previous chapter. In particular, SunOS wished to provide support for memory sharing, shared libraries, and memory-mapped files, which was not possible without major changes to the BSD design. Moreover, since SunOS ran on several different hardware platforms (Motorola 680x0, Intel 386 and Sun's own SPARC systems), it needed a highly portable memory architecture. The VM architecture became very successful. Later, when a joint team of engineers from AT&T and Sun Microsystems set out to design SVR4 UNIX, they based the SVR4 memory management on this design, rather than on the *regions* architecture that existed in SVR3.

The concept of *file mapping* is central to the VM architecture. The term file mapping is used to describe two different but related ideas. At one level, file mapping provides a useful facility to users, allowing them to map part of their address space to a file and then use simple memory access instructions to read and write the file. It can also be used as a fundamental organizational scheme in the kernel, which may view the entire address space simply as a collection of mappings to different objects such as files. The SVR4 architecture incorporates both aspects of file mapping.[1] Before

---

[1] These two ideas are independent. HP-UX 9.*x*, for instance, has user-level file mapping while retaining the traditional kernel organization. AIX 3.1, in contrast, uses file mapping as its fundamental I/O strategy, but does not export it to the user level (no *mmap* system call).

moving to the VM design itself, we discuss the notion of memory-mapped files and why it is useful and important.

14.2   Memory-Mapped Files

The traditional way of accessing files in UNIX is to first open them with the *open* system call and then use *read, write,* and *lseek* calls to do sequential or random I/O. This method is inefficient, as it requires one system call (two for random access) for each I/O operation. Moreover, if several processes are accessing the same file, each maintains copies of the file data in its own address space, needlessly wasting memory. Figure 14-1 depicts a situation where two processes read the same page of a file. This requires one disk read to bring the page into the buffer cache and one in-memory copy operation for each process to copy the data from the buffer to its address space. Furthermore, there are three copies of this page in memory—one in the buffer cache, plus one in the address space of each process. Finally, each process needs to make one *read* system call, as well as an *lseek* if the access was random.

Now consider an alternative approach, where the processes map the page into their address space (Figure 14-2). The kernel creates this mapping simply by updating some memory management data structures. When process **A** tries to access the data in this page, it generates a page fault. The kernel resolves it by reading the page into memory and updating the page table to point to it. Subsequently, when process **B** faults on the page, the page is already in memory, and the kernel merely changes **B**'s page table entry to point to it.

This illustrates the considerable benefits of accessing files by mapping them into memory. The total cost for the two reads is one disk access. After the mappings are set up, no further system calls are necessary to read or write the data. Only one copy of the page is in memory, thus saving two pages of physical memory and two in-memory copy operations. Reducing the demands on physical memory yields further benefits by reducing paging operations.

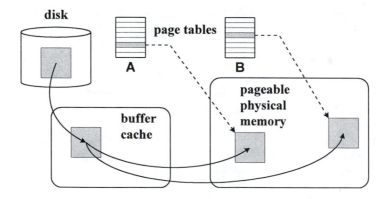

Figure 14-1. Two processes read the same page in traditional UNIX.

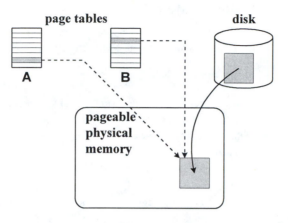

Figure 14-2. Two processes map the same page into their address space.

What happens when a process writes to a mapped page? A process may establish two types of mappings to files—*shared* and *private*. For a shared mapping, modifications are made to the mapped object itself. The kernel applies all changes directly to this shared copy of the page and writes them back to the file on disk when the page is flushed. If a mapping is private, any modification results in making a private copy of the page, to which the changes are applied. Such writes do not modify the underlying object; that is, the kernel does not write back the changes to the file when flushing the page.

It is important to note that private mappings do not protect against changes made by others who have shared mappings to the file. A process receives its private copy of a page only when it attempts to modify it. It therefore sees all modifications made by other processes between the time it establishes the mapping and the time it tries to write to the page.

Memory-mapped file I/O is a powerful mechanism that allows efficient file access. It cannot, however, fully replace the traditional *read* and *write* system calls. One major difference is the atomicity of the I/O. A *read* or *write* system call locks the inode during the data transfer, guaranteeing that the operation is atomic. Memory-mapped files are accessed by ordinary program instructions, so at most one word will be read or written atomically. Such access is not governed by traditional file locking semantics, and synchronization is entirely the responsibility of the cooperating processes.

Another important difference is the visibility of changes. If several processes have shared mappings to a file, changes made by one are immediately visible to all others. This is starkly different from the traditional model, where the other processes must issue another *read* to see these changes. With mapped access, a process sees the contents of a page as they are at the time of access, not at the time the mapping was created.

These issues, however, relate more to an application's decision to use mapped access to files. They do not detract from the merits and desirability of this mechanism. In fact, 4.3 BSD specified an interface for the *mmap* system call to perform file mapping, but did not provide an implementation. The next section describes the semantics of the *mmap* interface.

14.2.1 *mmap* and Related System Calls

To map a file into memory, it must first be opened using the traditional *open* system call. This is followed by a call to *mmap* [UNIX 92], which has the following syntax:

```
paddr = mmap (addr, len, prot, flags, fd, offset);
```

This establishes a mapping between the byte range[2] [offset, offset+len) in the file represented by fd, and the address range [paddr, paddr+len) in the calling process. The flags include the mapping, which may be MAP_SHARED or MAP_PRIVATE. The caller may set prot to a combination of PROT_READ, PROT_WRITE, and PROT_EXECUTE. Some systems, whose hardware does not support separate *execute* permissions, equate PROT_EXECUTE to PROT_READ.

The system chooses a suitable value for paddr. paddr will never be 0, and the mapping will not overlay existing mappings. *mmap* ignores the addr parameter unless the caller specifies the MAP_FIXED flag.[3] In that case, paddr must be exactly the same as addr. If addr is unsuitable (it either is not page-aligned or does not fall in the range of valid user addresses), *mmap* returns an error. The use of MAP_FIXED is discouraged, for it results in non-portable code.

mmap works on whole pages. This requires that offset be page-aligned. If MAP_FIXED has been specified, addr should also be page-aligned. If len is not a multiple of the page size, it will be rounded upward to make it so.

The mapping remains in effect until it is unmapped by a call to

```
munmap (addr, len);
```

or by remapping the address range to another file by calling *mmap* with a MAP_RENAME flag. Protections may be changed on a per-page basis by

```
mprotect (addr, len, prot);
```

14.3 VM Design Principles

The VM architecture [Ging 87] centers around the notion of a *memory object,* which is a software abstraction of a mapping between a region of memory and a backing store. The system uses several types of backing stores, such as swap space, local and remote files, and frame buffers. The VM system would like to treat these objects identically and perform the same set of operations on them, such as fetching a page from or flushing a page to the backing store. In contrast, each different type of backing store may implement these operations differently. Hence, the system defines a common interface, and each backing store provides its own implementation of it.

---

[2] We follow the standard convention for specifying ranges: square brackets indicate inclusive boundaries, while parentheses indicate exclusive boundaries.

[3] This is true of current implementations. The semantics of the call do specify that *mmap* will use addr as a hint if MAP_FIXED is not set.

> *Note: This chapter uses the word **object** in two different ways. A* ***memory object*** *represents a mapping, while a* ***data object*** *represents a backing store item, such as a file. The meaning is usually clear from the context; where it might be ambiguous, we specifically use the terms **memory object** or **data object**.*

The VM architecture is object-oriented. Section 8.6.2 explains the basic concepts of object-oriented design as they apply to UNIX systems. Using this terminology, the common interface to the memory object constitutes an *abstract base class* [Elli 90]. Each type of memory object (differentiated by its backing store type) is a *derived class,* or *subclass,* of the base class. Every specific mapping is an *instance,* or *object,* of the corresponding subclass.

The address space of a process comprises a set of mappings to different data objects. The only valid addresses are those that are mapped to an object. The object provides a persistent backing store for the pages mapped to it. The mapping renders the object directly addressable by the process. The mapped object itself is neither aware of nor affected by the mapping.

The file system provides the name space for memory objects and mechanisms to access their data. The *vnode layer* allows the VM subsystem to interact with the file system. The relationship between memory objects and vnodes is many-to-one. Each named memory object is associated with a unique vnode, but a single vnode may be associated with several memory objects. Some memory objects, such as user stacks, are not associated with files and do not have names. They are represented by the *anonymous object*.

Physical memory serves as a cache for data from the mapped objects. The kernel attempts to hold the most useful pages in physical memory, so as to minimize paging activity.

The memory is page-based, and the page is the smallest unit of allocation, protection, address translation, and mapping. The address space, in this context, is merely an array of pages. The page is a property of the address space, not of the data object. Abstractions such as regions may be implemented at a higher level, using the page as a fundamental primitive.

The VM architecture is independent of UNIX, and all UNIX semantics such as text, data, and stack regions are provided by a layer above the basic VM system. This allows future non-UNIX operating systems to use the VM code. To make the code portable to other hardware architectures, VM relegates all machine dependencies to a separate hardware address translation *(HAT)* layer, which is accessed via a well-defined interface.

Whenever possible, the kernel uses *copy-on-write* to reduce in-memory copy operations and the number of physical copies of a page in memory. This technique is necessary when processes have private mappings to an object, since any modifications must affect neither the underlying data object nor other processes sharing the page.

14.4   Fundamental Abstractions

The VM architecture [Mora 88] uses five fundamental abstractions to describe the memory subsystem:

- *page* (`struct page`)

- *address space* (struct as)
- *segment* (struct seg)
- *hardware address translation* (struct hat)
- *anonymous page* (struct anon)

These abstractions present object-oriented interfaces to each other, as well as to the rest of the kernel. Section 8.6.2 provides an introduction to the basic concepts of object-oriented systems. The VM system interacts closely with the file system through the vnode layer (see Section 8.6) and with the swap devices through the swap layer. Figure 14-3 shows the basic relationships between these layers.

14.4.1 Physical Memory

As in the 4.3BSD implementation, physical memory is divided into paged and non-paged regions. The paged region is described by an array of page structures, each describing one logical page (cluster of hardware pages). The page structure, shown in Figure 14-4, differs slightly from the BSD cmap structure. Because physical memory is essentially a cache of memory object pages, the page structure must contain standard cache management information. It also contains information required by the address translation mechanism.

Each page is mapped to some memory object, and each such object is represented by a vnode. Hence the *name,* or identity, of a physical page is defined by a *<vnode, offset>* tuple, which specifies the offset of the page in the object represented by the vnode. This allows a page to have a unique name even if it is being shared by several processes. The page structure stores the offset and a pointer to the vnode.

Every page is on several doubly linked lists, and the page structure uses three pairs of point-

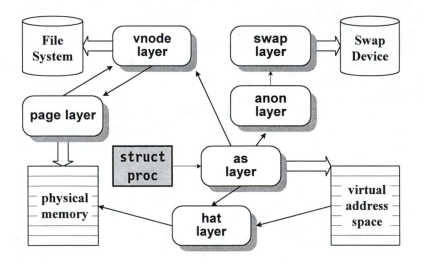

Figure 14-3. The SVR4 VM architecture.

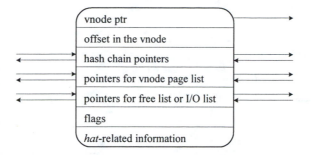

Figure 14-4. The page structure.

ers for this purpose. To find a physical page quickly, pages are hashed based on the vnode and off-set, and each page is on one of the hash chains. Each vnode also maintains a list of all pages of the object that are currently in physical memory, using a second pair of pointers in the page structure. This list is used by routines that must operate on all in-memory pages of an object. For instance, if a file is deleted, the kernel must invalidate all in-memory pages of the file. The final pair of pointers keeps the page either on a *free page list* or on a list of pages waiting to be written to disk. The page cannot be on both lists at the same time.

The page structure also maintains a *reference count* of the number of processes sharing this page using copy-on-write semantics. There are flags for synchronization *(locked, wanted, in-transit)* and copies of *modified* and *referenced* bits (from the HAT information). There is also a HAT-dependent field, which is used to locate all translations for this page (Section 14.4.5).

The page structure has a low-level interface comprising routines that find a page given the vnode and offset, move it onto and off the hash queues and free list, and synchronize access to it.

14.4.2 The Address Space

Figure 14-5 provides a high-level description of the data structures that describe the virtual address space of a process. The address space (struct as) is the primary per-process abstraction and pro-vides a high-level interface to the process address space. The proc structure for each process contains a pointer to its as structure. An as contains the header for a linked list of the mappings for the process, each of which is described by a seg structure. The mappings represent non-overlapping, page-aligned address ranges and are sorted by their base address. The hat structure is also part of the as structure. The as also contains a *hint* to the last segment that had a page fault, as well as other information such as synchronization flags and the sizes of the address space and resident set.

The *as layer* supports two basic sets of operations. The first consists of operations performed on the entire address space, including:

- as_alloc(), used by *fork* and *exec* to allocate a new address space.
- as_free(), called by *exec* and *exit* to release an address space.
- as_dup(), used by *fork* to duplicate an address space.

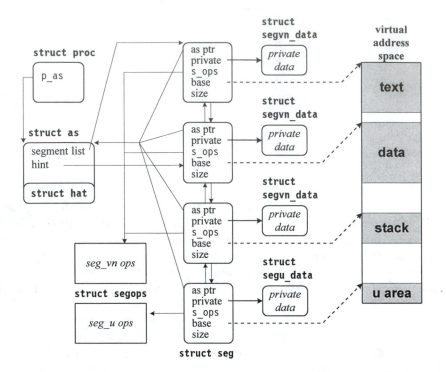

Figure 14-5. Describing the process address space.

The second set of functions operate on a range of pages within the as. They include the following:

- as_map() and as_unmap(), to map and unmap memory objects into the as (called by *mmap, munmap,* and several other routines).
- as_setprot() and as_checkprot(), called by *mprotect* to set and check protections on parts of the as.
- as_fault(), the starting point for page fault handling.
- as_faulta(), used for anticipatory paging *(fault ahead).*

Many of these functions are implemented by determining the mapping or mappings affected and calling lower-level functions in the mappings interface, which is described in the next section.

14.4.3 Address Mappings

The address space comprises a set of memory objects, which represent mappings between backing store items and process address regions. Each such mapping is called a *segment* and is represented by a seg structure. This term, however, is confusing, since these segments are not related to the hardware-recognized segments of segmented memory architectures. In the VM architecture, a *seg-*

ment is a memory object—a contiguous range of virtual addresses of a process mapped to a contiguous byte range in a data object, with the same type of mapping (shared or private).

All segments present an identical interface to the rest of the VM subsystem. In object-oriented terminology, this interface defines an *abstract base class*. There are several types of segments, and each specific segment type is a *derived class,* or *subclass,* of the base class. The VM system also provides a set of generic functions to allocate and free a segment, attach it to the address space, and unmap it.

The `seg` structure contains the public, or type-independent, fields of the segment, such as the base and size of the address range it maps, and a pointer to the `as` structure to which it belongs. All segments of an address space are maintained on a doubly linked list sorted by base address (segments may not overlap). The `as` structure has a pointer to the first segment, and each `seg` structure has forward and backward pointers to keep it on this list.

The `seg` structure has a pointer to a `seg_ops` vector, which is a set of *virtual functions* that define the type-independent interface of the segment class. Each specific subclass, that is, each segment type, must implement the operations in this vector. The `seg` structure contains a pointer (`s_data`) to a type-dependent data structure, which holds private, type-dependent data of this segment. This structure is opaque to the rest of the kernel and is only used by the type-dependent functions that implement the segment operations.

The operations defined in `seg_ops` include the following:

- *dup,* to duplicate a mapping.
- *fault* and *faulta,* to handle page faults for this segment.
- *setprot* and *checkprot,* to set and check protections.
- *unmap,* to unmap the segment and free all its resources.
- *swapout,* called by the *swapper* to swap out a segment.
- *sync,* to flush all pages of the segment back to the underlying data object.

Each segment also has a *create* routine. Although this routine is type-dependent, it is not accessed via the `seg_ops` vector, because it must be called before the segment, and hence the `seg_ops` vector, is initialized. The kernel knows the names and calling syntax of all *create* routines (the arguments to the *create* routine may also differ for each segment type) and calls the appropriate one for the segment it wants to create.

Note the distinction between a virtual function and its specific implementation by a subclass. For example, *faulta* is a virtual function, defining a generic operation on a segment. There is no kernel function called `faulta()`. Each subclass or segment type has a different function to implement this operation—for example, the segment type *seg_vn* provides the function `segvn_faulta()`.

14.4.4   Anonymous Pages

An *anonymous page* is one that has no permanent storage. It is created when a process first modifies a page that has a `MAP_PRIVATE` mapping to an object. The VM system must make a private copy of this page for the process, so that the modifications do not change the underlying object. Any subsequent access to this page must be resolved to the private copy, not to the original page. Such anonymous pages can be discarded when the process terminates or unmaps the page. Meanwhile, they may be saved on the swap device if necessary.

Anonymous pages are widely used by all segments that support private mappings. For example, although initialized data pages are initially mapped to the executable file, they become anonymous pages when first modified. The *swap layer* provides the backing store for anonymous pages.

A related but distinct concept is that of the *anonymous object*. There is a single anonymous object in the entire system. It is represented by the NULL vnode pointer (or in some implementations, by the file **/dev/zero**) and is the source of all zero-filled pages. The uninitialized data and stack regions of the process are MAP_PRIVATE mappings to the anonymous object, while shared memory regions are MAP_SHARED mappings to it.

When a page mapped to the anonymous object is first accessed, it becomes an anonymous page, regardless of whether the mapping was shared or private. This is because the anonymous object does not provide backup storage for its pages, so the kernel must save them to the swap device.

The struct anon represents an anonymous page. It is opaque to the other components of the VM system and is manipulated solely by a procedural interface. Because an anonymous page may be shared, the anon structures are reference-counted. A segment that has an anonymous page merely holds a reference to the anon structure for that page. If the mapping is private, then each segment holds a separate reference to that page. If the mapping is shared, then the segments share the reference itself. Sharing of anonymous pages is discussed further in Section 14.7.4.

The anon layer exports a procedural interface to the rest of VM. It includes the following functions:

- anon_dup() duplicates references to a set of anonymous pages. This increments the reference count of each anon structure in the set.
- anon_free() releases references to a set of anonymous pages, decrementing reference counts on its anon structures. If the count falls to zero, it discards the page and releases the anon structure.
- anon_private() makes a private copy of a page and associates a new anon structure with it.
- anon_zero() creates a zero-filled page and associates an anon structure with it.
- anon_getpage() resolves a fault to an anonymous page, reading it back from swap if necessary.

14.4.5   Hardware Address Translation

The VM system isolates all hardware-dependent code into a single module called the *HAT* (hardware address translation) *layer,* which it accesses through a well-defined, procedural interface. The HAT layer is responsible for all address translation. It must set up and maintain the mappings required by the MMU, such as page tables and translation buffers. It is the sole interface between the kernel and the MMU, and conceals the details of the memory architecture from the rest of the kernel.

The HAT layer's primary data structure is the `struct hat`, which is part of the `as` structure of each process. While this positioning underscores the one-to-one relationship between an address space and its set of hardware mappings, the HAT layer is opaque to the *as layer* and the rest of the VM system. It is accessed through a procedural interface, which includes three types of functions:

- Operations on the HAT layer itself, such as:
  - `hat_alloc()` and `hat_free()`, to allocate and free the `hat` structures.
  - `hat_dup()`, to duplicate the translations during *fork*.
  - `hat_swapin()` and `hat_swapout()`, to rebuild and release the HAT information when a process is swapped in or out.

- Operations on a range of pages of a process. If other processes share these pages, their translations are unaffected by these operations. They include:
  - `hat_chgprot()` to change protections.
  - `hat_unload()` to unload or invalidate the translations and flush the corresponding TLB entries.
  - `hat_memload()` and `hat_devload()` load the translation for a single page. The latter is used by *seg_dev* to load translations to device pages.

- Operations on all translations of a given page. A page can be shared by several processes, each having its own translation to it. These operations include:
  - `hat_pageunload()` unloads all translations for a given page. This involves operations such as invalidating its PTE and flushing its TLB entry.
  - `hat_pagesync()` updates *modified* and *referenced* bits in all translations for the page, using the values in its `page` structure.

All information managed by the HAT layer is redundant. It may be discarded at will and rebuilt from the information available in the machine-independent layer. The interface makes no assumption about what data is retained by the HAT layer and for how long. The HAT layer is free to purge any translation at any time—if a fault occurs on that address, the machine-independent layer will simply ask the HAT layer to reload the translation. Of course, rebuilding the HAT information is expensive, and the HAT layer avoids doing this as much as possible.

The `hat` structure is highly machine-dependent. It may contain pointers to page tables and other related information. To support operations such as `hat_pageunload()`, the HAT layer must be able to find all translations to a page, including those belonging to other processes sharing the page. To implement this, the HAT layer chains all translations for a shared page on a linked list, and stores a pointer to this list in the HAT-dependent field of the `page` structure (Figure 14-6).

The reference port for SVR4 is on the Intel 80x86 architecture [Bala 92]. Its HAT layer uses a data structure called a *mapping chunk* to monitor all translations for a physical page. Each active page table entry has a corresponding *mapping chunk entry*. Because non-active translations do not have mapping chunk entries, the size of the mapping chunk is much less than that of the page table. Each physical page has a linked list of mapping chunk entries, one for each active translation to the page. The struct page holds a pointer to this *mapping chain*.

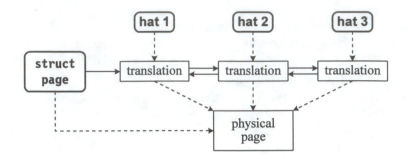

Figure 14-6. Locating all translations to a page.

14.5   Segment Drivers

There are several different segment types. The collection of routines and private data that implement each segment type is called its *segment driver*. The initial implementation included the following four segment types:

- *seg_vn*   Mappings to regular files and to the anonymous object.
- *seg_map*   Kernel internal mappings to regular files.
- *seg_dev*   Mappings to character devices (frame buffers, etc.).
- *seg_kmem*   Miscellaneous kernel mappings.

Later implementations added a *seg_u* driver for mapping the u area and a *seg_objs* driver to map kernel objects into user space. Specific implementations may add other drivers, such as *seg_kp* for multithreaded systems. *seg_vn* and *seg_map* are the most commonly used drivers.

The segment driver must implement all functions defined in the segment interface (Section 14.4.3). The driver is free to merge adjacent segments of the same type or break a segment into smaller segments, if dictated by efficiency considerations. Moreover, while a segment typically has the same protections for all its pages, the drivers permit protections to be specified on a per-page basis.

14.5.1   seg_vn

The *vnode segment*—also known as *seg_vn*—maps user addresses to regular files and to the anonymous object. The latter is represented by the NULL vnode pointer, or by the file **/dev/zero**, and maps zero-fill regions such as uninitialized *(bss)* data and the user stack. Initial page faults to such pages are handled by returning a zero-filled page. The text and initialized data regions are mapped to the executable file using the *seg_vn* driver. Additional *seg_vn* segments may be created to handle shared memory and files explicitly mapped with the *mmap* system call.

Figure 14-7 describes the data structures associated with vnode segments. Each vnode segment maintains a private data structure to store additional information used by the driver. This includes:

- *Current* and *maximum protections* for the pages of the segment.
- Mapping *type* (shared or private).
- Pointer to the vnode of the mapped file. This provides access to all the vnode operations on the file [Klei 86].
- *Offset* of the beginning of the segment in the file.
- *Anonymous map pointer,* for modified pages of private mappings (see Section 14.7.2).
- Pointer to a *per-page protections array,* if all pages do not have the same protection.

The *maximum protections* are set when the segment is initially mapped, depending on the protections required and the mode in which the file was opened. For example, a file initially opened in read-only mode cannot then be mapped MAP_PRIVATE with PROT_WRITE protection, even if the user has write permission to the file. The *current protections* are initially set equal to the maximum protections. Subsequently, they may be changed by calling *mprotect,* but they may never exceed the maximum protections.

Because *mprotect* may be called for any range of pages, it is possible for some pages of a segment to have protections that differ from those of the segment. The *per-page protections array* maintains this information and also allows locking of individual pages in memory (via *mlock*). The kernel ensures that the protections on any page cannot exceed the maximum protections of the segment.

The per-page protections are not unique to *seg_vn.* All segments that support *mmap* and *mprotect* use the same mechanism.

14.5.2 seg_map

UNIX files may be accessed in three ways—demand paging of executable files, direct access to *mmap*'ed files, and *read* or *write* calls to open files. The first case is similar to the second, since the

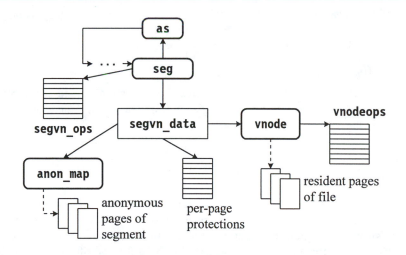

Figure 14-7. Data structures associated with a vnode segment.

kernel maps the text and data segments to the executable file, and the subsequent access is analogous to that of *mmap*'ed files. In both cases, the kernel uses the memory subsystem and page faults to access the data.

Treating *read* and *write* system calls differently from *mmap*'ed access can lead to inconsistency. Traditionally, the *read* system call reads the data from the disk into the block buffer cache, and from there to the process address space. If another process *mmap*s the same file, there will be two copies of the data in memory—one in the buffer cache and another in a physical page mapped into the address space of the second process. If both processes modify the file, the results will be unpredictable.

To avoid this problem, the VM system unifies the treatment of all three access methods. When a user issues a *read* system call on an open file, the kernel first maps the required pages of the file into its own virtual address space using the *seg_map* driver, then copies the data to the processes address space. The *seg_map* driver manages its own virtual address space as a cache, so only recently accessed mappings are in memory. This allows the VM system to subsume the role of the buffer cache, which now becomes largely redundant. It also allows full synchronization of all types of access to a file.

There is only one *seg_map* segment in the system. It belongs to the kernel and is created during system initialization. The driver provides two additional functions—segmap_getmap() to map part of a vnode to a virtual address, and segmap_release() to release such a mapping, writing data back to disk if modified. The role of these functions is similar to that of the traditional bread() and brelse()/bwrite() functions of the buffer cache, and is further described in Section 14.8. The *seg_map* driver is an optimized version of the vnode driver, providing quick but transitory mappings of files to the kernel.

14.5.3   seg_dev

The *seg_dev* driver maps character devices that implement an *mmap* interface. It is commonly used to map frame buffers, physical memory, kernel virtual memory, and bus memory. It only supports shared mappings.

14.5.4   seg_kmem

This driver maps portions of kernel address space such as kernel text, data, and *bss* regions and dynamically allocated kernel memory. These mappings are non-paged, and their address translations do not change unless the kernel unmaps the object (for example, when releasing dynamically allocated memory).

14.5.5   seg_kp

The *seg_kp* driver allocates thread, kernel stack, and light-weight process *(lwp)* structures for multithreaded implementations such as Solaris 2.*x* (see Section 3.6). These structures may be from swappable or non-swappable regions of memory. *seg_kp* also allocates *red zones* to prevent kernel stack overflow. The red zone is a single write-protected page at the end of a stack. Any attempt to write to this page results in a protection fault, thus protecting neighboring pages from corruption.

14.6   The Swap Layer

The *anon layer* manages anonymous pages and resolves page faults on them. It must maintain information necessary to locate the page. If the page is in memory, the anon structure stores a pointer to its page structure. If it has been swapped out, it must be retrieved from its backing store, which is managed by the swap layer. The swap_xlate() routine manages the mapping between anon structures and outswapped pages.

A system may be configured with several swap devices. Each is usually a local disk partition, but could also be a remote disk or even a file. A swap device may be added or removed dynamically, using the system call

> *swapctl* (int cmd, void *arg);

where cmd is SC_ADD or SC_REMOVE,[4] and arg is a pointer to a swapres structure. This structure contains the pathname of the swap file (for a local swap partition, this would be the device special file) and the location and size of the swap area in this file.

The kernel sets up a swapinfo structure for each swap device and adds it to a linked list (Figure 14-8). It also allocates an array of anon structures, with one element for each page on the device. The swapinfo structure contains the vnode pointer and starting offset of the swap area, as well as pointers to the beginning and end of its anon array. Free anon structures in the array are linked together, and the swapinfo structure has a pointer to this list. Initially, all elements are free.

Segments must both reserve and allocate swap space. When the kernel creates a segment that potentially will require swap space (typically, all writable private mappings), it reserves as much space as necessary (usually, equal to the size of the segment). The swap layer monitors the total available swap space and reserves the required amount from this pool. This does not set aside specific swap pages; it merely ensures that the reserved space will be available if and when needed.

This reservation policy is conservative. It requires that processes always reserve backing store for all anonymous memory, even though they may never use all of it. If the system will be used for large applications, it needs a large swap device. On the other hand, the policy guarantees that failures due to memory shortage only occur synchronously, that is, during calls such as *exec* and *mmap*. Once a process has set up its address space, it will always have the swap space it needs, unless it attempts to grow.

A segment allocates swap space on a per-page basis, whenever it creates a new anonymous page. Allocations may only be made against a previous reservation. The swap_alloc() routine allocates a free swap page and associates it with the anonymous page through an anon structure. It attempts to distribute the load evenly on the swap devices, by allocating from a different device after every few pages.

In SVR4, the position of the anon structure in the anon array equals the position of the swap page on the corresponding swap device. swap_alloc() returns a pointer to the anon structure. This pointer serves as the *name* of the anonymous page, since it can be used to locate the page on swap.

---

[4] There are two other commands—SC_LIST and SC_GETNSWP—for administrative purposes.

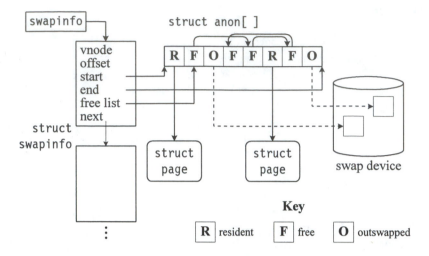

Figure 14-8. Swap layer data structures.

The anon array, and its relation to the swap device, are internal to the swap layer. The anon layer deals with a procedural interface, calling `swap_alloc()` and `swap_free()` to allocate and free the anon structure, and `swap_xlate()` to return the vnode and offset of the swap page corresponding to an anon structure. It then uses the `VOP_GETPAGE` operation on the vnode to retrieve the page from swap.

Segments that use anonymous memory refer to the anon structures indirectly. They maintain an *anon reference array,* which contains pointers to anon structures. The array has one element for each page in the segment. If a page is not anonymous (that is, if it is still managed by the segment driver), the corresponding entry is NULL. This permits operations to be performed on a range of pages, some of which may be anonymous.

Swap devices may be dynamically added or removed while the system is running. Adding a device increases the total available swap space, and removing a device decreases it. When removing a device, any pages currently stored on that device must be copied to another device, and new anon structures must be allocated for them. The remove operation fails if the other swap devices have insufficient room to relocate these pages.

The segments that own these pages, however, continue to refer to the old anon structures, and there is no way to trace back these references. Hence the anon structure has a field that stores a pointer to the new anon structure that maps the page. The anon structure also stores its reference count, and a pointer to the page structure if the page is resident or to the next free element if the anon structure is free.

14.7   VM Operations

Having described the data structures and interfaces that encapsulate the major VM abstractions, we now show how these components interact to provide the memory management functionality.

14.7.1 Creating a New Mapping

New regions are mapped into an address space either during *exec,* or when the process explicitly calls *mmap. exec* or *mmap* locates the vnode of the file being mapped and invokes its VOP_MAP function.[5] VOP_MAP performs file system specific argument checking. It then checks if the process has another mapping for this address range (as it might, if called from *mmap*), and if so, calls as_unmap() to delete that mapping. Finally, it calls as_map() to map the file into the address space. as_map() allocates a seg structure and calls the appropriate *create* routine to initialize the segment.

The *mmap* call ensures that permissions never exceed those with which the file was opened. This means that the user cannot modify a file through a shared mapping if the file was originally opened in read-only mode. The seg structure records the maximum permissions the segment can have. Functions such as *mprotect* that modify permissions check this field.

The *exec* system call establishes private mappings for the text, data, and stack regions.[6] It maps text and initialized data to the executable file, and *bss* data and stack to the anonymous object. It may also set up additional mappings to shared library regions. The text region is mapped with PROT_READ and PROT_EXECUTE protections, so any attempt to write to it generates a fault. The data regions are writable, but pages of initialized data that have not yet been modified may be shared by all processes running the program.

The as_unmap() and as_free() functions remove the mappings. as_unmap(), called by *munmap,* frees a range of addresses, which may include one or more partial or full segments. as_free(), called by *exit,* releases the entire address space. Both operate by looping through the involved segments and calling routines in the segment layer to unmap the pages.

14.7.2 Anonymous Page Handling

Anonymous pages are created in two situations:

- When a process first writes to a page that is mapped MAP_PRIVATE either to a file or to the anonymous object. This includes dirty pages of text, data, stack, and other explicitly created private mappings.
- On the first access to a shared memory page. This case is discussed in Section 14.7.6.

When a private mapping is initially created, the hardware translations for its pages are set to read-only. This is because changes to such pages must not modify the underlying data object. Hence the kernel must trap the first write to such a page and detach its mapping to the file. Because this removes the backup store for the page, the kernel must make alternative arrangements by allocating a backup location on the swap device. The page now becomes an anonymous page.

Figure 14-9 describes how the vnode segment implements anonymous pages. The private data structure of the segment contains a pointer to an anon_map structure. The anon_map contains a

---

[5] VOP_MAP, along with VOP_GETPAGE and VOP_PUTPAGE, was added to the vnodeops vector to support the VM system. These are virtual functions, as described in Section 8.6.2. The actual function invoked depends on the filesystem to which the vnode belongs.

[6] For ELF format files, *exec* maps in the interpreter that is specified in the program header. The interpreter, in turn, maps in the actual program.

pointer to, and the size of, an *anon reference array,* which has one entry for each page of the segment. Each entry is a reference to the anon structure for the corresponding page, or NULL if that page is not yet anonymous. The anon structure locates the page in physical memory or on the swap device and contains a count of the number of references to it. When the reference count falls to zero, the page and the anon structure may be deallocated.

These data structures are not created along with the segment. Rather, they are created and initialized when needed, that is, on the first write to a page in that segment. This lazy approach is beneficial, because many vnode segments may never create anonymous pages (text pages, for instance, are never modified unless the program is being debugged and the debugger deposits a breakpoint). By delaying the work, the kernel may avoid it altogether.

The first attempt to write to a privately mapped page causes a protection fault. The fault handler recognizes the situation, for the mapping type is MAP_PRIVATE and the *segment protections* are not read-only (as opposed to protections in the hardware address translation for the page, which have been deliberately set to read-only so as to trap this write attempt). It allocates an anon structure, thus allocating swap space (since each anon structure corresponds to a unique page on the swap device). It creates a reference to the anon structure (Section 7.9 explains object references in more detail) and stores it in the corresponding element of the anon reference array.

The handler then makes a new copy of the page, using a newly allocated physical page. It stores the pointer to the page structure for this page in the anon structure. Finally, the handler calls the HAT layer to load a new translation for the page, which is write-enabled, and translates to the new copy. All further modifications thus occur to this private copy of the page.

Some special cases require additional processing. If this is the first anonymous page created for the segment, the handler allocates and initializes the anon_map and the anon reference array. Also, if the faulting page was not in memory, the handler reads it in from its backing storage.

The kernel may eventually move this page to the swap device. This may cause the process to fault on it again. This time, the fault handler discovers that the segment has a reference to the anon structure for this page and uses it to retrieve the page from the swap device.

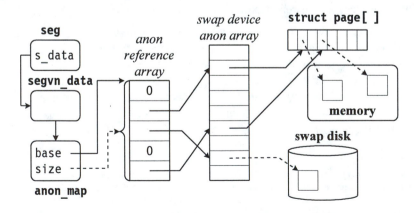

Figure 14-9. Anonymous pages of a vnode segment.

When a process *forks*, all its anonymous pages are shared copy-on-write with the child. The parent and the child have their own anon_map and anon reference array, but they refer to the same anon pages. This is described further in the next section.

14.7.3 Process Creation

The *fork* system call, after allocating and initializing the proc structure, calls the as_dup() function to duplicate the parent's address space. as_dup() first calls as_alloc() to allocate a new as structure for the child. It then goes through its segment list, and for each segment, invokes the *dup* operation of its driver to duplicate it.

The segment duplication starts by allocating a new seg structure, and a structure to hold the type-dependent private data. Many of the fields, such as base address, size, vnode pointer, offset, and protections are copied from the parent. In particular, the child inherits the seg_ops pointer and the mapping type from the parent. Mappings to text, data, and stack are MAP_PRIVATE in the parent and the child. Any MAP_SHARED mapping in the parent remains so in the child, preserving UNIX inheritance rules for shared memory regions. Other fields, such as the pointer to the as, are initialized to appropriate values in the child.

For MAP_PRIVATE mappings, the anon_map must be duplicated in a manner that allows copy-on-write sharing of the anon pages. The first step is to call hat_chgprot() to write-protect all anon pages. This ensures that any attempt to modify these pages by either the parent or the child will result in a page fault. The fault handler will make a new copy of that page and enable writes to it.

Once hat_chgprot() returns, the segment driver calls anon_dup() to duplicate the anon_map. anon_dup() allocates a new anon_map and anon reference array. It *clones* all the references in the array by copying the pointers and incrementing the reference counts of the associated anon structures. Figure 14-10 describes the situation after a segment has been duplicated.

After all segments have been duplicated, as_dup() calls hat_dup() to duplicate the hat structure and translation information. hat_dup() may allocate new page tables for the child and initialize them by copying from the parent.

This way, *fork* duplicates the address space without copying the pages themselves. It only copies the mappings and page tables. Although this seems to eliminate the need for *vfork*, SVR4 retains it for several reasons. First, *vfork* is even faster than copy-on-write, because it does not even copy the mappings. Second, several programs rely on the semantics of *vfork*, which allow the child to modify the parent address space. Eliminating *vfork* would break these programs. While *vfork* is not native to System V UNIX, it is incorporated in SVR4 along with the VM architecture.

14.7.4 Sharing Anonymous Pages

The anon_dup() function, called during *fork*, duplicates the references to all anonymous pages of the parent, so that they are shared copy-on-write by both parent and child. Even though anon_dup() operates on an entire segment, the sharing occurs on a per-page basis.

Figure 14-10 showed the state of a segment in the parent and child and the corresponding anon structures after the completion of anon_dup(). Figure 14-11 describes the same objects after some time has elapsed. During this time, the child has modified pages 0 and 1 of that segment. Page

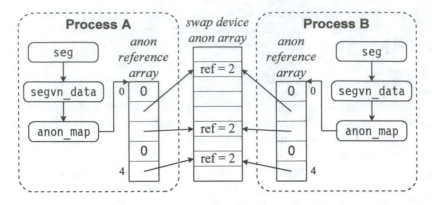

Figure 14-10. Sharing anonymous pages (part 1).

0 was initially not an anonymous page. When the child modified it, the kernel allocated a new anon structure and physical page, and added a reference to it in the child's anon reference array. Because the parent has not modified that page, it is still mapped to the vnode in the parent's address space.

Page 1, in contrast, was an anonymous page shared by both parent and child. It therefore had a reference count of 2. Since the mapping was private, the modifications by the child could not be applied to the shared copy. Thus the kernel made a new copy of the page and allocated a new anon structure for it. The child released its reference on the original anon structure and obtained a reference to the new one. As a result, the parent and the child now reference different anon structures for that page, and each has a reference count of 1.

This shows the sharing is indeed on a per-page basis. At this instance, as shown in Figure 14-11, the parent and the child are sharing the anonymous pages for pages 2 and 4 of the segment, but not for pages 0, 1, or 3.

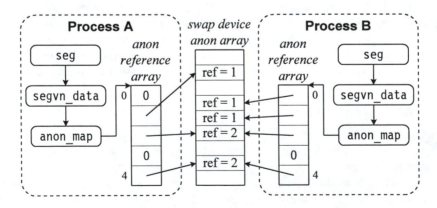

Figure 14-11. Sharing anonymous pages (part 2).

14.7.5 Page Fault Handling

The trap() routine is invoked for both protection and validation faults. It determines the type of fault, the type of access (read/write), the as structure of the faulting process, and calls as_fault() to handle the fault. as_fault() locates the segment containing the faulting address and invokes the *fault* operation of its driver. To facilitate this task, the *as layer* sorts the segments in order of increasing base address and also maintains a pointer to the last segment that had a fault. This pointer is used as a hint to begin the search, as the *locality of reference* principle suggests the next fault will also be in the same segment.

The actual fault handling differs for each segment type, and we restrict this discussion to the common case of vnode segments. The *seg_vn* driver's fault handler is segvn_fault(). It converts the fault address to a logical page number in the segment, which it uses as an index into the anon_map and into the per-page protections array, if one exists.

Protection faults are triggered by the protection settings in the hardware address translation entry and may be either real or spurious. segvn_fault() distinguishes the two types by checking the information in the segment's private data. The real protections for the page are contained in its entry in the per-page protection array, or if that is NULL, then in the segment's protection information. If this information confirms that access must be denied, segvn_fault() notifies the process by sending it a SIGSEGV signal.

Spurious protection faults are caused when the hardware has deliberately disabled protections in the hardware address translation for this page, in order to implement copy-on-write sharing or reference-bit simulation (see Section 13.5.3). For such faults, as well as for all validation faults, the further actions of segvn_fault() are based on the state of the page:

- If there is an anon_map entry, it calls anon_getpage() to obtain the anonymous page. anon_getpage() may find the page already in memory (in which case, the anon structure points to it) or may read it in from the swap device.
- If there is no anon_map entry for this page, and the segment is mapped to a file, it calls the VOP_GETPAGE operation on the file's vnode. VOP_GETPAGE may find the page already in memory (by searching the hash queues) or may read it in from disk.
- If there is no anon_map entry for this page, and the segment is mapped to the anonymous object, it calls anon_zero() to return a zero-filled page.

Many special cases are handled in VOP_GETPAGE and anon_getpage(). If the page is on the free page list, it must be reclaimed from this list. If the page has been marked invalid to perform reference-bit simulation, it is reclaimed by simply turning on the valid bit. If the page is in transit, the caller must wait for the I/O to complete. Text pages still in memory from previous invocations of the program may be retrieved by searching the hash queues based on *<vnode, offset>*. Any clustering or prepaging (read-ahead) is also handled in these routines.

At this point, the page is in memory, and segvn_fault() has a pointer to it. It now checks for the copy-on-write case. This is identified when

1. there is a write access attempted to a private mapping,
2. the segment protections (or per-page, if different) permit writes, and
3. (a) the page has no anon structure, or
   (b) its anon structure has more than one reference.

Case 3(a) involves a private mapping to a file, where modifications must be made to a private copy of the page. Case 3(b) deals with copy-on-write sharing of anonymous pages, as occurs after a *fork*. In either case, the fault handler calls anon_private() to make a private copy of the page.

Finally, the handler calls hat_memload() to load the new translation for the page into the hardware translation structures (page tables and TLBs).

14.7.6   Shared Memory

System V provides a shared memory mechanism as part of its interprocess communication (IPC) facility (see Section 6.3.4). After a process allocates a shared memory region, it and other cooperating processes may attach the region to a location in their address space. Each process may attach the region to a different address, and a process may also attach the same region to multiple locations in its address space. Once attached, the processes read and write to the region using ordinary memory access instructions, and any change made by one process is instantly visible to all processes sharing the region. The region remains in existence until it is explicitly removed, even if no processes are attached to it. This allows a process to create a shared memory region, leave data in it, and exit; another process could attach to this region at some point in the future and retrieve this information.

In this section, we describe how the VM architecture implements shared memory. Each shared memory region is represented by a vnode segment that is mapped MAP_SHARED to the anonymous object. Because the mapping is shared, all modifications are applied to the single, shared copy of the data, and hence are immediately visible to all processes. The anonymous object, however, does not provide backing store for these pages. Hence, when the pages are first written to, they are converted to anonymous pages and backed up on the swap device.

This form of sharing is fundamentally different from the copy-on-write sharing of anonymous pages between parent and child. In that situation, the two processes held separate references to the anon structures, and the sharing occurred at the individual page level.

Figure 14-12 describes the implementation of shared memory. The region is represented by a single anon_map, shared by all processes that have attached the region to their address space. Each process maintains its own seg structure for the region, which contains the base address, protections, and other pertinent information. The anon_map itself is reference counted—each process holds a reference to it, and the IPC subsystem retains another reference in a data structure associated with the region.

The IPC reference is created when the shared memory region is first allocated, and released when the region is explicitly deleted (by the IPC_RMID command to the *shmctl* system call). This ensures that the region does not disappear automatically when no processes have attached it.

The anon_map holds references to individual anonymous pages. When the reference count of the anon_map reaches zero (that is, when all processes have detached the region from their address spaces, and the region has been deleted), the kernel first releases all anonymous pages and then the anon reference array and the anon_map.

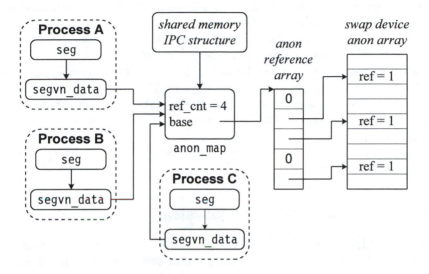

Figure 14-12. Implementing shared memory.

14.7.7   Other Components

Free Page Pool

The basic treatment is the same as that in BSD—a separate *pagedaemon* process implementing the two-handed clock algorithm (see Section 13.5.3). This has been adapted to the VM architecture. The following points must be noted:

- The front hand calls hat_pagesync() to turn off reference and modify bits in the hat structures.
- Dirty pages are flushed to disk by VOP_PUTPAGE, which handles any clustering.
- hat_pageunload() is called to invalidate pages that are moved to the free list.
- Reference-bit simulation must be performed if necessary.

Swapping

When a UNIX system boots, the initialization code creates the *swapper* process. This is a system process with no user context. Its PID is zero, and it executes a routine called sched(). It executes this routine forever (or until the system crashes or is shut down) and is normally asleep. It is awakened once every second, and also if certain other events occur.

When the swapper wakes up, it checks the amount of free memory and decides whether to perform any swapping activity. If the free memory is less than a tunable parameter named t_gpgslo, the swapper swaps out a process. To choose a process to swap out, it invokes the scheduling priority class-dependent CL_SWAPOUT operation of each class, which returns a candidate from that priority class (see Section 5.5). Similarly, the priority class routine CL_SWAPIN chooses the process to be swapped back in when sufficient memory is available.

The swapper swaps out a process by calling as_swapout(), which cycles through each segment and calls the *swapout* operation for each segment. The segment driver in turn must write out all in-memory pages of the segment to the backing store. Most segments are of type *seg_vn* and use the segvn_swapout() routine to implement this operation. Finally, the swapper swaps out the u area of the process.

To swap in a process, the swapper simply swaps in its u area. When the process eventually runs, it will fault in other pages as needed.

14.8   Interaction with the Vnode Subsystem

The file system provides the backing store for a large number of VM segments. Hence the VM subsystem constantly interacts with the file system to move data between files and memory. Conversely, the file system uses memory-mapped access to implement the *read* and *write* system calls. This section describes the interface between the VM and file subsystems, as well as some interesting problems that arise during its implementation.

14.8.1   Vnode Interface Changes

In systems such as 4.3BSD, the memory management data structures contain information about the physical locations of the file blocks (in the fill-on-demand page table entries). The drawback of this approach is that it compromises the modularity and independence of the file and VM subsystems. The VM architecture relegates all file system specific details to the vnode layer, accessing files solely through the procedural interface of the vnode. To enable this, SVR4 adds three operations to the vnode interface: VOP_MAP, VOP_GETPAGE, and VOP_PUTPAGE.

VOP_MAP is called from *mmap* to perform file-system-dependent initialization and parameter checking. It verifies, for instance, that the file being mapped is not locked and that the mapping does not extend beyond the end of the file. The file system may also choose to read in the information required to translate logical file offsets to physical block numbers (from the inode and indirect blocks), for reasons that are discussed below.

VOP_GETPAGE is called whenever the VM system must obtain pages from a file. The pages may still be in memory, but the VM system may not have a translation for them. VOP_GETPAGE will first look for the pages in memory. The kernel keeps all in-core pages in a global hash table, keyed by *<vnode, offset>*. It enters the page in the table when bringing it into memory and removes it from the table when reassigning or invalidating it. Although each file system implements VOP_GETPAGE differently, they all use a common function to search the hash table. If a page is not in the hash table, VOP_GETPAGE reads it in from the file in a file-system-dependent manner. A local file system such as *ufs* might determine the disk location from the inode and indirect blocks of the file, while a remote file system such as NFS might fetch the page from a server.

Because VOP_GETPAGE handles all file accesses, it is able to perform optimizations such as read-ahead. Moreover, since each file system knows its optimal transfer size and disk layout details, it may perform an optimization called *klustering*,[7] wherein it reads additional physically adjacent pages in the same disk I/O operation when suitable. It may also perform vnode operations such as updating the access or modify times of the underlying inode.

The VOP_PUTPAGE operation is called to flush potentially dirty pages back to the file. Its arguments include a flag that specifies whether the write-back is synchronous or asynchronous. When VOP_PUTPAGE is called by the *pagedaemon* to free some memory, a deadlock can occur. VOP_PUTPAGE needs to determine the physical location of the pages on disk. To do so, it may have to read in an indirect block (see Section 9.2.2), which it cannot do because no memory is available.

One way to avoid this deadlock is to store the translation information from the indirect blocks in memory as long as a file is mapped. This also improves performance of both VOP_GETPAGE and VOP_PUTPAGE, since they avoid having to read in the indirect blocks from disk. However, locking the information in memory incurs considerable space overhead.

14.8.2   Unifying File Access

The relationship between the memory and file subsystems is symbiotic. The file system provides the backing store for VM segments, and VM provides the implementation of file access (Figure 14-13). When a user issues a *read* or *write* system call on a file, the kernel temporarily maps that part of the file into its own address space using the *seg_map* segment, faults the data in, and then copies it to or

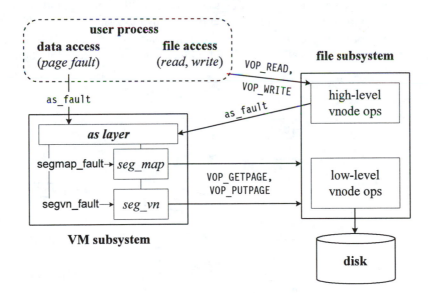

Figure 14-13. Relationship between file and VM subsystems.

---

[7] This should not be confused with *clustering*, which refers to the logical grouping of adjacent physical pages in memory.

from the user's address space. The *seg_map* driver reads file system blocks into paged memory; the buffer cache is no longer required for this purpose. This extends the mapped file access semantics to traditional access methods. Such a unified treatment of files eliminates consistency problems that may occur when the same file is accessed in different ways at the same time.

The *seg_map* driver is simply an optimized version of the vnode driver, providing quick but transitory mappings of files to the kernel. Figure 14-14 describes the data structures used. The private data (struct segmap_data) for the segment consists of pointers to an array of struct smap entries, as well as to a hash table and to a list of free smap entries. Each smap entry contains pointers to keep it on the hash queue and free list, the vnode pointer and offset for the page it represents, and a reference count that monitors how many processes are currently accessing the entry.

Each smap represents one page of the segment. The kernel virtual address of the page is determined by

```
addr = base + entrynum * MAXBSIZE;
```

where base is the starting address of the *seg_map* segment, entrynum is the index of the smap in the array, and MAXBSIZE is the (machine-dependent) size of each page. Because several file systems with different block sizes may coexist on the machine, one page in this segment may correspond to one file system block, several blocks, or part of a block.

When a process issues a *read* system call, the file system determines the vnode and offset for the data, and calls segmap_getmap() to establish a mapping for the page. segmap_getmap() checks the hash queues to find if a mapping already exists; if so, it increments the reference count for the smap. If there is no mapping, it allocates a free smap and stores the vnode pointer and offset in it. Finally, it returns the virtual address of the page represented by the smap.

The file system next calls uiomove() to copy the data from the page to the user address space. If the page is not in physical memory, or if its translation is not loaded in the HAT, a page

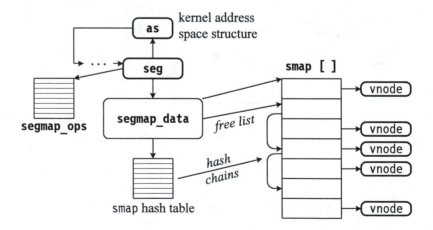

Figure 14-14. seg_map data structures.

fault occurs, and the fault handler calls `segmap_fault()` to handle it. `segmap_fault()` calls the `VOP_GETPAGE` operation of the file system to bring the page into memory and then calls `hat_memload()` to load a translation for it.

After copying the data to user space, the file system calls `segmap_release()` to return the smap entry to the free list (unless it has another reference). In case of a *write* system call, `segmap_release()` also writes the page back to the file, usually synchronously. The page remains mapped to the same vnode and offset until it is reassigned. This caches the translation, so the page may be found quickly the next time.

This may appear to be a complex set of operations merely to read a page from a file. However, it is necessary, because the role of the *seg_map* functions is to integrate file access through *read* and *write* system calls with mapped access. This ensures that even when a file is accessed simultaneously through both methods, only one copy of the page is in memory, and the behavior is consistent.

The `VOP_GETPAGE` operation performs the real work of fetching the page from the file. The page may already be in memory, as the *seg_map* hash table finds only those pages that are mapped into the *seg_map* segment (that is, those pages that have been recently accessed through *read* and *write* system calls). `VOP_GETPAGE` retrieves the page, either from memory or from the file, as described in Section 14.8.1.

An important requirement of unifying file access is to have a single name space for file and process pages. Traditional UNIX implementations identify a file system buffer by the <*device, block number*> pair. The VM architecture uses the <*vnode, offset*> pair to define its name space, and a global hash table to find a page by name. When disk access is needed, VM calls the file system to translate the name to the on-disk location of the page.

The buffer cache is not completely eliminated. We still need it to cache file system metadata (superblocks, inodes, indirect blocks and directories), which cannot be represented in the <*vnode, offset*> name space. A small buffer cache is retained exclusively for these pages.

14.8.3   Miscellaneous Issues

The page size may not be the same as the file system block size. Indeed, there may be several different file systems with different block sizes on the same machine. The VM system deals only with pages; it asks the file system to bring pages into memory and to write them out to disk. It is the vnode object manager's (file system's) task to read pages from disk. This may involve reading one block, several blocks, or part of a block. If the file does not end on a page boundary, the vnode manager must zero out the remainder of the last page.

The VM system deals with a name space defined by the <*vnode, offset*> pair. Thus, for each disk access, the file system must translate the offsets to the physical block number on disk. If the translation information (indirect blocks, etc.) is not in memory, it must be read from disk. When this occurs as part of a pageout operation, `VOP_PUTPAGE` must be careful to avoid deadlocks. Deadlock may occur if there is no free memory to read in the indirect block that has information about where the dirty page must be written.

14.9   Virtual Swap Space in Solaris

The SVR4 implementation of the swap layer has several drawbacks. The total anonymous memory that may be allocated in the system is limited to the total physical swap space. The backing store for a page is chosen randomly from the available swap space and cannot be changed thereafter unless the swap device is removed. The implementation does not allow intelligent swap space management, which would optimize paging and swapping.

To address these limitations, Solaris 2.x introduced the notion of a virtual swap space [Char 91]. The following were its primary goals:

- To increase the available swap space by including physical memory.
- To allow dynamic reallocation of swap locations.

To achieve this, Solaris introduced a new file system called *swapfs,* which provides a virtual backing store to the anon layer. This section describes the important features of the Solaris swap layer.

14.9.1   Extended Swap Space

Like SVR4, Solaris requires clients of anonymous memory to reserve all swap space at segment creation time.[8] In Solaris, however, the available space comprises all physical swap devices plus most of the available physical memory. A part of physical memory is kept aside to ensure that there will always be room to allocate kernel data structures. This allows Solaris to run with less swap space than SVR4.

Reservations against physical memory are permitted only when the space on the swap devices is exhausted. Any memory reserved for swapping is *wired down* (made nonpageable). When swap space is released, the system first releases any reservations made against main memory. Thus main memory is reserved as a last resort and freed as soon as possible.

Once reservations are made against main memory, the system may create anonymous pages that have no physical backing store. The *swapfs* provides names for these pages, as described in the following section. Because they are wired down, they cannot be paged out, and hence do not need physical swap space.

14.9.2   Virtual Swap Management

When a process tries to create an anonymous page, it must allocate swap space for it. Unlike reservation, the allocation assigns a specific swap location, or *name,* to the page. In SVR4, the location is always on a physical swap device. The position of the anon structure in the anon array for that device equals the position of the page on the swap device. Hence, the address of the anon structure implicitly serves as the name of the page. The *swap layer* routine swap_alloc() assigns the swap location and returns a pointer to the corresponding anon structure.

In Solaris, swap_alloc() assigns a virtual swap location to the page. It manages a single, system-wide, virtual file and allocates swap space from that file. The name of a virtual swap page is

---

[8] Reserving swap space does not set aside a specific area on a swap device; it merely guarantees that the space will be available somewhere when required.

described by the vnode of the virtual file and the offset of the page in that file. Instead of per-device anon arrays, swap_alloc() dynamically allocates anon structures. It explicitly stores the name (*<vnode, offset>* pair) of the page in the anon structure, instead of inferring it from the address of the structure. Note that to this point, the routine has not allocated and bound any physical swap space to this page (Figure 14-15(a)).

The page needs physical swap space only when it must be paged out. At that time, the *pageout daemon* obtains the name of the page and calls the VOP_PUTPAGE operator of the corresponding vnode. For an anonymous page, this invokes the corresponding *swapfs* routine, with the vnode and offset in the virtual file as arguments. This routine performs the following actions:

1. Calls the *swap layer* to allocate backing store for this page.
2. Calls the VOP_PUTPAGE operator of the physical swap device to write out the page.
3. Writes the new name of the page (the vnode and offset of the physical swap page) into both the anon and the page structures for the page (Figure 14-15(b)).

Eventually the page will be freed from main memory. Later, it may be read back from swap if needed, using the new information in the anon structure (Figure 14-15(c)).

Because *swapfs* allows allocations against main memory, it may not be able to find physical

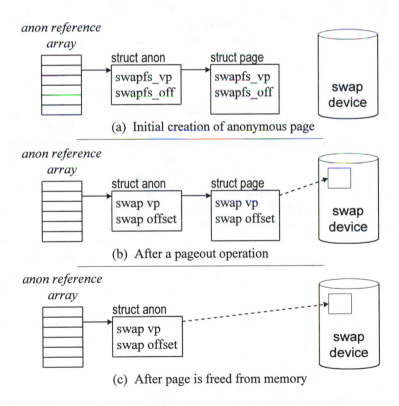

Figure 14-15. Allocating virtual and physical swap space.

swap space for a pageout operation. In that case, it simply wires down the page in memory and does not mark it as clean.

14.9.3   Discussion

The Solaris implementation allows the system to run with very little swap space (as low as 20% of main memory) without degrading performance. This is very useful when disk space is limited.

The Solaris framework allows enhancements to perform intelligent swap management. For instance, it is possible to have the *pagedaemon* batch its anonymous page writes. This permits the swap layer to allocate contiguous swap space for them and write them out in a single I/O operation. Alternatively, *swapfs* could define a separate vnode for each client process. It could then organize the backing store such that pages of the same process are allocated close together on the same device, resulting in better paging performance.

14.10   Analysis

The VM architecture is vastly different from the 4.3BSD memory management architecture. On one hand, it seems more complex, with a greater number of basic abstractions and data structures. On the other hand, the separation of responsibility within the different layers results in cleaner interfaces between the components. The bottom line, however, is functionality and performance. What have we gained with this approach, and at what cost? The VM architecture has the following major advantages:

- The design is highly modular, with each major component represented by an object-oriented interface that encapsulates its functionality and hides its inner implementation from the rest of the system. This brings with it the traditional advantages of object-oriented methods—each component may be easily modified or enhanced, and support for new functionality or new machines may be added fairly easily. One such example is the addition of a *seg_u* driver to manage u area allocation.

- In particular, isolating the hardware translation functionality into the HAT layer has made the architecture highly portable. It has already been ported successfully to many different systems, including Motorola 680*x*0, Intel 80*x*86, SPARC, AT&T 3B2, and IBM 370/XA.

- The architecture supports various forms of sharing—copy-on-write sharing of individual pages, MAP_SHARED mappings to the anonymous object for traditional shared memory regions, and shared access to files through the *mmap* interface. This sharing reduces the overall contention on physical memory and eliminates excess disk I/O to maintain multiple copies of the same page in memory.

- The *mmap* interface is particularly powerful, not only because of the sharing capabilities it offers, but also because it allows direct access to file data without system call overhead.

- Though shared libraries are not explicitly part of the kernel, they can be supported easily by mapping them into the process address space.

- Because the VM architecture uses vnode operations for all file and disk accesses, it can take advantage of all the benefits of the vnode interface. In particular, the VM system does not require special code to support the execution of files on remote nodes. Swap devices, likewise, may be specified on remote nodes, thus supporting truly diskless operation.

- Integrating the buffer cache with the VM system provides an automatic tuning of physical memory. In traditional architectures, the size of the buffer cache was fixed when the kernel was built at approximately 10% of physical memory. In reality, the ideal size of the buffer cache depends on how the system is used. An I/O-intensive system such as a file server requires a large buffer cache. A system used primarily for timesharing applications would prefer a small buffer cache, with much of the memory used for process pages. Even for a single machine, the ideal cache size varies in time as the usage pattern changes. The VM architecture dynamically changes the allocation of memory between process pages and file pages to reflect the actual demands on memory, and thus effectively addresses the needs of the users at all times.

- The problem with breakpoints in a shared text region (see Section 13.6) is solved neatly, because the text region is mapped MAP_PRIVATE. When a debugger tries to set a breakpoint by calling *ptrace,* the kernel makes a private copy of that page for the process and writes the breakpoint instruction to that copy. This ensures that other processes running this program do not see the breakpoint.

Although the advantages are impressive, they are not without cost. There are several important shortcomings of this design, primarily related to performance:

- The VM system has to maintain a lot more information about its fundamental abstractions. This results in many more data structures, and those having BSD counterparts are often larger in size. For example, the page structure is over 40 bytes in size, as opposed to the 16-byte cmap structure in BSD. This means that the VM system uses up more memory to maintain its own state, leaving less memory for user processes.

- The VM system does not save text and unmodified data pages to swap. Instead, it reads them back from the executable file when needed. This reduces the total swap space needed, and saves the expense of swapping out such pages. On the other hand, reading a page back from file is slower than retrieving it from swap, because of the greater overhead of the file system code and, in some cases, the need to read additional metadata blocks to locate the page. The effect of this policy on overall performance depends on how often such pages are retrieved.

- The algorithms are more complex and slower. The layering of components involves more function calls, many of them indirect via function table lookups. This has an impact on overall system performance. For example, [Chen 90] finds that function calls add a 20% overhead to page fault handling.

- The VM system has abandoned the BSD practice of computing disk addresses of all fill-from-text pages during *exec,* and storing them in the PTEs. This means that each disk address may have to be computed individually when there is a page fault on that page. If the indirect blocks for that file are no longer in physical memory, they must be read from disk. This slows down the demand paging of text and initialized data pages.

- The object-oriented method results in invariant interfaces to its abstractions, flexible enough to allow vastly different implementations of the underlying objects. This means, however, that the system is not tuned for a specific implementation. Optimizations such as those in the preceding paragraph are not possible in SVR4.

- Copy-on-write may not always be faster than anticipatory copying. When a page is shared copy-on-write, more page faults are generated, and the TLB entry also needs to be flushed when the page is initially write-protected. If pages need to be copied anyway, it is surely more efficient to do it directly rather than waiting for copy-on-write faults.
- Swap space is allocated on a per-page basis, randomly on the swap devices. This loses the clustering and pre-paging benefits of a BSD-like approach, which allocates contiguous chunks of swap space for each process. In contrast, the BSD approach wastes the unused space in each chunk.

These drawbacks are all performance-related and may be compensated for by the performance benefits of the new facilities such as memory sharing and file mapping. On balance, with the rapid increase in CPU speeds and memory sizes, performance considerations take are less important than functionality, and in that regard the VM architecture provides substantial advantages.

14.11   Performance Improvements

When the VM architecture was initially ported from SunOS to SVR4, it performed poorly compared to the *regions* architecture of SVR2 and SVR3 UNIX. In particular, it was observed that the VM system had a much higher page fault rate for typical multiuser benchmarks. A detailed analysis [Chen 90] suggested several enhancements, which were incorporated into SVR4.

14.11.1   Causes of High Fault Rates

One major problem concerns the treatment of hardware address translation maps. In the VM architecture, these maps are associated with an address space, not with individual segments. A segment may begin at any page boundary, and multiple segments may share a single translation map. Hence it is impossible for two processes to share the map, since they would have to share all segments mapped by it.

Because a page may be mapped by multiple translations, any change to the mapping must propagate to all translations. There are two types of changes, and both are propagated differently. The first is a valid-to-invalid change, which occurs, for instance, when the *pagedaemon* invalidates a page for reference-bit simulation (see Section 13.5.3). VM propagates this change immediately to all translations for the page, since failure to do so can lead to incorrect behavior.

The second type is an invalid-to-valid change. Suppose two processes are sharing a page that is currently not in memory. When the first process faults on the page, the fault handler brings the page into memory and establishes a valid translation to it for that process. The VM system adopts a *lazy approach* and does not propagate this change to the second process. If and when the second process faults on the same page, the handler will find the page in memory and create a valid translation at that time.

The advantage of the lazy approach (often called the *principle of lazy evaluation*) is that by deferring the task, we may avoid it altogether. The second process may never access the page, or may do so only after it has been paged out again. The drawback is that there are many more page faults. Many of these faults are spurious—the page is actually in memory, but the faulting process does not have a valid translation for it.

The original VM implementation also uses a lazy approach to initialize the translation maps. Unlike BSD, which allocates and initializes all page tables during *fork* or *exec*, VM defers the task as far as possible. It initializes each translation map entry only when the process first faults on that page. Likewise, it allocates each page of the map only when it is first needed. While this method eliminates some amount of work, it incurs many more page faults.

The lazy approach is beneficial if the total overhead of the extra page faults is less than the time saved by eliminating unnecessary operations. Under VM, the fault overhead is fairly large. Measurements on the AT&T 3B2/400 show that the cost of a *spurious validation fault* (one where the page is already in memory, but the system does not have a valid translation for it) is 3.5 milliseconds in the VM architecture, but only 1.9 milliseconds in the *regions* architecture. The difference is largely due to the modular design of VM, which results in many more function calls and longer code paths.

A similar tradeoff occurs in copy-on-write sharing during *fork*. Here, the objective is to copy only those pages that are modified by either the parent or the child. To do so, VM defers copying any page until the parent or the child faults on it. The drawback, once again, is that this causes additional page faults. On the 3B2, the cost of handling the protection fault and copying the page is 4.3 milliseconds, while that of copying alone is only 1 millisecond. Hence, for copy-on-write to be beneficial, less than one in four pages should need to be copied. If more than 1/4 of the in-memory pages are modified after a *fork*, it would have been better to copy all of them in advance.

The benchmarks also show that the initial VM implementation causes about three times the number of faults as the *regions* architecture. The critical activities are *fork* and *exec*, which are responsible for most of the address space set up and memory sharing. To reduce the fault rate, it is important to examine the paging behavior of these calls in typical situations.

Three important enhancements were made to VM based on these factors. They are described in the following section.

14.11.2   SVR4 Enhancements to the SunOS VM Implementation

The first and most beneficial change is to allocate and initialize the child's address translation maps in *fork*. Even though the child is likely to *exec* soon, in reality it always executes some user-level code (I/O redirection, closing some descriptors, etc.) between *fork* and *exec*, causing a few spurious page faults. The cost of these faults far exceeds that of building and copying the translation maps.

The second change is to partly initialize the translation maps during *exec*. Each segment is associated with a vnode, which maintains a linked list of all in-memory pages that belong to it. In the new version, *exec* traverses this list and initializes all translation map entries that map these pages. It also allocates any translation map pages required for these entries. This eliminates the spurious page faults caused by the lazy mapping approach.

In effect, this method estimates the working set of a segment by equating it to the number of pages of its vnode that are already in memory. Some of this work may be unnecessary, because the process may not access those pages while they are in memory. The overall benefit, again, is due to the fact that the cost of setting up the mappings is less than that of the page faults avoided.

The final change applies to copy-on-write sharing. Here, since the cost of copying all the pages is very high (which is why we do copy-on-write in the first place), it is important to guess which pages will need to be copied regardless. Copy-on-write occurs primarily because of *fork*, which is mostly called by the shells to implement command execution. An analysis of the memory access patterns of the different shells (*sh, csh, ksh,* etc.) shows that a single shell process will *fork* several times and will use *fork* in a similar way each time. The same variables are likely to be modified after each *fork* operation. In terms of pages, the pages that experience copy-on-write faults after one *fork* will probably do so after the next.

When a copy-on-write page is modified, it becomes an anonymous page. This provides an easy optimization. In the new implementation, *fork* examines the set of anonymous pages of the parent and physically copies each page that is in memory. It expects this set to be a good predictor of the pages that will be modified (and have to be copied) after the *fork*. The pre-copying eliminates the overhead of the copy-on-write faults.

14.11.3   Results and Discussion

These improvements substantially reduced the number of page faults. Table 14-1 [Chen 90] shows that with these enhancements, the fault rate is much lower than in the initial VM implementation, and also much lower than in the *regions* architecture.

The lazy evaluation strategy is widely used in SVR4 as well as in Mach. As this work shows, however, its benefits are questionable. It is important to use this approach carefully and only where it is efficient to do so.

14.12   Summary

This chapter describes the SVR4 VM architecture. It has several advanced features and functionality, and provides many forms of memory inheritance and sharing required for sophisticated applications. It must, however, be carefully optimized to yield good performance. The modern tendency is to concentrate on adding functionality and expect upgrades to faster hardware to compensate for the performance.

Kernel memory allocation in SVR4 is discussed in Section 12.7. The SVR4 treatment of

Table 14-1. Page faults with a multiuser benchmark on various implementations

Implementation	spurious validation faults	protection faults
SVR3 *regions* architecture	1172	1306
VM architecture, initial port	3040	1098
VM with *fork* enhancement	1116	1273
VM with *fork* and *exec* enhancements	840	1122
VM with *fork, exec,* and copy-on-write changes	640	142

translation buffer consistency is described in Section 15.11. The Mach memory management architecture, which has several parallels to SVR4 VM, is also discussed in Section 15.2.

14.13   Exercises

1.   In what ways is mapped file access semantically different from access through *read* and *write* system calls?
2.   Can *mmap* semantics be preserved by a distributed file system? Explain the effects of mapping files exported by NFS, RFS, and DFS servers.
3.   What are the differences between the page structure in SVR4 and the cmap structure in 4.3BSD?
4.   Why does the as structure have a hint to the segment that had the last page fault?
5.   What is the difference between an anonymous page and the anonymous object?
6.   Why do anonymous pages not need a permanent backing store?
7.   Why is there only one seg_map segment in the system?
8.   SVR4 delays the allocation of swap pages until the process creates an anonymous page, while 4.3BSD pre-allocates all swap pages during process creation. What are the benefits and drawbacks of each approach?
9.   Does each *mmap* call create a new segment? Is it always a vnode segment?
10.   When do processes share an anon_map?
11.   Why does the shared memory IPC structure acquire a reference to the anon_map for the segment?
12.   What support does the file system provide to the VM subsystem?
13.   Why does SVR4 not use the block buffer cache for file data pages?
14.   Why do both SVR4 and Solaris reserve swap space at segment creation time?
15.   In what situations does SVR4 use anticipatory paging? What are its benefits and drawbacks?
16.   What is lazy evaluation? When does SVR4 use lazy evaluation?
17.   What are the benefits and drawbacks of copy-on-write?

14.14   References

[Bala 92]   Balan, R., and Gollhardt, K., "A Scalable Implementation of Virtual Memory HAT Layer for Shared Memory Multiprocessor Machines," *Proceedings of the Summer 1992 USENIX Technical Conference,* Jun. 1992, pp. 107–115.

[Char 91]   Chartock, H., and Snyder, P., "Virtual Swap Space in SunOS," *Proceedings of the Autumn 1991 European UNIX Users' Group Conference,* Sep. 1991.

[Chen 90]   Chen, D., Barkley, R.E., and Lee, T.P., "Insuring Improved VM Performance: Some No-Fault Policies," *Proceedings of the Winter 1990 USENIX Technical Conference,* Jan. 1990, pp. 11–22.

[Elli 90]   Ellis, M.A., and Stroustrup, B., *The Annotated C++ Reference Manual,* Addison-Wesley, Reading, MA, 1990.

[Ging 87]   Gingell, R.A., Moran, J.P., and Shannon, W.A., "Virtual Memory Architecture in SunOS," *Proceedings of the Summer 1987 USENIX Technical Conference,* Jun. 1987, pp. 81–94.

[Klei 86]   Kleiman, S.R., "Vnodes: An Architecture for Multiple File System Types in Sun UNIX," *Proceedings of the Summer 1986 USENIX Technical Conference,* Jun. 1986, pp. 238–247.

[Mora 88]   Moran, J.P., "SunOS Virtual Memory Implementation," *Proceedings of the Spring 1988 European UNIX Users Group Conference,* Apr. 1988.

[UNIX 92]   UNIX System Laboratories, *Operating System API Reference, UNIX SVR4.2,* UNIX Press, Prentice-Hall, Englewood Cliffs, NJ, 1992.

15

More Memory
Management Topics

15.1 Introduction

This chapter discusses three important topics. The first is the Mach virtual memory architecture, which has some unique features such as the ability to provide much of the functionality through user-level tasks. The second is the issue of translation lookaside buffer consistency on multiprocessors. The third is the problem of using virtually addressed caches correctly and efficiently.

15.2 Mach Memory Management Design

The Mach operating system was developed in the mid-1980s at Carnegie-Mellon University, and its memory architecture evolved at about the same time as the SunOS/SVR4 VM design described in Chapter 14. While these two systems used very different terminology to describe their fundamental abstractions, they have many similarities in their goals, design, and implementation. Many VM objects and functions of SVR4 have almost identical counterparts in Mach. The following sections describe the design of the VM subsystem in Mach 2.5. The changes to this design in Mach 3.0 are relatively minor and not relevant to our description.

Due to the similarity of the Mach and SVR4 memory architectures, we avoid a lengthy explanation of all features of the Mach VM design. Instead, we present a comparative analysis and focus on those features of Mach VM that have no equivalent in SVR4.

15.2.1   Design Goals

Similar to SVR4, the Mach VM design is motivated by the limitations of 4.3BSD memory architecture, which is heavily influenced by the VAX hardware and hence is difficult to port. Moreover, the 4.3BSD functionality is primitive and restricted to demand-paging support. It lacks mechanisms for memory sharing other than read-only sharing of text segments. Finally, 4.3BSD memory management cannot be extended to a distributed environment. Although Mach provides full binary compatibility with 4.3BSD UNIX, it aims to support a richer set of features, including the following:

- Copy-on-write and read-write sharing of memory between related and unrelated tasks.
- Memory-mapped file access.
- Large, sparsely populated address spaces.
- Memory sharing between processes on different machines.
- User control over page replacement policies.

Mach separates all machine-dependent code into a small *pmap layer*. This makes it easy to port Mach to a new hardware architecture, since only the pmap layer needs to be rewritten. The rest of the code is machine-independent and is not modeled after any specific MMU architecture.

An important objective in the Mach VM design is to push much of the VM functionality out of the kernel. From its conception, Mach was intended to evolve into a microkernel architecture, with much of the traditional kernel functionality provided by user-level server tasks. Hence Mach VM relegates functions such as paging to external (user-level) tasks.

Finally, Mach integrates the memory management and interprocess communication (IPC) subsystems, to gain two advantages. The location-independence of Mach IPC (see Section 6.9) allows virtual memory facilities to be transparently extended to a distributed environment. Section 15.5.1 shows one example of how a user-level program can provide shared memory between applications on different machines. Conversely, the copy-on-write sharing supported by the VM subsystem allows fast transfer of large messages.

This discussion makes frequent references to the five fundamental abstractions of Mach, namely tasks, threads, ports, messages, and memory objects. A *task* is a collection of resources including an address space and some ports, in which one or more threads may run. A *thread* is a control point in a program; it is an executable and schedulable entity that runs within a task. Mach represents a UNIX process as a task with a single thread. Mach tasks and threads are described in Section 3.7. A *port* is a protected queue of messages. Many tasks may hold send rights to a port, but only one task has the right to receive messages from it. A *message* is a typed collection of data. Its size ranges from a few bytes to an entire address space. Mach ports and messages are described in Section 6.4. Memory objects provide the backing store for virtual memory pages and are described in this chapter.

15.2.2   Programming Interface

Mach supports a large number of operations related to memory management, which may be divided into four basic categories [Rash 88]:

- **Memory allocation** — A user may allocate one or more pages of virtual memory by calling *vm_allocate* for zero-filled pages or *vm_map* for pages backed by a specific *memory object* (for example, a file). This does not consume resources immediately, since Mach does not allocate physical pages until they are first referenced. The *vm_deallocate* call releases virtual memory pages.

- **Protection** — Mach supports read, write, and execute permissions for each page, but their enforcement depends on the hardware. Many MMUs do not recognize execute permissions. On such systems, the hardware will allow execute access to any readable page. Each page has a current and maximum protection. Once set, the maximum protection may only be lowered. The current protection may never exceed the maximum protection. The *vm_protect* call modifies both types of protections.

- **Inheritance** — Each page has an inheritance value, which determines what happens to that page when the task creates a child task using *task_create*. This attribute can take one of three values (Figure 15-1):

VM_INHERIT_NONE	The page is not inherited by the child and does not appear in its address space.
VM_INHERIT_SHARE	The page is shared between the parent and child. Both tasks access a single copy of the page, and changes made by one are immediately visible to the other.
VM_INHERIT_COPY	The child gets its own copy of the page. Mach implements this using copy-on-write, so the data is actually copied only if and when the parent or the child tries to modify the page. This is the default inheritance value of newly allocated pages.

The *vm_inherit* call modifies the inheritance value of a set of pages. It is important to note that this attribute is independent of how the task is currently sharing the page with others. For example, task **A** allocates a page, sets its inheritance to VM_INHERIT_SHARE, and then creates child task **B**. Task **B** sets the page's inheritance to VM_INHERIT_COPY and then creates task **C**. The page is thus shared read-write between **A** and **B**, but copy-on-write with **C** (Figure 15-2). This is in contrast to SVR4, where the inheritance method is identical to the current mapping type (*shared* or *private*) for the page in that process.

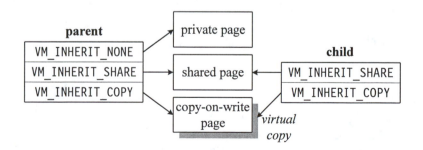

Figure 15-1. Inheriting pages through *task_create*.

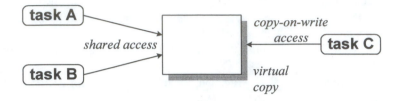

Figure 15-2. Multiple sharing modes on same page.

- **Miscellaneous** — The *vm_read* and *vm_write* calls allow a task to access pages belonging to other tasks. They are typically used by debuggers and profilers. The *vm_regions* call returns information about all the regions of the address space, and the *vm_statistics* call returns statistical data related to the virtual memory subsystem.

15.2.3   Fundamental Abstractions

Mach has been designed in an object-oriented manner, and its basic abstractions are represented by objects that are accessed by a well-defined interface. Figure 15-3 gives a high-level view of the important memory management primitives. The highest level object is the *address map,* described by the struct vm_map. It holds a doubly linked list of address map entries and a hint pointing to the last entry that resolved a page fault. Each *address map entry* (struct vm_map_entry) describes a contiguous region of virtual memory that has the same protection and inheritance properties, and is managed by the same memory object.

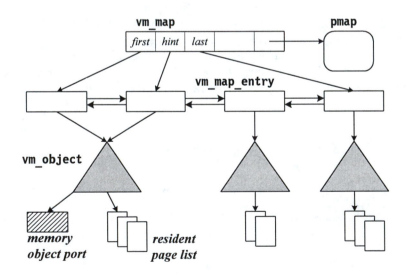

Figure 15-3. Objects that describe the Mach address space.

The *vm object* provides the interface to the pages of a memory object. The *memory object* [Youn 87] is an abstract object representing a collection of data bytes on which several operations, such as *read* and *write,* are defined. These operations are executed by the *data manager,* or *pager,* for that object. The *pager* is a task (user or kernel level) that manages one or more memory objects. Examples of memory objects are files, databases, and network shared memory servers (Section 15.5.1).

The memory object is represented by a port owned by the object's pager (that is, the pager has the receive rights to this port). The vm object has a reference, or *send right,* to this port and can use it to communicate with the memory object. This is described in more detail in Section 15.4.3. The vm object also maintains a linked list of all the resident pages of the memory object. This list speeds up operations such as deallocating the object or invalidating or flushing all of its pages.

Each memory object is associated with a unique vm object. If two tasks map the same memory object into their address space, they share the vm object, as described in Section 15.3. The vm object maintains a reference count to implement the sharing.

The similarity with SVR4 is striking. The vm_map corresponds to the `struct as`, and the vm_map_entry corresponds to `struct seg`. The pager's role is like that of the segment driver (except that the pager is implemented as a separate task), while the vm object and memory object together describe a specific data source such as a file. An important difference is the lack of a per-page protections array. If a user changes protections on a subset of pages of a region (the word region refers to the address range represented by an address map entry), Mach splits the region into two[1] different regions mapped to the same memory object. Other operations, likewise, could result in the merging of adjacent regions.

There are two other important data structures—the *resident page table* and the pmap. The *resident page table* is an array (`struct vm_page[]`) with one entry for each physical page. The size of a physical page is some power-of-two multiple of the hardware page size. Physical memory is treated as a cache for the contents of memory objects. The name space for these pages is described by the *<object, offset>* pair, which specifies the memory object the page belongs to and its starting offset in that object. Each page in this table is kept on three lists:

- A *memory object list* chains all pages of the same object and speeds up object deallocation and copy-on-write operations.
- *Memory allocation queues* maintained by the *paging daemon.* The page is on one of three queues—*active, inactive,* or *free.*
- *Object/offset hash chains* for fast lookup of a page in memory.

The vm_page[] array is very similar to the page[] array in SVR4. Finally, each task has a machine-dependent pmap structure (analogous to SVR4's *HAT layer*) that describes the hardware-defined virtual-to-physical address translation map. This structure is opaque to the rest of the system and is accessed by a procedural interface. The *pmap* interface assumes only a simple, paged MMU. The following are some of the functions it supports:

- pmap_create() is called when the system begins using a new address space. It creates a new pmap structure and returns a pointer to it.

---

[1] Or three different regions, if the subset is in the middle of the range of pages mapped by this region.

- `pmap_reference()` and `pmap_destroy()` increment and decrement reference counts on pmap objects.
- `pmap_enter()` and `pmap_remove()` enter and remove address translations.
- `pmap_remove_all()` removes all translations for a physical page. Since a page may be shared by multiple tasks (or be mapped to multiple addresses in the same task), it may have several translations.
- `pmap_copy_on_write()` lowers protections of all translations of that page to read-only.
- `pmap_activate()` and `pmap_deactivate()` are called during context switches to change the active pmap for the processor.

15.3   Memory Sharing Facilities

Mach supports read-write and copy-on-write sharing between related and unrelated tasks. Tasks inherit memory from their parent during *task_create*. This allows a task to share regions of its memory with its descendants. Unrelated tasks can share memory by mapping a region of their address space to the same memory object. Each of these facilities is described in this section.

15.3.1   Copy-on-Write Sharing

Copy-on-write sharing occurs when *task_create* duplicates a region marked as VM_INHERIT_COPY. Although this requires the child task to have its own separate copy of the region, the kernel optimizes the operation by not copying the page immediately. When either the parent or the child tries to modify a page in this region, it triggers a kernel trap. At that time, the kernel makes a copy of that page, and changes the address maps so that each process references its own personal copy of the page. This way, only those pages that are modified by either parent or child need to be copied, saving the kernel a lot of work.

The kernel implements such sharing by having the corresponding vm_map_entry in both tasks reference the same vm_object. It also sets a flag in the vm_map_entry to indicate that the region is shared copy-on-write. Finally, it calls `pmap_copy_on_write()` to write-protect the region for both the parent and the child, so as to trap any attempts to modify the pages. Figure 15-4 describes a typical scenario. Task **A** has created task **B**, and they both share a memory region copy-on-write. The region has three pages, currently managed by the shared vm object.

When either task attempts to modify a page, it results in a page fault, since the protections had been lowered to read-only. The fault handler allocates a new physical page and initializes it by copying from the faulting page. Furthermore, the handler must set up new mappings, so that each task references its own copy of that page while continuing to share the unmodified pages.

Mach uses a concept called *shadow objects* to implement such mappings. Figure 15-5 describes the situation after task **A** has modified page 1 and task **B** has modified page 3. Each task gets a shadow object, which manages the modified pages of that task. The shadow objects point back to the object that they shadow, which in this case is the original object.

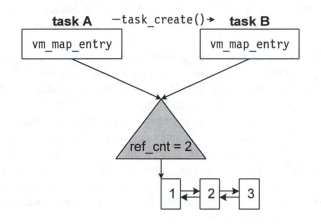

Figure 15-4. Copy-on-write inheritance.

To resolve a page fault, the kernel searches the shadow chain from the top down. Thus task **A** finds its page 1 from its shadow object, but pages 2 and 3 from the original object. Likewise, task **B** finds page 3 in its shadow object, but pages 1 and 2 from the original object.

As a task creates other children, it can build up a long chain of shadow objects. This not only wastes resources, but also slows down page fault handling since the kernel must traverse several shadow links. Mach therefore has algorithms to detect such situations and collapse shadow chains

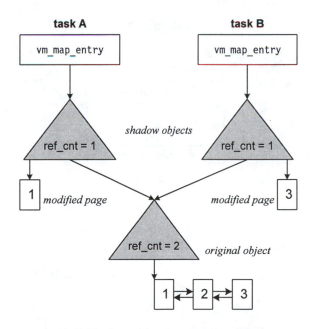

Figure 15-5. Shadow objects manage modified pages.

when possible. If all the pages managed by an object appear in objects above it in the chain, that object can be destroyed. This compaction method, however, is inadequate; if some of the pages of an object have been swapped out, the object cannot be deleted.

Copy-on-write sharing is also used for large message transfers. A task can send a message containing *out-of-line memory* (see Section 6.7.2). Applications use this facility to transfer a large amount of data without physically copying it if possible. The kernel maps such pages into the address space of the new process by creating a new vm_map_entry, which shares the pages copy-on-write with the sender. This is similar to copy-on-write sharing between parent and child.

One important difference is that while data is in transit, the kernel temporarily maps the data into its own address space. To do so, it creates a vm_map_entry in the kernel map and shares the pages with the sender. When the data has been mapped to the receiver's address space, the kernel destroys this temporary mapping. This protects against changes made to the data by the sender before the receiver retrieves the message. It also guards against other events such as termination of the sender.

15.3.2 Read-Write Sharing

Read-write sharing occurs when *task_create* duplicates a region marked as VM_INHERIT_SHARED. In this case, there is a single copy of this region, and any change is automatically visible to all processes sharing the page. This includes changes to the data, as well as to protections and other attributes. The latter may result in splitting the region into multiple subregions; each such region will be shared read-write by the tasks sharing the original region.

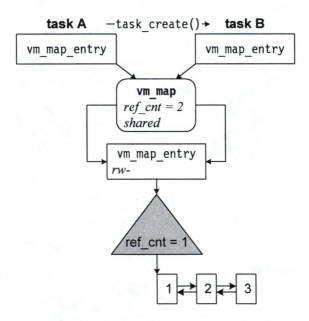

Figure 15-6. Read-write shared memory.

Since this is a fundamentally different form of sharing, the kernel needs a different way to implement it. Mach uses the notion of a *share map* to describe a read-write shared region. A *share map* is itself a vm_map structure, with a flag set to denote that it describes shared memory and a reference count of the number of tasks sharing it. It contains a list of vm_map_entrys; initially, the list contains a single entry.

Figure 15-6 illustrates the implementation of share maps. It requires that a vm_map_entry may point either to a vm_object or to a share map. In this example, the shared region contains three pages, initially with read and write permissions enabled. Subsequently, one of the tasks calls *vm_protect* to make page 3 read-only. This splits the region into two, as shown in Figure 15-7. Share maps allow such operations on shared regions to be implemented easily.

15.4   Memory Objects and Pagers

A memory object is a specific source of data, such as a file. A pager is a task that manages one or more memory objects and interacts with the kernel to move data between the object and physical memory. The interaction between the kernel, the pager, and user tasks takes place using well-defined, procedural interfaces.

15.4.1   Memory Object Initialization

To access the data in a memory object, a user task must first acquire send rights to the port repre-

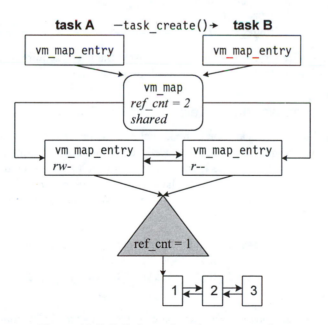

Figure 15-7. Splitting a shared memory region.

senting that object. It obtains the rights from the object's pager, since only the owner of a port may issue rights to it. This step is outside the scope of the VM subsystem and may involve some other interaction between the user task and the pager (and possibly other entities as well). For instance, the *vnode pager*[2] manages file system objects and provides a facility for user tasks to open files by name. When a user opens a file, the pager returns a send right to the port representing that file.

Once a task acquires a port (to acquire a port means to acquire send rights to it), it maps the memory object into its address space, using the system call

```
vm_map (pager_task, base_addr, size, mask,
         flag, memory_object_port, offset,
         copy, cur_prot, max_prot, inheritance);
```

This is similar to the *mmap* call in SVR4. It maps the byte range [offset, offset + size) in the memory object to the address range [base_addr, base_addr + size) in the calling task. The flag specifies whether the kernel may map the object to a different base address. The function returns the actual address to which the object was mapped.

The first time an object is mapped, the kernel creates two additional ports for the object—a *control port,* used by the pager to make cache management requests of the kernel, and a *name port,* which identifies the object to other tasks who may retrieve information about the object using the *vm_regions* call. The kernel owns these ports, and holds both send and receive rights to them. It then calls

```
memory_object_init  (memory_object_port,
                      control_port,
                      name_port,
                      page_size);
```

to ask the pager to initialize the memory object. This way, the pager acquires send rights to the request and name ports. Figure 15-8 describes the resulting setup.

15.4.2   Interface between the Kernel and the Pager

Once these channels have been established, the kernel and the pager use them to make requests of each other. Each request is made as a remote procedure call, by sending a message containing the parameters of the request to a port. The kernel sends messages to the pager through the memory object port, while the pager sends messages to the kernel using the pager reply port. A set of high-level functions provides a procedural interface to this message exchange. Some of the calls used by the kernel to communicate with the pager are:

```
memory_object_data_request (memory_object_port,
                             control_port, offset,
                             length, desired_access);
```

---

[2] Earlier releases of Mach used an *inode pager* and mapped the file with a *vm_allocate_with_pager* call [Teva 87]. The vnode pager was introduced to support the vnode/vfs interface [Klei 86].

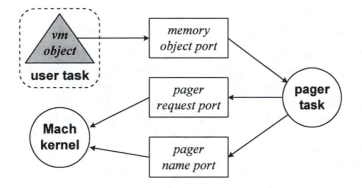

Figure 15-8. Communication with the pager.

```
memory_object_data_write    (memory_object_port,
                             control_port, offset,
                             data, data_count);

memory_object_data_unlock   (memory_object_port,
                             control_port, offset,
                             length, desired_access);
```

The kernel provides an interface used by the pager for cache management. It includes the following functions:

```
memory_object_data_provided    (control_port, offset, data,
                                data_count, lock_value);

memory_object_lock_request     (control_port, offset, size,
                                should_clean, should_flush,
                                lock_value, reply_port);

memory_object_set_attributes   (control_port, object_ready,
                                may_cache_object, copy_strategy);

memory_object_data_unavailable (control_port,
                                offset, size);
```

Each of these functions results in an asynchronous message. If the kernel makes a request of the pager, the pager responds by sending another message, using a kernel interface function. The following subsection shows some of the interactions between the kernel and the pager.

15.4.3   Kernel-Pager Interactions

There are four primary areas of interaction between the kernel and the pager:

- **Page faults** — When handling a page fault, the kernel traverses the address map to locate the appropriate vm object, which contains a reference to the memory object that can provide the required data. It then issues a `memory_object_data_request()` call, specifying the desired range of pages and type of access. The pager returns the data to the kernel by calling `memory_object_data_provided()`, giving it a pointer to the data in the pager's address space. The pager decides how to supply the required data—for instance, by getting it from a file or some network-based storage.

- **Pageouts** — When the kernel decides to write back a dirty page, it sends the page to the pager by calling `memory_object_data_write()`. When the pager has successfully saved the page, it calls *vm_deallocate* to release the cache resources.

- **Protection** — The kernel may request additional permissions to the page (such as write access to a page that is currently read-only) by calling `memory_object_data_unlock()`. Conversely, the pager may call `memory_object_lock_request()` to lower the access permissions on a page (for example, make a page read-only).

- **Cache management** — The pager calls `memory_object_lock_request()` with the `should_flush` flag to ask the kernel to invalidate its cached copy of the data, writing back any modifications. If the pager calls `memory_object_lock_request()` with the `should_clean` flag, it asks the kernel to write back any modified pages in the given range, but the kernel may continue to use the cached data. In both cases, the kernel responds by calling `memory_object_data_write()`, just as for pageouts.

15.5   External and Internal Pagers

The kernel-pager interface is very different from traditional implementations. Mach pagers are separate kernel or user-level tasks, and the kernel and the pager interact via message passing. Although this may seem cumbersome and complex, it offers some important advantages. User tasks can implement a variety of pagers to cater to different kinds of secondary storage objects. Although SVR4 also allowed multiple segment drivers, the kernel had explicit knowledge and control of each one. There was no way to add user-defined segment drivers. In Mach, the kernel has no specific knowledge of user-level pagers. It simply accesses the pagers through the vm objects.

Message passing brings with it the advantages of location transparency and extensibility. The pager task does not have to be on the same machine. It could run on any remote node on the network and be represented on the local machine by proxy ports for the memory objects. This allows Mach memory management to be extended to a multiple-processor configuration where machines share some of their memory via message passing. The next subsection describes such an example.

Pagers implemented as user tasks are known as external pagers. Mach also provides a *default pager,* which is internal (that is, implemented as a kernel task).[3] This pager manages all tempo-

---

[3] It is possible to have even the default pager run as a user task. [Golu 91] describes such an implementation.

rary memory objects, which have no permanent backing store. These objects may be divided into two types:

- Shadow objects, containing modified pages of regions that are shared copy-on-write.
- Zero-fill regions, such as stacks, heaps, and uninitialized data. Zero-fill regions are created by the call

> *vm_allocate* (target_task, address, size, flag);

The kernel creates the default pager during system initialization by calling `memory_object-_create()`. The objects it manages have no initial memory. The first time such pages are accessed, the kernel calls `memory_object_data_request()`, and the pager returns `memory_object_data-_unavailable()`, to indicate that the page must be zero-filled.

15.5.1 A Network Shared Memory Server

The *network shared memory server* has been frequently used to illustrate the versatility of the external pager interface. The server is a user-level task that allows a set of pages in its address space to be shared by client tasks anywhere on the network. It provides data to the clients when they page fault and synchronizes access to the shared data, making sure modifications made by one client are seen by all others. The clients must perceive no difference between sharing memory with other tasks on the same machine, or on different machines.

Memory sharing on a single machine is straightforward. There is only a single copy of the data, so that any changes made by one client are automatically and immediately visible to all others. Sharing data between tasks on different machines is complicated, since there may be copies of the same page on each machine, making it difficult to synchronize changes.

Let us consider the interactions that occur when two tasks on two different computers share a single page. The shared memory server may reside on either of these machines, or on a third machine. Figure 15-9 describes how the clients initially map the object into their address spaces. Each

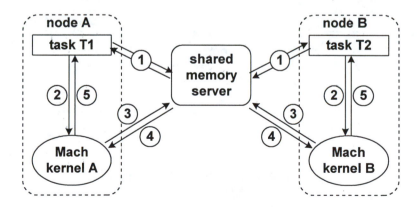

Figure 15-9. Two clients connect to the network shared memory server.

client task has the following interactions with the server:

1. The client acquires the memory object port from the server.
2. The client calls *vm_map* to map the object into its address space.
3. The kernel calls `memory_object_init()` to send a new object initialization message to the server. This gives the server the send rights to a control port to which the kernel listens.
4. The server calls `memory_object_set_attribute()` to inform the kernel that the object is ready.
5. The kernel completes the *vm_map* call and resumes the client.

Step 5 does not have to wait for step 4 to occur, but the client will not be able to access the data (attempted access will block) until the object is ready. Figure 15-10 shows what happens when task **T1** tries to write to the page:

1. Task **T1** write-faults, invoking the fault handler in the kernel.
2. The kernel calls `memory_object_data_request()` to request the server for a writable copy of the page.
3. The server returns the page via `memory_object_data_provided()`.
4. The kernel updates the address translation tables of task **T1** and resumes it.

Task **T1** can now modify the page. The server does not know yet of the changes made to the page. Consider what happens if task **T2** now wants to read this page (Figure 15-11):

1. Task **T2** read-faults and invokes the fault handler in kernel **B**.
2. Kernel **B** calls `memory_object_data_request()` to ask the server for a read-only copy of the page.
3. The server knows that node **A** has a writable copy of the page. So it calls `memory_object_lock_request()`, specifying the control port of kernel **A**, the `should_clean` flag, and a `lock_value` of `VM_PROT_WRITE`.[4]

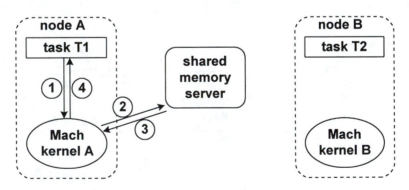

Figure 15-10. Task T1 tries to write to the page.

---

[4] If, instead, task **T2** were trying to write to the page, the server would use the `should_flush` flag, asking kernel **A** to invalidate its copy of the page.

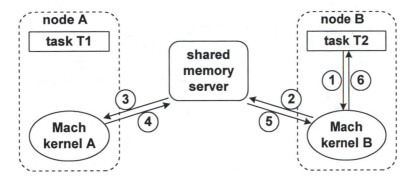

Figure 15-11. Task T2 tries to read the page.

4. Kernel **A** reduces the permissions on the page to read-only and writes back the modified page to the server via `memory_object_data_write()`.

5. Now the server has the most recent version of this page. It sends it to kernel **B** via `memory_object_data_provided()`.

6. Kernel **B** updates the address translation tables and resumes task **T2**.

Obviously, this is a slow process. If the two tasks frequently modify the page, they will re-peatedly go through this iteration, resulting in numerous IPC messages, repeatedly copying the page from one node to another. Much of this overhead is inherent in the problem of synchronizing data across a network. Note that each write fault causes the page to be copied over the network twice—first from the other client to the server, then from the server to the faulting client. We could think of reducing this to a single copy operation if the server could somehow ask one client to directly send the page to another. That, however, would break the modularity of the design and lead to quite complex interactions if there are more than two clients. Obviously, having the server reside on one of the clients would eliminate one copy operation and also reduce other message traffic on the net-work.

In spite of these shortcomings, the example illustrates how the close coupling of message passing and memory management allows us to build powerful and versatile applications. Another example [Subr 91] is an external pager that manages discardable pages, used by applications that perform their own garbage collection. The pager receives information from client tasks regarding which pages are discardable and influences page replacement by preflushing such pages. This frees up more memory for useful pages in the system.

15.6   Page Replacement

The Mach page replacement algorithm is different from those of SVR4 and 4.3BSD, both of which use the two-handed clock method (see Section 13.5.3). The algorithm is called *FIFO with second chance* [Drav 91]. It uses three FIFO (first-in, first-out) lists—*active, inactive,* and *free*—as shown in Figure 15-12.

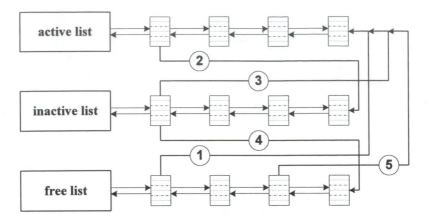

Figure 15-12. Page replacement.

Pages migrate from one list to another in the following ways:

1. The first reference to a page results in a page fault. The fault handler removes a page from the head of the free list and initializes it with the appropriate data (either fills it with zeroes or gets the data from the memory object). It then puts the page at the tail of the active list. Eventually, the page migrates to the head of this list, as pages ahead of it become inactive.
2. Whenever the free memory falls below a threshold value (vm_page_free_min), the *pagedaemon* is awakened. It moves some pages from the head of the active list to the tail of the inactive list. It turns off the reference bit in the hardware address translation mappings for these pages.
3. The *pagedaemon* also examines a number of pages at the head of the inactive list. Pages whose reference bits are set are returned to the tail of the active list.
4. If the *pagedaemon* finds a page whose reference bit is still clear, the page has not been referenced while on the inactive queue and can be moved to the tail of the free list. If the page is dirty, it is first written back to its memory object.
5. If the page is referenced while on the free list, it may still be reclaimed. In this case, it goes back to the tail of the active list. Otherwise, it will migrate to the head of the free list and eventually be reused.

On systems that do not support reference bits in the hardware, Mach simulates reference information by invalidating the mappings for the page, just as in BSD. Further, several parameters determine the amount of work done by the *pagedaemon* each time it awakens. These are described in Table 15-1.

Although the data structures and algorithms are somewhat different from the two-handed clock method used by SVR4 and 4.3BSD, the effect is somewhat similar. The inactive list is equivalent to the pages between the front and back hands. In the above description, step 2 is analogous to the function of the front hand, which clears the reference bits on pages to be scanned. The

Table 15-1. Mach *pagedaemon* parameters

Parameter	Usage	Default value (pages)
`vm_page_free_min`	Wake up pagedaemon when number of pages on free list falls below this value.	`25 + physmem/100`
`vm_page_free_target`	Move pages from inactive to free list until free list reaches this size.	`30 + physmem/80`
`vm_page_free_reserved`	Number of free pages reserved for the pagedaemon.	`15`
`vm_page_inactive_target`	Move pages from active to inactive list till inactive list reaches this size.	`physmem * 2/3`

function of the back hand is performed in steps 3 and 4, which examine the pages at the head of the inactive queue.

The major difference is in how the *pagedaemon* selects the active pages to move to the inactive queue. In the clock algorithm, the pages are picked sequentially based on their location in physical memory and not on their usage pattern. In Mach, the active list is also FIFO, so that the *pagedaemon* selects those pages that were activated the earliest. This is an improvement over the clock algorithm.

Mach does not provide alternative replacement policies. Some applications, such as databases, do not exhibit strong locality of reference and may find LRU-like policies inappropriate. [McNa 90] suggests a simple extension to the external pager interface that would permit a user-level task to choose its own replacement policy.

15.7   Analysis

Mach has a well-designed VM architecture with several advanced features. Much of its functionality is similar to that of SVR4, such as copy-on-write sharing, memory-mapped file access, and support for large, sparse, address spaces. Similar to SVR4, it also is based on an object-oriented approach, using a small set of objects that present a modular programming interface. It cleanly separates the machine-independent and dependent parts of the code and isolates the machine-dependent code in the pmap layer, which is accessed through a narrow, well-defined interface. When porting to a new hardware architecture, only the pmap layer needs to be rewritten.

Moreover, Mach VM offers many features not found in SVR4. It provides more flexible memory sharing facilities, by separating the notions of sharing and inheritance. It integrates memory management and interprocess communication. IPC uses VM to allow large messages (up to the entire address space of a task) to be transferred efficiently using copy-on-write. VM uses IPC to provide location independence for its objects and to extend the VM facilities to a distributed environment. In particular, user-level tasks may manage the backing store for memory objects, and the kernel communicates with these tasks through IPC messages. This coupling creates a highly flexible environment, allowing multiple user-level (external) pagers to coexist and provide different types of paging behavior. The network shared memory manager is an excellent example of how this interface may be used to add new functionality.

There are, however, some important drawbacks, many of them similar to those of SVR4. The VM system is larger, slower, and more complex than the BSD design. It uses more and larger data structures. Hence it consumes more physical memory for itself, leaving less available for the processes. Since the design keeps machine-dependent code to a minimum, it cannot be properly optimized for any particular MMU architecture.

In addition, the use of message passing adds considerable overhead. The cost is reduced in some cases by optimizing kernel-to-kernel message transfers. Overall, though, message passing is still a lot more expensive than simple function calls. Except for the network shared memory manager, external pagers are not used commonly. This raises questions about whether the external pager interface is useful enough to justify its high cost. Digital UNIX, the major commercial UNIX system based on Mach, does not support external pagers and does not export the Mach VM interface. Its VM subsystem has diverged from Mach in many respects.

15.8   Memory Management in 4.4BSD

In Section 13.4, we describe the 4.3BSD memory management model. This design is effective for the machines on which it was meant to run. When 4.3BSD was designed, a typical computer was a large, centralized time-sharing system that several users accessed concurrently through terminals connected by serial lines. It had a lot of local disk space (a few hundred megabytes), but a slow processor (1–2 mips) and small, expensive memory (4 megabytes was considered large). While UNIX supported networking, remote file systems had not yet become popular, and most systems used local disks for file systems and swap space. The 4.3BSD virtual memory model optimized memory consumption at the expense of extra storage or I/O.

This situation had changed dramatically by the early 1990s, when 4.4BSD was being developed. The typical user had exclusive use of a desktop workstation with a large memory (32 megabytes was not unusual) and fast processor (tens of mips). On the other hand, the proliferation of network file systems such as NFS allowed users to store their files on centralized file servers, and the workstation had either a small local disk or no disk at all. The 4.3BSD memory management design was quite unsuitable for this environment, and hence 4.4BSD replaced it with a new model [McKu 95].

The internal VM framework of 4.4BSD is based on that of Mach. Its external interface, however, is more like that of SVR4. Rather than exporting the notions of external pagers and memory objects, 4.4BSD provides an *mmap* system call, whose syntax is similar to that of SVR4 (see Section 14.2):

```
paddr = mmap (addr, len, prot, flags, fd, off);
```

This establishes a mapping between the locations [paddr, paddr+len) in the process and the byte range [off, off+len) in the file represented by fd.[5] As in SVR4, addr suggests what address to

---

[5]   We follow the standard convention for specifying ranges: square brackets indicate inclusive boundaries, while parentheses indicate exclusive boundaries.

map the file to, and prot specifies protections (combination of PROT_READ, PROT_WRITE, and PROT_EXECUTE). The flags MAP_SHARED, MAP_PRIVATE, and MAP_FIXED have the same meaning as in SVR4.

The 4.4BSD *mmap* has a few additional features. The flags argument must contain either MAP_FILE (mapping to a file or device) or MAP_ANON (mapping to anonymous memory). There are two additional flags—MAP_INHERIT, which specifies that the mapping should be retained after an *exec* system call, and MAP_HASSEMAPHORE, which specifies that the region may contain a semaphore.

Processes may share memory in two ways. They may map the same file into their address space, in which case the file provides the initial contents and backing store for the region. Alternatively, a process may map an anonymous region, associate a file descriptor with it, and pass the descriptor to other processes that wish to attach to the region. This avoids the overhead of a mapped file, and the descriptor is used only for naming.

4.4BSD allows fast synchronization between processes by allowing semaphores to be placed in a shared memory region. In traditional UNIX systems, processes use semaphores to synchronize access to shared memory (see Section 6.3). Manipulating semaphores requires system calls, which impose a lot of overhead and negate most of the performance benefits of shared memory. 4.4BSD reduces this overhead by placing semaphores in shared memory regions.

Empirical studies show that in most applications that use synchronization, when a process tries to acquire a shared resource, it finds the resource unlocked in a majority of cases. If cooperating processes place semaphores in a shared memory region, they can try to acquire the semaphore without making a system call, provided the system supports an atomic *test-and-set* or equivalent instruction (see Section 7.3.2). Only if the resource is locked does the process need to make a system call to wait for the resource to be unlocked. The kernel checks the semaphore again and blocks the process only if the semaphore is still locked. Likewise, a process freeing the resource can release the semaphore at the user level. It then checks if other processes are waiting for the resource; if so, it must make a system call to awaken them.

4.4BSD provides the following interface for semaphore management. The shared memory region containing the semaphore must be created with the MAP_HASSEMAPHORE flag. A process can acquire a semaphore using

```
value = mset (sem, wait);
```

where sem is a pointer to the semaphore and wait is a boolean that is set to true if the caller wants to block on the semaphore. On return, value is zero if the process has acquired the semaphore. To release a semaphore, a process calls

```
mclear (sem);
```

Systems that have an atomic *test-and-set* instruction implement *mset* and *mclear* as user-level functions. To block and unblock on the semaphore, 4.4BSD provides the following calls:

```
msleep (sem);
```

checks the semaphore, and blocks the caller if sem is still locked. The call *mwakeup* (sem);

wakes up at least one process blocked on this semaphore and does nothing if there are no blocked processes.

The semaphore interface in the System V IPC facility (see Section 6.3) is quite different from this. System V allows a set of semaphores to be manipulated in a single system call. The kernel ensures that all operations in a single call are committed atomically. This interface can be implemented in 4.4BSD by associating a single *guardian* semaphore with each such set. For any operation on the set, the process always starts by acquiring the guardian semaphore. It then checks if it can complete the desired operations; if not, it releases the guardian semaphore and blocks on one of the semaphores that it could not acquire. When it wakes up, it must repeat the whole process.

15.9   Translation Lookaside Buffer (TLB) Consistency

Memory traffic would be excessive if the processor had to access in-memory page tables for each address translation. Hence most MMUs contain a *translation lookaside buffer (TLB),* which is a cache of recent address translations. The TLB is implemented in hardware and consists of a small number of entries (typically, 64 to 256), each of which maps a virtual page to a physical page. The MMU checks this cache during each address translation operation. If it finds the translation in the cache, it can avoid looking up the in-memory address translation maps, which are costly to access.

The TLB is an associative cache, that is, the MMU simultaneously searches all the entries in the cache, trying to find one that matches the given virtual address. The entry contains the corresponding physical page number, as well as protection information about the page. The specific format of the entry is machine-dependent. Section 13.3 describes the format and access semantics of TLBs in the MIPS R3000, IBM RS6000, and Intel 80386 architectures.

The TLB supports two basic operations—*load,* and *invalidate* or *purge.* A TLB entry is loaded when there is a cache miss. On most architectures, this operation is performed by the hardware, which has explicit knowledge of the location and format of the second-order translation maps (such as page tables on many systems, or inverted page tables on systems such as IBM's RS6000). The MMU hardware locates the page table entry and loads a TLB entry for it before completing the address translation. The kernel is neither involved in nor aware of this operation.

Certain architectures, notably the MIPS R3000 [Kane 88], perform a *software reload.* On such systems, the MMU knows only about the TLB and generates a fault on each TLB miss. The kernel manages address translation maps, and the hardware neither knows about them nor defines their structure. Typically, the kernel uses traditional page tables, but this is not a requirement. When the MMU generates a TLB miss fault, the kernel must locate the translation and explicitly load a TLB entry containing the correct information.

All MMUs offer some way to invalidate TLB entries in software. The kernel may modify a page table entry for a variety of reasons, such as to change its protection or to invalidate it due to a pageout. This makes the associated TLB entry inconsistent, and it must be invalidated or purged from the cache. There are three ways in which the kernel may flush a TLB entry:

- Invalidate a single TLB entry, identified by the virtual address. If the TLB has no entry for that address, nothing is done. The TBIS (**T**ranslation **B**uffer **I**nvalidate **S**ingle) instruction on the VAX-11 is an example of this method.
- Invalidate the entire TLB cache. For instance, the Intel 80386 flushes the entire TLB any time the *Page Directory Base Register (PDBR)* is written to, either explicitly by a *move* instruction, or indirectly during a context switch. The VAX-11's TBIA (**T**ranslation **B**uffer **I**nvalidate **A**ll) instruction has the same effect.
- Load a new TLB entry, overwriting the previous entry for that address if one exists. This method is used by architectures such as the MIPS R3000, which allow software reloading of the TLB.

15.9.1 TLB Consistency on a Uniprocessor

On uniprocessor systems, the TLB is easy to manage. There are several events that may invalidate one or more TLB entries, such as:

- **Protection change** — A user may call *mprotect* to raise or lower protections on an address range. The kernel may change the protections on a page, either to simulate reference bits or to implement copy-on-write.
- **Pageout** — When a page is removed from physical memory, the kernel must invalidate all page table and TLB entries that refer to it.
- **Context switch** — When the kernel switches to a new process, all TLB entries for the old process become invalid. The entries mapping kernel addresses remain valid, since the kernel is shared by all processes. Some architectures support tagged TLBs, where each entry has a tag that identifies the process to which it belongs. For such systems, the TLBs are not invalidated by a context switch, since the new process will have a different tag.
- *exec* — When a process *execs* another program, all TLBs that map its old address space become invalid. The same virtual addresses now refer to pages of the new image.

TLB flushing is expensive, and the kernel tries to minimize its overhead in many ways. An important consideration is whether the inconsistency is benign. For instance, suppose the kernel reduces the protections on a page, changing it from read-only to read-write. The TLB entry is now inconsistent with the page table entry, but it is not necessary to invalidate it. In the worst case, the user will attempt to write to the page and find that the TLB entry still shows the page as read-only. At that time, the fault handler (or hardware) can reload a new TLB entry with the correct protections. By postponing the reload until absolutely necessary, we may often avoid it altogether (for instance, when the TLB entry is flushed by another event such as a context switch).

In situations involving multiple pages, the kernel may have to choose between flushing the entire TLB cache, and flushing a number of entries individually. The former is faster in the short run, since the whole cache is usually flushed in a single instruction. It might, however, lead to many more TLB misses, making it more expensive in the long run. The optimal solution usually depends on the number of entries that must be flushed.

15.9.2   Multiprocessor Issues

Maintaining TLB consistency on a shared-memory multiprocessor is a much more complex problem. Although all processors share main memory, each has its own TLB. Problems arise when one processor changes an entry in a page table that may be active on another processor. The latter may have a copy of that entry in its TLB and hence may continue to use the obsolete mapping. It is essential to propagate the change to the TLBs of any processor that may be using the page table.

A few machines synchronize TLBs in hardware. The IBM System/370, for instance, has an *ipte* instruction, which atomically changes the page table entry and flushes it from all TLBs in the system. More typically, the hardware provides no support for automatic synchronization of the different TLBs. Most systems do not even allow one processor to invalidate TLB entries on another.

There are many situations in which a change to one page affects TLBs on several processors:

- The page is a kernel page.
- The page is shared by multiple processes, each running on a different processor.
- On multithreaded systems, different threads of the same process may be running concurrently on different processors. If one thread modifies a mapping, all threads must see the change.

A related situation is where a process on one processor modifies the address space of a process running on another processor. Here, even though the change is to a single TLB, it is on a different processor from the one that initiated the change.

In the absence of hardware support, the kernel must solve the problem in software, using a notification mechanism based on cross-processor interrupts. For the purpose of this discussion, we define the terms *initiator* and *responder*. The initiator is the processor that modifies a mapping, thereby invalidating some remote TLBs. The responder is a remote processor that potentially holds a TLB for this mapping. The initiator sends an interrupt to the responder, who in turn invalidates the appropriate TLB.

The situation is complicated because we need to do two things at once—change the page table entry and invalidate the TLB entry. Suppose the responder flushes its TLB entry before the initiator changes the PTE. The process running on the responder may attempt to access the page in between, causing the hardware to reload the invalid TLB entry. Reversing the order also leads to problems. If the initiator first changes the PTE, the responder may write back an (obsolete) TLB entry to the page table in order to update *reference* or *modify* bits.

In order to perform the operation consistently, the responder must wait (in a busy loop) for the initiator to update the PTE before flushing its TLB. In the following section, we see the TLB synchronization algorithm used by Mach.

15.10   TLB Shootdown in Mach

The Mach *TLB shootdown* algorithm [Blac 89] involves a complex set of interactions between the initiator and the responder. The term *shootdown* refers to invalidating a TLB on another processor. To implement it, Mach uses a set of per-processor data structures:

- An *active* flag, which shows whether the processor is actively using some page table. If this flag is clear, the processor is participating in shootdown and will not access any modifiable *pmap* entry. (The *pmap* is the hardware address translation map for a task and usually consists of page tables.)
- A queue of invalidation requests. Each request specifies a mapping that must be flushed from the TLB.
- A set of currently active pmaps. Each processor usually has two active pmaps—the kernel pmap and that of the current task.

Each pmap is protected by a spin lock, which serializes operations on it. Each pmap also has a list of processors on which the pmap is currently active.

The kernel invokes the shootdown algorithm when one processor makes a change to an address translation that may invalidate TLB entries on other processors. Figure 15-13 illustrates the case of a single responder. The initiator first disables all interrupts and clears its own active flag. Next, it locks the pmap and posts TLB flush requests to every processor on which the pmap is active. It then sends cross-processor interrupts to those processors and waits for them to be acknowledged.

When the responder receives the interrupt, it also disables all interrupts. It then acknowledges the interrupt by clearing its active flag and spin-waits for the initiator to unlock the pmap. Meanwhile, the initiator has been waiting for all the relevant processors to become inactive. When they have all acknowledged the interrupt, the initiator flushes its own TLB, changes the pmap, and unlocks it. The responders now get out of their spin loop, process their request queue, and flush all obsolete TLBs. Finally, both the initiator and the responders reset their active flags, reenable interrupts, and resume normal operation.

15.10.1 Synchronization and Deadlock Avoidance

The shootdown algorithm uses several synchronization mechanisms, and the precise order of the operations is important [Rose 89]. It is important to disable all interrupts, otherwise a device interrupt can idle multiple processors for a long time. The lock on the pmap prevents two processors from simultaneously initiating shootdowns for the same pmap. The interrupts must be disabled before locking the page table, or a processor may deadlock when it receives a cross-processor interrupt (for another active pmap) while holding a lock.

The initiator clears its own active flag before locking the pmap, to avoid some deadlock conditions. Suppose two processors, **P1** and **P2**, attempt to modify the same pmap. **P1** disables interrupts, locks the pmap, and sends an interrupt to **P2**. Meanwhile, **P2** disables interrupts and blocks on the same lock. Now we have a deadlock, since **P1** is waiting for **P2** to acknowledge the interrupt, and **P2** is waiting for **P1** to release the pmap.

Clearing the active flag effectively acknowledges interrupts before they arrive. In the above example, **P1** will not block, since **P2** clears its flag before trying to lock the pmap. When **P1** unlocks the pmap, **P2** will resume and process the flush request posted by **P1**.

The shootdown algorithm has a subtle effect on all resource locking. It requires a consistent policy about whether interrupts are disabled before acquiring a lock. Suppose processor **P1** holds a resource with interrupts enabled, **P2** tries to acquire it with interrupts disabled, and **P3** initiates a

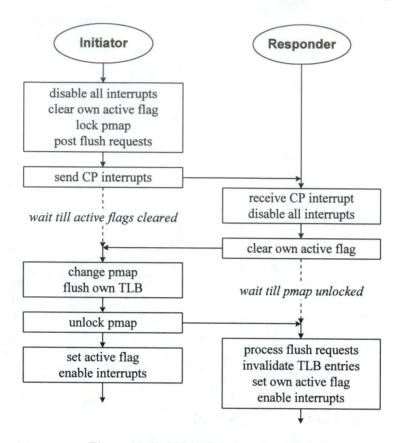

Figure 15-13. Mach TLB shootdown algorithm.

shootdown with **P1** and **P2** as responders. **P3** sends cross-processor interrupts to **P1** and **P2**, and blocks till they are acknowledged. **P1** acknowledges its interrupt and blocks until the pmap is released. **P2** is blocked on the lock with interrupts disabled and hence does not see or respond to the interrupt. As a result, we have a three-way deadlock. To prevent this, the system must enforce a fixed interrupt state for each lock: Either a lock should always be acquired with interrupts disabled or always with interrupts enabled.

15.10.2   Discussion

The Mach TLB shootdown algorithm solves a complex problem while making no assumptions about hardware features, other than support for cross-processor interrupts. It is, however, expensive, and does not scale well. All responders must busy-wait while the initiator changes the pmap. On a large multiprocessor with tens or hundreds of CPUs, shootdown can idle several processors at once.

The complexity is necessary due to two reasons. First, many MMUs write back TLB entries to the page tables automatically to update *modified* and *referenced* bits. This update overwrites the entire pmap entry. Second, the hardware and software page sizes are often different. Hence when the kernel changes the mapping of a single page, it may have to change several pmap entries. These changes must appear atomic to all processors. The only way to accomplish this is to idle all processors that may be using the pmap while making the change.

Many other TLB shootdown algorithms have been suggested and implemented. The next section describes some *ad hoc* solutions to reducing the frequency of TLB flushes. Other methods depend on some hardware characteristics that simplify the problem. For instance, [Rose 89] describes an efficient algorithm for the IBM Research Parallel Processor Prototype (RP3) [Pfis 85]. It uses the facts that the RP3 does not automatically write back TLB entries to main memory and that the large hardware page size (16 kilobytes) makes it unnecessary for a software page to span multiple hardware pages. Other research [Tell 88] suggests modifications to MMU architectures to assist in TLB shootdown.

15.11 TLB Consistency in SVR4 and SVR4.2 UNIX

The Intel Multiprocessor Consortium, comprising a group of computer companies, developed SVR4/MP, a version of SVR4 for the Intel family of multiprocessors. Subsequently, UNIX Systems Laboratories released SVR4.2/MP, a version of SVR4.2 that provided support for multiprocessors as well as for lightweight processes. In this section, we describe the TLB consistency algorithms of both releases.

15.11.1 SVR4/MP

The Mach shootdown algorithm solves the general TLB synchronization problem as efficiently as possible, while making no assumptions about hardware characteristics (other than the availability of cross-processor interrupts) or about the nature of the event that necessitates the shootdown. The SVR4/MP approach is to analyze the events leading to shootdowns and find better ways of handling them. There are four types of events that require TLB synchronization:

1. A process shrinks its address space, either by calling *brk* or *sbrk* or by releasing a region of memory.
2. The *pagedaemon* invalidates a page, either to free it or to simulate reference bits.
3. The kernel remaps a system virtual address to another physical page.
4. A process writes to a page that is shared copy-on-write.

In SVR4/MP, the hardware automatically flushes the TLB on each context switch [Peac 92]. Hence, case 1 is not a problem, unless the operating system supports multithreaded processes (which this release of SVR4/MP does not). SVR4/MP provides optimizations for cases 2 and 3.

To reduce TLB flushes in case 2, the *pagedaemon* batches a number of invalidate operations and flushes all TLBs in a single operation. This amortizes the cost of the global TLB flush over a number of page invalidations.

The major cause of TLB synchronization in SVR4 is the *seg_map* driver, used to support the read and write system calls. The kernel implements these calls by mapping the file into its own address space and then copying the data to the user process. It manages the *seg_map* segment to dynamically map and unmap file pages into its address space. As a result, the physical mapping of virtual addresses in this segment changes frequently. Since all processes share the kernel, it must ensure that such addresses are not accessed through obsolete mappings in the TLBs on other processors.

To track stale TLBs, the SVR4/MP kernel maintains a global generation count, as well as a local generation count for each processor. When a processor flushes its local TLB, it increments the global counter and copies the new value into its local counter. When *seg_map* releases the mapping for a page, the kernel tags the address with the global generation count. When *seg_map* reallocates the address to a new physical page, the kernel compares the saved generation count with the local counter of each processor. If any local counter has a lower value than the saved counter, the TLB may have stale entries, and the kernel performs a global TLB flush. Otherwise, all processors have done a local flush since this address was invalidated, and hence no stale TLBs exist for this page.

The SVR4/MP optimization for this situation is based on the assumption that once a *seg_map* mapping is invalidated, the kernel will not access that address until it is reallocated to a new physical address. To minimize the need for flushing, pages released by *seg_map* are reused in a first-in, first-out order. This increases the time between freeing and reallocating an address, making it more probable that other processors will flush their TLBs in the meantime.

15.11.2   SVR4.2/MP

SVR4.2/MP is a multiprocessor, multithreaded release of SVR4.2. Its TLB shootdown policies and implementation [Bala 92] have some features in common with the SVR4/MP work described in Section 15.11.1, but provide several important enhancements. All interactions with the TLB are restricted to the HAT layer (see Section 14.4), which is machine-dependent. The reference port for SVR4.2/MP is to the Intel 386/486 architecture, but the TLB consistency algorithms and interfaces are designed to be easily portable.

As in SVR4/MP, the kernel has complete control over its own address space, and hence can guarantee that it will not access invalid kernel mappings (such as those released by the *seg_map* segment). Hence the kernel may use a lazy shootdown policy for TLBs that map kernel addresses. SVR4.2/MP, however, supports lightweight processes (*lwps*, described in Section 3.2.2), and it is possible for multiple *lwps* of the same process to be running concurrently on different processors. Since the kernel does not control the memory access patterns of user processes, it uses an immediate shootdown policy for invalid user TLBs.

The global shootdowns used in SVR4/MP do not scale well for a system with a large number of processors, since the whole system idles while the shootdown proceeds. Hence SVR4.2/MP maintains a processor list for each hat structure. The hat of the kernel address space has a list of all on-line processors, since the kernel is potentially active on all of them. The hat of each user process has a list of all processors on which the process is active (an *lwp* of the process is running on it). This list is accessed through the following interface:

- hat_online() and hat_offline() add and remove CPUs to the list in the kernel hat structure.
- hat_asload (as) adds the processor to the list in the hat structure of the address space as and loads the address space into the MMU.

- `hat_asunload` (`as, flags`) unloads the MMU mappings for this process and removes the processor from the list of this `as`. The `flags` argument supports a single flag, which indicates whether the local TLB must be flushed after unloading the mappings.[6]

The kernel also uses an object called a *cookie,* which is visible only to the HAT layer. It may be implemented either as a timestamp or as a generation count (the reference port uses a timestamp), and must satisfy the condition that newer cookies are always greater in value. The routine `hat_getshootcookie()` returns a new cookie, whose value is a measure of the age of the TLB. The kernel passes the cookie to the `hat_shootdown()` routine, which is responsible for shootdown of kernel TLBs. If any other CPU has an older cookie, its TLB may be stale and needs to be flushed.

The following subsections explain how the kernel implements the lazy and immediate shootdown algorithms.

15.11.3   Lazy Shootdowns

As in SVR4/MP, the kernel uses lazy shootdown for *seg_map* pages. SVR4.2/MP also uses the lazy policy for the *seg_kmem* driver, which manages dynamically allocated kernel memory. When these drivers invalidate a page, they delay the shootdown until the page is about to be reused by the kernel. The *seg_map* driver, for instance, invalidates a page only when its reference count has gone down to zero, which means that no other process can access that page. Hence it is safe to let the stale and invalid translations for these pages remain in the TLBs. The kernel returns the page to a free list and calls `hat_getshootcookie()` to associate a new cookie with the page.[7]

When the kernel is going to reuse the page, it passes the cookie to `hat_shootdown()`, which compares it to the cookies on all the other CPUs. Any CPU having an older cookie has a TLB that is stale with respect to this page and is a candidate for shootdown.

The `hat_shootdown()` routine executes in the context of the initiator. It first acquires a global spinlock, so that only one shootdown can proceed at a time. It then sends cross-processor interrupts to all processors with an older cookie. Once each responding processor has begun processing the request, the initiator releases the spinlock and completes the reassignment of the page.

The responders do not need to wait for any synchronization upon receiving the interrupt. They simply flush their TLBs and resume normal processing. Since the initiator modifies the translations before the shootdown, any subsequent access to the page by the responder will load a valid TLB entry. The cross-processor interrupt runs at the highest interrupt priority level. No other interrupts should be allowed, since a deadlock can occur if a handler causes another shootdown.

The synchronization involved in this algorithm is simpler and more efficient than in the Mach shootdown algorithm. This is because the SVR4.2/MP kernel can guarantee not to access an invalid page, an assumption that Mach does not make.

---

6   The Intel context switch implementation does not ask `hat_asunload()` to flush the TLB, since the TLB is flushed anyway after the new u area is mapped in.

7   The treatment of *seg_kmem* pages is somewhat different. These pages are managed by a bitmap that is divided into zones (by default, a zone is 128 bits in size). A cookie is associated with each zone, and is set when an address in the zone is freed.

15.11.4   Immediate Shootdowns

When the kernel invalidates a user PTE, it must immediately shootdown the TLBs on all processors on which the process may be active. This is because the kernel has no control over the user's memory access pattern and cannot guarantee that the user will not attempt to access invalid pages. The algorithm, too, is more complex, since the responders must wait until the initiator modifies the PTEs before returning from the interrupt.

The SVR4.2/MP user TLB synchronization algorithm is essentially similar to that of Mach. The kernel uses an additional synchronization counter, which acts as a semaphore shared by the initiator and the responders. Figure 15-14 describes the sequence of operations.

When the kernel must invalidate a user PTE on a processor, it first locks the hat structure and then acquires the global spinlock (to avoid conflicts with other shootdowns). Next, it sends a cross-processor interrupt to each processor that shares this address space (using the list in the hat). When the responders receive the interrupt, they enter a loop waiting for the synchronization counter to be incremented.

When all the responders have begun looping, the initiator modifies the page table entries for the operation and then increments the synchronization counter. The responders exit the loop, flush their TLBs, and return from the interrupt. Finally, the initiator performs a local TLB flush and unlocks the spinlock and the hat structure.

This algorithm is further optimized for the Intel architecture in the case where the initiator must modify multiple PTEs in the same address space, such as when a process unmaps a segment. The 386 has a two-level page table (see Section 13.3.2), with the level 1 page table containing PTEs for the level 2 tables. In the multiple PTE case, the initiator simply invalidates the appropriate entries in the level 1 table, before incrementing the synchronization counter.

This allows the responders to complete their part of the shootdown and resume normal processing without waiting for the initiator to modify all the PTEs. If an *lwp* on the responder tries to access an invalid page, it will cause a page fault, since the level-1 PTE is invalid. The fault handler blocks, since the hat structure is still locked by the initiator. Thus, the responder will be unable to access invalid translations until the initiator has finished its work and loaded the correct mappings. This optimization, while elegant, is highly Intel-specific, and only applies in certain situations.

Another case that would normally require immediate shootdowns is in the pageout operation. Prior to SVR4.2/MP, the *pagedaemon* used a global replacement policy. It would scan a number of pages in the global pool and clear the reference bit (to collect reference information) or modify bit (after cleaning the page). Both these operations required a global shootdown. SVR4.2/MP has replaced this algorithm with one that uses local working set aging. The process to be aged is seized (all its *lwps* except the one running on the initiator are switched out) while the aging is performed. When the *lwps* are switched back in, the 386 context switch mechanism automatically flushes the TLB.

15.11.5   Discussion

SVR4/MP and SVR4.2/MP seek to optimize the TLB shootdown by taking advantage of the unique features of the hardware. Moreover, they treat each shootdown situation differently, taking advantage of the synchronization inherent in the functions that trigger the shootdown.

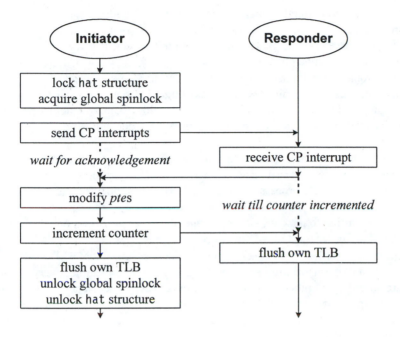

Figure 15-14. User TLB synchronization in SVR4.2/MP.

This approach achieves better performance than that of Mach, which uses a single, simple algorithm for all machines and all situations. However, the SVR4 approach is more difficult to port, since there are many dependencies on hardware and software specifics. For instance, the MIPS R3000, with its support for tagged TLB entries, presents a different set of problems, since there is no automatic TLB flush on each context switch. Section 15.12 presents a solution specific to such an architecture.

In brief, we again see a tradeoff between using a single solution that applies universally and using several *ad hoc* methods that tackle each situation optimally.

15.12   Other TLB Consistency Algorithms

A multiprocessor version of SVR3 for the MIPS R3000 target [Thom 88] provided yet another software solution for the TLB consistency problem. The MIPS architecture [Kane 88] features tagged TLBs (see Section 13.3.4). Each TLB entry has a 6-bit tag called *TLBpid,* which identifies the address space that owns the translation. This has some important consequences. There is no need to flush the TLB on a context switch, since the new process has a different TLBpid. As a result, a process may leave behind TLB entries on any processor on which it runs. If it later runs on the same processor again, it can reuse those entries, unless they have been flushed or individually replaced in the meantime.

Such a system needs to correctly handle the shrinking of an address space. Suppose a process runs first on processor **A** and then on processor **B**. While running on **B**, it shrinks its data region and flushes the invalid TLB entries on **B**. If it later runs on **A** again, it can access invalid pages through stale TLB entries left behind on **A**.

To solve this problem, the kernel assigns a new TLBpid to the process when it shrinks its address space. This automatically invalidates all its existing TLB entries on all processors.[8] The kernel must perform a global TLB flush when it reassigns the old TLBpid to another process. It reduces these events by reallocating TLBpids in first-in, first-out order, allowing stale entries to be flushed naturally.

The MIPS implementation also handles the case where a process writes to a copy-on-write page. The kernel makes a new copy of that page, and assigns it to the writing process. It also flushes the page from the local TLB. If the process had previously run on another processor, its TLB may have a stale translation for the page. The kernel maintains a record of the processors on which a process has run. If, after writing to the copy-on-write page, the process runs on one of those processors again, the kernel first flushes the TLB of that processor.

The optimizations described in this section reduce the need for global TLB synchronization and may improve system performance. In particular, the *seg_map* optimization is very useful, since kernel mappings are shared by all processors, and *seg_map* is heavily used. The solutions, however, are *ad hoc* and depend on specifics of both the hardware and the operating system function that triggers the synchronization. There is no single general algorithm (other than that of Mach) that is hardware-independent and caters to all situations.

15.13   Virtually Addressed Caches

Just as the TLB is a cache of address translations, computers also have high-speed caches for physical memory. Most machines have either separate caches for data and instruction or a common cache for both. Such a cache is usually 64-512 kilobytes in size and is accessed much faster than main memory. The cache is usually write-back, meaning that data writes change only the cache. The data is flushed to main memory only when the cache line needs to be replaced, perhaps to make room for other data.

Traditional hardware architectures provide a physically addressed cache (Figure 15-15). The MMU first translates the virtual address and then accesses the physical memory. All access to physical memory goes through the cache. If the data is found in the cache, the MMU does not need to access memory.

This has the advantage of simplicity. The hardware guarantees cache consistency, and the operating system is neither aware of nor responsible for the cache. The drawback is that the cache lookup can only happen after address translation, reducing the benefits of the cache. Moreover, if the TLB does not have a valid translation, the MMU has to fetch the page table entry from physical memory (or the cache). This requires additional cache and memory accesses.

---

[8]   This also flushes any valid TLB entries of that process.

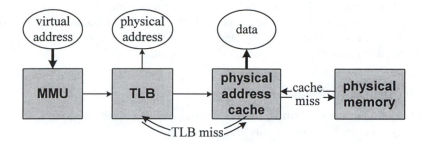

Figure 15-15. A physically addressed cache architecture.

Many modern architectures use a virtually addressed cache, in some cases eliminating the TLB altogether. Figure 15-16 shows a typical scenario. The MMU first searches for the virtual address in the cache. If found, there is no need to look further. If the data is not in the cache, the MMU proceeds with the address translation and obtains the data from physical memory.

It is also permissible to have both a virtual address cache and a TLB. In such architectures, such as the MIPS R4000 [MIPS 90] and the Hewlett-Packard PA-RISC [Lee 89], the MMU simultaneously searches the cache and the TLB. This has even better performance, at the cost of architectural complexity.

A virtual address cache is composed of a number of cache lines, each of which maps a number of contiguous bytes of memory. For instance, the Sun-3 [Sun 86] has a 64-kilobyte cache made up of 16-byte lines. The cache is indexed by virtual address, or optionally, by a combination of virtual address and a *process ID* or *context ID*. Since many virtual addresses (both from the same and different address spaces) map to the same cache line, the line must contain a *tag* that identifies the process and virtual address to which it maps.

Using the virtual address as a retrieval index has one important consequence—an *alignment factor* may be defined for the cache, such that if two virtual addresses differ by that value, they both map to the same cache line. This alignment factor usually equals the cache size or a multiple thereof. We use the term *aligned addresses* to refer to addresses that map to the same cache line.

Although physical address caches are completely transparent to the operating system, the hardware cannot guarantee consistency of virtual address caches. A given physical address may map

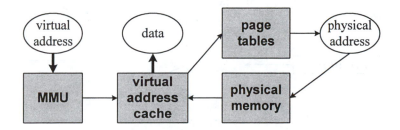

Figure 15-16. A virtual address cache.

to several virtual addresses and hence to multiple cache lines, causing an internal consistency problem. The write-back nature of the cache may cause main memory to become stale relative to the cache. There are three types of consistency problems—mapping changes or homonyms, address aliases or synonyms, and direct memory access (DMA) operations.

15.13.1   Mapping Changes

A mapping change occurs when a virtual address is remapped to a different physical address (Figure 15-17). This may occur in the following situations:

- **Context switch** — A context switch replaces one address space with that of the new process. In most architectures, the tag in the cache line identifies the process to which the line belongs. As a result, the context switch does not invalidate the entire cache. In many systems, however, the u area is in the kernel address space. When there is a context switch, the kernel remaps the u area addresses to the physical pages of the u area of the new process. Since the kernel is shared, its cache entries have a special tag that is valid for all processes. Hence the context switch invalidates all entries for the old u area in the cache.

- **Pageout** — When the *pagedaemon* removes a page from memory, it invalidates all cache entries for that page.

- **Protection changes** — Whenever the protections on a page change, the cache entries are affected. Protection changes may occur due to explicit *mprotect* calls or as a result of copy-on-write or reference-bit simulation by the kernel. When protections are reduced (for instance, when a read-only page is made writable), the change is benign and does not require updating the cache. When the process tries to access the data, it will page-fault and the fault handler will load the correct entry in the cache. When protections are increased (for instance, when a read-write page is made read-only), the change must be propagated to any cache entries for that data.

- **Copy-on-write** — When a process tries to write to a page that is currently shared copy-on-write, the kernel creates a new copy of the page, makes it writable, and changes the process's mappings to reference this copy. This invalidates any cache entries for this process that refer to the old page.

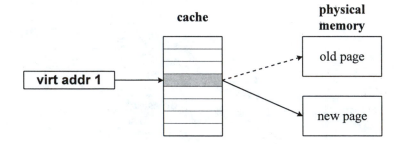

Figure 15-17. Mapping change invalidates a cache entry.

15.13.2   Address Aliases

Address aliases, or *synonyms,* are multiple virtual addresses for the same physical address (Figure 15-18). If a process modifies that location using one address, the change is not automatically propagated to the other cache line. If another process were to read the data using the other address, it would access stale data. Moreover, if two processes wrote to the location through the two different addresses, the order in which these writes will be flushed to memory is indeterminate. Synonyms occur due to several reasons:

- **Shared memory** — When many processes share a region of memory, each maps it into its address space. If these addresses are unaligned, they map to different cache lines, resulting in synonyms. Since processes are free to map shared memory regions to any location in their address space, the kernel usually cannot guarantee such alignment.
- **Mmap** — Processes may use *mmap* to map a file or memory object anywhere in their address space. If multiple processes map the same object to unaligned addresses, they create synonyms for it. A process may also map the same region into different parts of its address space, resulting in the same problem.
- **DVMA** — Systems that support *Direct Virtual Memory Access (DVMA)* allow devices to create a new virtual address mapping for a page that already has a virtual address. This requires one cache flush when establishing the new mapping and another upon completion.

15.13.3   DMA Operations

Many devices have the ability to transfer data to and from memory without involving the CPU. This feature is known as *Direct Memory Access* or *DMA* (not the same as DVMA, which is described in Section 15.13.2). DMA transfers usually bypass the cache and directly access main memory. Although this has the advantage of speed, it creates a cache consistency problem. Suppose the cache contains some modified data that has not been flushed to main memory. A DMA read will not receive these changes and, consequently, will read stale data. Likewise, a DMA write will not overwrite the cache, thus making its contents stale. At a later time, the stale cache line will be (incorrectly) flushed to memory, destroying the new data.

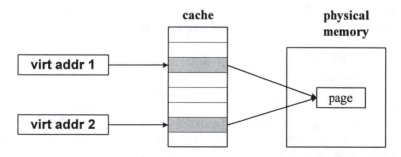

Figure 15-18. Synonyms lead to multiple cache entries for the same data.

15.13.4   Maintaining Cache Consistency

On systems with virtual address caches, the kernel must recognize events that might make the cache inconsistent and take some corrective action when they occur. The cache usually exports two operations to the kernel—*flush* and *purge*—both of which delete or invalidate an entry from the cache. The *flush* operation also writes back any changes to main memory; the *purge* operation does not. The kernel's action depends on the situation. Let us consider some specific examples.

When the mapping for a page changes, the kernel may have to flush all entries for that page. Cache flushes are expensive and must be avoided whenever possible. The kernel therefore flushes mappings only when they change from valid to invalid. For instance, during a context switch, the kernel flushes the cache entries for the u area of the old process when its mapping is invalidated. When the new u area is mapped in, no flushing is required, since this is an invalid-to-valid change.

The *pagedaemon* invalidates a page that is to be freed. At that time, its cache entries must be flushed, or else a process could continue to access the cached part of the page. When new data is read into a free page, however, no flushing is required.

During *fork,* many UNIX kernels map the pages of the child's u area temporarily to a region of kernel address space known as *forkutl*. The routine that uses *forkutl* does not explicitly release the mapping upon return. For virtual address cache systems, however, this routine must flush the relevant cache entries, since the region was implicitly unmapped.

The easiest way to handle address aliasing is to prevent it at the hardware level [Chao 90]. When a process faults on a page, the kernel checks to see if there is already another mapping for that page. If so, it invalidates that mapping, flushes the corresponding page from the cache, and then creates the new mapping for the faulting process. This way, memory sharing requires repeated re-mapping and cache flushing, since only one mapping is valid at a time.

This, however, is an expensive solution, due to the high costs of flushing the cache. In addition, there is the overhead of processing the traps as shared pages are faulted back and forth between the tasks. We need to consider cheaper alternatives. One immediate improvement is to allow aliases only for read-only access. When a process tries to write to such a page, the kernel invalidates all other mappings for the page.

Address aliases cause inconsistencies only when the two addresses are unaligned. Although UNIX allows applications to map shared memory regions or other memory objects to arbitrary, user-specified addresses, most applications do not rely on this feature. System calls such as *shmat* and *mmap* often provide options to let the kernel choose a convenient address for the mapping. Whenever possible, the kernel selects an aligned address, thus eliminating the cache consistency problem. For instance, on the Sun-3, if two addresses differ exactly by a multiple of 128 kilobytes, they map to the same cache entry. On this system, the kernel tries to find an address that is equal to, or different by a 128-kilobyte multiple from, the address of the region in other processes sharing it.

Many UNIX implementations are even more conservative, and either eliminate such facilities altogether or restrict their use. For instance, many versions of Hewlett-Packard's HP-UX operating system [Cleg 86] do not support *mmap* and only allow shared memory regions that are mapped to the same address in all processes. These systems implement shared text through a global shared virtual address segment rather than using memory mapping. SunOS [Chen 87] solves this problem by disabling caching on pages that may have multiple, nonaligned virtual addresses.

DMA operations, too, must be handled differently for virtual address caches. Before starting a DMA read, the kernel must flush from the cache any dirty data for the pages to be read. This ensures that main memory is not stale with respect to the cache. Similarly, in the case of a DMA write, the kernel must first purge any cache entries for the data to be overwritten. Otherwise, stale cache entries may later be written back to memory, destroying the more recent data from the DMA operation.

15.13.5   Analysis

A virtually addressed cache may improve memory access times substantially. However, it poses a variety of consistency problems that must be dealt with in software. Moreover, it changes the memory architecture in a fundamental way, which requires rethinking of several operating system design issues. Although it was designed to improve MMU performance, the cache conflicts with certain assumptions made by the operating system and may adversely affect overall system performance.

Modern UNIX systems support many forms of memory sharing and mapping, such as System V shared memory, memory-mapped file access, and copy-on-write techniques for memory inheritance and interprocess communications. In traditional architectures, these techniques reduce the amount of in-memory data copying and save memory by eliminating multiple resident copies of the same data. This results in substantial performance improvements.

On a virtual address cache architecture, however, such memory sharing results in synonyms. The operating system needs elaborate recovery procedures to ensure cache consistency, such as flushing the cache, making certain pages noncacheable, or eliminating or restricting certain facilities. These operations may reduce or eliminate any performance gains of memory sharing. [Chen 87] showed that while in typical benchmarks, the time taken by cache flushing was only 0.13% of total time, certain tests raised this value to 3.0%.

In many situations, several algorithms must be redesigned to perform efficiently on systems with virtual address caches. [Inou 92] describes several changes to operations in Mach and Chorus to address this problem. [Whee 92] describes many ways of eliminating unnecessary cache consistency operations, resulting in dramatic performance gains. Some of its suggestions are specific to the peculiarities of Hewlett-Packard's PA-RISC architecture. On that machine, the TLB lookup occurs in parallel with the address cache search, and the cache is tagged by the physical address. This allows it to detect many inconsistencies in software and take more efficient corrective measures.

15.14   Exercises

1.   How does memory inheritance in Mach differ from that in SVR4?
2.   In the example shown in Figure 15-2, what happens if task **A** tries to write to the page?
3.   Why does the Mach external pager interface result in poor performance?
4.   What is the difference between a *vm object* and a *memory object?*
5.   How does the network shared memory server behave if one of its clients crashes? What happens if the server crashes?
6.   Why does Mach not need a per-page protections array such as the one in SVR4?

7.   Suppose a vendor wished to provide System V IPC in a system based on a Mach kernel. How could he or she implement the shared memory semantics? What issues need to be addressed?

8.   What are the differences and similarities between the Mach *vm_map* call, the 4.4BSD *mmap* call, and the SVR4 *mmap* call?

9.   Section 15.8 mentions a guardian semaphore to implement System V-like semaphores in 4.4BSD. Would the guardian be allocated and managed by the kernel or a user library? Describe a skeletal implementation.

10. Why is the Mach page replacement policy called *FIFO with second chance?*

11. What is the benefit of having the operating system reload the TLB rather than the hardware?

12. Suppose the TLB entry contains a hardware-supported *referenced* bit. How will the kernel use this bit?

13. Since the UNIX kernel is nonpaged, what could lead to a change in a TLB entry for a kernel page?

14. Why is TLB shootdown expensive? Why is it more expensive in Mach than in SVR4/MP or SVR4.2/MP?

15. How do you think SVR4/MP and SVR4.2/MP handle TLB invalidations caused by writing a copy-on-write page?

16. What additional TLB consistency problems are caused by lightweight processes?

17. Why is lazy shootdown preferable to immediate shootdown in many cases? When is immediate shootdown necessary?

18. Does an MMU with a virtually addressed cache still need a TLB? What would be the benefits and drawbacks?

19. What is the difference between an address alias and a mapping change?

20. How does the kernel ensure consistency of the TLB and the virtual address cache during an *exec* system call?

15.15   References

[Bala 92]   Balan, R., and Golhardt, K., "A Scalable Implementation of Virtual Memory HAT Layer for Shared Memory Multiprocessor Machines," *Proceedings of the Summer 1992 USENIX Technical Conference,* Jun. 1992, pp. 107–115.

[Blac 89]   Black, D.L., Rashid, R., Golub, D., Hill, C., and Baron, R., "Translation Lookaside Buffer Consistency: A Software Approach," *Proceedings of the Third International Conference on Architectural Support for Programming Languages and Operating Systems,* Apr. 1989, pp. 113–132.

[Chao 90]   Chao, C., Mackey, M., and Sears, B., Mach on a Virtually Addressed Cache Architecture," *Proceedings of the First Mach USENIX Workshop,* Oct. 1990, pp. 31–51.

[Chen 87]   Cheng, R., "Virtual Address Cache in UNIX," *Proceedings of the Summer 1987 USENIX Technical Conference,* Jun. 1987, pp. 217–224.

[Cleg 86]   Clegg, F.W., Ho, G.S.-F., Kusmer, S.R., and Sontag, J.R., "The HP-UX Operating System on HP Precision Architecture Computers," *Hewlett-Packard Journal,* Vol. 37, No. 12, 1986, pp. 4–22.

[Drav 91]   Draves, R.P., "Page Replacement and Reference Bit Emulation in Mach," *Proceedings of the Second USENIX Mach Symposium,* Nov. 1991, pp. 201–212.

[Golu 91]   Golub, D.B., and Draves, R.P., "Moving the Default Memory Manager Out of the Mach Kernel," *Proceedings of the Second USENIX Mach Symposium,* Nov. 1991, pp. 177–188.

[Inou 92]   Inouye, J., Konuru, R., Walpole, J., and Sears, B., "The Effects of Virtually Addressed Caches on Virtual Memory Design and Performance," *Operating Systems Review,* Vol. 26, No. 4, Oct. 1992, pp. 14–29.

[Kane 88]   Kane, G., *Mips RISC Architecture,* Prentice-Hall, Englewood Cliffs, NJ, 1988.

[Klei 86]   Kleiman, S.R., "Vnodes: An Architecture for Multiple File System Types in Sun UNIX," *Proceedings of the Summer 1986 USENIX Technical Conference,* Jun. 1986, pp. 238–247.

[Lee 89]   Lee, R.B., "Precision Architecture," *IEEE Computer,* Vol. 21, No. 1, Jan. 1989, pp. 78–91.

[McKu 95]   McKusick, M.K., "A New Virtual Memory Implementation for Berkeley UNIX," *Computing Systems,* Vol. 8, No. 1, Winter 1995.

[McNa 90]   McNamee, D., and Armstrong, K., "Extending the Mach External Pager Interface to Accommodate User-Level Page Replacement," *Proceedings of the First Mach USENIX Workshop,* Oct. 1990, pp. 17–29.

[MIPS 90]   MIPS Computer Systems Inc., *MIPS R4000 Preliminary Users Guide,* 1990.

[Peac 92]   Peacock, J.K., Saxena, S., Thomas, D., Yang, F., and Yu, W., "Experiences from Multithreading System V Release 4," *Proceedings of the Third USENIX Symposium on Distributed and Multiprocessor Systems (SEDMS III),* Mar. 92, pp. 77–91.

[Pfis 85]   Pfister, G.F., Brantley, W.C., George, D.A., Harvey, S.L., Kleinfelder, W.J., McAuliffe, K.P., Melton, E.A., Norton, V.A., and Weiss, J., "The IBM Research Parallel Prototype (RP3): Introduction and Architecture," *Proceedings of the 1985 International Conference on Parallel Processing,* IEEE Computer Society, 1985, pp. 764–771.

[Rash 88]   Rashid, R.F., Tevanian, A., Young, M., Golub, D., Black, D., Bolosky, W., and Chew, J., "Machine-Independent Virtual Memory Management for Paged Uni-processor and Multiprocessor Architectures," *IEEE Transactions on Computing,* vol. 37, no. 8, Aug. 1988, pp. 896–908.

[Rose 89]   Rosenburg, B.S., "Low-Synchronization Translation Lookaside Buffer Consistency in Large-Scale Shared-Memory Multiprocessors," *Eleventh ACM Symposium on Operating Systems Principles,* Nov. 1987, pp. 137–146.

[Subr 91]   Subramanian, I., "Managing Discardable Pages with an External Pager," *Proceedings of the Second USENIX Mach Symposium,* Nov. 1991, pp. 201–212.

[Sun 86]   Sun Microsystems, Inc., "Sun–3 Architecture: A Sun Technical Report," Aug. 1986.

[Tell 88]   Teller, P., Kenner, R., and Snir, M., "TLB Consistency on Highly Parallel Shared Memory Multiprocessors," *Proceedings of the Twenty-First Annual Hawaii International Conference on System Sciences,* IEEE Computer Society, 1988, pp. 184–192.

[Teva 87]   Tevanian, A., Rashid, R.F., Young, M.W., Golub, D.B., Thompson, M.R., Bolosky, W., and Sanzi, R., "A UNIX Interface for Shared Memory and Memory Mapped Files Under Mach," Technical Report CMU–CS–1–87, Department of Computer Science, Carnegie-Mellon University, Jul. 1987.

[Thom 88]   Thompson, M.Y., Barton, J.M., Jermoluk, T.A., and Wagner, J.C., "Translation Lookaside Buffer Synchronization in a Multiprocessor System," *Proceedings of the Winter 1988 USENIX Technical Conference, Jan. 1988,* pp. 297–302.

[Whee 92]   Wheeler, R., and Bershad, B.N., "Consistency Management for Virtually Indexed Caches," *Proceedings of the Fifth International Conference on Architectural Support for Programming Languages and Operating Systems,* Oct. 1992.

[Youn 87]   Young, M.W., Tevanian, A., Rashid, R.F., Golub, D.B., Eppinger, J., Chew, J., Bolosky, W., Black, D., and Baron, R., "The Duality of Memory and Communication in the Implementation of a Multiprocessor Operating System," *Proceedings of the Eleventh ACM Symposium on Operating Systems Principles,* Nov. 1987, pp. 63–76.

16

Device Drivers and I/O

16.1   Introduction

The I/O subsystem handles the movement of data between memory and peripheral devices such as disks, printers, and terminals. The kernel interacts with these devices through *device drivers*. A driver controls one or more devices and is the only interface between the device and the rest of the kernel. This separation hides the intricacies of the device hardware from the kernel, which can access the device using a simple, procedural interface.

A comprehensive discussion of device drivers is beyond the scope of this book. Many books [Paja 92, Egan 88] devote themselves exclusively to this topic. Moreover, each UNIX vendor publishes detailed manuals [Sun 93] that explain how to write drivers for their platforms. This chapter simply provides an overview of the UNIX device driver framework. It deals primarily with the SVR4 interfaces, discusses their strengths and drawbacks, and describes some alternative approaches. It also describes the I/O subsystem, which is the part of the operating system that implements the device-independent processing of I/O requests.

16.2   Overview

A device driver is part of the kernel—it is a collection of data structures and functions that controls one or more devices and interacts with the rest of the kernel through a well-defined interface. In many ways, though, a driver is different and separate from the core components of the kernel. It is the only module that may interact with the device. It is often written by a third-party vendor, usually, the vendor of the device itself. It does not interact with other drivers, and the kernel may access it only through a narrow interface. There are many benefits to such an approach:

- We can isolate device-specific code in a separate module.
- It is easy to add new devices.
- Vendors can add devices without kernel source code.
- The kernel has a consistent view of all devices and accesses them through the same interface.

Figure 16-1 illustrates the role of the device driver. User applications communicate with peripheral devices through the kernel using the system call interface. The I/O subsystem in the kernel handles these requests. It, in turn, uses the device driver interface to communicate with the devices.

Each layer has a well-defined environment and responsibilities. User applications need not know whether they are communicating with a device or an ordinary file. A program that writes data to a file should be able to write the same data to a terminal or serial line without modification or recompilation. Hence the operating system provides a consistent, high-level view of the system to user processes.

The kernel passes all device operations to the I/O subsystem, which is responsible for all device-independent processing. The I/O subsystem does not know the characteristics of individual devices. It views devices as high-level abstractions manipulated by the device driver interface and takes care of issues such as access control, buffering, and device naming.

The driver itself is responsible for all interaction with the device. Each driver manages one or more similar devices. For example, a single disk driver may manage a number of disks. It alone knows about the hardware characteristics of the device, such as the number of sectors, tracks, and heads of a disk, or the *baud rates* of a serial line.

The driver accepts commands from the I/O subsystem through the device driver interface. It also receives control messages from the device, which include completion, status, and error notifications. The device usually gets the driver's attention by generating an interrupt. Each driver has an *interrupt handler,* which the kernel invokes when it fields the appropriate interrupt.

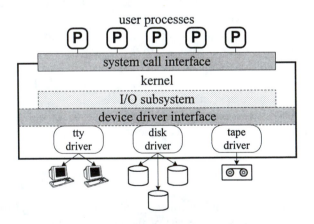

Figure 16-1. Role of a device driver.

16.2.1 Hardware Configuration

Device drivers are, by nature, extremely hardware-dependent. The driver framework takes into account how the CPU interacts with the device. Figure 16-2 is a simplistic view of the hardware setup in a typical system. The system bus is a high-speed, high-bandwidth interconnect, to which the CPU, MMU, and device controllers are attached. The Intel 80486 machines, for example, have ISA (Industry Standard Architecture) or EISA (Extended Industry Standard Architecture) buses.[1] On some machines, peripheral devices are connected to a separate I/O bus such as a MASSBUS or UNIBUS, which in turn is attached to the system bus through an *adapter*.

We can view a device as comprising two components—an electronic part, which is called a *controller* or *adapter,* and a mechanical part, which is the device itself. The *controller* is normally a printed circuit board that attaches to the computer and connects to the bus. A typical desktop computer may have a disk controller, a graphics card, an I/O card, and perhaps a network interface card.

Each controller may have one or more devices attached to it. The devices are usually of like type, but not necessarily so. For instance, a SCSI (Small Computer Systems Interface) controller [ANSI 92a] can control hard disks, floppy drives, CD-ROM (read-only compact disks) drives, and tape drives.

The controller has a set of *Control and Status Registers (CSRs)* for each device. Each device may have one or several CSRs, and their functions are completely device-dependent. The driver writes to the CSRs to issue commands to the device and reads them to obtain completion status and error information. These registers are very different from other general-purpose registers. Writing to a control register directly results in some device action, such as initiating disk I/O or performing a form-feed on a printer. Reading a status register may also have side effects, such as clearing the register. Hence the driver will not get the same results if it reads a device register twice in succes-

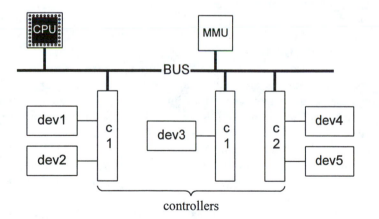

Figure 16-2. Hardware configuration in a typical system.

---

[1] Many 80486 machines also have a PCI (Peripheral Components Interconnect) local bus.

sion. Likewise, if it tries to read a register to which it has just written, the value read may be quite different from what was written.[2]

The I/O space of a computer includes the set of all device registers, as well as frame buffers for memory-mapped devices such as graphics terminals. Each register has a well-defined address in the I/O space. These addresses are usually assigned at boot time, using a set of parameters specified in a configuration file used to build the system. The system might assign a range of addresses to each controller, which in turn might allocate space for each device it manages.

There are two ways in which I/O space is configured in a system. On some architectures such as the Intel 80*x*86, the I/O space is separate from main memory and is accessed by special I/O instructions (such as `inb` and `outb`). Others, such as the Motorola 680*x*0, use an approach called *memory-mapped device I/O*. This approach maps I/O registers into a part of main memory and uses ordinary memory access instructions to read and write the registers.

Likewise, there are two ways of transferring data between the kernel and the device, and the method used depends on the device itself. We can classify devices into two categories based on their data transfer method—*Programmed I/O (PIO)* and *Direct Memory Access (DMA)*. PIO devices require the CPU to move data to or from the device one byte at a time. Whenever the device is ready for the next byte, it issues an interrupt. If a device supports DMA, the kernel may give it the location (source or destination) of the data in memory, the amount of data to transfer, and other relevant information. The device will complete the transfer by directly accessing memory, without CPU intervention. When the transfer completes, the device will interrupt the CPU, indicating that it is ready for the next operation.

Typically, slow devices such as modems, character terminals, and line printers are PIO devices, while disks and graphics terminals are DMA devices. Some architectures such as the SPARC also support *Direct Virtual Memory Access (DVMA),* where the device interacts directly with the MMU to transfer data to virtual addresses. In such a case, a device may directly transfer data to another device without going through main memory.

16.2.2   Device Interrupts

Devices use interrupts to get the attention of the CPU. Interrupt handling is highly machine-dependent, but we can discuss a few general principles. Many UNIX systems define a set of interrupt priority levels *(ipls)*. The number of *ipls* supported is different for each system. The lowest *ipl* is zero; in fact, all user code and most of the normal kernel code runs at *ipl* 0. The highest *ipl* is implementation-dependent: Some common values are 6, 7, 15, and 31. If the *ipl* of an arriving interrupt is lower than the current *ipl* of the system, the interrupt is blocked until the system *ipl* falls below that of the pending interrupt. This allows the system to prioritize different types of interrupts.

Each device interrupts at a fixed *ipl;* usually, all devices on a single controller have the same *ipl*. When the kernel handles an interrupt, it first sets the system *ipl* to that of the interrupt, so as to block further interrupts from that device (as well as others of the same or lower priority). Moreover,

---

2 A single register could server as a control and status register, allowing both reads and writes.

some kernel routines raise the *ipl* temporarily to block certain interrupts. For instance, the routine that manipulates the queue of disk block buffers raises the *ipl* to block out the disk interrupts. Otherwise, a disk interrupt may occur while the queue is in an inconsistent state, confusing the disk driver.

The kernel uses a set of routines to manipulate the *ipl*. For instance, `spltty()` raises the *ipl* to that of the terminal interrupt. The `splx()` routine lowers the *ipl* to a previously saved value. These routines are usually implemented as macros for efficiency.

Usually all interrupts invoke a common routine in the kernel and pass it some information that identifies the interrupt. This routine saves the register context, raises the *ipl* of the system to that of the interrupt, and calls the handler for that interrupt. When the handler completes, it returns control to the common routine, which restores the *ipl* to its previous value, restores the saved register context, and returns from the interrupt.

How does the kernel identify the correct interrupt handler? This depends on whether the system supports *vectored* or *polled* interrupts. In a completely vectored system, each device provides a unique *interrupt vector number,* which is an index into an *interrupt vector table.* The entries in the table are pointers to the appropriate interrupt handlers.

On some systems, the interrupt may only supply the *ipl*. Alternatively, it may supply a vector, but multiple devices may map to the same vector. In either case, the kernel may have to decide which of several interrupt handlers to invoke. It maintains a linked list of all handlers that share the same *ipl* (or the same vector). When an interrupt arrives, the common routine loops through the chain and polls each driver. The driver in turn checks if the interrupt was generated by one of its devices. If so, it handles the interrupt and returns success to the common routine. If not, it returns failure, and the common routine polls the next device.

It is possible to combine the two methods. Systems that support vectoring may also access the handlers through a linked list. This provides an easy way of dynamically loading a device driver into a running system. It also allows vendors to write *override drivers,* which are installed at the front of the linked list. Such a driver sits between the device and its default driver. It selectively traps and handles certain interrupts, and it passes the rest on to the default driver.

Interrupt handling is the most important task of the system, and the handler executes in preference to any user or system processing. Since the handler interrupts all other activity (except for higher priority interrupts), it must be extremely quick. Most UNIX implementations do not allow interrupt handlers to sleep. If a handler needs a resource that might be locked, it must try to acquire it in a nonblocking way.

These considerations influence what work the interrupt handler must do. On one hand, it must be short and quick, and hence do as little as possible. On the other hand, it must do enough work to make sure the device does not idle under a heavy load. For instance, when a disk I/O operation completes, the disk interrupts the system. The handler must notify the kernel of the results of the operation. It must also initiate the next I/O if a request is pending. Otherwise, the disk would idle until the kernel regained control and started the next request.

Although these mechanisms are common to a large number of UNIX variants, they are far from universal. Solaris 2.*x,* for instance, moves away from the use of *ipl*s except in a small number of cases. It uses kernel threads to handle interrupts and allows such threads to block if needed (see Section 3.6.5).

16.3   Device Driver Framework

In this section, we describe the framework for writing device drivers for UNIX. This includes the interface between the driver and the rest of the kernel, and the I/O subsystem's view of the devices and drivers.

16.3.1   Classifying Devices and Drivers

The I/O subsystem manages the device-independent part of all I/O operations. It needs a high-level, procedural view of devices. From its perspective, a device is a black box that supports a standard set of operations. Each device implements these operations differently, but the I/O subsystem is not concerned with that. In object-oriented terms (see Section 8.6.2), the driver interface forms an abstract base class, and each driver is a subclass, or specific implementation, of it. In practice, a single interface is not appropriate for all devices, since they vary greatly in functionality and access methods. UNIX therefore divides devices into two types—*block* and *character*—and defines a different interface for each.

A *block device* stores data and performs I/O in fixed-size, randomly accessible blocks. The block size is usually 512 bytes or a power-of-two multiple thereof. Examples of block devices are hard disks, floppy drives, and CD-ROM drives. Only block devices may contain a UNIX file system. The kernel interacts with block device drivers using buf structures, which encapsulate all details of the I/O operation.

Traditionally, the block drivers transferred data to and from an area of memory called the buffer cache (see Section 9.12). Each block of the cache has a buf structure associated with it. In modern UNIX systems, the memory subsystem provides much of the functionality of the buffer cache, and the latter is reduced both in size and in importance. Consequently, block devices do most of their I/O to paged memory. Nonetheless, block drivers continue to use buf structures to describe I/O operations. These structures are dynamically associated with the memory location of the data and passed to the driver. When the block driver reads or writes a buffer, it uses either a block in the buffer cache or an extent of memory described by a buf structure. This is further described in Section 16.6.

A *character device* can store and transfer arbitrary-sized data. Some character devices may transfer data one byte at a time, generating an interrupt after every byte. Others may perform some internal buffering. The kernel interprets the data as a continuous byte-stream that is accessed sequentially. The character device is not randomly addressable and does not permit a seek operation. Examples of character devices are terminals, printers, the mouse, and sound cards.

Not all devices fall neatly into one of these categories. In UNIX, every device that does not have the properties of a block device is classified as a character device. Some devices do no I/O at all. The hardware clock, for example, is a device whose job is merely to interrupt the CPU at fixed intervals, typically 100 times per second. Memory-mapped screens are randomly addressable, yet are treated as character devices. Some block devices, such as disks, also provide a character device interface, since that is more efficient for certain operations.

A driver does not have to control a physical device. It may simply use the driver interface to provide special functionality. The *mem* driver, for example, allows users to read or write locations in physical memory. The *null* device is a bit-sink—it only allows writes and simply discards all data written to it. The *zero* device is a source of zero-filled memory. Such devices are called *pseudodevices*.

One important advantage of a pseudodevice driver is that it is often the only way a third-party vendor can add functionality to a UNIX kernel. UNIX drivers support a general-purpose entry point called *ioctl*. This may be invoked with an arbitrary number of driver-specific commands. This allows a pseudodevice driver to provide a rich set of kernel functions to the user, without actually modifying the kernel itself.

Modern UNIX systems support a third class of drivers, called STREAMS drivers. STREAMS drivers typically control network interfaces and terminals, and replace character drivers used in earlier implementations for such devices. For compatibility reasons, the STREAMS driver interface is derived from that of character drivers, as described in Section 16.3.3.

16.3.2   Invoking Driver Code

The kernel invokes the device driver in several ways:

- **Configuration** — The kernel calls the driver at boot time to check for and initialize the device.
- **I/O** — The I/O subsystem calls the driver to read or write data.
- **Control** — The user may make control requests such as opening or closing the device, or rewinding a tape drive.
- **Interrupts** — The device generates interrupts upon I/O completion, or other change in its status.

The configuration functions are called only once, when the system boots. The I/O and control functions are *synchronous* operations. They are invoked in response to specific user requests and run in the context of the calling process. The block driver *strategy* routine is an exception to this (see Section 0). Interrupts are *asynchronous* events—the kernel cannot predict when they will occur, and they do not run in the context of any specific process.

This suggests partitioning the driver into two parts, usually called the *top half* and the *bottom half*. The top half contains the synchronous routines, and the bottom half contains the asynchronous routines. Top-half routines execute in process context. They may access the address space and the u area of the calling process, and may even put the process to sleep if necessary. Bottom-half routines run in system context and usually have no relation to the currently running process. They are therefore not allowed to access the current user address space or the u area. Also, they are not allowed to sleep, since that may block an unrelated process.

The two halves of the driver need to synchronize their activities with each other. If an object is accessed by both halves, then the top-half routines must block interrupts (by raising the *ipl*) while manipulating it. Otherwise, the device might interrupt while the object is in an inconsistent state, with unpredictable results.

In addition to the kernel accessing the driver, the driver may invoke kernel functions to carry out tasks such as buffer management, access control, and event scheduling. This part of the interface is described in Section 16.7. Before that, we discuss the specifics of the block and character driver interfaces.

16.3.3 The Device Switches

The *device switch* is a data structure that defines the entry points each device must support. There are two types of switches—struct bdevsw for block devices and struct cdevsw for character devices. The kernel maintains a separate array for each type of switch, and each device driver has an entry in the appropriate array. If a driver provides both a block and a character interface, it will have an entry in both arrays.

Example 16-1 describes typical switch data structures:

```
struct bdevsw   {
    int (*d_open)();
    int (*d_close)();
    int (*d_strategy)();
    int (*d_size)();
    int (d_xhalt)();
    ...
} bdevsw[];

struct cdevsw   {
    int (*d_open)();
    int (*d_close)();
    int (*d_read)();
    int (*d_write)();
    int (*d_ioctl)();
    int (*d_mmap)();
    int (*d_segmap)();
    int (*d_xpoll)();
    int (*d_xhalt)();
    struct streamtab* d_str;
    ...
} cdevsw[];
```

Example 16-1. Block and character device switches.

The switch defines the abstract interface. Each driver provides specific implementations of these functions. The next subsection describes each entry point. Whenever the kernel wants to perform an action on a device, it locates the driver in the switch table and invokes the appropriate function of the driver. For example, to read data from a character device, the kernel invokes the d_read() function of the device. In the case of a terminal driver, this might dereference to a routine called ttread(). This is further described in Section 16.4.6.

Device drivers follow a standard naming convention for the switch functions. Each driver uses a two-letter abbreviation to describe itself. This becomes a prefix for each of its functions. For instance, the disk driver may use the prefix *dk* and name its routines dkopen(), dkclose(), dkstrategy(), and dksize().

A device may not support all entry points. For instance, a line printer does not normally allow reads. For such entry points, the driver can use the global routine nodev(), which simply returns the error code ENODEV. For some entry points, the driver may wish to take no action. For instance, many devices perform no special action when closed. In such a case, the driver may use the global routine nulldev(), which simply returns 0 (indicating success).

As mentioned earlier, STREAMS drivers are nominally treated and accessed as character device drivers. They are identified by the d_str field, which is NULL for ordinary character drivers. For a STREAMS driver, this field points to a struct streamtab, which contains pointers to STREAMS-specific functions and data. Chapter 17 discusses STREAMS in detail.

16.3.4   Driver Entry Points

We now describe the device functions accessed through the device switch:

d_open()   Called each time the device is opened, and may bring device on-line or initialize data structures. Devices that require exclusive access (such as printers or tape drives) may set a flag when opened and clear it when closed. If the flag is already set, d_open() may block or fail. Common to both block and character devices.

d_close()   Called when the last reference to this device is released, that is, when no process has this device open. May shutdown device or take it off-line. A tape driver may rewind the tape. Common to both block and character devices.

d_strategy()   Common entry point for read and write requests to a block device. So named since the driver may use some strategy to reorder pending requests to optimize performance. Operates asynchronously—if the device is busy, this routine merely queues the request and returns. When the I/O completes, the interrupt handler will dequeue the next request and start the next I/O.

d_size()   Used for disk devices, to determine the size of a disk partition.

d_read()   Reads data from a character device

d_write()   Writes data to a character device

d_ioctl()   Generic entry point for control operations to a character device. Each driver may define a set of commands invoked through its *ioctl* interface. The arguments to this function include cmd, an integer that specifies which command to execute, and arg, a pointer to a command-specific set of arguments. This is a highly versatile entry point that supports arbitrary operations on the device.

d_segmap()   Maps the device memory into the process address space. Used by memory-mapped character devices to set up the mapping in response to the *mmap* system call.

d_mmap()   Not used if the d_segmap() routine is supplied. If d_segmap is NULL, the
                  mmap system call on a character device calls spec_segmap(), which in
                  turn calls d_mmap(). Checks if specified offset in device is valid and re-
                  turns the corresponding virtual address.

d_xpoll()   Polls the device to check if an event of interest has occurred. Can be used
                  to check if a device is ready for reading or writing without blocking, if an
                  error condition has occurred, and so on.

d_xhalt()   Shuts down the devices controlled by this driver. Called during system
                  shutdown or when unloading a driver from the kernel.

The switch structures vary a little between different UNIX versions. Some variants, for instance, expand the block device switch to include functions such as d_ioctl(), d_read(), and
d_write(). Others include functions for initialization or for responding to bus resets.

Except for d_xhalt() and d_strategy(), all of the above are top-half routines. d_xhalt()
is called during shutdown and, hence, cannot assume any user context or even the presence of interrupts. It therefore must not sleep.

The d_strategy() operation is special for several reasons. It is frequently invoked to read
or write buffers that are not relevant to the calling process. For instance, a process trying to allocate
a free buffer finds that the first buffer on the freelist is dirty, and invokes the strategy routine to
flush it to disk. Having issued the write, the process allocates the next free buffer (assuming it is
clean) and proceeds to use it. It has no further interest in the buffer that is being written, nor does it
need to wait for the write to complete. Moreover, disk I/O operations are often asynchronous (as in
this example), and the driver must not block the caller.

Hence d_strategy() is treated as a bottom-half routine. It initiates the I/O operation and
returns immediately without waiting for I/O completion. If the device is busy when the request arrives, d_strategy() simply adds the request to an internal queue and returns. Eventually, other
bottom-half routines invoked from the interrupt code will dequeue and execute the request. If the
caller needs to wait for the I/O to complete, it does so outside the d_strategy() routine.

The driver entry points for interrupt handling and initialization are typically not accessed
through the switch table. Instead, they are specified in a master configuration file, which is used to
build the kernel. This file contains an entry for each controller and driver. The entry also contains
information such as the *ipl,* interrupt vector number, and the base address of the CSRs for the driver.
The specific contents and format of this file are different for each implementation.

SVR4 defines two initialization routines for each driver—*init* and *start*. Each driver registers
these routines in the io_init[] and io_start[] arrays, respectively. The bootstrapping code invokes all *init* functions before initializing the kernel and all *start* functions after the kernel is initialized.

16.4   The I/O Subsystem

The I/O subsystem is the portion of the kernel that controls the device-independent part of I/O operations and interacts with the device drivers to handle the device-dependent part. It is also respon-

sible for device naming and protection, and for providing user applications with a consistent interface to all devices.

16.4.1 Major and Minor Device Numbers

The *name space* of devices describes how different devices are identified and referenced. There are three different name spaces for UNIX devices. The hardware name space identifies devices by the controller they are attached to and the logical device number on that controller. The kernel uses a numbering scheme to name devices. Users require a simple and familiar name space and use file system pathnames for this purpose. The I/O subsystem defines the semantics of the kernel and user name spaces and performs the mapping between them.

The kernel identifies each device by the *device type* (block or character), plus a pair of numbers, called the *major and minor device numbers*. The *major device number* identifies the type of device, or more specifically, the driver. The *minor device number* identifies the specific instance of the device. For example, all disks may have major number 5, and each disk will have a different minor number. Block and character devices have their own independent sets of major numbers. Thus major number 5 for block devices may refer to the disk driver, while that for character devices may refer to line printers.

The major number is the index of that driver in the appropriate switch table. In the previous example, if the kernel wants to invoke the *open* operation of a disk driver, it locates entry number *5* of bdevsw[] and calls its d_open() function. Usually, the major and minor numbers are combined into a single variable of type dev_t. The high-order bits contain the major number, and the low-order bits contain the minor number. The getmajor() and getminor() macros extract the respective parts. The code in the previous example looks something like this:

```
(*bdevsw[getmajor(dev)].d_open) (dev, ...);
```

The kernel passes the device number as an argument to the driver's d_open() routine. The device driver maintains internal tables to translate the minor device number to specific CSRs or controller port numbers. It extracts the minor number from dev and uses it to access the correct device.

A single driver may be configured with multiple major numbers. This is useful if the driver manages different types of devices that perform some common processing. Likewise, a single device may be represented by multiple minor numbers. For example, a tape drive may use one minor number to select an auto-rewind mode and another for no-rewind mode. Finally, if a device has both a block and a character interface, it uses separate entries in both switch tables, and hence separate major numbers for each.

In earlier UNIX releases, dev_t was a 16-bit field, with 8 bits each for the major and minor numbers. This imposed a limit of 256 minor devices for a major device type, which was too restrictive for some systems. To circumvent that, drivers used multiple major device numbers that mapped to the same major device. Drivers also used multiple major numbers if they controlled devices of different types.

Another problem is that the switch tables may grow very large if they contain entries for every possible device, including those that are not connected to the system or whose drivers are not linked with the kernel. This happens because vendors do not want to customize the switch table for each different configuration they ship, and hence tend to throw everything into the switches.

SVR4 makes several changes to address this problem. The dev_t type is 32 bits in size, usually divided into 14 bits for a major number and 18 for a minor number. It also introduces the notion of internal and external device numbers. The *internal device numbers* identify the driver and serve as indexes into the switches. The *external device numbers* form the user-visible representation of the device and are stored in the i_rdev field of the inode of the *device special file* (see Section 16.4.2).

On many systems, such as the Intel *x*86, the internal and external numbers are identical. On systems that support autoconfiguration, such as the AT&T 3B2, the two are different. On these systems, the bdevsw[] and cdevsw[] are built dynamically when the system boots and only contain entries for the drivers that are configured into the system. The kernel maintains an array called MAJOR[], which is indexed by the external major number. Each element of this array stores the corresponding internal major number.

The mapping between external and internal major numbers is many-to-one. The kernel provides the macros etoimajor() and itoemajor() to translate between the two numbers. The itoemajor() macro must be called repeatedly to generate all possible major numbers. There are also two minor numbers. For instance, if a driver supports two external major numbers with eight devices on each, they would internally map to minor numbers 0 to 15 for the single internal major number.

The getmajor() and getminor() macros return internal device numbers. The getemajor() and geteminor() macros return external device numbers.

16.4.2 Device Files

The *<major, minor>* pair provides a simple and effective device name space for the kernel. At the user level, however, it is quite unusable: users do not wish to remember a pair of numbers for each device. More important, users want to use the same applications and commands to read or write both to ordinary files and to devices. The natural solution is to use the file system name space to describe devices as well as files.

UNIX provides a consistent interface to files and devices by introducing the notion of a *device file*. This is a special file located anywhere in the file system and associated with a specific device. By convention, all device files are maintained in the directory **/dev** or a subdirectory thereof.

To users, a device file is not much different from an ordinary file. A user can open and close the device file, read or write to it, and even seek to a specific offset (only a few devices allow seeks). The shell can redirect *stdin, stdout,* or *stderr* to a device file. These operations translate to action on the device that the file represents. For instance, writing some data to the file **/dev/lpr** has the effect of printing the data on the line printer.

Internally, the device file is quite different from ordinary files. It has no data blocks on disk, but it does have a permanent inode in the file system in which it is located (usually, the root file system). The di_mode field of the inode shows that the file type is either IFBLK (for block devices) or IFCHR (for character devices). Instead of the list of block numbers, the inode contains a field called di_rdev, which stores the major and minor numbers of the device it represents. This allows the kernel to translate from the user-level device name (the pathname) to the internal device name (the *<major, minor>* pair). The translation mechanism is further described in the next section.

The device file cannot be created in the usual way. Only a superuser may create a device file, using the privileged system call

mknod (path, mode, dev);

where `path` is the pathname of the special file, `mode` specifies the file type (`IFBLK` or `IFCHR`) and permissions, and `dev` is the combined major and minor device number. The *mknod* call creates a special file and initializes the `di_mode` and `di_rdev` fields of the inode from the arguments.

Unifying the file and device name space has great advantages. Device I/O uses the same set of system calls as file I/O. Programmers may write applications without worrying about whether the input or output is to a device or to a file. Users see a consistent view of the system and may use descriptive character-string names to reference devices.

Another important benefit is access control and protection. Some operating systems such as DOS allow all users unrestricted access to all devices, whereas some mainframe operating systems allow no direct access to devices. Neither scheme is satisfactory. By unifying the file system and device name space, UNIX transparently extends the file protection mechanism to devices. Each device file is assigned the standard *read/write/execute* permissions for owner, group, and others. These permissions are initialized and modified in the usual way, just as for files. Typically, some devices such as disks are directly accessible only by the superuser, while others such as tape drives may be accessed by all.

16.4.3   The *specfs* File System

Modern UNIX systems use some form of the *vnode/vfs* interface [Klei 86], which allows multiple file system types in the same kernel. This approach associates an in-core object called a *vnode* with every open file. The interface defines a set of abstract operations on each vnode, and each file system supplies its own implementation of these functions. The `v_op` field in the vnode points to a vector of pointers to these functions. For example, the vnode of a *ufs* (UNIX file system) file points to a vector called `ufsops`, which contains pointers to the *ufs* functions such as `ufslookup()`, `ufsclose()`, and `ufslink()`. Section 8.6 describes this interface in detail.

Such a system needs a special way of handling device files. The device file itself resides on the root file system which, for the purposes of our discussion, may be assumed to be a *ufs* system. Thus its vnode is a *ufs* vnode and points to `ufsops`. Any operations on this file will be handled by the *ufs* functions.

This, however, is not the correct behavior. The device file is not an ordinary *ufs* file, but a special file that represents the device. All operations on the file must be implemented by corresponding action on the device, usually through the device switch. We therefore need a way to map all access to the device file to the underlying device.

SVR4 uses a special file system type, called *specfs,* for this purpose. It implements all vnode operations by looking up the device switch and invoking the appropriate functions. The *specfs* vnode has a private data structure called an *snode* (actually, the vnode is part of the snode). The I/O subsystem must ensure that, when a user opens a device file, he or she acquires a reference to the *specfs* vnode, and all operations to the file are routed to it.

To see how this happens, let us take an example where a user opens the file **/dev/lp**. The directory **/dev** is in the root file system, which is of type *ufs*. The *open* system call translates the pathname by repeatedly calling ufs_lookup(), first to locate the vnode for **dev**, then the vnode for **lp**. When ufs_lookup() obtains the vnode for **lp**, it finds that the file type is IFCHR. It then extracts the major and minor device numbers from the inode and passes them to a routine called specvp().

The *specfs* file system keeps all snodes in a hash table, indexed by the device numbers. specvp() searches the hash table and, if the snode is not found, creates a new snode and vnode. The snode has a field called s_realvp, in which specvp() stores a pointer to the vnode of **/dev/lp**. Finally, it returns a pointer to the *specfs* vnode to ufs_lookup(), which passes it back to the *open* system call. Hence *open* sees the *specfs* vnode and not the vnode of the file **/dev/lp**. The *specfs* vnode shadows the vnode of **/dev/lp**, and its v_op field points to the vector of *specfs* operations (such as spec_read() and spec_write()), which in turn call the device driver entry points. Figure 16-3 illustrates the resulting configuration.

Before returning, *open* invokes the VOP_OPEN operation on the vnode, which calls spec_open() in the case of a device file. The spec_open() function calls the d_open() routine of the driver, which performs the necessary steps to open the device. The term snode refers to shadow node. In effect, the *specfs* vnode shadows the "real" vnode and intercepts all operations on it.

16.4.4   The Common *snode*

The *specfs* system as described so far is incomplete and not quite correct. It assumes a one-to-one relationship between device files and the underlying devices. In practice, it is possible to have several device files, each representing the same device (their di_rdev fields will have the same value). These files may be in the same or different file systems.

This creates several problems. The device *close* operation, for instance, must be invoked only when the last open descriptor to the device is closed. Suppose two processes open the device using different device files. The kernel should be able to recognize the situation and call the device close operation only after both files are closed.

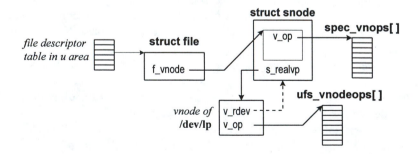

Figure 16-3. Data structures after opening **/dev/lp**.

Another problem involves page addressing. In SVR4, the name of a page in memory is defined by the vnode that owns the page and the offset of the page in the file. For a page associated with a device (such as memory-mapped frame buffers or disk blocks accessed through the raw interface), the name is ambiguous if multiple files refer to the same device. Two processes accessing the device through different device files could create two copies of the same page in memory, resulting in a consistency problem.

When we have multiple file names for the same device, we can classify device operations into two groups. Most of the operations are independent of the file name used to access the device, and thus can be funneled through a common object. At the same time, there are a few operations that depend on the file used to access the device. For instance, each file may have a different owner and permissions; therefore, it is important to keep track of the "real" vnode (that of the device file) and route those operations to it.

The *specfs* file system uses the notion of a *common snode* to allow both types of operations. Figure 16-4 describes the data structures. Each device has only one common snode, created when the device is first accessed. There is also one snode for each device file. The snodes of all files representing the same device share the common snode and reference it through the s_commonvp field.

The first time a user opens a device file for a particular device, the kernel creates an snode and a common snode. Subsequently, if another user opens the same file, it will share these objects. If a user opens another file that represents the same device, the kernel will create a new snode, which will reference the common snode through its s_commonvp field. The common snode is not directly associated with a device file; hence, its s_realvp field is NULL. Its s_commonvp field points to itself.

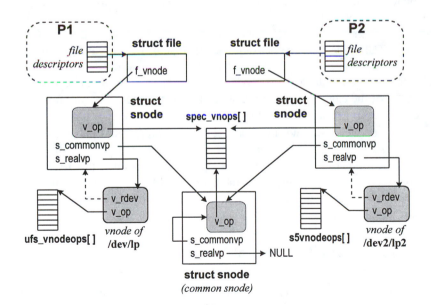

Figure 16-4. The common snode.

16.4.5   Device Cloning

In many cases, a user wants to open an instance of a device, but does not particularly want a specific minor number. For example, network protocols are usually implemented as device drivers and, if there are multiple active connections using the same protocol, each uses a different minor device number. A user who wants to establish such a connection does not care which minor number is used—any unused number will do. Although he or she could loop through all valid numbers searching for an unused one, that should not be the user's responsibility. It is desirable that the user specify that he wants any arbitrary minor device and that the kernel find an available device number.

This is achieved by the notion of *device cloning*. When a user opens a device file, the kernel initializes the snode and calls the spec_open() routine. spec_open() calls the d_open() entry point of the driver, passing it a pointer to the device number, stored in the s_dev field of the snode. One way a device can support cloning is by reserving one or more minor numbers for cloning. When a user opens a device file using such a number, the d_open() routine generates an unused minor number for this instance of the device. It modifies the s_dev field of the snode to reflect the new minor number (using the pointer passed to it) and updates internal data structures to reflect this mapping. In this way, multiple users can open the device by supplying the reserved minor number. The driver will return a different minor number (hence, a different logical instance of the device) to each caller.

In SVR4, most drivers that use cloning (e.g., network protocols and pseudoterminals) are implemented as STREAMS drivers. SVR4 provides special cloning support for STREAMS devices, using a dedicated *clone driver*. There is one device file for each STREAMS device that supports cloning. Its major device number is that of the *clone device,* and its minor number equals the major device number of the real device.

For instance, suppose the clone driver has major number 63. Then the device file **/dev/tcp** may represent all TCP (transmission control protocol) streams. If the TCP driver has a major device number 31, then the **/dev/tcp** file will have major number 63 and minor number 31. When a user opens **/dev/tcp**, the kernel allocates an snode and calls spec_open(). spec_open() invokes the d_open operation of the clone driver (implemented by the clnopen() routine), passing it a pointer to the device number (hence, a pointer to the s_dev field of the snode).

clnopen() extracts the minor number (31, in this example) and indexes it into cdevsw[] to locate the TCP driver itself. It then invokes the d_open operation of that driver, passing it the pointer to the device number, and a CLONEOPEN flag. In our example, this results in a call to the tcpopen() function. When tcpopen() sees the CLONEOPEN flag, it generates an unused minor device number and writes it back into the snode. This gives the user a unique TCP connection without having to guess which minor number to use.

16.4.6   I/O to a Character Device

The I/O subsystem plays a very small role in performing I/O to a character device. The driver does most of the work itself. When a user process first opens a character device, the kernel creates an snode and a common snode for it, as well as a struct file that references the snode. When the user makes a *read* system call, for example, the kernel dereferences the file descriptor to access the `struct file` and, from it, the vnode of the file (which is part of the snode of the device). It performs some validation, such as making sure the file is open for reading. It then invokes the `VOP_READ` operation on the vnode, which results in a call to `spec_read()`.

The `spec_read()` function checks the vnode type and finds that it is a character device. It looks up the `cdevsw[]` table, indexing by the major device number (which is stored in `v_rdev`). If the device is a STREAMS device, it calls `strread()` to perform the operation. For a character device, it calls the `d_read()` routine of the device, passing it the `uio` structure containing all the parameters of the read, such as the destination address in the user space and the number of bytes to be transferred.

Since `d_read()` is a synchronous operation, it can block the calling process if the data is not immediately available. When the data arrives, the interrupt handler wakes up the process, which copies it to user space. `d_read()` calls the kernel function `uiomove()` to copy data to user space. `uiomove()` must verify that the user has write access to the locations to which the data is being copied. Otherwise, a careless or malicious user could overwrite his or her text segment, or even the kernel address space. When the transfer completes, the kernel returns the count of bytes actually read to the user.

16.5   The *poll* System Call

The *poll* system call allows a user to multiplex I/O over several descriptors. Consider a server program that opens several network connections, each represented by a device file. It acquires a different file descriptor for each connection. If it wants to wait for an incoming message on a specific connection, it issues a read on that descriptor. The *read* system call will block the server until data arrives, then wake it up and return the data.

Suppose the server wants to wait for a message to arrive at any connection. Now the *read* system call is ineffective, since a read on one descriptor may block even though data is available on other connections. The server must use the *poll* system call, which allows it to wait simultaneously for events on a set of descriptors and return when any event occurs. Its syntax is

```
poll (fds, nfds, timeout);
```

where `fds` points to an array of size `nfds`, whose elements are described by

```
struct pollfd   {
    int fd;          /* file descriptor */
    short events;    /* events of interest */
    short revents;   /* returned events */
};
```

For each descriptor, `events` specifies which events are of interest to the caller, and on return, `revents` contains the events that have occurred. Both values are bitmasks. The types of defined events include `POLLIN` (data may be read without blocking), `POLLOUT` (data may be written without blocking), POLLERR (an error has occurred on the device or stream), POLLHUP (a *hang-up* has occurred on the stream), and others. Hence, in normal usage, *poll* checks if a device is ready for I/O or has encountered an error condition.

poll examines all the specified descriptors. If any event of interest has occurred, it returns immediately after examining all descriptors. If not, it blocks the process until any interesting event occurs. When it returns, the revents field of each pollfd shows which, if any, of the events of interest have occurred on that descriptor. *poll* also returns if timeout milliseconds expire, even if no events have occurred. If timeout is 0, *poll* returns immediately. If timeout is INFTIM or −1, *poll* returns only when an event of interest occurs (or the system call is interrupted). The return value of *poll* equals the number of events that have occurred, or 0 if the call times out, or −1 if it fails for another reason.

In our example, the server can issue a *poll* system call, specifying the POLLIN flag for each descriptor. When the call returns with a value greater than 0, the server knows that a message has arrived on at least one connection and examines the pollfd structures to find which ones. It can then read the message from that descriptor, process it, and poll again for new messages.

16.5.1   *poll* Implementation

Although the descriptors passed to *poll* may refer to any files, they are normally used for character or STREAMS devices, and we focus on this case here. The tricky part of *poll* is to block a process in such a way that it can be woken up when any one of a set of events occurs. To implement this, the kernel uses two data structures—pollhead and polldat. The struct pollhead is associated with a device file. It maintains a queue of polldat structures. Each polldat structure identifies a blocked process and the events on which it is blocked. A process that blocks on multiple devices has one struct polldat for each device, and they are chained together as shown in Figure 16-5.

The *poll* system call first loops through all the specified descriptors and invokes the VOP_POLL operation on the associated vnodes. The syntax for this call is

```
error = VOP_POLL (vp, events, anyyet, &revents, &php);
```

where vp is a pointer to the vnode, events is a bitmask of the events to poll for, and anyyet is the number of events of interest already detected by the *poll* system call on other descriptors. On return, revents contains the set of events that has already occurred and php contains a pointer to a struct pollhead.

In the case of a character device, the VOP_POLL operation is implemented by spec_poll(), which indexes the cdevsw[] table and calls the d_xpoll() routine of the driver. This routine checks if a specified event is already pending on the device. If so, it updates the revents mask and returns. If no event is pending and if anyyet is zero, it returns a pointer to the pollhead structure for the device. Character drivers typically allocate a pollhead for each minor device they manage.

On return from VOP_POLL on a device, *poll* checks revents and anyyet. If both are zero, no events of interest are pending on the devices checked so far. *poll* obtains the pollhead pointer from php, allocates a polldat structure, and adds it to the pollhead's queue. It stores a pointer to the

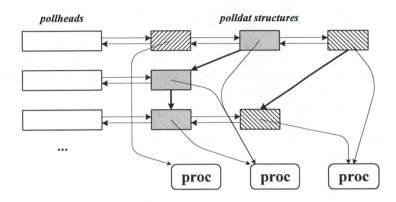

Figure 16-5. *poll* implementation.

proc structure and the mask of events for this device in the `polldat`, and chains it to other `polldat` structures for the same process.

If a device returns a nonzero value in `revents`, it means an event is already pending and *poll* does not need to block the process. In this case, *poll* removes all the `polldat` structures from the `pollhead` queues and frees them. It increments `anyyet` by the number of events set in `revents`. When it polls the next device, the driver will find `anyyet` to be nonzero and will not return a `poll-head` structure.

If no specified event is pending on any device, *poll* blocks the process. The drivers, meanwhile, maintain information about the events on which any process is waiting. When such an event occurs, the driver calls `pollwakeup()`, passing it the event and the pointer to the `pollhead` for that device. `pollwakeup()` goes through the `polldat` queue in the `pollhead` and wakes up every process waiting for that event. For each such process, it also traverses its `polldat` chain and removes and releases each `polldat` from its `pollhead` queue.

Each file system and device must implement polling. Ordinary file systems such as *ufs* and *s5fs* do so by calling the kernel routine `fs_poll()`, which simply copies the flags from `events` into `revents`, and returns. This causes *poll* to return immediately without blocking. Block devices usually do the same thing. STREAMS devices use a routine called `strpoll()`, which implements polling for any generic stream.

16.5.2   The 4.3BSD *select* System Call

4.3BSD provides a *select* system call that is functionally very similar to *poll*. The user calls select to wait for multiple events, using the syntax

select (nfds, readfds, writefds, exceptfds, timeout);

where `readfds`, `writefds`, and `exceptfds` are pointers to descriptor sets for read, write, and exception events respectively. In 4.3BSD, each descriptor set is an integer array of size `nfds`, with nonzero elements specifying descriptors whose events are of interest to the caller. For example, a user wishing to wait for descriptors *2* or *4* to be ready for reading will set elements *2* and *4* in readfds and clear all other elements in the three sets.

The timeout argument points to a struct timeval, which contains the maximum time to wait for an event. If this time is zero, the call checks the descriptor and returns immediately. If timeout itself is NULL, the call blocks indefinitely until an event occurs on a specified descriptor. Upon return, *select* modifies the descriptor sets to indicate the descriptors on which the specified events have occurred. The return value of *select* equals the total number of descriptors that are ready.

Most modern UNIX systems support *select,* either as a system call or as a library routine. Many of these implement the descriptor set in different ways, most commonly as a bitmask. To hide the details of the implementation, each system provides the following POSIX-compliant macros to manipulate descriptor sets:

```
FD_SET (fd, fdset)       /* sets descriptor fd in set fdset */
FD_CLR (fd, fdset)       /* clears fd in fdset */
FD_ISSET (fd, fdset)     /* checks if fd is set in fdset */
FD_ZERO (fdset)          /* clears all descriptors in fdset */
```

The constant FD_SETSIZE defines the default size of the descriptor set. It equals *1024* on most systems (including SVR4).

The implementation of *select* is similar to that of *poll* in some respects. Each descriptor of interest must correspond to an open file, otherwise the call fails. An ordinary file or a block device is always considered ready for I/O, and select is really useful only for character device files. For each such descriptor, the kernel calls the d_select routine of the appropriate character driver (the BSD counterpart of the d_xpoll entry point, to check if the descriptor is ready. If not, the routine records that the process has selected an event on the descriptor. When the event occurs, the driver must arrange to wake up the process, which then checks all descriptors once again.

The 4.3BSD implementation of select is complicated by the fact that the drivers can record only a single selecting process. If multiple processes select on the same descriptor, there is a collision. Checking for and handling such collisions may results in spurious wakeups.

16.6   Block I/O

I/O to block devices requires a lot more involvement of the I/O subsystem. There are two types of block devices—those that contain a UNIX file system, and *raw* or unformatted devices. The latter are only accessed directly through their device files. Although formatted devices may also be used in this way, they are normally accessed as a result of I/O to the files resident on them. Several different events may result in block I/O. These include:

- Reading or writing to an ordinary file.
- Reading or writing directly to a device file.
- Accessing memory mapped to a file.
- Paging to or from a swap device.

Figure 16-6 describes the various stages in the handling of a block read operation (the algorithm for writes is similar). In all cases, the kernel uses the *page fault* mechanism to initiate the read. The fault handler fetches the page from the vnode associated with the block. The vnode, in turn, calls the d_strategy() routine of the device driver to read the block.

A file may reside in many different places—on a local hard disk, on local removable media such as a CD-ROM or floppy disk, or on another machine on the network. In the last case, I/O occurs through network drivers, which are often STREAMS devices. This section only considers files on local hard disks. It begins by describing the buf structure, then examines the different ways in which the I/O subsystem accesses the block devices.

16.6.1 The buf Structure

The buf structure forms the only interface between the kernel and the block device driver. When the kernel wants to read or write to the device, it invokes the d_strategy() routine of the driver, passing it a pointer to a struct buf. This structure contains all the information required for the I/O operation, such as:

- Major and minor numbers of the target device
- Starting block number of the data on the device
- Number of bytes to be transferred (which must be a multiple of the sector size)
- The location of the data (source or destination) in memory
- Flags that specify whether the operation is a read or a write, and whether it is synchronous
- Address of a completion routine to be called from the interrupt handler

When the I/O completes, the interrupt handler writes status information in the buf structure and passes it to the completion routine. The completion status includes the following information:

- Flags that indicate that the I/O is complete, and whether it was successful
- An error code, if the operation failed
- The residual byte count, that is, the number of bytes not transferred

The buf structure is also used by the block buffer cache, to hold administrative information

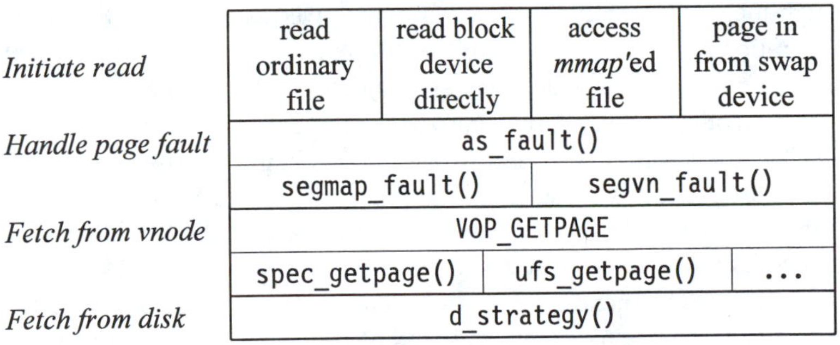

	read ordinary file	read block device directly	access *mmap*'ed file	page in from swap device
Initiate read				
Handle page fault	as_fault()			
	segmap_fault()		segvn_fault()	
Fetch from vnode	VOP_GETPAGE			
	spec_getpage()		ufs_getpage()	...
Fetch from disk	d_strategy()			

Figure 16-6. Different ways of initiating a block device read.

about a cached block. In modern UNIX systems such as SVR4, the buffer cache only manages file metadata blocks, such as those containing inodes or indirect blocks (see Section 9.2.2). It caches the most recently used blocks, in the expectation that they are more likely to be needed again soon, because of the *locality of reference* principle (see Section 13.2.6). A struct buf is associated with each such block; it contains the following additional fields used for cache management:

- A pointer to the vnode of the device file.
- Flags that specify whether the buffer is free or busy, and whether it is dirty (modified).
- The *aged* flag, which is explained in the following paragraph.
- Pointers to keep the buffer on an LRU freelist.
- Pointers to chain the buffer in a hash queue. The hash table is indexed by the vnode and block number.

The *aged* flag requires elaboration. When a dirty buffer is released, the kernel puts it at the end of the freelist. Eventually, it migrates to the head of the list, unless it is accessed in the interim. When the buffer reaches the head of the list, a process may try to allocate it and notice that it must be written back to disk first. Before issuing the write, it sets the *aged* flag on the buffer, indicating that the buffer has already traversed the freelist. Such an aged buffer must be reused before buffers that have been put on the freelist for the first time, since the aged buffers have been unreferenced for a longer time. Hence, when the write completes, the interrupt handler releases the aged buffer to the head of the freelist instead of the tail.

16.6.2   Interaction with the Vnode

The kernel addresses a disk block by specifying a vnode, and an offset in that vnode. If the vnode represents a device special file, then the offset is physical, relative to the start of the device. If the vnode represents an ordinary file, the offset is logical, relative to the start of the file.

Hence a data block of an ordinary file can be addressed in two ways—either by its file vnode and logical offset, or by the device vnode and physical offset. The latter is used only when a user directly accesses the underlying device. This could lead to two aliases for the same block in the kernel, resulting in two different copies of the block in memory. To avoid such inconsistencies, direct access to the block device file must be restricted to when the file system is not mounted.

Since each block is associated with a vnode (of a file or the device), the kernel channels all block I/O through the vnode (except for raw I/O, which we discuss in Section 16.6.4). The vnode provides two operations for this purpose—VOP_GETPAGE to fetch a page and VOP_PUTPAGE to flush it to disk. These correspond to the functions spec_getpage() and spec_putpage() for a device file, ufs_getpage() and ufs_putpage() for a *ufs* file, and so on.

This mechanism ensures consistency when a file is being accessed by multiple processes in different ways. In particular, it is possible for one process to map a file into memory, while another is accessing it through *read* and *write* system calls. To make sure the kernel sees a consistent view of the file, both access paths converge at the vnode.

The ufs_getpage() function, for example, checks to see if the page is already in memory, by searching a global hash table based on vnode and offset. If not, it calls the ufs_bmap() routine to convert the logical block number in the file to the physical block number on the disk. It then allocates a page in which to read the block and associates a buf structure with it. It obtains the disk's device number from the file's inode (which it accesses through the vnode). Finally, it calls the d_strategy() routine of the disk driver to perform the read, passing it a pointer to the buf, and waits for the read to complete (the calling process sleeps). When the I/O completes, the interrupt handler wakes up the process. ufs_getpage() also takes care of some other details, such as issuing read-aheads when necessary.

In the case when the block does not contain file data, it is associated with the vnode of the device file. Hence the spec_getpage() function is invoked to read the block. It too searches memory to check if the block is already there, and issues a disk read otherwise. Unlike a regular file, spec_getpage() does not need to convert from logical to physical block numbers, since its block numbers are already device-relative.

16.6.3   Device Access Methods

As discussed earlier, many different activities result in block I/O. Let us discuss each of them in turn, and examine the code path through the kernel.

Pageout Operations

Every page in the pageable part of memory has a struct page associated with it. This structure has fields to store the vnode pointer and offset that together name the page. The virtual memory subsystem initializes the fields when the page is first brought into memory.

The *pagedaemon* periodically flushes dirty pages to disk. It chooses the pages to flush based on their usage patterns (following a *not recently used* algorithm, described in Section 13.5.2), so as to keep the most useful pages in memory. There are several other kernel operations that result in writing pages out to disk, such as swapping out an entire process or calling *fsync* for a file.

To write a page back to disk, the kernel locates the vnode from the page structure and invokes its VOP_PUTPAGE operation. If the page belongs to a device file, this results in a call to spec_putpage(), which obtains the device number from the vnode and calls the d_strategy() routine for that device.

If the page belongs to an ordinary file, the operation is implemented by the corresponding file system. The ufs_putpage() function, for example, writes back pages of *ufs* files. It calls ufs_bmap() to compute the physical block number, then calls the d_strategy() routine for the device (getting the device number from the inode, which it accesses through the vnode). ufs_putpage() also handles optimizations such as *clustering,* where it gathers adjacent dirty pages and writes them out in the same I/O request.

Mapped I/O to a File

A process could map a file or part of a file to a segment of its address space using the *mmap* system call. Moreover, when *exec* loads a program, it maps the text and data into the process address space. Section 14.2 describes memory-mapped files in detail. Once the mapping has been established, when a process tries to read a page that is not already in memory (or not mapped in the *hardware address translation* tables), it causes a page fault. Since file-mapped pages belong to *vnode seg-*

ments (seg_vn), the fault is handled by the `segvn_fault()` routine. It invokes the `VOP_GETPAGE` operation on the vnode of the file, which is pointed to by the private data of the segment.

Likewise, when a process modifies a page to which it has a *shared* mapping, the page must be written back to the underlying file. This usually happens when the *pagedaemon* flushes the page, as previously described.

Ordinary File I/O

In SVR4, reads and writes to an ordinary file go through the *seg_map* driver. When a user invokes the *read* system call, for example, the kernel dereferences the file descriptor to get the `file` structure, and from it the vnode of the file. It invokes the `VOP_READ` operation on the vnode, which is implemented by a file-system-dependent function, such as `ufs_read()` for *ufs* files. `ufs_read()` performs the read as follows:

1. Calls `segmap_getmap()` to create a kernel mapping for the required range of bytes in the file. This function returns the kernel address to which it maps the data.
2. Calls `uiomove()` to transfer the data from the file to user space. The source address for the transfer is the kernel address obtained in the previous step.
3. Calls `segmap_release()` to free the mapping. The *seg_map* driver caches these mappings in LRU order, in case the same pages are accessed again soon.

If the page is not already in memory, or if the kernel does not have a valid hardware address translation to it, `uiomove()` causes a page fault. The fault handler determines that the page belongs to the *seg_map* segment, and calls `segmap_fault()` to fetch the page. `segmap_fault()` invokes the `VOP_GETPAGE` operation on the vnode, which retrieves the page from disk if necessary, as described above.

Direct I/O to Block Device

A user may directly access a block device, assuming he or she has the appropriate permissions, by issuing *read* or *write* system calls to its device file. In such a case, the kernel dereferences the file descriptor to access the `file` structure, and from that, the vnode. It then invokes the `VOP_READ` or `VOP_WRITE` operation on the vnode, which in this case, calls the `spec_read()` or `spec_write()` functions. These functions operate much like the corresponding *ufs* functions, calling `segmap_getmap()`, `uiomove()`, and finally `segmap_release()`. Hence the actual I/O occurs as a result of page faults or page flushes, just as in the previous cases.

Alternatively, a user could map a block device into its address space with the *mmap* system call. In that case, reads to mapped locations would cause page faults, which would be handled by the *seg_vn* (vnode segment) driver. The `segvn_fault()` routine would invoke the `VOP_GETPAGE` operation on the vnode, which would result in a call to `spec_getpage()`. This would call the `d_strategy()` routine of the device, if the page is not already in memory. Writes would be similarly handled by `spec_putpage()`.

16.6.4   Raw I/O to a Block Device

The problem with *read* and *write* system calls is that they copy the data twice—once between the user space and the kernel, and once between the kernel and the disk. This allows the kernel to cache the data, which is beneficial for typical applications. For applications that want to perform large data transfers to or from the disk, and whose access patterns do not benefit from caching, such an approach is inefficient and slow.

One alternative is to use *mmap* to map the data into the address space. While this eliminates the extra copy, its semantics are different from those of *read* and *write* system calls. Moreover, the *mmap* system call is a relatively new feature, not available on all implementations. UNIX provides a facility called *raw I/O,* which permits unbuffered access to block devices. It too avoids the extra copy, thus providing high performance. It is widely available, even on implementations that do not support *mmap.*

To allow raw I/O, the block device must also present a raw, or character interface. Hence it must have an entry in the character device switch. Applications perform raw I/O by issuing *read* or *write* system calls to the associated character device, which result in calling the d_read() or d_write() routines of that device. These routines directly call the kernel function physiock(), which does the following:

1. Validates the I/O parameters, such as making sure the I/O does not start beyond the end of the device.
2. Allocates a buf structure from a freelist.
3. Calls as_fault() to fault in the user pages involved in the operation.
4. Locks the user pages in memory so they cannot be paged out.
5. Calls the d_strategy() routine of the associated block device. The character driver passes the device number as an argument to physiock().
6. Sleeps until the I/O completes.
7. Unlocks the user pages.
8. Returns the results of the operation (transfer count, error status, etc.) to the caller.

16.7   The DDI/DKI Specification

Even though device drivers are part of the kernel, they are usually written independently by device vendors, frequently without access to the kernel source code. This is possible due to the switch-based, procedural interface between the kernel and the driver. To develop a driver for a UNIX kernel, the vendor simply supplies an implementation of the interface, which includes the switch functions, interrupt handler, and configuration and initialization functions. Entries are added to the appropriate configuration files (such as **conf.c**, which contains the bdevsw[] and cdevsw[] tables) and the kernel is rebuilt, linking the driver with the set of kernel object files provided by the operating system vendor.

The preceding sections discussed this part of the interface in detail. However, the interface described so far is incomplete, since it only covers the calls made by the kernel to the driver. The driver, too, must invoke several kernel functions to access services such as data transfer, memory allocation, and synchronization. Moreover, since multiple, independently written drivers coexist in the kernel and may be active concurrently, it is important that they not interfere with each other or with the kernel.

To reconcile the goals of independent driver development and peaceful coexistence, the interface between the kernel and the driver must be rigorously defined and regulated. To achieve this, SVR4 introduced the *Device-Driver Interface/Driver-Kernel Interface (DDI/DKI)* specification [UNIX 92b], which formalizes all interactions between the kernel and the driver.

The interface is divided into several sections, similar to the organization of the UNIX *man* pages. These sections are:

- **Section 1** describes the data definitions that a driver needs to include. The way in which the kernel accesses this information is implementation-specific and depends on how it handles device configuration.
- **Section 2** defines the driver entry point routines. It includes the functions defined in the device switches, as well as interrupt handling and initialization routines.
- **Section 3** specifies the kernel routines that the driver may invoke.
- **Section 4** describes the kernel data structures that the driver may use.
- **Section 5** contains the kernel #define statements that a driver may need.

The interface is divided into three parts:

- **Driver-kernel** — This is the largest part of the interface. It includes the driver entry points and the kernel support routines.
- **Driver-hardware** — This part describes routines that support interactions between the driver and the device. These routines are highly machine-dependent, but many of them are defined in the DDI/DKI specification.
- **Driver-boot** — This part deals with how a driver is incorporated into the kernel. It is not contained in the DDI/DKI specification, but is described in various vendor-specific device driver programming guides [Sun 93].

The specification also describes a number of general-purpose utility functions that provide services such as character and string manipulation. These are not considered a part of the DDI/DKI interface.

Each function in the interface is assigned a *commitment level*, which may be 1 or 2. A *level-1* function will remain in future revisions of the DDI/DKI specification and will only be modified in upward-compatible ways. Hence code written using level-1 functions will be portable to future SVR4 releases. The commitment to support *level-2* routines, however, is limited to three years after a routine enters level 2. Each such routine has an entry date associated with it. After three years, new revisions of the specification may drop the routine entirely or modify it in incompatible ways.

A level-1 routine may contain some features that are defined as level-2. Further, the entire routine may be moved to level 2 in a new release of the specification (for example, the rminit() function, discussed in Section 16.7.2). The date of that release becomes the entry date for that routine, and it will continue to be supported as defined for a minimum of three more years.

16.7.1   General Recommendations

The DDI/DKI specification makes a number of recommendations that help ensure the portability of drivers across different releases of SVR4:

- Drivers should not directly access system data structures, in particular the u area. Earlier versions of UNIX often required drivers to access the u area to read information such as the base address and byte count for a data transfer, or to return status and error values. As a result, the driver depended on the structure of the u area and had to be modified or rebuilt if the structure changed. SVR4 removes all such dependencies and passes information between the kernel and the driver through the data structures defined in section 4.
- While accessing section 4 structures, drivers should not access fields that are not described in the specification. These fields may not be supported in future releases.
- Drivers should not define arrays of the structures defined in section 4. Such arrays are not portable if the size of the structure changes in a future release. The iovec and uio structures are two exceptions to this rule.
- Some structure fields comprise a bitmask of flags. Drivers should only set or clear flags in such masks and never directly assign a value to the field. This is because the actual implementation may contain flags not listed in the specification.
- Structures intended to be opaque to the application are not specified in section 4, but are mentioned in the description of the routines that use them. Drivers should not access any members of such structures and should only use them by reference, passing pointers to them to those kernel routines.
- Drivers should use the section 3 functions to read or modify section 4 structures whenever possible. This protects the driver from changes made to the structures in future revisions.
- The driver should include the file **ddi.h** after all the system *include files,* but before any driver-specific *include files.* This is because many functions in the specification are implemented as macros by the rest of the kernel. The **ddi.h** file undefines the macros, forcing the drivers to use the function call forms of these routines, which are more portable. Including driver-specific files after **ddi.h** ensures that the driver only uses the DDI/DKI interface.
- The driver should declare as static any private routines or global variables that are used only by the driver.

16.7.2   Section 3 Functions

Section 3 forms the bulk of the DDI/DKI specification and contains kernel functions used by the device drivers. These routines may be divided into various functional groups:

- **Synchronization and timing** — The sleep() and wakeup() routines are described in Section 2.5.1. The delay() function blocks a process for a specified amount of time. The timeout() and untimeout() routines allow scheduling of tasks and are described in Section 5.2.1.

- **Memory management** — The kmem_alloc() and kmem_free() routines handle kernel memory allocation. The rminit(), rmalloc(), and rmfree() routines manage resource maps. These functions are described in Chapter 12. The functions physmap() and phys-mapfree() allocate and release virtual address mappings for physical addresses.
- **Buffer management** — geteblk() allocates a buffer, while brelse() releases one. The driver calls biowait() to wait for I/O completion, and the interrupt handler calls bio-done() to wake up waiting processes and release the buffer.
- **Device number operations** — The getemajor() and geteminor() functions extract the external major and minor device numbers from a dev_t. The itoemajor() and etoimi-nor() functions provide the translation between external and internal major numbers.
- **Direct memory access** — A set of machine-specific functions support DMA operations. The specification describes functions supported for the IBM PC-AT compatible architectures.
- **Data transfers** — The uiomove() move function copies data between kernel and user space or between two areas in kernel space. It is capable of scatter-gather I/O in any one direction. For instance, it can gather data from multiple user buffers into a single kernel buffer (see Figure 16-7). It uses a uio structure to describe the parameters of the transfer. The copyin() and copyout() routines transfer data between a driver buffer and a user buffer. Machine-specific routines, such as inb() and outb(), move data into or out of I/O space on architectures that do not support memory-mapped I/O (such as the Intel x86).
- **Device polling** — Routines to support device polling include phalloc() and phfree() to allocate pollhead structures and pollwakeup() to wake up polling processes.
- **STREAMS** — A number of routines support STREAMS device drivers. These are described in Chapter 17.
- **Utility routines** — The interface describes a set of string manipulation functions such as strcpy() and strlen(), byte manipulation functions such as bcopy(), bcmp() and bzero(), error handling functions such as ASSERT() and cmn_err(), and convenience functions such as max() and min().

16.7.3   Other Sections

Section 1 specifies that each driver must define a prefix, which it must use for all its global functions and data structures. The prefix is specified in the implementation-dependent configuration file and allows the kernel to identify the driver entry points. For example, a disk driver may define the prefix *dk,* and name its functions dkopen(), dkclose(), and so on. The section also specifies that the driver must define a global variable called *prefix*devflag and describes the flags that may be set in this variable. Some of the flags are:

D_DMA	The driver supports direct memory access.
D_TAPE	The driver controls a tape device.
D_NOBRKUP	The driver understands page lists, so the kernel does not need to break up a multipage transfer into multiple requests.

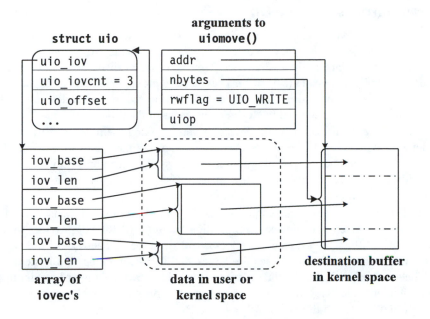

Figure 16-7. Data transfer using uiomove().

Finally, the section describes the *prefix*info structure that must be supplied by STREAMS drivers.

    Section 2 specifies the driver entry points described earlier in this chapter. These include all the switch functions, as well as the interrupt routine and the initialization functions *prefix*init() and *prefix*start().

    Section 4 describes data structures shared between the kernel and the drivers. These include the buf structure, described in Section 16.6.1, and the uio and iovec structures, described in Section 8.2.5. The rest of the structures are used by STREAMS (see Chapter 17) and by the machine-specific DMA interface.

    Section 5 contains the relevant kernel #define values. These include errno values (error codes), STREAMS messages, and signal numbers.

16.8   Newer SVR4 Releases

The initial SVR4 release has been followed by several upgrades that have added important new functionality. SVR4/MP added multiprocessor support, SVR4.1/ES added enhanced security, and SVR4.2 added support for dynamic loading of drivers.[3] Each of these features has affected the driver-kernel interface and placed new requirements on driver developers.

---

[3] Some vendors provided loadable drivers long before SVR4. Sun Microsystems, for instance, had them in SunOS4.1. OSF/1 has this feature as well.

16.8.1   Multiprocessor-Safe Drivers

Traditional single-threaded drivers do not work correctly in a symmetric multiprocessing (SMP) kernel. These drivers assume that they have exclusive access to data structures and that blocking interrupts is sufficient to protect these structures [Goul 85]. Such drivers need extensive modification to become multiprocessor-safe (MP-safe). They need to protect most global data by using multiprocessor synchronization primitives. In particular, they also need to protect device registers, since they could be simultaneously accessed by different instances of the driver.

The requirements for parallelizing device drivers (making them MP-safe) are no different from parallelizing the rest of the kernel. Section 7.10 discusses these issues in detail. To support such an effort, the kernel must export its multiprocessor synchronization primitives to the device drivers. In addition, it may modify or replace many interface functions that are not MP-safe, or place restrictions on their use.

SVR4/MP makes several changes to the DDI/DKI interface. First, it adds a set of functions that allow driver writers to use its new synchronization facilities. SVR4/MP provides three types of multiprocessor locks—basic locks, read-write locks, and sleep locks. These locks are not recursive, and a driver will deadlock if it tries to acquire a lock that it already holds. If a basic or read-write lock cannot be acquired immediately, the caller may wait either by blocking or by spinning, depending on the implementation. SVR4/MP also provides synchronization variables, which are similar to *condition variables,* described in Section 7.7.

SVR4/MP adds a set of functions to section 3 of DDI/DKI to allocate and manipulate the different synchronization objects. It also places new restrictions on several existing functions. In many cases, the restriction is that the function not be called while holding some or all types of locks.

In some cases, SVR4/MP replaces a non-MP-safe function with an equivalent MP-safe function with a slightly different interface. For example, the `timeout()` function is replaced by `itimeout()`, which takes an additional argument that specifies the interrupt priority level at which the specified function must be invoked. It also adds a function called `dtimeout()`, which will invoke the given function on a specific processor. The interface retains the `timeout()` function for compatibility, but moves it to level 2 (effective October 8, 1991). Hence the commitment to support `timeout()` expired on October 8, 1994.

Finally, SVR4/MP adds a D_MP flag to the *prefix*devflag of the driver. Drivers that set this flag declare themselves to be multiprocessor-safe. If the D_MP flag is not set, the kernel serializes, or single-threads, all operations of the driver. For instance, it may associate a global lock with the driver and acquire it before calling any of the driver's routines.

16.8.2   SVR4.1/ES Changes

SVR4.1/ES adds enhanced security features to the UNIX kernel. The main change to the driver interface is the addition of three flags to the *prefix*devflag variable. These flags are:

D_NOSPECMACDATA   The driver does not perform mandatory access control checking during data transfers and does not update the access time in inodes.

D_INITPUB   Devices controlled by this driver may be accessed by nonprivileged processes. This flag may be later modified by a security system call.

D_RDWEQ   Device accesses require strict equality under the mandatory access
                                 control policy.

16.8.3   Dynamic Loading and Unloading

Traditionally, the UNIX kernel is compiled and linked statically. Once the system boots, it is not
possible to modify the kernel, except for minor patches applied by debugging tools. This approach
is rigid and limiting. It encourages people to throw in every possible module and driver while
building the kernel, even though they are unlikely to be used. This results in an unnecessarily large
kernel. because the kernel is usually not pageable, it uses up a great amount of physical memory.
Any change to the kernel, such as upgrading a driver or adding a new driver requires building a new
kernel, then rebooting a system. While this may be only a minor inconvenience for an individual
workstation, it may be intolerable for a major commercial installation where high availability is
critical. It also slows down the driver development cycle, which requires constant debugging and
reloading of the driver.

Several modern versions of UNIX support dynamic loading of kernel modules. This means a
module (collection of objects) may be added to or removed from a running kernel. Dynamic loading
requires a runtime loader that performs final relocation and binding of addresses when the module is
loaded. This has several advantages. The system may boot with a small kernel, which contains only
a few, essential modules. It may add new modules when they are needed and remove them when
they are no longer in use. To upgrade a module, it is only necessary to disable the current version of
the module in the kernel, unload it, and load the new version. The entire system does not have to be
rebooted.

Dynamic loading may be used for several different types of modules. Those supported in
SVR4.2 are:

- Device drivers.
- Host bus adapter and controller drivers.
- STREAMS modules.
- File systems.
- Miscellaneous modules, such as those containing common code shared by multiple dy-
  namically loaded modules.

Although the mechanisms and considerations for dynamic loading are similar for all these
types, this section concentrates on device drivers. Loading a driver into a running kernel requires
several operations:

1. Relocation and binding of the driver's symbols. The runtime loader is responsible for this.
2. Driver and device initialization.
3. Adding the driver to the device switch tables, so that the kernel can access the switch
   routines.
4. Installing the interrupt handler, so that the driver can respond to device interrupts.

Likewise, unloading a driver requires undoing most of these tasks—releasing memory allocated
to the driver, performing shutdown operations on the driver and device, uninstalling the interrupt

handler and the switch table entries, and removing all references to the driver from the rest of the kernel.

SVR4.2 provides a set of facilities to perform all the above tasks. It adds the following routines to the DDI/DKI specification:

*prefix*_load()

This section 2 routine must be provided by the driver. It performs driver initialization, and the kernel invokes it when the driver is loaded. It handles the tasks usually performed by the *init* and *start* routines, since those functions are not invoked when a driver is dynamically loaded. It allocates memory for private data, initializing various data structures. It then calls the mod_drvattach() routine to install the interrupt handler and, finally, initializes all devices associated with this driver.

*prefix*_unload()

This section 2 routine must be provided by the driver. The kernel invokes it to handle driver cleanup when unloading the driver. Typically, it undoes the actions of the *prefix*_load() routine. It calls mod_drvdetach() to disable and uninstall interrupts for this driver, releases memory it had allocated, and performs any necessary shutdown on the driver or its devices.

mod_drvattach()

This is a kernel-supplied, section 3 routine. It installs the interrupt handler for the driver and enables interrupts from the driver's devices. It must be called from *prefix*_load() with a single argument, a pointer to the driver's *prefix*attach_info structure. This structure is defined and initialized by the kernel's configuration tools when the driver is configured. It is opaque to the driver, and the driver must not attempt to reference any of its fields.

mod_drvdetach()

This is a kernel-supplied, section 3 routine, which disables interrupts to the driver and uninstalls its interrupt handler. It must be called from *prefix*_unload() with the *prefix*attach_info pointer as an argument.

Wrapper Macros

The DDI/DKI specification supplies a set of macros that generate wrapper code for a loadable module. There is one macro for each type of module, as follows:

MOD_DRV_WRAPPER	for device drivers
MOD_HDRV_WRAPPER	for Host Bus Adapter drivers
MOD_STR_WRAPPER	for STREAMS modules
MOD_FS_WRAPPER	for file systems
MOD_MISC_WRAPPER	for miscellaneous modules

Each macro takes five arguments. For MOD_DRV_WRAPPER, the syntax is

```
MOD_DRV_WRAPPER (prefix, load, unload, halt, desc);
```

where prefix is the driver prefix, load and unload are the names of the *prefix*_load() and *prefix*_unload() routines, halt is the name of the driver's *prefix*_halt() routine, if any, and desc is a character string that describes the module. The wrapper code arranges to call *prefix*_load() when the driver is loaded and *prefix*_unload() when the driver is unloaded. The **moddefs.h** file defines the wrapper macros.

There are two ways in which a driver may be loaded into the SVR4.2 kernel [UNIX 92a]. A user, typically the system administrator, may explicitly load and unload the driver using the *modload* and *moduload* system calls. Alternatively, the system may automatically load the driver on first reference. For instance, the kernel loads a STREAMS module (see Section 17.3.5) the first time it is pushed onto a stream. If a module remains inactive for a time greater than a tunable parameter called DEF_UNLOAD_DELAY, it becomes a candidate for unloading. The kernel may unload such a module automatically if there is a memory shortage. Modules may override DEF_UNLOAD_DELAY by specifying their own unload delay value in the configuration file.

The SVR4.2 dynamic loading facility is powerful and beneficial, but it has some limitations. It requires explicit support in the driver; hence, older drivers cannot use this facility transparently. [Konn 90] describes a version of dynamic loading that does not suffer from these limitations. It allows transparent loading of the driver when first opened, and optionally, transparent unloading on the last close. When the system boots, it inserts a special *open* routine in the cdevsw[] and bdevsw[] for all major numbers that have no driver configured. When the device is first opened, this routine loads the driver, then calls the driver's real *open* routine. Since the loading process updates the device switch table, subsequent *open*s will directly call the driver's *open* routine. Likewise, the *autounload on close* feature uses a special *close* routine that is installed in the device switch entry if the driver specifies an *autounload* flag in the configuration file. This routine first calls the real *close* routine, then checks to see if all the minor devices are closed. If so, it unloads the driver.

The [Konn 90] implementation is transparent to the driver, since it uses the driver's *init* and *start* routines instead of special *load* and *unload* routines. It works with well-behaved drivers that satisfy certain requirements. The driver should not have any functions or variables directly referenced by the kernel or other drivers. On the last *close*, it should perform complete cleanup and leave no state behind. This includes releasing any kernel memory, canceling pending timeouts, and so on.

16.9 Future Directions

One of the limitations of the UNIX device driver framework is that it offers little support for sharing code between drivers. Any given class of devices, such as ethernet controllers or hard disks, has several different manufacturers, each with their own controller board or chip. Only a fraction of the driver code, however, is controller or ASIC-dependent.[4] The rest is dependent on the class of the device and the specifics of the processor and operating system on which it runs.

---

[4] ASIC stands for Application-Specific Integrated Circuit.

In spite of this, each device manufacturer must provide his or her own drivers. Each must implement all the entry points for the driver, which constitute a very high-level interface. Each driver contains not only the ASIC-dependent code, but also the high-level, ASIC-independent code. As a result, different drivers of the same device class duplicate much of the functionality. This leads to a lot of wasted effort and also increases the size of the kernel unnecessarily.

UNIX has addressed this problem in several ways. STREAMS provides a modular way of writing character drivers. Each stream is built by stacking a number of modules together, each module performing a very specific operation on the data. Drivers can share code at the module level, since multiple streams may share a common module.

SCSI devices offer another possibility for code sharing. A SCSI controller manages many different types of devices, such as hard and floppy disks, tape drives, audio cards, and CD-ROM drives. Each SCSI controller has a number of controller-specific features and thus requires a different driver. Each device type, too, has different semantics and hence must be processed differently. If we have m different types of controllers and n different types of device, we may have to write $m \times n$ drivers.

It is preferable, however, to divide the code into a device-dependent and a controller-dependent part. There would be one device-dependent module for each device type, and one controller-dependent driver for each controller. This requires a well-defined interface between the two pieces, with a standard set of commands that is understood by each controller and issued by each device-dependent module.

There are several efforts to create such a standard. SVR4 has released a Portable Device Interface (PDI), consisting of the following:

- A set of section 2 functions that each host bus adapter must implement.
- A set of section 3 functions that perform common tasks required by SCSI devices, such as allocating command and control blocks.
- A set of section 4 data structures that are used by the section 3 functions.

Two other interfaces aimed at a similar layering are SCSI CAM (Common Access Method) [ANSI 92b], supported by Digital UNIX [DEC 93] and ASPI (Adaptec SCSI Peripherals Interface), popular in the personal computer world.

The I/O subsystem in Mach 3.0 [Fori 91] extends such layering to all devices on a case-by-case basis. It optimizes the code sharing for each device class, providing device-independent modules to implement the common code. It also moves the device-independent processing to the user level, thereby reducing the size of the kernel. It also provides location transparency by implementing device interactions as IPC (interprocess communication) messages. This allows users to transparently access devices on remote machines. This interface, however, is incompatible with the UNIX driver framework.

16.10   Summary

This chapter examines the device driver framework and how the I/O subsystem interacts with the devices. It describes the SVR4 DDI/DKI specification, which allows vendors to write drivers that will be portable across future SVR4 releases. In addition, it describes several recent features in the driver framework, such as support for multiprocessors and dynamic loading and interfaces for sharing code between drivers.

16.11 Exercises

1. Why does UNIX use device switch tables to channel all device activity?
2. What is the difference between DMA and DVMA?
3. When is it necessary to poll the devices rather than rely on interrupts?
4. Why are pseudodevices such as mem and null implemented through the device driver framework?
5. Give some examples of hardware devices that are not used for I/O. Which functions of the driver interface do they support?
6. Give some examples of hardware devices that do not map well to the UNIX driver framework. What aspects of the interface are unsuitable for these devices?
7. Why do top-half routines need to protect data structures from bottom-half routines?
8. What are the advantages of associating a device special file with each device?
9. How does the *specfs* file system handle multiple files associated with the same device?
10. What is the use of the common snode?
11. What functionality must the driver implement to support cloning? Give some examples of devices that provide this feature.
12. In what ways is I/O to a character device treated differently than I/O to a block device or a file?
13. What are the differences in functionality between the poll and select system calls? Describe how each may be implemented as a library function using the other and the problems that may arise in doing so.
14. What does it mean for a device to support memory mapped access? What kind of devices benefit from this functionality?
15. The DDI/DKI specification discourages direct access to its data structures and requires drivers to use a procedural interface instead. Why? What are the advantages and drawbacks of using function calls to access fields of a data structure?
16. What are the main problems in writing a multiprocessor-safe driver?
17. What are the benefits of loadable drivers? What problems must the driver writer be careful to avoid?

16.12 References

[ANSI 92a]   American National Standard for Information Systems, *Small Computer Systems Interface—2 (SCSI-2)*, X3.131–199X, Feb. 1992.

[ANSI 92b]   American National Standard for Information Systems, *SCSI-2 Common Access Method: Transport and SCSI Interface Module,* working draft, X3T9.2/90–186, rev. 3.0, Apr. 1992.

[DEC 93]   Digital Equipment Corporation, *Guide to Writing Device Drivers for the SCSI/CAM Architecture Interfaces,* Mar. 1993.

[Egan 88]   Egan, J.I., and Texeira, T.J., *Writing a UNIX Device Driver,* John Wiley & Sons, 1988.

[Fori 91]   Forin, A., Golub, D., and Bershad, B.N., "An I/O system for Mach 3.0," Technical Report CMU–CS–91–191, School of Computer Science, Carnegie Mellon University, Oct. 1991.

[Goul 85]   Gould, E., "Device Drivers in a Multiprocessor Environment," *Proceedings of the Summer 1992 USENIX Technical Conference,* Jun. 1992, pp. 357–360.

[Klei 86]   Kleiman, S.R., "Vnodes: An Architecture for Multiple File System Types in Sun UNIX," *Proceedings of the Summer 1986 Usenix Technical Conference,* Jun. 1986, pp. 238–247.

[Konn 90]   Konnerth, D., Bartel, E., and Adler, O., "Dynamic Driver Loading for UNIX System V," *Proceedings of the Spring 1990 European UNIX Users Group Conference,* Apr. 1990, pp. 133–138.

[Paja 92]   Pajari, G., *Writing UNIX Device Drivers,* Addison-Wesley, Reading, MA, 1992.

[Sun 93]   Sun Microsystems, *Writing Device Drivers,* Part No. 800–5117–11, 1993.

[UNIX 92a]   UNIX System Laboratories, *Device Driver Programming—UNIX SVR4.2,* UNIX Press, Prentice-Hall, Englewood Cliffs, NJ, 1992.

[UNIX 92b]   UNIX System Laboratories, *Device Driver Reference—UNIX SVR4.2,* UNIX Press, Prentice-Hall, Englewood Cliffs, NJ, 1992.

17

STREAMS

17.1 Motivation

The traditional device driver framework has many flaws. First, the kernel interfaces with the drivers at a very high level (the driver entry points), making the driver responsible for most of the processing of an I/O request. Device drivers are usually written independently by device vendors. Many vendors write drivers for the same type of device. Only part of the driver code is device-dependent; the rest implements high-level, device-independent I/O processing. As a result, these drivers duplicate much of their functionality, creating a larger kernel and greater likelihood of conflict.

Another shortcoming lies in the area of buffering. The block device interface provides reasonable support for buffer allocation and management. However, there is no such uniform scheme for character drivers. The character device interface was originally designed to support slow devices that read or wrote one character at a time, such as teletypewriters or slow serial lines. Hence the kernel provided minimal buffering support, leaving that responsibility to individual devices. This resulted in the development of several *ad hoc* buffer and memory management schemes, such as the *clists* used by traditional terminal drivers. The proliferation of such mechanisms resulted in inefficient memory usage and duplication of code.

Finally, the interface provides limited facilities to applications. I/O to character devices requires *read* and *write* system calls, which treat the data as a FIFO (first-in, first-out) byte stream. There is no support for recognizing message boundaries, distinguishing between regular data and control information, or associating priorities to different messages. There is no provision for flow control, and each driver and application devises *ad hoc* mechanisms to address this issue.

The requirements of network devices highlight these limitations. Network protocols are designed in layers. Data transfers are message- or packet-based, and each layer of the protocol performs some processing on the packet and then passes it to the next layer. Protocols distinguish between ordinary and urgent data. The layers contain interchangeable parts, and a given protocol may be combined with different protocols in other layers. This suggests a modular framework that supports layering and allows drivers to be built by combining several independent modules.

The STREAMS subsystem addresses many of these problems. It provides a modular approach to writing drivers. It has a fully message-based interface that contains facilities for buffer management, flow control, and priority-based scheduling. It supports layered protocol suites by stacking protocol modules to function as a pipeline. It encourages code sharing, as each stream is composed of several reusable modules that can be shared by different drivers. It offers additional facilities to user-level applications for message-based transfers and separation of control information from data.

Originally developed by Dennis Ritchie [Ritc 83], STREAMS is now supported by most UNIX vendors and has become the preferred interface for writing network drivers and protocols. Additionally, SVR4 also uses STREAMS to replace the traditional terminal drivers, as well as the *pipe* mechanism. This chapter summarizes the design and implementation of STREAMS and analyzes its strengths and shortcomings.

17.2   Overview

A *stream* is a full-duplex processing and data transfer path between a driver in kernel space and a process in user space. STREAMS is a collection of system calls, kernel resources, and kernel utility routines that create, use, and dismantle a stream. It is also a framework for writing device drivers. It specifies a set of rules and guidelines for driver writers and provides the mechanisms and utilities that allow such drivers to be developed in a modular manner.

Figure 17-1 describes a typical stream. A stream resides entirely in kernel space, and its operations are implemented in the kernel. It comprises a *stream head,* a *driver end,* and zero or more optional *modules* between them. The stream head interfaces with the user level and allows applications to access the stream through the system call interface. The driver end communicates with the device itself (alternatively, it may be a *pseudodevice* driver, in which case it may communicate with another stream), and the modules perform intermediate processing of the data.

Each module contains a pair of *queues*—a *read queue* and a *write queue*. The stream head and driver also contain such a queue pair. The stream transfers data by putting it in *messages*. The write queues send messages *downstream* from the application to the driver. The read queues pass them *upstream,* from the driver to the application. Although most messages originate at the stream head or the driver, intermediate modules may also generate messages and pass them up or down the stream.

Each queue may communicate with the next queue in the stream. For example, in Figure 17-1, the write queue of module **1** may send messages to the write queue of module **2** (but not vice-versa). The read queue of module **1** may send messages to the read queue of the stream head. A queue may also communicate with its *mate,* or companion queue. Thus, the read queue of module **2**

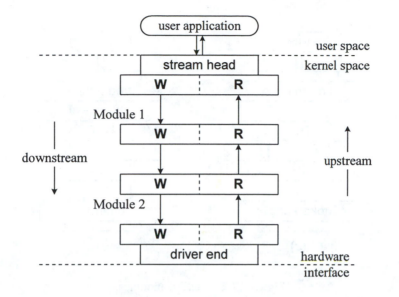

Figure 17-1. A typical stream.

may pass a message to the write queue of the same module, which may then send it downstream. A queue does not need to know whether the queue it is communicating with belongs to the stream head, the driver end, or another intermediate module.

Without further explanation, the preceding description shows the advantages of this approach. Each module can be written independently, perhaps by different vendors. Modules can be mixed and matched in different ways, similar to combining various commands with pipes from a UNIX shell.

Figure 17-2 shows how different streams may be formed from only a few components. A vendor developing networking software may wish to add the TCP/IP (Transmission Control Protocol/Internet Protocol) suite to a system. Using STREAMS, he develops a TCP module, a UDP (User Datagram Protocol) module, and an IP module. Other vendors who make network interface cards independently write STREAMS drivers for ethernet and token ring.

Once these modules are available, they may be configured dynamically to form different types of streams. In Figure 17-2(a), a user has formed a TCP/IP stream that connects to a token ring. Figure 17-2(b) shows a new combination, featuring a UDP/IP stream connected to an ethernet driver.

STREAMS supports a facility called *multiplexing*. A multiplexing driver can connect to multiple streams at the top or bottom. There are three types of multiplexors—upper, lower, and two-way. An upper, or fan-in, multiplexor can connect to multiple streams above it. A lower, or fan-out, multiplexor can connect to multiple streams below it. A two-way multiplexor supports multiple connections both above and below it.

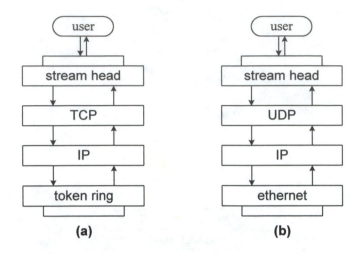

Figure 17-2. Reusable modules.

By writing the TCP, UDP, and IP modules as multiplexing drivers, we can combine the above streams into a single compound object that supports multiple data paths. Figure 17-3 shows a possible layout. TCP and UDP act as upper multiplexors, while IP serves as a two-way multiplexor. This allows applications to make various kinds of network connections and enables several users to access any given combination of protocols and drivers. The multiplexor drivers must manage all the different connections correctly and route the data up or down the stream to the correct queue.

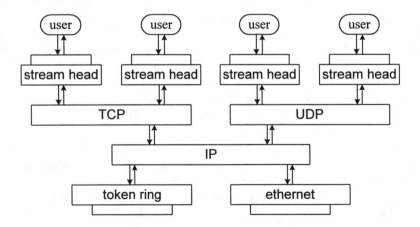

Figure 17-3. Multiplexing streams.

17.3 Messages and Queues

STREAMS uses message passing as its only form of communication. Messages transfer data between applications and the device. They also carry control information to the driver or a module. Drivers and modules generate messages to inform the user, or each other, of error conditions or unusual events. A queue may handle an incoming message in several ways. It may pass it to the next queue, either unchanged or after some processing. The queue may schedule the message for deferred processing. Alternatively, it may pass the message to its mate, thus sending it back in the opposite direction. Finally, a queue may even discard the message.

In this section, we describe the structure and function of messages, queues, and modules.

> *Note — Extended Fundamental Types: SVR4 uses larger sizes for several fundamental data types. For example, the dev_t type is 16 bits in SVR3, but 32 bits in SVR4. The new types are called* Extended Fundamental Types (EFT). *Likewise, many structures in SVR4 contain additional fields that are absent in SVR3. When these changes affect public data structures and interfaces, they create backward compatibility problems, preventing interoperability with drivers and modules written for earlier releases. To ease this transition, SVR4 provides a compilation option that allows a system to be built using the old data types. When compiled without EFT, these fields are packed differently to ensure that the old drivers work correctly. Some fields are placed in different structures depending on the compilation option. In some cases, certain structures are used only for one compilation option. Support for the old data types may not be included in future releases. This chapter assumes the system uses the new data types.*

17.3.1 Messages

The simplest message consists of three objects—a `struct msgb` (or type `mblk_t`), a `struct datab` (type `dblk_t`), and a data buffer. A multipart message may be constructed by chaining such triplets together, as shown in Figure 17-4. In the `msgb`, the `b_next` and `b_prev` fields link a message onto a queue, while `b_cont` chains the different parts of the same message. The `b_datap` field points to the associated `datab`.

Both the `msgb` and the `datab` contain information about the actual data buffer. The `db_base` and `db_lim` fields of the `datab` point to the beginning and end of the buffer. Only part of the buffer may contain useful data, so the `b_rptr` and `b_wptr` fields of the `msgb` point to the beginning and end of the valid data in the buffer. The `allocb()` routine allocates a buffer and initializes both the `b_rptr` and `b_wptr` to point to the beginning of the buffer (`db_base`). As a module writes data into the buffer, it advances `b_wptr` (always checking against `db_lim`). As a module reads data from the buffer, it advances `b_rptr` (checking that it does not read past `b_wptr`), thus removing the data from the buffer.

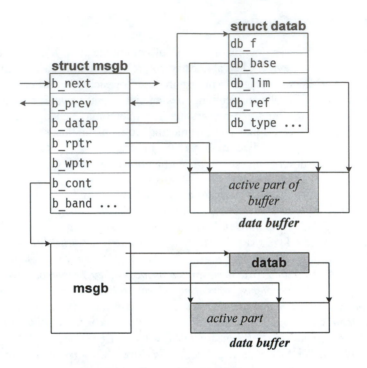

Figure 17-4. A STREAMS message.

Allowing multipart messages (each a msgb-datab-data buffer triplet) has many advantages. Network protocols are layered, and each protocol layer usually adds its own header or footer to a message. As the message travels downstream, each layer may add its header or footer using a new message block and link it to the beginning or end of the message. This way, it is unnecessary for higher-level protocols to know about lower-level protocol headers or footers or leave space for them while allocating the message. When messages arrive from the network and travel upstream, each protocol layer strips off its header or footer in reverse order by adjusting the b_rptr and b_wptr fields.

The b_band field contains the priority band of the message and is used for scheduling (see Section 0). Each datab has a db_type field, which contains one of several message types defined by STREAMS. This allows modules to prioritize and process messages differently based on their type. Section 17.3.3 discusses message types in detail. The db_f field holds information used for message allocation (see Section 17.7). The db_ref field stores a reference count, which is used for *virtual copying* (see Section 17.3.2).

17.3.2   Virtual Copying

The datab is reference counted, and its db_ref field is used for that purpose. Multiple msgb's may share a single datab, thus sharing the data in the associated buffer. This allows efficient *virtual*

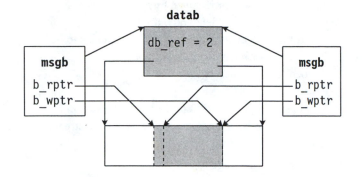

Figure 17-5. Two messages sharing a datab.

copying of the data. Figure 17-5 shows an example where two messages share a datab. Both share the associated data buffer, but each maintains its independent read and write offset into it.

Normally, such a shared buffer is used in read-only mode, for two independent writes to it may interfere with each other. Such semantics, however, must be enforced by the modules or drivers processing these buffers. STREAMS is neither aware of nor concerned with how or when modules read or write the buffers.

One example of the use of virtual copying is in the TCP/IP protocol. The TCP layer provides reliable transport, and hence must ensure that every message reaches its destination. If the receiver does not acknowledge the message within a specified period of time, the sender retransmits it. To do so, it must retain a copy of each message it sends until the message is acknowledged. Physically copying every message is wasteful, hence TCP uses the virtual copying mechanism. When the TCP module receives a message to send downstream, it calls the STREAMS routine dupmsg(), which creates another msgb that references the same datab. This results in two logical messages, each referencing the same data. TCP sends one message downstream, while holding on to the other.

When the driver sends the message and releases the msgb, the datab and data buffer are not freed, because the reference count is still non-zero. Eventually, when the receiver acknowledges the message, the TCP module frees the other msgb. This drops the reference count on the datab to zero, and STREAMS releases the datab and the associated data buffer.

17.3.3 Message Types

STREAMS defines a set of message types, and each message must belong to one of these. The db_type field in the datab identifies the type. The type of a message relates to its intended purpose and its queuing priority. Based on the type, messages may be classified as normal or high-priority. High-priority messages are queued and processed before normal messages. Section 17.4.2 describes message priority in greater detail.

SVR4.2 defines the following normal message types [USL 92a]:

M_BREAK   Sent downstream; asks the driver to send a *break* to the device.
M_CTL   Intermodule control request.

M_DATA	Ordinary data sent or received by system calls.
M_DELAY	Requests a real-time delay on output.
M_IOCTL	Control message; generated by *ioctl* commands to a stream.
M_PASSFP	Passes a file pointer.
M_PROTO	Protocol control message.
M_RSE	Reserved.
M_SETOPTS	Sent upstream by modules or drivers to set stream head options.
M_SIG	Sent upstream by a module or driver; asks the stream head to send a signal to the user.

The following are the high-priority message types:

M_COPYIN	Sent upstream; asks stream head to copy data in for an *ioctl*.
M_COPYOUT	Sent upstream; asks stream head to copy data in for an *ioctl*.
M_ERROR	Sent upstream; reports error condition.
M_FLUSH	Asks module to flush a queue.
M_HANGUP	Sent upstream; sets hangup condition on stream head.
M_IOCACK	*ioctl* acknowledgment; sent upstream.
M_IOCNACK	Negative *ioctl* acknowledgment; sent upstream.
M_IOCDATA	Sends *ioctl* data downstream.
M_PCPROTO,	High-priority version of M_PROTO.
M_PCSIG	High-priority version of M_SIG.
M_PCRSE	Reserved.
M_READ	Read notification; sent downstream.
M_START	Restart stopped device output.
M_STARTI	Restart stopped device input.
M_STOP	Suspend output.
M_STOPI	Suspend input.

The message type allows modules to recognize special processing requirements of a message without having to understand its contents. For multipart messages, the first datab contains the type of the entire message. There is one exception to this rule. When an application uses a high-level service interface (such as *TPI,* the *Transport Provider Interface*), its data messages consist of a single M_PROTO block, followed by one or more M_DATA blocks in the same message.

17.3.4 Queues and Modules

Modules are the building blocks of the stream. Each module comprises a pair of queues—a read queue and a write queue. Figure 17-6 illustrates the queue data structure. It has the following important fields:

| q_qinfo | Pointer to a qinit structure (described in the following paragraph) |
| q_first, q_last | Pointers to manage a doubly linked list of messages queued for deferred processing. |

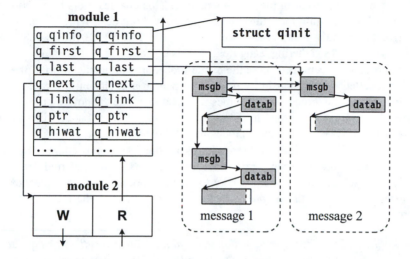

Figure 17-6. The queue structure.

q_next	Pointer to the next queue upstream or downstream.
q_hiwat, q_lowat	High- and low-watermarks for the amount of data the queue may hold, and are used for flow control (Section 17.4.3).
q_link	Pointer used to link the queue to a list of queues that need to be scheduled (Section 0).
q_ptr	Pointer to a data structure that holds private data for the queue.

The q_qinfo field points to a qinit structure, which encapsulates the procedural interface to the queue. Figure 17-7 shows the data structures accessed through q_qinfo. Each queue must supply four procedures—*put, service, open,* and *close.* These are the only functions required for other STREAMS objects to be able to communicate with the queue. The module_info structure contains default high and low watermarks, packet sizes, and other parameters for the queue. Some

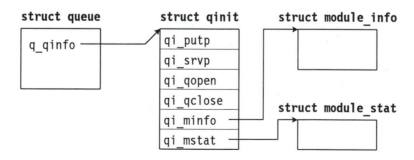

Figure 17-7. Objects accessed through q_qinfo.

of these fields are also present in the queue structure. This enables users to override these parameters dynamically by changing the values in the queue, without destroying the defaults saved in the module_info. The module_stat object is not directly used by STREAMS. Each module is free to perform its own statistics gathering using fields in this object.

The subsequent sections discuss the queue procedures in detail. In brief, the *open* and *close* procedures are called synchronously by processes opening and closing the stream. The *put* procedure performs immediate processing of a message. If a message cannot be processed immediately, the *put* procedure adds the message to the queue's message queue. Later, when the *service* procedure is invoked, it will perform delayed processing of these messages.

Each queue must provide a *put* procedure,[1] but the *service* procedure is optional. If there is no *service* procedure, the *put* procedure cannot queue messages for deferred processing, but must immediately process each message and send it to the next module. In the simplest case, a queue will have no *service* procedure, and its *put* procedure will merely pass the message to the next queue without processing it.

> **Note:** *There is some confusion in terminology because the word* queue *refers both to the queue object and to the queue of messages contained within it. This book uses the term* queue *to refer to the queue object, and* message queue *to refer to the linked list of messages in the queue.*

17.4   Stream I/O

The stream performs I/O by passing messages from one queue to another. A user process writes to the device using the *write* or *putmsg* system calls. The stream head allocates a message (a msgb, datab, and data buffer) and copies the data into it. It then sends it downstream to the next queue, and eventually the data reaches the driver. Data from the device arrives asynchronously, and the driver sends it upstream toward the stream head. A process receives data through *read* and *getmsg* calls. If there is no data available at the stream head, the process blocks.

A queue passes a message to the next queue in the stream by calling putnext(). The putnext() function identifies the next queue through the q_next field, and invokes the *put* procedure of that queue. A queue should never directly call the next queue's *put* procedure, as the q_next field is internal to the queue and may be implemented differently in future releases. A queue may send a message in the reverse direction by passing it to its mate. The read queue, for example, does so by calling

```
WR(q)->put (WR(q), msgp);
```

Stream I/O is asynchronous. The only place where an I/O operation may block the process is at the stream head. The *put* and *service* procedures of the module and driver are non-blocking. If the

---

[1] Except for multiplexors (see Section 17.8.3)

put procedure cannot send the data to the next queue, it places the message on its own message queue, from where it may be retrieved later by the *service* procedure. If the *service* procedure removes a message from the queue and discovers that it cannot process it at this time, it returns the message to the queue and tries again later.

These two functions complement each other. The *put* procedure is required for processing that cannot wait. For instance, a terminal driver must immediately echo the characters it receives, or else the user will find it unresponsive. The *service* procedure handles all non-urgent actions, such as canonical processing of incoming characters.

Because neither procedure is allowed to block, they must ensure that they do not call any routine that may block. Hence STREAMS provides its own facilities for operations such as memory allocation. For instance, the `allocb()` routine allocates a message. If it cannot do so for any reason (it may not find a free `msgb`, `datab`, or data buffer), it returns failure instead of blocking. The caller then invokes the `bufcall()` routine, passing a pointer to a callback function. `bufcall()` adds the caller to a list of queues that need to allocate memory. When memory becomes available, STREAMS invokes the callback function, which usually calls the stream's *service* routine to retry the call to `allocb()`.

The asynchronous operation is central to the design of STREAMS. On the read side (upstream), the driver receives the data via device interrupts. The read-side *put* procedures run at interrupt level, and hence cannot afford to block. The design could have allowed blocking in the write-side procedures, but that was rejected in the interest of symmetry and simplicity.

The *service* procedures are scheduled in system context, not in the context of the process that initiated the data transfer. Hence blocking a *service* procedure could put an innocent process to sleep. If, for example, a user shell process is blocked because an unrelated transfer cannot complete, the results would be unacceptable. Making all *put* and *service* procedures non-blocking solves these problems.

The *put* and *service* procedures must synchronize with each other while accessing common data structures. Because the read-side *put* procedure may be called from interrupt handlers, it may interrupt the execution of either *service* procedure, or of the write-side *put* procedure. Additional locking is required on multiprocessors, since the procedures may run concurrently on different processors [Garg 90, Saxe 93].

17.4.1   The STREAMS Scheduler

When the *put* procedure defers the processing of data, it calls `putq()` to place the message onto the queue and then calls `qenable()` to schedule the queue for servicing. `qenable()` sets the QENAB flag for the queue and adds the queue to the tail of the list of queues waiting to be scheduled. If the QENAB flag is already set, `qenable()` does nothing, since the queue has already been scheduled. Finally, `qenable()` sets a global flag called `qrunflag`, which specifies that a queue is waiting to be scheduled.

STREAMS scheduling is implemented by a routine called `runqueues()` and has no relation to UNIX process scheduling. The kernel calls `runqueues()` whenever a process tries to perform an I/O or control operation on a stream. This allows many operations to complete quickly before a context switch occurs. The kernel also calls `runqueues()` just before returning to user mode after a context switch.

The `runqueues()` routine checks if any streams need to be scheduled. If so, it calls `queuerun()`, which scans the scheduler list, and calls the *service* procedure of each queue on it. The *service* procedure must try to process all the messages on the queue, as described in the next section.

On a uniprocessor, the kernel guarantees that all scheduled *service* procedures will run before returning to user mode. Because any arbitrary process may be running at the time, the *service* procedures must run in system context and not access the address space of the current process.

17.4.2   Priority Bands

Many network protocols support the notion of out-of-band data [Rago 89], which consists of urgent, protocol-specific control information that must be processed before regular data. This is distinct from high-priority messages recognized by their message types. For example, the *TELNET* protocol provides a *Synch* mechanism to regain control of a process by sending an urgent message. Usually, a special data mark denotes the end of out-of-band data (also called expedited data) in a stream.

STREAMS treats out-of-band messages as ordinary data messages, as their treatment is protocol-dependent. However, it provides a feature called *priority bands,* which allows modules to prioritize messages and process them in order of priority. Specific protocols may use these bands to implement different classes of data messages.

Priority bands apply only to normal message types. Each such message is assigned a band priority value between 0 and 255. Band 0 is default, and most protocols only use bands 0 and 1. High-priority message types (such as M_PCPROTO) have no band priority and are considered to be more urgent than all band priority messages.

Within a queue, STREAMS maintains separate queues for each priority band in use. To do so, it uses a set of qband structures, one for each priority band. STREAMS allocates qband structures dynamically when needed. When `putq()` queues a message, STREAMS adds it to the tail of the list on the appropriate qband structure (allocating a new qband if needed). When the *service* procedure retrieves a message from the queue by calling `getq()`, STREAMS returns a message from the highest-priority band that has a pending message.

Hence the *service* procedure first processes all pending high-priority messages, then the normal messages in order of band priority. Within each priority band, it processes the messages in FIFO order.

17.4.3   Flow Control

The simplest flow control is no flow control. Consider a stream where each module has only a *put* procedure. As data passes through the stream, each queue processes the data and sends it to the next by calling `putnext()`. When data reaches the driver end, the driver sends it to the device immediately. If the device cannot accept data, the driver discards the message.

Although this is an acceptable method for some devices (trivially, the *null* device can be implemented this way), most applications cannot afford to lose data because the device is not ready, and most devices cannot always be ready for data. This requires that the stream be ready for a

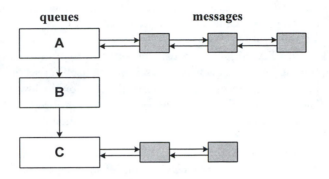

Figure 17-8. Flow control between two queues.

blockage in one or more of its components and handle the situation correctly without blocking a *put* or *service* procedure.

Flow control is optional in a queue. A queue that supports flow control interacts with the nearest modules on either side that also support it. A queue without flow control has no *service* procedure. Its *put* procedure processes all messages immediately and sends them along to the next queue. Its message queue is not used.

A queue that supports flow control defines low- and high-water marks, which control the total amount of data that may be queued to it. These values are initially copied from the module_info structure (which is statically initialized when compiling the module), but may be changed later by *ioctl* messages.

Figure 17-8 shows the operation of flow control. Queues **A** and **C** are flow-controlled, while queue **B** is not. When a message arrives at queue **A**, its *put* procedure is invoked. It performs any immediate processing that is necessary on the data and calls putq(). The putq() routine adds the message to the queue **A**'s own message queue, and puts queue **A** on the list of queues that need to be serviced. If the message causes the queue **A**'s high-water mark to be exceeded, it sets a flag indicating that the queue is full.

At a later time, the STREAMS scheduler selects queue **A** and invokes its *service* procedure. The *service* procedure retrieves messages from the queue in FIFO order. After processing them, it calls canput() to check if the next flow-controlled queue can accept the message. The canput() routine chases the q_next pointers until it finds a queue that is flow-controlled, which is queue **C** in our example. It then checks the queue's state and returns TRUE if the queue can accept more messages or FALSE if the queue is full. Queue **A**'s *service* procedure behaves differently in the two cases, as shown in Example 17-1.

```
if (canput (q->q_next))
    putnext (q, mp);
else
    putbq (q, mp);
```

Example 17-1. Message handling in the *service* procedure.

If canput() returns TRUE, queue **A** calls putnext(), which passes the message to queue **B**. This queue is not flow-controlled and immediately processes the message and passes it to queue **C**, which is known to have room for the message.

If canput() returns FALSE, queue **A** calls putbq() to return the message to its message queue. The *service* procedure now returns without rescheduling itself for servicing.

Eventually, queue **C** will process its messages and fall below its low watermark. When this happens, STREAMS automatically checks if the previous flow-controlled queue (**A** in this example) is blocked. If so, it reschedules the queue for servicing. This operation is known as *back-enabling* a queue.

Flow control requires consistency on the part of the module writer. All messages of the same priority must be treated equally. If the *put* procedure queues messages for the *service* procedure, it must do so for every message. Otherwise, messages will not retain their sequencing order, leading to incorrect results.

When the *service* procedure runs, it must process every message in the queue, unless it cannot do so due to allocation failures or because the next flow-controlled queue is full. Otherwise, the flow control mechanism breaks down, and the queue may never be scheduled.

High-priority messages are not subject to flow control. A *put* procedure that queues ordinary messages may process high-priority messages immediately. If high-priority messages must be queued, they are placed in front of the queue, ahead of any ordinary messages. High-priority messages retain FIFO ordering with respect to one another.

17.4.4   The Driver End

The driver end is like any module, but with a few important differences. First, it must be prepared to receive interrupts. This requires it to have an interrupt handler and make the handler known to the kernel, in a machine-dependent manner. Devices generate interrupts upon receiving incoming data. The driver must package the data into a message and arrange to send it upstream. When the driver receives a message coming down from the stream head, it must extract the data from the message and send it to the device.

Drivers usually implement some form of flow control, as most devices require it. In many cases, especially for incoming data, the driver resorts to dropping messages when it cannot manage the load. Hence, if the driver cannot allocate a buffer, or if its queues overflow, it silently discards incoming or outgoing messages. It is the responsibility of applications to recover correctly from dropped packets. Higher-level protocols such as TCP ensure reliable transport by retaining a copy of each message until it reaches its destination; if the receiver does not acknowledge the message within a certain period of time, the protocol retransmits it.

The driver end also differs from the module in the way it is opened and initialized. STREAMS drivers are opened by the *open* system call, while modules are *pushed* onto streams by *ioctl* calls. Section 17.5 describes these operations in detail.

17.4.5   The Stream Head

The stream head is responsible for system call handling. It is also the only part of the stream where an I/O operation may block the calling process. While each module or driver has its own *put, service, open,* and *close* procedures, all stream heads share a common set of routines internal to STREAMS.

A process writes data to a stream using the *write* or *putmsg* system calls. The *write* system call allows only ordinary data to be written and does not guarantee message boundaries. It is useful for applications that have a byte-stream view of the stream. The *putmsg* system call allows the user to supply a control message and a data message in one call. STREAMS combines them into a single message whose first datab has type M_PROTO and the next has the type M_DATA.

In either case, the stream head copies the data from the user address space into STREAMS messages and then calls canput() to see if the stream has room for the data (the next flow-controlled module or driver is not full). If so, it sends the data downstream by calling putnext() and returns control to the caller. If canput() returns FALSE, the calling process blocks on the stream head until the head is back-enabled by the next flow-controlled module.

Hence, when the *write* or *putmsg* system call returns, the data has not necessarily reached the device. The caller is guaranteed that the data has safely been copied into the kernel and has either reached the device or been queued at a module or driver.

A process reads data from the stream using *read* or *getmsg*. The *read* system call only reads ordinary data. A module may send a M_SETOPTS message to the stream head, asking it to treat M_PROTO messages as ordinary data. After this, the *read* call reads the contents of both M_DATA and M_PROTO messages. In any case, the *read* system call does not preserve message boundaries or return information about message types. It is primarily used when the application has a byte-stream view of the data.

The *getmsg* system call, in contrast, retrieves both M_PROTO and M_DATA messages. It preserves message boundaries and returns the two types of messages in separate return arguments. If an incoming message consists of an M_PROTO block followed by one or more M_DATA blocks, *getmsg* will separate the two parts correctly.

In either case, if data is already available at the stream head, the kernel extracts it from the message, copies it into user space, and returns control to the caller. If there is no message waiting at the head, the kernel blocks the caller until a message arrives. Several processes may attempt to read from the same stream. If no message is waiting, all will block. When a message arrives, the kernel will give it to one of these processes. The interface does not define which process will receive the message.

When a message reaches the stream head, the kernel checks if a process is waiting for it. If so, the kernel copies the message into the process's address space and wakes up the process, which then returns from the *read* or *getmsg*. If no process is waiting, the kernel queues the message at the stream head. If the stream head's queue becomes full, further messages will be queued at the preceding flow-controlled queue, and so on.

17.5   Configuration and Setup

This section examines the steps required to configure a STREAMS driver or module into the system and to create and set up a stream in a running kernel. STREAMS configuration consists of two phases. First, when the kernel is built, the STREAMS modules and drivers must be linked with the kernel, and the appropriate kernel routines must know how to find them. Second, the appropriate device files must be created and set up so that applications may access streams as they access ordinary files. STREAMS setup is dynamic and occurs when a user opens a stream and pushes modules onto it.

17.5.1   Configuring a Module or Driver

STREAMS modules and drivers are usually written by device vendors, independently of the kernel. They must then be linked with the rest of the kernel, such that the kernel knows how to access them. STREAMS provides a complete set of facilities to achieve this.

      Each STREAMS module must supply three configuration data structures—module_info, qinit, and streamtab. Figure 17-9 describes their contents and relationship. The streamtab structure is the only publicly visible object; the others are usually declared as static, and hence are not visible outside the module.

      The streamtab contains pointers to two qinit structures—one for the read queue, and one for the write queue. The other two fields are only used by multiplexing drivers, to store pointers to an additional queue pair. The qinit structure contains pointers to the set of functions (*open, close, put,* and *service*) that forms the procedural interface to the queue. The *open* and *close* routines are common to the module and are defined only in the read queue. All queues have a *put* routine, but only flow-controlled queues have a *service* routine. The qinit structure also contains a pointer to a module_info structure for the queue.

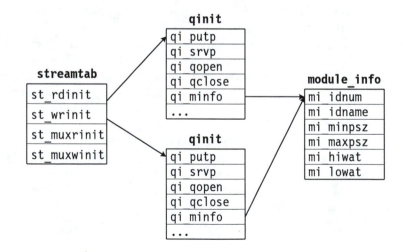

Figure 17-9. Data structures for configuring a module or driver.

The module_info structure contains default parameters of the module. When the module is first opened, these parameters are copied into the queue structure. A user may override them by subsequent *ioctl* calls. Each queue may have its own module_info structure, or both may share a single object, as in the previous example.

The rest of the configuration is different for modules and drivers. Many UNIX systems use an fmodsw[] table to configure STREAMS modules. Each entry in the table (Figure 17-10(a)) comprises a module name and a pointer to the streamtab structure for the module. Modules, therefore, are identified and referenced by name. The module name should be the same as the mi_idname in the module_info structure, though STREAMS does not enforce this.

STREAMS device drivers are identified through the character device switch table. Each cdevsw entry has a field called d_str, which is NULL for ordinary character devices. For STREAMS devices, this field contains the address of the streamtab structure for the driver (Figure 17-10(b)). To complete the configuration, it is necessary to create the appropriate device files, with the major number equal to the index of the driver in the cdevsw[] array (except for clone opens, which are described in Section 17.5.4). STREAMS drivers must handle device interrupts and need an additional mechanism to install their interrupt handlers into the kernel. This procedure is system-dependent.

Once the driver or module is configured, it is ready to be used by applications when the kernel is booted. The following subsections describe how that happens.

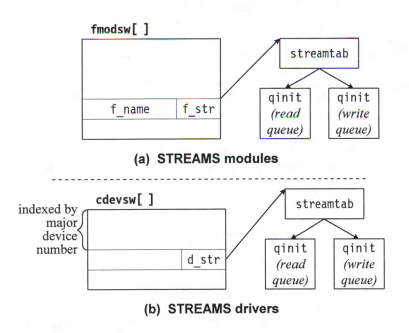

Figure 17-10. Module and driver configuration.

17.5.2   Opening a Stream

A user opens a stream by opening the corresponding device file. The first time a user opens a particular STREAMS device, the kernel translates the pathname and discovers that it is a character device file. It calls specvp(), which allocates and initializes an snode and a common snode for this
file (as described in Section 16.4.4). It then invokes the VOP_OPEN operation on the vnode (the
vnode associated with the common snode acts as the vnode for this stream), which is handled by the
spec_open() function. spec_open() indexes the cdevsw[] array using the major device number
and finds that the device is a streams device (d_str != NULL). It then calls the stropen() routine,
passing it pointers to the vnode and to the device number, as well as the open flags and credentials.
When called for a new stream (one that is not already open), stropen() performs the following actions:

1. Allocates a queue pair for the stream head.
2. Allocates and initializes a struct stdata, which represents a stream head.
3. Sets the stream head queues to point to the strdata and stwdata objects, which are
   qinit structures (for the read and write queue respectively) that contain the generic
   stream head functions.
4. Stores the vnode pointer in the sd_vnode field of the stdata structure.
5. Stores a pointer to the stream head in the vnode (v_stream field).
6. Stores a pointer to the streamtab structure for this driver (obtained from the cdevsw
   entry) in the sd_streamtab field of the stream head.
7. Makes the private data pointer (q_ptr) of the stream head queues point to the stdata
   structure.
8. Calls qattach() to set up the driver end, as described in the following paragraph.
9. Pushes any *autopush* modules specified by the device onto the stream by calling
   qattach(). This is described in the next section.

Figure 17-11 shows the relevant data structures after stropen() returns.

The qattach() function attaches a module or driver below the stream head by performing
the following actions:

1. Allocate a queue pair and link it below the stream head.
2. Locate the streamtab structure, via the cdevsw[] array for a driver or the fmodsw[] array
   for a module.
3. From the streamtab, obtain the read and write qinit structures and use them to initialize
   the q_qinfo fields of the queue pair.
4. Finally, call the *open* procedure of the module or driver.

Now suppose another user opens the same stream, either through the same device file or
through another device file that has the same major and minor numbers (the common snode handles
the latter case). The kernel discovers that the v_stream field of the common snode's vnode is not
NULL, but points to the stdata structure of the stream. This indicates that the stream is already
open, and stropen() simply calls the *open* procedure of the stream driver and every module in the
stream, to inform them that another process has opened the same stream.

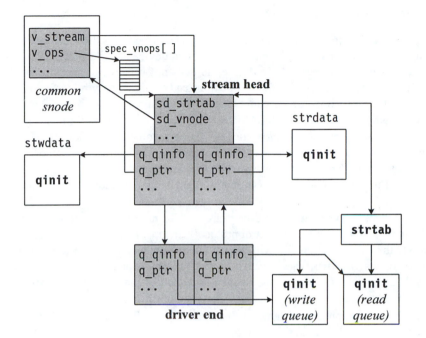

Figure 17-11. Data structures after `stropen()`.

17.5.3   Pushing Modules

A user may push a module onto an open stream by making an *ioctl* call with the I_PUSH command. The kernel allocates a queue pair and calls qattach() to add it to the stream. qattach() initializes the module by locating its strtab entry from the fmodsw[] table. It links the module into the stream immediately below the stream head and calls its *open* procedure.

A user may remove a module from the queue using the I_POP *ioctl* command. This always removes the module nearest to the stream head. Thus modules are popped in last-in, first-out (LIFO) order.

STREAMS provides an *autopush* mechanism, using *ioctl* commands for a special driver called the *STREAMS administrative driver (sad(8))*. Using this, an administrator may specify a set of modules to push onto a given stream when it is first opened. The stropen() routine checks if autopush has been enabled for the stream, and finds and pushes all specified modules in order.

There are two other common mechanisms for pushing modules onto a stream. One is to provide library routines that open the stream and push the correct modules onto it. Another is to start up a daemon process during system initialization to perform this task. Thereafter, whenever applications open the device file, they will be connected to the same stream, with all the right modules already pushed onto it.

17.5.4   Clone Devices

Section 16.4.5 described the notion of device cloning. The principle is that certain device types may have multiple, equivalent instances. Each instance of that device needs a unique minor device number. When a user wants to open such a device, he does not care which instance of the device he opens, as long as it is not one that is already open. Instead of the user trying to find an unused minor device number, it is better if the driver could supply one for him.

Cloning is used mostly by STREAMS devices such as network protocols and *pseudoterminals*. Hence STREAMS provides a *clone driver,* which automates the cloning of STREAMS devices. The *clone device* has its own major device number and is implemented as a STREAMS driver. It provides one device file for each STREAMS device that supports cloning. Its major device number is that of the *clone device,* and its minor number equals the major device number of the real device.

For instance, suppose the clone driver has a major number of 63. The device file **/dev/tcp** may represent all TCP (transmission control protocol) streams. If the TCP driver has a major device number of 31, then the **/dev/tcp** file will have a major number of 63 and a minor number of 31. When a user opens **/dev/tcp**, the kernel allocates an snode and a common snode, then calls spec_open(). spec_open() invokes the d_open operation of the clone driver, passing it a pointer to the device number (hence, a pointer to the s_dev field of the common snode).

The clnopen() routine implements the d_open operation for the clone driver. clnopen() extracts the minor number (31, in this example) from s_dev and indexes it into cdevsw[] to locate the TCP driver. It then invokes the d_open operation of this driver, passing it a CLONEOPEN flag and the device number. In our example, this results in a call to the tcpopen() function. When tcpopen() sees the CLONEOPEN flag, it generates an unused minor device number and writes it back to the snode.

When clnopen() returns, spec_open() discovers that a clone open had occurred. Because the common snode was the one associated with the clone device (**/dev/tcp**), spec_open() must allocate a new vnode and snode for this connection. It initializes the v_stream field of the new vnode to point to the stream head and copies the new major and minor device numbers (from s_dev) into the new vnode and snode. It then calls stropen() to open the new stream.

Finally, spec_open() zeroes the v_stream field of the original common snode (that associated with **/dev/tcp**). This makes it appear as though the device had never been opened. Subsequently, if another process tries to open **/dev/tcp**, the kernel performs the same series of operations and builds a new stream and device number for it. This gives the user a unique TCP connection without having to guess which minor number to use.

17.6   STREAMS *ioctl*s

STREAMS needs special mechanisms to deal with *ioctl*s. Though some *ioctl* commands are handled entirely at the stream head, others are targeted at the driver or at intermediate modules. These are converted to messages and sent downstream. This causes problems in two areas—process synchronization and data transfer between user and kernel space.

The stream head is responsible for synchronization. If it can handle the command itself, it does so synchronously and in process context, and there is no problem. If the stream head must send the command downstream, it blocks the process and sends down an M_IOCTL message containing the command and its parameters. When a module handles the command, it returns the results in an M_IOCACK message. If no module or driver can handle the message, the driver generates an M_IOCNACK message. When the stream head receives either of these messages, it wakes up the process and passes the results to it.

The data movement problem is concerned with the exchange of arguments and results between the user program and the module or driver that handles the *ioctl*. When a user issues an *ioctl* command to an ordinary character device, the driver processes the command in the context of the calling process. Each *ioctl* command is usually accompanied by a parameter block, whose size and contents are command-specific. The driver copies the block from user space into the kernel, processes the command, and copies the results to user space.

This method breaks down for STREAMS drivers and modules. The module receives the command as an M_IOCTL message, asynchronous to the process and in system context. Because the module does not have access to the process's address space, it cannot copy in the parameter block, or copy the results back to the user space.

STREAMS provides two ways of overcoming this problem. The preferred solution involves a special type of *ioctl* command called I_STR. The other method handles ordinary *ioctl* commands and is necessary to maintain compatibility with older applications. It is called *transparent ioctl* handling, as it does not require modification of existing applications.

17.6.1   I_STR *ioctl* Processing

The normal syntax of the *ioctl* system call is

```
ioctl (fd, cmd, arg);
```

where fd is the file descriptor, cmd is an integer that specifies a command, and arg is an optional, command-specific value, which often contains the address of a parameter block. The driver interprets the contents of arg based on the cmd and copies the parameters from user space accordingly.

A user may issue a special STREAMS *ioctl* message by specifying the constant I_STR as the cmd value, and setting arg to point to a strioctl structure, which has the following format:

```
struct strioctl {
    int ic_cmd;        /* the actual command to issue */
    int ic_timeout;    /* timeout period */
    int ic_len;        /* length of parameter block */
    char *ic_dp;       /* address of parameter block */
};
```

If the stream head cannot handle the *ioctl,* it creates a message of type M_IOCTL and copies the ic_cmd value into it. It also extracts the parameter block (specified by ic_len and ic_dp) from user space and copies it into the message. It then passes the message downstream. When the module that handles the command receives the message, it contains all the information required to process the command. If the command requires data to be returned to the user, the module writes it into the same message, changes the message type to M_IOCACK, and sends it back upstream. The stream head will copy the results to the parameter block in user space.

Hence the stream head passes the message downstream until it reaches a module that can recognize and handle it. That module sends back an M_IOCACK message to the stream head, indicating that the command was successfully intercepted. If no module can recognize the message, it reaches the driver. If the driver cannot recognize it either, it sends back a M_IOCNACK message, upon which the stream head generates an appropriate error code.

This solution is efficient, but imposes some restrictions on the commands it can handle. It will not work with older applications that do not use I_STR commands. Moreover, since the stream head cannot interpret the parameters, they must be contained directly in the parameter block. For example, if one parameter is a pointer to a string stored elsewhere in user space, the stream head will copy the pointer but not the string. Hence it is essential to have a general solution that will work in all cases, even if it is slower or less efficient.

17.6.2   Transparent *ioctl*s

Transparent *ioctl*s provide a mechanism to handle the data copying problem for commands that do not use the I_STR framework. When a process issues a transparent *ioctl*, the stream head creates an M_IOCTL message and copies into it the *cmd* and *arg* parameters. Usually, the *arg* value is a pointer to a parameter block, whose size and contents are known only to the module that handles the command. The stream head sends the message downstream and blocks the calling process.

When the module receives the message, it sends back an M_COPYIN message, passing the size and location (same as arg) of the parameter block. The stream head wakes up the process that had issued the *ioctl*, to handle the M_COPYIN message. The process creates a new message of type M_IOCARGS, copies the data from user space into it, sends the message downstream, and blocks again.

When the module receives the M_IOCARGS message, it interprets the parameters and processes the message. In some cases, the module and the stream head may need to exchange several messages to read in all parameters correctly. For example, if one of the parameters is a pointer to a string, the module sends an additional message to extract the string itself.

Finally, the module receives all the parameters it needs and services the message. If results must be written back to the user, the module issues one or more M_COPYOUT messages, passing back the results and specifying the location to which they must be written. Each time, the stream head wakes up the process, which writes them to its address space. When all results have been copied, the module sends an M_IOCACK message, and the stream head wakes up the process for the last time and completes the *ioctl* call.

17.7   Memory Allocation

STREAMS memory management has very special requirements, and hence is not handled by the regular kernel memory allocator. Modules and drivers constantly use messages and require an efficient mechanism to allocate and free them. *put* and *service* procedures must be non-blocking. If the allocator cannot supply the memory immediately, they must handle the situation without blocking, perhaps by retrying at a later time. In addition, many STREAMS drivers allow direct memory access (DMA) from device buffers. STREAMS allows such memory to be directly converted into messages instead of copying it into main memory.

The main memory management routines are `allocb()`, `freeb()`, and `freemsg()`. The syntax for `allocb()` is

```
mp = allocb (size, pri);
```

`allocb()` allocates a `msgb`, a `datab`, and a data buffer at least `size` bytes long; it returns a pointer to the `msgb`. It initializes them so that the `msgb` points to the `datab`, which contains the beginning and end of the data buffer. It also sets the `b_rptr` and `b_wptr` fields in the `msgb` to point to the beginning of the data buffer. The `pri` argument is no longer used and is retained only for backward compatibility. The `freeb()` routine frees a single `msgb`, while `freemsg()` traverses the `b_cont` chain, freeing all `msgbs` in the message. In both cases, the kernel decrements the reference count of the associated `databs`. If the count falls to zero, it also releases the `datab` and the data buffer to which it points.

Allocating three objects individually is inefficient and slow. STREAMS provides a faster solution using a data structure called `mdbblock`. Each `mdbblock` is 128 bytes in size and includes a `msgb`, a `datab`, and a pointer to a *release handler,* which is discussed in the next section. The remaining space in the structure may be used for a data buffer.

Let us examine what happens when a module calls `allocb()` to allocate a message. `allocb()` calls `kmem_alloc()` to allocate a `struct mdbblock`, passing it the `NO_SLP` flag. This ensures that `kmem_alloc()` returns an error instead of blocking if the memory is not available immediately. If the allocation succeeds, `allocb()` checks if the requested size is small enough to fit into the `mdbblock`. If so, it initializes the structure and returns a pointer to the `msgb` within it Figure 17-12. Hence a single call to `kmem_alloc()` provides the `msgb`, `datab`, and data buffer.

If the requested size is larger, `allocb()` calls `kmem_alloc()` once more, this time to allocate the data buffer. In this case, the extra space in the `mdbblock` is not used. If either call to `kmem_alloc()` fails, `allocb()` releases any resources it had acquired and returns `NULL`, indicating failure.

The module or driver must handle an `allocb()` failure. One possibility is to discard the data with which it is working. This approach is used by many network drivers when they are unable to keep pace with incoming traffic. Often, though, the module wants to wait until memory is available. Because *put* and *service* procedures must be non-blocking, it must find another way of waiting for memory.

STREAMS provides a routine called `bufcall()` to handle this situation. When a module cannot allocate a message, it calls `bufcall()`, passing it a pointer to a callback function and the size of the message it wanted to allocate. STREAMS adds this callback to an internal queue. When sufficient memory becomes available, STREAMS processes this queue and invokes each callback function on it.

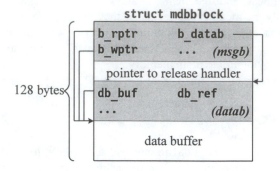

Figure 17-12. Small message allocation.

Often, the callback function is the *service* procedure itself. The callback may not, however, assume that enough memory is indeed available. By the time the callback runs, other activity may have depleted the available memory. In that case, the module typically reissues the bufcall().

17.7.1   Extended STREAMS Buffers

Some STREAMS drivers support I/O cards containing *dual-access RAM* (also called *dual-ported RAM*). The card has memory buffers which may be accessed both by the device hardware and by the CPU. Such a buffer may be mapped into the kernel or user address space, allowing an application to access and modify its contents without copying it to or from main memory.

STREAMS drivers place their data into messages and pass them upstream. To avoid copying the contents of the I/O card's buffers, STREAMS provides a way to use them directly as the data buffer of the message. Instead of using allocb(), the driver calls a routine called esballoc(), passing it the address of the buffer to be used. STREAMS allocates a msgb and datab (from a mdbblock), but not a data buffer. Instead, it uses the caller-supplied buffer and adjusts the msgb and datab fields to reference it.

This causes a problem when the buffer is freed. Normally, when a module calls freeb() or freemsg(), the kernel frees the msgb, datab, and the data buffer (assuming no other references to the datab). The kmem_free() routine releases these objects and recovers the memory. Driver-supplied buffers, however, cannot be released to the general memory pool since they belong to the I/O card.

Hence esballoc() takes another parameter, which is the address of a *release handler* function. When the message is freed, the kernel frees the msgb and datab, and calls the release handler to free the data buffer. The handler takes the necessary actions to mark the buffer as free, so that the I/O card may reuse it. The syntax for esballoc() is

```
mp = esballoc (base, size, pri, free_rtnp);
```

where base and size describe the buffer to be used, and free_rtnp is the address of the release handler. The pri argument is for compatibility only and is not used in SVR4. esballoc() returns a pointer to the msgb.

17.8 Multiplexing

STREAMS provides a facility called *multiplexing,* which allows multiple streams to be linked to a single stream, called a *multiplexor.* Multiplexing is restricted to drivers and is not supported for modules. There are three types of multiplexors—upper, lower, and two-way. An upper multiplexor connects multiple streams at the top to a single stream at the bottom. It is also known as a fan-in, or M-to-1, multiplexor. A lower multiplexor, also called fan-out or 1-to-N, connects multiple lower stream below a single upper stream. A two-way, or M-to-N, multiplexor supports multiple streams above and below. Multiplexors may be combined in arbitrary ways to form complex configurations, such as the one shown earlier in Figure 17-3.

STREAMS provides the framework and some support routines for multiplexing, but the drivers are responsible for managing the multiple streams and routing data appropriately.

17.8.1 Upper Multiplexors

Upper multiplexing is simply a result of opening multiple minor devices to the same driver. STREAMS provides no special support except the processing in the *open* and *close* system calls. Any driver that supports multiple minor devices is an upper multiplexor.

The first time a user opens a particular STREAMS device, the kernel creates a stream for it and references it through the snode and common snode. Subsequently, if another (or the same) process opens the same device file, the kernel finds that the file is already streaming (a stream is set up), and the new process uses the same stream. The same holds if the second process opens a different device file having the same major and minor device numbers. The kernel recognizes that the same device is being opened (since it will go through the same common snode), and the two processes will share the same stream. So far, we have no multiplexing.

If, however, the second process uses a different minor device number, the kernel will create a separate stream for it, and also a separate snode and common snode. Since the two streams have the same major device number, they will be handled by the same driver. The *open* procedure of the driver will be called twice, once for each stream. The driver will manage two sets of queues, perhaps with different modules pushed on them. When data comes in from the device, the driver examines the data and decides which stream should receive it. The decision is usually based on information contained in the data, or on which port on the controller card the data arrived.

For example, Figure 17-13 describes an ethernet driver acting as an upper multiplexor. The two streams may contain different modules. For instance, one stream may be using an IP module and another an ICMP module. When data arrives from the network, the driver examines its contents to decide which stream should receive the data.

STREAMS provides no special support for upper multiplexors. The driver maintains data structures to keep track of the streams connected to it. It stores pointers to the different read queues,

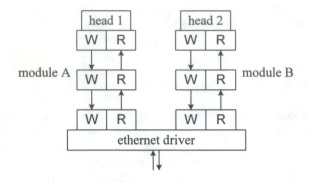

Figure 17-13. An upper multiplexor.

so that it can send the data to any stream. It manages its own flow control, since *STREAMS does not provide flow control for multiplexors*.

17.8.2   Lower Multiplexors

A lower multiplexor driver is a pseudodevice driver. Instead of controlling a physical device, it interfaces with one or more streams below it. To build such a configuration, a user creates the upper and lower streams, and links the upper stream to each of the lower streams. STREAMS provides special *ioctl* commands called I_LINK and I_UNLINK to set up and dismantle lower multiplexors.

Consider a system that has both an ethernet and an FDDI card, and a STREAMS driver for each. The system could implement the IP layer as a multiplexing driver and connect it to both network interfaces. Example 17-2 shows how such a configuration is built.

```
fd_enet = open ("/dev/enet", O_RDWR);
fd_fddi = open ("/dev/fddi", O_RDWR);
fd_ip = open ("/dev/ip", O_RDWR);
ioctl (fd_ip, I_LINK, fd_enet);
ioctl (fd_ip, I_LINK, fd_fddi);
```

Example 17-2. Building a lower multiplexor.

The example omits the statements to check the return values and handle errors. The first three statements open the *enet* (ethernet), *fddi,* and *ip* drivers, respectively. Next, the user links the *ip* stream onto the *enet* stream and then onto the *fddi* stream. Figure 17-14 shows the resulting configuration.

The next section examines the process of setting up the lower multiplexor in detail.

17.8.3   Linking Streams

A lower multiplexor driver must provide two queue pairs, as opposed to a single pair for ordinary STREAMS drivers. The two pairs are called upper and lower. In the streamtab structure for a

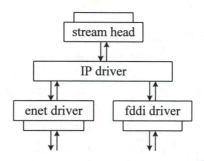

Figure 17-14. An IP driver as a lower multiplexor.

multiplexor, the st_rdinit and st_wrinit fields reference the qinit structures for the upper queue pair, while the st_muxrinit and st_muxwinit fields point to the lower queue pair. In the queues, only some procedures are required. The upper read queue must contain the *open* and *close* procedures. The lower read queue must have a *put* procedure, and so must the upper write queue. All other procedures are optional.

Figure 17-15 describes the *ip* and *enet* streams before the I_LINK command. The strdata and stwdata are shared by all stream heads and contain the read and write qinit structures, respectively. Only the *ip* driver has a lower queue pair, and it is not used as yet.

Now let us look at what happens when the user issues the first I_LINK command. The strioctl() routine does the initial processing of all *ioctl* requests. For the I_LINK case, it takes the following actions:

1. Checks that both upper and lower streams are valid and that the upper stream is a multiplexor.
2. Checks the stream for cycles. A cycle could occur if the lower stream was already connected above the upper stream, directly or indirectly. STREAMS fails any I_LINK call that results in such a cycle.
3. Changes the queues in the *enet* stream head to point to the lower queue pair of the *ip* driver.
4. Zeroes out the q_ptr fields in the *enet* stream head, so that they no longer point to its stdata structure.
5. Creates a linkblk structure, containing pointers to the queues to be linked. These are q_top, which points to the write queue of the *ip* driver, and q_bot, which points to the write queue of the *enet* stream head. The linkblk also contains a *link ID,* which later may be used in routing decisions. STREAMS generates a unique link ID for each connection and also passes it back to the user as the return value of the I_LINK *ioctl*.
6. Sends the linkblk downstream to the *ip* driver in an M_IOCTL message and waits for it to return.

Figure 17-16 shows the connections after the I_LINK completes. The heavy arrows show the new connections set up by STREAMS.

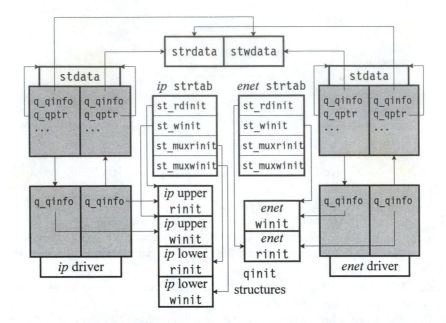

Figure 17-15. *ip* and *enet* streams before linking.

The *ip* driver manages other details of the multiplexor configuration. It maintains data structures describing all streams connected below it and, when it receives the M_IOCTL message, adds an entry for the *enet* stream to them. This entry, at a minimum, must contain the lower queue pointer and link ID (from the linkblk structure passed in the message), so it can pass messages down to the lower stream. In the next section, we describe the data flow through the multiplexor.

17.8.4 Data Flow

The *fddi* stream is linked below the *ip* driver just like the *enet* stream. The *ip* driver receives a second M_IOCTL message and adds an entry for the *fddi* stream. Once the configuration is set up, it must be able to route incoming and outgoing messages correctly.

When a user sends data downstream, the *ip* driver must decide whether the data should be sent to the ethernet or the FDDI interface. This decision may be based on the destination IP address of the packet, if the two interfaces are serving different subnets. It then looks up the address of the write queue of the appropriate lower stream in its private data structures. It then calls canput() to make sure the lower stream can accept the message and, if so, sends it down by calling the *put* procedure of the lower write queue.

The plumbing set up by STREAMS takes care of the upstream routing. When data comes in over the ethernet or the FDDI, the driver sends it upstream. When it reaches the stream head, it is handled by the *put* procedure of the stream head's read queue. This queue, however, now points to

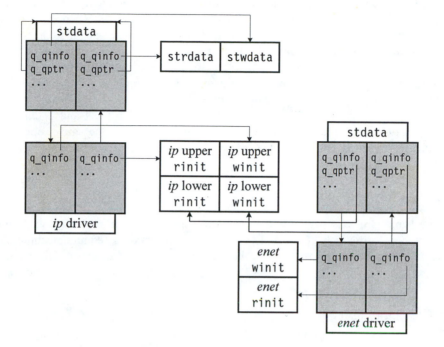

Figure 17-16. IP and *enet* streams after linking.

the `qinit` structure of the lower read queue of the multiplexor. Hence the message is processed by the *ip* driver, which sends it up toward the *ip* stream head.

STREAMS does not directly support flow control for multiplexors. Hence the *ip* driver must handle any flow control it requires.

17.8.5   Ordinary and Persistent Links

Ordinarily, a link stays in place until the last open instance of that stream is closed. Alternatively, a user may explicitly unlink a stream below a multiplexor by using the I_UNLINK *ioctl* command, passing it the link ID returned by I_LINK.

For a multiplexor configuration, the stream to the upper driver is the controlling stream for that configuration. For a multilevel configuration involving several multiplexors, the controlling stream for each multiplexor at each level must be linked under the next higher level multiplexor. If the streams are set up correctly in this way, the final *close* of the topmost controlling stream dismantles the entire configuration.

Consider a complex configuration such as the one described in Figure 17-3. It is desirable to set up this configuration once and for all and to leave it in place indefinitely for applications to use. One way to do it is to have a daemon process open and link all the streams and push any required modules. This daemon process then blocks indefinitely, holding an open descriptor to the controlling streams. This prevents the setup from being dismantled when no other process is using it.

Other processes may now use this configuration by issuing *open* calls to the topmost drivers (TCP or UDP in the example of Figure 17-3). These are typically clone devices and opening them creates new minor devices and, correspondingly, new streams to the same driver.

This solution requires a process to be dedicated to keeping the streams open. It does not protect the system against accidental death of that process. STREAMS provides an alternative solution, using the I_PLINK and I_PUNLINK commands in place of I_LINK and I_UNLINK. I_PLINK creates *persistent links,* which remain active even if no process has the stream open. Such a link must be explicitly removed by I_PUNLINK, passing it the link ID returned by I_PLINK.

17.9 FIFOs and Pipes

One of the benefits of STREAMS is that it offers a simple way of implementing FIFO files and pipes. Section 6.2 described FIFOs and pipes from an interprocess communications perspective. This section shows how SVR4 implements these objects and the advantages of this approach.

17.9.1 STREAMS FIFOs

FIFO files are also called *named pipes.* A user creates a FIFO by the *mknod* system call, passing it the pathname, permissions, and the S_IFIFO flag. The file may reside in a directory of any ordinary file system such as *s5fs* or *ufs.* Once created, any process that knows its name may read or write the file, as long as it has the appropriate permissions. The file continues to exist until explicitly deleted through the *unlink* system call. I/O to the file obeys first-in, first-out semantics. Thus, once opened, the file behaves a lot like a pipe.

SVR4 uses a separate file system type called *fifofs* to handle all operations on the FIFO file. It uses a stream with a *loopback* driver to implement the functionality. When a user calls *mknod* to create a FIFO, the kernel parses the pathname to obtain the vnode of the parent directory. It then invokes the VOP_CREATE operation on the parent vnode, to create a file in that directory. It sets the IFIFO flag in the inode, which marks it as a FIFO file.

Figure 17-17 describes how SVR4 sets up a FIFO. To use the FIFO, a process must first open it. When the *open* system call sees the IFIFO flag in the inode, it calls specvp(), which in turn calls the *fifofs* routine fifovp(). This routine creates a *fifonode,* which is much like an snode. The vnode contained in the fifonode points to the vector of *fifofs* operations. *fifofs* returns this vnode to the *open* call, so that all further references to the file use the *fifofs* operations.

The *open* system call then invokes the VOP_OPEN operation on the new vnode. This results in a call to the fifo_open() routine. Since the file is being opened for the first time, there is no stream associated with it. fifo_open creates a new stream head, and simply connects its write queue to its read queue. It stores the pointer to the stream head (struct stdata) in the v_stream field of the vnode. On subsequent opens, fifo_open() will find that the stream already exists, and all users will share access to the stream.

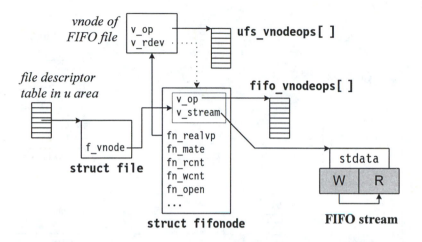

Figure 17-17. STREAMS-based FIFO.

Whenever a user writes data to the FIFO, the stream head sends it down the write queue, which immediately sends it back to the read queue, where the data waits until it is read. Readers retrieve data from the read queue and block at the stream head if no data is available. When no processes have the FIFO open, the stream is dismantled. The stream will be rebuilt if the FIFO is opened again. The FIFO file itself persists until explicitly unlinked.

17.9.2 STREAMS Pipes

The *pipe* system call creates an unnamed pipe. Prior to SVR4, data flow in the pipe was unidirectional. The *pipe* call returned two file descriptors, one for writing and the other for reading. SVR4 reimplemented pipes using STREAMS. The new approach allows bidirectional pipes.

As before, *pipe* returns two file descriptors. In SVR4, however, both are open for reading and writing. Data written to one descriptor is read from the other, and vice versa. This is achieved by using a pair of streams. The *pipe* system call creates two fifonodes and a stream head for each of them. It then fixes the queues such that the write queue of each stream head is connected to the read queue of the other. Figure 17-18 describes the resulting configuration.

This approach has some important advantages. The pipe is now bidirectional, which makes it much more useful. Many applications require bidirectional communication between processes. Prior to SVR4, they had to open and manage two pipes. Moreover, implementing the pipe via streams allows many more control operations on it. For instance, it allows the pipe to be accessed by unrelated processes.

The C library routine *fattach* provides this functionality [Pres 90]. Its syntax is

```
error = fattach (fd, path);
```

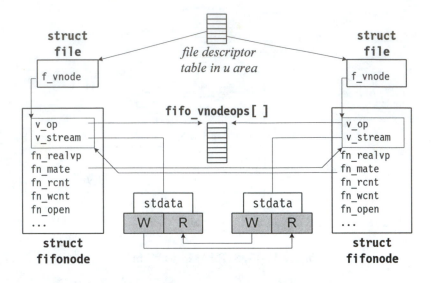

Figure 17-18. STREAMS-based pipe.

where fd is a file descriptor associated with a stream, and path is the pathname of a file owned by the caller (or the caller must be root). The caller must have write access to the file. *fattach* uses a special file system called *namefs* and mounts an instance of this file system onto the file represented by path. Unlike other file systems, which may only be mounted on directories, *namefs* allows mounting on ordinary files. On mounting, it binds the stream file descriptor fd to the mount point.

Once so attached, any reference to that pathname accesses the stream bound to it. The association persists until removed by *fdetach,* at which time the pathname is bound back to the original file associated with it. Frequently, *fattach* is used to bind one end of a pipe to a filename. This allows applications to create a pipe and then dynamically associate it with a filename, thus providing unrelated processes with access to the pipe.

17.10   Networking Interfaces

STREAMS provides the kernel infrastructure for networking in System V UNIX. Programmers need a higher-level interface to write network applications. The sockets framework, introduced in 4.1cBSD in 1982, provides comprehensive support for network programming. System V UNIX handles this problem through a set of interfaces layered on top of STREAMS. These include the *Transport Provider Interface (TPI),* which defines the interactions between transport providers and transport users, and the *Transport Layer Interface (TLI),* which provides high-level programming facilities. Since the sockets framework came long before STREAMS, there are a large number of applications that use it. To ease the porting of these applications, SVR4 added support for sockets through a collection of libraries and STREAMS modules.

17.10.1 Transport Provider Interface (TPI)

A transport provider is a network module such as TCP that implements layer 4 (transport layer) of the OSI protocol stack [ISO 84]. A transport user is an application such as the *file transfer protocol (ftp)*, which uses the module. TPI is built on top of STREAMS, and defines the format and contents of messages that govern interactions between the transport provider and the transport user.

TPI messages originate both from the application and from the transport provider. Each message is contained in a STREAMS message block of type M_PROTO or M_PCPROTO. The first field of the message is its TPI message type. This type determines the format and contents of the rest of the message. For instance, the application issues a T_BIND_REQ message to bind the stream to a port. It contains the port number to which the stream must be bound, as well as other parameters specific to the request. The transport provider replies by sending a T_BIND_ACK message, which contains the results of the operation.

Similarly, TPI defines the format for sending data up or down the stream. The application creates a message headed by a T_DATA_REQ or T_UNITDATA_REQ block, followed by one or more M_DATA blocks containing the body of the message. The header contains the destination address and port number in protocol-specific format. When data comes in over the network, the transport provider prepends a header, which is a T_DATA_IND or T_UNITDATA_IND message block.[2]

The role of TPI is to standardize interactions between the transport provider and the transport user. For instance, an application uses the same message to bind to a port, whether using a TCP or a UDP connection. This allows a greater degree of transport independence. TPI does not, however, provide a simple programming interface. That is taken care of by sockets and the transport layer interface.

17.10.2 Transport Layer Interface (TLI)

The TLI [AT&T 89] is native to System V UNIX and was introduced in SVR3 in 1986. It provides a procedural interface to open and use a network connection. TLI functions are particularly suitable for implementing client-server interactions. They may be used both for connection-oriented and connectionless services. Internally, they are implemented as STREAMS operations.

In a connection-oriented protocol (Figure 17-19), the server opens a transport endpoint by calling t_open(), then binds it to a port through t_bind(). It then calls t_listen(), in which it blocks until a client requests a connection. Meanwhile, a client program, usually on a different machine, calls t_open() and t_bind(), followed by a t_connect() to connect to the server. The client blocks in t_connect() until the connection is established.

When the connect request arrives at the server machine, t_listen() returns, and the server calls t_accept() to accept the connection. This sends a reply to the client, which returns from t_connect(). The connection is now established. The server sits in a loop, calling t_rcv() to receive a client request, processing it, and calling t_snd() to send the reply. The client calls t_snd() to send a request and t_rcv() to receive the reply.

---

[2] The T_UNITDATA_REQ and T_UNITDATA_IND types are used for datagrams, while T_DATA_REQ and T_DATA_IND are used for byte-stream data.

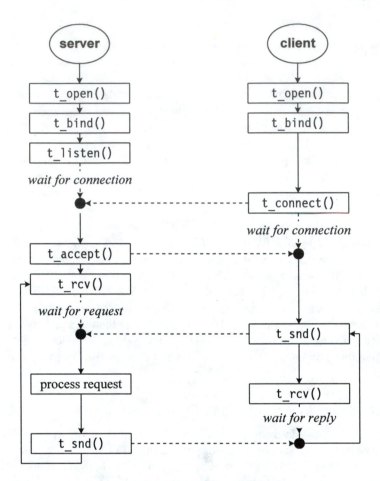

Figure 17-19. TLI functions for a connection-oriented protocol.

Connectionless protocols operate differently (Figure 17-20). Both the server and the client call t_open() and t_bind(), just as before. Since there are no connections to be made, we do not need t_listen(), t_connect(), or t_accept() calls. Instead, the server sits in a loop, calling t_rcvudata(), which blocks until a client sends a message. When a message arrives, the call returns to the server with the address and port number of the sender, along with the body of the message. The server processes the message and replies to the client calling t_sndudata(). The client likewise calls t_sndudata() to send messages and t_rcvudata() to receive replies.

17.10.3 Sockets

Sockets [Leff 86], introduced in 4.1BSD in 1982, provide a programming interface, which may be used both for interprocess and network communications. A *socket* is a communication endpoint and

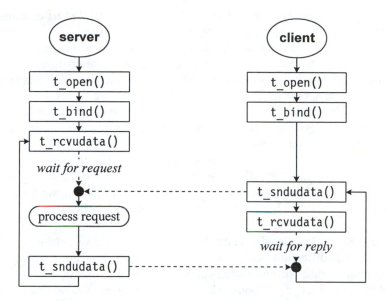

Figure 17-20. TLI functions for a connectionless protocol.

represents an abstract object that a process may use to send or receive messages. Although sockets are not native to System V UNIX, SVR4 provides full BSD socket functionality in order to support the huge number of applications written using the socket interface.

The socket interface is similar to TLI in several respects. There is almost a one-to-one correspondence of socket and TLI functions. Table 17-1 shows the common TLI functions and the equivalent socket calls.

Table 17-1. Correspondence between TLI and socket calls

TLI functions	Socket functions	Purpose
t_open()	socket()	Open a connection endpoint
t_bind()	bind()	Bind endpoint to port
t_listen()	listen()	Wait for a connection request
t_connect()	connect()	Send a connection request
t_accept()	accept()	Accept a connection
t_rcv()	recvmsg()	Receive message from connection
t_snd()	sendmsg()	Send message to connection
t_rcvudata()	recvfrom()	Receive message from any node
t_sndudata()	sendto()	Send message to specified node

There are, however, substantial differences in the arguments to and semantics of the TLI and socket calls. Although TLI and STREAMS were designed to be mutually compatible, there were several problems in adding sockets support to STREAMS [Vess 90]. Let us examine some of the important factors that cause incompatibility between the two frameworks.

The sockets framework is procedural, not message-based. When an application calls a socket function, the kernel sends the data to the network by directly calling lower-level transport functions. It finds the transport-specific functions through a table lookup and routes the data to them. This allows higher layers of the socket interface to share state information with transport layers through global data structures. In STREAMS, each module is insulated from others and has no global state. Although such a modular framework has many advantages, it is difficult to duplicate some socket functionality that depends on shared state.

Socket calls execute in the context of the calling process. Hence any errors can be synchronously reported to the caller. STREAMS processes data asynchronously, and calls such as *write* or *putmsg* succeed as soon as the data is copied in by the stream head. If a lower-level module generates an error, it can only affect subsequent write attempts; the call that caused the error has already succeeded.

Some problems are associated with the decision to implement sockets on top of TPI. Certain options are processed in different places by sockets than by TPI. For instance, socket applications specify the maximum number of unaccepted connect indications (backlog) in the listen() call, after the socket has been opened and bound. TPI, however, requires the backlog to be specified in the T_BIND_REQ message, sent during the bind operation itself.

17.10.4   SVR4 Sockets Implementation

Figure 17-21 describes the implementation of sockets in SVR4. The sockets functionality is provided jointly by a user-level library called **socklib** and a STREAMS module called **sockmod**. The two play complementary roles. The **socklib** library maps socket functions to STREAMS system calls and messages. The **sockmod** module mediates **socklib**'s interactions with the transport provider and supports socket-specific semantics.

When a user calls *socket* to create a socket, **socklib** maps the arguments to the device file name using the SVR4 *Network Selection Facility* [AT&T 89]. It opens the file, thus creating a stream, and calls the I_PUSH *ioctl* to push the **sockmod** module just below the stream head. Once this configuration is set up in this way, **sockmod** and **socklib** cooperate to handle user requests.

For example, consider what happens when the user calls *connect* to connect a TCP stream to a remote server. **socklib** creates a T_CONN_REQ TPI message, and sends it downstream by calling *putmsg*. It then calls *getmsg* to wait for the reply. When **sockmod** intercepts the message, it stores the destination address for later use and passes the message to TCP. The TCP module processes the request and sends an acknowledgment upstream. When getmsg returns, **socklib** extracts the results from the message, and returns control to the application.

Subsequently, the user may send data to the connection by calling *sendmsg*. Again, **socklib** sends it downstream by calling *putmsg*. When **sockmod** receives the message, it prepends a header containing the destination address, which it had remembered when establishing the connection.

Both **socklib** and **sockmod** need to maintain some state about the socket. When a connection is established, for example, **socklib** records the connection's status and destination address.

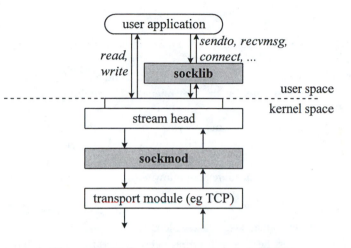

Figure 17-21. Implementing sockets in SVR4.

This way, it can reject *sendmsg* calls to unconnected sockets. If **sockmod** alone maintained the connection information, there would be no way to return the correct error status to the caller.

Likewise, it is not sufficient to maintain state in **socklib** alone. This is because a process may create a socket and then call *exec,* wiping out any state maintained in **socklib**. The socket implementation detects this because *exec* initializes **socklib** to a known state. When a user tries to use a socket after an *exec,* **socklib** sends an *ioctl* to **sockmod** to recover the lost state. Since **sockmod** is in kernel space, its state is not wiped out by the *exec* call.

There are many interesting issues and problems concerning the SVR4 sockets implementation. They are discussed in detail in [Vess 90].

17.11   Summary

STREAMS provides a framework for writing device drivers and network protocols. It enables a high degree of configurability and modularity. STREAMS does for drivers what pipes do for UNIX shell commands. It allows the writing of independent modules, each of which acts as a filter and performs some specific processing on a data stream. It then allows users to combine these modules in different ways to form a stream. This stream acts like a bidirectional pipe, moving data between the application and the device or network interface, with appropriate processing in between.

The modular design allows network protocols to be implemented in a layered manner, each layer contained in a separate module. STREAMS are also used for interprocess communication, and SVR4 has reimplemented pipes and FIFOs using streams. Finally, many character drivers, including the terminal driver subsystem, have been rewritten as STREAMS drivers. Some of the recent enhancements to STREAMS include multiprocessor support [Garg 90, Saxe 93].

17.12   Exercises

1. Why does STREAMS use separate `msgb` and `datab` data structures, instead of having a single buffer header?
2. What is the difference between a STREAMS module and a STREAMS driver?
3. What is the relationship between the two queues of a module? Must they perform similar functions?
4. How does the presence or absence of a *service* procedure affect the behavior of a queue?
5. Both the *read* and the *getmsg* system calls may be used to retrieve data from a stream. What are the differences between them? For what situations is each of them more suitable?
6. Why are most STREAMS procedures not allowed to block? What can a *put* procedure do if it cannot process a message immediately?
7. Why are priority bands useful?
8. Explain how and when a queue is back-enabled.
9. What functionality does the stream head provide? Why do all stream heads share a common set of routines?
10. Why are STREAMS drivers accessed through the `cdevsw` table?
11. Why do STREAMS devices require special support for *ioctl?* Why can there be only one active *ioctl* on a stream?
12. Why is it often reasonable to discard incoming network messages if there is a memory shortfall?
13. What is the difference between a multiplexor and a module that is used independently in two different streams?
14. Why does STREAMS not provide flow control for multiplexors?
15. In Figure 17-14, why is the IP layer implemented as a STREAMS driver and not as a module?
16. What are the benefits of persistent links?
17. STREAMS pipes allow bidirectional traffic, while traditional pipes do not. Describe an application that takes advantage of this feature. How would you provide this functionality without using STREAMS pipes?
18. What is the difference between TPI and TLI? What interactions does each of them pertain to?
19. Compare sockets and TLI as frameworks for writing network applications. What are the advantages and drawbacks of each? Which features of one are not easily available in the other?
20. Section 17.10.4 describes how SVR4 implements sockets on top of STREAMS. Could a BSD-based system implement a STREAMS-like interface using sockets? What important issues will need to be addressed?
21. Write a STREAMS module that converts all newline characters to "carriage-return + line-feed" on the way up and the reverse transformation on the way down. Assume the messages contain only printable ASCII characters.
22. A user may configure a stream dynamically by pushing a number of modules on the stack. Each module does not know what module is above or below it. How then, does a module know how to interpret the messages sent by the neighboring module? What restrictions does

this place on which modules may be stacked together and in what order? In what way does TPI address this problem?

17.13 References

[AT&T 89]   American Telephone and Telegraph, *UNIX System V Release 4 Network Programmer's Guide,* 1991.

[AT&T 91]   American Telephone and Telegraph, *UNIX System V Release 4 Internals Students Guide,* 1991.

[Garg 90]   Garg, A., "Parallel STREAMS: A Multi-Processor Implementation," *Proceedings of the Winter 1990 USENIX Technical Conference,* Jan. 1990.

[ISO 84]   International Standards Organization, *Open Systems Interconnection—Basic Reference Model,* ISO 7498, 1984.

[Leff 86]   Leffler, S., Joy, W., Fabry, R., and Karels, M., "Networking Implementation Notes— 4.3BSD Edition," University of California, Berkeley, CA, Apr. 1986.

[Pres 90]   Presotto, D.L., and Ritchie, D.M., "Interprocess Communications in the Ninth Edition UNIX System," *UNIX Research System Papers, Tenth Edition,* Vol. II, Saunders College Publishing, 1990, pp. 523–530.

[Rago 89]   Rago, S., "Out-of-band Communication in STREAMS," *Proceedings of the Summer 1989 USENIX Technical Conference,* Jun. 1989, pp. 29–37.

[Ritc 83]   Ritchie, D.M., "A Stream Input-Output System," *AT&T Bell Laboratories Technical Journal,* Vol. 63, No. 8, Oct. 1984, pp. 1897–1910.

[Saxe 93]   Saxena, S., Peacock, J.K., Verma, V., and Krishnan, M., "Pitfalls in Multithreading SVR4 STREAMS and Other Weightless Processes," *Proceedings of the Winter 1993 USENIX Technical Conference,* Jan. 1993, pp. 85–95.

[USL 92a]   UNIX System Laboratories, *STREAMS Modules and Drivers, UNIX SVR4.2,* UNIX Press, Prentice-Hall, Englewood Cliffs, NJ, 1992.

[USL 92b]   UNIX System Laboratories, *Operating System API Reference, UNIX SVR4.2,* UNIX Press, Prentice-Hall, Englewood Cliffs, NJ, 1992.

[Vess 90]   Vessey, I., and Skinner, G., "Implementing Berkeley Sockets in System V Release 4," *Proceedings of the Winter 1990 USENIX Technical Conference,* Jan. 1990, pp. 177– 193.

Index

Note: Page numbers in bold face indicate primary reference or definition